THE LETTERS OF JOHN MURRAY TO LORD BYRON

THE LETTERS OF JOHN MURRAY TO LORD BYRON

Edited by Andrew Nicholson

LIVERPOOL UNIVERSITY PRESS

First published 2007 by
Liverpool University Press
4 Cambridge Street
Liverpool L69 7ZU

British Library Cataloguing-in-Publication data

A British Library CIP record is available

ISBN 978-1-84631-069-0 cased

Typeset by Carnegie Book Production, Lancaster
Printed and bound in the European Union by Bell and Bain Ltd, Glasgow

for John and Ginnie
and
The House of Murray

Contents

THE LETTERS

PART I
Murray to Byron in England (1811–16)

1811   3

Letter 1: September. JM sends first proof of *CHP* I – his remarks thereupon – asks B to soften political and religious expressions – 'Orthodox' – urges completion – two further Cantos (1)

Interim Note: September 1811 to September 1812. B's movements – *CHP* I and II published – JM and B meet

1812   8

Letters 2–7: September: B is Cheltenham – JM sends reviews of *CHP* I and II – unprecedented sales – 4th edition – Meyer's engraving – George Thomson applies for songs – Lucien Buonaparte's *Charlemagne* – Scott's *Rokeby* (2). September–October: opening of Drury Lane Theatre – *Rejected Addresses* – B's 'Address' – its reception – 5th edition of *CHP* I and II (3–4); Busby episode – 'Parenthetical Address' – *Waltz* (5). November: JM removes to Albermarle Street – 'A Critique' on B's 'Address' – B returns to London – JM sends letters and reviews of *CHP* I and II (6–7)

PART II
Murray to Byron abroad (1816–22)

bust (162–163). November: JM sends MSS of *DJ* III–V – defends himself against misprints – B directs to Pisa but remains in Ravenna – proofs of *Cain* and *The Vision of Judgment* sent to Pisa – B signs agreement for Memoirs – prose tracts – payment for tragedies and *DJ* III–V – pirated editions (164)

Interim Note: November 1821–April 1822: *Cain* – Gifford's opinion – Moore's opinion – published with *Sardanapalus* and *The Two Foscari* – attacked and defended – *DJ* III–V misprints – B's comments in the Mawman copy – JM offended – squabbles with Hobhouse over B's bust – *Heaven and Earth* – proofs

Acknowledgements

I owe my first and greatest debt of gratitude to John R. Murray for his unsparing generosity to me throughout this venture, for allowing me frequent and unrestricted access to the Murray Archives, and for his kind permission to publish the material collected in this volume. It was under his auspices that this work was begun and by whom it was originally to have been published. I owe a huge debt also to Virginia Murray for her patient and invaluable assistance to me in the course my researches, and for her energetic burrowing around in the Murray Archives to trace stray manuscripts. Without their liberal cooperation this work could not have been accomplished, and to them it is dedicated as the only fitting expression of my sincere thanks to them for their friendship and many other kindnesses over all these years.

For access to, and for permission to include, material in this volume I have to thank the following institutions: the Bodleian Library, Oxford; the British Library, London; Cheltenham Ladies College, Gloucestershire; the Huntington Library, San Marino, California; Jarndyce Antiquarian Booksellers, London; Princeton University Library, Princeton. For the illustrations, I am grateful to the National Library of Scotland, the John Murray Collection at Albermarle Street, and a Private Collector.

I should like to thank the following for helping me with my inquiries: Robin Myers of the Stationers' Company; Rita Gibbs and Peter Hunter of the Vaughan Library, Harrow School; Brian Lake of Jarndyce Antiquarian Booksellers, London; Stephen Wagner of the Pforzheimer Library, New York; Stephen Crook of the Berg Collection, New York Public Library; Barbara Smith-Laborde and Tara Wenger of the Harry Ransom Humanities Research Center, University of Texas; Robert E. Parks and Christine Nelson of the Pierpont Morgan Library, New York; Gayle M. Barkley of the Huntington Library, San Marino, California; Carol A. Sommer of the William Andrews Clark Memorial Library, University of California, Los Angeles; Laetitia Yeandle of the Folger Shakespeare Library, Washington, DC; Mark Farrell and Margaret Sherry Rich of Princeton University Library; Lorna Knight of Cornell University Library, Ithaca; Sarah

Hartwell of Dartmouth College Library, Hanover, New Hampshire; Adrian Henstock of the Nottinghamshire Archives, Nottingham; Iain G. Brown and Ruth Boreham of the National Library of Scotland; Marie Paccard of Galignani, Paris; Claudia Giuliani of the Biblioteca Classense, Ravenna; M. Marconcini of the Biblioteca Universitaria, Genoa; the librarian of the Scuola Normale Superiore, Pisa; Julie Ramwell of the John Rylands Library, Manchester; Christopher Sheppard of Leeds University Library; Colin Harris of the Bodleian Library, Oxford; and Sally Brown, Frances Harris and Chris Fletcher of the Manuscript Room at the British Library. I am also grateful to the staff of the University of London Library and of the Rare Books and Manuscripts Reading Room at the British Library, who have been uniformly courteous and helpful beyond their call.

I have met with considerable kindness and encouragement during the course of my researches, and many people have expressed their interest in this work. In particular, I should like to mention the following: Katy Allen; Robin Alston; Bernard Beatty; Andrew Bennett; Barbara Boissard; Drummond Bone; the late Humphrey Carpenter; Stephen Cheeke; Peter Clifford; John Clubbe; Peter Cochran; Howard Davies; Paul Douglass; Clement Tyson Goode; Warwick Gould; Alistair Hamilton; Malcolm Hardman; Peter Isaac; Dilwyn Knox; Fiona MacCarthy; the late Leslie Marchand; Jerry McGann; Grant McIntyre; David Matthews; Donald and Kathleen Mitchell; Diana Murray; Michael Rees (Brother Teilo); Charlie Robinson; Gloria Speke Dever; Jane Stabler; William St Clair; Deirdre Toomey; Tim Webb; Tom Winnifrith; and Bill Zachs.

Thanks of a very special kind go to Bernard Beatty and Paul Douglass, and to my editors at Liverpool University Press, Robin Bloxsidge, Anthony Cond, Andrew Kirk and Helen Whiteley, who have taken such care in seeing this work through the press.

I am sorry that my mother, Rosemary Nicholson, and Humphrey Carpenter, for whom I was researching during his last year, did not live to see this work in print. To them, and to Tim Webb, who has been a constant support and encouragement to me, I owe more than I can ever repay. On a final note, this work has been a privilege to undertake and I hope that I have fulfilled my duties as an editor both to the reader and to Murray and Byron themselves, whose companionship has been such a grateful pleasure to me over all these years.

A. N.
Bloomsbury and Twickenham
19 April 2007

Preface

This correspondence is the record of a relationship that lasted exactly 11 years and is unique in the annals of publishing. It began in the autumn of 1811, shortly after Byron's return from his first visit to Greece, and continued until the winter of 1822, when a number of factors compounded to break off all communication between them whatsoever.[1]

John Murray was exactly 10 years older than Byron and was already a publisher of some standing by the time they met.[2] Although he was not amongst those booksellers recommended to bibliomaniacs by Thomas Dibdin in 1811 (William Miller led the field in this respect),[3] with the *Quarterly Review* behind him, he had a wide circle of friends and influential connections in London and Edinburgh (Constable, Ballantyne, Blackwood, Scott),[4] many of whom – in particular William Gifford, Isaac D'Israeli, John Wilson Croker and John Hookham Frere – advised him on literary matters (Murray's 'Synod', as Byron was to call it – though this gives the false impression of fixity to what was in fact a fluctuating, ad hoc body).

Situated as he was for the first year of their acquaintance in Fleet Street, Murray was at a rather inconvenient distance from Byron, whose quarters at the time were in St James's, Piccadilly. When exactly they first met has not been recorded (though they certainly did so once in June 1812), and neither has the frequency – if such was the case – of their subsequent meetings during that time; and the absence of any surviving letters from Murray to Byron for exactly a year between Letters 1 and 2 does not help matters. (The anecdote recorded by Murray's son – that Byron used to come to the shop and spar at Murray's books with his swordstick, punctuating his thrusts with such remarks as "You think that a good idea, do you Murray?" and so forth – is profoundly questionable.)

However, their very first exchange about *Childe Harold* (Letter 1) is a fair example of the sort of rapprochement they established from the outset, and of the way their correspondence would, at least initially, proceed: Murray – deferential and complimentary without being sycophantic, forthright but diplomatic, eager though reserved, writing with the authority of experience and knowledge whilst appealing to Byron's self-esteem and best interest; Byron – flattered, agreeable, bantering, but firm and unyielding, transmuting Murray's very objections to various passages into reasons for their retention, and – an imprint of many future exchanges – immortalizing Murray's use of the word 'Orthodox'.

When Murray removed to Albemarle Street late in 1812, he and Byron became close neighbours and thenceforth kept in constant touch with each other, exchanging notes and letters on a regular basis by hand or by messenger, sometimes twice or thrice daily. Such proximity and immediacy of communication were crucial elements in the publishing process of Byron's works, facilitating as they did, and as these letters attest, the accommodation of last-minute revisions or additions, or alterations suggested by others (Murray himself, Gifford or Frere, for instance).

Childe Harold I and II were published in March 1812 and their success for both of them was immediate and immense. Apart from other considerations, the poem became an emblem for their literary alliance, not only in the eyes of others but also in their own – even at the very end of their connection with each other (see Letter 171). This was followed successively, and as successfully, throughout 1813 and 1814 by *The Giaour, The Bride of Abydos, The Corsair* and *Lara*, and much of the correspondence at the time traces the tortuous production of these compositions – sometimes in rather technical though highly illuminating detail, serving to clarify certain textual matters that have hitherto remained obscure.

Once he was established in Albemarle Street, Murray began to keep open house, and his drawing-room became a forum where authors, politicians, travellers and casual visitors might drop in and meet and talk freely together (Washington Irving gives a wonderful vignette of one of these occasions).[5] This gave his business a distinct and homogeneous identity, rather like a club, and soon 'Albemarle Street' and 'John Murray' became synonymous and interchangeable terms not only for each other, but also for a standard of book production and publishing practice that Murray himself had set and represented – and was expected to live up to. It was here that Scott and Byron were first introduced to each other by Murray in April 1815 and formed a lasting friendship; it was here too that Byron expanded his circle of friends so that his social and literary life overlapped, and he found himself in the evening amongst those with whom he had mingled during the day.

This overlap between private and business relations went much deeper for both of them. Being 10 years older than Byron and a family man, Murray took an almost fatherly interest in Byron's personal welfare. His solicitude for his safety during the severe winter of 1813–14, for instance, his visit to Newstead in the autumn of 1814, the delight he took in Byron's friends and family and the news of his marriage, and his generosity (which

Byron was never to forget) at the time of its collapse, indicate a concern for his author beyond that of mere trade. Similarly, Byron's sending Murray game, cider and perry and cheese, and recommending such Drury Lane pieces as *The Magpie* to him, and Hunt's *The Story of Rimini* and Coleridge's *Kubla Khan* and *Christabel*, suggest a wish to serve the interests (and the appetite) of Murray both as a man and as a publisher.

These same concerns become even more apparent after Byron had left England in 1816, with his sending Murray presents (stones, bones and the spoils of Waterloo), recommending publications and introducing book-dealers (Missiaglia) to him, sending him manuscripts (the Algarotti collection), interesting him in the Armenian Grammar, and offering to get Murray's publications republished for him in Italy. This is an aspect of their relationship that has scarcely been recognized before – almost as if Byron were acting as Murray's agent abroad; and it says much for the goodwill, trust and understanding that subsisted between them.

Their correspondence too takes on a new and livelier colour after Byron had left England. It is quite true that he rarely wrote a dull letter and could enliven even those to his Attorneo, but his letters to Murray from abroad are unquestionably the best he ever wrote: they are the longest, the most interesting, the most entertaining, the most confidential (much to the disgust of his friends occasionally), the most literary, and even the most poetic (Ruskin singles out two such for special attention in *Praeterita*[6]); in short, they are the most self-revealing – those in which Byron is most *himself*. And Murray responded in full measure: he becomes more expansive, self-confident and easy-going; his letters are anecdotal, informative, playful and teasing, occasionally discursive – even hesitantly argumentative; he sends Byron the latest publications, and always obliges his constant requests for soda powders, corn-rubbers and dental supplies (no publisher can have been quite so intimate with the personal hygiene of his author). In an important way too Murray knew how to *read* Byron, to read beyond the written word and catch at his humour: his anxieties, frustrations, anger, illnesses or depressions; he gauged and understood these shifts often much better than some of Byron's own friends, and bore much in return that was exaggerated, unfair, or merely the vent of spleen, with admirable patience. Occasionally too he was more protective of Byron's own interest than Byron was himself.

Their correspondence reaches its zenith around 1820–21, when Byron cheerfully addresses Murray as 'Moray' or 'High-minded Moray' or the like (borrowed from Scott), and Murray addresses Byron by name rather than the formal 'My Lord', and concludes his letters with such endearments as 'most dear', and 'dearest Lord Byron'. Such familiarity is quite unprecedented and, so far as I have been able to discover, is not to be found in Murray's letters to others of the nobility. Sadly this was to end all too abruptly.

Naturally enough, Byron's poetry developed in new directions during his years abroad. *Childe Harold* III and IV are very different in character from Cantos I and II, though they retain certain familiar, if loose, connections with them. *Manfred*, however, and the dramatic monologues, explore new terrain, as do the historical dramas and *Cain*. But *Beppo* (1818) was something wonderful – a revelation – and Murray was astonished and delighted. As his letters show, he constantly urged Byron to pursue this happy vein – suggesting a series of such stories on the character and manners of the Italians. Although *Don Juan* I and II were not quite what he meant or what he was expecting, they did not shock him – contrary to what is generally thought, he was keen to publish them forthwith; it was Frere, Hobhouse, Scrope Davies and Kinnaird who objected.

Byron was never averse to omitting or altering passages in his poetry, provided he was consulted beforehand. Whilst he was in England he was on hand and this could be done easily and swiftly enough; but once abroad distance inhibited the process. To the first sign of Murray's meddling with his poetry without consulting him – the removal of two lines from *The Prisoner of Chillon* and of a note to *Childe Harold* III – Byron reacted with restraint; but when this began to be repeated in 1821 he was furious. He was further infuriated by Murray's delays (to which he himself contributed by telling Murray to direct to him at Pisa whither he did *not* immediately go) and by the appalling misprints in *Don Juan* III–V. Moreover, he did not think that Murray was being altogether candid in his financial proposals for his poetry. To make matters worse, he began operating through Kinnaird who was frequently absent from London and not entirely reliable, and with whom Murray did not feel at ease.

Unfortunately for us, many crucial letters of this time – covering at least two critical moments in the decline of relations between Murray and Byron – do not survive (though I have done my best to try to piece together what appears to have occurred). But once Byron had decided to withdraw from Murray as a publisher – partly, it must be remembered, because he was aware that his poetry was becoming unsuitable or uncomfortable for Murray to publish (*The Vision of Judgment* is the prime example here) – and with the advent of John Hunt on the scene, and the mislaying of manuscripts and proofs (again, *not* Murray's fault), the correspondence soon descends into a miserable exhibition of false accusations and rancour from which it was never to rise again.

Notes to the Preface

1. For the circumstances as to how Murray became Byron's publisher, see Appendix A.

2. He was born on 27 November 1778, the second – though first legitimate – son of John McMurray (1737–93) of Edinburgh, who had started life in the Navy before setting up the bookselling business (and dropping the 'Mc') at 32 Fleet Street in 1768. His mother, Hester (née Weemss), was his father's second wife, the younger sister of his first wife, Nancy, who had died childless of ill health in 1776 after a stormy marriage of 13 years. During that time, Murray's father – who was of a gallant and genial nature and, like Don Juan's father, 'a lineal son of Eve' – 'Went plucking various fruit without her leave.' The fruit of one such plucking was Murray's elder half-brother, Archie, who was born of mother unknown in 1770 and was destined to serve in the Navy. Murray no less was intended for the Navy; but during his school-days he suffered a severe head injury, and then in an accident at the Royal Naval Academy at Gosport he lost the sight of his right eye.* On his father's death, therefore, he was apprenticed to his father's former shopman, Samuel Highley, who continued the business under the supervision of his mother. On her remarriage a year later to Captain Henry Paget, a co-partnership was formed between Murray and Highley, which was dissolved at Murray's desire in 1803. Thereafter he built up the business by himself, following his own preference for literature, history, travels and memoirs, establishing links in Edinburgh with Ballantyne, Blackwood, and Constable – for whom he published six numbers of the *Edinburgh Review* (X, xix [April 1807] to XII, xxiv [July 1808]), and eventually setting up the *Quarterly Review* in 1808. In 1807 he married Anne Elliot, the daughter of an Edinburgh publisher, Charles Elliot. Their first child, the future John Murray III, was born the following year.

---

* It is much to Murray's credit that he never once complains of the loss of his eye, nor does he allude to it in his correspondence with Byron. Neither does Byron in his correspondence with him – though he does on three occasions in his correspondence with others, but then only very tangentially and with no cruel intent (he would never taunt another with their infirmity). Writing to Kinnaird on 13 September 1821 in connection with his copyright negotiations with Murray, he quotes (incorrectly) two lines from *Paradise Lost* (II, 943–44) and continues, 'Follow the Arimaspian Murray – who seems as reluctant to part with "Gold" as the rest of his Nation' (*BLJ* VIII, 208; by 'Nation' Byron means Scotland). The Arimaspians were a one-eyed tribe from the far north of Scythia who warred with the griffins over the gold they guarded (Herodotus, *Histories*, III, 116 and IV, 27). The allusion therefore – however appropriate perhaps – is directed less at Murray's one-sightedness than at what Byron then considered to be his greediness and meanness in his financial dealings with him. Similar allusions in two later letters – to Moore of 28 October 1821, and to Procter of 5 March 1823 – continue the same piece of spleen (*BLJ* VIII, 250 and X, 116).

3. See the Rev. Thomas Frognall Dibdin, *Bibliomania* (1811), 405–07.

4. For the founding and subsequent history of the *Quarterly Review*, see Samuel Smiles, *A Publisher and His Friends: Memoir and Correspondence of the late John Murray*, 2 vols, 2nd edn (London: John Murray, 1891), I, 91–204; John O. Hayden, *The Romantic Reviewers 1802–1824* (London: Routledge & Kegan Paul, 1969), 22–38; Roy Benjamin Clark, *William Gifford: Tory Satirist, Critic, and Editor* (New York: 1930); and Hill Shine and Helen Chadwick Shine, *The Quarterly Review Under Gifford: Identification of Contributors 1809–1824* (Chapel Hill: University of North Carolina Press, 1949). I will merely add that the first six numbers (I, i [February 1809] to III, vi [May 1810]) were published in conjunction with John Ballantyne, the next 18 (IV, vii [August 1810] to XII, xxiv [January 1815]) with William Blackwood; and thereafter (from XIII, xxv [April 1815] onwards), Murray was the sole publisher.

5. See Ben Harris McClary, ed., *Washington Irving and the House of Murray* (Knoxville: University of Tennessee Press, 1969), 3–9; see also, Crabbe's Journal entry for 30 June 1817 (Thomas C. Faulkner, ed., *Selected Letters and Journals of George Crabbe* [Oxford: Clarendon Press, 1985], 211), and Mrs Bray's account of her visit in the autumn of 1819 (John A. Kempe, ed., *Autobiography of Anna Eliza Bray* [London: Chapman and Hall, 1884], 145–47).

6. See John Ruskin, *Praeterita: The Autobiography of John Ruskin* (Oxford: Oxford University Press, 1978), 136–38.

Editorial Introduction

This edition collects together for the first time all John Murray's extant letters to Byron. Apart from one or two, printed not always very accurately by Smiles in his *Memoir* of John Murray, none of these letters has been published before.

Text and Notes

Unless otherwise stated, the manuscripts of these letters are in the Murray Archives (MA), now lodged in the National Library of Scotland, Edinburgh. Wherever this is not the case, or where no original manuscript survives, I have stated the present location or the source of the text in the headnote to the letter concerned.

All letters are so designated even though many, particularly those written to Byron while he was in England, are merely brief communications or covering notes accompanying proofs, books or some other enclosure (such as another correspondent's letter).

Each letter is preceded by the day, date, month and year in full, whether or not Murray himself has supplied these (those parts not supplied by him being placed within square brackets), and at the head of the notes to each letter, where extant, the cover direction (<u>Cover</u>), postmark (<u>pm</u>) and date of arrival (<u>arrived</u>). Conjectural datings are enclosed within square brackets with a question mark and are stated to be so conjectured in the headnote to the relevant letter.

I have reproduced the text of each letter exactly as Murray wrote it – punctuation (or lack of it), misspellings, inconsistent use of upper or lower case, and other idiosyncrasies. All deletions are enclosed within angle brackets (<>) and are retained within the body of the letter rather than relegated to an apparatus at the foot of the page. All <u>underlinings</u> appear as such in both Murray's letters and other manuscript sources quoted in the notes. Any query or other detail arising from textual matters I have endeavoured to cover in the Notes.

The Notes follow each letter. I am aware that these are somewhat extensive in places, and I hope they do not prove an encumbrance. My aim has been to provide the reader with as much information as possible for appreciating each letter in its fullest context and in that of the continuing dialogue between Murray and Byron, to whom I refer hereinafter as JM and B respectively. I have tried to illuminate obscurities and identify references, and have quoted freely from Byron's letters and from contemporary documents and other sources both published and unpublished. Many letters from other correspondents and several new letters or fragments of letters of Byron's will also be found in the Notes, and I have taken the opportunity to correct any errors I have come across that have crept into the Byron corpus elsewhere (including my own).

The letters fall naturally into two periods: those written to Byron while he was in England (1811–16), and those written to him when abroad (1816–22). To signal this, I have divided the volume into Part I and Part II. Regrettably, many of Murray's letters to Byron have been lost or destroyed, and there are at least two major gaps in the correspondence in Part II. Where these occur, I have attempted to reconstruct from available material what took place in the interim and have assembled the information as an 'Interim Note' between the last surviving letter and the next.

In the Appendices will be found a brief note on how Murray became Byron's publisher (Appendix A), the newspaper attacks on Byron in February 1814 following the publication of *The Corsair* (with 'Lines to a Lady Weeping') (Appendix B), and Byron's book Sale Catalogue of 1813, a rare copy of which is in the Murray Archives (Appendix C).

Forgeries

I have come across no forgery of a Murray letter. Amongst Byron's letters, however, there are two printed in *BLJ* that are forgeries. The first is '[To John Murray (*a*)]', dated '*Decr. ye. 14th. 1813*', printed in *BLJ* III, 197. The manuscript of this letter is in the Murray Archives and is written in three different styles of handwriting as if as a joke (a very ill-timed one too). This is almost certainly the work of Major Byron. The second is to Douglas Kinnaird, dated 'Pisa – March 15th. 1822', printed in *BLJ* XIII, 59–60. The manuscript of this letter is in the Rauner Special Collections Library at Dartmouth College, Hanover, New Hampshire, USA, and is by Major Byron. (It is curious that this was allowed to enter the canon when it had already been listed as a forgery in *BLJ* IX, 230.)

Abbreviations

BB	*Byron's Bulldog: The Letters of John Cam Hobhouse to Lord Byron*, ed. Peter W. Graham (Columbus: Ohio State University Press, 1984)
BL	The British Library (followed by the catalogue or manuscript number)
BLJ	*The Letters and Journals of Lord Byron*, ed. Leslie A. Marchard, 13 vols (London: John Murray, 1973–94)
Bodleian	The Bodleian Library, Oxford (followed by the name of the Deposit: Lovelace Byron)
Byron's Life and Works	*The Works of Lord Byron: with His Letters and Journals, and His Life by Thomas Moore* [ed. John Wright], 17 vols (London: John Murray, 1832–33)
CHP	*Childe Harold's Pilgrimage*
CMP	*Lord Byron: The Complete Miscellaneous Prose*, ed. Andrew Nicholson (Oxford: Clarendon Press, 1991)
Coleridge	*The Works of Lord Byron: A New, Revised and Enlarged Edition, with illustrations. Poetry*, ed. Ernest Hartley Coleridge, 7 vols (London: John Murray, 1898–1904)
CPW	*Lord Byron: The Complete Poetical Works*, ed. Jerome J. McGann, 7 vols (Oxford: Clarendon Press, 1980–93)
Dallas, *Correspondence*	R. C. Dallas, *Correspondence of Lord Byron with a Friend*, 3 vols (Paris: A & W. Galignani, 1825)
Dallas, *Recollections*	R. C. Dallas, *Recollections of the Life of Lord Byron* (London: Charles Knight, 1824)
Dep. Lovelace Byron	The Lovelace Byron Deposit at the Bodleian Library, Oxford
DJ	*Don Juan*

EBSR   *English Bards and Scotch Reviewers*

Hobhouse,   John Cam Hobhouse (Lord Broughton), *Recollections of*
   Recollections   *a Long Life*, ed. Lady Dorchester (his daughter), 6 vols
                    (London: John Murray, 1909–11)

LBLI   Teresa Guiccioli, *Lord Byron's Life in Italy (Vie de Lord*
                    Byron en Italie), trans Michael Rees, ed. Peter Cochran
                    (Newark: University of Delaware Press, 2005)

LLLM   *Byron's "Corbeau Blanc": The Life and Letters of Lady*
                    Melbourne, ed. Jonathan David Gross (Houston: Rice
                    University Press, 1997)

Lockhart, *Life of*   J. G. Lockhart, *The Life of Sir Walter Scott, Bart*, New
   Scott   Popular Edition (London: Adam & Charles Black, 1893)

MA   The Murray Archives at the National Library of
                    Scotland, Edinburgh

Marchand   Leslie A. Marchand, *Byron: A Biography*, 3 vols (London:
                    John Murray, 1957)

Medwin,   *Medwin's Conversations of Lord Byron*, ed. Ernest J. Lovell,
   Conversations   Jr (Princeton: Princeton University Press, 1966)

Moore, *Journal*   *The Journal of Thomas Moore*, ed. Wilfred S. Dowden, 6
                    vols (Newark: University of Delaware Press, 1983–91)

Moore, *Letters*   *The Letters of Thomas Moore*, ed. Wilfred S. Dowden, 2
                    vols (Oxford: Clarendon Press, 1964)

Prothero   *The Works of Lord Byron: A New, Revised and Enlarged*
                    Edition, with illustrations. Letters and Journals, ed. Rowland
                    E. Prothero, 6 vols (London: John Murray, 1898–1901)

Scott, *Letters*   *The Letters of Sir Walter Scott*, ed. H. J. C. Grierson, 12
                    vols (London: Constable, 1932–37)

Shelley, *Letters*   *The Letters of Percy Bysshe Shelley*, ed. Frederick L. Jones,
                    2 vols (Oxford: Clarendon Press, 1964)

Smiles   Samuel Smiles, *A Publisher and His Friends: Memoir and*
                    Correspondence of the late John Murray, with An Account
                    of the Origin and Progress of the House, 1768–1843, 2 vols,
                    2nd edn (London: John Murray, 1891)

Wise   T. J. Wise, *A Bibliography of the Writings in Verse and Prose*
                    of George Gordon Noel, Baron Byron, 2 vols (London:
                    Printed for Private Circulation Only, 1932–33)

Chronology

1811   14 July: B returns from Greece with *Childe Harold* I and II, *Hints from Horace* and *The Curse of Minerva*; puts up at Reddish's Hotel, St James's Street.

1 August: B's mother dies.

2 August: B goes down to Newstead, having placed *Childe Harold* I and II in Dallas's hands.

21 August: B accepts Dallas's offer to mediate between himself and JM.

23 August: B writes first letter to JM.

5 September: JM writes first letter to B.

28 October: B returns to town; lodgings at 8 St James's Street.

4 November: B dines with Rogers, Moore and Campbell.

19 December: B at Newstead with Frances Hodgson and William Harness.

1812   11 January: B returns to London.

27 February: B's Maiden Speech in House of Lords ('Frame Work Bill Speech').

10 March: *Childe Harold* I and II published.

April: B's liaison with Lady Caroline Lamb begins.

21 April: B's second Speech in House of Lords ('Roman Catholic Claims Speech').

June: B introduced to the Prince Regent; B calls on JM at 32 Fleet Street (first known meeting).

August–October: B in Cheltenham.

10 October: B's 'Address' delivered at the opening of the Drury Lane Theatre.

23 October: B's 'Parenthetical Address' printed in *Morning Chronicle*.

24 October: B visits the Oxfords at Eywood, near Presteign.

October–November: JM removes from 32 Fleet Street to 50 Albemarle Street.

21 November: B returns to Cheltenham.

24–30 November: B at Middleton, Oxford, with the Jerseys.

30 November: B returns to London; puts up at Batt's Hotel.

December: B at Eywood with the Oxfords.

1813   19 January: B returns to London; takes lodgings at 4 Bennet Street, St James's, Piccadilly.

May: JM becomes bookseller to the Admiralty and Board of Longitude.

June: Madame de Staël arrives in England (stays until May 1814).

1 June: B's final Speech in House of Lords ('Presentation of Major Cartwright's Petition').

5 June: *The Giaour* published.

11 September: 5th edn of *The Giaour* published.

2 December: *The Bride of Abydos* published.

1814   January–February: B at Newstead with Augusta.

1 February: *The Corsair* and the 7th edn of *Childe Harold* I and II published.

28 March: B moves into Albany, Piccadilly.

9 April: News of Napoleon's abdication received in England.

16 April: *Ode to Napoleon Buonaparte* published.

July–August: B at Hastings with Augusta.

August: Claughton forfeits Newstead.

6 August: *Lara* and Rogers' *Jacqueline* published together.

August–September: B at Newstead with Augusta.

9 September: B proposes to Annabella.

18 September: B receives Annabella's acceptance.

23 September: B returns to London.

October: JM visits Newstead on way to Edinburgh.

29 October: B leaves for Seaham to visit Annabella.

30 October: JM returns from Edinburgh.

24 November: B returns to London.

24 December: B leaves London to be married at Seaham.

1815   2 January: B married at Seaham.

29 March: B and Annabella at 13 Piccadilly Terrace.

5 April: *A Selection of Hebrew Melodies* published by Nathan.

7 April: B and Scott meet at JM's.

May: *Hebrew Melodies* published by JM; B appointed to the Sub-Committee of Management of Drury Lane Theatre.

7 June: JM mugged on return from Stoke Newington.

18 June: Napoleon defeated at Waterloo.

14 July–8 August: JM visits Paris.

November: Bailiffs enter 13 Piccadilly Terrace.

10 December: B's daughter, Augusta Ada, born.

1816   15 January: Annabella leaves for Kirkby Mallory, Leicestershire, with Ada; B remains in London. They never meet again.

2 February: B receives Sir Ralph Milbanke's proposal for an amicable separation.

13 February: *The Siege of Corinth* and *Parisina* published together.

4 April: 'A Sketch from Private Life' privately printed.

5–6 April: B's library sold at auction.

8 April: 'Fare Thee Well' privately printed.

21 April: B signs Deed of Separation.

23 April: B leaves London for the Continent accompanied by Dr John Polidori.

June–October: B at Diodati; Shelley, Mary and Claire Clairmont nearby at Montalègre.

26 August: Hobhouse and Scrope Davies join B at Diodati.

28 August: Shelley, Mary and Claire return to England with Claire Clairmont's fair copy of *Childe Harold* III, and with *The Prisoner of Chillon*, 'Darkness', 'The Dream' and 'Prometheus'.

5 September: Scrope Davies returns to England with B's fair copy of *Childe Harold* III.

10 November: B and Hobhouse arrive at Venice.

18 November: *Childe Harold* III published.

5 December: *The Prisoner of Chillon and Other Poems* published.

1817   April: Polidori returns to England.

February–March: B sends *Manfred*.

17 April: B leaves for Rome.

23 April: B sends *The Lament of Tasso*.

5 May: B sends revised Act III of *Manfred*.

28 May: B returns to Venice.

6 June: *Manfred* published.

17 July: *The Lament of Tasso* published.

August: Madame de Staël dies in Paris.

19–27 September: the Kinnairds and Rose visit B and Hobhouse in Venice.

1818   8 January: Hobhouse returns to England with *Childe Harold* IV.

19 January: B sends *Beppo*.

24 February: *Beppo* published.

28 April: *Childe Harold* IV published.

August: JM takes share in *Blackwood's Edinburgh Magazine*.

11 November: Hanson arrives in Venice.

26 December: Lauderdale delivers *Don Juan* I, *Mazeppa* and *Ode on Venice* to JM.

1819   January: JM pulls out of *Blackwood's Edinburgh Magazine*.

2–3 April: B meets Teresa (née Gamba), Countess Guiccioli.

3 April: B sends *Don Juan* II.

1 June: B leaves Venice to join the Guicciolis in Ravenna.

28 June: *Mazeppa* published.

15 July: *Don Juan* I and II published anonymously; JM at Wimbledon.

9 August: B follows the Guicciolis to Bologna.

16 August: Peterloo Massacre in Manchester.

23 August: B sends 'Letter to the Editor of the *British Review*'.

12 September: B leaves Bologna with Teresa for Venice.

7–11 October: Moore visits B in Venice; B gives him his Memoirs (written up to 1816 only).

13 December: Hobhouse in Newgate.

24 December: B returns to Ravenna to join the Guicciolis.

1820   29 January: George III dies.

February: B moves into the Palazzo Guiccioli.

19 February: B sends *Don Juan* III and IV.

28 February: B sends translation of *Morgante Maggiore*; Hobhouse released from Newgate.

14 March: B sends *The Prophecy of Dante*.

20 March: B sends 'Francesca of Rimini'.

28 March: B sends 'Some Observations upon an Article in *Blackwood's Edinburgh Magazine*'.

6 June: Queen Caroline arrives in London.

July: Neapolitan uprising.

July–August: B sends *Marino Faliero*.

August–November: Trial and acquittal of Queen Caroline.

9 December: Shooting of military Commandant of Ravenna.

28 December: B sends *Don Juan* V to Kinnaird.

1821   12 February: B sends *Letter to John Murray* (the Bowles/Pope Controversy).

31 March: *Letter to John Murray* published.

21 April: *Marino Faliero* and *The Prophecy of Dante* published together.

25 April: First performance of *The Doge of Venice* (*Marino Faliero*) at Drury Lane Theatre.

5 May: Napoleon dies at St Helena.

2 June: B sends *Sardanapalus*.

July: B promises Teresa to discontinue *Don Juan*; the Gambas banished from the Romagna.

14 July: B sends *The Two Foscari*.

19 July: Coronation of George IV.

7 August: Queen Caroline dies; *Don Juan* III–V published; B sends *The Blues*.

31 August: B receives *Don Juan* III–V; enraged by misprints; relations deteriorate.

10 September: B sends *Cain*.

4 October: B sends *The Vision of Judgment*.

29 October: B leaves Ravenna to join Teresa, the Gambas, and the Shelleys at Pisa.

1 November: B arrives in Pisa; residence at Casa Lanfranchi.

14 December: B sends *Heaven and Earth*.

19 December: *Sardanapalus*, *The Two Foscari* and *Cain* published together.

1822   January?: B resumes *Don Juan*.

28 January: Lady Noel, B's mother-in-law, dies; B takes name of Noel Byron.

29 January: B sends *Werner* to Moore in Paris.

24 March: The 'Pisan Affray' with Sergeant-Major Masi.

16 April: Moore arrives in London with *Werner*.

20 April: Death of Allegra.

July: Leigh Hunt and family arrive in Pisa.

8 July: Shelley and Williams drown in Bay of Spezia.

7 and 10 September: B sends *Don Juan* VI–IX to Kinnaird.

10 September: JM attends burial of Allegra at Harrow Church.

27 September: B leaves Pisa for Genoa.

October: B arrives in Genoa; residence at Casa Saluzzo, Albaro; JM refuses to publish *Don Juan* VI–IX.

15 October: The first number of *The Liberal* published, containing *The Vision of Judgment* (without the Preface) and 'Letter to the Editor of the *British Review*'.

8 November: JM's final letter.

22 November: *Werner* published.

Plate 1. John Murray II, by H. W. Pickersgill.
(*John Murray Collection*)

Plate 2. Byron, by Thomas Phillips, 1814.
(*John Murray Collection*)

Plate 3. Gifford, by W. H. Watts.
(*John Murray Collection*)

Plate 4. Thomas Moore, by Thomas Lawrence.
(*John Murray Collection*)

Plate 5. Scott by Stewart Newton.
(*John Murray Collection*)

Plate 6. Hookham Frere, engraving.
(*John Murray Collection*)

Plate 7. Croker sketch by J. Jackson, n.d.
(*John Murray Collection*)

Plate 8. Foscolo sketch by Febre.
(*John Murray Collection*)

Lord Byron and Sir Walter Scott at No 50 Albemarle Street, 1815.

Plate 9. Drawing room at 50 Albemarle Street.
(*John Murray Collection*)

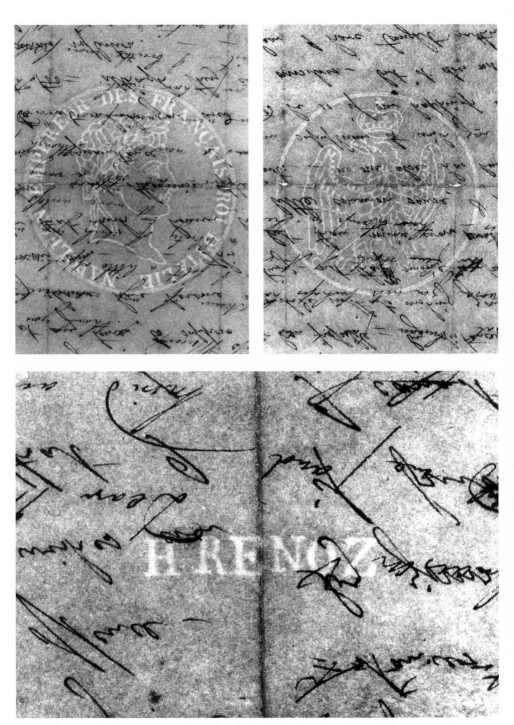

Plate 10. Writing paper with Napoleon watermark, on Byron's letter to Mercer Elphinstone, 11 April 1816. See Letter 73.

(*Private Collection*)

Plate 11. Waterloo spoils. See Letters 88, 92 and 94.
(*John Murray Collection*)

Plate 12. Skull Cup watercolour, n.d.
(*John Murray Collection*)

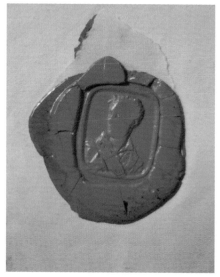

Plate 13. Wax seal based on Phillips' portrait of Byron, and used by John Murray on his letters to Byron in 1817. See Letter 106.
(*John Murray Collection*)

Wimbledon Common
July 16. 1819

My Lord

La Sort est jetée – Don Juan was published yesterday, and having fired the Bomb – here I am out of the way of its explosion – its publication has excited a very, very great degree of interest – public opinion & expectation having risen up like the surrounding breakers the Thames when a first rate is struck from its Stocks – as yet my Scouts & dispatches afford little clue to public opinion, it certainly does not appear, to be what they had chosen to anticipate a work of Satyre in which every man of note – it was hoped – would be abused – fathers forbid it their families – and its beauties, may not be talked about – but as soon as these breakings find their way in words & vent in news papers & reviews – by the Lord you shall have them all – that you may repel them & those who are calling every half hour, I understand – sorry that McMurray has had any thing to do with it" – To you I look for protection against all this, & for a mighty effort – and an early one too, that shall burst the fences of present disapprobation – and carry again the Castle of Admiration on which you have stood so long preeminent & alone – Gifford who never ceases his fatherly estimation of your Genius says that he has lived to see three men equally great in them and unequalled in their line – Pitt – Nelson – Wellington – & that you are – or were – or may yet be the fourth – if you will not entirely break the feelings of a nation which are yet entirely with you – as to hear thro' many the most minute particle of the least Tale – yet I rise & fall with it – & my interest in your soaring above the other Stars – & continuing to create wonder even in your aberrations – is past calculation – I wish you would let the

London March 7. 1820
Tuesday

My dear Lord (Kinnit)

   Your most kind and valuable packets, which have put fresh vigour, if not new life into me, arrived (4 in number) very safely half an hour ago. I am truly rejoiced in the receipt of them, these Cantos I shall announce instantly, & publish fearlesly. My eyes have scarced in to over for the pleasure of finding a Letter inclosed - but I shall look for this by the earliest post, in the mean time I shall send these two Cantos to the Printer. Probably you will tell me if we shall print the Translation from Pulci, with its facing Italian at the end of the Volume. × With regard to what your lordship says as to what was permitted in a Catholic & bigoted age to a Clergyman - I humbly conceive & am surprised that you do not perceive that - religion had nothing to do with it - It was Manners - and they have changed - as man might as coolly appear without Cloaths - and quite over Saxon Ancestors - The Comedies of Charles's Seconds days are not tolerated now - and even in my own times I have gradually seen my favourite Love for Love absolutely pushed by public feeling from the Stage - It is not affectation of morality but the real

× This would make a Volume of equal bulk with the former. The Prophecy is it come to hand?

369ª   Prothero   45   Ravenna. Septr 12th 1821.

Dear Sir/

     By Tuesday's post – I forwarded to you three packets – the drama of "Cain" in three acts – of which I request the acknowledgement when arrived. — — To the last speech of Eve in the last act (i.e. where she curses Cain) add these three lines, as the concluding ones. —

"May the Grass wither from thy feet! the Woods
"Deny thee shelter! Earth a home! the Dust
"A Grave! the Sun his light! and Heaven her God!

There is no prettier a piece of Imprecation for you, when joined to the lines already sent – as you may wish to meet with in the course of your business. — But don't forget the addition of the above three lines which are clinchers to Eve's speech. — — —

Let me know that Gifford thinks (if the new the piece as Poetry — it is in my way metaphysical style in the Manfred line. — yrs

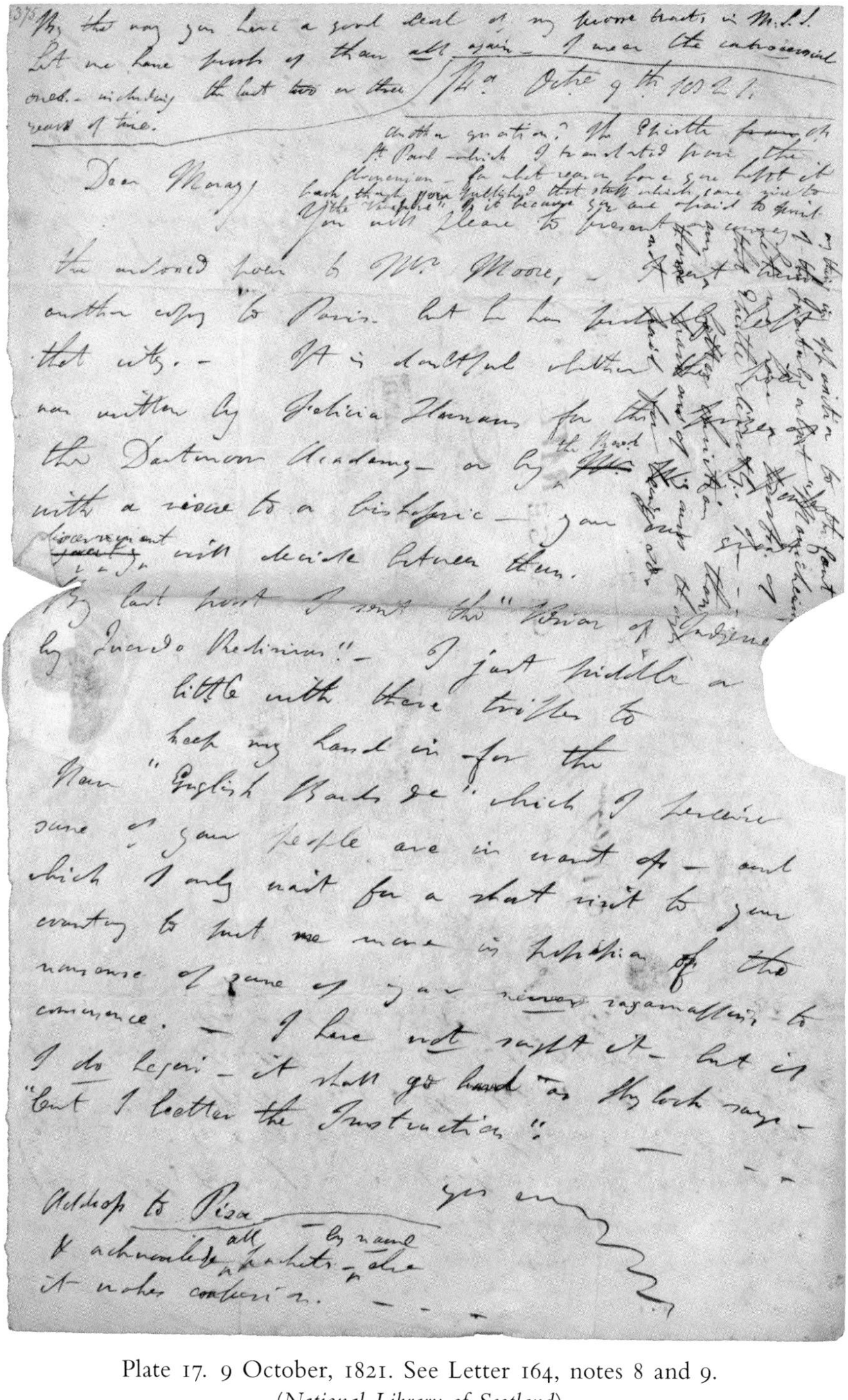

Pisa. Octr 9th 1821.

Dear Murray

The enclosed letter to Mr. Moore, —

Address to Pisa

Plate 17. 9 October, 1821. See Letter 164, notes 8 and 9.
(*National Library of Scotland*)

Plate 18. Westall watercolour illustration for *Don Juan*, Canto I, Stanza 181.
(*John Murray Collection*)

Letter 1) Wednesday 4 September 1811

London Sepr. 4. 1811
Wednesday

My Lord

An absence of some days passed in the country,[1] has prevented me from writing earlier in answer to your obliging Letter – I have now, however, the pleasure of sending under a separate cover, the first proof sheet of your Lordships Poem – which is so good as to be entitled to all your care to render perfect<ionate> – besides its general merits, there are parts, which I am tempted to believe, far excel anything that your Lordship has hitherto published, and it were therefore grievous indeed, if you do not condescend to bestow upon it, all the improvement of which your Lordships mind is so capable; every correction already made is valuable, and this circumstance renders me more confident in soliciting for it your further attention – There are some expressions too concerning Spain & Portugal – which however just, and particularly so at the time they were conceived, yet, as they do not harmonize with the general feeling, they would so greatly interfere with the popularity which the Poem is, in other respects, so certainly calculated to excite, that, in compassion to your publisher, who does not presume to reason upon the subject, otherwise than as a mere matter of business, I hope your Lordships goodness will induce you to obviate them – and, with them, perhaps, some religious feelings which may deprive me of some customers amongst the <u>Orthodox</u>[2] – could I flatter myself that these suggestions were not obtrusive I would hazard another, in an earnest solicitation that your Lordship would add the two promissed Cantos,[3] – and complete the Poem – – it were cruel indeed not to perfect a work which contains so much that is excellent – your Fame my Lord demands it – you are raising a Monument that will outlive your present feelings,[4] and it should therefore be so constructed as to excite no other associations than those of respect and admiration for your Lordships Character and Genius.

I trust that you will pardon the warmth of this address, when I assure your Lordship that it arises, in the greatest degree, in a sincere regard for your lasting reputation, with, however, some view to that portion of it, which must attend the Publisher of so beautiful a Poem, as your Lordship is capable of rendering,

"The Romaunt of Childe Harold."[5]

I have the honour to be, My Lord,
your Lordships
obedient and faithful Servant.
John Murray

Notes to Letter 1)

In his very first letter to JM, written from Newstead on Friday 23 August 1811, B told him that he had heard from Dallas that JM was willing to publish the first two Cantos of *CHP*, which Dallas had placed in his hands at the beginning of the month, but that he also intended showing the manuscript to Gifford – to which B strongly objected, regarding it as 'a kind of petition for praise' (*BLJ* II, 78). However, his objection went unheeded and JM avoids alluding to it here. Indeed, by this time Gifford had apparently already seen the manuscript, and the culprit for his having had occasion to do so looks suspiciously like Dallas who wrote to B on Thursday 5 September:

> I saw Murray yesterday – if he has adhered to his intention you will receive a proof of "Childe Harold's Pilgrimage" before this letter. I am delighted with its appearance. Allowing you to be susceptible of the pleasure of genuine praise you would have had a fine treat could you have been in the room, with Gyges's ring on your finger, while we were discussing the publication of the Poem, not perhaps from what I or Mr Murray said, but from what he reported to have been said by <u>Aristarchus</u> [i.e., Gifford], into whose hands "the childe" had somehow fallen, between the time of Murray's absence and return. This happening unknown to you, and indeed contrary to your intention, removes every idea of courting applause; but it is not a little gratifying to me to know that what struck me on the first perusal to be admirable has also forcibly struck M^r. Gifford – Of your Satire [*EBSR*] he spoke highly, but this Poem he pronounces not only the best you have written, but equal to any of the present age, allowing however for its being unfinished, which he regrets. Murray assured me that he expressed himself very warmly. With the <u>fiat</u> of such a judge will not your Muse be kindled to the completion of a work that would if completed irrevocably fix your fame? In your short preface you talk of adding concluding cantos if encouraged by public approbation – This is no longer necessary, if Gifford approves, who shall disapprove? or what disapprover be cared for? (MA; cf. Dallas, *Correspondence*, II, 91–92)

1. Where exactly JM had gone to I have been unable to discover; perhaps to Brighton with the D'Israelis, or to Chichester where his mother lived – his usual venues at this time of year. In a letter to B of Monday 26 August, Dallas had told him: 'I went to town on Saturday [24 August] and hoped to have arranged all particulars relative to Childe Harold with Murray – I was rather disappointed on finding that he had left London, and was to be absent ten days or a fortnight', but he does not say where (MA).

2. In his reply of Thursday 5 September, B accepted JM's 'compliments', but refused to alter 'the political & metaphysical parts' of the poem or to recant his views on 'Spanish affairs'; and he added: 'As for the "*Orthodox*" let us hope they will buy on purpose to abuse, you will forgive the one if they will do the other' (*BLJ* II, 90–91). The use of the word 'Orthodox' in fact originates with B who told Dallas on Tuesday 21 August: 'I fear Murray will be in a Scrape with the Orthodox, but I cannot help it, though I wish him well through it' (ibid., 76, 'him' omitted; corr. Dallas, *Correspondence*, II, 79, *Byron's Life and Works* II, 53 and Prothero, I, 336).

3. In his letter of Friday 23 August, B had not 'promised' two further Cantos, but had said that if JM determined on publication he would add 'some smaller poems (never published) a few notes, & a short dissertation on the Literature of the modern Greeks (written at Athens)' which would 'come in at the end of the volume' (*BLJ* II, 78). He reiterated this in his reply of Thursday 5 September, and added: 'You tell me to add 2 Cantos, but I am about to visit my *Collieries* in Lancashire on the 15th. Inst. which is so *unpoetical* an employment that I need say no more' (*BLJ* II, 91). However, in his Preface to the first two Cantos B had intimated that the public's reception of them would determine whether he would proceed further in the poem (*CPW* II, 3).

4. JM glances at Horace, *Odes* III, xxx, 1: 'Exegi monumentum aere perennius' (I have finished a monument more lasting than bronze). However, he may very well have in mind more nearly the climactic conclusion to the series of reviews of Gibbon's *Decline and Fall* in the *Critical Review*, LXVII (March 1789), p. 182: 'We must now leave this vast work, and rest from our labours, with a consciousness of having discriminated the merits and defects of the historian with a steady and impartial hand. He has erected a monument to his fame, which will be probably as durable as the English language; and, if empire, as has been predicted, shall travel westward, he may, after intestine wars, and another period of barbarian darkness, be rescued from oblivion, and received by a very distant age, as another Livy, unexpectedly recovered, and proportionally prized; as an author who could render the dark annals of a rude age interesting, and add a lustre even to the classical elegance of the most refined æra.'

5. The first two editions of *CHP* I and II were entitled *Childe Harold's Pilgrimage. A Romaunt*. For full details of the background and publication of the poem,

see *CPW* II, 265–71; see also, *The Manuscripts of the Younger Romantics. Lord Byron. Volume VI. Childe Harold's Pilgrimage: A Critical, Composite Edition*, eds. David V. Erdman and David Worrall (New York & London: Garland Publishing, 1991). There are, however, three documents relating to the copyright agreement between B, JM and Dallas in MA. The first is a copy in JM's hand of a letter to him from B dated Tuesday 17 March 1812:

> Sir
>   I desire that you will settle any account for Childe Harold with Mr R. C. Dallas to whom I have presented the Copy Right
> yr. obedt. Servt.
> Byron
> To Mr John Murray
> Bookseller
> 32 Fleet Street
> London Mar 17 – 1812

The second is a receipt, dated Wednesday 1 April 1812, written in Dallas's hand:

> Received April 1st. 1812 of Mr. John Murray the sum of One Hundred & One pounds 15/8 – being my entire half share of the profits of the 1st. Edition of Childe Harolds Pilgrimage 4to
>
> RC Dallas –
>
> £101 – 15 – 8   Mem: This Receipt is for the above Sum in part
> of five hundred Guineas agreed to be paid by
> Mr Murray for the Copyright of Childe Harold's
> Pilgrimage –
>
> RC Dallas –

The third is the Copyright agreement, dated Monday 6 April 1812, which is written in JM's hand and signed by himself and Dallas:

> Mr Murray agrees to pay to R. C. Dallas Esqr the Sum of Five Hundred Guineas for the entire & perpetual Copy Right of Childe Harold's Pilgrimage & such other Poems as <may be> are included in the 4to Edition and in the first 8vo Edition by Lord Byron & the said R.C. Dallas Esqr agrees to accept the same
>
> John Murray
> RC Dallas –
>
> Fleet Street,
> London
> April 6th. 1812.

Interim Note

Although B wrote again on 14 September, remonstrating with JM for having shown the MS of *CHP* I and II to Gifford, and on 16 September returned him 'the proof',[1] he had still 'heard nothing of Murray' after his return from Lancashire in early October, though he subsequently learnt he was 'making a tour in Middlesex'.[2] Thereafter and for the remainder of the year he moved between London, Newstead and Cambridge; and apart from four brief letters to JM in mid-1812, there is no further correspondence between them extant until almost exactly a year later.[3] By the time their correspondence resumes, *CHP* I and II had been published (10 March 1812); B had become famous overnight and was moving much in Society; his liaison with Lady Caroline Lamb had blazed and burnt out; Newstead had been put up for sale, and Thomas Claughton had made an offer which he was eventually unable to honour.

In the interim, however, JM and B had certainly met each other personally – at least on one occasion at some point during the week commencing Sunday 21 June 1812. For, writing to Scott on Saturday 27 June 1812, JM told him that B had been to 'an evening party at Miss Johnson's [*sic*] – this week' at which the Prince Regent was present and to whom he had been introduced.[4] They had conversed 'for more than ½ an hour' on poetry and poets, in the course of which the Prince had expressed his particular admiration for Scott whom 'he preferred ... far beyond every [*sic*] other poet of the time': 'Lord B called on me, merely to lett of [*sic*] the raptures of the Prince respecting you, thinking as he said, if I were likely to have occasion to write to you that it might not be ungrateful for you to hear'.[5] The news was certainly not 'ungrateful' for Scott to hear: it elicited a grateful reply from him to JM enclosing a gracious letter for B which prompted their subsequent correspondence and friendship.[6]

Notes

1. *BLJ* II, 98–99 and 100.

2. B to Dallas, 26 September and 11 October 1811, and to Hodgson, 13 October 1811 (*BLJ* II, 107, 111 and 113).

3. In fact, only three: letters (a) and (b), conjecturally dated May 1812 (*BLJ* II, 174), and the letter misdated 12 June 1812 in the text, but correctly dated 20 June 1812 in the Sources, enclosing 'a corrected copy of some lines already sent ... with directions where to insert them' (*BLJ* XIII, 22 and 93; MS Pforzheimer Library), which almost certainly concerns the 4th edn of *CHP* I and II which was announced in the *Monthly Literary Advertiser*, No. 88 (10 August 1812), 61. Letter (c), conjecturally dated May 1812 (*BLJ* II, 175), is in fact two letters belonging to 1814 (see Letter 34 below).

4. For further details of this meeting between the Prince and the Poet, see

Andrew Nicholson, 'Byron's Introduction to the Prince Regent in 1812',
The Byron Journal 34, 2 (2006), 147–54.

5. MA (Letter Books); cf. Smiles, I, 212–14: in addition to concocting an
   elaborate introduction to this letter, and reading 'every' as 'any', Smiles
   has amended 'lett of' to 'let off'; but 'tell of' might equally have been
   intended.

6. See Scott, *Letters*, III, 134–39; see also, *BLJ* II, 182–83.

Letter 2   Monday 7 September 1812

London Sep[r]. 7th. 1812
Monday

My Lord

I had the honour of receiving a letter from you this day, and by the
Mail, I have sent,

> 2 Letters
> 2 Parcels
> 2 Reviews[1]

M[r] Ridgway assures me that it is impossible to complete a Copy of the
new Edition of Adair on Diet before tomorrow or the day following.[2]
I have written to M[r] Thomson in obedience to your Lordships
wishes[3] –

The tardy Engraver promises the portrait in ten days,[4] and I shall
do myself the pleasure of sending a copy, for your Lordships remarks,
before it is prefixed to the Poem;[5] – the demand for which, proceeds
with undiminished vigour – I have now sold, within, a few copies of
Four Thousand, Five Hundred – and, in less than six months – a sale so
unprecedented, except in one instance,[6] that your Lordship should cease
to reproach the public and the publisher for "tardy editions"[7] – Your
Lordship will readily believe that I am delighted to find you thinking
upon a new Poem, for which I should be proud to give A Thousand
Guineas – and I should ever gratefully remember the fame it would
cast over my new establishment, upon which I enter at the close of the
present month[8] –

Since I had the pleasure of seeing your Lordship[9] I have had occasion
to visit Lucien Bonaparte, to make arrangements for <u>his</u> Poem, which,
with the translation will form Two Volumes in Quarto, and which I am
to publish immediately, if his brother will permit its circulation on the
Continent – Lucien is commanding and interesting in his person and

address[10] –

Walter Scott, has, I am informed my Lord, by his intimate friend M[r] Heber,[11] retained very closely the <u>subject</u> of his new Poem,[12] which is perhaps not impolitic, – the name of Rokeby is that of his friend M[r] Morritt's (who had the dispute with Briant about the Troad)[13] estate in Yorkshire, to whom it is no doubt intended as a compliment – The poem, a letter from the publisher this day, informs me, will not be published before Christmas –

Indeed my Lord I hope that you will cut the tugging strings of care and allow your mind to soar into its congenial element of Poesy

From a delirious Earth avert thine eyes
And dry thy fruitless tears, and seek fictitious Skies.

<u>D Israeli</u>[14]

Your Lordship will easily conceive my contempt for any thing in the Anti Jacobin Review when I venture to send you their vituperative criticism without previous<l> notice[15] –

I am ashamed to see how long I may have trespassed upon your Lordships patience –

I am ever My Lord
your faithful humble Servant
John Murray

Notes to Letter 2)

B had arrived in Cheltenham for an extended stay on 23 August 1812. Writing from thence on Saturday 5 September, he had acknowledged a letter (not extant) of 'enquiries' from JM concerning his health, and had asked him (clearly in response to JM's having mentioned them in his letter) 'to send those dispatches & a No. of the E[dinburgh] R[eview] with the rest' (*BLJ* II, 190, 'those' misread 'these'; corr. MS MA). He hoped JM had 'written to Mr. Thompson [*sic*]', thanking him 'for his present' and telling him he would be 'truly happy to comply with his request', and had enquired after his 'graven image "with *bays & wicked rhyme upon't*"', which were 'to grace or disgrace some of our tardy editions' (ibid., 190–91, quoting Butler, *Hudibras*, Pt I, I, 656). He had requested *Rokeby*, querying 'who the deuce is he?' (referring to the title, *not* the author of the poem), and closed by asking, 'What will you give *me* or *mine* for a poem of 6 Cantos (*when complete …*) … ?' (ibid., 191). (Although *The Giaour* – not in Cantos but 'disjointed fragments' [*CPW* III, 39] – may indeed have been gestating at this period [see ibid., 413], this last question is in part a jest, each of Scott's three major poems – *The Lay of the Last Minstrel* [1805], *Marmion* [1808] and *The Lady of the Lake* [1810] – as well as his new poem *Rokeby*, being designated 'A Poem in Six Cantos' [cf. also, *DJ* III, 86]. Moreover, rumours were in circulation as to the remuneration Scott was to receive for *Rokeby*; for instance *The Gentleman's Magazine*, LXXXII, Pt II

[October 1812], 344, reported: 'Mr. WALTER SCOTT has a poem in six cantos in the press, called "ROKEBY," for the copy-right of which his publishers have agreed to give him three thousand guineas. Excepting the travels edited by Dr. Hawkesworth, for which six thousand guineas were paid, instances of so liberal a price for a work of any kind in English literature can very rarely be produced.') In the postscript to his letter B added: 'Send me Adair on Diet & regimen just republished by Ridgway' (*BLJ* II, 191).

1. In his reply of Monday 14 September B told JM that the parcels

> contained some letters & verses all (but one) anonymous & compli-
> mentary and very anxious for my conversion from certain infidelities
> into which my goodnatured correspondents conceive me to have
> fallen. – The Books were presents of a <u>convertible</u> kind also,
> "Christian Knowledge" & the "Bioscope" a religious dial<,> of life
> explained. To the author of the former (Cadell publisher) I beg you
> will forward my best thanks for his letter, his present, & above all,
> his good intentions. – The "Bioscope" contained an M.S.S. copy
> of very excellent verses, from whom I know not, but evidently the
> composition of some one in the habits of writing & of writing well,
> I do not know if he be yͤ. author of the "Bioscope" which accom-
> panied them, <wh> but whoever he is if you can discover him,
> thank him from me most heartily (text from MS [MA]; cf. *BLJ* II,
> 196–97).

The first of these items was *Christian Knowledge* (1795), which appears as part of lot 247 in B's Sale Catalogue (1813) (see Appendix C; it does not appear in his later Sale Catalogues), but of which I have been unable to trace a copy. Fortunately, however, it was reviewed in the *Monthly Review*, XVIII (October 1795), p. 232, its full title being there given as: '*Christian Knowledge*, in a Series of Theological Extracts and Abridgments; affection-ately addressed to Philosophical Deists, Socinians, Christians, and Jews. By a Lover of true Philosophy. Volume the First. 8vo. pp. 400. 6s. Boards. Cadell jun. and Davies. 1795.' The reviewer observed that the extracts 'in defence of religion, contained in this volume, are chiefly made from three works long ago published' ('a learned introduction to a book entitled Horæ Solitariæ', 'Dr. Scott's Christian Life', and 'Stackhouse's History of the Bible'), and concluded: 'The Editor's intention is laudable; but we have our doubts whether these extracts will engage the attention of many readers, who are not already inclined to study the subjects in the original authors; and to such as *are*, abridgments of this kind are of little use.' The second item was *The Bioscope, or Dial of Life, Explained. To which is added, a Translation of St. Paulinus's Epistle to Celantia, on the Rule of Christian Life: and an Elementary View of General Chronology; with a Perpetual Solar and Lunar Calendar.* By the Author of 'The Christian Survey', &c., which was published by William Miller in June 1812 (a slip case containing the Bioscope itself, engraved by Charles Heath, accompanied the volume; the second edition was published by JM in 1814). The author was Granville Penn, F.S.A. (1761–1844), of Stoke Park, Colnbroke in Buckinghamshire, son of the Hon. Thomas Penn and grandson of William Penn, the founder of Pennsylvania. His *A Christian's Survey of all the Primary Events and Periods of the World; from the Commencement of History, to the Conclusion of Prophecy* was published without his name by William Miller in 1811 (a second, corrected and improved edition with his name appeared in 1812; the third edition was published by JM in 1814). He was indeed the writer of the 'excellent verses' (16 Spenserian stanzas entitled 'To Harold' exhorting him in a very charitable manner to have faith), the manuscript of which is in MA, and the following year sent B and JM a printed copy of them each. His letter accompanying the copy to B, expressing his pleasure of having met him at JM's, is dated 4 June 1813 from Tunbridge Wells and is in the Bodleian (Dep. Lovelace Byron 155, f. 112). His letter accompanying the copy to JM, and asking him to thank B for having sent him a copy of *The Giaour* (1813), is dated 24 June 1813 from Tunbridge Wells and is in MA. The poem itself, 'To Harold' (dated Stoke Park, September 1812), eventually appeared in Penn's anonymous *Original Lines, and Translations*, published by JM in 1815 (pp. 15–27), with a generous acknowledgement to B for the 'kind and courteous manner' in which he had received the lines 'from a stranger' (p. 17). One of the two 'Reviews' JM here mentions may have been the *Edinburgh Review*, XX, xxxix (July 1812), which was presumably the number B had requested in his letter of 5 September, but which contains nothing about him and to which he does not allude in his reply of 14 September. Otherwise, the two seem to have been the *Quarterly Review*, VII, xiii (March 1812), pp. 180–200 of which carried George Ellis's favourable though not uncensorious review of *CHP* I and II, and the *Antijacobin Review, and True Churchman's Magazine*, XLII, 170 (August 1812), pp. 343–65 of which carried a very unfavourable review, particularly of its religious views, of the 3rd edn of *CHP* I and II – to the latter of which JM refers more largely at the end of this Letter, and to both of which B refers in his reply of 14 September (*BLJ* II, 197; see also, n. 15 below).

2. James Ridgway (1745–1838), bookseller of Piccadilly, and 'well known pamphlet publisher', sentenced to four years imprisonment in 1793 for publishing Paine's *Rights of Man* (1792) and other anti-government pamphlets, also supplied B with his newspapers (*BLJ* II, 254; see also, C. H. Timperley, *Encyclopaedia of Literary and Typographical Anecdote*, 2 vols, 2nd edn [London, 1842], II, 953, and Joseph O. Baylen and Norbert J. Gossman, eds., *Biographical Dictionary of Modern British Radicals, Vol. I: 1770–1830* [1979], 409–10). B would have seen the following advertisement in the *Courier* (the only newspaper that carried it at that time) for Friday 4 September 1812: '*An Essay on Diet and Regimen, as indispensable to the Recovery and Enjoyment of strong, firm health; especially to the Studious, the Delicate, the Indolent, the Sedentary, and Invalid, with appropriate Cases; and an efficient Mode of Exercise for both Sexes*. By J. M. Adair, M.D. Printed for James Ridgway, Piccadilly, opposite Bond-street.' Although B reiterated his request in his reply to JM of 14 September 1812 (*BLJ* II,

197), and although the above advertisement was repeated in the *Morning Chronicle* for Monday 30 November 1812 and a year later in the same paper on Monday 18 October 1813, he does not appear to have received the work and it is not listed in the Sale Catalogues of his books: perhaps therefore it was never in fact republished. James Makittrick Adair (1728–1801) was a well-respected Scottish physician and dietician whose lively and anecdotal *Essay* was first published in Bath in 1786 under the title *Medical Cautions, for the consideration of Invalids; those especially who resort to Bath: Containing Essays on Fashionable Diseases; Dangerous Effects of Hot and Crowded Rooms; Regimen of Diet, &c.*, and was very favourably reviewed in the first John Murray's *English Review*, VI (May 1786), 348–51. The second edition appeared under the title *Essays on Fashionable Diseases. The Dangerous Effects of Hot and Crouded Rooms. The Cloathing of Invalids. Lady and Gentlemen Doctors. And on Quacks and Quackery* in 1790, and was again well reviewed in the *English Review*, XVI (November 1790), 337–41. Although Marchand records an 1804 edition under the above advertised title (*BLJ* II, 191n), the latest edition held in the BL that Ridgway sold is dated 1799 and entitled *An Essay on Regimen, for the Preservation of Health, especially of the Indolent, Studious, Delicate and Invalid; illustrated by Appropriate Cases.*

3. George Thomson (1757–1851), Clerk to the Board of Trustees for Manufactures and Improvements in Scotland and a close friend of Burns, was an amateur musician and collector of Scottish, Welsh and Irish airs, to whom we must be grateful for Beethoven's settings of B (see Barry Cooper, *Beethoven's Folksong Settings: Chronology, Sources, Style* [Oxford: Clarendon Press, 1994], esp. 69–71, 80–81 and 89–92, and J. Cuthbert Hadden, *George Thomson, The Friend of Burns: His Life and Correspondence* [London: Nimmo, 1898], esp. 187–93). His mode of procedure was to invite a poet (Burns, Scott, Joanna Baillie, William Smyth, B) to write the lyrics for an original folk melody, which he would then ask a composer (Pleyel, Kozeluch, Haydn, Beethoven) to harmonize. Emboldened by 'admiration of the lyric pieces in Childe Harold's pilgrimage', he had written to B care of JM on 10 July 1812, explaining that he spent his leisure hours 'in collecting the national Melodies, Scottish, Welsh, & Irish, worthy of preservation, and in getting Accompaniments composed for these by the greatest musical professors, and Songs written for them by the most distinguish'd Poets', but that 'in the concluding volume of the Scottish and Irish Collection, now in preparation', 'A few of the Melodies remain yet unprovided for, and if I could prevail on your Lordship to take three or four of them into favour, and to match them with congenial Verses, I would be the happiest of men'. And he concluded: 'In order that your Lordship may see that your name would not be discredited by appearing in my Work, I take the liberty to send a copy, and humbly <h> beg that you will be pleased to accept of it, even though you should deny me the great favour I am soliciting. I owe this tribute to your Lordship, for the exquisite pleasure I have had in perusing Childe Harold' (MA; for the 'copy' of the 'Work' Thomson sent, see *CMP*, 244, lots 369 and 370).

B did not eventually fulfil his undertaking (see Letter 3, n. 5, and Letter 35 below).

4. This was an engraving by Henry Meyer of George Sanders' portrait of B, which JM intended to prefix to the forthcoming edition of *CHP*, but to which (when finished) B strongly objected. See Letter 4 below.

5. The 4th edn of *CHP*, published on 14 September 1812 (*CPW* II, 269), now entitled (as with the 3rd and subsequent editions up to the 10th), *Childe Harold's Pilgrimage, A Romaunt: and Other Poems*. Its contents were the same as with edns 2 and 3, but with the addition of 'Addition to the Preface'.

6. This may be Mrs Maria Eliza Rundell's *A New System of Domestic Cookery, formed upon Principles of Economy, and adapted to the Use of Private Families. To which are prefixed Miscellaneous Observations for the Use of the Mistress of a Family. By a Lady*, which was first published by JM in 1805, and went through numerous editions, making it one of his most successful publications. Cf. B's Journal entry for Monday 13 December 1813: '"The *Harold* and *Cookery* are much wanted." Such is fame' (*BLJ* III, 238).

7. JM echoes B's 'tardy editions' in his letter to him of 5 September (*BLJ* II, 191; see headnote above).

8. For the 'new Poem', see the close of B's letter of 5 September (*BLJ* II, 191; see headnote above). At the beginning of October 1812 JM removed from 32 Fleet Street to 50 Albemarle Street where the firm remained until 2002 (see Letter 6 below). In his reply of 14 September, B acknowledged this information by remarking, 'in winter we shall be nearer neighbours' (*BLJ* II, 197).

9. Perhaps this refers to when B called on JM to tell him the Prince's opinion of Scott (see Interim Note above); otherwise, no other meeting is recorded or known.

10. Lucien Buonaparte (1775–1840), younger brother of Napoleon with whom he had quarrelled, had been captured by the English on his way to America and now lived in exile in England. JM did not in the event become the publisher of his epic poem *Charlemagne; ou l'Église Délivrée*, which was published by Longmans in 1814 (see Letter 12 below). In his reply B jocularly asked JM for 'a letter of introduction' to Lucien, questioning whether it was not 'somewhat treasonable' for JM to have dealings with him (*BLJ* II, 197).

11. Richard Heber (1773–1833), book collector and editor of editions of Persius (1790), Silius Italicus (1792) and Claudian (1793–96), was the half-brother of Reginald Heber (1783–1826), the future bishop of Calcutta (1822–26), and an intimate friend of Scott whom he assisted in collecting border minstrelsy.

12. Scott's new poem, *Rokeby: A Poem, in Six Cantos*, first announced in the *Morning Chronicle* for Saturday 29 August 1812 'to be published speedily', was not in fact completed until December 1812, and was eventually published by

Ballantyne in January 1813. It was dedicated to his old friend John Bacon Sawrey Morritt (1771–1843), classical scholar and traveller, after the name of whose estate in Yorkshire the poem was entitled and in which its scene is laid. It met with a somewhat tepid reception, though George Ellis, after a 'second perusal', eventually gave in its favour in the *Quarterly Review*, VIII, xvi (December 1812), 485–507.

13. Jacob Bryant (1715–1804) (whose name JM misspells here), classical scholar, had denied the existence of Troy and the event of the Trojan war in his *Observations upon A Treatise, entitled a Description of the Plain of Troy, by Monsieur le Chevalier* (1795), and his *Dissertation concerning the War of Troy, and the Expedition of the Grecians, as described by Homer, shewing That no such Expedition was ever undertaken and that no such City of Phrygia existed* (1796; 2nd edn, corr., 1799), which had caused a furore, and had also earned B's deepest indignation (see, for example, his Ravenna Journal entry for 11 January 1821 [*BLJ* VIII, 21–22], and *DJ* IV, 76 & 101 [*CPW* V, 227 & 235]). During his travels in Greece and Asia Minor in 1794–96, Morritt had surveyed the site of the *Iliad*, and in 1798 published *A Vindication of Homer and of the Ancient Poets and Historians, who have recorded the Siege and Fall of Troy. In Answer to Two Late Publications of Mr. Bryant*. In its review of this, the *British Critic* (XII [Dec. 1798], 632–45, & XIII [Feb. 1799], 116–35) had supported Morritt against Bryant, who then responded with *An Expostulation, addressed to the British Critic* (1799), and replied to Morritt with *Some Observations upon the Vindication of Homer...* (1799). To these in his turn Morritt replied with *Additional Remarks on the Topography of Troy, ... in answer to Mr. Bryant's last Publications* (1800).

14. Isaac D'Israeli (1766–1848), poet, man of letters and father of the future prime minister and novelist, Benjamin Disraeli, was a close intimate and literary adviser of JM's. These lines were probably an extemporary effusion; they appear neither in his correspondence with JM nor in his numerous publications.

15. See n. 1 above. In his reply B remarked, 'The Antijacobin Review is all very well, & not a bit worse than the Quarterly, & at least less harmless [*sic*]' (*BLJ* II, 197).

Letter 3   [Monday 28 September 1812]

My Lord
   I feel much honoured by the confidential communication in the Letter which I had the pleasure of receiving this morning, and I trust that your Lordship will do me the favor to believe that I shall entertain it with discretion[1] – I shall now go to the Theatre on its opening, with

a double anxiety, but with incalculable interest, and I hope that the faithful[2] report which I propose to send of your Lordships reception by Dramatic Critics will be as grateful to you as the applause which you have already anticipated from the Public at large − − indeed I shall thrill with delight at the favourable reception of the address − I will get it printed in an hour or two after I am favored with a Copy −

There will be many ironical Addresses published, <as the rejected ones>+ − I was solicited to publish a collection written by two very respectable young men of the name (in confidence) of Smith who wrote "Horace in London" & made some tolerable translations from Horace in the Monthly Mirror[3] & who had lately as I conceived sent two or three very neat translations that appeared in the M. Chronicle − but I have been told since that these were by T. Moore[4] −

I inclose a communication from Mr G. Thomson of Edinburgh[5] −

I am provoking the Engraver of your Lordships portrait to make every exertion[6] −

I received your Lordships former Letter & the inclosure which will do no discredit to the new Edition of Childe Harold[7] − which will be published as soon as we can add the Prologue −

I am ever

My Lord

your obedient & faithful Servt.

John Murray

+ I forgot to mention that <u>One</u> − is intended to be in imitation of your Lordships Style − I did not see them

Notes to Letter 3

1. Drury Lane Theatre had been destroyed by fire in February 1809. It had been rebuilt under the auspices of Samuel Whitbread who, together with Lord Holland, had formed a Committee which, in August 1812, had announced a competition for an Address to be spoken at its reopening on Saturday 10 October 1812. The closing date for submissions was 10 September; but, as none of the entries was deemed acceptable, Lord Holland had asked B to write one. Although B had told JM in a postscript to his letter of 14 September that he had been 'applied to', but disrelished 'contending against all Grubstreet & threw a few thoughts on the subject into the fire' (*BLJ* II, 197), he had later complied with Lord Holland's request and was soon in the throes of exchanges with him (see *BLJ* II, 203–24). Rehearsing these '*confidential*' circumstances to JM on Sunday 27 September, B told him he had 'written a prologue which *has* been received & will be spoken' and would, whatever its fate, be published 'in the next [the 7th] Edition of C[hilde]

H[arol]d', but in the meantime begged him to keep his name a secret (*BLJ* II, 211–12; see also, *CPW* III, 394).

2. JM's underlining suggests he intends a pun: a true and faithful report by one of the 'faithful'.

3. The brothers James (1775–1839) and Horatio (Horace) (1779–1849) Smith poked fun at the Drury Lane Address competition by writing a collection of parodies of the chief authors of the day whose entries were supposedly rejected by the committee. This was *Rejected Addresses: or The New Theatrum Poetarum*, which was published by John Miller on 12 October 1812 and was an instant success. Their parody of B was 'Cui Bono? [What's the point?] *By Lord B*', 12 Spenserian stanzas in imitation of the mood and manner of *CHP*. B thought the whole affair huge fun, and 'the *C. H.* [*Childe Harold*] imitation one of the best' (*BLJ* III, 7; see also, II, 228 and 235). They followed this with *Horace in London: consisting of Imitations of the First Two Books of the Odes of Horace, By the Authors of Rejected Addresses, or the New Theatrum Poetarum*, published by John Miller in 1813, which imitations had previously appeared in the *Monthly Mirror* in 1810 and 1811.

4. In the *Morning Chronicle* for Tuesday 8 September 1812 appeared 'Horace, Ode 11, Lib. 2. Freely translated by G.P. Esq', prefaced by the following letter to the Editor:

> Sir, I was, some time ago, entrusted with the publication of a Work, entitled, "*Odes of Horace, done into English by several Persons of Fashion*," and the printing of it is, at present, very far advanced; but, perceiving that the great Quarto Leviathan of Poetry is about to make another plunge in the ocean, I know how dangerous it is for *small fry* to come in contact with him, and shall, therefore, reserve my Work for some more halcyon season. In the mean time I shall, now and then, give the public a *prelibation* of its merits, through the medium of your very respectable Journal. As it is done by persons of the *very first fashion*, you may depend upon its containing nothing offensive to the higher powers; indeed I know the character of your Journal too well, to suppose that it would admit any allusions of that nature into its columns, I am, Sir, your's, &c. BIBLIOPOLA TRYPHON.

The following week, in the same paper on Wednesday 16 September, appeared 'Horace, Ode 22, Lib. I. Freely translated by Lord Eld-n', with a short prefatory letter promising more 'another time', signed by 'BIBLIOP. TRYPHON'. Both these were by Moore, whose pseudonym is borrowed from the Roman bookseller who sold Martial's books (see Martial, *Epigrams*, IV, lxxii, and XIII, iii). They were first published without their prefatory letters, and with the former more pointedly subtitled 'Freely translated by G.R. [i.e., George Rex]', in his *Intercepted Letters; or, The Twopenny Post-Bag. To which are added, Trifles Reprinted. By Thomas Brown, the Younger* (1813),

70–74 and 75–78 respectively. B was to quote the penultimate line of the first ode, 'All gentle and juvenile, curly and gay', on more than one occasion (see, for example, *DJ* X, 19, and *BLJ* X, 29; Marchand mistakenly ascribes it to Moore's *Epistles, Odes, and Other Poems* [1806] [ibid., 29n]).

5. See Letter 2, n.3 above. George Thomson had written again to B care of JM on 22 September 1812, delighted to have learnt through JM that B had 'consented to grant the favour' he had 'lately presumed to solicit', and sending 'Five Airs' for which he wished B 'to invoke the Muse', with some instructions as to the technicalities (MA). However, B had second thoughts, which he must have asked JM to pass on to Thomson. For, replying to a letter from JM of 23 January 1813 (no longer extant), Thomson expressed his deep disappointment at learning 'that his Lordship now entertains some doubts whether he should write for the Airs I sent, because M^r. Moore wrote verses for the same Airs'; but undismayed he sent a further five which again in the event elicited nothing from B (BL Add. 35267, ff. 66–69).

6. For the 'Engraver', see Letter 4 below.

7. Between his letters of 14 and 27 September as printed in *BLJ* II, 196–97 and 211–12, there is the following unpublished letter of Tuesday 22 September 1812 from B to JM in MA, which has somehow escaped the notice of previous editors. There is no cover and B does not give his address, though he was in Cheltenham at the time; I transcribe it exactly and as completely as it appears in the MS:

> Dear Sir,
>   I send you a few things to be added to the Lyric part of our next Edition, (when we come to it) & perhaps I may have a few others which I will send accordingly. –
>   y^rs. truly
>   <u>B</u>
> Sep^tr. 22^d. 1812 –

Fortunately it is endorsed on verso in another hand (not JM's): '1812 Septr 22^d Byron. Lord Inclosing two Poems to be added to the 5th Edition'. JM was preparing the 5th edition of *CHP* I and II which, however, when it appeared was no different in content from editions 2–4. The 7th was the next edition to include additional poems, and of these the most likely that B may have sent with this letter are 'Lines inscribed upon a Cup formed from a Skull' and 'To Time', uncorrected proofs of both of which are bound up with various proofs of the 5th edition of *CHP* (see *CPW* I, 391, and III, 390 respectively). Alternatively, 'From the Portuguese' and 'On Being Asked What Was the "Origin of Love"?' may have been sent instead (but see *CPW* III, 404 and 425–26).

Letter 4)   Thursday [15 October 1812]

My Lord

    As soon as I was favoured with your letter, this morning, I sent
for the engraved portrait, with which the artist did not part without
a sigh – he had promised himself much increased reputation from its
publication – and had laid aside the portrait of Lady Jersey, to complete
it[1] – There were no more than three Copies taken off, the One sent
to your Lordship, and other two remaining with me – One of these,
I venture to entreat your Lordship to allow me to retain – a favour,
which I shall ever consider as a mark of your Lordships confidence[2]
– For the Plate itself, as I had not courage to violate your Lordship even
in effigy, I trust that I shall be pardoned for evading this part of your
commands by sending it to your own custody, trusting that you will be
content to banish it to the family archives, there to rest, until a happy
occasion shall draw it forth again –

    I was present during the first recitation of the address and can assure
your Lordship that is [sic] was received, throughout, with applauding
satisfaction – I have inclosed the Copy of the address which I had in my
hand, and on which I marked, with my pencil <u>at the time</u>, those parts
at which the warmest approbation was loudly expressed – there was not
the <u>slightest</u> <appea> demonstration or appearance of dissatisfaction, at
any <u>one point</u> – there were many important variations in Mr Ellistons
delivery, which was, throughout, exceedingly bad – indeed his acting
exhibits nothing but conceit – I was surprised to find your Lordships
name given up at once to the public, I confess – & the appendage to the
address, stating the <u>reward</u> offered for the best copy of verses, appeared
to reflect discredit & ridicule in what ever way it was viewed[3] –

    I have just exhausted one, of three thousand, which were printed of
Childe Harold, for the <u>second time</u>, – & <so> this I have justly called
a <u>fifth</u> edition[4] – when we shall have disposed of these two thousand
– I shall print an <u>entirely</u> New Edition, &, in it, I would solicit your
Lordships obliging permission to insert the address & the two other
Poems, of which I inclose a proof in the parcel containing the Copper
Plate,[5] and any others, that your Lordship may deem completely worthy
of <the> your high reputation, wch it will be my <highes> best
gratification to see perpetuated, in your Lordships future writings –

    I have inclosed the <u>Satyrist</u>[6] & the "Rejected addresses" – wch I
announced to your Lordship some time ago – & One – really a rejected
address – dedicated to your Lordship, & wch offers the best apology
for the Managers[7] – Your Lordship will I hope do me the kindness to

pardon my circumlocution –
  With the highest esteem
  I have the honour to be My Lord
  Your Lordships
  obedient & faithful Servant
  John Murray

Fleet Street
Thursday

The Parcel is sent by the Mail[8]

Notes to Letter 4)

Between this letter and Letter 3 above, JM had clearly sent B a proof of the engraved portrait, which was to have been prefixed to the 5th edn of *CHP*. Writing from Cheltenham on Monday 12 October, B told him he had 'a '*very strong objection* to the engraving', and requested that it would 'on no account be prefixed', and that '*all* the proofs be burnt, & the plate broken' (*BLJ* II, 224).

1. The 'artist' was Henry Meyer (1782?–1847), portrait painter and engraver, a pupil of Bartolozzi and nephew of John Hoppner, RA (1758–1810), who later became a founding member (1824) and president (1828) of the Society of British Artists. His engraving was of the portrait of B by the Scottish portrait painter and miniaturist, George Lethbridge Sanders (or Saunders) (1774–1846), to whom Lady Jersey had also sat for her portrait – at the same time, it seems, as had Princess Charlotte (much to the displeasure of the Prince Regent) (*Letters of the Princess Charlotte 1811–1817*, ed. A. Aspinall [London: Home and Van Thal, 1949], 62), and from which portrait Meyer was also making an engraving (see Freeman O'Donoghue, *Catalogue of Engraved British Portraits Preserved in the Department of Prints and Drawings in the British Museum*, 4 vols [London, 1908–14], II, 642, no. 4). For further details, see Annette Peach, *Portraits of Byron* (London: The Walpole Society, 2000), esp. 38–39.

2. Having received the parcel containing 'the Plate itself', B wrote to JM on Friday 23 October saying 'The *plate* is *broken*' (clearly by himself), adding that JM might keep '*one* of the two remaining copies', but that 'the other must be *burned peremptorily*' (*BLJ* II, 234). This '*one*' copy has survived in MA and is reproduced in Peach, *Portraits of Byron*, Fig. 14.

3. B's 'Address, Spoken at the Opening of Drury-lane Theatre Saturday, October 10th, 1812' was delivered on that occasion (after the national anthem and 'Rule Britannia' and prior to a performance of *Hamlet*) by Robert William Elliston (1774–1831), the Hamlet of the subsequent performance.

Unfortunately JM's 'marked' 'Copy of the address' has not survived – it is not that described as 'an amanuensis copy' in MA (*CPW* III, 393). However, Lord Holland sent his immediate impressions from the theatre itself that very night (though his note is undated): 'I write from the box, to catch the post – It has succeeded admirably – Elliston repeated it well, at least that part of it which he was <u>perfect</u> in – his only fault was not knowing it by <u>heart</u> & the cry for silence put him out – He <mad> substituted here & there some vile epithets – but it succeeded admirably & will more & more every night ... the more perfect Elliston gets in it – the more it will be approved of' (BL Add. 51639 f. 109; he was to amplify these reservations more severely a week later). The *Morning Chronicle* for Monday 12 October gave its verdict as follows: 'Mr. Elliston then came forward and delivered the following *Prize* Address. We cannot boast of the eloquence of the delivery. It was neither gracefully nor correctly recited. The merits of the production itself we submit to the criticism of our readers. We cannot suppose it was selected as the most poetical composition of all the scores that were submitted to the Committee. But, perhaps by its tenor, by the allusions to the fire, to GARRICK, to SIDDONS, and to SHERIDAN, it was thought most applicable to the occasion, notwithstanding its being in parts unmusical, and in general tame.' It then printed the Address, and added somewhat maliciously: 'The Committee of Drury-Lane Theatre, to invite competition, offered 20gs. for the best written Address.' B had seen this report before receiving this letter (4) from JM (see *BLJ* II, 225); perhaps he had also seen in the *Morning Chronicle* for Wednesday 14 October its observation on his parodist in *Rejected Addresses*, 'certainly he has assigned to the pen of Lord B. a superior *poem* to that which has gained the prize'.

4. The 4th edn of *CHP* was still being advertised in November; the publication of the 5th edn was first announced in the *Morning Chronicle* on Saturday 5 December 1812. It bore the same title and contents as the 4th edn, except for the omission of the facsimile and the alteration in the title-page of the place of publication: 'John Murray (*removed to*) Albemarle-Street' (see Letter 6 below).

5. The 'Copper Plate' was of Henry Meyer's engraving (see n. 1 above); for 'the two other Poems', see Letter 3, n. 7 above.

6. In his letter of Monday 12 October, B told JM that he had heard that *CHP* had been reviewed in the *Satirist* (which JM here misspells) and wished to know whether 'old personalities' had been revived (*BLJ* II, 225). His reason for wishing to know this was that its editor, Hewson Clarke (1787–1832?), miscellaneous hack-writer and sometime sizar of Emmanuel College, Cambridge, had persistently attacked him personally and poetically in both that periodical and *The Scourge* during his time at Trinity and thereafter (see *BLJ* I, 136 and 167, and II, 65, 67 and 68). The review of *CHP* appeared in *The Satirist, or Monthly Meteor*, New Series, XI, 3 (October 1812), 344–58, and was continued and concluded in XI, 5 (December 1812), 542–50. However,

although deploring B's misanthropy, melancholy and lack of patriotism, the review was otherwise very favourable, the bullfight stanzas and the descriptions of Greece being singled out for special praise. In his reply to JM of Saturday 17 October, B remarked that *The Satirist* had 'taken a *new* tone' and that the Editor 'almost ought to be thanked for his revocation it is done handsomely after five years warfare' (*BLJ* II, 228 and 229).

7. JM refers to *Rejected Addresses* and in particular – and with some jocularity – to the parody of B, 'Cui Bono?' (see Letter 3, n. 3 above). B replied that he thought them 'by far the best thing of the kind since the Rolliad [1784]', and wished JM had published them, telling him to 'Tell the author "I *forgive* him were he twenty times our satirist"' (*BLJ* II, 228, B himself parodying *Richard II*, V, ii, 101–02: 'Away fond woman! were he twenty times my son/I would appeach him.').

8. That is, the 'Parcel' containing the plate of the engraving and the proof of the two poems.

Letter 5)   Thursday [22 October 1812]

My Lord

    I was not fortunate enough to meet with Mr Perry <early enou> in time to inform you, by yesterdays post, that he will most joyfully insert the lively parody in tomorrows paper[1] – it would have appeared this morning had he not actually printed that which appeared today[2] – I met him again this moment & he tells me he has received <u>another</u> & a very good one[3] – I am distracted at this time between two houses & am forced to write in haste[4] – I had a sale, to the Booksellers, on Tuesday when I sold no less than 878 Copies of the <u>Fifth</u> Edition of Childe Harold,[5] from which your Lordship will judge of the opinion of the booksellers respecting its <u>continuing</u> success – I am anxious to be favoured with the "Waltzing [*sic*][6] –

    With great respect
    I remain
    Your Lordships
    Most obedient Servant
    John Murray

Fleet Street
Thursday

Notes to Letter 5)

<u>Cover</u>: The R^t Honble Lord Byron/Cheltenham <u>pm</u> 22 October 1812 <u>endorsed by B at the head of the page</u>: Octr. 22^d. 1812

B's 'Address' continued to be recited by Elliston every night prior to the main performance at Drury Lane Theatre till Tuesday 20 October. On Wednesday 14 October, after a performance of the *Hypocrite*, George Frederick Busby – the son of Dr Thomas Busby (1755–1838), composer, organist, editor, musicologist and translator of Lucretius, *The Nature of Things* (2 vols, 1813), to which B was a subscriber – had tried unsuccessfully to deliver his father's real rejected Address ('Monologue') in order to show its superiority to B's. The following evening (Thursday 15 October), Dr Busby himself had attempted to do so. He had harangued the audience in the interval between the acts and even during the performance itself (the play was suitably entitled *Turn Out* and the audience made the most of it). He had eventually been allowed to deliver it after the performance, but such was the uproar that he remained inaudible. This was reported in full in the *Morning Chronicle* on Friday 16 October with the following editorial comment: 'An explanation is certainly due for the adoption of this flimsy Address [i.e., B's], after the pledge given that the best of all the essays anonymously sent should be impartially chosen. The high respect in which the names of Lord HOLLAND, Mr. WHITBREAD and Mr. CRAUFURD are held protects them from any suspicion of a breach of integrity – and we trust it will be found, in compliment to their judgment, that, with all its deficiencies, Lord BYRON's was the best.' On Saturday 17 October, the *Morning Chronicle* charitably printed Busby's 'Monologue', as well as an 'explanatory communication' concerning B's position in the Address proceedings signed 'CANDIDUS'. This has been mistakenly ascribed to B himself (*BLJ* XI, 181–82), but its author was either Lord Holland or Samuel Whitbread. For, to B's enquiry of Wednesday 14 October as to whether the Committee intended offering any explanation of their proceedings (ibid., II, 225–26), Lord Holland replied the following day (Thursday 15): 'the Committee … have not yet thought it proper to answer the nonsense that has appeared in the papers because they did not wish to give the publication of their proceedings in a controversial form – What happened last night when Dr Busby's son jumped on the stage to read his papa's nonsense may make a detail necessary & Whitbread promised me to compose a paragraph thereupon – I write to remind him … <u>Ede tua</u> will be the best answer to the poetasters & then they will see what the publick thinks of them' (BL Add. 51639, ff. 113–14). He wrote again to B on Tuesday 20 October saying, 'Busby who is your Milbourne is excellent & I think must give you an itching for a Satire or an epigram' (ibid., f. 118). The references to Luke Milbourne, Dryden's critic, and Martial (*Epigrams*, I, xci: 'Cum tua non edas, carpis mea carmina, Laeli./carpere vel noli nostra vel ede tua' [Although you don't publish your poems, Laelius, you carp at mine; either don't carp at mine or publish yours]), strongly suggest that Holland was (also?) the author of the following much more forthright and serious explanation, dated 19 October, which appeared in *The*

Times for Tuesday 20 October:

> Sir, – It is necessary to correct some misstatements respecting the
> Address spoken at the opening of Drury-Lane Theatre.
>
> No pecuniary reward was ever offered. Lord BYRON's Prologue
> was not among those submitted to the Committee before the 10th of
> September last. It was not till those so submitted had been exam-
> ined, and judged unfit by the persons to whom the decision was
> referred, that Lord BYRON was *requested* to furnish the Address
> which has been spoken with so much success, and criticised with
> so much acrimony. Lord BYRON entered into competition with
> nobody. When *requested* to write an Address, he liberally undertook
> that difficult task; and executed it in a manner gratifying to the
> Managers, and, I firmly believe, satisfactory to the public.
>
> The Committee acknowledged considerable merit in some of the
> rejected Addresses, and have recorded, in a resolution, their favour-
> able opinion of two. On such as arrived too late to be accepted, viz.
> after the time specified, and subsequent to the application made to
> Lord BYRON, they expressed no opinion. These, Sir, are facts on
> which you may depend; and, in my judgment, neither the Noble
> Author, nor the Managers, have reason to blush at the result. The
> scheme and competition failed. Recourse was had to a Writer whose
> poetical reputation stands justly high, and a work was produced,
> which, with some imperfections, is nevertheless remarkable for the
> harmony of its versification, and for more novelty, as well as poetry,
> than could reasonably have been expected in so hacknied a theme. A
> candid consideration of the difficulties the writer had to encounter,
> and a fair review of the beauties the Address really possesses, will
> place Lord BYRON's merit in this composition, at no great distance
> from the most successful of his predecessors; and, with respect
> to his contemporaries, the few specimens of rejected Addresses
> which we have hitherto seen, have gone far indeed to prove the
> Committee correct in their judgment, when they pronounced what
> was submitted to them, *altogether unfit to be spoken at the opening of
> Drury-Lane.*
>
> These disappointed writers have it, however, still in their power,
> to adopt the generous example of Dr. MILBOURNE, recently
> sanctioned by Dr. BUSBY's imitation, and to publish their own
> compositions. Such an appeal to the public may possibly reconcile
> the most fastidious to the Address which was spoken; and till it has
> been made, all censure of the Committee for their condemnation of
> the works submitted to them, must be founded in conjecture only:
> for *carpere vel noli nostra, vel ede tua.*
>
> I am, Sir, your constant reader, PETRONICULUS.

It is possible that this episode came to the attention of the Lord Chamberlain,

Francis Ingram Seymour, second Marquis of Hertford (1743–1822), Lord Chamberlain (1812–1821), who desired some explanation. For on 23 October 1812 Thomas Dibdin sent B's Address to John Larpent (1741–1824), examiner of plays in the Lord Chamberlain's Office (1778–1824), with the accompanying note: 'I am directed by the Manager to send, for your inspection, the inclosed address, as spoken by Mʳ Elliston on the opening of the Theatre Royal Drury Lane' (Larpent Collection 1737, Huntington Library; BL microfiche copy 254/463). The Address, together with *Marino Faliero* (1821), were the only works of B's submitted to the Lord Chamberlain's Office during his lifetime (see Letter 154, n. 5 below).(Incidentally, in a postscript to his letter to Lady Melbourne of Tuesday 20 October B wrote: 'Thanks for your "Examiner" Hunt is a clever man & I should like to know his opinion – pray send it' [*BLJ* II, 233]. None of Lady Melbourne's surviving letters to B helps illuminate this; but it almost certainly refers to *The Examiner*, No. 251, Sunday, Oct. 18, 1812, in pp. 663–64 of which Hunt printed B's Address and commented on it at some length, not altogether favourably, but fairly and with great generosity of spirit.)

1. James Perry (1756–1821) was the editor of the *Morning Chronicle*. B reacted to Busby's exhibition of himself by parodying his 'Monologue' with 'Parenthetical Address, by Dr. Plagiary', which he sent to JM on Monday 19 October (not 17 October) asking him to get it 'inserted in several of the papers ... particularly the M[orning] Chronicle' (*BLJ* II, 227–28; date corr. MS MA). Accordingly it appeared anonymously in the *Morning Chronicle* on Friday 23 October (see *CPW* III, 32–33 and 403–04). At the same time B must also have sent a copy with a similar request to George Raymond, the stage manager at Drury Lane Theatre. No letter from B is extant, but Raymond's reply, written from the Theatre Royal Drury Lane on Tuesday 20 October, is in MA and runs as follows:

T: R: D: Lane
Ocᵗʳ – 20 –

My Lord/

Doctor Busby has recᵈ the punishment due to so contemptible a Coxcomb. He most earnestly entreated the Audience to hear his Son repeat his sublime production, the clamour of the ignorant prevailed, and his son began – but alas! never was grub-Street vender of Verses, so handled – he was groaned off the Stage in disgrace, and was only preserved from further wrath by my <u>politeness</u> in leading him to the door. The Doctor, full of dire revenge, threatened to send your Lordship, Manager, & Committee, to Stygean glooms – He swore he would publish it – he has kept his Oath – and the punishment of the Knout could not have been half so severe. Had the riot which this pedantic reciter of Lucretius created continued till the present moment, your Lordships batoon [*sic*] of Satire would doubtless have done that good which the Doctor's insignificance has done – but good order having been restored, I think he is unworthy of further

notice – At the Same time I think it would be a good slap in his
face if your Lordship would allow me to insert it, with a good head-
piece in the Mor\[g] Chronicle. If this should meet your Lordships
approbation, on hearing from you I will take care it shall be inserted
in a conspicuous place. Our success since the opening has been
wonderful – Your address received little aid from the reciter.
I have the honour to be
Lordships [*sic*] &c &c &c.
J G Raymond.

2. In the *Morning Chronicle* for Thursday 22 October there appeared an excep-
tionally clever parody entitled 'The Lamentations of Dr. B—. An Heroic
Poem. Occasioned by a Recent Occurrence at Drury-Lane Theatre', dated
'Lambeth, Oct, 17, 1812' and signed 'P.M.', consisting of 76 lines written in
heroic couplets and founded on the opening of the *Aeneid* (the judgement of
Paris) with numerous allusions to Milton, Dryden, Gray and others. It is so
good that one might be forgiven for claiming it as B's (see n. 3 below). Its
author, however, was Philip Martineau, a brewer of King's Arms Stairs (or
Yard) in Lambeth, a regular contributor of such similarly signed ephemera to
the *Morning Chronicle* and himself a rejected addresser (Drury Lane Rejected
Addresses, BL Add. 27899, ff. 34 and 213–15). Philip Martineau was almost
certainly, as Roger Fulford tentatively suggests, 'a connexion of Whitbread's
partner', John Martineau (Roger Fulford, *Samuel Whitbread 1764–1815: A
Study in Opposition* [London: Macmillan, 1967], 284n).

3. In his reply to JM of Friday 23 October B told him, 'The other parody which
P[erry] has received is *mine* also (I believe), it is Dr. B[usby]'s speech versified'
(*BLJ* II, 235). This is puzzling. It could of course be a misunderstanding on
B's part – a covert reference, perhaps, to his having sent another copy of his
'Parenthetical Address' to Raymond (see n. 1 above). But it is extremely
curious that on his return to Cheltenham, after a month at Eywood with
the Oxfords, he should write to JM on Sunday 22 November saying that the
public 'must be tolerably sick of the subject, & except the parod*ies* I have not
interfered nor shall, indeed I did not know that the Dr. [Busby] had published
his apologetical letter & postscript [which appeared in the *Morning Chronicle*
on the very same day as did B's 'Parenthetical Address'] or I should have
recalled *them*' (*BLJ* II, 250, emphases added). This certainly suggests that he
wrote more than one parody; but of the almost daily squibs that had appeared
in the *Morning Chronicle* since the episode, none appears to be by him. Of these,
however, one in particular captured his attention. Continuing his letter of
22 November, B writes: 'I see some mountebank has stolen Alderman Birch's
name to vituperate the Doctor; he had much better have pilfered his pastry
– which I should imagine the more valuable ingredient at least for a Puff'
(*BLJ* II, 250; Alderman Samuel Birch [1757–1841] was a well-known dramatist
and pastry-maker in Cornhill). This refers to the following epigram which
appeared in the *Morning Chronicle* for Saturday 31 October 1812:

THE TWO BUSBYS

"Use every man according to his *deserts* and who shall
escape *whipping.* – HAMLET."
        Erst Doctor BUSBY the terrific *Virga*,
        Applied with vigour to each Urchin's *Terga*.
        Now (tit for tat!) let every Urchin come,
        And tickle up the modern BUSBY's B—.
Cornhill, Oct. 23, 1812.   SAMUEL BIRCH.

Why this should have struck B so forcibly is curious. Obviously it gives him
the opportunity of making a witty pun on 'Puff' and pastry, and his attention
may have been drawn to it by the editorial statement in the *Morning Chronicle*
for Tuesday 3 November denying Samuel Birch's authorship, or by Samuel
Birch's own denial in the *Morning Chronicle* for Wednesday 18 November
– which would have appealed to his Swiftian Bickerstaff-Partridge sense
of fun. Moreover, despite its crudity, the epigram is cleverer than it may
seem to be. The epigraph is from *Hamlet*, IV, ii, 2, and 'Virga' is Latin for
a cane or whip (picked up in the attribution to Samuel *Birch*), and 'Terga'
for the backside. The lines themselves appear to be an imitation of Juvenal
Satire VII, 210–13: 'metuens virgae iam grandis Achilles/cantabat patriis
in montibus et tui non tunc/eliceret risum citharoedi cauda magistri;/sed
Rufum atque alios caedit sua quemque iuventus' (When Achilles was already
grown up and taking music lessons in his native hills, he feared the cane of
his lyre-playing teacher [Chiron – half man, half horse] and would never
laugh at his tail. But nowadays Rufus and the others are beaten by their
young pupils); and whoever the author was seems to have known something
of the history of Westminster School, for Lambert Osbaldston (1594–1659),
the School's headmaster from 1622 to 1638, fell foul of Archbishop Laud for
referring to some unspecified person as a 'little urchin', and was relieved of
his post to be succeeded by Dr. Richard Busby (1606–95), headmaster from
1638 until his death, who was renowned for the severity of his discipline and
well known as a 'flogger' (see John Sargeaunt, *Annals of Westminster School*
[London: Methuen, 1898], 67, and John Field, *The King's Nurseries: The Story
of Westminster School* [London: James & James, 1987], 32). The 'Two' Busbys
therefore are not Dr. Thomas Busby and his son, George, but Dr. Thomas
and Dr. Richard Busby.

4. JM was in the very process of moving to Albemarle Street; this was the last
   letter he was to address to B from his Fleet Street premises.

5. Tuesday would have been 20 October when the 5th edn of *CHP* would have
   been sold to the trade (at what may have been one of JM's sale dinners at
   the Albion Tavern, for which see Letter 91, n. 9 below). It was not, however,
   announced as published until Saturday 5 December (see also, Letter 4, n. 4
   above).

6. In his letter to JM of Saturday 17 October, B had told him that he had 'in *hand* a *satire* on *Waltzing* which you must publish anonymously, it is not long, not quite 200 lines, but it will make a very small boarded pamphlet – in a few days you shall have it' (*BLJ* II, 229). He reiterated this in his letter of Monday 19 October (*BLJ* II, 228, where it is conjecturally dated '[17th?]'), but by the time of his reply on Friday 23 October it had extended to 'rather above 200 lines with an introductory letter to the Publisher' (*BLJ* II, 234). When exactly he sent it to JM is unclear.

Letter 6)   Wednesday 4 November 1812

My Lord

I had the pleasure of receiving safely your obliging Letter dated the 23rd.[1] but was unwilling to intrude an answer upon you until something important should cast up – and the occasion<ed> is now furnished, by the tremendous "Critique upon Lord Byrons Address"[2] which I have the honour to inclose, under this and another cover – Your Lordship declined writing the address originally, because "you would not contend with all" "Grub Street"[3] – but you did not suspect, at that time, that success would induce all Grub Street to contend against you – but this is the present state of the war – your Lordship will have seen by the Chronicle of today & yesterday, that it is in contemplation to collect & publish in one volume the whole of the rejected addresses[4] – which would be an excellent subject of fun for an article in the Review, & Mr G – would I think join forces with you[5] –

I shall be careful to give your Lordship full notice of the new Edition of Childe Harold – which has been very much assisted in sale by the admiration of it, forced from the Ragamuffins who are abusing the address[6] – – I would be delighted, if your Lordship had had a new Poem ready for publication <a> about the same time (this month I believe) that Walter Scotts is expected[7] – but I will sacrifice my right arm (your Lordships friendship) rather than publish any poem not equal to Childe Harold – without a conscriptive Command – <las> like that which I lately executed in committing your Lordships Portrait to the Flames, but where I had some consolation in seeing it ascend in sparkling brilliancy to Parnassus[8]

Neither I, nor Mr Gifford, I can venture to assure you, upon honour, have any notion, who the author is of the admirable article on Horne Tooke <–> is [*sic*][9] –

Does your Lordship yet think of migrating to the Metropolis

I am most anxious in the hope that your Lordships health is
improving –
I ever remain
Your Lordships faithful
Servant
John Murray

Albemarle Street
Wednesday Nov. 4. 1812

I do not mention "Waltzing" from the hope that it improves,
Geometrically, as to the time it is retained[10]

Notes to Letter 6)

This is JM's first letter to B from Albemarle Street; the full date and address at
the close and the extremely neat orthography throughout perhaps register his
feelings on this momentous occasion. In the *Morning Chronicle* for Saturday 5
December 1812 he announced: 'MR. MURRAY, Publisher of the QUARTERLY
REVIEW, acquaints his Friends, that he has removed from Fleet-street, to No.
50, Albemarle-street (lately Mr. Miller's)'; and on Friday 11 December, he wrote
to Sir Robert Wilson, boasting himself the publisher of Scott and Campbell (but
not of B), saying his new situation was 'peculiarly favourable for the dissemination
of any work of eminence among the fashionable & literary part of the Metropolis'
(BL Add. 30106 f. 366*v*).

1. JM acknowledges B's letter from Cheltenham of Friday 23 October (*BLJ*
   II, 234–35). The very next day B set off for Eywood, and this letter of JM's
   evidently not having been forwarded to him, he did not receive it until his
   return to Cheltenham a month later, replying to it on Sunday 22 November
   (ibid., 249).

2. This was an undated, 18-page pamphlet, written in halting anaphora, entitled *A Critique on the Address written by Lord Byron, Which was spoken at the
   opening of the New Theatre Royal, Drury Lane, October 10, 1812*, by Lord — —,
   in which the anonymous noble author, whilst conceding occasional beauties,
   deplored 'the glaring faults, and general insipidity' of B's Address, instancing
   its poor rhymes, grammatical solecisms, unintelligibilities and inconsisten-
   cies, and concluded with the observation that its selection did little credit
   to the Committee's 'judgment or their honour'.

3. In his letter to JM of Monday 14 September, B had told him that, though he
   had been 'applied to, to write ye. address for Drury Lane', the moment he had
   heard of the contest he 'gave up the idea of contending against all Grubstreet
   & threw a few thoughts on the subject into the fire' (*BLJ* II, 197).

4. B. M'Millan, printer and publisher in Bow Street, announced his intention of collecting and publishing the unsuccessful Addresses in the *Morning
Chronicle* for Wednesday 4 November, which also carried a notice by the
editor stating: 'As Mr. Mac Millan [*sic*] has undertaken to print the *Rejected
Addresses* in a volume, we request of the Correspondents who have favoured
us with copies of their verses, to state to us their pleasure, whether or not
we shall transmit them to that gentleman.' The volume, entitled *The Genuine
Rejected Addresses presented to the Committee of Management for Drury-Lane
Theatre; preceded by that written by Lord Byron, and adopted by the Committee,*
was published by B. McMillan (*sic*) on Thursday 19 November 1812. In his
reply to JM of Sunday 22 November, B observed: 'How came Mr. Mac-
somebody without consulting you or me, to prefix the address to his volume
of "dejected Addresses" is not this somewhat larcenous? I think the ceremony
of leave might have been asked' (*BLJ* II, 249; Marchand's *note* should not
read 'Macmillan' or 'Dejected Addresses').

5. *The Genuine Rejected Addresses* and *Rejected Addresses* were favourably, if somewhat pedantically, reviewed by John Wilson Croker in the *Quarterly Review*,
VIII, xv (September 1812), 172–81; in the case of the former, he thought
the Committee's judgement at fault in many instances, but to the latter he
accorded high praise.

6. Not least amongst these 'Ragamuffins' was the reviewer in *The Antijacobin*,
XLIII, 174 (November 1812), 359–73, of *The Genuine Rejected Addresses* and
A Critique on the Address written by Lord Byron, who, concurring with the
opinions expressed in the latter, added that B's Address was 'infinitely below,
in point of genius, taste, or poetical beauty, any thing which we should
have expected from his Lordship's pen. It is laboured, unharmonious, and
affected' (360).

7. B did not contrive to oblige JM before Scott's *Rokeby* was at last published
in early January 1813.

8. For the incineration of the engraving of B's portrait, see Letter 4 above.

9. In his letter to JM of Friday 23 October, B had asked, 'Did Mr. Ward write
the review of H. Tooke's life? – it is excellent' (*BLJ* II, 235). John William
Ward and Edward Copleston reviewed W. Hamilton Reid's *Memoirs of the
Public Life of John Horne Tooke* in the *Quarterly Review*, VII, xiv (June 1812),
313–28. They demolished the work in their opening two sentences – 'This
is the only Life of Mr. Tooke we have yet seen. It is a miserable performance, below contempt as to style, information, and talent' – and proceeded
to rectify the deficiency with a balanced account of Tooke's life.

10. In his letter of Friday 23 October, B had told JM that *Waltz* would be
'prepared', but had increased to 'rather above 200 lines' (*BLJ* II, 234; see
also, Letter 5, n. 6 above); in his reply of Sunday 22 November, he made no
reference to the poem. JM must have sent another note (not extant) under

the same cover as the *Critique* (see n. 2 above); for in his reply of Sunday 22 November, B asked him 'to retain the letters & any other subsequent ones to the same address till I arrive in town to claim them which will probably be in a few days' (*BLJ* II, 249; see Letter 7 below).

Letter 7)   Monday [30 November 1812?]

My Lord

I have the greatest pleasure in hearing of your safe arrival –

I have the pleasure of sending Twenty Nine Letters – and a packet of Newspapers – & a Volume containing the best of all criticisms upon Childe Harold[1] – Extracts from it – for the instruction of the rising generation –

I am ever your Lordships
bounden Servant
Jno Murray

Monday

Notes to Letter 7)

The date of this letter is conjectural. B had written to JM from Cheltenham on Sunday 22 November asking him to retain all letters for him until his return to London 'which will probably be in a few days' (*BLJ* II, 249; see Letter 6, n. 10 above). On his arrival in London on Monday 30 November – the day of the opening of the new session of Parliament (though B did not resume his seat until Thursday 3 December) – he put up at Batt's Hotel and immediately wrote to Lady Melbourne that he had 'received exactly 36 letters notes &c. (as I write a 37th!) of all descriptions' (*BLJ* II, 252). Perhaps JM had anticipated that B would return in time for the opening of the new session or had been alerted to his imminent arrival by Hobhouse (see B to Hobhouse, Friday 27 November 1812 [*BLJ* II, 251], and Hobhouse to B, Nov.–Dec., 1812 [*BB*, 106]).

1. In his letter to JM of Monday 14 September, B had told him somewhat facetiously: 'I want all the Reviews, at least the Critiques, quarterly monthly &c. Portuguese & English extracted & bound up in one vol. for my *old age*' (*BLJ* II, 197).

Letter 8)   [Late February – early March 1813?]

My Lord
  in coming home I found the [*sic*] Mr Wynne had returned me <u>The
Book</u> – when your Lordship has read it do me the kindness to let me
have it again
  ever yr Lordships
  Obliged
  J. M.

I will send the Packet in a minute

Notes to Letter 8)

<u>Cover</u>: The Lord Byron

The conjectural dating of this letter is suggested by the collocation of 'Mr Wynne'
and 'The Book', and involves the following somewhat convoluted circumstances.
Charles Watkin Williams Wynn (1775–1850), politician and barrister, MP for
Montgomeryshire and close friend of Southey (of whose *Madoc* [1805] he is the
dedicatee), was under-secretary for the Home Office in 1806–07. In 1806 an
Inquiry took place into the conduct of the Princess of Wales, and particularly the
allegation that she had had a child by Admiral Sir Sidney Smith in 1802 – the
'Delicate Investigation' as it came to be known. Although entirely exonerated from
the charges, she was censured for her levity and irregularity of conduct and for the
company she kept, in the light of which the Prince imposed various restrictions
upon her intercourse with their daughter, Princess Charlotte. The following year,
Spencer Perceval (1762–1812), the future Prime Minister (1809–12), but at the time
Chancellor of the Exchequer and counsel for the Princess, privately printed but
did not publish the secret proceedings of the Inquiry under the title *The Proceedings
and Correspondence, Upon the Subject of the Inquiry Into the Conduct of Her Royal
Highness the Princess of Wales. Faithfully Copied from Authentic Documents*, printed by
Richard Edwards, Crane Court, Fleet-Street, for J. Cawthorn, Catherine-Street,
Strand, and W. Lindsell, Wimpole-Street, Cavendish-Square. 1807. (An unbound
copy, endorsed on its pink cover by Perceval himself 'Most <u>secret</u> & Confidential
/ It is earnestly requested that this Book may be lockd [*sic*] up when not in
hand, and that it may be returned as soon as read / Sp Perceval', is in the BL
[B/p.8/3].) He later ordered all copies save six of the original 2,000 printed to be
burnt; but several were surreptitiously purloined and escaped the conflagration.
To one of these a certain unscrupulous miscellaneous writer and editor, traveller
and one-time soldier, Thomas Ashe (1770–1835) – whom we meet in B's letters
of 14 December 1813 and 5 January 1814 (*BLJ* III, 197–98 and IV, 15) – claimed
to have had 'access', and in 1811 published as its editor *The Spirit of "The Book"*;

or, *Memoirs of Caroline Princess of Hasburgh* [*sic*], *A Political and Amatory Romance*, 3 vols, of which a 4th edn appeared in 1812. This purported to be the memoirs of the Princess of Wales written in the form of letters from herself to her daughter, Princess Charlotte, sympathetic to her cause and supporting that of Perceval's book. With the increasingly embattled domestic relations of the royal family and concomitant questions concerning the 'Delicate Investigation' proceedings occupying both public and parliamentary attention throughout February and March 1813 (and indeed involving B, Hobhouse, Sir Francis Burdett and the Oxfords), as well as the many and various 'impositions practised on public credulity with regard to "The Book"' (as the *Annual Register for 1813* [1814] puts it in its coverage of the whole affair in its General History section, pp. 16–23), it was deemed advisable to publish the full proceedings, which accordingly appeared under the title of *The Genuine Book. An Inquiry, or Delicate Investigation into the Conduct of Her Royal Highness The Princess of Wales; before Lords Erskine, Spencer, Grenville, and Ellenborough, The Four Special Commissioners of Inquiry, Appointed by His Majesty in the Year 1806. Reprinted from an Authentic Copy, Superintended through the Press By the Right Hon. Spencer Perceval*; London: printed by R. Edwards, Crane Court, Fleet Street; and published by W. Lindsell, Wigmore [*sic*] Street; Reprinted and sold by M. Jones, 5 Newgate-Street. 1813. (This is indeed an exact reprint of the 1807 imprint – in format, layout, contents, pagination, and even errata page.) Although its publication was first announced in the *Morning Post* for Monday 15 March 1813, extracts from it had been appearing in that same paper since Wednesday 10 March. This explains B's reference in his letter to Lady Melbourne of Saturday 13 March 1813: 'I shall make you blush by asking you if you have read the *perjuries* in the Morning Post – with the immaculate deposition of the Lady Douglas – much good will the publication add to the rising marriageables of this innocent metropolis – & I doubt not that for the rest of ye. 19th Century every body will be "satisfied with *only* Sir John"' (*BLJ* III, 25; for Lady Melbourne's reply, see *LLLM*, 137). Lady Douglas, wife of Sir John Douglas, was the principal witness against the Princess in the proceedings of 1806. The *Morning Post* for Saturday 13 March extracted her deposition in which she stated: 'The Princess of Wales has told me, that she got a bed-fellow whenever she could, that nothing was more wholesome; she said that nothing was more convenient than her own room: it stands at the head of the staircase which leads into the Park, and I have bolts in the inside, and have a bed-fellow whenever I like. I wonder you can be satisfied only with Sir John. – She said this more than once. She has told me that Sir Sydney [*sic*] Smith had lain with her. That she believed all men liked a bed-fellow, but Sir Sydney better than any body else.' This appears verbatim in *The Genuine Book* (1813), Appendix (A), No. 2, p. 203. In Appendix (A), No. 16, p. 223 of the same work appears an extract from the Birth Registration, which effectively confirmed that the child to which the Princess was supposed to have given birth was in fact born to Sophia Austin who had claimed to be its mother all along. This information was supplied by Charles Watkin Williams Wynn. However, whether 'The Book' which he had now returned to JM and which B evidently wished also to see (and which JM presumably sent him in 'the Packet') refers to Ashe's fabrication or to *The Genuine Book* is not altogether clear. In his letter to Ashe of Tuesday 14 December 1813, B told him, 'your name is not unknown to me', and commended his resolution to 'abjure & abandon the publication & composition of works such as those to which you have alluded. – Depend upon it – they amuse *few* – disgrace both *reader & writer* – & benefit *none*' (*BLJ* III, 198).

Letter 9)   [Monday 14 June 1813?]

I am grateful for your Lordships obliging note –
I wrote to Mr Heber last night –
Childe Harold is entirely out of print everywhere.

2 o Clock   J. M

Notes to Letter 9)

The dating of this letter is entirely conjectural. In a letter of Sunday 13 June 1813, written from Maidenhead on his way to Portsmouth for a short stay, B asked JM whether he had 'got back Ld. Brooke's M.S.? & what does Heber say of it? – Write to me at P[ortsmout]h' (*BLJ* III, 62). This concerns 'a curious & very long MS. poem' written by Fulke Greville, Lord Brooke (1554–1628), found in the library of Lord Oxford in 1812, which B thought might be unpublished and had therefore wished Gifford to see it (*BLJ* II, 249). Perhaps on Gifford's advice JM consulted Richard Heber, the bibliophile, whose opinion B was now anxious to learn; but there is no further reference to the matter. There is no immediate reference either to *CHP* being 'out of print everywhere' (cf. *BLJ* IV, 30).

Letter 10)   Thursday [17 June 1813]

My Lord
    I have the pleasure of sending the inclosed Letter from Mr Gifford –
    ever faithfully
    Your Lordships Servt.
    Jno Murray

Thursday
6½ o Clock

I have sent the 3 Copies of the Giaour to Dr Clarke[1]

Notes to Letter 10)

<u>Cover</u>: The Lord Byron/Bennet S^t. <u>location</u>: Bodleian, Dep. Lovelace Byron, 155, f. 108

At this time B was intending to set forth on his travels again to the East (though he eventually abandoned the project after a number of false starts over the next few months). On learning this, Gifford wrote him the following letter of well-wishing and advice, which he clearly sent via JM who now enclosed it to B:

> James S^t
> June 15th. 1813.

> My dear Lord
>   You are going, as Murray tells me, to leave England for some months. Perhaps I may not have the pleasure of seeing you before you set out, and I therefore take the only mode in my power of expressing my high opinion of your poetical excellence, and of intreating you, as a sincere but humble friend, not to squander your extraordinary powers in common efforts. It is my deliberate conviction that you may choose your station in the temple of Fame; but it must be, in some measure, by concentrating your powers on one point. If I might venture to advise, this point should be, in the first instance, Child [sic] Harold. A little pains might bring him again on the scene, and render him at once the object of tender interest and regard. His fixed melancholy might be shaken, and glimpses of delight break in occasionally upon his habitual gloom. This will not tax your abilities very highly – in the moral descriptive you have no equal: deep feeling, pathos, harmony are all your own – Here, then, is more than is wanted for the purpose. With respect to the sentiment – men & manners of every description are before you, & free for use; but where religion is concerned, some retention is necessary and even wise. I say this, because I have observed that posterity seldom, if ever, quote passages of an irreligious tendency with any applause; while the writer, as he advances in life, almost always views them with increasing disregard or displeasure.
>   In the weak state of my health, I can scarcely hope to witness your future fame, which yet I do not the less confidently anticipate, provided you be not greatly and, let me add, inexcusably wanting to yourself and the world.
>   With my best and most fervent wishes for your health and safety while abroad, and happiness on your return, I am, my dear Lord
>   your very faithful
>   and obed^t serv^t
>   W^m. Gifford

[Bodleian Library, Dep. Lovelace Byron 155, ff. 39–41. <u>Cover</u>: To/ The Right Honble/Lord Byron.]

B was deeply affected by this letter (some of the advice of which might be said to have borne fruit three years later with the resumption of *CHP* in 1816) and replied to it with great feeling and gratitude on Friday 18 June, enclosing his letter with a covering note to JM on the same day saying: 'Will you forward the enclosed answer to the kindest letter I ever received in my life – my sense of which I can neither express to Mr. G[ifford] himself nor to any one else' (*BLJ* III, 63–64).

1. *The Giaour* had been published on Saturday 5 June 1813 (*CPW* III, 413; see also, the *Monthly Literary Advertiser*, No. 98 [10 June 1813], 43). In a letter of Thursday 17 June 1813 to Edward Daniel Clarke (1769–1822), traveller and antiquary and Professor of Mineralogy at Cambridge, to whom B had already sent one of the privately printed copies of *The Giaour*, B told him that he had ordered JM to send him '*three* copies' of the 1st edn, 'two for yourself & any friend – & the other for Mr. Smyth' (*BLJ* III, 63). This was William Smyth (1765–1849), Professor of Modern History at Peterhouse, Cambridge, author of the enormously popular *English Lyrics* (1797) and one of the major contributors to George Thomson's collections of Airs.

Incidentally, on Saturday 5 June 1813 was also published the 6th edn of *CHP* I and II (the *Monthly Literary Advertiser*, No. 98 [10 June 1813], 43). On its title-page the place of publication read for the first, and it seems only time in connection with a work of B's: 'London: *Printed by T. Davison, Whitefriars*, For John Murray, Bookseller to the Admiralty, and to the Board of Longitude, 50, Albermarle-Street' (cf. B's letter to JM of 11 April 1818 containing his verses '[To Mr. Murray]'; *BLJ* VI, 29; see also, *CPW* IV, 172 and 493). By this appointment, which he had secured through John Barrow of the Admiralty, JM became the official publisher of the *Navy List*, which had originally been published at Steel's Navigation-Warehouse in Cornhill under the title of *Steel's Original and Correct List of the Royal Navy, and Hon. East-India Company's Shipping*. JM's first number was advertised in February 1814: 'NAVY LIST, Feb. 1, *Price* 1s 6d./A LIST of his MAJESTY'S NAVY; compiled by Authority of the LORDS COMMISSIONERS of the ADMIRALTY, from original and authentic Documents, &c.' (the *Monthly Literary Advertiser*, No. 106 [10 February 1814], 11). It was a monthly publication and continued for some years in competition with Steel's. For further details, see W. G. Perrin, 'The Navy List. I. The Forerunners of the Official Navy List', *The Mariner's Mirror*, I, 10 (October 1911), 257–64, and W. G. Perrin, 'The Navy List. II. – The Official Navy List and Its Competitors', *The Mariner's Mirror*, I, 12 (December 1911), 321–29.

Letter 11)   [Tuesday 22 June *or* Thursday 1 July 1813?]

My Lord

There <can be> (though by striking out I lessen the <u>general</u> for the <u>personal</u> feeling) <u>is</u> no trouble & no doubt about the <u>Improvements</u> which your truly Noble Pen prepares for me – –

I think what you now send is admirable & I will cancel all there is worked off hitherto –

J. M.

Notes to Letter 11)

<u>Cover</u>: <M>the Lord Byron

The dating of this letter is conjectural. *The Giaour* had been published on Saturday 5 June 1813 (*CPW* III, 413). In preparation for the 2nd edn (published in early July) B wrote to JM on Tuesday 22 June: 'I send you a *corrected copy* of the lines with several *important* alterations – so many that this had better be sent for proof rather than subject the other to so many blots. – You will excuse the eternal trouble I inflict upon you – as you will see I have attended to your Criticism & softened a passage you proscribed this morning' (*BLJ* III, 66). On Thursday 1 July he wrote again saying: 'There is an error in my dedication – the word "my" must be struck out "my" admiration &c. – it is a false construction & disagrees with the signature. I hope this will arrive in time to prevent a *cancel* & serve for proof – recollect it is only the "*my*" to be erased throughout' (ibid., 69). The wording in these two letters ('eternal trouble', 'struck out' and '*cancel*' and the repetition of the possessive pronoun) and that of JM's ('striking out', 'the <u>general</u> for the <u>personal</u>, 'no trouble' and 'cancel') suggest that each is deliberately drawing on the vocabulary of the other. To what lines or '<u>Improvements</u>' they may be referring is very uncertain; McGann notes that the earliest addition to the 2nd edn of *The Giaour* 'is dated 19 June, the latest 24 June' (*CPW* III, 412; see also, ibid., 409, no. 9). In the privately printed copies and the 1st edn of the poem the dedication is worded: 'To Samuel Rogers, Esq. As a slight but most sincere token of my admiration of his genius; my respect for his character, and gratitude for his friendship; this production is inscribed by his obliged and affectionate servant, Byron.' In MA there is an undated proof of the Dedication page in which both 'my's are cancelled in pencil; and in the 2nd and all subsequent editions neither 'my' appears – the dedication reading as printed in *CPW* III, 39, where this little detail is not recorded (nor is it there noted that in line 1 of what forms the 'Advertisement' to the 2nd edn 'tale' reads 'story' in the 1st edn).

Letter 12)   [Sunday 22 August 1813?]

My Lord

Mr Hodgson can not, I am sorry to say, accompany me to Mad. de Staels today, and as I mentioned my intention of inviting him, I have been the means, I fear, of preventing your Lordship from procuring two or three Stanzas of <u>Charlemagne</u>, which I am very anxious to carry with me – should Mr H. call before 4 – at which time I have ordered the Chaise – your Lordship will greatly oblige me by obtaining from him what I want – & I will engage to bring the individual pages back – uncopied –

<Th> The Article upon the <u>Giaour</u> is replete with feeling & delicacy both of taste & criticism and is every thing that the authors bookseller – or friend could desire – the praise is high and is delicately interwoven with the criticism – not too prominent or abrupt, to deprive it of effect – they have picked out with taste & displayed not without art almost all the striking passages – – Their Review of Grimm your Lordship will find – or I presume <have> has already found, to be admirably skilful & entertaining – this is Jeffery [sic] – Sir Jas Mackintoshs Essay on Suicide is really very beautiful –

Your Servant has interrupted me with your Lordships obliging attention[1] – for which my nonsense is not a very grateful return –

I am
Your Lordships
faithful Servant
John Murray

Notes to Letter 12)

<u>Cover:</u> The Lord Byron

The date of this letter is conjectural. Madame de Staël had arrived in England in mid-June 1813 and remained until May 1814. She stayed in London for her first six weeks or so, signing a contract with JM on 12 July for her book *De l'Allemagne* (Simone Balayé, *Les Carnets de voyage de Madame de Staël* [Genève: Libraire Droz, 1971], 357n), and on 10 August retired to Richmond whence she returned to London again on 24 September and remained until 23 October (ibid., 371–73). She visited JM or invited him to dine with her on many occasions. In MA there is a letter to him of Tuesday 17 August in which she says she looks forward to seeing him accompanied by James Perry on Sunday. This would have been Sunday 22 August, on which day B wrote to Moore: 'In a "mail-coach copy" of the Edinburgh, I perceive the Giaour is 2d article ... The said article is so very mild and sentimental, that it must be written by Jeffrey *in love* ... There is an excellent review of Grimm's Correspondence and Made. de Staël (*BLJ* III, 94 and 96). B had received an early copy of the *Edinburgh Review*, XXI, xlii (July 1813) – first announced as published in the *Morning Chronicle* for Wednesday 4 September – which contained a review by Jeffrey of Grimm and Diderot's *Correspondance Littéraire* (5 vols, Paris: 1812) (Art. I, pp. 263–99); a very favourable review, also by Jeffrey, of the 1st edn of *The Giaour* (Art. II, pp. 299–309), and a deeply thoughtful (and respectful) review by Sir James Mackintosh of Madame de Staël's *Réflexions sur le Suicide* (1813) (Art. VIII, pp. 424–32; Marchand incorrectly states this review was of Madame de Staël's *Germany* [*BLJ* III, 96n]). In the same letter to Moore, B also mentions that he had seen much of Lucien Buonaparte's poem 'in MS, and he really surpasses every thing beneath Tasso. Hodgson is translating him *against* another bard' (ibid., 97).

Lucien Buonaparte's *Charlemagne; ou l'Église Délivrée. Poème Épique, en Vingt-Quatre Chants* was eventually published by Longman in two volumes quarto in 1814. Its English translation, *Charlemagne; or the Church Delivered. An Epic Poem, in twenty-four books*, also published by Longman in two volumes quarto in 1815, was made jointly by the Rev. Samuel Butler and Francis Hodgson. At this time, however (August 1813), Hodgson and Butler were translating the poem independently of each other (only in mid-October 1813 did they begin to collaborate, after B had recommended Hodgson to Butler [see *BLJ* III, 150]), and JM was eager to have a specimen of Hodgson's translation with a view to publishing the poem; but it seems he was not to be supplied with one until November. Writing to Butler on Saturday 30 October 1813 from Searle Street, Lincoln's Inn, Hodgson told him: 'I have had an interview with Murray, but nothing satisfactory passed. He wishes to see some of the Translation at least, before he enters into any agreement as to the purchase of the work. I would not show him any without your permission; but, as it appears reasonable that he should see a specimen of what he is to buy, I have written to ask whether I may show him the translation of the 9th. Canto ... Lord Byron went with me to him, & joined in my eulogies of the poem, as far as he was acquainted with it' (BL. Add. 34584 f. 63; BL misdates this letter 1814). And the following month, in an undated letter from Cambridge (postmarked Cambridge, Saturday 20 November 1813), he wrote again saying: 'I am proceeding with Charlemagne – hitherto but slowly – Now, I trust, my progress will be rapid – I could not get anything satisfactory from Murray upon the agreement for publication – He is evidently disposed to make as good a bargain as he can, & talks of the comparatively small sale of the French in this country. Lord Byron & myself have equally refused to listen to this; but really fear this sorry Sosius★ will not b[e] brought to a sufficient estim[ation] of this unique work to give a just consideration for it's property. The Question is, will any other bookseller give more than he will? – I doubt this; & as I have no doubt he takes the opinion of some one or more of the numerous literati who frequent his shop, & that such opinion will induce him to value the prize offered him more as he ought to do, I think in justice to Lucien (notwithstanding my private indignation on the subject) that Murray should be allowed to see a specimen of the translation, and further treated with in the business' (BL Add. 34583 ff. 451–52 [square brackets indicate words torn off with seal]; ★Sosius: the Socii were famous booksellers in Rome; see Horace, *Epistles*, I, xx, 2, and esp. *Ars Poetica*, 345, 'hic meret aera liber Sosiis' [That is the book to make money for the Sosii]).

    1. There is no indication as to what B's 'obliging attention' concerned.

Letter 13)   Sunday [29 August 1813]

5 Pavilion Parade
Sunday

My dear <Lord and> Lord[1]

    I inclose a Letter[2] not without most serious compunctions which shall not be excited upon any similar occasion –

    I rejoice to hear that your Lordship is yet making improvements upon the Giaour – it is a series <of> of Gems that well deserve the finest polish.[3]

    We are rather dull here though the place is quite full for the Prince Regents appearance or behaviour either prevented from coming or drove away from the Place – all respectable people – he was more outrageously dissipated the short time he was here than ever – & has sunk into the vilest of his former associates – Lord Barrymore &c[4]

    Lord Sheffield has been so good as to invite me to pass some days at his house where I shall go on Wednesday[5] in case your Lordship has occasion to honour me with any Letter, which I shall be gratified by if it assure me of your Lordships health – & inform me of your address in the country – where I would like, if you please, to send the Proof of the small Edition of the Giaour[6]

    Your Lordship will see that I could not refrain from asking after you or from presenting my hasty compliments –

    I dine today with three of my Authors – D'Israeli Prince Hoare – and Northcote[7] –

    I am ever
    Your Lordships
    Affectionate & grateful
    humble Servant
    John Murray

My address is
Post Office

Notes to Letter 13)

JM had gone to Brighton for ten days and was probably writing from the D'Israelis, who may have taken a house at 5 Pavilion Parade. As B wrote to him on Thursday 26 August saying, 'I was quite sorry to hear you say you staid in town on my account – & I hope sincerely you did not mean so superfluous a piece of politeness' (*BLJ* III, 100), JM must have left London on Friday 27 or Saturday 28. He had returned to London by Thursday 9 September (see B's letter to Moore of that date; *BLJ* III, 112).

1. JM was about to write 'My dear Lord and Master' but clearly had second thoughts and reserved the address for a later occasion (see Letter 23 below).

2. I regret I have been unable to trace any such letter, but it seems very probable that it was the same as that for which JM gives his long explanation in his letter to B of 22 September 1813 (see Letter 15 and n. 1 below).

3. This would have been in preparation for the 5th edn of *The Giaour*, which B told Moore on Wednesday 1 September he had 'added to a good deal; but still in foolish fragments. It contains about 1200 lines, or rather more – now printing' (*BLJ* III, 105), and which was first announced as published in the *Morning Chronicle* for Saturday 11 September 1813.

4. The Prince Regent and his entourage made two visits to Brighton in August 1813: from 4 to 11 August (returning to London in time for his birthday on Thursday 12), and from 17 to 27 August. JM refers to his second visit when Lord Barrymore – Henry Barry, 8th and last Earl of Barrymore (1770–1823) – was in attendance. *The Times* of Friday 27 August reports that on Monday of that week the Prince had taken 'an extended ride through Shoreham and over the Downs by the Dyke, accompanied by Lord BARRYMORE and others', and on Tuesday had given 'a magnificent supper and ball, to which all those who move in the present Pavilion circle were invited, and a number of people of fashion now here and in adjacent places of summer resort. The company amounted to about 150, and remained in much gaiety and hilarity till a late hour, abundantly delighted with the splendour of the banquet, the festivity of the amusements, and the charms of the vocal and instrumental music. The whole suite of apartments were [*sic*] lighted up with the utmost possible brilliancy.' Among the royal, ducal and noble guests specifically mentioned as being present was Lord Barrymore. Again, on Monday 30 August *The Times*, reporting the Prince's departure from Brighton on Friday 27, summed up his visit as follows: 'During the residence of the PRINCE at the Pavilion, the evening parties have been uniformly splendid and festive, and continued with much gaiety to a late hour: but the public have been merely auditors, and in no instance spectators of the sumptuous festivals and exhibitions that have enlivened and embellished this summer excursion of royalty ... The royal amusements and hospitalities

have been entirely confined within the walls of the Pavilion.' Among those 'conspicuous' at his parties had been Lord Barrymore. According to Gronow, Lord Barrymore was club-footed, one of the founders of the Whip Club and among the leading members of the Four-in-hand Club, had a taste for pugilism and cock-fighting, was 'an accomplished musician, a patron of the drama, and a great friend of Cooke, Kean, and the two Kembles', and said 'to be a man of literary talents'. Although a 'boon companion' of the Prince, assisting 'at the orgies that used to take place at Carlton House, where he was a constant visitor', he was eventually 'discarded, in accordance with that Prince's habit of treating his favourites', and 'left Carlton House ruined in health and reputation', dying 'a martyr to the gout and other diseases' (John Raymond, ed., *The Reminiscences and Recollections of Captain Gronow* [London: Bodley Head, 1964], 274 and 348–50; see also, John Robert Robinson, *The Last Earls of Barrymore, 1769–1824* [London: Sampson Low, Marston & Co., 1894], esp. 227–52).

5. John Baker Holroyd, 1st Earl of Sheffield (1735–1821), statesman and writer on social and commercial affairs, was a great friend of Gibbon and edited his *Miscellaneous Works* (1796), the 2nd edn of which JM was to publish and to give B as a wedding present in 1814 (see Letter 61 below). Wednesday would have been 1 September; but how long JM remained with him is difficult to say. He lived at Sheffield Place, Sussex from where he wrote to JM at Brighton on Tuesday 7 September 1813 regretting JM's having to leave him so soon and saying that his horse was very welcome but had a bad cough (MA).

6. B may have told JM that his movements were to be a little uncertain, but he was still in town when JM returned. He did not 'honour' JM with 'any Letter' either at Sheffield Place or at the 'Post Office' in Brighton. For 'the small Edition of the Giaour', see n. 3 above; by 'small', JM means small in the quantity printed, not in the size of the book (see *CPW* III, 413).

7. Prince Hoare (1755–1834) ('Prince' being his first name, not a title), author and artist and Secretary for Foreign Correspondence to the Royal Academy where he had exhibited between 1781 and 1785. Of his writings, JM published his *Epochs of the Arts* (1813), dedicated to the Prince Regent, and a collection of miscellaneous essays by various writers edited by Hoare entitled *The Artist*, 2 vols (1810). Of his numerous plays, from which many songs were extracted and published separately, *No Song, No Supper: an opera* (1790) was his most popular. James Northcote, RA (1746–1831), author and artist and regular exhibitor at the Royal Academy, was the assistant of Sir Joshua Reynolds and published (not with JM, but with Henry Colburn) *Memoirs of Sir Joshua Reynolds, Knt.* (1813) and *Supplement to the Memoirs … of Sir Joshua Reynolds, Knt.* (1815). He was commissioned by the engraver John Boydell (1719–1804) to paint nine of the pictures for his Shakespeare Gallery, which Boydell engraved and produced in his edn of Shakespeare's works (1802). B had a set of these plates (see his Sale Catalogue for 1816; *CMP*, 244, lot

374). In 1830 William Hazlitt published *Conversations of James Northcote*, the very first conversation of which concerns B.

Letter 14)   Monday [20 September 1813], Tuesday [21 September 1813]

Albemarle St.
Monday

My most dear Lord

Some time ago I mentioned that I had sent the fifth Edition of the Giaour to Mr Gifford which I did not expect him to touch except for the purpose of sending it to our Reviewer, (who has totally disappointed us)[1] – . I called to day upon M^r G and as soon as a Gentleman was gone & he was to begin upon business he fell back in his largest Arm Chair and exclaimed – upon my honour Murray Lord Byron is – <the most extrad> a most extraordinary Man – the new Edition of his Poem contains passages of exquisite – extraordinary beauty^+ equal to any thing that I have ever read – what is he about will he not collect all his force <fo> for one immortal Work – – His subject is an excellent one – we never had descriptions of eastern Manners before – all that has been hitherto attempted was done without actual knowledge – I told him that Moore was writing an Eastern Story – Moore said he will do only what has been already done – & he is incapa<p>ble of writing any thing like Lord Byron[2] – M^r G – speaks too of the vigour of all your Additions[3] – Speaking of Scott he said you did not interfere with each other but that he had completely settled in his mind your certain superiority – a Genius of a higher order – I told him how rejoiced <he> I was to hear him speak thus of you & added that I knew you cherished his Letter to you[4] – he again deplored your wandering from some great object & regretted that you would not follow his recommendation of producing something worthy of you for highly as he thinks of your Lordships talents in both poems[5] & I believe most particularly in the last, still he thinks you have by no means stretched your pinions to the full & taken the Flight to which they are equal –

I would apologize to Your Lordship for detail – what superficially appears mere praise but I am sure your Lordship will go deeper in to it and see in it my anxiety after your Fame alone – In our next number there will be an able review of the Fifth Edition – for the Edinb. Rev. had anticipated our extracts[6] –

At Mad. de Staëls yesterday you were much the subject of

conversation with Sir Ja^s Mackintosh – Conversation Sharp & Sir Ja^s asked, and was astonished at, the Number of Copies sold of the Giaour – a Lad<ay>y (another Lady) (not very young though) <to> took away a Copy of the Giaour by the talismanic effect of the enclosed Card[7] –

Do me the Kindness to tell me when your Lordship proposes to return – I am At Home[8] – for the remainder of the Season & until the termination of All Seasons

your Lordships
faithful Servant
John Murray

+I <remem> recollect now that he said they astonished him –

I have ventured to address at – rather than to your Lordship & if it find you I hope you will pardon my thus breaking in upon your retreat.
Murray

Tuesday[9]

Notes to Letter 14)

Cover: The R^t Honble Lord Byron/Ashton Hall/Yorkshire pm: 21 September 1813

This letter has been redirected 'supposed Warrington/Lancaster'. Here it was endorsed 'No such Person at the Duke of Hamiltons/Ashton Hall/Lancaster', and was forwarded (postmarked Warrington 25 September 1813) to London where it eventually arrived on 16 October 1813. B had gone to stay with James Wedderburn Webster at Aston Hall, Rotherham where he remained for a week, from about Friday 17 to Saturday 25 September (see *BLJ* III, 115 and 118). By JM's unfortunate misspelling of Ashton for Aston, B would not have received this letter until his return to London from his second visit to the Websters on Wednesday 20 October.

1. The publication of the 5th edn of *The Giaour* (now increased to 1215 lines) was announced in the *Morning Chronicle* for Saturday 11 September. The 'Reviewer, (who has totally disappointed us)' was George Ellis, to whom Gifford had written on Wednesday 30 June 1813 (in a cover addressed, dated and franked by B, '1813/London July fifth –/George Ellis Esqre/Sunning Hill/Staines/Byron'): 'I had some thoughts of asking you to say a few words on the Giaour You pleased Lord Byron mightily before, and he seems to me worth some pains. He is in bad hands, and is therefore gloomy and perverse, and sees every thing thro' a vile medium: but he has great powers, and had his good fortune thrown him into respectable society, they might have been

turned to good account. Should you like to give a page or two on his little poem? If not, it must be passed over, for I know no one else, to whom I could trust it' (BL Add. 28099, ff. 115–16). Evidently Ellis declined; for Gifford wrote again on Monday 1 November (in a cover addressed, dated and franked by B, '1813/London November second/G – Ellis Esqre./Sunning Hill/Staines/Byron.'): 'And then there is the Giaour – I have examined like Mrs Quickly man by man boy by boy [*I Henry IV*, III, iii, 55], & cannot get a substitute for you – so you must march like poor Deshayes. True it is, that I rec^d long since a couple of voluntary reviews of this poem; but rejected them both, with the plea that the work was already in hand. Lord Byron, as Murray conceits [*sic*], only stays in England till we dismiss him in peace' (ibid., ff. 117–18. Deshayes is presumably André Des Hayes, the choreographer and dancer at the King's Theatre, to whom B refers in *EBSR*, 622–23; see *CPW* I, 248, 411). This clearly persuaded Ellis; for Gifford wrote on Monday 13 December (in a cover addressed, dated and franked by B, '1813/London Decr. thirteenth/G. Ellis Esqre./Sunning Hill/Staines/Byron'): 'Your letter has made me very happy – and I mean to proceed to Murray's forthwith, & dispatch the bride of Abydos to you – who, by the way, is not a <u>bride</u> – unless after the manner of Monk Lewis's spectres "Since Death, not Romeo, hath her maidenhead"' (ibid., ff. 119–20, adapting *Romeo and Juliet*, III, ii, 137). See also n. 6 below.

2. Moore had in fact been working since 1812 at what would eventually become *Lalla Rookh* (1817); but progress was slow and he was discouraged by the publication of *The Giaour*. In a letter to Mary Godfrey of July or August 1813 he told her: 'I confess I feel rather down-hearted about it. Never was anything more unlucky for me than Byron's invasion of this region, which when I entered it, was as yet untrodden, and whose chief charm consisted in the gloss and novelty of its features; but it will now be over-run with clumsy adventurers, and when I make my appearance, instead of being a leader as I looked to be, I must dwindle into an humble follower – a Byronian. This is disheartening, and I sometimes doubt whether I shall publish it at all; though at the same time, if I may trust my own judgment, I think I never wrote so well before' (Moore, *Letters*, I, 275). B certainly knew Moore was intending a '*grand coup*' at least as early as 22 August 1813, lending him books for that purpose (*BLJ* III, 97 and 104), and it was probably he who gave JM this information. For he wrote to Moore 'from Murray's, and I may say, from Murray,' on 9 September 1813, expressly to tell him that JM 'would be happy to treat with you, at a fitting time', and recommending him as a 'fair, liberal, and attentive' publisher (*BLJ* III, 112). It may have been in response to this, or to a subsequent enquiry of JM's concerning the progress of the poem, that Moore wrote to JM on a Sunday evening in late 1813: 'It is only very lately that I have applied with any degree of earnestness to the poetical Work I am employed upon, and I hope to be ready for the *hammer* before the end of Spring' (*Letters*, I, 291).

3. For the specific additions, see *CPW* III, 411.

4. For Gifford's letter to B, see Letter 10 above.

5. That is, *CHP* I and II and *The Giaour*.

6. In the event it was not the 5th but the 11th edn of *The Giaour* that, together with *The Bride of Abydos*, was favourably reviewed by George Ellis in the *Quarterly Review*, X, xx (January 1814), 331–54 (see also, n. 1 above). For Jeffrey's review in the *Edinburgh Review*, see Letter 12 above.

7. In his Journal for Monday 20 September 1813, Lord Glenbervie records that he, Lady Glenbervie and Frederick North were at Madame de Staël's in Richmond 'yesterday' (i.e., Sunday 19 September), where her own family, 'Raucourt' (*sic* for Rocca), Sir James Mackintosh and Richard 'Conversation' Sharp, 'formed the rest of the party at dinner' (Walter Sichel, ed., *The Glenbervie Journals* [London: Constable, 1910], 189–90). He does not say that JM was there, nor that any of the conversation concerned the sale of *The Giaour*, nor that Lady Glenbervie 'took away a Copy' of it, though she was almost certainly the 'Lady' who did so.

8. JM's underlining of 'At Home' suggests that he may be glancing at his own – perhaps new – visiting card, which itself may be 'the enclosed Card', though none has been forthcoming.

9. 'I have … Tuesday': this postscript is written on the inside of the cover.

Letter 15)   Wednesday [22 September 1813]

My Lord

I did not know to what your Letter referred until I had examined my people – I find that the day on which I left town I sent a Letter for the indulgence of your Lordships frank and that my superior clerk asked me to solicit a frank for him also[1] – I therefore wrote upon his address my compliments – – The Letter contained a note which the poor fellow, who is on the point of beginning business for himself, was sending to his friend to discount. As I went away in the evening I knew nothing further about the affair – but the Man says that he ordered his inferior in office to go directly & state that the letters had been safely received – of mine I know nothing but I dare say it has arrived safely and my only anxiety is about the uneasiness – or rather trouble which it appears to have occasioned your Lordship – to say nothing of the misery I suffer at receiving a Letter from your Lordship without one word of that kindness which has made all the former ones so dear to My Lord

Your Lordships
faithful Servant
Jno Murray

Wednesday

I addressed a Letter to your Lordship yesterday – simply Ashton Hall
– Yorkshire[2]

Notes to Letter 15)

B was still with the Websters at Aston Hall (see Letter 14 above). There is no
letter extant from him to JM to which JM might be referring, and the exact
nature of his complaint is not altogether clear. The suggestion seems to be that
B had rather brusquely taken exception to JM's apparent freedom with his frank
– of which postal procedure I give the following explanation.

'Franking' was a term used for the right of sending letters or packages post-free
(Fr. 'franc'). By an Act of Parliament of 1764, every peer and every member of
the House of Commons was allowed to send 10 free letters a day, not in excess
of an ounce, to anywhere in the Kingdom, and to receive 15 letters free (see,
for example, B to Hodgson, 13 October 1811: 'as my letters are free, you will
overlook their frequency' [*BLJ* II, 111]). As the Act did not restrict this privilege
to letters actually written by or to those so privileged, they frequently sent or
received letters for their friends – the only requirement being their signature in
the corner of the envelope or cover. Hence they supplied friends with envelopes
already signed to be used at any time. So matters stood and abuses prospered until
stricter regulations came into force in 1837. (For an amusing play on 'franking',
see B's letter of 28 July 1813 to Moore who, having neglected writing properly
to B himself for some time, had asked him to forward yet another letter of his to
Rogers upon which B expostulated in his best Shylockian manner: 'I shall send
you verse or arsenic, as likely as any thing, – four thousand couplets on sheets
beyond the privilege of franking; that privilege, sir, of which you take an undue
advantage over a too susceptible senator, by forwarding your lucubrations to every
one but himself. I won't frank *from* you, or *for* you, or *to* you – may I be curst if
I do' [*BLJ* III, 82].)

1. It seems very likely that either JM's 'Letter' or that of his 'superior clerk' is
   the one JM refers to at the opening of his letter to B of Sunday 29 August,
   written just after his arrival in Brighton (see Letter 13 and n. 2 above).

2. The postscript refers to Letter 14 above. What JM does not mention either
   in this Letter (15) or in Letter 14 above is that he had received B's letter to
   him of Wednesday 15 September asking him to enquire after any ship bound
   for the Mediterranean (*BLJ*, III, 115). That JM had received it is evident from
   a letter in MA from him to Croker, dated simply 'Friday N[t].' but clearly

Friday 17 September, passing on B's request, and recommending him as 'a personal friend ... an entertaining Companion ... a Man of Genius ... good hearted & simple hearted'. He assured Croker that B knew nothing and would know nothing of the present application, and nothing seems to have come of it.

Letter 16)   [Thursday 21 October 1813?]

My Lord

I am glad to find by your Lordships note that you are safe & well – & hope for the pleasure of seeing you here today –

Mr Glover (Son of the Author of Leonidas) is just exclaiming that Lord Byron is a very extraordinary Man –

Amen

J. M

Notes to Letter 16)

Cover: The Lord Byron.

The date of this letter is conjectural: there is no extant 'note' from B to which it is an obvious response, though he had returned from the Websters the preceding day (Wednesday 20 October) and may have informed JM of his arrival (cf. *BLJ* III, 148–51). Richard Glover (*c*.1750–1822), MP for Penryn and intimate friend for 30 years of the fifth Duke of Leeds (d. 1799), was the son of Richard Glover (1712–85), the author of *Leonidas* (1737), and may have been with JM at the time for reasons connected with his father's *Memoir* which JM was to publish in December 1813 (see Letter 24, n. 3 below). He lived in St James's Street and was, according to Lord Glenbervie, 'a prosing boring old bachelor' (Francis Bickley, ed., *The Diaries of Sylvester Douglas (Lord Glenbervie)*, 2 vols [London, 1928], II, 120; see also, *The Gentleman's Magazine*, XCII, Pt II [September 1822], 284).

[Between this Letter (16) and the next Letter (17) there is the following note from B to JM (MS Cheltenham Ladies College) not included in *BLJ*.]

> [Saturday] 13 November 1813. Cover: To – /Jno. Murray Esqre./50 Ae. Street/Byron. Endorsed in JM's hand: Novr 13 – 1813
>
> Dear Sir –
>
> Will you send me once more the Gour [*sic*] proof – it shall be returned tomorrow morning – or before – & excuse the plague I have given you this day. –
>
> ever yrs.
>
> B

B was by this time back in London and was preparing the 7th edn of *The Giaour*. The most likely proof he here requests to see again is the partial proof of *The Giaour* dated by JM 10 November 1813 (see *CPW* III, 410, no. 25). B had also only just completed *The Bride of Abydos*, which he had sent to JM the day before (Friday 12) and of which he had already received a proof (see *BLJ* III, 161–64 and *CPW* III, 433, nos 1–3). However, he was still undecided as to whether to publish the poem separately or with *The Giaour*. This needs to be stressed. On Friday 12 November he told JM that Rogers and Sharpe (neither of whom had seen *The Bride*) had advised him 'not to risk at present any single publication separately', and therefore suggested she should 'steal quietly into the world' with 'any new edition' of *The Giaour* (*BLJ* III, 162–63). On Monday 15, however, he reported that though he liked 'the *double* form better', Hodgson 'contrary to some others – advises a *separate* publication' (ibid., 166). Nevertheless, on Wednesday 17, he continued to inform Lord Holland that 'The Bride is to be appended to the G[iaou]r' (ibid., 168). Eventually, on Tuesday 23 November, he wrote leaving the decision 'as to printing' to JM: 'print as you will & how you will – by itself if you like – but let me have a few copies in *duets*' (ibid., 173). (As a corollary to this, readers may care to know that the word 'Giaour' occurs only once in *The Bride of Abydos* [I, 459], and in every proof and in the first ten editions inclusive of the poem, is misprinted ['Giour']: the 11th edn [1815] is the first to read 'Giaour' – the reading in all subsequent editions. This has not been recorded elsewhere.)]

Letter 17)   Thursday 18 November 1813

London Nov\. 18\. 1813
Thursday

My dear Lord

I am very anxious that our business transactions should occur frequently, and that they should be settled immediately – for short accounts are favourable to long friendships[1] –

I restore the Giaour to your Lordship entirely, and, for <u>it</u> – the Bride of Abydos – and the miscellaneous Poems, intended to fill up the volume of the small edition[2] – I beg leave to offer your Lordship the sum of One Thousand Guineas – and I shall be happy if your Lordship perceive that my estimation of your talents in my character <as> of a man of business – is not much under my admiration of them, as a man.[3]

I do most heartily accept the offer of your Lordships Portrait, as the most noble mark of friendship with which your Lordship could, in any way, honour me[4] – I do assure your Lordship that I am truly proud of being distinguished as your publisher – and that it will be my anxious endeavour to preserve, through life, the happiness of your Lordships steady confidence.

I shall ever continue
My Lord
your Lordships faithful servant
John Murray

Notes to Letter 17)

Following a 'conversation' on the same subject that they had evidently had together the previous day (Wednesday 17), B had written to JM to confirm his view that the arrangement regarding payment for the copyrights of *The Giaour* and *The Bride of Abydos* should be postponed until after Easter (1814), by which time JM would know how the latter had taken and could then make an offer for the two (*BLJ* III, 166–67).

1. This phrase is proverbial, but cf. Maria Edgeworth, 'Out of Debt Out of Danger', ch. 1 (Mrs Ludgate speaking): 'short accounts make long friends' (Maria Edgeworth, *Popular Tales*, 4th edn, 3 vols [London, 1811], I, 295).

2. The 'miscellaneous Poems' were eventually added to the 7th edn of *CHP* I and II, and comprised: 'From the Portuguese' (no. 194), 'Impromptu, in Reply to a Friend' (no. 216), 'Address, Spoken at the Opening of Drury-lane Theatre' (no. 190), 'To Time' (no. 180), 'Translation of a Romaic Love Song' (no. 154), 'A Song' (no. 221), 'On Being Asked What Was the "Origin of Love"?' (no. 210), 'Remember Him' (no. 217), and 'Lines inscribed upon a Cup formed from a Skull' (no. 124). (B's fair copy of 'Impromptu' is endorsed by JM 'Rec\[d\] Sep. 26 – 1813'; the fair copy, 'not in B's hand, which was used as copy text for the proof' [*CPW* III, 427], is in JM's hand – with the reading 'bleed', later corrected by B in the proof to 'droop', in the final line). See also, Letter 29, n. 1 below.

3. In his Journal for 22 November 1813 B records: 'Mr. Murray has offered me one thousand guineas for the "Giaour" and the "Bride of Abydos." I won't – it is too much, though I am strongly tempted, merely for the *say* of it' (*BLJ* III, 212); and in a letter to JM of Sunday 27 November he repeated his own proposal outlined in the headnote above: 'I shall not trouble you on any arrangement on the score of "the Giaour & Bride" ... before *May* – 1814 – that is six months from hence – and before that time you will be able to ascertain how far your offer may be a losing one – if so – you can deduct proportionally – & if not I shall not at any rate allow you to go higher than your present proposal which is very handsome & more than fair' (ibid., 176–77; see also, Letter 24 n. 2 below).

4. B had made this offer the previous day: 'The pictures of Phillips I consider as *mine* all three – & the one (not the Arnaut) of the two best – is much at

your service if you will accept it as a present' (*BLJ* III, 167). He fulfilled his promise after the Summer Exhibition at the Royal Academy had closed in July 1814 (see Letter 49 below).

Letter 18)   [Saturday 20 November 1813?]

My Lord

Turn to Page 374 of Mad. de Staels <u>Translation</u> Vol 1^{+1} & you will find to my mind a \<c\> still clearer explanation of "The <u>Music</u> of the Face"

I will call tomorrow between 1 & 2^2 –

ever your Lordships

Ser^t.

J. M

at ye Bottom of ye Page

Notes to Letter 18)

<u>Cover</u>: The Lord Byron

The date of this letter is conjectural. In a letter to JM of '[Nov. 20, 1813]' B told him: 'You will cut out the *last half* of the *note* I sent you – & only print down to "*for us both*" – these words will conclude the note'; and he added in a postscript: 'If I could see you for 5 minutes about 1 or 2 – you would oblige me – there is a parcel I cant send' (*BLJ* III, 169). The note in question is that to line 179 of *The Bride*, I ('The mind – the Music breathing from her face!'). The MS of the passage in which this line occurs (lines 170–81) B first sent to JM with a revised proof of the poem dated by JM 'Nov. 19 – 1813'. In this proof, between received lines 169 ('Who met the maid with tears – but not of grief') and 182, originally numbered 170 ('Her graceful arms in meekness bending'), B has made a marginal insertion mark with the direction: 'there is \<an\> an M.S. sent for insertion here. – '. These lines (received lines 170–81) were first printed in a proof dated by JM '1813 Nov. 21', together with the *whole* note (of which there is no MS extant) which remained unaltered thereafter and appears in full in *CPW* III, 436. Immediately following 'for us both.', the note continues: 'For an eloquent passage in the latest work of the first female writer of this, perhaps, of any age, on the analogy (and the immediate comparison excited by that analogy) between "painting and music," see vol. iii. cap. 10. DE L'ALLEMAGNE.' The passage to which this refers in Madame de Staël's *De L'Allemagne*, 3 vols (Londres: John Murray, 1813), III, ch. x, 'Influence de la Nouvelle Philosophie sur les Sciences', runs as follows: 'Sans cesse nous comparons la peinture à la musique, et la musique à la peinture, parceque [*sic*] les

émotions que nous éprouvons nous révèlent des analogies où l'observation froide
ne verroit que des différences' (p. 149). In the English translation this is slightly
abbreviated to: 'We incessantly compare painting to music; because the emotions
we feel discover analogies where cold observation would only have seen differences' (*Germany*; By the Baroness Staël Holstein. Translated from the French. 3
vols [London: John Murray, 1813], III, ch. x, 'Influence of the new Philosophy on
the Sciences', p. 152). However, the passage to which JM directs B's attention here,
and which – though never adopted – does indeed seem 'a still clearer explanation of "The Music of the Face"', occurs in *Germany*, Vol. I, ch. xiii, 'Of German
Poetry', in which, discussing Schlegel's poem *Mélodies de la vie* (a dialogue between
an Eagle and a Swan – the former symbolizing active life, the latter contempla-
tive life), Madame de Staël writes: 'the true beauties of harmony are also found
in this piece, not imitative harmony, but the internal music of the soul. Our
emotion discovers it without having recourse to reflection; and reflecting genius
converts it into poetry' (pp. 374–75; p. 351 in the French edition). When *The Bride*
was published, B's note elicited 'a very pretty billet from M. la Baronne de Staël
Holstein', who was 'pleased to be much pleased' with his mention of her, and
flattered him 'very prettily' (*BLJ* III, 226–27). This is so. Her 'billet' is in the
Bodleian (Dep. Lovelace Byron 155, ff. 139–40), and although it is undated B has
pencilled on the cover: 'Tuesday – Nov 30 – 1813' – the same date as his reply to
her (*BLJ* III, 184–85). She told him in somewhat extravagant terms how deeply
honoured she was to be noticed in the note to his poem, 'et de quel poëme!',
and how she now felt for the first time assured of lasting fame; and she hoped to
see him sometime.

1. JM's cross here refers to his closing direction, 'at ye Bottom of ye Page'
   – which is indeed where the passage to which he alludes in *Germany* begins
   (p. 374; see headnote above).

2. If the dating of this letter is correct, 'tomorrow' would have been Sunday
   21 November (the same date as the first proof of *The Bride* to contain both
   the lines and the note discussed above).

Letter 19)   Saturday [20 November 1813?]

My Dear Lord –
   I declare to God the more I have occasion to read the Poem the
more it delights me – Giffords word <was> conveyed a just Criticism
– it is

Beautiful

Mr Heber agrees entirely with Mr Gifford[1] –
– So My Lord let me print it <u>separately</u> – and allow the <prop>

Venturous Proposal in my Letter to Stand accepted[2] – & then I may
boldly congratulate you upon having passed in Copy Right even
Scott[3] –

  ever faithfully
  your Lordships friend
  & Servant
  Jno Murray

Saturday
11 at N[t].

Notes to Letter 19)

Cover: The Lord Byron

The date of this letter is conjectural. B was still hesitant as to publishing *The Bride*
separately, but first gave JM leave to print as he wished on Tuesday 23 November
(*BLJ* III, 173; see endnote to Letter 15 above).

  1. That is, Richard Heber who, together with Gifford, must have made these
     comments viva voce.

  2. JM's 'Venturous Proposal' was that contained in Letter 17 above.

  3. JM is not quite correct. For the poems of which he had sold the copy-
     right, Scott received £770 for *The Lay of the Last Minstrel* (1805), 1,000
     guineas for *Marmion* (1808), 2,000 guineas for *The Lady of the Lake* (1810)
     and 3,000 guineas for *Rokeby* (1813) (see John Sutherland, *The Life of Walter
     Scott* [Oxford: Blackwell, 1995], 105, 120, 144 and 170).

Letter 20)   Monday [22 November 1813?]

My Lord
  M[r] Canning returned the Poem today with very warm expressions
of delight – I told him your delicacy as to a separate publication – of
which, he said, you should you should [*sic*] remove every apprehension.
  I expect to be able to send the Proof to yr Lordship presently[1] –
  J. M

Monday

Notes to Letter 20)

<u>Cover</u>: The Lord Byron

The dating of this letter is conjectural. However, in his letter to JM of Tuesday 23 November B writes: 'Mr. C[anning]'s approbation (*if* he did approve) I need not say makes me proud' (*BLJ* III, 173). George Canning (1770–1827), statesman, barrister and MP for Liverpool (1812–22), had served in the Pitt and Portland administrations but refused office under Spencer Perceval and Lord Liverpool. His 'warm expressions of delight' with *The Bride* were clearly made prior to its publication and to JM personally. The comment Marchand quotes in his note (*BLJ* III, 173n) was made in a later letter to JM dated (Tuesday) 21 December 1813 written from Hinckley, the pertinent part of which runs as follows: 'I received the Books, & among them the Bride of Abydos. – It is very, very beautiful. – Lord Byron (when I met him one day at dinner at Mr Ward's) was so kind as to promise to give me a Copy of It. I mention this, not to save my purchase – but because I really should be flattered by the present' (MA). The dinner with Ward, where B 'met Canning & all the wits' (including Frere; see Letter 23 below), took place on Tuesday 23 November 1813 (see B's letter to Lady Melbourne of Thursday 25 November, and his Journal entries for Tuesday 23 and Wednesday 24 November [*BLJ* III, 173, 216 and 219]).

1. The proof in question seems most likely to be that dated by JM '1813 Nov. 21', which was the first to contain received lines 170–81 of Canto I of *The Bride* and the note on Madame de Staël (see Letter 18 above).

Letter 21) [Tuesday 23 November 1813?]

Your Lordship may rely upon the careful insertion of the beautiful addition wch I have just received.
    Murray

Notes to Letter 21)

<u>Cover</u>: The Lord Byron

The dating of this letter is conjectural; but in his letter of Tuesday 23 November to JM B told him: 'You wanted some *reflections* – and I send you *per Selim* (in his speech in Canto 2d. page 46) eighteen lines in decent couplets of a pensive if not *ethical* tendency – One more revise poz the *last* if decently done – at any rate the *pen*ultimate' (*BLJ* III, 172–73; cf. also Letter 22 and headnote below). B seems to refer to Selim's speech in *The Bride*, Canto II, 19, 398-[416?] (see *CPW* III, 136 and apparatus, and 432).

Letter 22)   [Tuesday 23 November 1813?]

Genl. Sir To^s. Grahame commands the Expedition to Holland

My Lord

I forgot to tell you that Rogers Poems are a very leading Article in the Edinb. Rev. wch I saw for ten minutes today – L'Allemagne is the last Article in High Praise[1] –

> ever yr Lordships
> Servt.
> J. M

N.B. Mr Hammond[2] tells me Mr Wards hour is 6 poz

Notes to Letter 22)

Cover: The Lord Byron

Although the dating of this letter is conjectural, it was clearly written prior to B's dinner with Ward, where he had been invited this very day to dine in the evening (see *BLJ* III, 173, 216 and 219), and probably just after JM had received B's letter to him of this same date (cf. JM's doubly emphatic 'poz' and B's 'One more revise poz' [*BLJ* III, 173]). Further confirmation comes from the following (see also, n. 2 below). After a distinguished career in the military, General Sir Thomas Graham (1748–1843), soon to be created Baron Lynedoch (1814), was appointed to lead the British Expedition to Holland to support the Dutch effort for independence from the French, his appointment being confirmed at a sitting of the Cabinet Council on Tuesday 23 November 1813. This news did not become public until Wednesday 24 November on which day *The Times* reported: 'Sir Thomas Graham was in the Foreign-office during the sitting of the Cabinet Council yesterday [i.e., Tuesday 23 November]. At the breaking up of the Council he went to the Commander in Chief's office, and had a long interview with the Duke of York. It is said he is to command the troops in Holland.' The *Morning Post* for the same date (Wednesday 24 November), however, announced less tentatively: 'Lieutenant General Sir Thomas Graham has accepted the appointment, which was offered to him in a manner the most flattering, and at the same time in terms so pressing as to amount almost to a command. It is needless to add, that his departure may be hourly expected.' Perhaps it was not quite so 'needless to add' after all, since, according to *The Times* for Monday 6 December, Sir Thomas had still 'not yet left town' on that date; and according to the *Morning Post* for Tuesday 14 December, he did not finally embark from Deal until Sunday 12 December (see also, B to Dr William Clark, 29 November 1813; *BLJ* III, 180). To avoid any confusion, however, it needs to be said that, although the liberation of Holland had taken place on Monday 15 November 1813, the event was not reported in the English newspapers until Monday 22 November, on which date *The Times* announced (with 'Gratitude to the Almighty Disposer of events') the restoration of the Dutch Republic through its own 'spontaneous' efforts, and scattered the page with '*Orange Boven!*' ('up with Orange!') and 'HOLLAND is free!'; the *Morning Post* reported the event, with similar apostrophes, the following day (cf. also B's Journal entry for Tuesday 23 November; *BLJ* III, 218).

1. Rogers' *Poems* ['Including Fragments of a Poem called the *Voyage of Columbus*'] (1812), and Madame de Staël's *De l'Allemagne* (1813), were both very favourably reviewed by Sir James Mackintosh in the *Edinburgh Review*, XXII, xliii (October 1813), Art. II, 32–50, and Art. XII, 198–238 respectively. In a letter of 24 December 1813 to his family, Sir James told them: 'In the last Edinburgh Review you will find two articles of mine, one on Rogers, and the other on Madame de Staël; they are both, especially the first, thought too panegyrical. I like the praises which I bestowed on Lord Byron and Thomas Moore. I am convinced of the justness of the praises given to Madame de Staël' (Mackintosh, II, 271). Without directly naming either of them, Sir James refers with great sensitivity and penetration first to B and then to Moore in his survey of literature during the course of his review of Rogers (pp. 37–38; cf. B's Journal entry for Saturday 27 November 1813 [*BLJ* III, 224]):

> Greece, the mother of freedom and of poetry in the west, which had long employed only the antiquary, the artist, and the philologist, was at length destined, after an interval of many silent and inglorious ages, to awaken the genius of a poet. Full of enthusiasm for those perfect forms of heroism and liberty, which his imagination had placed in the recesses of antiquity, he gave vent to his impatience of the imperfections of living men and real institutions, in an original strain of sublime satire, which clothes moral anger in imagery of an almost horrible grandeur; and which, though it cannot coincide with the estimate of reason, yet could only flow from that worship of perfection, which is the soul of all true poetry.
>
> The tendency of poetry to become national, was in more than one case remarkable. While the Scottish middle age inspired the most popular poet perhaps of the 18th century, the national genius of Ireland at length found a poetical representative, whose exquisite ear, and flexible fancy, wantoned in all the varieties of poetical luxury, from the levities to the fondness of love, from polished pleasantry to ardent passion, and from the social joys of private life to a tender and mournful patriotism, taught by the melancholy fortunes of an illustrious country; – with a range adapted to every nerve in the composition of a people susceptible of all feelings which have the colour of generosity, and more exempt probably than any other from degrading and unpoetical vices.

2. George Hammond (1763–1853) had held various diplomatic posts in Paris, Vienna and Washington, and had been under-secretary for foreign affairs (1795–1806 and 1807–09). He was an intimate friend of Lord Grenville and George Canning and joint editor of *The Anti-Jacobin*. It was undoubtedly he, with his close political associations, who gave JM the as yet unpublicized information concerning Sir Thomas Graham's appointment. See also, Letter 42 below.

Letter 23)   [Wednesday 24 November 1813?]

My dear Lord – & Master[1]

I am so very anxious to procure the best criticism or opinion upon the Bride – that I ventured last night[2] to introduce her to the protection of – Mr Frere – He has just returned – delighted – he is <u>quite</u> delighted – he read several passages to Mr Heber[3] – as exquisitely beautiful he says there is a simplicity runs through the whole that reminds him of the Ancient Ballad[4] – He thinks it equal to any thing your Lordship has produced – I asked if it was equal to the Giaour – he said that the Giaour contained perhaps a greater number of Splendid Passages – but that the mind carries something to <u>rest</u> <u>upon</u> after rising from the Bride of Abydos – it is more perfect – He made one or two remarks – He says that – such words as <u>Gul</u> – & Bulbul though not unpoetical in themselves – but that it is in bad Taste wch ought not to receive the Sanction of yr Lordships example[5] – on the same plan our language might be stripped to the Pronoun –

& scarcely in the chace could <u>cope</u>

with Timid <u>Fawn</u> –

Cope is to meet in conflict[6]

In the passage Stanz [*sic*] IX p 12–13 – wch M^r F though [*sic*] <u>particularly</u> fine he thinks that the dimness of sight occasion [*sic*] by abstraction of mind is rendered less complete by defining the Sabre Stroke as <u>right</u> Sharply dealt.

At page 38 the Parenthesis renders the sense less intelligible

He dont like the arrangement of

and one was red – perchance of guilt –

Ah! <u>how without</u> can blood be spilt?[7]

    it is easily changed

one was red, with Guilt no doubt

Ah how could blood be spilt without[8]

Notes to Letter 23)

Although the dating of this letter is conjectural, Frere was certainly in London and at Ward's dinner on Tuesday 23 (see Letter 20 above and *BLJ* III, 216). Moreover, in MA there is a proof of *The Bride* dated by JM '1813 Nov. 24' (Wednesday), in which the word 'Gul' (Canto I, 1, 8) has been underlined, and both it and the verb 'cope' (Canto I, 5, 136) marked in the margin – all in pencil and in another hand from that of JM, who has himself in pen underlined the adjective 'right' (Canto I, 9, 249) and written beside it in the left margin 'Qy' (i.e., 'Query'), and in the right margin 'too distinct & critical'. He has also marked with a large pen cross in the margin the parenthesis at Canto II, 15, 251–52 (p. 38 in the 1st edn), and on the end fly-leaf written in pen, 'something equal & reminding one of the simplicity of the Ant. Ballad'. Clearly this Letter reflects those proof annotations.

1. Cf. JM's cancelled appellation of B at the opening of Letter 13 above.

2. If the dating of this letter is correct, 'last night' would have been Tuesday 23 November.

3. This would have been Richard Heber again.

4. By 'the Ancient Ballad' Frere means the ballad genre generally rather than any specific ballad.

5. 'Bulbul' ('Lover of the rose', or 'Nightingale') occurs in Cantos I, 10, 288 and II, 28, 694. Lord Holland – to whom *The Bride* is dedicated – after an earlier reading of the poem also questioned the propriety of B's vocabulary. Writing to B on Tuesday 16 November he observed: 'There is somewhere an expression of a sword which <u>sunk keener</u> – It may cut keener or it may sink deeper – but can it <u>sink keener</u>? ... The word <u>Blench</u> I never recollect ... nor can I, truth to say, tell what is the meaning of it ... The sound of some of your Turkish words is not calculated to remove my aversion to them – <u>Wulwulhey</u> [*sic*] is a devil of a word & even in reading your obliging note on my Uncles opinions about the Nightingale's song I could not help regretting that Philomela had so inharmonious a name in the East as <u>Bulbul</u>' (BL Add. 51639, ff. 149–50; B's note referring to Holland's uncle, Fox, is appended to the first occurrence of 'Bulbul' [see *CPW* III, 438, where '"errare mallem", &c.', incidentally, refers to Cicero, *Tusculan Disputations*, I, xvii, 39: 'Errare mehercule malo cum Platone ... quam cum istis vera sentire' ('By heaven I'd rather err with Plato ... than be right with those others')]; 'The loud Wul-wulleh' appears in Canto II, 27, 627). In his reply to Holland of Wednesday 17 November, B answered only the two first of his objections: 'I have altered *Sunk* to *Cut* – "blench" is to grow pale – to shrink – but is a vile word nevertheless' (*BLJ* III, 168). In fact B altered the word to 'Pierced keener than a Christian's sword' in Canto I, 5, 108 (see *CPW* III, 111 and apparatus); 'blench' appears unaltered in Canto I, 12, 353.

6. JM quotes *The Bride* I, 5, 136–37 to which B made no alteration. This

pedantic observation does not have the full authority of Johnson (to whom JM will defer on a later occasion), whose synonyms for 'cope' include to contend, struggle or strive with, to oppose, to encounter, and even 'to interchange kindness or sentiments' (Samuel Johnson, *A Dictionary of the English Language*, 2 vols, 5th edn [London: W. & A. Strahan, 1784], 'Cope').

7. JM slightly misquotes *The Bride* II, 8, 125–26 ('of guilt' for 'with guilt') to which again B made no alteration.

8. The somewhat abrupt ending here may suggest that there should be more to this letter; but JM has written on the recto and verso of the first page only of a folded sheet and could have filled the second page at his leisure had he so wished.

Letter 24)   Monday [29 November 1813]

My dear Lord

I write, chiefly, to assure you that the errata was instantly sent to the printer & that it shall be inserted in every future Copy – I had determined, at first, to cancel the leaf, but, your Lordship will readily perceive, that the insertion would disarrange the figures denoting the number of the lines – but in the next batch of Copies (after the first 1500) it shall be regularly inserted – in the first Instance, I submit to your Lordship, if we might not insert the Errata opposite to the opening of the Poem, by wch means, the reader will be provided against the omission &, probably, will insert the two lines with his pen so as not to disturb him when he comes to the place – if inserted at the end, the two lines will lose their effect[1] –

Although nothing can alter my determination as to the sum I had the honour of offering to your Lordship for the two Poems – yet I am no less sensible to your Lordships extreme liberal<l>ity & kindness[2] –

I have sent the Mem^r. to Lady H. & Copies of the Bride to the two other persons named in your lordships obliging note[3] –

I send yr Lordship a Note wch I have just received from Lord Melvilles private Sect^y Mr Hay, a gentleman of whose taste I have a high opinion.[4]

   ever faithfully
   yr Lordships Ser^t
   Jno Murray

Monday
1 o Clock

Notes to Letter 24)

At 3 o'clock in the morning of Monday 29 November, in his *'doublet & hose
– swearing'*, B sent JM 'an Errata page' containing two additional lines to the
passage imitative of Ovid's Medea which would be 'incomplete without these
two lines' (*BLJ* III, 181; see also, ibid., 183, to JM (a), '[November 30, 1813]'
which should be dated '[Monday 29 November 1813]'). An hour later, 'at 4 in
the morning' and still in his 'doublet & *hosen*' (but not 'swearing'), he sent Lord
Holland a copy of the poem with the same two lines added in his own *'scrawl'*,
which he said he had written in compliance with Holland's suggestion to 'fill up
the *Ovidian* hiatus' (ibid., 189; Marchand conjecturally dates this letter '[Dec. 2,
1813?]', but it should be dated '[Monday 29 November 1813]'). The two lines in
question are what McGann calls the 'D6' version (i.e., the first version) of *The
Bride*, II, 456–57, the proof of which B was to revise to the received 'second D6
version' the following day (see *CPW* III, 138 and apparatus, and 433 and 434;
see also, to JM (b), 'Tuesday Even. [November 30 1813]' [*BLJ* III, 183]). The
lines specifically paraphrase Ovid, *Metamorphoses*, VII, 67–68: 'nihil illum amplexa
verebor/aut, siquid metuam, metuam de coniuge solo' ('in his embrace I shall fear
nothing, or if I fear at all, it shall be for my husband only').

1. When sending JM the errata page, B had told him to print it 'at the end of
   All that is of [the] *"Bride of Abydos"'* (*BLJ* III, 183; see above for correction
   of date): in his reply to this letter later the same day he agreed with JM's
   suggestion: 'You are right about the Er[rata] Page – place it at the beginning' (ibid., 182), and accordingly it was prefixed to the 1st edn, tipped in
   between the Dedication page and the first page of the text (page 1). In the
   second issue and all subsequent editions the lines were incorporated into the
   text.

2. In his letter to JM of Sunday 28 November, B had reiterated his own
   earlier counter-proposal that he would not trouble JM with any arrangement concerning the copyrights of *The Giaour* and *The Bride* 'before *May
   – 1814*' (*BLJ* III, 176–77; see also, Letter 17, headnote and n. 3, and Letter
   19 above).

3. In his letter of Sunday 28 November, B had asked JM to 'Send another copy
   (if not too much of a request) to Ly. Holland of the *Journal* in my name when
   you receive this – it is for *Earl Grey* – and I will relinquish my *own*. – Also to
   Mr. *Sharpe* – Ly. H[ollan]d and Ly. C[aroline] L[amb] copies of "the Bride"
   as soon as convenient' (*BLJ* III, 176; see also, B to Lord Holland, [Monday
   29 November 1813] [ibid., 189, and headnote above for correction of date]).
   I regret to say that Marchand's annotation to 'the *Journal*' here (176, n. 1
   and 189, n. 2), and on one other occasion (ibid., 182 and n. 3; see below), is
   incorrect (see Letters 55 and 56 below). The *'Journal'* in question was *Memoir
   of a Celebrated Literary and Political Character, from the Resignation of Sir Robert
   Walpole, in 1742, to the Establishment of Lord Chatham's Second Administration,*

in 1757; containing Strictures on Some of the Most Distinguished Men of that time. Written by Himself, which was published by JM on Thursday 2 December 1813 (the same day as *The Bride*). The anonymous Memoirist was Richard Glover (1712–85), poet, MP for Weymouth, and author of among other works the celebrated epic poem *Leonidas* (1737) (see Letter 16 above; see also, *CMP*, 165, 199, 462–63 and 513); his anonymous editor was Richard Duppa, FSA (1770–1831), artist and author whose *The Life and Literary Works of Michel Angelo Buonarotti* was first published by JM in 1806 (2nd edn, 1807). In his Preface to the *Memoir*, Duppa suggested that no one had a better claim to be Junius than 'the author of these Memoirs' (p. vi) – a claim he attempted in vain to substantiate in his anonymous *An Inquiry concerning the Author of The Letters of Junius, with reference to the Memoirs by a Celebrated Literary and Political Character*, published by JM in 1814 (B possessed both the *Memoir* and *An Inquiry*; see *CMP*, 243, lot 326). In an undated letter, most probably written *c.*27 November 1813, thanking B for what must have been an earlier copy of the *Memoir* than that requested for Lady Holland, Lord Holland wrote: 'Many thanks for the book – Except your poem I have not seen so interesting a production for some time – It is not like Junius but it is a very curious <docum> memoir of times so confused that it requires many such works to understand them – Surely our Ancestors were yet greater rogues or at least Yet meaner dogs than the race of Politicians of this day even including all the roses blown or blowing' (BL Add. 51639, ff. 186–87). In his reply to JM of Monday 29 November, B observed: 'Mr. Perry is a little premature in his compliments ... though I see the next paragraph is on the *Journal* which makes me suspect *you* as the author of both' (*BLJ* III, 182). In the *Morning Chronicle* for Monday 29 November 1813, there appeared as two successive paragraphs: 'Lord BYRON's Muse is extremely fruitful. He has another Poem coming out, entitled "the Bride of Abydos," which is spoken of in terms of the highest encomium. A new Candidate is to be started, out of an old Trunk, for *Junius*, in the Memoirs of a celebrated literary and political character – another BUBB DODDINGTON [*sic*]'. (George Bubb Dodington, Baron Melcombe [1691–1762], wit, political pamphleteer, and time-serving politician holding offices in the Treasury under various admin-istrations, recorded the venal intrigues of his time in what was first published posthumously in 1784 as *The Diary of the late George Bubb Dodington, Baron of Melcombe*).

4. Robert Saunders Dundas, 2nd Viscount Melville (1771–1851), statesman, schoolfellow and lifelong friend of Scott, was Lord Privy Seal for Scotland and First Lord of the Admiralty from 1812 to 1827 (in which capacity he encouraged exploration in the Arctic where 'Melville Sound' is named after him). The 'Note' of Robert William Hay (1786–1861), his private secretary and contributor to the *Quarterly Review*, is not extant – although B returned it to JM 'with thanks to him & you' on Monday 29 November (*BLJ* III, 182).

Letter 25)   Tuesday [7 December 1813?]

My Lord

I send the MSS – which, anticipating your desire to see it again (I suppose) you will find in the same <u>arrangement</u> as when I received it

I trust your Lordship will favor me with it again as I am desirous to bind it up hereafter with the papers which I have already.

J. M

Tuesday N^t.

Notes to Letter 25)

<u>Cover</u>: The Lord Byron

The date of this letter is conjectural, but it seems to be in response to B's request of '*Tuesday Even. – Decr.* 7 1813' when he wrote to JM: 'Among the heap of blotted M.S.S. I gave you are some which don't belong to the *mass* – & some left out – I shall be obliged to you to let me have ye. *bundle* early *tomorrow* – & if you would like to have it again it shall be sent' (*BLJ* III, 192). There appears to be no further reference to this exchange.

The following unpublished letter from B to JM is in MA. It is undated but was almost certainly written at about this time (December 1813?):

> An enquiry into the true parentage of Jesus Christ by M^r. Taylor of Norwich – it is sold (<u>privately</u>) by Pople Chancery Lane –
> Get me a copy as a <u>favour</u> at any price or in any manner. –

(The dating of this letter is conjectured from Marchand's conjectural dating of 'Dec.? 1813' of B's letter to JM requesting *Ecce Homo! or, A Critical Enquiry into the History of Jesus Christ; being a Rational Analysis of the Gospels*, an anonymous second edition of which was printed, published, and sold in London by D. I. Eaton in 1813 [see *BLJ* III, 185–86]). William Taylor of Norwich (1765–1836) was largely responsible for introducing German literature into England and was well known for his translations of Bürger, Goethe, Lessing and Wieland. He contributed many articles to the *Monthly Magazine*, the *Critical Journal* and other periodicals and was a close friend of Southey (see Jack Simmons, *Southey* [London, 1945], esp. 64, 72–73 and 80). His religious views were highly unorthodox, and his 'enquiry' (which appeared anonymously in 1811 as *A Letter Concerning the Two First Chapters of Luke, addressed to An Editor of the Improved Version*. Printed for the Author at Norwich, and sold by W. Pople, 67, Chancery-Lane, London) is a 'Rational' interpretation of the first two chapters of Luke, in which – grounding his argument on the testimonies of Zacharias, Mary, Elizabeth and Christ himself

– he claims that Zacharias was the father of Christ. B makes no further reference to this work.

Letter 26)   Friday [17 December 1813]

My dear Lord

I send you a proof of the corrections &c which you sent me yesterday & if you are so good as to let me have them soon today it will oblige an impatient <u>Public</u>.

I have to ask a favor of your Lordship which is <u>particular</u> because of its obvious delicacy –

A Mr Dallas (whom I take to be <u>our</u> friends) Nephew has just come over from America[1] & has brought with him an exceedingly humorous work called <u>Scotch Fiddle</u> by Kickerbocher [sic][2] – which I am most anxious to get and to Print here – if your Lordship feel that you could obtain this by an early application – or I shall be anticipated – it would do me a great Service though it can not add to the brimming Cup of my obligation to your Kindness[3]

Jno Murray

Friday

Notes to Letter 26)

On Thursday 16 December B sent JM two lines together with a note to be added to the 4th edn of *The Bride* (*BLJ* III, 201). These form received lines 662–63 of Canto II, stanza 27 (*CPW* III, 145 and apparatus, 434 and 442 n. 663).

1. In a letter of Thursday 2 December 1813 thanking B for *The Bride* and *The Giaour*, which he had received two days earlier, Dallas told him: 'I find you are the Bard of American idolatry [cf. *Romeo and Juliet*, II, i, 110] – I have a nephew just arrived in this country from St Petersburg, where he was sent as Secretary to the American Mission, and it is from him I hear that your name fills the trump of Transatlantic Fame [cf. *EBSR*, 400]. You are read from one end of the United States to the other, and universally placed foremost in the list of Poets' (MA; cf. B's Journal entry for Sunday 5 December 1813; *BLJ* III, 229–30). Dallas's nephew was George Mifflin Dallas (1792–1864) – 'son to the American Attorney-general', as B noted in his Journal (ibid., 229), Alexander James Dallas (1749–1817) – who in 1813 was appointed Secretary to the diplomat Albert Gallatin (1761–1849), the leader of the American peace mission to Russia who had offered to mediate between Britain and the United States in their continuing hostili-

ties. (In the event the mission proved fruitless as Britain refused mediation, and peace was not restored until the ratification of the Treaty of Ghent in February 1815.) The *Morning Post* for Saturday 27 November 1813 reported that 'Mr. Dallas, Secretary to the Commissioners from the United States to St. Petersburgh, arrived in town this morning from Gottenburgh, with dispatches for his Majesty's Ministers.' *The Times* for Monday 29 November 1813, however, reported that 'A Sunday paper says, "We are authorised to state, that the rumour of Mr. DALLAS being the bearer of pacific overtures on the part of America is utterly without foundation. That Gentleman's journey to this country is purely for the purpose of visiting an uncle and other relations, and to facilitate this object he obtained a courier's passport. The mission to Russia, to which Mr. DALLAS was attached as Secretary, has long since terminated."'

2. This was a burlesque of Scott's *The Lay of the Last Minstrel* entitled *The Lay of the Scottish Fiddle: A Tale of Havre de Grace. Supposed to be written by Walter Scott, Esq. First American, from the Fourth Edinburgh Edition*, first published in Philadelphia by Inskeep and Bradford in 1813. (Written in irregular stanzas, with gothic machinery, pirates and freebooters, and one hundred pages of notes, it is set in New York and burlesques the war between Britain and America. I do not know if the pun was intended but, according to the *Dictionary of the Vulgar Tongue* [London: C. Chappel, 1811], 'Scotch Fiddle' was slang for 'the itch'.) The author was not in fact Washington Irving – whose pseudonym (Diedrich Knickerbocker) JM misspells here, and to whom nonetheless it was universally ascribed – but his fellow-countryman and satirist, James Kirke Paulding (1778–1860), author of *The Diverting History of John Bull and Brother Jonathan* (1812), who together with Washington and William Irving had founded and edited the satirical periodical, *Salmagundi; or, the Whim-whams and Opinions of Launcelot Langstaff, and Others* (New York, 1807–08), which was reprinted in London by J. W. Richardson in 1811, edited by John Lambert, and favourably reviewed in the *Monthly Review*, LXV (August 1811), 418–24.

3. In his reply to JM of Friday 17 December, B told him: 'I shall be seeing Mr. Dallas today at 5 – & for particular reasons think & hope that I shall be able notwithstanding your *feud* to settle what you wish – at any rate I will do my best' (*BLJ* III, 201). It appears, however, that he did not see Dallas that day, for writing to him the following day, Saturday 18 December, he asked him to let Murray 'have the publication of the S. F. if not absolutely impracticable ... This will not only be a *triumph* to yourself, but will set all right between you and him, and I hope be of eventual service to both ... You can easily dispose of Cawthorn, if he has already arranged with you' (*BLJ* III, 202–03). The '*feud*' to which B refers here arose from what Dallas in a rather confused letter to JM of 8 June 1813 called a 'misunderstanding between us ... relative to my own publication'; a 'note' of his 'for twenty guineas ... included in the Purchase of Childe Harold's Pilgrimage', and a

further note for 'another hundred pounds as a loan', of which JM had said he would probably 'not require the repayment'; and last but not least, JM's failure to pay him 'the compliment of the last Editions of Childe Harold's Pilgrimage' despite his 'promise that if the work had an extensive sale' he 'would make some further advance' (Dallas to JM, 8 June 1813 [MA]); Dallas had also written to B complaining of JM's behaviour in much the same vein two months earlier on 14 and 20 April 1813 [MA]. The 'note for twenty guineas' seems to refer to a loan JM made to him in late 1811 when, having been arrested (presumably for debt), Dallas wrote to JM on 1 November 1811 begging him to lend him 'twenty guineas for a couple of months', which letter JM has endorsed: 'Mem sent the £21 – P^r M^r D's Nephew – DB. 9 – 316 – though vexatiously inconveniencing to me' [MA]; but there is no indication in the copyright agreement or elsewhere that this sum was 'included in the Purchase of Childe Harold's Pilgrimage'. Of this letter (that of 8 June 1813), however, JM apparently took no notice, as is evident from what Dallas now said in his reply to B of Sunday 19 December 1813: 'I would not hesitate a moment to put aside the kind of resentment I feel against Murray for the pleasure of complying with the desire you so strongly express, if it were in my power – but judge of the impracticability when I assure you that a considerable portion of the Poem is in the Printer's hands, and that the publication will soon make its appearance ... I wish for no triumph over Murray, my dear Lord – His money would have been accept-able – I hold him to be considerably in my debt at present, in spite of which he keeps a note of hand of mine in his possession, after treating me with contempt of not noticing a letter in which I desired it might be given up' (MA). JM's application was therefore unsuccessful, and the poem (of which B had a copy; see *CMP*, 240, lot 251) was published by James Cawthorn in February 1814 under the title of *The Lay of the Scottish Fiddle. A Poem. In Five Cantos. Supposed to be Written by W— S—, Esq. First American, from the Fourth Edinburgh Edition*, and was adversely reviewed by John Wilson Croker in the *Quarterly Review*, X, xx (Jan. 1814), 463–67. Scott himself, however, in a letter to Matthew Weld Hartstonge of 18 July 1814, told him he thought it 'a piece of tolerable dull Trans-Atlantic Wit, A Parody on the Lay of the Last Minstrel, which however I take to be the highest compliment I ever received, since it blends me with the Naval reputation of my country' (Scott, *Letters*, III, 466).

Letter 27) Thursday 30 December 1813

My Lord

I feel nearly as little able to write to you, as I was to speak. – without motive, or object, & merely from caprice, to place me at the mercy of one, whom your Lordship told me, but a few days ago, would <u>never</u>

forgive me – <is> were an act of consummate Cruelty which I can
not conceive it possible for you seriously to <im> meditate – but it has
produced the entire effect upon me – for I never felt <more> so bitterly
unhappy <than> as at this moment – – If you really meant to give the
Stab, you gave, to my feelings, may God, harden my heart against man,
for never, never, will I attach myself to another –

Indeed, my Lord, this is not worthy treatment of one whom you have
suffered to absorb – the humble servant in the
    faithful friend
    John Murray

Thursday 7 o Clock
Decr 30 – 1813

Notes to Letter 27)

Cover: To/The R^t Honble Lord Byron/Bennet Street/St James's

This inaugurates the first major hiccup in the relations between B and JM, which
was largely due to the already strained relations between Dallas and JM (see
Letter 24 above). On 17 December 1813 Dallas had written to B informing him
that his nephew Charles would lose his commission in the army (which Dallas
had succeeded in obtaining 'without purchase') if he did not join his regiment in
Cavan in Ireland by the end of the month; and that, as it was beyond his power
'at this time to supply him with the means', he begged B to 'assist this good lad
with forty or fifty pounds', saying he would call on him that day 'about the time
you come home to dress' (MA). This would account for B's saying to JM in his
letter of 17 December that he had 'particular reasons' for thinking he would be
able to settle the '*feud*' between him and Dallas when he saw Dallas at 5 that day
(*BLJ* III, 201); but whether or not he did see him that day is open to question
(see Letter 26, n. 3 above). According to Doris Langley Moore, B 'paid Dallas
£50 over and above the copyright fees to help in equipping his son [*sic*] for the
army' (*Lord Byron: Accounts Rendered* [London: John Murray, 1974], 202); but it
seems very odd that Dallas should not have thanked B for the sum, or otherwise
alluded to it in his letter to B of 19 December. Nevertheless, knowing Dallas's
straightened circumstances, B did present him with the copyright of *The Corsair*;
and this was the immediate reason why JM was now so deeply hurt and offended.
Dallas himself tells us that B gave him the copyright with liberty to treat with
any publisher he chose; but there is no confirmation of this elsewhere. His version
of events is as follows: 'On the 28th of December [1813] I called in the morning
on Lord Byron, whom I found composing "The Corsair." He had been working
upon it but a few days, and he read me the portion he had written. After some
observations he said, "I have a great mind – I will." He then added he should
finish it soon, and asked me to accept of the copyright. I was much surprised ...

But as he continued in the resolution of not appropriating the sale of his works to his own use, I did not scruple to accept that of the Corsair, and I thanked him' (Dallas, *Correspondence*, III, 58–59). Without disputing whether B 'asked' Dallas to accept the copyright, or whether Dallas 'asked' B for it (as he had done in the case of *CHP* I and II), so far this is plausible enough; but the remainder of his story is extremely suspect: 'He gave me the poem complete on new-year's day, 1814, saying, that my acceptance of it gave him great pleasure, and that I was fully at liberty to publish it with any bookseller I pleased, independent of the profit ... I must however own, that I found kindness to me was not the sole motive of the gift. I asked him if he wished me to publish it through his publisher? "Not at all," said he; "do exactly as you please: he has had the assurance to give me his advice as to writing, and to tell me that I should out-write myself. – I would rather you would publish it by some other bookseller." – The circumstance having lowered the pride of wealth, a submissive letter was written, containing some flattery, and, in spite of an awkward apology, Lord Byron was appeased. He requested me to let the publisher of the former poems have the copyright, to which I of course agreed' (ibid., 59–60).

From what we know, B began *The Corsair* on 18 December 1813, and completed his fair copy between 27 December 1813 and 1 January 1814 (*CPW* III, 442). On Wednesday 29 December 1813 Dallas wrote to him: 'The delight I felt in hearing you read such exquisite Poetry, not diminished you will believe by the manner in which it was bestowed, made me forget to say that I wished if you thought practicable to save you the labour of copying it. I did mean to call again today to make the offer, though I confess I fear I should be longer about it than I could wish unless I could be near you while I wrote, and indeed I shall prize it the more in your handwriting, for I purpose to have it recopied for the Press ... If I wished a triumph over Murray, you have given me <an> such an opportunity as I might be proud to make use of, but I shall feel much more pleasure in showing you with what moderation I can use the power you have put into my hands' (MA; not in Dallas). The following day, Thursday 30 December, having seen B again he wrote: 'When I left you this morning, in thinking that it was hardly possible for you to write out the Poem this week, I forgot that in receiving from you as much as you may have written would expedite my fair copy of it, I shall therefore come to town on Saturday [1 January 1814], and will call in Bennett Street. – If I should find the whole done, it will be a pleasure indeed – in which case I think I should be able to bring you my fair Copy on Monday [3 January 1814]. – I cannot tell you with what delight my family have received the information of this new proof of your kindness' (MA; not in Dallas). These letters seem to corroborate part of Dallas's story (though in Dallas he does not mention any of these copying proposals); and it must have been after Dallas had left B in the morning of 30 December that B told JM he had given him the copyright. But there is no indication that he had given Dallas leave to treat with any other publisher. Indeed, quite the reverse; for, in his reply to JM, which Marchand conjecturally dates '[January 3? 1814]' but which seems to have been written immediately in response to this letter (27) of JM's, and should rather be dated '[Saturday 1 January 1814?]', B told

him: 'I will answer your letter this evening – in the mean time it may be sufficient to say – that there was no intention on my part to annoy you – but merely
to *serve* Dallas – & also to rescue myself from a possible imputation that I had
other objects than fame in writing so frequently – whenever I avail myself of any
profit arising from my pen – depend upon it it is not for my own convenience …
I shall answer this evening – & will set all right about D[alla]s – – – – I thank
you for your expressions of personal regard – which I can assure you I do not
lightly value' (*BLJ* IV, 14–15); and again, in a letter (which may well have been
his 'answer' here promised) of Sunday 2 January 1814, B told JM: 'The Corsair
is copied & now at Ld. Hol[land]'s but I wish Mr. G[iffor]d to have it tonight.
– Mr. D[alla]s is very *perverse* – so that I have offended both him & you – when
I really meaned to do good at least to one – & certainly not to annoy either'
(*BLJ* IV, 14). Thus JM's present anxiety seems to have arisen not from Dallas's
unsubstantiated claim that B had allowed him to treat with another publisher, but
from B's having placed JM at 'the mercy of one' who would not use what Dallas
sanctimoniously calls 'moderation' in his dealings with him.

Furthermore, on Monday 3 January 1814, Dallas wrote again to B saying: 'I
am come here to go to rest, but cannot till I write a few lines to tell you I have
thought again & again of your letter of dedication. It cannot add to the beauty of
the Poem, but I do not think you are aware of the value it adds to the publication. Independent of intrinsic elegance, the dedication of it to Moore will make
thousands buy who would have confined their pleasure to perusal – thousands in
England, and myriads in Ireland, where every young man that can buy a dinner,
and read, will fast a day rather than not read and possess the praises of their Poet
so emphatically & beautifully recorded. Thanks, and Good night!' (MA).

With regard to the original (and, in the event, printed and received) version
of the Dedication to Moore, B certainly found Dallas's support useful; for when
he sent both it and the second version (written at JM's solicitation) to Moore for
him to choose between the two, he told him: 'Take your choice; – no one, save
he [JM] and Mr. Dallas, has seen either, and D. is quite on my side, and for the
first' (to Moore, Saturday 8 January 1814; *BLJ* IV, 18). With regard to the copyright agreement of *The Corsair*, there is in MA the following letter, of which the
signature and closing address to JM are in B's hand, but the remainder in another
hand, which does not appear to be that of Dallas:

> 4, Bennet Street, St. James's
> Tuesday Jany. 4th. 1814 –
>
> Sir,
> I have given the Copyright of my new poem to be called the
> Corsair (the Manuscript of which I delivered into your hands on
> Sunday last [2 January 1814]) to Mr. R. C. Dallas and desire that he
> may have all the benefit of it. You will therefore agree with him for
> the purchase of it and I will ratify and confirm whatever agreement
> he may make with you on the subject and for transferring the whole
> Copyright thereof to you
>
>   Byron

To
J. Murray Esq^e.
50 Albemarle Street
London

In what seems to be a response to this (and perhaps a subsequent meeting between JM and either Dallas or B), is the following clerk's copy of a letter from JM to Dallas of Thursday 6 January 1814, which is also in MA:

> Dear Sir
>
> I was no less surprised than concerned to hear a few days ago that you complained of my having said something which you considered as hurtful to your feelings. I do assure you that nothing was ever more distant from my intention or thoughts and I have therefore no hesitation in saying that this imagined slight must have arisen in a misconception which I very much regret.
>
> As I do not desire to keep you waiting for the Settlement of the Corsair Poem which Lord Byron inform\<ed\>s me he has presented to you, I have the pleasure of inclosing 3 bills at 2, 4 & 6 Mo^{ths}. payable at my Bankers, amounting to five Hundred Guineas for the Copy-right, and I shall feel happy if this transaction, prove the occasion for the renewal of our acquaintance.
>
> With Compliments I beg leave to offer the assurance of the continued regard, in which I remain
>
> Dear Sir
> Your faithful Servant
> John Murray
> Albemarle Street
> Do me the favor to return the Receipt which is inclosed when it is signed

A 'Copy' in a clerk's hand of that 'Receipt' is also in MA:

> Received this Tenth day of January 1814 – by the Consent and Desire of the Right Honorable Lord Byron of M^r. John Murray the Sum of five hundred Guineas for the entire Copy-right of the "Corsair", a Tale by Lord Byron and I promise a further Assignment if required
>
> R. C. Dallas
>   By my Consent and Desire
>   Byron

£525. 0. 0

Letter 28)   [Monday 3 January 1814?]

Some part of Childe Harold in <u>this</u> Copy is wrong & I send it only for the New Poem –

My Lord
 I will attend you this evening between 9 & 10 if agreeable –
 I send the Corsair <u>corrected</u> <&> from the Copy I got last night & Childe Harold with the <u>New</u> & very beautiful Poem
 Jno Murray

Notes to Letter 28)

<u>Cover</u>: The Lord Byron

The date of this letter is conjectural. On Sunday 2 January 1814 B told JM that *The Corsair* was copied and was at Lord Holland's, but that he wished Gifford to have it that night (*BLJ* IV, 14). The following day, Monday 3 January, he repeated twice that he would 'answer' JM's letter (27) 'this evening' (ibid., 14–15). As there is no letter extant that might be taken as such an 'answer', the suggestion seems to be that B would so 'answer' when he and JM met in the evening – which would thus account for JM's opening sentence here specifying the time he would 'attend' him.

With this present letter JM clearly sent B two proofs. Of these the one was evidently a partial of a proof of *CHP* (7) containing the 'New Poem', which would have been 'To Ianthe' (originally entitled 'To the Lady Charlotte Harley'), which was first printed as the introductory stanzas to that edition. This is the only 'New Poem' that would have affected the text of *CHP*. In MA there is an undated proof of 12 pages (six leaves), paginated from 3 to 14, which contains the texts of 'To Ianthe' (pp. 3–5) and *CHP* I, 1–13, including the first four stanzas of Childe Harold's 'Good Night' (pp. 6–14), which is endorsed by JM 'Correct & Press/<u>immediately</u>/J.M', beside which he has jotted 'p. 90 Corsair/broken f'. The proof is very grubby and contains numerous directions by the printer to the typesetter concerning the layout of the texts – which in the case of 'some part of Childe Harold' is indeed 'wrong'. The whole proof is unmarked by B, but it incorporates corrections made by him in an earlier proof of 'To Ianthe' which McGann designates '*MI proof*' (*CPW* II, 6–8, apparatus).

The other proof must have been that of *The Corsair* endorsed by JM as the first proof with author's corrections and dated by him 4 January 1814 (presumably the date he received it from B, after this letter [28] and after their meeting in the evening), on the title-page of which is a comment by Gifford saying the title 'is placed too high – It does not look well'. This is designated '*Proof 1*' by McGann (*CPW* III, 443).

[At some point after this Letter (28), Gifford wrote JM the following undated letter in MA which JM clearly forwarded to B who has annotated it (B's underlinings and crosses; his comments in square brackets in text):

> I send the Corsair – the only thing which I have attended to is the pointing, <u>having done what I wished before in the proof</u>+ [+ this I have not seen/<u>B</u>n.] – Lord B. uses dashes for commas – this gives the work a very singular appearance, & in some places, mars the sense
>
> I have remedied this in some degree – but he should see it. It took me the whole of yesterday – I am sorry no use was made of the <u>former remarks</u>+ [+ where are these?/B]

With this letter JM must have sent the undated proof McGann designates '*Proof 7a*' (*CPW* III, 444), in which Gifford has converted almost every single dash on every page into some other punctuation mark (which certainly would have taken him 'the whole of yesterday'). B's reply to JM, specifically alluding to this proof and to Gifford's letter (which B retained whilst reiterating his annotated queries), is dated simply 'Tuesday', which Marchand has expanded to 'Tuesday [January 4, 1814]' (*BLJ* IV, 15). But this should almost certainly be dated Tuesday 11 January 1814, and was probably written a little earlier in the day than that correctly dated by Marchand 'Tuesday [11 January 1814]', which alludes to the same matters and in which B repeats his thanks to Gifford (*BLJ* IV, 24–25).]

Letter 29)   Thursday 20 January [1814]

My Lord

I am truly anxious to know of your personal safety during this weather of turbulence & disaster – only three Mails had arrived at 3 o Clock today.

I called upon Mr Gifford today & he expresses himself quite delighted with the annexed Poems most particularly with – the Song from the Portuguese & the Stanzas to a "Lady weeping" the latter however he thinks you ought to slip quietly amongst the Poems in Childe Harold for <this is> the present work is to be read by women & the lines would disturb the political feeling – & as it has been already published in a Newspaper it does not accord with your character to appear to think much of it – If you will allow me I should transfer it to Childe Harold & place the Impromptu in its place.[1]

Mr Dallas has sent his proofs with about 200 alterations of the pointing merely now as Gifford made nearly as many – I could not venture so direct an affront upon him as to overturn all that his care had taken[2]

Allow me the pleasure of hearing from your Lordship as early as convenient – Mr Moore returned his proof to me without a correction[3]

I hope to go to press immediately upon receipt of Your Lordships Letter – Mr Gifford is really delighted

I remain in haste

most faithfully

Yr Lordships

Servant

Jno Murray

Thursday

Jan 20

Notes to Letter 29)

<u>Cover</u>: The R^t Honble Lord Byron/Newstead Abbey/Notts <u>pm</u>: 20 Jan 1814

B had left town for Newstead on Monday 17 January 1814 intending to return 'in a week' (*BLJ* IV, 35); but the weather was so appalling – one of the hardest winters on record – that he was constrained to remain until 6 February, by which time *The Corsair* and *CHP* (7) had been published (Tuesday 1 February 1814). B received this letter in the course of writing to JM on Saturday 22 January, his twenty-sixth birthday (*BLJ* IV, 36–38).

1. 'From the Portuguese' (no. 194), written in 1812, and 'Impromptu, in Reply to a Friend' (no. 216), were first published in *CHP* (7) (*CPW* III, 34 and 404, and 92 and 427; see also, Letter 17 above). 'Lines to a Lady Weeping' (no. 182) was first printed anonymously in the *Morning Chronicle* for Friday 7 March 1812 (and noticed 'with disgust' in the *Courier* for that date). In his reply to JM of 22 January, B insisted that 'Lines to a Lady Weeping' 'must go with the Corsair – I care nothing for consequences on this point' (*BLJ* IV, 37), and accordingly it was published – together with the five further supplementary poems – at the end of the 1st edn of *The Corsair* (*CPW* III, 10, 391 and 444; see also, Letters 30 and 31 below).

2. B's reply was emphatic: 'In all points of difference between Mr. G[ifford] & Mr. D[allas] – let the first keep his place – & in all points of difference between Mr. G[ifford] & Mr. anybody else I shall abide by the former – if I am wrong – I can't help it – but I would rather not be right with any other person' (*BLJ* IV, 38).

3. *The Corsair* was dedicated to Moore to whom B had sent a proof on Thursday 13 January asking him to return it 'by the post' (*BLJ* IV, 30); Moore must have returned it direct to JM.

Letter 30) Wednesday [2 February 1814]

My Lord

I have been unwilling to write until I had something to say, an occasion to which I do not always restrict myself –

I am most happy to tell you that your Lordships last Poem <u>is</u> – what Mr Southey's is <u>called</u> – a <u>Carmen Triumphale</u>¹ – never in my recollection has any work since the Letter of Burke to the Duke of Bedford excited such a ferment² – a ferment which I am happy to say will subside into lasting fame – I sold on the Day of Publication, a thing perfectly unprecedented, 10,000 Copies – and I suppose Thirty People who were purchasers (strangers) called to tell the people in the Shop how much they had been delighted & satisfied – Mr Ward says it is masterly – wonderful performance – Mr Hammond – Mr Heber – D Israeli every one who comes & too many call for me to enumerate declare [sic] their unlimited approbation³ – Mr Ward was here with Mr Gifford yesterday & mingled their admiration – Mr Ward is much delighted with the unexpected change of the Dervise – Up rose the Dervise with that burst of light &c⁴ – and Gifford did, what I never knew him do before he repeated several passages from memory Particularly the closing Stanza his death yet dubious – deeds too widely known⁵ – indeed from what I have observed from the very general & unvarying sentiment which I have now gathered the suffrages are descidedly [sic] in favor of this Poem in preference to the Bride of Abydos – & are even now balancing with the Giaour – I have heard no one pass without notice & with expressed regret the idea thrown out by your Lordship of writing no more for a considerable time⁶ – I am really marking down without suppression or extention [sic] literally what I have heard – I was with Mr Shee⁷ this morning to whom I had presented the Poem – he declared himself to have been delighted & that he had long placed Your Lordship far beyond any contemporary Bard – and indeed the [sic] your last Poem does in this is the opinion of almost all that I have conversed with – indeed men women & Children are delighted⁸ – I have the highest encomiums in Letters from Croker & Mr Hay⁹ – but I rest most upon the warmth it has created in Giffords Critic heart – and I do most sincerely congratulate your Lordship – confessing that when you first told me that you were writing another Poem – that heart quaked for your fame – The versification is thought highly of indeed – After Printing the Poems at the End of the first edition I transplanted them to Childe Harold conceiving that your Lordship would have the goodness to pardon this <u>ruse</u> to give additional impetus to that poem &

to assist in making it a more respectable thickness[10] – I <would> sent previous to Publication Copies to all your Lordships friends containg [sic] the Poems at the End & one of them has provoked a great deal of discussion, so much so that I expect to sell off the whole Edition of Childe Harold merely to get at it –

Lord Holland	Mr Gifford
Lady Holland	— Frere
— Melbourne	— Rogers
— Jersey	— Canning
Mr Lewis	— W Scott

— Ward – Mackintosh – Hodgson Hammond – D Israeli – Merivale – Moore &c &c &c[11] – All had them – I sent your Lordship on Sundays [sic] Sundry Reviews &c wch would amuse you[12]

I really think that I may venture to congratulate your Lordship upon the Publication of a Poem wch has set up your fame beyond all assailment – You have no notion of the sensation which it has occasioned and my only regret is that you were not present to witness it[13] –

I earnestly trust that Your Lordship is well & with ardent compliments I remain

My Lord
Your obliged &
faithful Servant
John Murray

Wednesday Night

I have very strong reason to believe that the Bookseller at Newark continues to <u>reprint</u> – not altering the Edition – your Lordships early Poems – Perhaps yr Lordship would ascertain this fact.[14] I am really so dreadfully busy as to be forced to ask yr Lordships forgiveness for writing in this haste

Notes to Letter 30)

<u>Cover</u>: R^t Honble/Lord Byron/Newstead/Notts <u>pm</u>: 3 Feb 1814

1. The Corsair was published on Tuesday 1 February 1814; Southey's first publication on assuming the Laureateship, *Carmen Triumphale for the Commencement of the Year 1814*, appeared on New Year's Day 1814 and was very unfavourably reviewed in the *Edinburgh Review*, XXII, xliv (January [pub. April] 1814), Art. XII, pp. 447–54, and *The Scourge* (see n. 12 below).

2. This was Burke's vigorously written defence of his pension granted by the Crown on his retirement, *A Letter from the Right Honourable Edmund Burke to A Noble Lord, on Attacks made upon him and his Pension, in The House of Lords, by The Duke of Bedford and the Earl of Lauderdale* (Dublin, 1796), in which he reviews and justifies his career and especially his antagonism to the French Revolution. It was addressed to Lord Grenville and is still considered unequalled in English prose (see Edmund Burke, *On Empire, Liberty, and Reform: Speeches and Letters*, ed. David Bromwich [New Haven & London: Yale University Press, 2000], 464–514).

3. These opinions must have been verbal. B replied delightedly on Friday 4 February thanking JM for his 'very welcome' and 'unexpected' news, saying he had also had 'a very kind' letter from D'Israeli (not extant) and that he particularly valued Ward's 'approbation', not to mention Gifford's (*BLJ* IV, 44–45).

4. *The Corsair*, II, 142 (*CPW* III, 175).

5. *The Corsair*, III, 694 (*CPW* III, 214).

6. In his dedication to *The Corsair*, B had stated that it would be 'the last production' with which he would 'trespass on public patience ... for some years' (*CPW* III, 148); he reiterated his 'Good Night' to his 'Authorship' in his reply to JM (*BLJ* IV, 44–45).

7. Martin Arthur Shee, RA (1769–1850), poet, novelist and portrait painter, founder of the British Institution in 1807 and President of the Royal Academy from 1830 to 1850. For B's single extant letter to Shee, see *BLJ* IV, 96–97.

8. Perhaps not quite as complimentary as intended. JM echoes Johnson's dismissal of *Ossian*: when asked by Dr Blair on Tuesday 24 May 1763 'whether he thought any man of a modern age could have written such poems? Johnson replied, "Yes, Sir, many men, many women, and many children"' (James Boswell, *The Life of Samuel Johnson, LL.D.*, 2 vols [London: Dent, 1949], I, 245).

9. Both these letters are in MA. That of John Wilson Croker (1780–1857), First Secretary to the Admiralty and frequent contributor to the *Quarterly Review*, is dated 21 January 1814 from the Admiralty and runs as follows:

> Dear Murray
>   I am extremely obliged to you for the early perusal of the Corsair which I return – It is "me judice" [in my opinion] much the best of Lord B's. I sincerely wish that he had not <written> published the Giaour or the Bride of Abydos as I fear they will have deaden'd the public taste to the enjoyment of this the last & best – There is, there must be something of repetition when one writes three poems all of archipelagic story & scenery; & the appearance of tautology <will be> is increased by the similarity of the characters & catastrophe<,>

in each of the three poems. for [sic] these reasons I do not pretend
to say that "the Million" [Hamlet, II, ii, 428] will like the Corsair as
well as they did the Giaour, tho' I think it, a long shot of Phœbus's
bow, better, & I repeat it, I think there would be but one cry of
admiration if this were the first <& if [the expression?] as well> of
its class in point of time as well as of merit, & if Conrade [sic] &
Gulnare were not (tho' first of their names) the third of their respective characters.

There are half a dozen <u>feeble</u> lines & a <u>dozen</u> which are <u>obscure</u>;
but there are hundreds of the most striking beauty & effect.

There are one or two new words very well coin'd, & one or two
old words very well revived. – on the whole I have read it, tout
d'un trait [at one stretch], with the greatest interest & if the conclusion had been a little <u>clearer</u>, I should have said that I had nothing
more to wish for in a poem of its kind

Yours ever

JW Croker

That of Robert William Hay (for whom see Letter 24, n. 4 above), is dated
31 January 1814 from St James Place, the relevant part of which runs as
follows:

L^d. Byron has much to answer for. His "Corsair" kept me from
Church yesterday, & I have felt a foreboding & lawless disposition
ever since. Schiller's "Robbers" is said to have increased the banditti
of Germany. Should we shortly relapse into the "dull & piping times
of Peace" [Richard III, I, i, 24], we shall now see our young men of
ardent minds & adventurous Spirits hoisting "the blood Red Flag"
[The Corsair, I, 529, and III, 492] on their Yachts & Pleasure Boats &
exacting the maritime rights of this Country according to their own
interpretation. Our females too will begin to imagine that "Killing
is indeed no Murder" [proverbial] – & proceed to slay with other
weapons than their eyes. Gulnare is the first female homicide that I
remember to have met with, who retains after ye Deed is done, any
degree of feminine softness & loveliness, – & I confess I do not see
why she should not, – though the Ladies who are represented by
the Greek Tragedians as taking such bloody business in hand, are
described afterwards as completely lost to all sense of what is amiable
in woman, it is not the case, if I recollect right, with those whose
splendid deeds in that way are recorded in Scripture. The Pirate's
horror at the prowess of Gulnare forms a striking feature in his
character, & operates most providentially in preserving his fidelity to
Medora at some critical moments.

I feel anxious to know the end of Gulnare, she might have been
described like perturbed Spirits on the Banks of Styx, wandering
as a sort of penance, round the shores of the Isle, in expectation of

the return of Conrad's Boat, but it is perhaps better to leave her fate uncertain, though those who delight in tittle tattle may not improbably set it about that she is gone off with the Pirate, & may become M^rs. Conrad the 2^d. in another Island. I shall say no more on the subject of the Poem, till I have read it again; a thing, I assure you, which I very rarely do.

10. This is the first instance of JM's tampering with B's intentions and directions to secure a good sale; later ones were to have disastrous effects. On this occasion – although he had not read the attack on him in the *Courier* for Tuesday 1 February, but was aware of it from the *Morning Chronicle*'s rebuff to it on Thursday 3 February – B was at first indulgent (*BLJ* IV, 45; see also, Appendix B herein); but the following day he wrote saying he thought 'the withdrawing the small poems from the Corsair (even to add to C[hil]de H[arol]d) looks like shrinking & shuffling – after the fuss made upon one of them by the tories'; and while regretting that *CHP* (7) required 'such allotments to make him move off', he told JM to 'replace them in the Corsair's appendix' (*BLJ* IV, 46; see also, Letter 29 n. 1 above, and Letter 31 below). That JM does indeed mean that 'Lines to a Lady Weeping' appeared in both *The Corsair* and *CHP* (7) is confirmed by his next two letters and is, in the light of his reiteration and the absence of any known copy of the latter containing them, an extraordinary revelation (see Letter 31 and n. 2, and Letter 32 below). However, without going into bibliographical minutiae, it must be stressed that the edition of *The Corsair* without the supplementary poems, which has unfortunately been designated the 'first issue' of the first edition, did not reach public circulation (cf. *CPW* III, 444, and Wise, I, 92). The first edition of *The Corsair* contained the supplementary poems.

11. Matthew Gregory ('Monk') Lewis (1775–1818), author of the Gothic novel *The Monk* (1796) which gained him his nickname, and John Herman Merivale (1779–1844), author of *Orlando in Roncesvalles*, upon the manuscript of which B had recently commented (*BLJ* IV, 12), which was published in April 1814.

12. Sunday would have been 30 January 1814. Although JM's 'parcel' containing 'the *Mags*' had not arrived by Friday 4 February nor by Tuesday 8, when B had got as far as Wandsford on his return to London (*BLJ* IV, 46 and 49), the 'Sundry Reviews' may well have included the following, all of which were published on 1 February: *The British Critic (New Series)*, I (Jan. 1814), Art. III, pp. 34–50 of which contained a review of *The Bride of Abydos*; the first number of *The New Monthly Magazine and Universal Register*, I, i (Feb. 1814); *The Satirist*, New Series, 19 (Feb. 1814), pp. 145–59 of which contained a review of *The Bride of Abydos*; and *The Scourge*, VII (Feb. 1814), pp. 122–30 of which contained a scathing review of Southey's *Carmen Triumphale*.

13. B replied to this: 'I thank you for wishing me in town – but I think one's success is most felt at a distance – & I enjoy my solitary self importance – in

an agreeable sulky way of my own – upon the strength of your letter for
which I once more thank you' (*BLJ* IV, 46).

14. The Newark bookseller was John Ridge who had published *Hours of Idleness*
in 1807 and a 'Second Edition', retitled *Poems Original and Translated*, in
1808 (see *CPW* I, 362). The BL has two copies of an unauthorized edition
of the latter, bearing the same date of publication but printed on paper
watermarked 'SALMON/1811' (Ashley 306 and 11646ccc9; for a full description, see Wise, I, 12–13). B reprimanded Ridge on his way back to London
on Sunday 6 February (see *BLJ* IV, 46 and 47), which, unless JM had also
complained to him, elicited the following letter to JM which is in MA
(altered and abbreviated in Wise, I, 12–13):

> Dear Sir,
>   We beg Leave to assure you that it is far from our Intention to
> injure the Feelings of any one, and more especially those of so good
> a Friend as Lord Byron
>   On mustering all the Copies of his early Poems on hand we find
> only 10, four of which are bound calf extra [*sic*]. The Quantities in
> London on Sale must also be very trifling. Immediate Application
> shall be made for them when we shall have no Objection to
> exchange the Whole for your own Publications to the same Amount.
> We had the Pleasure of seeing his Lordship at Newark on Sunday
> last [6 February] when he seemed to think the few Copies we have
> of trifling Consequence
> We are, Sir,
> Your obt. Servts,
> Saml & Jno. Ridge.
> Newark, Feb 10. 1814

Letter 31)   [Saturday] 5 February [1814]

I have saved two other Couriers for your Lordship

My Lord
    I send <by> this nights Courier in which is commenced a series of
strictures upon you[1] – I thought it my duty to reprint all the poems
as they stand in the Copy of the Corsair sent to your Lordship – the
moment the first Poem was the subject of attack – so that they will
appear now both in the Corsair & Childe Harold.[2] Every man here
reprobates exceedingly these injudicious attacks upon you – and your
Fame has absolutely received an impetus from this last poem which
has not yet subsided – I declare to you I hear nothing but continued

unlimited praise – Mr Gifford is delighted that his prognostic was just & speaks of you with the most ardent feelings of regard –

I remain in haste – & in great anxiety to hear from your Lordship
My Lord
Your obliged & faithful Servant
John Murray

Feby. 5

I forgot to mention that it was the <u>Turkish</u> Song wch M^r G so much liked[3]

Notes to Letter 31)

<u>Cover</u>: R^t Honble Lord Byron/Newstead Abbey/Notts <u>redirected</u> <Nottingham> No. 4 Bennet Street/St. James's/<u>London</u> <u>pm</u>: 10 Feb 1814

B did not receive this letter until after his return to town on Wednesday 9 February.

1. The *Courier* attacked the 'Lines to a Lady Weeping' the very day *The Corsair* was published (Tuesday 1 February), and persisted in its antagonism over the next few days before commencing an even more virulent series of strictures on B, entitled '*BYRONIANA*', on Saturday 5 February. For this and related material, see Appendix B (JM would have sent item 7, and had probably 'saved' items 1 and 4).

2. The 'first' of the supplementary poems in *The Corsair* volume immediately following the notes to *The Corsair* was 'Lines to a Lady Weeping'. Although apparently a proof of those lines, together with the five other poems included in *The Corsair*, was pulled for *CHP* (7) (*CPW* III, 391), no copy of that edition or any other of *CHP* survives containing the poem (see also, Letter 30, n. 10 above, and Letter 32 below).

3. The 'Song' being 'From the Turkish', printed with *The Corsair* (see *CPW* III, 6–7 and 390).

Letter 32)   Tuesday [8 February 1814]

Tuesday

My Lord
I have allowed myself to indulge in the pleasure I derived from the expression of your Lordships satisfaction, because I have anticipated the

point upon which there was likely to be some uneasiness − As soon as
I perceived the fuss that was made about certain Lines − I caused them
to be immediately re-instated[+] and I wrote on Saturday[1] to acquaint
your Lordship that I had done so − a conviction of duty towards your
Lordship made me do this − −

I can assure your Lordship with the most unreserved sincerity
that Childe Harold did not require the insertion of the Lines which
have made so much noise, to assist its sale but they made it still more
attractive & my sordid propensities got the better of me[2] − I sold my
Lord at once nearly a Thousand Copies of this New Edition − and I
am convinced by the collected & unshaken opinions of the best Critics
that it is just as certain of becoming a Classic as Thomson or Beattie[3]
− what delights me is that amidst the most decided applause − there
is a constant difference at [sic] to which is the best of your Lordships
poems − Gifford declared to me again the other day that you would
last far beyond any poet of the present day − I tried him particularly
as to Campbell[4] − but he had not a doubt about the certainty of your
passing him − Although therefore I may concur with your Lordship
in feeling some little surprise at such unprecedented triumph over
peoples prejudices − yet I can differ upon very solid reasons in your
Lordships notion of "temporary reputation"[5] − I declare to God I have
not heard One expression of disappointment or doubtful satisfaction
upon reading the Corsair − which bids fair to be the most popular
of your Lordships Poems − I believe I have now sold 13,000 Copies a
thing perfectly unprecedented & the more grateful to me too as every
buyer returns with looks of satisfaction & expressions of delight − & one
more confirmative expression I always hear <from all> is − of heartfelt
regret at <a> the hint in the dedication of leaving off writing for a time
however short. − You can not meet a man in the Street − who has not
read or heard read the Corsair.

The Fac Simile is restored to Childe Harold only 200 Copies having
been sent out without it[6] − The Poem on the Skull Cup[7] − is introduced
− I long to have the pleasure of congratulating yr Lordship personally
− Your Noble conduct to a Schoolfellow[8] does not lessen the admiration
with which I remain

    My Lord
    Your faithfully attached
        Serv[t]
  Jno Murray

<[+]I wrote>

Notes to Letter 32)

B was already on his return journey to London at the time of JM's writing this letter.

1. See Letter 31 above.

2. See Letter 30, n. 10 above. In his letter of Saturday 5 February B had regretted 'that C[hil]de H[arol]d requires some & such allotments to make him move off ... I told you his popularity would not be permanent' (*BLJ* IV, 46).

3. JM would have been thinking in particular of James Thomson's *The Castle of Indolence* (1748), and James Beattie's *The Minstrel* (1771–74), both written in Spenserian stanzas.

4. That is, Thomas Campbell (1777–1844), author of the immensely successful *The Pleasures of Hope* (1799).

5. JM echoes B's letter of 5 February in which he had said that it was lucky he had made up his mind 'to a temporary reputation in time', and that the success he had enjoyed seemed singular as it had been 'in the teeth of so many prejudices' (*BLJ* IV, 46–47).

6. As B had pointed out in his letter of 5 February (*BLJ* IV, 46), the facsimile of the letter from the Bey of Corinth, though listed in the table of contents, was omitted from *CHP* (6). It was restored in *CHP* (7) (though not listed in its table of contents). For a discussion and translation of the facsimile, see Petros Peteinaris, 'The Bey Apologises', *The Newstead Byron Society Review* (July 2000), 13–19.

7. This seems very odd. B sent his 'Skull cup' lines on 5 February saying JM could 'add them to C[hild]e H[arol]d if only for the sake of another outcry' (*BLJ* IV, 47); yet *CHP* (7), in which the lines first appeared, was published by this time and the lines had already been parodied in the *Courier* for 1 February (see Appendix B, item 1; see also, *CPW* I, 225–26 and 391).

8. JM is making merry with B's 'Skull cup' lines in the manner of Hamlet or the grave-digger; perhaps he also has in mind that according to Herodotus the Scythians made ornamented drinking bowls out of the skulls of both their enemies and their kinsmen (*Histories*, IV, 65–66).

Letter 33)   Saturday 26 February 1814

My Lord

    Your Lordship appeared to be so satisfactorily convinced that silence would be most becoming – that I wrote the note to Mr Dallas late on

Saturday evening with the hope of preventing the publication of his Letter.

The meaning of the "expressions" pointed out by your Lordship in my note, is, that having formerly told M[r] Gifford – M[r] Hammond M[r] Frere – M[r] Ward – M[r] Canning & many other of my friends that your Lordship had given me the Copyright of the Giaour &, having had occasion, subsequently, to unsay this – it was placing my assertions in a very doubtful light – if I allowed to be insinuated, publicly, that I was to pay nothing for this Poem or for the Bride of Abydos.[1]

Your Lordship does not seem <that I> to be aware that I feel as much bound, by my promise, to pay your Lordship a Thousand Guineas for the Copyright of the Giaour & Bride of Abydos in May next – as I am, by my Bond, to give Lord Sheffield a similar sum for Gibbon[2]

My expression to Mad. de Staël was, not that I had actually "paid" but that I had "given" your Lordship 1,000 G[s] for these two Poems[3] – because it is as much so as the 500 G[s] for the Corsair which I am to pay in 2 – 4 & 6 Mos. – And I must confess that at the time I stated this circumstance to Mad de Staël I was not aware of your Lordships liberal intentions with regard to this sum – for I did not then conceive it possible that your Lordship would have resumed your Gift of the Giaour to me – to bestow it on another – & therefore the "explanation" of that part of Mr Dallass Letter which refers to me, is – that although Lord Byron has not actually received any thing for the "Giaour & Bride" – yet I am under an engagement to pay his Lordship a Thousand Guineas for them in May – But as <Da> M[r] Dallass Letter <wa> was published & as your Lordship appeared to approve of it – I said nothing – nor should I have said anything further if your Lordship had not commanded this explanation

— I declare to God I think these things are very unworthy a place in your Lordships mind – why allow a Blight on One Blade – to prevent you from reaping & revelling in the Rich & superabundant Harvest of Fame which your Inspired Labours have created[4]

I am sure my Lord if you will give it but a reflection my conduct towards you has uniformly been that of a very humble – but very faithful friend –

I have the honour to be
My Lord
Your Lordships obliged
& obedient Servant
John Murray

Saturday
Feb[y] 26 – 1814

Notes to Letter 33)

On Thursday 17 February, the *Courier* had charged B with having 'received and pocketted' sums for his poetry (see Appendix B, item 10). That same evening B wrote to Dallas saying that JM was 'going to contradict this', but that Dallas's '*name*' would not be mentioned and he could therefore act as he wished (*BLJ* IV, 63). The following day, however, he wrote again saying that he and JM had now decided to keep quiet and recommended that Dallas should do the same (ibid., 64). Dallas took the first of these letters as a covert request, which B 'was too delicate to ask', to interfere on his behalf; and the second as evidence of B's 'hurt' that JM should say nothing. Having therefore written a letter in reply to the *Courier*'s charge, he evidently read it to B, whom it 'greatly pleased', before sending it with his concurrence to the newspapers (Dallas, *Correspondence*, III, 63–64). JM's 'note' of Saturday 19 (of which Dallas makes no mention) failed to forestall its publication, and the letter was printed in the *Morning Chronicle* and *Morning Post* on Monday 21 February 1814 (see Appendix B, item 14). In that letter, Dallas acknowledged B's gift of the copyrights of *CHP* I and II and *The Corsair*, and stated that JM could testify that 'no part of the sale' of *The Giaour* and *The Bride of Abydos* had ever touched B's hands or been disposed of for his use. This 'insinuated', as JM here complains, that he had got the two poems for nothing.

Of what happened thereafter between Dallas and JM, Dallas makes no mention; but on Thursday 24 February he received what must have been JM's 'note' of Saturday 19 which prompted the following letter to B (MA):

> My dear Lord
> I must send you the enclosed copy of a letter from Murray, which I received this evening on my return home. I mean to take no notice of it, because I think you would not like what I should write. Every line of it contains a gross insult – His surprise at learning that I meant to act contrary to your opinion – his hint as to the <u>whole truth</u>, which he dashes with his pen – his inference of my want of judgment – his desire that what I write should not be such as he should contradict. –
> My dear Lord, I am afraid lest any word should drop from me at this moment that might by the slightest inference convey an idea that I took any merit in what has, in its own nature, done me much honour, I will not therefore take this occasion to say any thing about either <u>Gifford</u> or <u>Murray</u>, for I mean to preserve terms with the latter while he is your Publisher or Bookseller, and with the judiciousness of the former I will not dispute the point – but though I am not by many the most judicious of your friends, be assured I am among the most ardent.
> I am
> My dear Lord
> Your truly attached

RC Dallas –
Worton House
Thursday Feb. 24th. 1814 –

B evidently sent this letter, with its enclosure annotated by him, to JM with his own letter of Friday 25 February asking, 'what the Devil may all this be?' and seeking clarification (*BLJ* IV, 70–71).

1. For the arrangements over the copyrights of *The Giaour* and *The Bride of Abydos*, see Letters 17, 19 and 24 above.

2. JM published a new and enlarged edition in 5 vols of Lord Sheffield's *The Miscellaneous Works of Edward Gibbon* in late 1814 (see Letter 61 below). According to a note in MA he paid Sheffield £1,000 on 9 June 1815.

3. In his letter of Friday 25 February B had said: 'Do you mean to tell *me* as you told Me. de Stael that you actually *paid* the sum you *offered* or that *I* received it – or that any one else did – if so – Bravo!' (*BLJ* IV, 71; B had heard of this assertion to Madame de Staël as early as Wednesday 1 December 1813; see *BLJ* III, 187).

4. Replying to JM the same day as this letter, B told him that his 'distinctions' seemed 'without a difference', and that he did not altogether understand the remainder of his 'explanation'; however, he too suggested their dropping the matter (*BLJ* IV, 71–72).

Letter 34) Wednesday [2 March 1814]

My Lord
    I accept your donation with Melancholny [*sic*] for really I must confine myself to Cyder for ever, if you restrain your self, from writing –
    I will send all the Boxes of Letters and would advise the indiscriminate & Chaotic publication of the whole by way of immolation –
    ever My Lord
    Your faithful Servt
    Jno Murray

Wednesday

Notes to Letter 34)

Cover: The Lord Byron

Sometime earlier this same day B had enquired: 'Are you fond of Cyder & Perry? – I have a hogshead of each in Worcestershire which I don't know what to do with & if you like it it shall be sent Carriage free – & presented to you for your "bye drinkings" without expence and as little trouble as I can give you with it'; and he added, 'I want all my *boxes* of papers & trunks that may contain others ... let them be sent down when convenient' (*BLJ* IV, 76). JM regularly misspelt 'melancholy' 'melancholny'; and he was so on account of B's announcing in the dedicatory preface to *The Corsair* that it would be 'the last production' with which he would 'trespass on public patience ... for some years' (*CPW* III, 148).

[See note 3 to Interim Note between Letters 1 and 2 above.

The following two letters from B to JM in MA are misplaced and printed incorrectly in *BLJ* II, 175 as a single letter ('To John Murray (*c*) [May, 1812?]'). The first letter should be conjecturally dated '[Tuesday 1 March 1814?]':

> Dᵣ. Sir/
>   Could you get me a copy of yᵉ. British Rᵂ. & send it here – it is or is to be out? –
>
>   yʳˢ. evʳ.
>   Bn
>   [Cover] To Jⁿᵒ Murray Esqʳᵉ. –

The *British Review*, V, x (February 1814) was announced in *The Times* for Tuesday 1 March 1814 as that day published. It contained an unfavourable review of *The Bride of Abydos* (pp. 391–400), in which the reviewer expressed his disappointment that B was not living up to the promise of *CHP* I and II; he disliked *The Giaour*, and *The Bride* pleased him even less (subject, style, metre). He thought B too prolific and suggested that 'the real and radical reason of his late failures' was 'his pruriency for the press' (p. 400).

The second letter may have been sent at about the same time as the above, but should be conjecturally dated '[March–October 1814?]':

> Pray is the <u>North</u> British Rᵂ out? – if it is send it me – if not – when it appears. – you need not trouble yourself at any rate to answer this. –

The *North British Review* was a somewhat ill-fated journal, which ran for only three numbers (no copies of which are extant), whose commencement was first announced in *The Sun* for Wednesday 16 February 1814: 'A NEW REVIEW is immediately to be commenced in Edinburgh, under the title of THE NORTH BRITISH REVIEW, or CONSTITUTIONAL JOURNAL; to be published every two months' (see also, the *Morning Post* for Thursday 17 February 1814, and *The Gentleman's Magazine*, LXXXIV, Pt I [February 1814], 144). On Thursday 3 March 1814 *The Times* announced that the first number had been published on 'the first of March' and, on

Saturday 2 April 1814, that the first number 'is arrived' (in London). The second number (tantalizingly containing reviews of *The Corsair* and *Ode to Napoleon Buonaparte*) was announced as just published in *The Times* for Friday 5 August 1814; and the third number (apparently containing nothing on B) was announced in *The Times* for Thursday 20 October 1814.]

Letter 35)   [December 1813 – March 1814?]

My Lord

During your absence I was solicited by a <m> Composer to allow him to set to Music One of your Lordships Songs, which, as your Lordships Literary ViceGerent, I ventured to accord – & I now send you the produce.

J M.

Friday N^t.

Notes to Letter 35)

<u>Cover</u>: The Lord Byron/4 Bennet S^t/St Jamess

The dating of this letter is conjectural. George Thomson had written to JM on 2 September 1813 asking permission to set to music three of B's poems: 'Loch na Garr, particularly the first three stanzas; ... Oh! had my fate been join'd with thine. – & The kiss dear maid thy lip has left' (MA). Evidently JM informed B who replied directly to Thomson on 10 September 1813, but without exactly answering his request (*BLJ* III, 113–14). This elicited another letter from Thomson to JM of Friday 8 October 1813, thanking him for procuring an answer from B, 'even tho' it puts an end to the hope he gave me of writing Songs for me, and vexes me sorely', but pointing out that B 'forgot to say a word pro or con to my application for leave to set to music <u>three</u> of the Songs printed in his works. Will you have the kindness to ask his Lordship whether I have his consent to this? I am very much pleas'd with "<u>Oh had my fate been join'd with thine</u>," and wish to join it to a beautiful Welsh air which Beethoven has harmonised in a most exquisite manner' (MA). By this time B was out of town again with the Websters at Aston Hall, and JM must have granted the permission on his behalf; the 'produce' of which being the setting of 'Oh! had my Fate' (for Voice and Piano Trio accompaniment), eventually published by Thomson in his *A Select Collection of Original Scottish Airs*, Vol. 5 (1818) and forming number 12 of Beethoven's Op. 108 (see Cooper, *Beethoven's Folksong Settings*, 70, 85, 115–16 and 146). There is no reply to this letter.

Letter 36)   Saturday [26 March 1814?]

My Lord.

I have <reff> refrained from calling upon you with the hope that you would have written me your opinion <about t> of the <u>Wanderer</u> – of which I am exceedingly anxious for a criticism – you may remember – warm from the brain how exceedingly just your opinion was of Patronage – – When you <read> have read the Novel & I will have the pleasure of sending something else (in confidence)[1]

I asked today after your Lordships Cold which I regretted to hear was not much lessened.[2]

Your Lordships faithful

Servant ever

J. Murray

Saturday 10

Notes to Letter 36)

<u>Cover</u>: The Lord Byron

The dating of this Letter is conjectural. On Monday 27 December 1813 B had asked JM to send Lord Holland and himself (if possible), 'Me. D'Arblay's (or even Miss Edgeworth's thing) new work' (BLJ III, 203–04). These were Patronage, by Maria Edgeworth (4 vols, London: J. Johnson, 1814), and The Wanderer; or, Female Difficulties, by Fanny Burney (Madame D'Arblay) (5 vols, London: Longman, 1814) – neither of which had yet been published (the first was published on Tuesday 25 January 1814; the second on Monday 28 March 1814). JM seems to have obliged B, who thanked him for certain unspecified 'books' on Sunday 2 January 1814, and gave him his adverse opinion of Patronage ten days later on 'Wednesday – or Thursday' (12 or 13 January) (BLJ IV, 14 and 24–25). With regard to The Wanderer, B had in fact been asked by Cawthorn to read the manuscript – if he got it (which he did not) – as early as December 1811 (BLJ II, 143 and 146). By the end of January 1814 and still two months prior to its publication, not only B and Lord Holland but several other literati had read the first volume, which fact had come to the dismayed attention of Fanny Burney herself (see The Journals and Letters of Fanny Burney (Madame d'Arblay), 1791–1840, ed. Joyce Hemlow, 12 vols [Oxford: Clarendon Press, 1972–84], VII, 236 and 239–40; see also, VII, 260, and VIII, 317–18). The first intimation B himself gives of having read any part of the novel is in his letter of Wednesday 30 March 1814 to Lady Melbourne – who had evidently sent or returned him the first two volumes and drawn attention to the 'coincidence' between Lady Caroline Lamb's 'dagger scene' and what, given the context, is clearly the heroine's publicly 'staged' suicide attempt in Vol. II,

chap. xxxviii, not the earlier, more private attempt in the summerhouse in Vol.
I, chap. xviii (*BLJ* IV, 86–87, and cf. 86n). (Although neither Lady Melbourne
nor B actually mentions the name of the work they are discussing, the 'two more
Vol^s' she sent him on 1 April 1814 with the promise of 'the fifth to morrow',
can only refer to *The Wanderer* [*LLLM*, 169].) However, B gave no indication of
his opinion to JM until Sunday 24 July 1814 when he wrote from Hastings that
he liked *Waverley* as much as he hated *Patronage* and *The Wanderer* 'and all the
feminine trash of the last four months' (*BLJ* IV, 144).

1. What the 'something else' was remains unidentified.

2. B gives no hint of having a 'Cold' at this particular time, but in his Journal
   for Monday 28 March 1814 he records: 'The last few days, or whole week,
   have been very abstemious, regular in exercise, and yet very *unwell*' –
   though after a good night out with Scrope Davies the previous evening,
   and having 'sparred with Jackson *ad sudorem*' during the day, he felt 'much
   better in health than for many days' (*BLJ* III, 255; see also, *BLJ* IV, 86). B's
   abstemiousness soon became public knowledge. The *St James's Chronicle* for
   Thursday 7 to Saturday 9 April 1814 announced wittily: 'Lord Byron has
   recently adopted the most abstemious regimen of diet, eating no animal food
   whatever, and living principally upon boiled potatoes, moistened only with
   vinegar, using even no salt but that which he *attically* compounds in his new
   Epic preparing for the press.'

Letter 37)   [Saturday 2 April 1814?]

My Lord
   I trust to your confidence what a peculiar sort of sensation upon
this point, could not be extorted from me, by any other being – it is
<u>nothing</u> & yet it is every thing¹ –

                    +   +

   I entreat you to tell me when you have read the wanderer what you
really think of it²

            +   +   +

   I beseach you not for <u>my whole honour</u>, to mention what I send &
please to be so kind as to leave it out for me at <u>night</u> to be sent over in
the Morning³

                          J. M
   I was mad with Ridgway whom you have served – (or rather who
has served your Lordship) & will make him ashamed⁴

Notes to Letter 37)

The date of this Letter is conjectured from the following letter in MA from James Ridgway to B, dated 3 April 1814:

> My Lord
>
> If I am to Credit what took Place in a Conversation last last [*sic*] Night between Mr Murry [*sic*] and my Son, your Lordship is Very Angrey [*sic*] at being Pointed out as the <u>supposed author</u> of a Poem or two Contained in the Spirit of the Journals for the last year.
>
> After what had happened respecting the Corsair – and the Scandalous Abuse Poured forth against your Lordship – By an unprincipled Hireling Anti-Jacobin gang little better than literary Assassins – and the Public anxiety occasioned by it, to be informed of the Treason Committed – I Certainly did feel it a duty due to your Lordship, Not only to find an Assilum [*sic*] for the fugitives, but also to Point out where it [*sic*] might be seen and judged off [*sic*]. This is the true Stape [*sic*] of the Case, and I can only further assure your Lordship if what Mr Murry said be true; after what may apper [*sic*] in the Times; the Advertisement shall be altered. I beg to assure your Lordship, I am not Capable of Wilfully or intentionally Committing an Outrage against your Lordship? [*sic*] In the hope that this explanation will be Sattisfactory [*sic*], and that your Lordships Kindness to me will be Continued. I have the Honor to be [...]

The Spirit of the Public Journals for 1813: Being an Impartial Selection of the Most ingenious Essays and Jeux d'Esprits that appear in the Newspapers and Other Publications (James Ridgway, 1814), XVII, contained 'To a Lady Weeping. By Lord Byron' (p. 363), and 'Inscription on the Monument of a Newfoundland Dog. (By the Same.)' (p. 364). With the exception of one by John Mitford, all the other selections are anonymous or pseudonymous, and each is accompanied by its original source (e.g., from the *Morning Herald* of such-and-such a date). *The Times* for Saturday 9 April 1814 carried the following advertisement (repeated verbatim on Wednesday 13 April 1814, but not thereafter): 'This day is published, price 7s. in boards, THE SPIRIT of the PUBLIC JOURNALS for 1813. Several of the much admired Pieces, contained in this volume, are said to be written by Lord Byron.' B does not appear to have replied either to Ridgway or to JM; and, if the dating of this present Letter (37) is correct, he was on the point of leaving town and, indeed, may not have received it or Ridgway's letter until his return. He told Lady Melbourne on Friday 8 April that he had been 'out of town since Saturday [2 April] & only returned last Night [Thursday 7 April]' (*BLJ* IV, 90). He had been on a visit to Augusta, who was expecting a child (Elizabeth Medora), and in fact seems to have left London on Sunday 3 April, as he wrote to Hanson's clerk on that day (*BLJ* IV, 89). On Tuesday 12 April B told JM: 'A "Goodnatured friend" tells me there is a most scurrilous attack on *us* in the Anti-jac[obin] R[evie]w – which you have *not* sent – send it'; and later the same day: 'I have read the

Anti-jac[obin] it is a bagatelle & reprint of Courier' (*BLJ* IV, 95 and 96). It may well be that the '"Goodnatured friend"' refers to Ridgway and his allusion to the 'unprincipled Hireling Anti-Jacobin gang'. *The Antijacobin Review*, XLVI, 190 (March 1814), 207–37 contained a scathing review of *The Bride* and *The Corsair*, rehearsing approvingly the attacks by the *Courier* on B's dedications and 'impudent doggrel', refusing to believe his promise to write no more, and expressing its disgust with his religious sentiments.

1. Although B wrote to JM on Saturday 2 April, his letter would hardly have elicited this response (*BLJ* IV, 89); perhaps he had told JM confidentially of his intended visit to Augusta or of her imminent parturition.

2. See headnote to Letter 36 above.

3. There is no indication as to what this might have been.

4. See headnote above.

Letter 38)   [Saturday 9 April 1814]

NB The Old <u>Pope</u> – is safely with the Allies[1]

My Lord
Buonaparte has either solicited or accepted a retirement upon a <u>Pension</u> in the Island of Elba – He has formally abdicated – Ney, Victor, Mortier Oudinot – ha<ve>d all forsaken him – Boulogne is opened – the <u>Deputies</u> are from Dunkirk & not from Paris – All this My Lord is true[2] –
A Fine Subect [*sic*] for an Epic[3]
J. Murray

past 5.
I cant procure One Courier[4]

Notes to Letter 38)

<u>Cover</u>: The Lord Byron

With evident excitement JM announces the first news to reach England of Napoleon's abdication, the official confirmation of which was reported in the afternoon papers (the *Courier* and *The Star*) for that day.

1. The Allies had entered Paris on 31 March 1814. The 'Old Pope' was the 74-year-old Pope Pius VII (1740–1823), who held the Pontificate from 1800

until his death. He had been kidnapped by Napoleon in 1809 and detained at Savona and Fontainebleau. *The Star* for Saturday 9 April 1814 reported that the Pope, the Cardinals and the Spanish prisoners had been released.

2. Between them, the *Courier* and *The Star* for Saturday 9 April announced that two Deputies from Dunkirk had arrived at the Admiralty (to invite Louis XVIII to return to France), bringing with them all the English prisoners in the neighbourhood; that Napoleon had accepted the Emperor Alexander's offer and had abdicated and was to retire with his family to the Island of Elba on a pension rumoured to be six million francs (£240,000) (but which was in fact two million francs); that Dunkirk, Calais, Boulogne and all the other ports along that line of the coast (which were closed to the English during the wars) had been reopened and had declared for the Bourbons; that Marshals Victor, duc de Bellune (1766–1841), Mortier, duc de Trévise (1768–1835), Marmont, duc de Raguse (1774–1852), and indeed all the Generals in the vicinity of Paris, had sent in their adherence to the newly constituted provisional Government which was to be administered by a committee of five (under Talleyrand). Michel Ney, duc d'Elchingen and Prince de la Moskova (1769–1815), Napoleon's 'brave des braves', was the most famous and popular of his marshals at whose counsel, and through whose nego-tiation with Alexander, Napoleon had agreed to abdicate. Nicolas-Charles Oudinot, duc de Reggio (1767–1847) was another of his Marshals whose ability to survive numerous woundings earned him renown.

3. JM clearly intends to prompt B to write that 'Epic'; but the poem he embarked upon the following day (Easter Day) was his *Ode to Napoleon Buonaparte* (*BLJ* III, 257).

4. Perhaps there had been a run on copies of the *Courier*; but the latest confirm-atory reports were in *The Star*, the third edition of which came out at 4 p.m. that day.

Letter 39)   [Saturday 9 April 1814]

My Lord

Being at home – it is unnecessary for me to add that I shall attend your summons in less than 15 minutes

As to the Books ————— You behave as Napoleon did to a Woman who had lost her beauty – – even Mad de – S – was his Enemy[1]

J M.

Notes to Letter 39)

<u>Cover</u>: The Lord Byron

In response to JM's letter (38) B had written: 'All these news are very fine – but nevertheless I want my books … if only to lend them to N[apoleo]n in the "island of Elba" during his retirement'; he also asked JM 'to step down' for a few minutes that evening as he wished to speak to him about the publication of Moore's *Lalla Rookh* (*BLJ* IV, 91). B had moved from Bennet Street into Albany on Monday 28 March 1814, on which date he noted in his Journal: 'shall get in all my books to-morrow' (*BLJ* III, 255). But what with all the 'hammering – and teaching people the left hand from the right', and then being out of town for a week from Saturday 2 to Thursday 7 April, this had clearly been delayed, and he was still pining for them on Monday 11 April: 'Oh my books! my books! will you never find my books?' (*BLJ* IV, 87, 90 and 94).

1. JM may have seen the article that Hobhouse certainly saw (*Recollections*, I, 104) by Jean-Charles-Dominique de Lacretelle (1766–1855), publicist, author and Professor of History at the Sorbonne, which appeared in different translations in *The Times* and the *Morning Post* for Saturday 9 April 1814, in which he claimed that Napoleon 'was always insulting in his conduct towards females, and even rallied them in a rude and unfeeling manner on the decline of their beauty' (*The Times*, Saturday 9 April 1814). As for the enmity between Napoleon and Madame de Staël, B hardly needed to be told what he and everybody else already knew. For instance, in an undated letter of late 1813 or early 1814 Lady Holland told Mrs Creevey that 'She [Mme. de Staël] is violent against the Emperor, who, she says, is not a man – "ce n'est point un homme, mais un système" – an Incarnation of the Revolution. Women he considers as only useful "pour produire les conscrits"; otherwise "c'est une classe qu'il voudroit supprimer"' (*The Creevey Papers*, ed. the Right Hon. Sir Herbert Maxwell, 3rd edn (London: John Murray, 1905), 189; cf. *DJ* XVII, Unincorporated Stanza [*CPW* V, 662 and 771]).

Letter 40)   [Monday 11 April 1814]

My Lord

I have sent the MSS to M^r G – but having got a proof[1] I can not refrain from communicating it to you before I get his answer – All the first part is at least equal to any thing you have written after Stanza IX I think it wants your attention & the closing lines are not good[2] – it is a subject <u>certainly every way worthy of you</u> – I think any degrading notice of Kings should not be in a poem which will otherwise find universal admirers – & this I ask of you for your Booksellers Sake – You will hear

or see me as soon as I have heard from or seen M^r G –
     J. M.

Notes to Letter 40)

On Sunday 10 April, B wrote to JM: 'I have written an ode on the fall of
Nap[oleo]n which if you like I will copy out & make you a present of ... you may
shew it to Mr. G[iffor]d & print it or not as you please ... There are ten stanzas
of 90 lines in all' (*BLJ* IV, 94). This was the first draft of his *Ode to Napoleon
Buonaparte* which is no longer extant (*CPW* III, 456), and which he clearly did
not send with this letter. Whether or not he waited for any reply from JM, he
copied it out, increasing it to 12 stanzas in the process, and sent it to JM a little
later in the day (*BLJ* III, 257, IV, 94 and *CPW* III, 456). At this point the poem
comprised received stanzas 1, 4, 6–12 and 14–16 (*CPW* III, 259–65), for a facsimile
of which in their original numbered sequence, see *The Manuscripts of the Younger
Romantics. Lord Byron, Volume XI: Ode to Napoleon Buonaparte*, ed. Cheryl Fallon
Giuliano (New York & London: Garland Publishing, 1997), pp. 12–29.

   1. This was either '*Proof A*', dated by JM 11 April 1814, or the undated '*Proof B*',
   corrected copies of which B returned to JM on Monday 11 April (*CPW* III,
   456).

   2. The stanzas 'after Stanza IX' (received stanza 12) to which JM recommends
   B's attention would have been received stanzas 14, 15 and 16 (*CPW* III,
   263–65), which may be seen in their draft state in pp. 24–29 of Giuliano's
   facsimile edition.

Letter 41)   Tuesday [12 April 1814]

My Lord
     I have sent your last note to the printer –
     All your alterations appear to me great improvements – the last I like
exceedingly – & in the previous one the Quotation from Gibbon is
happiness itself
     If the thing be complete it will be read in every Part of the kingdom
– I think your alterred [*sic*] stanza just received will be very popular & is
really a just tribute to the Nation – Patriotism is the universal sentiment
at this time –
     most faithfully
     Your Lordships increasing Admirer –
     J. M.

Tuesday

Notes to Letter 41)

<u>Cover</u>: The Lord Byron

In his letter of Monday 11 April B said he hoped JM had 'got a note of alterations sent this Matin', and told him to 'Alter "*potent* spell" to "*quickening* spell"'
(*BLJ* IV, 94; this latter alteration is not recorded in the apparatus to line 65 in
CPW III, 261). The following day (the date of this letter) he sent 'a few notes and
trifling alterations and an additional motto from Gibbon' (*BLJ* IV, 95), which last
he directed to be placed 'as a 2ᵈ motto <u>not</u> on the title page – but immediately
before stanza 1ˢᵗ.' (MS bound in with proofs in the Vaughan Library, Harrow
School). This was the motto from Gibbon's *Decline and Fall* concerning the abdication of the Emperor Nepos which was first incorporated in *Proof A* (*CPW* III,
259, apparatus), and most certainly did appear with the published poem (cf. *BLJ*
IV, 95n). Again, at some point on this same day he also sent '2 new Stanzas to
the 2d and third' (*BLJ* IV, 96; Marchand's note here is misplaced), which were
clearly received stanzas 2 and 3 of the *Ode* which were first incorporated in *Proof
D* (*CPW* III, 259–60 and 456), and may be seen in their draft state in pp. 36–39 of
Giuliano's facsimile edition (see headnote to Letter 40, above). The 'thing' was not
quite 'complete' however; for before the first edition of 15 stanzas was published
anonymously on Saturday 16 April B added received stanza 13; and for the third
edition, published on Wednesday 20 April, added received stanza 5 which he sent
to JM on Sunday 17 April, and the corrected proof of which he returned the
following day (*BLJ* IV, 98 and 99, and XI, 187; *CPW* III, 260–61, 263 and 456;
Giuliano's facsimile edition, pp. 30–31 and 34–35).

Letter 42)   Monday [25 April 1814]

My Lord
    I am exceedingly obliged by your kindness in sending the Letter wch
Mʳ Hammond desires me to thank you for & to say that he thinks it
excellent¹ –
    I want to occupy One more page at the end of the <u>Ode</u> in order to
escape the <u>necessity</u> of paying a Stamp Duty & of having every Copy
Stamped it being only One Sheet² – May I print the beautiful poem you
sent me on Saturday?³
    I beg the favor of two franks – May I send the <u>Letter</u> to Mʳ G – I
will get it back to you this evening⁴ –
    Most faithfully
    Yr Lordships Seʳ
    Jno Murray

Monday

Notes to Letter 42)

Cover: The Lord Byron

1. In a note to JM, conjecturally dated by Marchand '[*April, 1815?*]', but which should be dated Monday 25 April 1814, B wrote: 'Perhaps the enclosed from Paris may amaze Mr. Hammond or some of *your* knowing ones – let me have it again this Evening' (*BLJ* IV, 287). For George Hammond, see Letter 22, n. 2 above. The 'Letter' in question was Hobhouse's letter to B of Wednesday 20 April 1814, written from Paris on his arrival there, and giving his first impressions of the city since the fall of Napoleon (see *BB*, 122–24).

2. This has given rise to all sorts of ingenious explanations; however, there was no such 'Stamp Duty' nor was any copy of the *Ode* ever 'Stamped'. JM was either misinformed, or was hoodwinking B into allowing him to print the 'beautiful poem' (see n. 3 below). For further details concerning this and Letter 43 below, see Andrew Nicholson, 'Napoleon's "last act" and Byron's *Ode*', *Romanticism*, 9:1 (2003), 68–81.

3. 'Saturday' would have been 23 April, on which day JM must have received B's letter of Friday 22 enclosing a poem 'for the small Edition' JM 'intended some time or other to print' (*BLJ* IV, 102). This was almost certainly '[Translation From the Romaic. I Wander Near That Fount of Waters]', the manuscript of which is dated 15 April 1814, but which in the event was not published during B's lifetime (*CPW* III, 266–67 and 458, and *BLJ* IV, 97n). B was doubtful about the lines 'being worth printing' anyhow, and suggested instead – though not very enthusiastically – that he could 'knock off a stanza or 3 for the Ode that might answer the purpose better' (*BLJ* IV, 104; note that this particular suggestion came from B himself and not, as is generally supposed, from JM). Although he did indeed compose three further stanzas (for which see *CPW* III, 265–66 and 456; Giuliano's facsimile edition, pp. 40–45), he wrote the following day (Tuesday 26 April) saying 'I don't like the additional stanzas *at all* – and they had better be left out' (*BLJ* IV, 107). They were first published by Moore in 1830.

4. For 'franking' see the headnote to Letter 15 above. JM almost certainly wanted one of these franks to send the 'Letter' (Hobhouse's) to Gifford, to whom B willingly consented to its being sent in his reply of the same day (*BLJ* IV, 103).

Letter 43)   Sunday [1 May 1814]

My Lord

I really could not believe that you were serious until I received your formidable note – you are not aware of the mischief you would dash into my affairs – it is I fear impossible for me to <to> resist any wish of yours, although my ruin & <u>utter</u> <u>dejection</u> of <u>Spirits</u> would be the consequence of your present demand – I declare to God I am half determined to <giv> throw up my business altogether I entreat that your Lordship will take a few days to reflect upon a conduct which will occasion so much misery of Mind to one who looks up to you as a patron & who would go to the worlds end to serve you – You have not my Lord the slightest conception of the unhappiness you would occasion me for the fame of your Genius is invaluable to me

I really do not know what to say if your Lordship will have no feeling for one who would really become

your attached & devoted Servant

Jno Murray

Sunday

Notes to Letter 43)

Without offering any explanation other than his own 'caprice', B had written peremptorily to JM on Friday 29 April terminating their publishing relationship, releasing him from all contractual obligations and demanding the destruction of all but 'two copies each for *yourself* only' of *The Giaour* and *The Bride of Abydos* (*BLJ* IV, 107–08). Although this order may have been connected with JM's request in the second paragraph of the preceding letter (42 above), B revoked it on Sunday 1 May on receipt of this letter (43) and told JM to 'go on as usual' (*BLJ* IV, 112; see also, Letter 42, n. 2 above).

Letter 44)   Tuesday [24 May 1814]

My Lord

I am really ashamed to call upon you – will it interfere with your Lordships objects if I send a note payable in Two months for the 1000 G^s – if left at your Lordships Banker – it will cost no further trouble – if this <really> (under the circumstances) not very modest request, would disarrange your Lordships plans I entreat your Lordship to say so, & my convenience will instantly yield to your wishes − I must repeat that I feel ashamed to have had occasion to say a word upon the matter[1] −

+   +   +

The author of "Buonaparte" has just returned from Paris & when I communicated to him your Lordships particular & repeated praise of his poem he desired me to assure you that he feels more gratified by your opinion than by any other − He begs me to present a Copy if it be worthy your Lordships acceptance, in the name of the author M[r] Stratford Canning[2]

I am my Lord
your faithful Servant
Jno Murray

Tuesday

Notes to Letter 44)

1. Publishing arrangements having resumed their former footing (see Letter 43 above), JM was now due to pay B 1,000 guineas for *The Giaour* and *The Bride of Abydos* in fulfilment of his offer in Letter 17 above. Replying the same day, B willingly complied with JM's request saying the readjustment would 'do very well' (*BLJ* IV, 117). B's bankers were Hammersley's.

2. On Tuesday 26 April B had said that he could not guess at the author of the anonymous poem JM had sent him, but that he thought it 'a noble poem − & worth a thousand odes of anybody's' (*BLJ* IV, 106−07). This was *Buonaparte. A Poem*, published by JM in early May 1814, whose author was Stratford Canning (1786−1880), first Viscount Stratford de Redcliffe (1852), diplomat, who had co-edited *The Miniature* while at Eton (cf. 'Lines Associated with *English Bards and Scotch Reviewers*'; *CPW* I, 264), played against B in the first Eton and Harrow cricket match in 1805, became acquainted with him at Constantinople in 1810, and was at this time a disappointed suitor of Annabella's (whom he called 'Princess Nonparelia'). He and B were not intimates. Evidently JM passed B's letter of 26 April on to Canning, who replied from Grillon's Hotel in Albemarle Street on 'Monday Evening' (almost certainly 23 May 1814): 'I thank you for Lord Byron's Note making allusion to me. Whatever opinion I may entertain of his character, it cannot but be agreeable to me to find that a poetical composition of mine has met with the approbation of the most celebrated English Poet of the time' (MA). To this letter of JM's B replied the same day saying he did 'not think less highly' of the poem for knowing its author, and reiterated his high opinion of it even more strongly to JM on 2 September 1814 (*BLJ* IV, 117 and 164). The poem may be found in Stanley Lane-Poole, *The Life of the Right*

Honourable Stratford Canning, Viscount Stratford de Redcliffe (2 vols [London, 1888], I, 214–221), where there are many other references to B.

Letter 45)   [Tuesday 14 – Tuesday 21 June 1814?]

My Lord
    I called to take leave & to receive yr commands & <u>possibly</u> the first Canto – but hearing that you had certain People[1] with You I thought the meeting might prove too Dramatic for Your taste & so I send over my <u>dutiful</u> Compliments instead having the great pleasure of delivering them in Person
    Jno Murray

Noon

Notes to Letter 45)

<u>Cover</u>: The Lord Byron

The date of this letter is conjectural, but JM seems almost certainly to refer to *Lara*, the last of the Turkish tales to be written in cantos, which B had begun in May. On Tuesday 14 June he told Moore it was finished and that he was in the process of fair-copying it (*BLJ* IV, 126); and by Tuesday 21 June he had given JM the fair copy of the first canto (*BLJ* IV, 129; see Letter 46 below).

    1. Possibly Caro Lamb who was besieging B again at this period (Marchand, I, 458).

Letter 46)   [Tuesday 21 June 1814?]

My Lord
    Lara is I declare to God more evenly great from first to last as far as I have read than any of his relations[1] – I copied the <u>whole</u> in order to preserve the MSS & this evening I expect the first proof[2] – & I have waited only for this to call & tell you how much I am surprised & delighted by this new Poem. I am truly anxious to receive the remainder which I hoped to do when I brought the first proof – wch will not be of the <u>whole</u> – because nothing but exertion <to> could retain even two men at their work –
    J. M.

Notes to Letter 46)

Cover: The Lord Byron

The date of this letter is conjectural. Not having heard from JM since giving him the fair copy of the first canto of *Lara* (see Letter 45 above), B wrote on Tuesday 21 June wishing to know whether, as he supposed, it had 'gone to the Devil', as it would spare him the trouble of 'copying the rest' (i.e., Canto II) (*BLJ* IV, 129).

   1. Specifically *The Corsair*, to which *Lara* is the sequel, but also the two earlier Turkish Tales.

   2. It is evident from this and the next letter (47) that the amanuenses' copy of B's fair copy was copy text for the first edition, not B's fair copy itself (cf. *CPW* III, 452): hence, no doubt, the blunders in proof (see Letter 47 below).

Letter 47)   [Friday 24 June 1814?]

My Lord
   I send a proof of the whole of Lara but I have to entreat the favor of your pardon for the <u>gross</u> incorrectness wch will be found in the two last sheets owing to my desire of preserving the original MSS & the haste with which the Copy of it was made by 6 people in order to retard as little as possible the means of sending the proof to Your Lordship –
   I think the close of the <fig> Battle & the Death of Lara are the finest things that were ever penned particularly the first of these two & as a whole I will venture my Life that it does your Lordship honour[1] –
   Amen
   J. M.

Notes to Letter 47)

The date of this letter is conjectural, but B received the first proof of *Lara* on Friday 24 June, and returned it corrected the same day, appalled at 'the most *horrible* blunders that ever crept into a proof' and hoping the next one would be better (*BLJ* IV, 132; see also, Letter 46, n. 2 above).

   1. The close of the battle and Lara's death in *Lara*, II, stanza 16ff. (see also, Letter 53, n. 4 below).

Letter 48)   [Monday 27 June 1814?]

My Lord
  I have received your communication & am delighted by your mode of giving Battle – of which your Lordship shall receive a proof tomorrow.
    JM

Notes to Letter 48)

Perhaps prompted by JM's reference to 'the Battle' at the close of his previous letter (47), B added stanza 15 to the battle scene in *Lara*, Canto II, which he sent to JM on Monday 27 June saying, 'You demanded more *battle* – there it is' (*BLJ* IV, 134; see also, *CPW* III, 452).

Letter 49)   Monday [11 July 1814]

My Lord
  The Exhibition having closed, I entreat the favor of your kind recollection of a promise, made some time ago, to honour me, with the highest mark of personal <h> esteem, by presenting me with your Lordships Portrait – a favor my Lord upon which if I have no increased claim – I am sure I stand in greater need when the room in which I should place <the portrait> it is no longer honoured with the presence of the Original to whose continued friendship I owe so much.
  I am my Lord
  "your poor servant ever"[1]
  John Murray

Albemarle Str
Monday

Notes to Letter 49)

The Summer Exhibition at the Royal Academy opened on Monday 2 May and closed on Saturday 9 July 1814. Hazlitt in the *Morning Chronicle* for Tuesday 3 May reported that among paintings by Lawrence, West, Stothard, Haydon, Raeburn, Reinagle and Turner, the '*Portrait of a Nobleman in the Dress of an Albanian*, by T. PHILLIPS, No. 84; and *Portrait of a Nobleman*, 172, seem to be the same individual. They are both fine. They are said to be the portrait of Lord Byron, though in that case we do not see why they should be incognito. They are too smooth, and seem, as it were "barbered ten times o'er," [*Antony and Cleopatra*, II, ii, 228] both in the face and in the expression. There is, however, much that conveys the idea of the softness and the wildness of character of the popular poet of the East.' B had promised JM one of the two portraits as early as Wednesday 17 November 1813 (*BLJ* III, 167; see also, Letter 17 above). He reiterated his pledge in his reply of Monday 11 July 1814 (*BLJ* IV, 140), and the latter of the two portraits now hangs with some irony above the fireplace where his Memoirs were burnt in the drawing-room at 50 Albemarle Street.

    1. JM casts himself as Horatio to B's Hamlet: *Hamlet*, I, ii, 162 (see also, Letter 65 below).

Letter 50)   [Tuesday 12 July 1814?]

your Lordship is yet in good time – I send <u>another</u> copy of the Proofs which I have by me[1] –

    I have sent Childe Harold & the Giaour to Stothard to read previously[2] –

    I send yr Lordship a Letter which comes to me very flatteringly.[3]
    J. M.

Notes to Letter 50)

<u>Cover</u>: The Lord Byron

The dating of this letter is conjectural.

    1. In his letter of Monday 11 July, B had asked JM to send the proof of *Lara* to Moore, who wanted to read it before he left for the country the following day (*BLJ* IV, 140). The next morning (Tuesday 12 July) Moore sent B a note saying, 'I got Lara at three o'clock this morning – read him before I slept, and was enraptured. I take the proofs with me' (*Byron's Life and Works*, III, 96n). Informing JM of this, B requested another proof 'exactly the same' (*BLJ* IV, 140–41).

    2. A set of 12 Plates, illustrative of B's works, engraved by Finden and others from designs by Thomas Stothard (1755–1834), was published by JM on 1 December 1814, and may now be seen in *CPW* II and III. They were reviewed in *The Examiner*, No. 399, Sunday, August 20, 1815 (pp. 238–39): 'Mr. STOTHARD's pictures are always parts of his author's character ... It is the same with the Works of Lord BYRON, just published. The characteristics of this author are passion, melancholy, a fondness for the mysterious, an intense feeling both of the painful and the voluptuous. All these, and these

only, are to be found in the designs for his productions by Mr. STOTHARD. We ... must content ourselves with pointing out to the reader the evident mystery of the print in *Lara*; the striking contrast between the two pictures in the *Giaour*; and lastly, our two favourite ones, the Spanish dance in *Childe Harold*, and the love scene in the *Bride of Abydos*. Mark the nice distinction, in these last, between the pleasing and not vulgar, though still not lady-like, gracefulness of the girl dancing, and the accomplished perfection of the exquisite creature who is pressing her flower upon *Selim*' (359). JM presented Annabella with a set in May 1815 (*BLJ* IV, 292), and one set was sold at the sale of B's books in 1816 (*CMP* 243, lot 332). In a letter to an unidentified recipient dated by Marchand '[January 14, 1814]', B says: 'C[hilde] H[arold] is at present out of print, but Mr. Murray talks of an illustrated edition, and in that case I should wish my friends to have Stothard's designs' (*BLJ* IV, 30). The recipient can almost certainly be identified as Edward Daniel Clarke, the traveller, and his 'harmonious namesake' as John Clarke (or John Whitfeld or John Clarke Whitfeld as he also called himself) (1770–1836), composer, organist and Professor of Music at Cambridge, whose *Twelve Vocal Pieces*, 2 vols (n.d.; entered at the Stationers' Hall, 13 May 1817) contained settings of poems by B (see *CPW* III, 472, 473 and 475; the second volume also included 'Zuleika' – a setting of *The Bride of Abydos*, II, 621–61). Clarke later issued 'One struggle more, and I am free' (i.e., 'To Thyrza') as a separate Canzonet (n.d.; entered at the Stationers' Hall, 15 September 1819), which is considered as rising 'well above the mediocrity of the contemporary English ballad' (Nicholas Temperley in *The New Grove Dictionary of Music and Musicians*). It may or may not be significant that B mentions that JM's 'parcel of Clarke & letters has not arrived yet' in his letter to him from Hastings of Thursday 28 July 1814 (*BLJ* IV, 146).

3. This letter is unidentified.

Letter 51)   Wednesday [6 or 13 July 1814?]

My Lord

Mr Rogers called today with his Poem to be printed with yours – I send the first Sheet of Giffords Copy of the Proof – the rest I will get (if not today) tomorrow –

Mr Ward has read the Proof & admires the Poem greatly – I suggested if it were not too <u>semblable</u> – he said it shewed uncommon talent to exhibit the same Portrait in as many lights &c &c[1]

I am obliged to go to the Country ¼ before 3 – but return at night. faithfully yr Lordships Servt

Jno Murray

Wednesday

Notes to Letter 51)

Cover: The Lord Byron

The latter of these conjectural dates is the more likely of the two. Unfortunately
no proofs of *Lara* survive (*CPW* III, 452). Rogers had sent B the manuscript of his
poem *Jacqueline* on Monday 27 June, and on Friday 8 July B told Moore that they
had 'almost coalesced into a joint invasion of the public', though there was still
some uncertainty as to whether they would (*BLJ* IV, 138). *Lara* and *Jacqueline* were
eventually published together anonymously on Saturday 6 August 1814 (*Morning
Chronicle*, Friday 5 and Saturday 6 August 1814).

　1. Ward seems to have been particularly impressed by the description of night
　　　in *Lara*, I, 155–80. Writing to Mrs Stewart on 29 August 1814 from Paris he
　　　told her: 'Mackintosh is here on his way to Switzerland ... He has got Rogers
　　　with him who, as you know, has published a new poem entitled "Jacqueline"
　　　for which Murray has been goose enough to give him a guinea a line. But
　　　then "Lara" precedes it, and I suppose he has been obliged to buy the lean
　　　rabbit along with the fat one, according to ancient usage. Tell me whether
　　　you don't think the 10th stanza of the 1st canto of "Lara" as fine a thing as
　　　you ever read' (*Letters to 'Ivy' from the First Earl of Dudley*, ed. S. H. Romilly
　　　[London, 1905], 256; see also, Letter 53, and Letter 79, n. 2 below).

Letter 52)   Wednesday [20 July 1814]

My Lord

　I have the pleasure of sending you the fragment which Sir John
Malcolm repeated to you in part the other day – he will feel obliged if
in returning it you would favor him with any critical Comments[1] –

　It should have been given to your Lordship yesterday[2] but I was so
much broken in upon that it unfortunately escaped me.

　I beg leave to offer my Compliments & remain
　<Dear> My Lord
　your faithful Servant
　John Murray

Wednesday

Notes to Letter 52)

B left London accompanied by Augusta and her children and his cousin, Captain
George Anson Byron, for a holiday in Hastings, where Hodgson had arranged

for their taking Hastings House (see *BLJ* IV, 137–40, 142–43). *The Champion* for 31 July 1814 announced: 'Lord Byron has taken the beautiful mansion, called Hastings-house, at Hastings, where his Lordship arrived on Wednesday last.' They stayed for three weeks, from Wednesday 20 July to Tuesday 9 August. B did not receive this letter (52) until Sunday 31 July, when the parcel it accompanied arrived after considerable delay (see *BLJ* IV, 146–48).

1. In a letter to JM dated merely 'Wednesday', Sir John Malcolm told him: 'You will have 225 Copies of the little Poem on Saturday morning. I beg you will send a Copy immediately to Lord Byron' (MA). The poem was *Persia: A Poem* (380 lines in heroic couplets, with extensive notes, descriptive of Persia, its inhabitants and literature – especially, Hafiz, Ferdausi and Sadi), published by JM on Saturday 6 August (*Morning Chronicle*, Friday 5 and Saturday 6 August 1814). In his reply to JM of Sunday 31 July, B wrote: 'Many thanks for Sir J. Malcolm – I wish to the skies – he had been of the party with R[ogers] & me' (that is, had formed a third in the Byron-Rogers joint publication of *Lara* and *Jacqueline*); and in his letter of Wednesday 2 August asked JM to 'present my best thanks to Sir Jno. Malcolm for a very beautiful poem' (*BLJ* IV, 147–48 and 150; Marchand's note referring us to Malcolm's *History of Persia* is incorrect). According to Moore, B had also proposed that Moore himself 'should make a third in this publication; but the honour was a perilous one, and I begged leave to decline it' (*Byron's Life and Works*, III, 95n).

2. That would have been Tuesday 19 July, the day before B left London.

Letter 53)   Saturday [6 August 1814]

My Lord

I am really grateful for your obliging sufferance of my desire to publish Lara, for, I am sure, your Lordship knows the respect I bear you in every way, would not have allowed me to do this without your consent[1] – I had anticipated this and had done every thing but actually deliver the Copies of Lara and the moment I received your Lordships Letter, for, for it I waited – I cut the last Cord of my aerial work[2] – and at this instant Six Thousand Copies are gone!!![3] I had sent copies, I believe, to every one of your Lordships friends and without an exception they are delighted and their praise is most particularly and rootedly confirmed on a second perusal – which proves to them that your researches into the human heart and character are at once wonderful & just – Mr Frere likes the Poem greatly & admires mostly the first canto – I mentioned the passage in the second canto descriptive of the morning after the battle, which delighted me so

much[4] – and, indeed Mr Wilmot[5] & many other persons, and his
remark was that he thought it rather too shocking – this is perhaps
a little fastidious – Sir Jno. Malcolm, whom I have not seen since,
called to express his satisfaction, & by the way, I may <just> add, that
Mr Frere has been here this moment to take another Copy with him
<in> to read again in his carriage – he told me that Mr Canning liked
it equally – Mr Frere and, in his report,[6] Mr Canning, are the only
persons whom I can have the pleasure of hearing speak in praise of
Jacqueline – but they say it is beautiful & this is a Host[7] – there is an
obvious tendancy [sic] to disparage Jacqueline but I think it is unjust &
will be overcome.[8]

With regard to the portrait, the advertisement which your Lordship
notices,[9] was sent to the papers immediately after you had, at first, not
disapproved of it – but as this was a a [sic] point of realy [sic] delicacy
towards your Lordship I did not think of giving out a Copy of it until
I should have obtained permission – which I venture to entreat for – as
a matter in which you need not care to concern yourself – & the next
I make shall be with every endeavour to render it more worthy of the
original – upon the score then of indifference – I solicit your Lordships
Fiat.

Against the formidable attack upon my Advertisement I feel perfectly
secure[10] – Imprimis – the<y> words are Giffords[11] – in the second
place Mr Frere denies that they are not Grammar & in the third place
no other persons or person have [sic] noticed them & those to whom I
suggested the <incorre> alledged [sic] incorrectness agree that they can
be noticed noly [sic] by fastidiousness and Hypercriticism of Friendship[12]
– who, in such a poem, would stop for a moment at a word in the
preface – Moreover here is Johnson for you – and (thank God) for your
Publisher – who, now that his author is found out to be Dryden is, I
suppose, to be treated like Tonson[13] – but to Johnson

That – 1 not this

2 Which: relating to an antecedent thing

The mark that is set before him
                                                            Perkins
The time that clogs me

                                                    Shakespeare
Bones that hasten to be so

                                                            Cowley
Judgment that is equal

                                                    Wilkins[14]

Are you Answered?

Mr Merivale is here & subscribes to \<my\> the opinion in favour of <u>That</u>

I felt more about the publication \<about\> of those lines than I could
express & therefore I said nothing – it was most shameful to print at
all – but with the <u>name</u> it was villanous [*sic*] – I saw them only in the
Chronicle & I rejoice that they did not originate with out friend Perry[15]
– they spoil that tone of harmony towards your Lordship which had
been so powerfully struck into the Public Mind by <u>Jeffery</u> [*sic*] – every
body thinks highly of the talent of the Article in the E. R and accord
[*sic*] with its sentiments throughout.[16]

I must remain some days yet to watch the progress of the demand
for Lara &, therefore, as I could not attend my family to Scotland I
rather think of going to Paris first – and afterwards to the North.[17] Your
Lordship does not tell me & perhaps cannot the time of your return
– Do me the favor to say if I shall have the pleasure of forwarding
your Lordships Letters? —— I have now decyphered the last part of your
Lordships note – made obscure by the erasure of some valuable remarks
– and rejoice that I shall have the pleasure of seeing your Lordship in
Town – <u>next week</u>[18] –

> With assurances of the highest esteem I have the honour to remain
> My Lord
> Your faithful Servant
> John Murray

Albemarle S^t
Saturday

Notes to Letter 53)

<u>Cover</u>: The R^t Honble/Lord Byron/Hastings <u>pm</u>: 6 Aug 1814

1. B had written several times from Hastings instructing JM to postpone the
   publication of *Lara* until his return to London; but having seen it advertised
   in the papers, he resisted no longer, and wrote on Friday 5 August: 'Out
   with Lara – since it must be – the tome looks pretty enough – on the outside'
   (*BLJ* IV, 154–55; see also, IV, 144–54).

2. Perhaps glancing at B's remark in his letter of Sunday 24 July: 'the country
   is not Spain but the Moon' (*BLJ* IV, 146).

3. JM reiterated this figure to Hobhouse on Thursday 11 August (BL Add.
   47232, f. 9), and to Annie, his wife, at Edinburgh in a letter of Monday 29
   August: 'I have now sold the whole 6.000 of Lara – Longman who took 500
   at first sent for 250 more on Saturday – after a time I will print it alone &
   hope to sell at least 10,000 more – tell Blackwood by a short Note to ship

for me 250 of his if he finds them not certain of immediate sale, I have not got <u>One Copy left</u> (MA).

4. Lara, II, stanza 16 (see Letter 47 above).

5. Robert Wilmot (1784–1841), B's first cousin, later mediator in the Separation proceedings.

6. By 'in his report' JM means 'according to him', or 'as Frere tells me', and not a written report by Frere or Canning.

7. JM means that between them Canning and Frere constitute 'a Host'.

8. R. W. Hay, for instance, wrote to JM on Wednesday 3 August: 'Many thanks for your attention in sending me Lara &c. unequal as they be' (MA); and see also, Ward's unflattering reference to *Jacqueline* in n. 1 to Letter 51 above.

9. At the end of the volume containing *Lara* and *Jacqueline* are four pages of Advertisements for JM's publications, the first of which is for a portrait of B, engraved by J. S. Agar, from 'the spirited and faithful Likeness' by Thomas Phillips. B had objected to the engraving, and had told JM very firmly on Thursday 28 July: 'Remember – *we positively will not have that same print* by Phillips' engraver' (*BLJ* IV, 146; see also, IV, 144 and 145–46). In his letter of Friday 5 August, B observed with some exasperation: 'It seems also that the "spirited & faithful likeness" is another of your publications – I wish you joy of it – but it is no likeness – that is the print' (*BLJ* IV, 154).

10. Both the 'Advertisement' and the note on Lara's name prefixed to *Lara* (p. iv and vii of the 1st edn respectively) were written by Hobhouse, the latter on Friday 29 July at the suggestion of Lady Holland (BL Add. 47232, f. 8r). On Thursday 4 August Hobhouse had written indignantly to B: 'Murray has been cutting at the advertisement and made it bad English – It stood originally thus. "The reader of Lara may probably regard it as a sequel to *The Corsair.*" As it now stands, it is, "The reader of Lara may probably regard it as a sequel to a poem *that recently appeared*[.]" You will see instantly that the underlined words should be, "*which has* recently appeared." It is a downright vulgarism to use "*that*" for "which" and unless the *has* is prefixed the relative verb is not of the same tense as the antecedent sentence. I tell you it's bad grammar altogether therefore dont lose a moment in writing to Murray and *ordering* him *peremptorily* to put "*which has* recently appeared." I have made strong representation to him but perhaps he may not care for me – Diable I never saw such a spectaculo as they have made of my bit of prose' (*BB*, 132). B enclosed this letter with his to JM of Friday 5 August commenting: 'witness the grammar of H[obhouse]'s "bit of prose" which has put him & me into a fever' (*BLJ* IV, 154).

11. As JM says, '<u>Imprimis</u> [in the first place] – the words are Giffords'. Writing from Ryde on 26 July 1814, and referring solely to the 'Advertisement' to

Lara, Gifford told JM: 'I wish the mention of the <u>Corsair</u> could be overided [*sic*]. Might you not say "as a sequel" to a poem "that recently appeared["]? It is better to suppress the name. – line 6 read ["]is left to his determination["], & omit <u>following</u> line 10. The remainder will do very well.' (MA). It is clear from this that the 'Advertisement' was written prior to 26 July, not 'between 31 July and 3 Aug.' (*CPW* III, 452). However, 'is left to his determination' was not adopted in place of 'shall be left to his determination' (line 6 in the 'Advertisement' on p. iv of the 1st edn); but as the two closing words only ('the attempt.') occupy line 10 of the 'Advertisement' (the last line on p. iv), leaving space enough for a few more words or a further short sentence, it is possible that Gifford's final instruction was followed (the 'Advertisement' for *Jacqueline* occupies the following page v).

12. JM's underlining of '<u>Friendship</u>' glances ironically at Hobhouse's grammatical 'fastidiousness'. Indeed, Gifford, Frere and Hobhouse were still arguing the point (on slightly different grounds) on Thursday 11 August when Hobhouse noted in his Diary: 'Gifford ... & H. Frere say the following sentence is good English – "The reader of Lara may probably regard it as a sequel to a poem that lately appeared" I say it is not & that it ought to be – "that has lately appeared". It is in the advertisement to Lara – which was written by myself – with the exception of the words "a poem that recently appeared" which was put by Gifford instead of "the Corsair" my reading' (BL Add. 47232, f. 9*v*).

13. Jacob Tonson (1656–1737), the leading publisher and bookseller of the day who was both the publisher and the satirical butt of Dryden and Pope. JM's parallel is high praise of B (if not covertly and perhaps unintentionally of himself).

14. JM cites the first four examples of 'that' used as 'which' in the entry for 'That' in Johnson, *A Dictionary of the English Language*.

15. In his letter of Tuesday 2 August, B had said he was 'sorry to see that the papers have by some means obtained & published a copy (an imperfect one by the bye) of some lines – I cannot divine how – as none were ever given except to the person to whom they were addressed' (*BLJ* IV, 149). He followed this up on Friday 5 August saying: 'You don't condole with me about the Champion's seizure & publication of the lines on the picture – of which I knew nothing and am in a very bad humour at the proceeding – I gave no copy whatever (except to Ly. J[ersey]) and had not even one of my own' (*BLJ* IV, 154). The lines were '[Condolatory Address to Sarah, Countess of Jersey, On the Prince Regent's Returning Her Picture to Mrs. Mee]' which B had written and sent to Lady Jersey on 29 May 1814 (*BLJ* IV, 120). They were first printed without B's authority in *The Champion* on Sunday 31 July 1814, entitled simply 'LINES BY LORD B—.', and reprinted from there in the *Morning Chronicle* on Monday 1 August 1814 (hence JM's relief 'that they did not originate with our friend Perry'). See *CPW* III, 272–73 and 459–60; see also, Letter 54 below.

16. B had been in daily expectation of the *Edinburgh Review* which at last arrived on Friday 5 August. Issued late (in July), the *Edinburgh Review*, XXIII, xlv (April 1814), Art. IX, pp. 198–229, contained Jeffrey's extremely favourable review of *The Bride of Abydos* (6th edn) and *The Corsair* (5th edn).

17. Evidently in response to some remark in JM's covering letter (not extant) sent with the *Edinburgh Review*, B had apologized in his reply of Friday 5 August: 'if I *have* delayed your journey to S[cotland] I am sorry you carried your complaisance so far' (*BLJ* IV, 154). In the event, JM did not go to Paris, but went first to Brighton for ten days, and then, after a week in London, set out to join Annie and his family in Edinburgh.

18. As Marchand indicates, there are nine lines crossed out at the end of B's letter of Friday 5 August (*BLJ* IV, 155). These are very heavily erased and indecipherable, and are partly written crosswise up the page so that even the legible final words 'I shall be in town next week – & in the mean time wish you a pleasant journey' are 'made obscure'. JM is not suggesting he could read B's erased lines, but that any 'remarks' B might make were necessarily 'valuable'. B returned to town on Tuesday 9 August.

Letter 54)   Sunday [14 August 1814?]

My Lord

Will your Lordship be so very kind as to allow me to have a Copy of the Lines to Lady J today – that is to say, provided your Lordship \<has\> have no disinclination to accord me this favor – for I have some literary friends to dine with me today & I would be glad to read them – I pledge my word to allow no copy to be taken – or, if yr Lordship lent me your own Copy by Six o Clock, I would return it this night –

ever yr Lordships
bounden Servant
Jno Murray

Sunday

Notes to Letter 54)

<u>Cover</u>: The Lord Byron

B had returned to London from Hastings on Tuesday 9 August (*BLJ* IV, 155). He remained in town for ten days and left for Newstead with Augusta on Sunday 21 August. JM wrote to Annie on Monday 15 August saying he had dined with D'Israeli the preceding evening (Sunday 14 August), and that he was to have

Blackwood and John Cumming, the Dublin bookseller, to dine with him that day (Monday 15 August) (MA). He must have forgotten that B had told him he had no copy of his '[Condolatory Address to Sarah, Countess of Jersey, On the Prince Regent's Returning Her Picture to Mrs. Mee]' in his letter from Hastings of Friday 5 August (BLJ IV, 154). If B did in fact have a copy, there is no indication as to whether or not he complied with this request, which seems an odd one to have made when the lines had already been printed in the *Morning Chronicle* where indeed JM had read them – though, of course, he may have mislaid or disposed of that paper (see Letter 53, n. 15 above).

Letter 55)   [Wednesday 17 August 1814?]

My Lord

    I entreat you shew it not to anyone, until I shall exchange this copy for a perfect one –

    J M.

Upon my honour No other Personage or Person has a line – but you – Pray do not leave it <u>about</u> I will relieve you from this <u>some</u> time tomorrow

Notes to Letter 55)

<u>Cover</u>: The Lord Byron

The date of this letter is conjectural. In a letter to JM conjecturally dated by Marchand '[Dec. 1813?]', but which should be dated Wednesday 17 August 1814, B had written: 'Will you have the kindness to lend me your Buccaneer's Journal for the Evening?' (BLJ III, 186). This Letter (55) seems to have accompanied that 'Journal'; see Letter 56 below.

Letter 56)   Saturday [20 August 1814]

My Lord

    Any time this evening will y^r Lordship do me the favor to say

    If Newstead is satisfactorily settled –

    Does your Lordship go there tomorrow?

    Have you done with Penrose whom I wish to convey to Scotland tomorrow by Blackwood to have it printed there –

    Most Devotedly

yr Lordships Servant
John Murray

Saturday
¼ past 5

Notes to Letter 56)

Cover: The Lord Byron

See Letter 55 above. Writing to Annie on Thursday 18 August, JM told her (quoting verbatim from B's letter to him of that same morning): 'I have got at last Mr Eagles MSS Journal of Penrose the Seaman which you may remember I am to pay £200 in 12 Mos for 1,000 Copies too dear perhaps – but Lord Byron sent me word this morning by Letter – for he borrowed the MSS last night "Penrose is most amusing – I never read so much of a book at one sitting in my life – he kept me up half the night & made me dream of him the other half – it has all the air of truth – and is most entertaining & interesting in every point of view"' (MA; cf. *BLJ* IV, 160). B must have returned the manuscript when he saw JM in the evening (Saturday 20 August), when he would also have answered JM's other enquiries. *The Journal of Llewellen Penrose, A Seaman*, ed. John Eagles, 4 vols, was published by JM in London and by Blackwood in Edinburgh in 1815. Blackwood was in London on business for a fortnight in August. On Saturday 13 August JM wrote to Annie: 'Lord Byron was here yesterday & I introduced him to Blackwood to whom he was very civil'; and on Monday 22 August: 'I went down to the Wharf of the Old Shipping Company yesterday [Sunday 21 August] to see Blackwood off, in the Lord Wellington ... Lord Byron set out for Newstead ... it is finally settled to be his again the man forfeiting £25,000' (MA).

Letter 57)   Monday 5 September [1814]

My Lord
    I am greatly obliged by your Letter which enables me to stettle [*sic*] my plan of proposals with Mr Hogg as with the associated view which your Lordship has judiciously given it may prove an interesting and valuable publication – though I can not help wishing that it had a more tasteful Editor – but I shall write to him immediately.[1]
    I had not heard of Campbells little poem or I would have tried at least to have seduced him into Publication[2] – he is now at Rouen or Paris –
    Your Lordship will observe in the Chronicle of today a curious, if not completely satisfactory, obstetrical Epistle from the renowned Dr

Sims which will destroy <u>Joanna's</u> Happiness & remove your Lordships wonder at its protuberant cause[3] – though affter [sic] the happy & successful amours of the Hottentot Venus – with a Drummer our scepticism upon this mystic subject might naturally subside[4] – Sharpe has long been her devoted admirer & has actually ruined his fortune by its immediate & collateral effects.[5]

Does your Lordship perceive M[r] Hunts announcement "The Descent of Liberty" & the now Hebdom<i>adal incense of Sonnets to keep his name & misfortunes before a heartless Public?[6] – Gifford thinks there are some fine things in <the> Wordsworths new Poem.[7]

I trust that your Lordship is not Idle[8] – The plan which you propose for the arrangement of your Poems shall be adopted as soon as we have sold the small edition now nearly compleated [sic] which runs as follows –

> Vol I –   Childe Harold
> II   Giaour – Bride
> III   Corsair – Lara
> IV   Poems – Ode

they will be ready in November & by March I expect to have demand for a new Edition[9] – I have not – nor do I hear of any new book to interest your Lordship or I should venture to send it.

I have been confined to the house by a cold & fever for the last fortnight but I hope to be able to leave town for Scotland or Paris on Tuesday or Wednesday in next week[10] – but I shall take the liberty of writing again before I go – I had a Letter from M[r] Ward at Paris last week – Mad. de Stael has returned there by this time[11] –

The publication of the English Bards in Ireland was only of the first Edition a Copy of which I have & they have promissed to sin no more.[12]

I hope that M[rs] Leigh & the family are well[13] & with respectful compliments remain

My Lord
your faithful Servant
John Murray

Monday
Sep 5.

Notes to Letter 57)

1. In a letter to B from Edinburgh of 17 August 1814, James Hogg had written: 'May it please your lordship Look over the inclosed and after you have drawn your pen thorough [*sic*] every word of it that you disapprove either put it to Mr. Murray or not as you please … I was very sorry I could not mention your name <u>positively</u> as a supporter to Mr. Murray for which cause I mentioned none' (Bodleian, Dep. Lovelace Byron 155, f. 49*r*). The 'inclosed' was a letter to JM, also of 17 August, in which Hogg told him he had been arranging materials for an intended periodical work of which he then proceeded to give him the plan:

> "On the 1st of Nov*r*. next will be published price 5/ to be continued half-yearly <u>The Edin. Poetical Repository</u> To consist of <u>Original Poetry</u> by most of the eminent British Poets of the present day – and likewise a character or Analysis of every new poetical work of distinction so as to form not only a Repository for Original Poetry of merit, but for every thing connected with the poetry of the era to which it belongs. The names of those noblemen and gentlemen who have so liberally tendered their support to the work and under whose patronage it is <published> commenced will be afterwards published" This is my projected plan and for this I am now at full liberty to treat; but I must likewise inform you that on laying the plan before Con.*e* [Constable] and Miller they disapproved of the latter part of the plan thinking it should consist of good classical poetry alone and to be a small elegant post 8*vo.* for the drawing room table – But when I consented to this they proposed that it should be only once a year which I would in nowise consent to the adventure being so trifling I thought the spirit of keeping up the thing would lag and finally die away About this sir – I shall be very happy to treat with you and particularly to be advised <about the> about the plan name size &c I know that an author's or editor's share of any such thing must be ruled by the sale therefore of that there is little to be said but I like above all things punctuality and fairness I am the reverse of greedy but the first time I discovered aught of over-reaching or imposition in a publisher I would change him next day. If you enter into it you are free to chuse at the end of every year

(MS National Library of Scotland). B did not draw his pen through any of this, but forwarded it to JM on Friday 26 August, telling him he had done so the next day and hoping it would 'lead to a lucrative alliance between you' (*BLJ* IV, 162): he encouraged JM even further in his reply of Wednesday 7 September (*BLJ* IV, 167). James Hogg, the Ettrick Shepherd (1770–1835), poet, author of *The Forest Minstrel* (1810), *The Queen's Wake* (1813) and, under the name of J. H. Craig of Douglas, *The Hunting of Badlewe, a Dramatic Tale*

(1814). *The Pilgrims of the Sun*, dedicated to B, was published in 1815; and, in 1816, the subject of his present negotiation was published by JM under the title of *The Poetic Mirror*.

2. B had written again to JM on Friday 2 September recommending his 'alliance' with Hogg and suggesting that among other contributors he 'might coax Campbell too into it': '*he* has an unpublished (though printed) poem on a Scene in Germany (Bavaria, I think) which I saw last year – that is perfectly magnificent' (*BLJ* IV, 163). This was 'Lines on Leaving a Scene in Bavaria', written in 1800, from which B quotes three very pertinent lines in *Some Observations* (1820) (see *CMP*, 97).

3. Joanna Southcott (1750–1814), the Methodist prophetess of the new Messiah, Shiloh, to whom she was to give birth, and whose 'accouchement' was imminent, had been the subject of much discussion (and mirth) in the papers since the beginning of August. B himself had jocularly referred to the matter in his letter to JM of Friday 2 September (*BLJ* IV, 164). In the *Morning Chronicle* for Monday 5 September 1814 there appeared a long letter from Joanna Southcott herself defending her pregnancy on the testimony of Dr. Reece; and one from Dr. Sims who had examined her and denied it on medical grounds (which he detailed with considerable explicitness), adding however, that 'this poor woman is no impostor, but ... labours under a strong mental delusion'. She died of brain disease on 27 December 1814.

4. 'The Hottentot Venus' was an African woman called Sartje who was brought over from South Africa in 1810 and exhibited as a steatopygous prodigy at the Liverpool Museum in Piccadilly. In November 1810, her case was brought before Lord Ellenborough in the Court of King's Bench on the grounds of inhumanity and indecency when among other particulars of her history it transpired that 'She had a child by a drummer at the Cape, where she lived two years' (*The Times*, Thursday 29 November 1810, and *The Examiner*, No. 152, Sunday 25 November 1810, p. 745; see also, *The Times*, Monday 26 November 1810, and *The Examiner*, No. 153, Sunday 2 December 1810, pp. 767–68). She was the subject of a number of prurient cartoons and epigrams, but also of much compassion – Kemble's, for instance (see Mrs Mathews, *Memoirs of Charles Mathews, Comedian*, 4 vols [London, 1839], IV, 136–39). Having toured the provinces she was taken to Paris where Cuvier examined her and where she died of 'the small pox' in December 1815 (see the *Morning Chronicle*, Saturday 6 January 1816, and for an epigram 'On the Death of the Hottentot Venus', the *Morning Chronicle*, Tuesday 9 January 1816). See also, Richard D. Altick, *The Shows of London* (Cambridge, Mass.: Harvard University Press, 1978), 268–72.

5. William Sharp (1749–1824), the engraver, was one of Joanna Southcott's most fervent disciples. B had referred to him in his letter to JM of Friday 2 September (*BLJ* IV, 164). See also, Letter 62, n. 1 below.

6. The *Morning Chronicle* for Monday 5 September printed a sonnet 'To LEIGH

HUNT, Esq. Occasioned by the Perusal of his Second Sonnet to Hampstead',
'By a Lady' (who signed herself 'M'), and carried an advertisement for Hunt's
The Descent of Liberty, to be published by Cawthorn 'at the beginning of
the season', upon which B commented wryly in his reply: 'I have not seen
Hunt's sonnets nor descent of Liberty – he has chosen a pretty place wherein
to compose the last' (Hunt being in prison at the time) (*BLJ* IV, 167).

7. Wordsworth's 'new Poem' was *The Excursion,* published in August 1814. It
   was favourably reviewed by Charles Lamb in the *Quarterly Review* (XII, xxiii
   [October 1814], 100–11), and damned outright by Jeffrey in the *Edinburgh
   Review* (XXIV, xlvii [November 1814], 1–30) with the famous opening
   sentence: 'This will never do.' B replied to JM on Wednesday 7 September:
   'There must be many "fine things" in Wordsworth – but I should think it
   difficult to make 6 quartos (the amount of the whole) all fine' (*BLJ* IV, 167).

8. B replied: 'I *am* "very idle" – I have read the few books I had with me – &
   been forced to fish for lack of other argument' (*BLJ* IV, 167; glancing at
   Henry V, III, i, 21).

9. JM was preparing his first collected edition of B's works, for which in
   his letter to JM of Friday 2 September B had recommended the following
   arrangement: 'Childe H[arold] – the smaller poems – Giaour – Bride –
   Corsair – Lara – the last completes the series' (*BLJ* IV, 165). In the event
   The Works of the Right Honourable Lord Byron. In Four Volumes, published in
   octavo in 1815, followed JM's arrangement exactly, but with the addition of
   Hebrew Melodies in Vol. IV. Four further volumes were added to this collection between 1817 and 1820.

10. JM had been afflicted with rather more than 'a cold & fever'. Writing irri-
    tably to his wife Annie on Friday 2 September, he told her: 'I have torn up
    three Letters on Wednesday & today for I am in a confounded ill temper
    – troubled with Bowell Complaint – Piles – & a Law Suit with Brewster &
    Professor Robinsons Executors – & if I write out I should say that I shall
    not be able to get to Scotland or anywhere else ... I may perhaps go for a
    week to Brighton but this is I fear all I can effect indeed I am in such a
    vile disposition at present that I can do nothing' (MA). Eventually he went
    to Brighton with D'Israeli, and later joined Annie in Edinburgh.

11. There is no extant letter from Ward; but, writing to Annie on Monday 29
    August, JM told her: 'I learn from a message left <at> by Lady Mackintosh
    that Mad. de Stael is again at Paris at least I am led to this inference & this
    would certainly rather accelerate & determine my motions there' (MA).
    Madame de Staël had returned to Paris in May 1814, and in mid-July
    retired to Coppet for the rest of the summer. She was back in Clichy by 30
    September 1814.

12. In his letter to JM of Friday 2 September, B had written: 'Cawthorne writes
    that they are publishing '*E[nglish] B[ards]* in *Ireland* – pray enquire into this

– because *it must* be stopped' (*BLJ* IV, 165). JM quotes John 8.11: 'go, and sin no more' (Christ to the woman taken in adultery).

13. This particular enquiry elicited a response from B which arrived just in the nick of time to save Annie from the wrathful pen of her husband, who wrote to her on Thursday 8 September: 'If I had not, luckily for you, received and read, after yours a Letter from Lord Byron which concludes with the following PS I should most certainly have exercised all my literary wrath upon your audacious temerity – "P.S – Mrs Leigh & the Children are very well – I have just read to her a sentence from your epistle – and her remark was 'how <u>well</u> he writes' – so you see – you may set up as Author in person whenever you please" – no man is a prophet in his own country [Mark 6.4] & thus it is that you are insensible to the value of my correspondence merely because you have the happiness of having me for a husband' (MA; cf. *BLJ* IV, 167).

Letter 58)   Saturday 10 September [1814]

My Lord

I have just received the accompanying MSS which I think it may be interesting to you to read & afterwards I will beg the favor of its remission to me as I intend to urge very strongly to its author the splendid advantages of the Theatre.[1]

I am just setting out for Brighton until Wednesday in order to put off my tour, this year, to the Continent – for I find it indispensable for me to shew myself in Scotland – whither I propose to set out in Ten days[2] –

I do not mean this as an answer to your Lordships obliging Letter[3] which I delay until my return from Brighton –

I suspect I have to acknowledge your Lordships various kindness in the Shape of some Birds which have this moment arrived & which I shall put into the chaise with me.[4]

With Compliments
I remain
My Lord
your faithful Servant
Jno Murray

Sep. 10 –
Saturday

Notes to Letter 58)

Cover: The Lord Byron

1. There is no indication as to what this 'MSS' may have been or who may have been its author; but JM's intention 'to urge ... the splendid advantages of the Theatre' suggests some amusement at it.

2. In a letter to Annie of this same date (Saturday 10 September) JM told her he had 'determined to set off at 3 oClock today by a Coach that gets to Brighton in 6 Hours & to stay there until Tuesday or Wednesday ... & by the Monday following I may hope to set off for my good old wife' (MA). On Wednesday 14 September he wrote from Brighton saying he had put up at 'the Ship, our old quarters, & there with tolerable attention, I put up with an intolerable bed – I pass all my time with the D Israelis with whom I board altogether, and who are particularly kind to me', and who – the Paris expedition now abandoned – pressed him to stay for another week (MA). He returned to London on Tuesday 20 September (letter to Annie of Wednesday 21 September 1814; MA).

3. B's letter to JM of Wednesday 7 September (*BLJ* IV, 167).

4. In his letter of Friday 2 September B had said: 'If you were not going to Paris – or Scotland I could send you some game – If you remain – let me know' (*BLJ* IV, 164–65). JM told Annie: 'I have just received two brace of Partridges from Lord Byron which I shall take with me to D Israeli' (letter of Saturday 10 September; MA). When JM had returned from Brighton, B sent him 'a Hare & two Brace of Partridges', of which JM gave Gifford half the latter, 'the Hare I roasted yesterday & upon it with two slices of the most delicious crumped Cod I ever ate Dr Black & I dined' (letter to Annie of Monday 26 September; MA).

Letter 59)   [Monday 24 October 1814]

My Lord

If I have been too long in availing myself of your obliging permission to address you, on my travels, it has been occasioned less, I believe, from the want of objects to write about, than from their hurried succession.

Your Lordship will smile to be told how much your name has mingled in every stage of my journey & of my stay – Nottingham, the first place of my rest, became so, only from the magic of the Letter which your Lordship had so kindly given me <for> to your steward, for every part of the "Blackmoors Head"[1] (as well as its Landlords,)

was filled with the People, from all surrounding parts, who had come
to the Fare [sic], &, in the noble market Place, where it was held, I
saw Forty Thousand well dressed men & women. The next morning I
rode over to Newstead Abbey, into every corner of which I obliged my
worthy namesake to carry me, & to repeat its individual history – it was
indeed "a vast and venerable pile" – but now, "so old it seemeth only
not to fall"[2] I can not describe to your Lordship the anxiety, & instant
vexation, with which I viewed every spot & <to> heard M[r] Murrays[3]
description of what it had once been & what it now is; to have seen it
in all its antique splendour and to have experienced, inch by inch, all its
sad changes, as he has done, reflected to my mind a picture of human
existance [sic] so miserable that I was thrown into a state of despondence
[sic] which I could not shake of [sic] until the day after, when I <gave>
lost my melancholny [sic] reflections <to> amongst the delightful scenery
of Matlock. I, now, less wonder at your Lordships philosophy in parting
with it – than admire the noble feelings which have induced you to
retain a Place which constantly reflects upon the barbarity which could
have despoiled it to a degree that absolutely annihilates every hope,
even in possibility, of any means by which it could be re instated – to
have torn from within every remnant of its Monastic splendour, to have
sucked its waters dry & to have shorn the land of the noble wood which
surrounded it – are things as impossible to be forgotten or <to be>
forgiven – as they are to be restored – –

At Darlington where the Mail Coach stopped to breakfast – the room
was preoccupied by a most respectable man who was very polite to us
& with whom I had a good deal of conversation – when the passengers
had assembled in the Mail again I learnt that my late friend was Steward
to – Sir Ralph Millbanke [sic] – this gave rise to a discourse upon a
reported marriage & upon the merits of both parties in which they were
loud & <without> unanimous – – ever since my arrival in this City,
where I have incessantly breakfasted in one place, dined in another &
passed the evening in a third – I have supported myself literally upon
the interest which all ranks are possessed with, of making enquiries
about your Lordship & really the people here are so confoundedly
intelligent that if it had not been for this fortunate source of Literary
wealth I could not have supported my place in society here – but I may
assure your Lordship of the pride which I feel in perceiving your fame
so deeply rooted in the estimation of such a people & so universally
– as to Hogg – he is out of the question for you have intoxicated him
– but you will not be dissatisfied to learn how much you are esteemed
by Dugald Stewart[4] & his accomplished wife who dined with me at
my mothers, on Sunday last & who were minute in their enquiries &

vehement in their commendation − M^rs S had heard a great deal also of
the accomplished & amiable character of — & rejoiced with maternal
kindness at the prospect of so auspicious a union − There is a Lady
Williamson here just now, who is my only rival, for she is a particular
friend of Miss — & has delighted every one here with her character[5]
− Ballantyne − Walter Scotts particular friend[6] gave me a full account
of the delightful manner in which Scott speaks of you & in a very kind
invition [sic] to pass some days with Scott, of which I am about to avail
myself, the cause of his desire to see me is let out in the concluding
line of his letter in which he says "as I want to hear about Ellis Gifford
− but especially about Lord Byron"[7] − I am neither chagreened [sic] nor
vain at my spurious importance, but I do assure your Lordship I am
very Proud to see so completely realized all that my own mind & heart
have felt for you −

To trouble your Lordship with business in which I know your
kindness is not uninterested I am happy to say that I am actually
printing Hoggs new poem wch he has parted with as we thought
irreparably & that we are arranging for his collection & moreover that
we are very good friends.[8] − I am very sanguine in my expectation of
carrying off with me a slice of Mr Scotts new Poem − of which I just
saw the MSS of the first part, wch is now beginning to be printed[9] &
that in every other respect I have solid reason to rejoice at my visit to
this Land of Literature & to regret an absence wch has deprived me of
Waverley & of other things − Waverley is universally given to Scott &
Hogg can prove logically that the Bridal of Triermain is by the same by
the same [sic] author.[10]

If your Lordship meditate any excurtion [sic] upon a certain event,
I most earnestly entreat you to think of this place, where, both you &
yours, will be received with delight, and, I am certain, that you will,
both, be charmed with this intellectual Swerga[11] − as to the City itself, it
surpasses every thing that can be imagined, & I stop whenever I go out
to breathe out my extacy [sic] at the pleasure its architecture & situation,
afford [sic] me at every Step. M^r & Mrs Stewart would give you an
introduction to every thing, &, it is sufficient to tell you respecting the
latter, that she is the confidential correspondent of Mr Ward.[12]

I am grievously disappointed with Lord Thurlow in which, I do avow
there is not more than one tolerable thing, − but I can assure you that
it is upheld here "by those concerned" as the most inimitable piece of
wit.[13]

I know your Lordships goodness will excuse the openness with which
I write & I shall be most anxious in the hope of finding you in London
upon my return on Tuesday (if not Monday) next, that I may tell you

all that passes during my visit with Mr Scott, at whose house I shall sleep the day after tomorrow. (Wednesday)[14]

I sent 500 Lara here the day it was published & they have not had a Copy for a month – it is in high estimation here –

Allow me to assure your Lordship that wherever I <am> go I carry with me the highest esteem for your Lordship & that I ever remain
My Lord
Your grateful & affectionate
humble Servant
John Murray

Notes to Letter 59)

Cover: The R^t Honble Lord Byron/Albany/Piccadilly/London pm: 24 Oct 1814 received: 27 Oct 1814

By this time JM had rejoined Annie in Edinburgh where they were staying together at her mother's, Mrs Elliot's house in Northumberland Street. He had been there for a good fortnight before writing this letter. B, now engaged to Annabella (of which B had informed JM on Friday 23 September), was preoccupied with matters material to their marriage and there is no reply to this or the next letter (Letter 60).

1. The Blackmoor's Head Inn in Pelham Street, the main inn in Nottingham.

2. JM quotes *CHP* I, 7: 'It was a vast and venerable pile;/So old, it seemed only not to fall' (*CPW* II, 10; cf. also, *DJ* XIII, 66).

3. Joe Murray, B's old and trusted steward at Newstead.

4. Dugald Stewart (1753–1828), philosopher, whose works included *Elements of the Human Mind*, 3 vols (1792–1827) and *Outlines of Moral Philosophy* (1793), both of which B possessed (see *CMP*, 242–43, lots 297, 298, 343 and 344). See also n. 12 below, and Letter 76 below.

5. The two blanks here ('character of —' and 'Miss —') stand for Annabella. Lady Maria Williamson (1767–1848) was the widow of Sir Hedworth Williamson, 6th baronet (d. 14 March 1810), of Whitburn Hall, Whitburn (just up the coast from Seaham), High Sheriff of County Durham (1788–1810). She was 'very intimate with Lady Noel', according to Hobhouse (BL Add. 43748, f. 118; see also, *Recollections*, VI, 174–75), and according to Moore, an accomplished singer – her voice, even in old age, being 'one of great power and truth' (Moore, *Journal*, V, 2012–13). It was at one of her Edinburgh dinner parties that James Hogg first tasted ice cream – much to his disgust and whereupon he immediately requested 'whuskey'. She died at Aske in Yorkshire aged 81 on 10 January 1848 (see *The Gentleman's Magazine*, LXXX, Pt I [April 1810], 396 and 665–66; ibid., XXIX, New Series [March

1848], 333; and R. P. Gillies, *Memoirs of a Literary Veteran*, 3 vols [London, 1851], II, 130; see also, Malcolm Elwin, *The Noels and the Milbankes* [London: Macdonald, 1967], 338 and 347).

6. James Ballantyne (1772–1833) and his brother John (1774–1821) were friends and publishers of Walter Scott; the former, who had been with him at Kelso Grammar School, was his 'particular friend'.

7. In a letter to JM from Abbotsford of Thursday 20 October, sent care of Blackwood, Scott wrote: 'I am happy to find I shall have an opportunity of seeing you at this place on Wednesday or Thursday next week which <wh> will give me great pleasure as I want to hear about Ellis Gifford but especially about Lord Byron' (MA; see also, Scott, *Letters*, III, 509 and 510–11).

8. Hogg had written to B on Friday 14 October saying he had angrily withdrawn the MS of his new poem, *The Queen's Wake*, from Constable and Miller because they had neglected it: 'if Murray and I do not agree I am in a fine scrape' (MA). Writing again on Tuesday 18 October he wrote cheerfully: 'I have had a very pleasant crack with Mr. Murray and we have sorted [got on] very well I hope we shall long do so; he has made me a present of a proof copy of your picture and seems indeed very much attached to you' (MA).

9. Scott's 'new Poem', still in MS and not completed till December, was *The Lord of the Isles* published by Ballantyne in 1815. JM did not get a share in its publication. Blackwood wrote to commiserate on 8 November 1814, saying JM 'should feel it much less than any man living – having such a poet as Lord Byron' whose *Lara* he had just reread with increased admiration (Smiles, I, 258).

10. JM had not had a share in *Waverley*, published anonymously in July 1814 and now in its third edition. It was 'universally given to Scott' who denied his authorship until 1827. His poem, *The Bridal of Triermain*, was published anonymously in March 1813, and was believed to be an 'imitation' of him (cf. *CMP*, 117 and 396).

11. Indra's Paradise in Southey's *The Curse of Kehama* (1810). B never returned to Scotland after he had left it in 1798.

12. Dugald Stewart's wife, Helen d'Arcy Stewart (née Cranstoun) (1765–1838) was the addressee of Ward's *Letters to 'Ivy'*.

13. By '"by those concerned"' JM means the conductors of the *Edinburgh Review*, in vol. XXIII, xlvi (September 1814), Art. VIII, pp. 411–24, of which appeared Moore's facetious and dismissive review of four volumes of poetry by Lord Thurlow (1781–1829). See also, *BLJ* III, 54–55 and *CPW* III, 88–90.

14. JM returned to London on Sunday 30 October only to find that B had left for Seaham the day before (see Letter 60 below). Wednesday would have been 26 October.

Letter 60)   [Monday 31 October 1814?]

My Lord

It is no small addition to my vexation at finding that I came to town only <u>one</u> day after your Lordship had left it; to be deprived of the means of addressing you. I do confess I guess where you are – but am I at liberty to <add> write to you where my imagination – & wishes have placed you? – You see my Lord I am under the necessity of committing the trespass before I can be certain that it is imprivileged land –

Walter Scott, my Lord, (you see I put my best foot foremost) commissioned me to be the bearer of his warmest greetings to you. His house was full the day I passed with him, & yet, both in corners and at the surrounded table he talked incessantly of you, & unwilling that I should part without bearing some mark of his love (a <u>Poets</u> love) for you he gave me a superb Turkish Dagger to present to your Lordship as the only rem͂brance which at that moment, he could think of to offer you[1] – He was greatly pleased with a Portrait which I recollected to carry with me[2] & during the whole dinner when all were admiring the peculiarity & taste in which Scott has fitted up a sort of Gothic Cottage[3] he expressed his anxious wishes that your Lordship might honour him with a visit, which I ventured to assure him <that> you would feel no less happy than certain in effecting when you should go to Scotland & I am sure he would hail your Lordship as "yet more than brother."[4]

The – the [sic] Quarterly Review – my Lord (have patience!) has ventured during my & your Lordships absence to put forth a voluminous criticism <m> upon certain poems entitled – The Corsair & Lara – which I wish to introduce to your Lordship – presuming that, upon the whole, you will not be displeased with the acquaintance[5] And now, I rise to the real <object> purpose of this Letter – Your Lordship has often performed, in my favour, <promisses [sic] which you did> what you did <promise> not promise – but there is one promise, which yet remains to be performed – I shall never feel satisfied until your Lordship is so very good as to send me an order upon Phillips – for the <u>Portrait</u> which I do entreat of you again even at the heavy risque of being thought troublesome[6] –

I am advancing in the Fourth Volume of <u>The Works</u> – wch will consist of

Ode to Buonaparte
Poems at End of Child Harod [sic]
Dᵒ   – Corsair
Death of Sir P. Parker ?

Any thing unpublished ?[7]

Allow me to hope that your Lordship will find a<n> vacant moment
to write a few lines to
My Lord
your grateful & faithful
humble Servant
John Murray.

Notes to Letter 60)

B left for Seaham on Saturday 29 October; JM arrived in London the very next
day.

1. This is the only instance in JM's correspondence with B of his use of a
   contraction sign (for 'remembrance'). In return for this Turkish Dagger, B
   gave Scott an ornamental urn, or 'vase', when they met in London in April
   1815 (see Letters 67 and 68 below).

2. JM took several copies of the prints of B's portrait to distribute among his
   friends in Edinburgh (see also, Letter 59, n. 8 above).

3. Abbotsford.

4. JM quotes *The Bride of Abydos*, II, xxii, 502: 'yet now my more than brother!'
   Smiles (I, 257) alters the phrase to '"a very brother"', thus substituting Burns,
   Tam O'Shanter, 43: '*Tam* lo'ed him like a vera brither'.

5. *The Corsair* and *Lara* were favourably reviewed by George Ellis in the
   Quarterly Review, XI, xxii (July 1814), 428–57.

6. See Letter 49 above.

7. See Letter 57, n. 9 above (for B's lines 'On the Death of Sir Peter Parker,
   Bart.', see *CPW* III, 276–77 and 461).

Letter 61)   Friday [23 December 1814?]

My Lord
  I take the liberty of presenting to you the first and only Copy
that can be ready for some weeks of Gibbons Miscellaneous works
– containing all the New Matter & a copious Index –
  With the most anxious hopes for your Lordships happiness I beg leave
to renew the assurance of my unabated gratefulness & fidelity.
  I would beg the favor of your Lordship to offer my respectful

compliments to M^rs. Leigh
  Adieu
  J. Murray.

Friday N^t.
Nov. 12. [*sic*]

Notes to Letter 61)

The original of this letter is not forthcoming; the present text is from a copy made by one of Smiles' amanuenses, whose reading of the date cannot be correct (12 November was a Thursday). The letter accompanied JM's wedding present to B of Lord Sheffield's *The Miscellaneous Works of Edward Gibbon. New Edition, with considerable additions*, 5 vols, published by JM in 1814 (the 1st edn of which had appeared in 2 vols in 1796). B set out from London with Hobhouse for his wedding at Seaham on Friday 23 December 1814, and spent the weekend en route with Augusta at Six Mile Bottom. On Tuesday 27 December Hobhouse noted in his Diary: 'read: the new Gibbon – delightful!!' (BL Add. 47232, f. 48*r*). Having arrived at Seaham, B wrote to JM on Wednesday 31 December: 'A thousand thanks for *Gibbon* – all the additions are very great improvements' (*BLJ* IV, 248).

Letter 62)   Monday [2 January 1815]

My Lord
  It is done – the Plate has been obtained from the Printer & shall never be used again – I will immediately commence a new one which shall be submitted through various stages to the judgment of your Lordships Critical friends.[1]
  I trust your Lordship will do me the favor by a <u>word</u> to "advise" of a certain important Day[2] –
  Does your Lordship wish or not to incorporate the Melodies in your collected works – the publication of which is delayed only for your Lordships <Veto> opinion on this subject – in case it be your desire perhaps your Lordship will inclose a note to Mr Kinnaird.[3]
  I beg leave to offer your Lordship every good wish.
  I remain
  My Lord
  Your faithful Servant
  John Murray

Albemarle St.

Monday

I trust that your Lordship received the Edinburgh Review[4]

Notes to Letter 62)

1. In his letter to JM of Wednesday 31 December 1814, B had insisted on the print from Phillips' picture being destroyed: 'burn the plate – and employ a new *etcher* from the other picture' (*BLJ* IV, 248). The 'new *etcher*' was William Sharp (see Letter 57, n. 5 above); 'the other picture' was '*Portrait of a Nobleman*' (see Letter 49 above), '*not* the Albanian' as B firmly reiterated in his reply thanking JM for 'the abolition of the print' and adding he would wish Augusta and Annabella 'to decide upon the next' (*BLJ*, IV, 250). For further details, see Peach, *Portraits of Byron*, 49–65.

2. The 'certain important Day' was in fact the very day on which JM was writing. B replied on Friday 6 January 1815 (on which day it was also reported in the *Morning Chronicle*): '*The* marriage took place on the 2d. Inst. so pray make haste & congratulate away' (*BLJ* IV, 250).

3. B's *Hebrew Melodies* were written specifically for the composer Isaac Nathan (1790–1864) at the request of Kinnaird, whose protégé Nathan was. But JM was eager to publish them himself, without the music, and thus deprive Nathan of what was his by right and pre-empt his publication and market. In an undated note to Nathan, probably of Friday 6 January 1815, B asked him whether he would allow JM the 'privilege' of including them in the collected edition, 'without considering it an infringement on your copyright', but adding that although he wished to 'oblige' JM, it was 'against all good fashion to give and take back[.] I therefore cannot grant what is not at my disposal' (*BLJ* IV, 249). To JM he replied: 'Mr Kinnaird will I dare say have the goodness to furnish copies of the Melodies if you state my wish upon the subject – you may have them if you think them worth inserting' (*BLJ* IV, 250). On receiving this, JM wrote a note (not extant) to Kinnaird, who promptly enclosed it in a letter to B of Tuesday 10 January, written 'From the Merchant's Book-shop', saying that Nathan and the tenor John Braham (1774–1856) had 'enter'd into a partnership in the publishing' and that Braham was to sing them in public: 'I cannot bring myself to give up <these> Your words to Murray without your direction for me so to do – I will venture to say now that not one of Nathan's golden dreams will have carried him beyond the truth – & I cannot but think that the printing of these poems wd destroy the effect of the publication <->of the music'; and he concluded bluntly: 'As for the merchant Murray, I could silence him by speaking to his interest – Let him reserve these for the next whole edition of your works – But this Scotchman considers you as his property' (MA; see Letter 63, nn. 1 and 2 below).

4. This would have been the *Edinburgh Review*, XXIV, xlvii (November 1814),
containing the damning review of Wordsworth's *Excursion* (see Letter 57,
n. 7 above) and a very favourable review of *Waverley* (pp. 208–43).

Letter 63)   [Wednesday] 11 January 1815

My Lord

I was not <out> wrong in suspecting that Mʳ Kinnaird would
not allow us to have the Melodies – but Mʳ Hobhouse thinks it
unreasonable that they should not be included in the edition of your
Lordships works collected[1]
 — We had agreed that they should not be printed separately – nor
even <u>announced</u> as contained in the works – but those who had the
works would find them there with a note stating that they had been
set to music very beautifully by so & so[2] – which we supposed might
operate as an advantageous announcement of the Music – & they would
just have filled up our rather meagre Vol 4 –

I am delighted with the extract, appropriate in every way, from
Gibbon – and I send a Proof of it in print – The original paper on
which it came I will consider, if your Lordship will allow me, as a far
more valuable remembrance than either the Cake or the Gloves – which
I was promised & which I will now cease to regret – the Hand-writing
& by association the Hand which wrote[3] – is more valuable even than
the "Glove upon that hand"[4] – and it was inclosed in yours as I trust it
ever will be during your lives.

I beg leave to offer to Lady Byron the assurance of my faithful
services. Remaining forever My Lord

Most gratefully yours.

John Murray

Janʸ. 11ᵗʰ. 1815

Notes to Letter 63)

<u>Location:</u> Bodleian, Dep. Lovelace Byron 155, ff. 110–11

1. Writing to B again on Thursday 12 January 1815, Kinnaird informed him: 'I
   have just seen Braham, who protests, albeit humbly, against the printing of
   your <u>Psalms</u> in the edition of your works, unless it be intended to spoil the
   sale of the Musical Work – It now appears that Murray wanted to purchase
   the poetry of Nathan – & failing in that, he endeavours to persuade you that

it would be doing no harm to those whom you intended sh^d be benefitted, provided they were worthy of your words – I hope you think that Braham is ... Murray set Hobhouse on me – who wrote me a hasty note – but I have not yet seen him' (MA; see also, Letter 62, n. 3 above, and B to Hobhouse, *BLJ* IV, 260). JM was clearly nettled by Kinnaird's refusal to allow him to have *Hebrew Melodies*. Writing on 1 March 1815 to George Thomson, who had sent him the first volume of his *Irish Songs* regretting that B had not fulfilled his promise to contribute to it, JM told him: 'I am more grieved that [*sic*] you imagine at the omission of one great writer amongst them – where he had far better appeared than in some Stupid Hebrew Melodies to which as a sort of Charity Lord Kinnairds brother induced him to write no less than 12 exquisite poems – I have not the most distant connexion with the publication & although I am now publishing a compleat collection of Lord B's Works – they will not be contained in them' (MA). Eventually they were (see n. 2 below). Thomson himself, applying yet again to B 'on the subject of Song' on 24 August 1815, told him 'how pre-eminently you succeed in that species of Poetry; the Hebrew Songs being Diamonds of the first water, of which I have not words to express my admiration' (MA).

2. In the event *A Selection of Hebrew Melodies* was published by Nathan on Wednesday 5 April 1815 (advertisement in *The Times* for that date), and towards the end of May JM published *Hebrew Melodies. By Lord Byron*, with the following advertisement to the reader on p. v: 'The subsequent poems were written at the request of the author's friend, the Hon. D. Kinnaird, for a Selection of Hebrew Melodies, and have been published, with the music, arranged, by Mr. BRAHAM and Mr. NATHAN.' They were included in Vol. IV of *The Works of the Right Honourable Lord Byron. In Four Volumes* (1815), which appeared in June. For further details, see *CPW* III, 465–66; Catherine MacKerras, *The Hebrew Melodist. A Life of Isaac Nathan* (Sydney: Currawong Publishing, 1963); Thomas L. Ashton, *Byron's Hebrew Melodies* (London: Routledge & Kegan Paul, 1972); and Frederick Burwick and Paul Douglass, eds, *A Selection of Hebrew Melodies, Ancient and Modern, by Isaac Nathan and Lord Byron* (Tuscaloosa and London: University of Alabama Press, 1988).

3. In a second letter, dated Friday 6 January, B sent JM an additional note to the conclusion of *The Corsair* saying, 'it is from Gibbon – a quotation – and you will think it not mal apropos' (*BLJ* IV, 250–51). The note is from JM's wedding present to B, Sheffield's *Miscellaneous Works of Edward Gibbon* (see Letter 61 above; see also, *CPW* III, 445 and 451); it was written in Annabella's hand and was thus a more 'valuable remembrance' than 'Cake' or 'Gloves', the usual presents given to friends at weddings.

4. JM quotes *Romeo and Juliet*, II, ii, 23.

Letter 64)   [Friday] 17 February 1815

London
Feby. 17 – 1815

My Lord

I have paid frequent attention to your wish that I should ascertain
if all things appeared to be safe in your Lordships Chambers & I am
happy in being able to report that the whole establishment carries an
appearance of Security wch is confirmed by the unceasing vigilence [sic]
of your Lordships faithful & frigid Duenna.[1]

Every day I have been in expectation of receiving a Copy of Guy
Mannering of which the reports of a friend of mine who has read
the two first Volumes is [sic] such as to create the most extravagant
expectations of an extraordinary combination of wit humour & pathos
– I am certain of receiving one of the first Copies & this your Lordship
may rely upon receiving with the utmost expedition.[2]

I hear many interesting Letters read to me from the Continent &
one in particular from Mr Fazackerly [sic] describing his interview of
four hours with Buonaparte was peculiarly good – he acknowledged
at once the poisoning of the Sick prisoners in Egypt – they had
the Plague & would have communicated it to the rest of his army
if he had carried them on with him & he had only to determine
if he should leave them to a cruel death – by the Turks – or to
an easy one – by poison – When asked his motive for becoming a
Mahomedan he replied, that there were great political reasons for
this – and gave several – but, he added – the Turks would not admit
me at first unless I submitted to two indispensable ceremonies – the
first was, Circumcision – the other, a solemn oath to taste no more
wine – <the> To the first, he assured them, he could by no means
submit, as he had nothing to spare – &, for the other, he engaged to
drink as seldom as possible – They agreed at length to remit the first
& to commute the other for a solemn vow, for every offence to give
expiation by the performance of some good Action – Oh Gentlemen
says he for good Actions – you know you may command me – and
his first good action was, to put to instant death an hundred of their
Priests, whom he suspected of intrigues against him – not aware of his
summary justice they sent a deputation to beg the lives of these people
on the score of his engagement – he answered that nothing would have
made him so happy as this opportunity of shewing his zeal for their
religion – but that they had arrived too late – their friends had been
dead nearly an hour.

He asked Lord Ebrington, of which party he was, in Politics – The Opposition – The Opposition? – then can your Lordship tell me the reason why the Opposition are so unpopular in England? – with something like presence of mind – on so delicate a question, Lord Ebrington instantly replied – Because, Sir, we always insisted upon it, that you would be successful in Spain[3] –

Your Lordship will have heard that Lady Westmorland has made a conquest of the Pope – and that, next in estimation, at Rome, is – Lady Davy[4] – The King of Prussia has interfered & the marriage of the beautiful unfortunate Miss Rumbolds – even a la main gauche – is not to take place – Sir Sidney is compleatly done up – the Duchess of Oldenberg is positively to be married to the Prince of Wurtemberg [sic].[5] – <Your L>

Walter Scott sent your Lordship a Copy of the Lord of the Isles but as it arrived, at least a month after I had forwarded a "Mail Coach" Copy to your Lordship – I took that Copy in exchange (there was no writing in it) & thus balanced my Account – <It> There are not two opinions about it being his worst poem.[6]

I am delaying the publication of our edition in four Volumes – only until your Lordship find a leisure moment to strike off the dedication to your valuable friend Mr Hobhouse who still thinks that it is not precisely the same thing to have <ones poems set to> music made to ones poems <as> and to <s> write poetry for Music – and I advise your Lordship most <u>conscientiously</u> to abide by the determination of Mr Hobhouses Good Sense.[7]

I have been, with all my family to view Lady Byrons Carriage which is equally tasteful & <beautiful> & [sic] handsome[8]

I hope if I can serve your Lordship in London (or its antipodes) you will not deny me the only consolation under your long absence, the pleasure of receiving your commands –

Mrs Wilmots Tragedy is to be brought forward at Drury Lane immediately after Easter[9]

I have the honour to remain My Lord
your faithful Servant
John Murray

I sent your Lordship D Israeli – a fine book of light reading, the Day before yesterday – To Hannaby [sic][10]

Notes to Letter 64)

Cover: The R^t Honble/Lord Byron/Seaham/Stockton on Tees pm: 17 Feb 1815

B had written to JM on Thursday 2 February 1815 asking him to keep an eye on his chambers in Albany and report 'how far my old woman continues in health and industry', adding that he had not yet received *Guy Mannering* (*BLJ* IV, 264).

1. Mrs Mule, 'Your grim white woman', as Kinnaird refers to her in a letter to B of 15 September 1814 (MA; quoting the title of 'Monk' Lewis's poem in *Tales of Wonder* [1801]). See also B's Journal entry for Sunday 27 February 1814 (*BLJ* III, 246), and Moore's wonderful description of her (*Byron's Life and Works*, III, 7n–8n).

2. Scott's *Guy Mannering, By the Author of Waverley*, was published on 24 February 1815 (see Letter 65 below).

3. JM tells these stories remarkably well (for the 'Circumcision' proposal, cf. *DJ* V, 69–72). During his exile in Elba, Napoleon was interviewed by a number of visitors among whom were George V. Vernon, Fazakerley and Lord Ebrington. Reports of their conversations were soon circulating in England: those of Fazakerley and Lord Ebrington were recorded by Hobhouse in his Diary for Thursday 16 February and Saturday 25 March 1815 (BL Add. 47232, ff. 67 and 81–82; see also, Lady Melbourne to B, 11 January 1815; *LLLM*, 276). Lord Ebrington later published his interview as *Memorandum of Two Conversations between the Emperor Napoleon and Viscount Ebrington at Porto Ferrajo, on the 6th and 8th of December 1814* (London, 1823); that of Vernon and Fazakerley was printed in G. V. Vernon, *Sketch of a Conversation with Napoleon at Elba* [an account addressed to the Marquis of Lansdowne, dated 1 March 1815], first published in *Miscellanies of the Philobiblion Society*, VIII, 6 (1863–64). See also, *The Times*, Wednesday 15 February 1815.

4. In a letter of 13 February 1815, Lady Anne Romilly informed Maria Edgeworth: 'There is a colony of English at Rome. The Hollands, Davys, and Lady Westmorland, keep open house one night in the week each', adding 'Lady Davy has been obliged to quit her House in the Corso because her admirer the Pope has reastablished [*sic*] the punishment of la Corda exactly before her windows. Lady Westmorland however has braved it ... she gets the House for half price in consequence' (Samuel Henry Romilly, *Romilly-Edgeworth Letters 1813–1818* [London: John Murray, 1936], 104–05). Hobhouse wrote to B on 9 February 1815 telling him: 'Our friend Lady Westmoreland is kept by the Pope' (*BB*, 161).

5. The *Morning Chronicle* for Friday 6 January 1815 had announced: 'It is said that the daughter of an English Baronet, deceased (she who was considered as the most *beautiful woman* in England when the Potentates were here), and who accompanied her mother and father-in-law [i.e., stepfather] to Vienna, is married *a la main gauche* [i.e., morganatic] to Prince Augustus of Prussia.'

The rumour was false. Prince Augustus of Prussia (1779–1843), a cousin of the King of Prussia, Frederick William III (1770–1840), died unmarried. Miss Rumbold ('a Lydia Languish but most luxurious', according to Hobhouse; BL Add. 56530, f. 19v), was the 'beautiful' daughter of Sir George Berriman Rumbold (1764–1807), diplomat, whose widow Admiral Sir Sidney Smith (1764–1840), the hero of the Siege of Acre, married in 1810. The *Morning Post*, for Wednesday 11 January 1815 reported that the marriage between Crown Prince William of Wurtemberg (1781–1864) and Catherine, the Grand Duchess of Oldenburg (1788–1819), sister of Czar Alexander, would be celebrated at St Petersburg 'in the course of the next spring' (this was confirmed in *The Times* and the *Morning Chronicle* for Friday 17 February 1815). These two snippets of news were of such interest at the time because they affected the succession of the English Crown: both Princes had been considered as prospective husbands for Princess Charlotte.

6. According to the *Morning Chronicle* for Friday 13 January 1815, Scott's *The Lord of the Isles* was published that day. However, B told Moore on Tuesday 10 January: '"the mail-coach copy" I have, by special licence of Murray' (*BLJ* IV, 252; see also, IV, 280 n. 2). It was not very favourably reviewed by Jeffrey in the *Edinburgh Review*, XXIV, xlviii (February 1815), 273–94, and adversely reviewed by George Ellis in the *Quarterly Review*, XIII, xxvi (July 1815), 287–309.

7. In his letter to JM of Friday 6 January, B had said: 'The vols. in their collected state must be inscribed to Mr. Hobhouse – but I have not yet mustered the expressions of my inscription – but will supply them in time' (*BLJ* IV, 250). In the event the collected edition contained no dedication whatsoever.

8. Longacre was the home of coachbuilding (see also, Letter 65 below).

9. *Ina, A Tragedy; in Five Acts*, by Mrs Wilmot, with a Prologue by the Hon. William Lamb and an Epilogue by Thomas Moore, was published by JM in 1815, and at its first performance at Drury Lane on Saturday 22 April 1815 was, as B says, 'damned' (*BLJ* IV, 290).

10. JM must have sent D'Israeli's *Quarrels of Authors* (1814) (cf. *BLJ* IV, 297); Halnaby was pronounced 'Hannaby'.

Letter 65) [Wednesday] 8 March 1815

"My Lord, I fear,
"Has forgot, Britain.
– he comes not – sends not —[1]

Albemarle Street
Mar. 8 – 1815

My Lord

I have today sent by the Mail to Seaham, the first Copy of D[r]
Hollands Tour in Albania – & which I think will prove interesting to
your Lordship whose name is quoted with appropriate honour – passim[2]
– The first part appears to me to be dull – but the Account of Ioannina
is exceedingly interesting & to you – ament meminisse periti[3] – it will
be delightful.

I sent your Lordship "Guy Mannering" on Thursday[4] – the Book
is not yet in London – but "what a falling off is there"[5] – there is but
One good Scene in the whole – the retreat of the Gipsey [sic] & Meg
Merillies curse – the whole Story before & after & its details are little
– a very little – beyond a common Romance[6] – It is really cruel my
Lord to reward my sleepless anxiety to send you the first literary Game
of the season with no line of thanks or Criticism and I am absolutely
forced to offer my respects daily to your New Carriage in Long Acre
as the only regulator of my expectations of your speedy arrival in town[7]
– Indeed my Lord you who now feel how much our happiness depends
upon the kindness of others should a little [sic] upon the pains arising
from its sudden privation.

I remain My Lord
thy poor Servant ever[8]
John Murray

Notes to Letter 65)

1. B had not written now for over a month; JM aptly quotes *Cymbeline*, I, vi,
   111–12, and *The Corsair*, III, 69 (his long blank standing for 'faithless one!')
   (cf. also, *Lara*, I, 31).

2. Dr (later Sir) Henry Holland (1788–1873) had travelled in Greece with
   Sir William Gell and Richard Keppel Craven, and was to accompany the
   Princess of Wales as her physician during her Continental travels (1814–20).
   His *Travels in the Ionian Isles, Albania, Thessaly, Macedonia, &c. during the
   Years 1812 and 1813*, was published by Longman in March 1815. There are
   numerous complimentary references to B throughout, especially in connec-

tion with Albania and Ali Pasha, from whom Holland brought B a letter in June 1815 (*BLJ* IV, 299). After his return from Greece, he frequently met B in London, later recalling his impressions in *Recollections of Past Life* (London, 1872).

3. JM quotes from the motto that first appeared on the title-page of the 2nd edn of the *Encyclopedia Britannica*, 10 vols (Edinburgh: Bell, 1778): 'Indocti discant, et ament meminisse periti' (Let the unlearned learn, and the learned delight to remember).

4. 'Thursday' would have been 2 March.

5. JM quotes *Hamlet*, I, v, 47.

6. For Scott's *Guy Mannering*, see also, Letter 64, n. 2 above. JM refers in particular to Meg Merrilies' 'curse' in Chapter VIII. His opinion of the book was shared by John Wilson Croker in the *Quarterly Review*, XII, xxiv (January 1815), 501–09.

7. See Letter 64, n. 8 above. B and Annabella left Seaham on Thursday 9 March, stayed en route at Six Mile Bottom, and arrived in town on Tuesday 28 March.

8. JM quotes *Hamlet*, I, ii, 162 again (see Letter 49 above).

Letter 66)   Thursday [6 April 1815]

My Lord

I have the pleasure of sending <the first> a proof of the first portion of the valuable poems which you were so good as to confide to me yesterday[1] – Sotheby[2] read them from the Folio today to Gifford & they <me> both expressed a satisfaction too full of praise for one, so interested as myself, to venture to detail to you – "He is an extraordinary Man"!

The General Title & the foot Note (as Scott would call it)[3] <&> are mere fill ups – until your Lordship place what is appropriate.

A propos of Scott – he called upon me today[4] & will be with me tomorrow or – (and) – the day after about 3 – if your Lordships convenience permitted the favor of a call on either day – it would be adding to your kindness to allow me the pleasure of seeing you together – & perhaps your Lordship may Say if you propose so to honour me.[5]

I venture to offer my respectful compliments to Lady Byron, Remaining

ever My Lord
your grateful Servant
John Murray

10
Thursday

Notes to Letter 66)

1. This evidently refers specifically to those Hebrew melodies most recently written at Seaham for Nathan, but which were first published by JM, the fair copies of which were made by Annabella and the proofs of which are no longer extant (see *CPW* III, 466 and 469–72, and Letter 68, n. 2 below). They would have been particularly 'valuable' to JM as they gave his edition of *Hebrew Melodies* the immediate and unjust advantage over Nathan's, whose first number (1815) did not contain them, and whose second number first containing them was not published until 1816 (see Letter 62, n. 3, Letter 63, nn. 1 and 2 above, and esp. Ashton, *Byron's Hebrew Melodies*, 33–34 and 36–44).

2. William Sotheby (1757–1833), the translator and writer of tragedies, whom B later dubbed 'Botherby' (*Beppo*, 72) and 'Solemnboy' (see *CMP*, 86 and 355–56).

3. The first recorded use of 'foot-note' in the *Oxford English Dictionary* is 1841; Scott via JM must now claim the precedent.

4. Scott, his wife and daughter sailed from Edinburgh on 31 March and arrived in London on Wednesday 5 April 1815. They stayed with the Dumergues on the corner of Whitehorse Street, Piccadilly, just down the way from No. 13 Piccadilly, which B and Annabella had rented from the Duchess of Devonshire, and from JM in Albemarle Street. They remained until 11 June.

5. Perhaps this proposal prompted B to write to Scott on Friday inviting him to dinner and the theatre on Saturday 8 April. For in a letter to B of 'Friday' (7 April), congratulating him on his 'late change of condition', Scott regretted that he could not disengage himself 'so soon as tomorrow evening' (Saturday 8 April), but that JM had told him B would 'be in his shop by three o clock when I hope to have the pleasure I have long wished <to>of making your personal acquaintance' (MS, Huntington Library; misdated by Grierson in Scott's *Letters*, XII, 424–25). Accordingly, the famous first meeting between the two poets, which JM told Hogg he regarded 'as a commemorative event in literary history' (Smiles, I, 347), took place in JM's drawing-room on Friday 7 April 1815, and was recorded much later by his son: '1815/ April 7 W Scott & Ld Byron met first at Nº 50 Albemarle Sᵗ & were introduced to each

other by JM. They conversed together 2 hours – Met at N⁰ 50 often' (MA; for a rather more elaborate version of dubious authority, see Smiles I, 267). For Scott's recollections of his meetings with B, see Lockhart, *Life of Scott*, 311–12, and *Byron's Life and Works*, III, 162–67. Incidentally, Henry Crabb Robinson records that in a conversation with Annabella on 12 February 1854 she remarked that B 'once went out to dinner where Wordsworth was to be; when he came home, I said, "Well, how did the young poet get on with the old one?" "To tell the truth," said he, "I had but one feeling from the beginning of the visit to the end – *reverence!*" She mentioned the warm admiration Lord Byron expressed of Wordsworth's dignified manners' (Edith J. Morley, ed., *Henry Crabb Robinson on Books and their Writers*, 3 vols [London: Dent, 1938], II, 736). I believe Annabella's memory is at fault here and that she has confounded Wordsworth with Scott. There is no evidence that B dined in Wordsworth's company or saw anything of him in 1815; and besides other details the manner in which he speaks of him to Hunt later on in the year hardly suggests he ever felt '*reverence*' for him (see *BLJ* IV, 317 and 324–26). Yet, from his meeting with Scott to the end of his life, B always spoke of Scott with veneration and affection.

Letter 67)   [Sunday 9 April 1815]

My [*sic*]

I write one line to say that the Vase has safely arrived[1] –

Now I submit to you & from hence to higher Authority – three Items which occur to me

Having <u>seen</u> the person to whom it is to be presented – it will be a greater compliment to have seen a little more of him

II. That there are two vacant Tablets at the Bottom which if occupied by a few Words – a simple inscription if nothing poetical arise out of further acquaintance – will render it hereditary in his family[2]

III. I will make a case for it in Four days during which time all the utsupra [*sic*][3] may be cogetated [*sic*] upon.

I hope your Lordship will pardon all this & if I have not a "yes" from you tomorrow which shall mean "Delay" I send it off immediately – x x x [*sic*]

After the extraordinary effect produced by Keanes [*sic*] personification of Richard – perhaps your Lordship may like to Verify by Hume & the Notes to Shakespeare, & as I believe you have not your Books around you, which are only the Stars of Life of which a Beautiful & Intelligent wife is the Sun – I send my Volumes for your evenings perusal[4] –

J. M.

Notes to Letter 67)

The original MS of this letter is not extant; the present text is taken from a poor copy made by Smiles' amanuensis. The date is conjectural, but almost certain.

1. See also Letter 66, n. 5 above. To commemorate their meeting, B presented Scott with a silver sepulchral urn. Had B's library been sold in 1813, Scott might not have been quite so fortunate in his gift; the urn forms lot 151 in the 1813 Sale Catalogue of B's books (for which see Appendix C herein). See also n. 2 below.

2. In his reply B thanked JM for the books (see n. 4 below), but objected to his inscribing the urn as he felt 'it would appear *ostentatious* on my part' (*BLJ* IV, 287). In the end it bore two inscriptions: on the one face, 'The bones contained in this urn were found in certain ancient sepulchres within the long walls of Athens, in the month of February, 1811'; and on the other, 'Expende — quot libras in duce summo invenies?/ — Mors sola fatetur quantula sint hominum corpuscula./Juv. X.' (Put in the balance, how many pounds' weight will you find in the greatest commanders? ... Death alone tells us how paltry are our human bodies [Juvenal, *Satire*, X, 147–48 and 172–73 – the first part of which B had used as a motto to his *Ode to Napoleon Buonaparte*]). Scott later added a third inscription: 'The gift of Lord Byron to Walter Scott'. Accompanying this urn was a letter from B (no longer extant), which Scott regarded as 'more valuable to me than the gift itself, from the kindness with which the donor expressed himself towards me', and for the later theft of which he suspected, not 'a mere domestic' but 'the inhospitality of some individual of a higher station' (Lockhart, *Life of Scott*, 311–12; see also, *Byron's Life and Works*, III, 164–65, and Malcolm Elwin, *Lord Byron's Wife* [London: Macdonald, 1962], 312). The result of this gift was the following letter from Scott to B, which I transcribe verbatim from the original MS in the Bodleian, Dep. Lovelace Byron 155, ff. 134–35 (cf. Lockhart, *Life of Scott*, 312):

> My dear Lord
>   I am not a little ashamed of the value of the Shrine in which your Lordship has inclosed the Attick reliques. But were it yet more costly the circumstance could not add value to it in my estimation when considered as a pledge of your Lordships regard and friendship. The principal pleasure which I have derived from my connection with literature has been the access which it has given me to those who are distinguishd [*sic*] by talents and accomplishd [*sic*] and standing so high as your Lordship justly does in that distinguishd [*sic*] rank my satisfaction in making your acquaintance has been proportion-ally great. It is one of those wishes which after having been long & earnestly entertained I have found completely gratified upon <making> becoming personally known to you, & I trust you will

permit me to profit by it frequently during my stay in town
    I am my dear Lord
    Your truly obliged & faithfull [*sic*]
    Walter Scott
    Piccadilly
    Monday [10 April 1815]
    [On cover] The Right Honble/Lord Byron/&c &c &c

3. 'ut supra' = the above, the aforementioned.

4. *King Richard the Second*, with Kean as Richard, was performed at Drury
   Lane Theatre on Saturday 8 April 1815 (*The Times* for that date). B's edition
   of Shakespeare was *Bell's Edition: The Dramatic Writings of Will. Shakspere.*
   With the Notes of all the various Commentators; Printed Complete from the Best
   Editions of Sam. Johnson and Geo. Steevens, 20 vols (1788), where the play
   appears in Vol. XI. The Annotations are principally by Johnson, Steevens,
   Malone and Warburton, but there are none by David Hume, whose balanced
   and impartial account of Richard II appears in his *The History of England,*
   from the Invasion of Julius Caesar to the Revolution in 1688, 8 vols (1807), III,
   chap. xvii. Both these works were sold in the sale of B's books in 1816 and
   both were bought by JM (see *CMP*, 236, lot 126, and 241, lot 282). Kean's
   performance was reviewed by Hazlitt in *The Examiner*, No. 377 (Sunday
   19 March 1815), 190–92, who without the slightest grounds for doing so
   objected to his 'dashing the glass down with all his might, in the scene with
   Hereford [IV, i, 268–91], instead of letting it fall out of his hands, as from
   an infant's' (p. 191). The stage direction in *Bell's Edition* is '[*Dashes the Glass*
   against the Ground]' (p. 92), and in the performing version itself, '[*Dashing it*
   to the ground]' (*Shakespeare's King Richard the Second; An Historical Play. Adapted*
   to the Stage, with Alterations and Additions, by Richard Wroughton, Esq. And
   Published as it is Performed at The Theatre-Royal, Drury-Lane [John Miller,
   1815], p. 57). As B makes much of his own mirror scene in *Sardanapalus*,
   III, i, 145–47, 163–65 (see *CPW* VII, 74–75 and 619–20), it may be that he
   was peculiarly struck by this scene and wished to 'Verify' whether or not
   Hazlitt's objection was valid. The Commentators do not gloss the episode,
   nor does Hume record it as a historical fact. However, in an earlier edition
   of the play published by Bell, Richard's lines are glossed: 'This idea of the
   glass is odd, and the reflections on it very inferior to the former ideas of
   his situation. We think therefore, in action, the circumstance had better
   be omitted' (*Bell's Edition of Shakespeare's Plays, As they were performed at the*
   Theatres Royal in London; Regulated from the Prompt Books of each House ... with
   Notes Critical and Illustrative; by the Authors of the Dramatic Censor [1774], Vol.
   VII, p. 68).

Letter 68)   Sunday [9 April 1815]

My Lord

I have put a mark in the Volume of Percy which contains the beautiful fragment of "Hardy Knute"[1] –

I inclose proofs of <u>all</u> the Melodies[2] –

Might one tablet of the Vase contain simply –

— April 7. —

— 1815 —

in commemoration of the day on which you first met & of the commencement of your personal friendship – on the other

Lord Byron

to

Walter Scott Esqr.

I have my doubts if your Lordship may not think this unpardonably obtrusive?[3]

J. M.

Sunday

Notes to Letter 68)

No MS forthcoming; this is taken from a copy made by Smiles' amanuensis. JM almost certainly wrote it very shortly after Letter 67 above and before he had received B's reply of the same date (*BLJ* IV, 287).

1. 'Hardyknute. A Scottish Fragment', written by Sir John Bruce of Kinross and first published in Edinburgh in 1719, was collected in Allan Ramsay's *Tea-Table Miscellany* (1724) and in Percy's *Reliques of Ancient English Poetry*, of which B possessed the third edition, published in three volumes by Dodsley in 1775, where it appears in Vol. II, Bk. I, pp. 96–112 (see *CMP*, 240, lot 252). Scott recalled that it was the first poem he ever learnt – 'the last I shall ever forget'. He had recited it to B who 'was so much affected, that some one who was in the same apartment asked me what I could possibly have been telling Byron by which he was so much agitated' (Lockhart, *Life of Scott*, 23 and 311; see also, *Byron's Life and Works*, III, 163–64).

2. JM's emphasis on '<u>all</u>' here seems to confirm that the proof he had sent with Letter 67 above contained only those poems B had most recently supplied him with; whereas now he sends proofs of the entire collection of *Hebrew Melodies* (see Letter 67, n. 1 above).

3. See Letter 67, n. 2 above.

Letter 69)   Saturday [29 April or 6 May 1815]

My Lord
   I shall take my chance at finding you at home tomorrow forenoon
   J. Murray
Saturday

Notes to Letter 69)

This is written at the top of a letter from Gifford to JM dated simply 'Friday' but
in which he says that 'To-morrow' (i.e., Saturday) he would 'preside at the Wheel
of Fortune'. Richard Cumberland's comedy *The Wheel of Fortune* (with Kean as
Penruddock – the part B had taken in his Southwell days) was performed at Drury
Lane Theatre on Saturday 29 April and Saturday 6 May 1815. Gifford's letter must
therefore have been written on Friday 28 April or Friday 5 May 1815. It concerns
Hebrew Melodies, and specifically 'To Belshazzar' and 'Vision of Belshazzar' (*CPW*
III, 283–84 and 303–04). Gifford writes: 'The additions are good like the rest. I
think, however, that Belshazars [*sic*] vision might be brightened by a few touches
– There is nothing in description more striking than the passage in Daniel [Daniel
5, esp. 5–7] beginning "In the same hour" – and ending the king <u>cried</u> <u>aloud</u>
to bring in the astrologers." Something might be made of this. And a Hebrew
might allude with propriety to the vengeance taken for profaning the vessels of
their Temple. If one of the two melodies 193 195 must be omitted let it be the
former [i.e., 'To Belshazzar'], the latter [i.e., 'Vision of Belshazzar'] is above all
praise' (MA). In the event, 'Vision of Belshazzar' was indeed adopted, while 'To
Belshazzar' remained unpublished during B's lifetime (*CPW* III, 462 and 471).
JM's 'tomorrow' would have been Sunday 30 April or Sunday 7 May 1815; there
is no reply from B to this letter.

Letter 70)   Friday [9 June 1815]

I would beg the favour of a Frank to professor Monk.

My Lord
   I regret that I am unable to attend you with the inclosed Letter from
Professor Monk,[1] but if your Lordship would permit me to convey your
assent by this nights post, to the request made in the second page of the
Letter,[2] it would go far in effecting my cure & the more so if it would
be accompanied with any opinion in favour of <u>Helga</u>[3] –
   With compliments I remain ever my Lord – sick or well

Your Lordships
faithful Servant
John Murray

Albemarle S^t.
Friday

Notes to Letter 70)

No MS extant; this is taken from a copy made by Smiles' amanuensis.

1. JM was 'unable to attend' B because he had been mugged on his way home from dining with the D'Israelis on Wednesday 7 June. This was first reported in the *Morning Herald* for Saturday 10 June 1815: 'Mr. MURRAY, the respectable bookseller of Albemarle-street, on his return to town from Stoke Newington over the fields, on Wednesday last [7 June], was assailed by two ruffians, who knocked him down and robbed him of his money, but declined taking his watch.' The report subsequently appeared in the *Morning Chronicle* for Monday 12 June, which is probably where B first read it and after which he promptly sent JM his condolences – making rather more sport of it to Moore that same day (*BLJ* IV, 294 and 297). There is no reply to this letter.

2. James Henry Monk (1784–1856), classical scholar at Trinity when B and Hobhouse were there, and now successor to Porson as Regius Professor of Greek at Cambridge, had written to JM on Thursday 8 June asking him ('in the second page of the Letter') to remind B that the Trinity College Anniversary dinner, which B had promised to attend, was to take place at Willis's Rooms the following Wednesday (14 June) and adding: 'It is a sentiment very general amongst Trinity men, that Ld B. is one of the greatest living ornaments of our Society, one of whom we ought to be most proud' (MA). This compliment did not induce B to fulfil his promise, and he did not attend. In a letter to B of 6 October 1810, Hobhouse referred to Monk as 'Davies great enemy' and 'a great teller of lies' (*BB*, 52).

3. *Helga. A Poem. In Seven Cantos* was published by JM in 1815. Its author was the son of the Earl of Carnarvon, the Hon. William Herbert (1778–1847), classical scholar and translator to whom B gives a couplet in *EBSR*, 509–10 (*CPW* I, 245). What B thought of *Helga* is unknown; a copy was sold at his book sale in 1816, and he later referred to its author rather unflatteringly as 'Helga Herbert' (see *CMP*, 236, lot 136, and *BLJ* VII, 114; see also, Letter 131, n. 2 below).

Letter 71)   Thursday [Wednesday 13 September 1815?]

My Lord

Walter Scott has this moment arrived and will call today between 3 & 4 for the chance of having the pleasure of seeing your Lordship before he sets out tomorrow for Scotland[1] – I will shew your Lordship a beautiful Miniature of Buonaparte[2] –

your Lordships dutiful Servant

Jno. Murray

Mr Scott talked of going to the Theatre this evening[3]

Thursday

Notes to Letter 71)

JM must have mistaken the day when writing this letter, which has been misdated and mistranscribed by Smiles (I, 267–68). Scott and his fellow-traveller, John Scott of Gala, arrived in London from their visit to Paris and the field of Waterloo on Wednesday 13 September. They called on B, who was out, and proceeded to Albemarle Street, which is when JM would have written this letter. Eventually they caught up with B, and the three of them dined together with Daniel Terry and Charles Mathews, after which Scott, John Scott and Mathews set out for Leamington in the early hours of Thursday 14 September. For further details, see especially Donald Sultana, *From Abbotsford to Paris and Back: Sir Walter Scott's Journey of 1815* (Stroud: Alan Sutton, 1993), 124–34; see also, John Scott, *Journal of a Tour to Waterloo and Paris, in company with Sir Walter Scott in 1815* (London, 1842), 238–45, and Mrs Mathews, *Memoirs*, II, 376–80.

1. Smiles omits 'tomorrow' (i.e., Thursday 14 September).

2. This 'Miniature' (misread by Smiles as 'caricature') was probably a trophy brought back by Scott from France; but no such known one survives in MA.

3. Omitted by Smiles. They had dinner only instead.

Letter 72)   [Tuesday] 26 September 1815

Chichester Sep. 26. 1815

My Lord

I send a draft for the lowest sum mentioned for "the said" Magpie
and I shall think myself very fortunate if I <do not> lose only Ten
pounds more by its Publication,[1] we are very late and there are at
least Two Magpies, (I cant say how many Maids) in the field before us
already, but still, we will publish it for the honour of Old Drury,[2] & I
trust that your Lordship will do me the favour to draw up an ingenious
advertisement, to be issued fourthwith [sic], knowing that ours is the
true Magpye [sic] and the real Maid[3] and that all others are Jays and
Peacocks[4] – And moreover I hope to be registered as Bookseller &
Publisher to the Theatre Royal Drury Lane – and expect to be favoured
with a deep Tragedy during the winter[5] –

If your Lordship will have the goodness to obtain the MSS I will
order my printer Mr Dove – a more appropriate one could not be
found[6] – to take it from you with any directions & he will print it in
three days.

I am glad to find that the drawings have been found & sent to your
Lordship, I hope, in time – I conjecture that they are for Theatrical
purposes – I have five folios of Costumes of Russia Austria China &c
&c for which your Lordship has only to apply to my people, if either
your curiosity or need require them.[7]

If your Lordship have occasion to communicate any more upon the
subject of the Magpye do me the favour to address me at H. Pagets Esqr
Chichester.

I have the honour to remain
My Lord
your faithful Servant
John Murray

Notes to Letter 72)

At the beginning of the month, JM had gone down to Chichester to visit his
mother, Mrs Paget, who was seriously ill and who sadly had died by the time he
arrived. He remained in Chichester to comfort his stepfather, Henry Paget, and
to help deal with family affairs. Meanwhile, back in London, B was occupied as
a member of the Subcommittee of Drury Lane Theatre, where the season had
opened with what turned out to be an immensely popular 'new Melo-dramatic
Romance, called THE MAGPIE; or the Maid of Palaiseau' (*The Times*, Tuesday

12 September 1815). This had first been presented as a musical at the Lyceum on 2 September under the title *The Maid and the Magpie, or Which is the Thief?* (trans. S. J. Arnold; music by Smart), where it ran until the theatre closed on Friday 15 September, when yet another version (trans. I. Pocock; music by Bishop) opened under the same title as that of Drury Lane at Covent Garden. Thereafter, the two theatres fought it out between them until well into the New Year. For B's involvement with the Subcommittee generally, see Richard Lansdown, *Byron's Historical Dramas* (Oxford: Clarendon Press, 1992), chap. 1. See also, Elwin, *Lord Byron's Wife*, 318–20. The following fragment of a letter from Annabella to Augusta, referring to *The Magpie* and the Committee under Douglas Kinnaird ('DK.'), and also to certain domestic strains both as a wife and as an expectant mother, is in the British Library (BL Add. 31037, f. 21). It is franked by Annabella '1815/London Sepr. twenty Eighth/To the Honble./M^rs. Leigh/Newmarket/Byron', and bears a postmark of the same date:

The Magpie –

The fame of Old Drury must surely revive
Mis-managed by such a Committee of Five! –
Their labours already bring forth – not a Mouse –
For 'twas thought there were too many cats in the house –
Nor a Goose – Though perhaps you would guess it the bird,
As the offspring of Wit has been often absurd.
But an emblem most just of the eloquent things
Which the Green-room applauds from its Manager Kings –
Their Tyrant,* at least, ably mimics the part,   *DK.
And seems to be formed by the very same art
As the Magpie which chatters so mal-à-propos,
Too foolish the mischiefs it causes to know –
Then there's Byron, ashamed to appear like a Poet,
He talks of Finances, for fear he should show it –
And makes all the envious Dandys despair,
By the cut of his shirt, and the curl of his hair! –

I have not got the others down yet – I believe B– will go to the Theatre to-night, but you seem to have mistaken – for the mischief has not lately taken place there but after his return – when alone – I grow more unable to sit up late –

1. On Monday 25 September, B had written: 'Will you publish the Drury Lane Magpye? or what is more will you give fifty or even forty pounds for the copyright of the said? – I have undertaken to ask you this question on behalf of the translator – and wish you would – we can't get so much for him by ten pounds from any body else' (*BLJ* IV, 315).

2. 'Old Drury' was the fond and familiar sobriquet for Drury Lane Theatre.

3. See headnote; on Friday 15 September there would have been three Maids and Magpies to choose from.

4. An improvement on 'apes, and peacocks' (I Kings 10.22); but JM may also have in mind William Wagstaffe's 'Character' of Richard Steele, as quoted by D'Israeli in *Quarrels of Authors*, 3 vols (1814), II, 302: 'For his literary character we are told that "STEELE was a Jay, who borrowed a feather from the Peacock, another from the Bullfinch, and another from the Magpye; so that *Dick* is made up of borrowed colours ..."'.

5. JM jocularly aspires to being 'Bookseller & Publisher to the Theatre Royal Drury Lane' as he was already to the Admiralty and Board of Longitude (see Letter 10, n. 1 above). B was delighted with this response and replied on Wednesday 27 September: 'That's right − & splendid & becoming a publisher of high degree − Mr. Concanen (the translator) will be delighted − & pay his washerwoman − & in reward for your bountiful behaviour in this instance − I won't ask you to publish any more for D[rury] L[ane] or any Lane whatever again. − − You will have no tragedy or anything else from me I assure you' (*BLJ* IV, 315). He forwarded 'Murray's bill (£40) for the Magpye' to Thomas Dibdin the same day (*BLJ* IV, 316).

6. This is superb. *The Magpie; or, The Maid of Palaiseau. A Melo-dramatic Romance. In Three Acts. Performed at The Theatre Royal, Drury Lane, on Tuesday, September 12, 1815,* published by JM in 1815, was 'Printed by J. F. Dove, St. John's Square' (p. 48; there is no mention of Matthew Concanen, the Younger (fl. 1795–1818) being the translator, though as B somewhat jocularly implies, he was indeed indigent; see n. 5 above). In a letter to JM of 29 September 1815, Gifford said he preferred Roworth as a printer to Dove who gave 'rather too much trouble' (MA).

7. This is curious; B mentions no 'drawings', 'for Theatrical Purposes' or otherwise, nor do the reviewers of *The Magpie* draw attention to any of the costumes, and it is hardly likely that JM could be referring to the 'drawings' he gave Annabella in May (*BLJ* IV, 292).

Letter 73)   Faturday [Saturday 4 November 1815?]

Albemarle S[t]
Faturday [*sic*]

My Lord

The inclosed note will explain the contents of the accompanying volume − in Sheets wch if returned to me I will put in such dress as your Lordships taste shall direct[1] −

I picked up the other day some of Napoleons own writing paper − all

the remains of which has [sic] been burnt – as it has his portrait & Eagle
– as your Lordship will perceive by holding a Sheet to the light – either
of Sun or Candle – so I thought I would take a little for your Lordship
– hoping in return that you will just write me a poem upon any 24
Quires of it in return [sic]² –

I beg the favor of your Lordship to offer my thanks to Lady Byron
for some Game which came opportunely to fatten Southey & Sotheby
– Malcolm with sundry other Poeticals & Historicals who dined with
me on Thursday.³

I am really more grieved than I can venture to say that I so rarely
have an opportunity of seeing your Lordship – but I trust that you are
well – <& remain> With Compliments I remain

    My Lord
    your faithful Servant
    John Murray

Notes to Letter 73)

The date of this letter is conjectural. 'Faturday' is JM's choice spelling which he
has not attempted to alter nor seems even to have noticed. JM had been in Paris
from 14 July to 8 August 1815; Sir John Malcolm from 15 July to 25 September;
Southey from 22 September to 28 October; and, in a letter to Scott of 8 November
1815, JM told him Sotheby was in London 'recovering from the loss of his son in
the bustle attending the preparation for "Ivan"' (Smiles, I, 286; see also, *BLJ* IV,
311–12, 313–14 and 323). The present dating therefore seems the most likely.

1. This was Sir John Malcolm's *History of Persia*, 2 vols (1815), of which a
   copy 'bound in *russia*' was sold at the sale of B's books in 1816 and bought
   by Fletcher (*CMP*, 243, lot 327; see also, Letter 74 below); 'in Sheets' =
   unbound.

2. JM's 'the other day' is somewhat casual; it would have been at least three
   months earlier when he was in Paris. B does not appear to have obliged him
   by writing 'a poem upon any 24 Quires of it'; but he did use the paper when
   writing to Miss Mercer Elphinstone on Thursday 11 April 1816, explaining
   that it was 'part of the spoils of Malmaison & the imperial bureau – (as it
   was told me)' and asking her to 'accept a few sheets of it which accompany
   this – their stamp is the Eagle' (*BLJ* V, 65; in Marchand's note Hobhouse
   should now read Murray). This letter was sold as lot 15 in the auction of
   the Bowood Archives on Wednesday 12 October 1994, and the purchaser
   and present owner has been kind enough to allow us to photograph the
   watermark. This is reproduced in Plate 10.

3. 'Thursday' would have been 2 November, the day Annabella finished the
   fair copy of *The Siege of Corinth*, and on which day B sent it to JM (*CPW*

III, 476 and 480; see also, Letter 74 below). Hence by 'Game' JM may mean literary (legible) rather than literal (edible) 'Game' with a reading of which he was able to entertain the company at dinner.

Letter 74) [Saturday 4 November 1815?]

My Lord

I assure you my conscience has not been without its compunctions at not calling or writing although incessant business and interruptions have prevented both.

Mr Gifford has read with great delight the siege of Corinth in which <the> from the apparition which is exquisitely conceived and supported to the end he says you have never written better the battle in the Streets and the catastrophe all worthy of their author – He makes three critical remarks – we are rather too long in coming to the interesting Part – the Scene immediately before the Apparition is rather too frightful – and there are perhaps too many minutiæ after the catastrophe – all very easy of reparation if your Lordship feel their force which certainly I <u>do</u> – and then it as [sic] beautiful a little poem as was ever written.[1]

Your Lordship would have received a proof before this had I not been anxious to preserve the MSS – but a portion will be sent this night and the rest on Monday.

Coleridge is will [sic] & fanciful & will make much talk and I will gladly make a bidding when I can have the remainder as well to judge of <u>quantity</u> as quality.[2]

I am very anxious to receive Mr Hunts poem of which your Lordships opinion is perfectly satisfactory[3]

I have put up for your Lordship the Sheets of Sir Jno Malcolms Persia wch will not be published until December – but I am anxious that you should have the first reading of it – & I will give you a better Copy hereafter – with its 20 Plates &c.[4]

Mr Ward was with me yesterday & enquired most warmly after yr Lordship – we are filling now – if you are out about 4 – will your Lordship look in & see us.[5]

Pardon my haste

J. M.

Notes to Letter 74)

This seems to have been written on the same day as Letter 73 above.

1. See Letter 73, n. 3 above. Gifford seems to object to stanzas 16 and 17, which are particularly grisly and embattled and occur just prior to the 'Apparition' in stanza 19. He reiterated his complaints later (see Letter 75 below). B replied the same day saying: 'I will attend to the remarks when I have the proofs – of which there is no hurry' (*BLJ* IV, 331).

2. In a letter to B of 17 October 1815, Coleridge told him he was having two volumes of his works printed at Bristol, which he would send B, and if B's opinion of them was favourable he would then offer them to the London Booksellers. B replied the following day hoping his 'unpublished poem' (*Christabel*, written in 1797 and 1800), which Scott had repeated to him in the spring, was to be included. Thereupon Coleridge sent a transcription, which B received safely on Friday 27 October and was pleased to find only 'a little effort would complete' (see *BLJ* IV, 318–19 and 321, and *Collected Letters of Samuel Taylor Coleridge*, ed. Earl Leslie Griggs, 6 vols [Oxford: Clarendon Press, 1956–71], IV, 601–02 and VI, 1037). Replying to JM on Saturday 4 November, B said he was 'anxious that you should be ye. publisher' (*BLJ* IV, 331), which in the event he was, and accordingly *Christabel* was published by JM in 1816 in a uniform volume with *Kubla Khan* and *The Pains of Sleep*.

3. Leigh Hunt's poem was *The Story of Rimini*, which B had recommended to JM and urged even more strongly in his reply (*BLJ* IV, 331). For further details, see *CMP*, 213–17 and 536–42.

4. See Letter 73, n. 1 above.

5. In his letter to Scott of 8 November 1815, JM told him that Ward had just returned from Italy (Smiles, I, 286). It is unlikely that B did 'look in' at the customary afternoon gathering at JM's, for he told Moore he was dining with Kinnaird, Sheridan and Colman that day (*BLJ* IV, 330).

Letter 75)   Sunday [5 November 1815]

My Lord
    The Printer disappointed me in not sending a proof last night, & now, that it is come this morning, I find that he has not taken it off in the way I <wish> had directed which was, only one column on the right hand half of a page of foolscap writing paper – leaving the left for emendations – I expect to receive it thus tomorrow, but I send you what is already done, rather than send nothing.[1]

+

    In this Days Observer – the last Column of the third Page your Lordship will find rather an interesting account of an unfortunate traveller.[2]

+

Gifford asks why you should change the measure in the Poem he says
he does not see any thing gained by it[3] – He told me again yesterday
that too much can not be said in Praise of all from Stanza 18 to the end
– except that the <ef> grand effect of the explosion is rather weakened
by too much detail afterwards – but we must close with the Eagle[4]

Can your Lordship without inconvenience, spare me admission for
half a dozen to see Tamerlane on Monday & oblige[5]

My Lord
your faithful Servant
John Murray

Sunday

Notes to Letter 75)

1. As promised in Letter 74 above, JM now sends the first proof of *The Siege
   of Corinth*, of which only one (later) proof survives (*CPW* III, 478).

2. In the last column of the third page of the *Sunday Observer* for 5 November
   1815 there appeared an article entitled 'Some Particulars of the Travels and
   Death of Dr. Seetzen', who had last been heard of in 1811 and, it now transpired, had been poisoned by the local inhabitants during his researches in
   Yemen. Dr Ulrich Jasper Seetzen (1767–1811) was a traveller, researcher and
   antiquary in Africa, Asia Minor and other countries in the East, whose *A
   Brief Account of the Countries adjoining the Lake of Tiberias, the Jordan, and the
   Dead Sea* had been published by the Palestine Association of London in Bath
   in 1810 at the instigation of Sir Joseph Banks. In Burckhardt's view, Seetzen
   applied his researches with such 'indefatigable zeal to countries the most
   difficult of access', that had he lived to publish all his travels they 'would
   have far excelled all travellers, who ever wrote on the same countries' (John
   Lewis Burckhardt, *Travels in Nubia* [1819], lxxiii-lxxiv).

3. Although basically tetrametric, the measure is daringly irregular. Gifford's
   objection was shared by the critic in the *Monthly Review*, LXXIX (February
   1816), 196–208, who, in an otherwise favourable review of *The Siege of
   Corinth* and *Parisina*, deplored B's 'unpardonable licence both of phraseology
   and of versification' (197).

4. The 'explosion' occurs in the final stanza of *The Siege of Corinth* and is
   followed by much grisly detail closing with 'the Eagle' (1028–34). When
   D'Israeli read the poem he was overwhelmed by it. In a letter to JM dated
   simply 'Tuesday', but which was clearly written at about this time, he
   confessed:

   I am anxious to tell you, that I find myself this morning so strongly affected by the perusal of the poem last night that I feel that it is one, which stands quite by itself. I know of nothing of the kind which is worthy of comparison with it; There is no scene – no incident – nothing so marvellous in pathos and terror in Homer – or any bard of antiquity – It impresses one with such a complete feeling of utter desolation – mental and scenical – that when Minotti touched that last spark which scattered its little world into air, he did not make it more desolate than the terrible and affecting energy of the poets imagination. But Homer had not such a sort of spirit as the mistress of Alp – he had wolves & vultures & dogs but Homer has never <drawn> conveyed his reader into a vast golgotha, nor harrowed us with the vulture flapping the back of the gorged wolf, nor the dogs – <so terrible, so true> <with the> <so real> the terror, the truth and the loneliness of that spot will never be erased from my memory. Alp by the side of the besieged wall – that Column which only appears when he sought who was addressing him – that <celestial> ghost-like manner of giving him a minute's reflection by observing one of the phenomena of Nature – that is a stroke of a Spirit's character never before imagined – and can never be surpassed – and <Alp>after the most sublime incident that ever poet invented still to have the power to agitate the mind by that Eagle, who flies nearer the Sun mistaking the cloud of destruction for night – in a word, I could not resist to assure you that I never read any poem Exceed [*sic*] in power this to me, <wonderful> most extraordinary production. I do not know where I am to find any which can excite the same degree of Emotion – Now when you have read this hasty Effusion, throw it into the fire, only recollect that I cannot get rid of the recollections which are still agitating my fancy, & <kept me from let me be> would not subside till I wrote this (MA; cf. Smiles, I, 358).

5. The first performance of Rowe's *Tamerlane*, with Kean as Bajazet, took place at Drury Lane Theatre on Monday 6 November 1815. No doubt B did oblige JM, but there is no reply to this letter.

Letter 76)   Thursday [and] Friday [28 and 29 December 1815?]

Albemarle Street
Thursday

My Lord
  I send you two donations from authors – a <u>poem</u> from <u>Stephen Weston</u> – and, a Dissertation <by> From Dugald Stewart which

was sent to Mr Ward to be presented to your Lordship with suitable compliments from the author, whose good feelings towards you I have more than once announced.[1]

I wish your Lordship to do me the favour to look at and to consider with your usual kindness the accompanying note to Mr Leigh Hunt respecting his poem for which he requires £450 which would presuppose a sale of, at least 10,000 Copies – now if I may trust to my own experience in these matters, I am by no means certain that the sale would do more than repay the expensaes of Paper & Print – but <it> the Poem is peculiar & may be far more successful, in which event, the proposition which I have made to the author will secure to him all the advantages of such a result. I trust that your Lordship will see in this an anxious desire to serve Mr Hunt although, as a mere matter of business, I can not avail myself of his offer. I would have preferred calling upon your Lordship today were I not confined by a temporary indisposition, but I think your Lordship will not be displeased at a determination founded upon the best judgment I can form of my own business – I am really uneasy as [sic] your feelings in this affair but I think I may venture to hope that your Lordship knows <the principles of> me sufficiently to allow me to trust my decision entirely to your usual kindness.[2]

I am writing a Farce merely to gain admission to the Green room, as the only means of having an opportunity of seeing your Lordship – though I shall certainly be d—d – if I succeed in my object.[3]

I remain My Lord
Your dutiful Servant
John Murray

concluded on
Friday

Tell me if Mrs Leigh & your Lordship admire Emma?[4]

Notes to Letter 76)

1. Stephen Weston (1747–1830), 'an old, tottering clergyman', according to Hobhouse (*Recollections*, I, 119), and antiquary, whose numerous publications included *Remains of Arabic in the Spanish and Portuguese Languages* (1810), *Persian Distichs* (1814) and *Episodes from the Shah Nameh; or Annals of the Persian Kings; by Ferdoosee* (1815), which last was probably what JM sent B. Dugald Stewart's 'Dissertation', *A General View of the Progress of Metaphysical, Ethical, and Political Philosophy, since the Revival of Letters in Europe*, was prefixed to the Supplement of the *Encyclopaedia Britannica* (Edinburgh, 1816), and

reviewed, not altogether sympathetically, in the *Edinburgh Review*, XXVII, liii (September 1816), 180–244. Ward told Mrs Stewart on 7 January 1816: 'I sent the copy of Mr. S's book to Lord Byron through Murray with the message you wished to accompany it' (*Letters to 'Ivy'*, 293).

2. Hunt was negotiating for the publication of *The Story of Rimini*, which he had recently sent to JM. In a letter to Hunt of 27 December 1815, JM suggested that he first try other publishers, failing which he would undertake 'to print an Edition of 500 or 750 Copies, as a trial, at my own risk and give you one half of the profits; after this edition the Copyright shall be entirely your own property – By this arrangement I mean, in case the work turn out a prize as it may do, that you should have every advantage of success, for its popularity once ascertained, I am sure you will find no difficulty in procuring purchasers, even if you should be suspicious of my liberality from this specimen of fearfulness in the first instance' (MA). This was clearly the 'accompanying note' that JM now sent B, who was not impressed by JM's 'liberality' (cf. *BLJ* V, 13). Hunt, however, was perfectly satisfied and wrote to JM accepting his offer on 29 December (MA).

3. JM alludes spiritedly to B's preoccupation with theatrical matters at Drury Lane Theatre, although he was also aware that B was now not only a father (Ada was born on Sunday 10 December 1815), but in dire financial straits, with bailiffs occupying his home where marital relations were already under considerable strain.

4. Jane Austen's *Emma* (1816) was published by JM in December 1815. There is no indication as to what Augusta, who was staying at 13 Piccadilly, thought of it, and B nowhere refers to it. Readers may like to know, however, that *Sense and Sensibility* (1811) and *Pride and Prejudice* (1813) formed part of lot 154 in the Sale Catalogue of B's books for 1813 (see Appendix C herein).

Letter 77) Tuesday 2 January 1816

My Lord

I tore open the packet you sent me and have found in it a Pearl – it is very interesting – pathetic beautiful – do you know I would almost say Moral – I am really writing to you before the billows of the passions you have excited are subsided – I have been most agreeably disappointed (a word I can not associate with the poem – at the Story which what you hinted to me and wrote – had alarmed me for [*sic*] & I should not have read it aloud to my wife – If my eye had not traced the delicate hand that transcribed it[1] – This poem is all action & interest not a line but what is necessary – now I do think that you should – <u>fragmentize</u>[2]

the first hundred & <con> condense the last 30 − of Corinth & then
you have in words of the highest compliment "Two poems (as M^r H
− said as good as any you have written)³

I admire the fabrication of the "big Tear" which is very fine − much
larger by the way than Shakesperes [sic]⁴

I do think you thought of <u>Ney</u> in casting off the bandage⁵

The Close is exquisite − & you know alls well that ends well − with
which I stop − I will answer for Mr Gifford⁶ − and to conclude (a
Bargain) say that they are mine for the inclosed <Six hundred and
Sixty g>⁷ & add to the obligations of

My Lord
your faithful Servant
John Murray

Albemarle St
Tuesday Even^g Jany 2nd. 181<5>6

Notes to Letter 77)

1. The 'Pearl' was *Parisina*, which JM was 'agreeably disappointed' to find was
   less obviously incestuous than he had feared, the sight of the fair copy in
   Annabella's 'delicate hand' reassuring him. Replying the same day, however,
   B warned him: 'I am very glad that the handwriting was a favourable omen
   of the morale of the piece − but you must not trust to that − for my copyist
   would write out anything I desired in all the ignorance of innocence' (*BLJ*
   V, 13).

2. JM underlines '<u>fragmentize</u>' with a wry glance at *The Giaour* but meaning
   abridge or 'condense' (not literally make into fragments).

3. 'Mr H' is almost certainly R. W. Hay (see Letter 79 below).

4. The exact phrase 'big Tear' does not occur in *Parisina*; but stanza 14 contains
   a moving description of Parisina's convulsion, esp. lines 336–45: 'But every
   now and then a tear/So large and slowly gathered slid/From the long dark
   fringe of that fair lid' (336–38). By comparison, JM may have in mind *As
   You Like It*, II, i, 38–40: 'the big round tears/Cours'd one another down
   his innocent nose/In piteous chase' (cf. also, *The Merchant of Venice*, II, viii,
   46–49).

5. See *Parisina*, 475–76: 'He claimed to die with eyes unbound,/His sole adieu to
   those around.' Michel Ney and Joachim Murat, Napoleon's closest marshals,
   had recently been shot (7 December and 13 October 1815 respectively). Both
   had refused to be bandaged. B may very well have argued that, if he was
   thinking of either, it was of Murat; see his letter to Moore of Saturday 4

November 1815 (the very day the report of Murat's execution appeared in the *Morning Chronicle*): 'Poor, dear Murat, what an end! ... He refused a confessor and a bandage; – so would neither suffer his soul or body to be bandaged' (*BLJ* IV, 330–31).

6. JM plays on the title of Shakespeare's play; for Gifford's reaction, see Letter 78 below.

7. JM's erasure is interesting; perhaps the figure was for *Parisina* only. What he actually 'inclosed' was a draft for 'one thousand & fifty pounds' to cover both *The Siege of Corinth* and *Parisina*, which B returned '*torn*', saying: 'Your offer is *liberal* in the extreme ... & much more than the two poems can possibly be worth – but I cannot accept it – nor will not' (*BLJ* V, 13 and 16). A little more light is thrown on this exchange by the following letter from JM to Blackwood – dated 5 December 1815 by Mrs Oliphant, but almost certainly of Friday 5 January 1816:

> Lord Byron is a curious man. He gave me, as I told you, the copyright of his two new poems, to be printed only in his works. I did not receive the last until Tuesday night [2 January 1816]. I was so delighted with it that even as I read it I sent him a draught for a 1000 guineas. The two poems are altogether no more than twelve hundred and fifteen hundred lines, and will together sell for five and sixpence. But he returned the draught, saying it was very liberal – much more than they were worth; that I was perfectly welcome to both poems to print in his (collected) works without cost or expectation, but that he did not think them equal to what they ought to be, and that he would not admit of their separate publication. I went yesterday [Thursday 4 January 1816], and he was rallying me upon my folly in offering so much, that he dared to say I thought now I had a most lucky escape. "To prove how much I think so, my lord," said I, "do me the favour to accept this pocket-book" – in which I had brought with me my draught changed into two bank-notes of £1000 and £50; but he would not take it. But I am not in despair that he will yet allow their separate publication, which I must continue to urge for mine own honour. These poems are not by any means equally finished as the "Corsair," but the "Siege of Corinth" contains two or three of the finest scenes he ever conceived, and the other, called "Parisina," is the most interesting and best conceived and best told story I ever read. I was never more affected; and you may be sure, from habit, I can tell when a thing is very good, and, moreover, that I have, according to our respective situations, as much to resign in my property in his name and fame as he has (Mrs Oliphant, *Annals of a Publishing House. William Blackwood and His Sons, Their Magazine and Friends*, 2 vols, 2nd edn [1897], 48–49; see also, 52–53).

Letter 78)   [Thursday 4 January 1816]

My Lord,

I send the manuscript, of which Gifford says: "I read the manuscript, and with great pleasure. It is indeed very good, and the plan is ingenious. The poetry is in the best manner."[1] Nothing can be more ingeniously framed and more interestingly told than this story. I liked it ten times better on the third reading than on the first. I read it last night to D'Israeli and his family, and they were perfectly overcome by it. The gradual madness of Parisina, the preparation and death of Hugo, and the subsequent description of Azo, by which, after all the story is over, you recreate a new and most tender interest, are all most attractive and touching, and in your best manner. In these matters I always liken myself to Molière's "old woman"; and when I am pleased I know our readers will be pleased.[2] Where you can strengthen expressions or lines, I entreat you to do so, but otherwise nothing can be added or retrenched for its improvement, though it is a gem truly worth polishing. These two tales form an invaluable contrast, and display the variety of your power. For myself, I am really more interested by the effect of the story of 'Parisina' than by either, I think, of the former tales.[3] I will call upon you from two to three. Depend upon it you beat them all; you have allowed plenty of time for any to take the field and equal your last 'Lara,' which I find, from the opinion of Rose and Ellis, is thought by poets to be your *best poem*.[4] I really am convinced that there is not any volume, the production of one man, to be picked out that will be so interesting and universally popular as that which your six tales would make. Formed upon human passions, they can never pass away.

John Murray.

Notes to Letter 78)

No MS survives of this letter which is taken from Smiles, I, 359–60.

1. JM slightly abbreviates Gifford's remarks in a letter to him dated merely 'Wednesday' (3 January 1816): 'I read the ms. & with great pleasure – it is, indeed, very good, & the plan is ingenious. The poetry is in the best manner. I have not touched Corinth, because I hope that the author will do something to it first, to fit it for the perusal of his fair admirers – its conclusion is enfeebled by <u>minutiæ</u> – Look the [*sic*] fine spirited ending of the last poem, & mark the difference' (MA).

2. JM refers to the story recorded by Boileau and rehearsed by Addison in *The Spectator*, No. 70, Monday 21 May 1711: '*Moliere*, as we are told by Monsieur *Boileau*, used to read all his Comedies to an old Woman who was his House-keeper, as she sat with him at her Work by the Chimney-Corner; and could foretel the Success of his Play in the Theatre, from the Reception it met at his Fire-Side: For he tells us the Audience always followed the old Woman, and never failed to laugh in the same Place' (*The Spectator*, ed. G. Gregory Smith, 4 vols [London: Dent, 1945], I, 215). The reference is to Boileau's *Réflexions Critiques sur quelques passages du rheteur Longin*, 'Réflexion Première': 'je me souviens que Moliere m'a montré aussi plusieurs fois une vieille Servante qu'il avoit chez lui, à qui il lisoit, disoit-il, quelquefois ses Comedies; il m'asseuroit que lorsque des endroits de plaisanterie ne l'avoient point frappée, il les corrigeoit, parce qu'il avoit plusieurs fois éprouvé sur son Théâtre que ces endroits n'y reüssissoient point' (*Oeuvres Complètes de Boileau*, ed. Françoise Escal [Éditions Gallimard, 1966], 493–94).

3. By 'either' JM may mean 'any'; otherwise he may have in mind specifically *The Corsair* and *Lara*.

4. George Ellis, who had reviewed *The Corsair* and *Lara* very favourably in the *Quarterly Review* for July 1814 (see Letter 60, n. 5 above), and William Stewart Rose (1775–1843), the translator of Casti's *Animali Parlanti* (1819), which B much admired.

Letter 79)   Wednesday [10 January 1816?]

Albemarle Street
Wednesday

My Lord
   Though I have not written to you – you have occupied my thoughts –

Gifford declared to me that you never surpassed Parisina[1]
   I inclose Ward's note after reading the Siege of Corinth – I lent him Parisina also & he called yesterday to express his wonder at your hesitation about their merits – he particularly struck [*sic*], in this, with the Sons reply to Azo[2] –
   I lent <u>Parisina</u> to Mr Hay (Mr Willmots friend) who is ill last night & I inclose his note[3]
   I send the Proof – if you are <u>sure</u> that you can improve it – do – otherwise touch it not[4]
   I will send a revise of Corinth[5] – this night or tomorrow Gifford thinks if the Narrative were put into the mouth of one of the Turks (if

it did not choak him) would give it additional interest.[6]
I hope your Lordship is well?
J. M.

Notes to Letter 79)

The date of this letter is conjectural; but see n. 4 below.

1. Gifford must have said this to JM; see also, Letter 78, n. 1 above.

2. Ward's note is not extant; but in his letter to Mrs Stewart of 7 January 1816 he told her B 'has written two new poems; one of them I have seen. It is as usual quite magnificent, but the same portrait, and the same scenery. This extreme barrenness of subjects and this extreme fertility in adorning them form a most singular contrast' (*Letters to 'Ivy'*, 294). For 'the Sons reply to Azo', see *Parisina*, stanza 13.

3. Hay's note is not forthcoming (cf. Letter 77 above); Robert Wilmot, B's cousin, soon to be involved in the separation proceedings on Annabella's side.

4. This must have been the first separate proof of *Parisina*, which B corrected and gave to JM in person on Saturday 13 January 1816 (*CPW* III, 488).

5. The only surviving proof of *The Siege of Corinth* is the corrected proof of both it and *Parisina*, dated by JM 19 January 1816 (*CPW* III, 478 and 488).

6. Presumably it did 'choak him', for no 'Turk' narrates *The Siege of Corinth*.

Letter 80)   Monday [22 January 1816?]

Albemarle Street, Monday, 4 o'clock.
My Lord.
I did not like to detain you this morning, but I confess to you that I came away impressed with a belief that you had already reconsidered this matter, as it refers to me. Your Lordship will pardon me if I cannot avoid looking upon it as a species of cruelty, after what has passed, to take from me so large a sum – offered with no reference to the marketable value of the poems, but out of personal friendship and gratitude alone, – to cast it away on the wanton and ungenerous interference of those who cannot enter into your Lordship's feelings for me, upon persons who have so little claim upon you, and whom those who so interested themselves might more decently and honestly enrich from their own funds, than by endeavouring to be liberal at the cost

of another, and by forcibly resuming from me a sum which you had generously and nobly resigned.

I am sure you will do me the justice to believe that I would strain every nerve in your service, but it is actually heartbreaking to throw away my earnings on others. I am no rich man, abounding, like Mr. Rogers, in superfluous thousands, but working hard for independence, and what would be the most grateful pleasure to me if likely to be useful to you personally, becomes merely painful if it causes me to work for others for whom I can have no such feelings.

This is a most painful subject for me to address you upon, and I am ill able to express my feelings about it. I commit them entirely to your liberal construction with a reference to your knowledge of my character.

I have the honour to be, &c.,

John Murray.

Notes to Letter 80)

No MS survives of this letter, which is taken from Smiles, I, 355–56. The date is conjectural, but almost certain. According to Smiles, before sending it to B, JM submitted it to Gifford who remarked: 'I have made a scratch or two, and the letter now expresses my genuine sentiments on the matter. But should you not see Rogers? It is evident that Lord Byron is a little awkward about this matter, and his officious friends have got him into a most *unlordly* scrape, from which they can only relieve him by treading back their steps. The more I consider their conduct, the more I am astonished at their impudence. A downright robbery is honourable to it. If you see Rogers, do not be shy to speak: he trembles at report, and here is an evil one for him' (Smiles, I, 356; no MS extant). On learning that B had refused JM's offer of 1,000 guineas for *The Siege of Corinth* and *Parisina*, Sir James Mackintosh wrote Rogers the following extraordinarily ill-advised letter (dated simply 'Weedon Lodge: Friday', but almost certainly Friday 19 January 1816):

> Dear Rogers, – It is said that Lord Byron has refused a very large sum from Murray for permission to publish separately two new poems which his lordship wishes only to be added to the collection of his works. Knowing the noble use which he has hitherto made of the produce of his works, I venture to point out to you poor Godwin as a person whom Lord Byron could save from ruin by granting the permission on condition of Murray's giving Godwin such part of the sum spoken of as Lord Byron may be pleased to direct. Godwin is a man of genius, likely, for his independence of thinking, to starve at the age of sixty for want of a few hundred pounds necessary to carry on his laborious occupation. If you agree with me I am certain that the benevolence of your heart will need no solicitor. But if you should not make any application to Lord B.,

I shall conclude that it would be improper. Say yes or no in writing
(P. W. Clayden, *Rogers and His Contemporaries*, 2 vols [London, 1889],
I, 211).

As ill-advisedly, Rogers forwarded this letter to B with a covering note (no longer
extant), evidently urging B's compliance with the proposal, to which B replied
'hastily ... by Murray' in the morning of Saturday 20 January. Later the same day
he wrote again to Rogers saying that he had 'closed with M[urray] in consequence
of Sir J's & your suggestion', and proposed that 'the sum of six hundred pounds'
should be 'transferred to Mr. Godwin in such manner as may seem best to you';
the 'remainder', he said, he would reserve 'for other purposes' (Coleridge and
Maturin) (*BLJ* V, 16 and n). To this Rogers replied with a 'note' (not extant),
asking B to 'pause', which B sent on to JM on Sunday 21 January, promising to
see him the following day 'at about three' (*BLJ* V, 17). After that meeting, JM
wrote this letter (80). B replied sharply the same day, withdrawing both works
from publication and demanding the return of the manuscripts (*BLJ* V, 17). The
matter soon dropped and harmony was restored, and the poems were eventually
published on 13 February 1816. For this whole messy business, see *BLJ* V, 16–18,
Clayden, op. cit., I, 210–14, and Marchand, II, 565–66.

Letter 81)   [Saturday 3 February 1816?]

<Dea> My Lord.
   I shall have the pleasure of attending to your desire – I sent the MSS
the first thing this morning to Mʳ G – and I rather anxiously await his
Opinion of it – for I am very sanguine – <being> having been much
interested –
   You are a Strange Man – and to have your own way no one can
be more stoically determined[1] – I will send the proofs of the Siege
tomorrow or next day & go on –
   I write with the Room full – & hope you will excuse my haste &
impudence
   J. M.

Notes to Letter 81)

Cover: The Lord Byron location: BL Add. 31037, f. 38

The date of this letter is conjectural, but it seems to be a response to B's letter
of Saturday 3 February, returning Scott's *Marmion* to JM, convinced, as he had
thought, that there was an unintentional resemblance between *Parisina* (stanza xiv)
and *Marmion* (II, xxi). He wished JM to ask Gifford whether he should mention

the fact (presumably Gifford thought not, as there is no such mention of it), adding: 'There are a few word & phrases I want to alter in the M.S. & should like to do it − before you print − I will return it in an hour' (*BLJ* V, 22).

1. JM seems to translate Madame du Parc's exclamation in Molière's *L'Impromptu de Versailles*, scene iv: 'Mon Dieu, que vous êtes une étrange personne! Vous voulez furieusement ce que vous voulez.'

Letter 82)   Friday [29 March 1816?]

Albemarle St
Friday

My Lord

I have met with so many interruptions this forenoon that I must trust to your kindness to excuse my not attending your Lordship according to my appointment.[1]

I inclose in two notes at 2 & 3 Months the Sum of 1000G^s for the Copyright of the Siege of Corinth & Parisina which is the utmost profit which can possibly be derived from its Sale.

I have sent an account for Books merely that it may be ascertained to be correct & it is to be paid only when you return from your Travels & succeed to a new Estate.[2]

As your Lordship spoke of giving me some assignment for the Ode & Melodies I have extended it to the whole works & the thing will then be safe − if your Lordship approve of this − I will thank you to allow some friend to see you sign it & you must <del> afterwards use the words I deliver this as my Act & Deed − & your friend will sign it also

The other paper is a Power of Attorney to enable me to act for<ma> your Lordship in case of any spurious Edition of the Bards &c[3]

I will attend your Lordship at any hour tomorrow. I have the honour to be My Lord
your obedient Servant
John Murray

Notes to Letter 82)

1. There is no indication elsewhere that B and JM had arranged any 'appoint-ment' between them.

2. B replied to this letter the same day, returning JM's 'bills ... and the papers concerning the copyrights', and adding: 'I must remain your debtor for the

present on the book account − and will take my chance from Evans's sale − returning you your note which is not due till the 12th. of April' (*BLJ* V, 57−58; see also, Letter 84, n. 3 below). It should be remembered that B's exile from England at this point was not seen as permanent.

3. By an Indenture dated 27 March 1816 and in consideration of £3,925, B assigned to JM the copyrights of all his works published by JM (but not, e.g., *EBSR*). The witness was James Holmes (1777−1860), the painter and engraver, who also witnessed B's Power of Attorney made the same day, empowering JM to suppress the publication and sale of *EBSR* and *Hints from Horace*, to which B appended an additional endorsement (see *CMP*, 218 and 543−45, and *BLJ* XIII, 39 − though there, '*my*' should read 'my').

Letter 83)   Monday [1 April 1816]

It is tremendously exquisite − the most astringent dose that was ever presented to female Character[1] −

I inclose our friends remarks[2] −

I made a Copy for the Printer & shall have proofs by 3 − 4 o Clock − − I therefore trust that you will return me the original wch I inclose −

I shall be with you before you have read this −

J. Murray

Monday
2 o Clock

Notes to Letter 83)

1. This was B's bitter satire against Mrs Clermont, *A Sketch from Private Life*, the MS of which is dated Saturday 30 March (*CPW* III, 494), and which B appears to have sent JM the same day, saying: 'I send you my last night's dream − and request to have *50* copies (for *private distribution*) struck off − and a proof tomorrow if possible − I wish Mr. Gifford to look at them − they are from life' (*BLJ* V, 58). According to a memo by JM's son, when B saw JM later in the day he said: 'I could not get to sleep last night, but lay rolling & tossing about, till this morning when I got up & wrote that, and it is very odd Murray after doing that I went to bed again & never slept sounder in my life' (MA).

2. This was Gifford, who commented in an undated note to JM: 'It is a dreadful picture − Caravagio [*sic*] outdone in his own way I have hinted at the

removal of one couplet – if its sense be wanted it may be compressed into one of the other lines. Its powers are unquestionable – but can any human being deserve such a delineation? I keep my old opinion of Lord Byron – he may be what he will – why will he not <u>will</u> to be the first of poets and of men? I lament bitterly to see a great mind run to seed, & waste itself in rank growth' (MA; Smiles [I, 357] incorrectly applies this to *The Siege of Corinth*). Gifford's allusion to the Italian painter Michelangelo Merisi da Caravaggio (1571–1610) refers to the striking chiaroscuro, dramatic story-telling and detailed realism for which Caravaggio is renowned (cf. also, *DJ* XIII, 72).

Letter 84)   [Monday 1 April 1816?]

My Lord

Mr Rogers – Frere & Stratford Canning have all seen & admired this – <y> they agree that you have produced nothing better – that Satire is your fort [*sic*] – & so is each Class as you choose to adopt it.[1]

Mr F. suggests that in the last line <u>weltering</u> does not accord – <u>hang on high</u> wch preceeds [*sic*] it[2] –

I have sent a Proof to M^r G –

Pray leave out the <u>Catalogue</u> – for the Auctioneer wants it instantly[3]

–

Ever My Lord
your faithful Servt
Jno Murray

8 o Clock

Notes to Letter 84)

This seems to have been written on the same day as Letter 83 above and accompanying the first proof of *A Sketch from Private Life* sent to B on this date (*CPW* III, 495).

1. This may have been Stratford Canning's *initial* reaction, but ten days later, on receiving copies of both 'A Sketch' and 'Fare Thee Well' from JM on Thursday 11 April, he wrote with pointed insolence: 'I thank you for the three pieces of poetry which I received from you this morning. M^r. Frere's translation has given me great pleasure in the perusal. The two others I beg leave to return. I happen to have heard too much of the real state of the circumstances to which they refer to have any pleasure in reading, much less in keeping them' (MA).

2. In the final line of 'A Sketch' (line 104) the word 'festering' originally read 'weltering', which Frere evidently felt did not accord with 'hang on high' two lines earlier in the poem (line 102). Although not entirely convinced, B altered the word to the present reading, which he felt was 'perhaps in any case ... the best word of the two', and returned the proof and the 'Catalogue' on Tuesday 2 April (*BLJ* V, 60; see also, n. 3 below).

3. The 'Catalogue' was of B's books, which were to be auctioned at the house of R. H. Evans in Pall Mall on Friday 5 and Saturday 6 April 1816 prior to his departure from England (see *CMP*, 231–45 and 566).

Letter 85)   [Tuesday 2 April 1816?]

I expected it & am more pleased than surprised[1]
Mr Frere has just read your corrected proof & thinks it excellent
– He says you always remind him of Archilochus[2]
I expect a pacquet in the Morning[3]

Notes to Letter 85)

Cover: The Lord Byron

1. This seems to be JM's response to B's own speedy correction and return of the first proof of 'A Sketch', who himself had closed his accompanying letter 'Be *quick*' (*BLJ* V, 60; see also, Letter 84 above).

2. Frere's praise is extraordinarily apt. Archilochus, early 7th century BC Parian poet, was the father of iambic (i.e., abusive, scornful, bitter) poetry. His invective against his prospective father-in-law and daughter was so extreme that they committed suicide; while he himself was condemned by the Spartans for the indelicacy of his verses and banished from Sparta as a dangerous citizen. Horace regarded himself as his follower and boasts that he was the first to introduce him to Rome (see *Epodes*, 6, and *Epistles*, I, xix, 23–25; see also, the Loeb Classical Library editions of *Greek Iambic Poetry*, ed. and trans. Douglas E. Gerber [Cambridge, Mass.: Harvard University Press, 1999] 14–293 and *The Greek Anthology*, trans. W. R. Paton, 5 vols [London: Heinemann, 1927], esp. bks VII, Epigrams 69–71, 351, 352, 664 and 674, IX, Epigram 185 and XI, Epigram 20, and Anne Pippin Burnett, *Three Archaic Poets: Archilochus, Alcaeus, Sappho* [Bristol: Bristol Classical Press, 1998], 15–104). Incidentally, in his note to line 271 of *CHP* IV, Hobhouse deplores the 'hornets and wasps' that beset the otherwise luxuriant site of Petrarch's tomb, adding: 'No other coincidence could assimilate the tombs of Petrarch and Archilochus' (*CPW* II, 231). His reference is to Gaetulicus's Epigram on Archilochus in the Palatine Anthology, which concludes: 'Wayfarer, pass by

quietly lest you stir up the wasps that have settled on his grave' (see *The Greek Anthology*, bk VII, 71 and *Greek Iambic Poetry*, 50–51).

3. Probably containing the final proof of 'A Sketch'.

Letter 86)   Saturday [13 April 1816]

Albemarle S^t
Saturday 11/¾ N^t

My Lord

Except during a walk to my banker I have not had a moment uninterrupted by incessant visits for the farewell[1] – I had more than once my hat on to proceed to you & had twice began [*sic*] to write – until I sunk into my Dinner Chair at 7 – I can not however refrain from communion –

I inclose a proof – Rogers & Frere think the lines you gave me last night very good – making one or two remarks wch I will communicate tomorrow – the Subject certainly deserves your best Verses[2] – the Bills I can turn into Cash next week[3] – I will call between two & three – I hope you had a Good Supper last night for really the weather was inclement & & [*sic*] proved nearly the Death of an Actress a Painter & My Lord

Your faithful Publisher[4]
Jno Murray

Notes to Letter 86)

1. B's poem to Annabella, 'Fare Thee Well', was printed for private circulation on Monday 8 April 1816 (*CPW* III, 494).

2. The 'lines' B gave JM 'last night' were 'To [Augusta]' ('When all around grew drear and dark'), on the MS of which JM has written: 'Given to me (& I believe composed) by Ld B. Friday April 12th 1816' (MA; see also, *CPW* III, 496). The 'proof' to which JM refers was undoubtedly of this poem, although no proof survives nor is one known to have existed (see *CPW* III, 496). However, the meeting 'tomorrow', Sunday 14 (Easter Day), evidently not having taken place, B wrote to JM on Monday 15 stating very firmly: 'Of the copies of late things written by me – I wish more particularly the *last* not to be circulated – at present – (you know which I mean – those to A[ugusta])' (*BLJ* V, 67–68).

3. The 'Bills' may relate to the sale of B's books, 'whatever little profit' from which B had insisted on Saturday 6 April JM should keep; otherwise, they

may relate to B's 'account' which he asked JM at the same time to let 'stand over for the present' (*BLJ* V, 62).

4. JM may be making some obscure allusion to the Last Supper, as 'last night' was Good Friday. Otherwise he must refer to the 'Supper' which took place on Thursday 11 April, for which day Hobhouse recorded in his Diary: 'dined at the Clarendon with Burdett – Byron – S. B. Davies & the two Kinnairds – we had a pleasant day – though Davies was obliged to walk off – he went to bed – got up again went to the Union & won 3.700£' (BL Add. 47232, f. 114*r*). However, he does not mention any peculiar severity in the weather, neither does B and nor do the papers; and, as for the near deaths of 'an Actress' and 'a Painter' and JM himself, this sounds suspiciously like a joke.

Letter 87)   Monday [22 April 1816]

My Lord

I have just received the inclosed Letter from Mrs Maria Graham[1] – to whom I had sent the Verses – it will shew you that you are thought of in the remotest corners, and furnishes me with an excuse for repeating that I shall not forget you – God bless your Lordship

Fare Thee well[2]

J. Murray

Monday
4 0 Clock

Notes to Letter 87)

This appears to be JM's last letter to B in England. On the following day, Tuesday 23 April, B left London for Dover, accompanied by Hobhouse, Scrope Davies, Fletcher, Polidori and Berger.

1. Maria Graham, later Lady Callcott (1785–1842), was a great Byron enthusiast, but no such letter from her of this date appears to survive. In a lively letter to JM of 2 March 1816, however, she had complained of the carnage in stanza 16 of *The Siege of Corinth*, and of the poem's metre which she was angry she could not defend as she was 'so great an admirer of his lordship that I cannot bear people to find true fault with him'; accordingly, she made her husband 'read the Corsair to me to put me in good humour' (MA; see also, Rosamund Brunel Gotch, *Maria, Lady Callcott* [London: John Murray, 1937], esp. 160 and 210, and Smiles, I, 381).

2. A touching borrowing of the title of B's poem.

PART II
Murray to Byron abroad

Letters 88–171:
11 July 1816 to 8 November 1822

Letter 88)   [Thursday] 11 July 1816

London July 11th.
1816

My Lord

Should no earlier opportunity have occurred for the safe Conveyance of the important MSS which your Lordship has allowed me, (most anxiously) to look for, I should feel gratified in receiving it by the hands of my friend Mr Brown one of the principal Merchants in this City, and who has most obligingly undertaken, to take charge of it.

I venture also to present Mr Brown to the favour of your Lordships attentions which will add much to the kindness which has already rendered me My Lord

your Lordships
Obliged & faithful Servant
John Murray

To
The Rt Honb
Lord Byron

Notes to Letter 88)

Location: Jarndyce Antiquarian Booksellers, London.

A facsimile of the MS of this letter may also be seen in the Jarndyce Catalogue CLV, *The Romantics: Part One. Byron &c.* (Winter 2003–2004), lot 158. In his first letter to JM since leaving England, written from Ouchy on Thursday 27 June 1816 during his tour round the Lake of Geneva with Shelley, B had informed him of the completion of *CHP* III and said that he would 'send it by the first safe-looking opportunity' (*BLJ* V, 82). Replying to this letter (88) on Wednesday 28 August from Diodati, he said he had consigned the MS 'to the care of my friend Mr. Shelley', as Mr Brown (who is otherwise unidentified) had 'returned by Brussels – which is the longest route' (*BLJ* V, 90). The MS was Claire Clairmont's fair copy of *CHP* III (see Letter 90, n. 3 below). However, JM had also been kept informed of B's movements by Dr John William Polidori (1795–1821), B's physician and secretary, from whom he had received two letters prior to this Letter (88); a third, written the day before, would cross with it. All three letters are in MA and are given here.

The first letter, dated 'Brussels 6 May 1816', has no cover:

> Sir
> By Lord Byrons desire I wish you would take this heap of trophies under your care paying for us what is due for Customs &c – We had a Delightfull [sic] ride over Waterloo on a Cossack horse & flemish steed – We are well in health &c
>
> > Yours &c
> > J Polidori
>
> Brussels 6 May 1816
> PS LB will account to you for it he would pay himself but cannot ascertain the amount LB will write in a day or two – Mr Gordon a friend of LB's is the bearer.

For the 'trophies' consigned to Mr Gordon, see Letter 92, n. 21 and Letter 94 below. For B's feelings about his ride over Waterloo, see *BLJ* V, 76 and 82, and his note to *CHP* III, line 270 (*CPW* II, 303). Polidori was rather more illuminating when writing to Hobhouse five days later from Coblenz on 11 May, telling him that they counted on being at Geneva in '10 days at best' and that B and he were 'both well & hearty': 'Lord Byron's health is greatly improved his stomack [sic] returning rapidly to its natural state. Exercise & peace of mind making great advances towards the amendment of his corps delabré [debilitated body] leave little for medicine to patch up. His spirits I think are also much improved He blythely [sic] carols thro the day "Heres to you tom brown" & when he has done says that's as well as Hobhouse does it – You & his other friend Mr Scroop davies [sic] form a great subject of conversation. God! here I am at the end of all my thoughts oh no waterloo was ridden over by Mylord on a Cossack horse accompanied by myself on a Flemish steed – L B singing turkish or Arnaout riding tunes & your L S [Lordship's Servant?] listning [sic]. We had a very good day of it L B visited Howards I think Colonel burying place twice ...'; and on the outside cover he added: 'Excuse the bad writing &c. for I am in a fever of digestion after my ride' (BL Add. 36456, ff. 337–38v; for Hobhouse's reference to this letter, see *BB*, 221; for B's visiting Howard's grave, see his note to *CHP* III, line 270 [*CPW* II, 303], and for the deteriorating state of Polidori's health, see *BLJ* V, 76).

The second letter, written from Diodati on 18 June 1816, is addressed to 'John Murray Esqr/Albemarle Street/London' and arrived in London on 27 June 1816:

> Dear Sir
> We are at Campagne Diodati near Geneva. Has Mr Gordon remitted into your hands the spoils of Waterloo Lord Byron has ready to pass you by the first safe hand a third canto of Childe Harold. We should be much oblidged [sic] to you if you would send us

Kubla Khan &c Cristabel [sic] & other poems of Coleridge Esqʳ
Holcrofts Memoirs
Bertram of Mathurin [sic]
The Antiquary by Guy Mannering [sic]
Taylors Translation of Pausanias
Common red tooth powder from Waith<s> [sic] the dentist
& if you would send to 38 Gʳᵗ Pulteney Sᵗ my fathers to ask for 3
vols of Crabbe all which if [sic] you would pack immediatly [sic]
together <to> directed to

<Mʳ> P. B. Shelly [sic] Esqʳ
at Messʳˢ Longdills & Co
5 Grays inn Square

in whose name it will be forwarded hither as he is <with us> our
neighbour. – We have heard of the success of Bertram with great
pleasure & saw <up> a commentary in the french papers upon your
giving 12 times as much to Mʳ Mathurin that would <ple> flatter
you

I remain
Yours truly
J Polidori
Campagne Diodati
Pres de Geneva
June 18 1816

On the blank third page of this letter, JM has written in list form: 'Ilderim/
Adolphe/Tripoli'. Before he left England, B had recommended *Bertram; or, The
Castle of St. Aldobrand*, by the Rev. Charles Robert Maturin (1782–1824), to Drury
Lane Theatre where it was first performed on Thursday 9 May 1816 and ran with
great success for 14 nights (*The Times*, Thursday 9 May 1816, and *BLJ* IV, 336–37;
see also, Letter 94, n. 7 below). On 27 May 1816, B had also told Hobhouse he
had heard of its success 'by the French papers' (*BLJ* V, 79). On 1 May, B had
asked Hobhouse to bring out with him a Pausanias and '(Taylor's ditto)', which
he repeated, with the addition of 'some of Waite's *red* tooth powder', and asking
him to tell JM that he had 'a 3d. Canto of Childe Harold finished' on 23 June
(*BLJ* V, 74 and 80; the reference is to Thomas Taylor's *The Description of Greece by
Pausanias*, 3 vols [1794]). B had read Henry Gally Knight's *Ilderim: A Syrian Tale*
(1816) by 5 October, and Benjamin Constant's *Adolphe* (1816) by 29 July (*BLJ* V,
86 and 111), but he does not mention 'Tripoli'. This was *Narrative of a Ten Years'
Residence at Tripoli in Africa: from the Original Correspondence in the possession of the
Family of the late Richard Tully, Esq. The British Consul* (Henry Colburn, 1816),
which he was to exploit in *DJ* III (see *BLJ* VIII, 186, *CPW* V, 699, n. 481ff.,
and *The Manuscripts of the Younger Romantics: Lord Byron. Vol. VIII: Don Juan,
Cantos III–IV Manuscript*, ed. Andrew Nicholson [New York & London: Garland
Publishing, 1992], pp. xviii–xix). He had received Scott's *The Antiquary* (1816), and
Coleridge's *Christabel* (1816) by 30 September (*BLJ* V, 108–09), and had read the
former, together with *Memoirs of the late Thomas Holcroft, Written by Himself, and*

continued to the time of his Death, from his Diary, Notes and Other Papers [by William Hazlitt] 3 vols (London: Longman, 1816), by 5 October (*BLJ* V, 112). Longdills were Shelley's solicitors.

Polidori's third letter, written from Diodati on 10 July 1816, is addressed 'A Monsieur/Monsieur Murray/Albemarle Street/Londres.' and arrived in London on 22 July 1816, thus crossing with JM's present letter (88), and indicating that JM had written at least two letters (no longer extant) prior to it:

Campagne Diodati July 10 1816

Dear Sir

Your letter to me was received <with> both by myself & Lord Byron with great pleasure. Yours of tuesday following has not arrived which is a pity as in your last you talk of a journal in it which to Lord Byron who hears nothing but reports of insurrection in the east Rebellions in the west & murders north & south would be a great gratification. Lord Liverpool resigned Lord Wellington blown up & half a dozen greatly lettered names with some pleasant accident after them is all we hear to keep us newspaperly alive. we [*sic*] are also quite ignorant of all literary news <w> some thing of some poems by Coleridge Mathurins [*sic*] play the Antiquary & Glenarvon has reached us.

Since it has given you hopes entering [*sic*] well into the lit<t>erary field next winter, that childe Harold has got another Canto of 118 Stanzas you will be more pleased to hear of another poem of 400 lines called the castle [*sic*] of Chillon the feeling of a third of 3 brothers in prison on the banks of the Genevan lake. I think very beautifull [*sic*] containing more of his tender than Sombre poetry. Indeed Childe Harold himself is a little altered more philo-sophic less blackly misanthropic than before.

With regard to the books you were so good as to send according to direction we wish you would send to enquire if a clerk is coming out to Mr Shelly [*sic*] if not that you would send them quam cito [as soon as possible] to us by the shortest conveyance adding (if a number of the Pampheteer [*sic*] has come out since the 1st of July) it with them for me

Lord Byron desires me to say that it was my neglectfull [*sic*] hurry in writing my last that hindered me repeating to you his compts which he now sends you thrice repeated. At the same time I beg leave to assure You I am your

very obtidged [*sic*] & humble Servant

John Polidori.

P.S. Lord Byron is well has not fixed upon a corrector of Childe Harold says has written to you the other day from Ouchy short not much consequence.

B himself occasionally referred to *The Prisoner of Chillon* as 'the Castle of Chillon'

(*BLJ* V, 83 and 90), and had read Lady Caroline Lamb's *Glenarvon* (Henry Colburn, 1816) by 29 July (*BLJ* V, 86). *The Pamphleteer*, VIII, xiv (August 1816), which contained Polidori's essay 'On the Punishment of Death' (pp. 281–304), would have been the same issue that B told JM he had read on 5 October (*BLJ* V, 111). B's 'short' letter from Ouchy was that of 27 June 1816 (*BLJ* V, 81–82; see also, above). In his next letter to JM of 22 July 1816, B told him: 'I wrote to you a few weeks ago – and Dr. P[olidori] received your letter – but ye. packet has not made its appearance nor ye. epistle of which you gave notice therein' (*BLJ* V, 84). Incidentally, B's letter of 30 July 1816 to an unidentified correspondent thanking him for 'the details with regard to Bonnivard' (*BLJ* V, 87), was to John Rocca, Madame de Staël's husband and the 'citizen' to whom B refers in his note to line 394 of *The Prisoner of Chillon* (*CPW* IV, 453; see also, 448–51 for commentary). His letter to B, dated 29 July 1816 from Coppet, is in MA and runs as follows:

Mylord
J'ai l'honneur de vous envoyer cy incluse la notice que vous m'avez fait l'honneur de me demander. Il me semble que Bonnivard doit être le héros principal d'un poême sur chillon – je crois que sans s'écarter de la plus exacte vérité historique on peut peindre Bonnivard homme fier entreprenant éclairé, martyr de sa résistance au tyran de sa patrie, se croyant condamné à passer le reste de ses jours dans le même cachot creusé dans le rocher audessous du niveau du lac, n'entendant que le rétentissement de ses pas sous la voûte et quelquefois et seulement pend[an]t la tempére, les gémissemens des vagues qui venaient se briser contre le roc dans le sein du quel il était enfermé. Bonnivard n'ayant personne à qui se plaindre soutenu contre les horreurs d'une solitude absolu et qu'il croyoit éternelle par la seule conscience de son inébranlable vertu – son étonnement ses incertitudes lorsqu'après six années passées sans espérance il entend au travers <des brises> des flots, les coups de canon des barques des Genevois et des Bernois qui attaquent et battent en brêche le château de chillon – enfin les bruits des assaillants venant à cesser tout-à-coup la porte de son cachôt [*sic*] s'ouvre et il verse bientôt après des larmes de joie <et de délivrance> lorsque des concitoyens ses libérateurs lui apprennent que sa patrie qu'il croyait gémissante sous la plus dure oppression est libre – qu'elle a chassé ses tyrans – je ne me permettrois pas Mylord de vous envoyer tous ces détails, si je ne savais pas que vous avez le don de tout illustrer par vôtre belle poésie, et si je ne souhaitois pas au plus vertueux citoyen de ma patrie l'honneur d'être consacré dans vos vers –
J'ai l'honneur d'être Mylord
v[ôtre] t[rès] h[umble] s[ervant].
A[lbert] J[ean] de Rocca
Coppet ce 29 Juillet 1816

[My Lord

I have the honour of enclosing herewith the account you favoured me by requesting. It seems to me that Bonnivard should be the principal hero of a poem on Chillon. I think that without departing from the strictest historical truth, one might paint him as a proud, bold and enlightened man, the martyr of his resistance to the tyrant of his country, who believes himself condemned to pass the rest of his days in the same dungeon hollowed in the rock beneath the level of the lake, hearing only the echoes of his own footsteps under the vault, and sometimes – and then only during calm weather – the wash of the waves breaking against the rock in which he is incarcerated. Having no one with whom to commiserate, Bonnivard bears himself up against the horrors of a solitary confinement he imagines will last for ever solely by the consciousness of his own unshakeable virtue; the astonishment and uncertainty he feels when after six hopeless years he hears over <the winds> the waters the sound of canon-fire from the ships of the Genevese and Bernese as they attack and storm the Castle of Chillon. At last the noise of the assault ceases, his prison door suddenly opens, and soon he is shedding tears of joy <and of deliverance> as his fellow citizens, his liberators, inform him that his country, which he believed was groaning under the harshest oppression, was free, and that its tyrants had been driven out.

I would not presume to send you all these details, My Lord, did I not know that you had the power of doing honour to everything in your noble poetry, and did I not wish the bravest citizen of my country to be consecrated in your verse –

I have the honour to be, My Lord,
Your very humble servant
A[lbert] J[ohn] de Rocca
Coppet 29 July 1816]

Letter 89) Thursday 12 September 1816

My most particular compliments
to Mr Hobhouse – & to Mr Davies
& Dr Polidori

London 12 Sepr. 1816
Thursday

My Lord

I have rarely addressed you with more pleasure than upon the present occasion – I was thrilled with delight yesterday by the announcement

of Mr Shelley with the MSS of Childe Harold[1] – I had no sooner got
the quiet possession of it, than trembling with auspicious hope about
it, I carried it direct to Mr Gifford, who has been exceedingly ill with
a Jaundice, unable to write or do any thing, he was much pleased by
my attention & I promissed to call the next day – but in the evening
of yesterday I received from him, most unexpectedly the note which I
inclose[2] – it speaks volumes – I called upon him today – he said that
he was unable to leave off last night as his note intimated and that
he had sat up until he had finished every line of the Canto – it had
actually agitated him into a fever and he was exceedingly worse when I
called – he had persisted this morning in finishing the Volume and he
pronounced himself to be infinitely more delighted than when he first
wrote to me – He says <w> that what you have heretofore published is
nothing to this effect – he says also, besides its being the most splendid
original & interesting – it is the most finished of your writings and
he has undertaken to correct the press & to point it, with a glow of
pleasure that I never saw equalled – he says there are not three words in
the whole, of which he would recommend the alteration – never since
my intimacy with Mr Gifford did I ever see him so heartily pleased or
give one fiftieth part of his commendation with one thousandth part
of the warmth. Harold is exquisite – but he thinks the Tale no less so
– and he speaks in extacy [sic] of the Dream – the whole volume beams
with Genius[3] – With such opinions I would beg the favour of your
Lordship to write to me immediately empowering me to give the entire
exclusive reading of the Proofs to Mr Gifford alone and he will attend
to it with all his mind[4] – I am sure he loves you in his heart – & when
the [sic] called upon me some time ago & I told him that your Lordship
was gone he instantly exclaimed in a full room – "Well he has not left
his equal behind him that I will say" – perhaps you will write – a line
for him.[5] Now for this said Volume I propose to pay into your Lordships
Banker the sum of <Fifteen> Twelve Hundred Guineas and should this
proposal happen to be honoured by your Lordships approbation I would
venture to solicit as a mark of your favour, that you would present to
me the Original MSS with every scrap belonging to it.[6] Your Lordship
will let me know <if> by a word if 2. 3 & 4 Mos Bills would be
inconvenient & I can easily manage it, in any Other way. This will be
a glorious triumph for you upon my Soul – and set me forward in such
force that I shall keep possession of the field during the whole campaign
– I shall place it in the hands of the printer immediately, if any addition,
correction or emendation of any kind occur, do me the favour to dash it
off immediately – Respecting the Monody I extract from a Letter wch I
received this morning from Sir J^s. Mackintosh

"I presume that I have to thank you for a Copy of "the Monody
on Sheridan" received this morning – I wish it had been
accompanied by the additional favour of mentioning the name of
the writer, at which I only guess & which it is difficult to read the
Poem without desiring to know"[7]

Generally speaking it is not I think popular, and spoken of rather for
fine passages than as a whole – how could you give so trite an image as
in the last two lines[8] – Gifford does not like it – Frere does – a propos
of Mr Frere – he came to me whilst at breakfast this morning and
<with> between some Stanzas wch he was repeating to me of a truly
Original Poem of his own – <sa> he said carelessly – by the way about
half an hour ago I was so silly (taking an immense pinch of Snuff &
priming his nostrils well with it) – as to get Married!!! – perfectly true
– he set out for Hastings about an hour after he left me – and upon my
conscience I very [sic] believe that if I had had your MSS to have put
into his hands – as sure as fate he would have sat with me reading it all
the morning & totally forgotten his late engagement.[9]

You have heard that Brougham has got into a Crim Con scrape with
the wife of G. L – the trial is to come on[10] – I saw Lord Holland today
looking very well – I wish I could send you Gifford's Ben Jonson it
is full of fun & interest & allowed on all hands to be most ably done,
and would I am sure amuse you[11] – I have very many new important
& interesting works of all kinds in the Press, wch I should be happy to
know any means of sending – My Review[12] is improving in sale beyond
my most sanguine expectations I now sell nearly 9,000 even Perry says
the Edinb Rev is going to the Devil. I was with Mrs Leigh today who
is very well, she leaves town on Saturday – her eldest Daughter – I
fancy – is a most engaging girl[13] – But yours my Lord is unspeakably
interesting & promising & I am happy to add that Lady B is looking
well.[14] God Bless you my best wishes & feelings are always with you & I
sincerely wish that your happiness may be as unbounded as your Genius
which has rendered me so much My Lord your obliged Servant
    J. M.

Notes to Letter 89)

Cover: The Rt Honble/Lord Byron/Diodati/Genéve

Hobhouse and Scrope Davies had joined B at Diodati on Monday 26 August;
Scrope left for England ten days later. B found this letter (89) and the next letter
(90) awaiting him at Diodati on his return from his Alpine tour with Hobhouse,
which lasted from Tuesday 17 September to Sunday 29 September.

1. Within three days of his arrival in England, Shelley wrote to B on Wednesday 11 September saying he had 'just seen Murray and delivered the poem to him. He was exceedingly polite to me; and expressed the greatest eagerness to see the Poem' (Shelley, *Letters*, I, 505).

2. The 'note' is not forthcoming, but JM rehearsed Gifford's 'raptures' and 'unbounded commendation' to Sir James Mackintosh in a letter of this same day (BL Add. 52452, ff. 218–19). Replying on Sunday 29 September, B said he was 'very much flattered by Mr. Gifford's good opinion', and hoped the poem would justify his 'kindness' (*BLJ* V, 105).

3. With Claire Clairmont's fair copy of *CHP* III Shelley had also brought the MSS of *The Prisoner of Chillon*, 'The Dream' and various other poems.

4. In his letter of Wednesday 28 August, B had said he did not know 'to whom to consign the correction of the proofs' and suggested Moore, failing whom 'Mr. S[helley] will take it upon himself' who 'in any case ... is authorized to act for me in treating with you' (*BLJ* V, 90). JM's emphasis here is on 'entire exclusive reading of the Proofs to Mr Gifford alone': he did not like Shelley, of whose history he was probably well aware and who was a rather more punctilious businessman than JM had bargained for (see Letter 90, n. 1, and Letter 92 below; see also, Shelley, *Letters*, I, 508–14). B did not, however, give a direct answer to this request (though see Letter 90, n. 4 below).

5. B merely replied, 'My best remembrances to Mr. G[ifford] – pray say all that can be said from me to him', repeating these wishes the following day (*BLJ* V, 106 and 108).

6. 'Fifteen' is rubbed out (not struck through) and barely visible beneath 'Twelve'; the alteration was clearly a strategic manoeuvre on JM's part (see Letter 90 below). B replied on Sunday 29 September: 'With regard to the price – *I* fixed *none* but left it to Mr. Kinnaird – & Mr. Shelley & yourself to arrange' (*BLJ* V, 105–06; see also, Letter 90 below).

7. B's *Monody on the Death of The Right Honourable R. B. Sheridan*, written at Kinnaird's request and sent to him by B on Saturday 20 July, was published anonymously by JM on Monday 9 September 1816 (*CPW* IV, 454). Sir James Mackintosh's letter is not forthcoming, but JM told him that B was the author when writing to him this same day (BL Add. 52452, f. 219).

8. The 'last two lines' of the *Monody* run: 'Sighing that Nature formed but one such man/And broke the die – in moulding Sheridan!' (*CPW* IV, 22). Replying on Sunday 29 September, B told JM the circumstances of the poem's composition adding: 'I did as well as I could – but where I have not my choice – I pretend to answer for nothing'; he received his copy of the poem the next day (Monday 30 September) (*BLJ* V, 106 and 107).

9. John Hookham Frere married Jemima Elizabeth, Dowager Countess of Erroll, in the morning of the day of this letter (W. E. and Sir Bartle Frere,

The Works of John Hookham Frere, in Verse and Prose ... with a prefatory Memoir, 2 vols [1872], I, clv). JM told this story just as entertainingly to Sir James Mackintosh in his letter of this same day (BL Add. 52452, ff. 219–20). The 'truly Original poem of his own' was almost certainly *Whistlecraft*, published by JM in 1817 (see Letter 109, n. 17 below).

10. Henry Brougham (who was actually in Switzerland at the same time as B and spreading gossip about him) was having an affair with Mrs George Lamb ('Caro George' of the Devonshire House set); it did not come before the courts, but it did do him considerable political damage.

11. Gifford's *The Works of Ben Jonson, In Nine Volumes. With Notes Critical and Explanatory, and a Biographical Memoir* was published jointly by JM and others in 1816.

12. That is the *Quarterly Review*; James Perry was the editor of the *Morning Chronicle*.

13. Georgiana, Augusta's eldest daughter and B's favourite niece, was eight years old.

14. B's daughter Ada, whom he had last seen in January and was never to see again, was now nine months old. B had been anxious about Annabella's health ever since he had first heard of her 'illness' in late August (see *BLJ* V, 87–88; see also, 'Lines On Hearing That Lady Byron Was Ill' [*CPW* IV, 43–45]). In his letter of Wednesday 11 September, Shelley also told B: 'Murray tells me that Lady Byron is in London, and that her health has materially improved' (Shelley, *Letters*, I, 505).

Letter 90)   Friday 20 September 1816

London Sepr. 20 – 1816
Friday

My Lord

As soon as I had read the third Canto <myself> of Childe Harold myself I made no hesitation in telling Mr Kinnaird that I should make my Offer Fifteen Hundred Guineas – but he has called today to say that Two Thousand are expected by your Lordships friends – I told him that hitherto I believed that no one had impugned my estimations, and that with regard to your Lordship I had no other feeling that [*sic*] a desire to give all that was possible <&> – on the present occasion I thought I had anticipated any notions and that I suspected it be rather from my own data than from fair estimation that this extra demand was put upon me.[1] The Poem however is so much beyond any thing in Modern days that I may be out in my Calculation – it requires an etherial mind like its Authors to cope with it – he was so obliging as to wish the addition [sic] 500£ eventual but I have preferred to settle it at once at the £2100 – and now the Lord (Not you) have Mercy upon me[2] – It appears to me that you have compleatly distanced every Modern Poet & when I read you I wander in the regions of Spencer [sic] Milton or Shakespeare – it really [sic] a Triumph over the whole world which I do from my heart glory in, & congratulate you upon. Remember I do stipulate for All the MSS Original, Copies, or Scraps.[3]

I am thinking more seriously than ever of establishing a Monthly Literary Journal and am promised the Contributions of the greater Characters here & if I succeed I will venture to solicit the favour of your powerful Assistance in the shape of Letters, Essays, Characters Facts Travels Epigrams & other, to you, small Shot, & to entreat <that> the favour of your influence amongst your friends – every One can communicate something, fact – or perhaps some curious Letter &c.[4]

I heartily wish your Lordship joy of this production of your intellect – and with best compliments, I remain

My Lord
Your faithful Servant
John Murray

When I know exactly where you are I will send the Proofs to you[5] – I have already set up Canto 3 – wch is this day gone to Mr G. whose Second reading only confirms the first.

I offer my best comp^s to Mr Hobhouse & Mr Davies – the latter of whom I look for every day[6]

Notes to Letter 90)

Cover: The R^t Honble/Lord Byron/Diodati/Genéve

Between Letter 89 above and the present Letter (90), JM had sent the third Canto of CHP to Croker from whom he had received the following reply, dated 18 September 1816 from the Admiralty, which is in MA (cf. Louis J. Jennings, ed., *The Croker Papers. The Correspondence and Diaries of the late Right Honourable John Wilson Croker*, 3 vols [London: John Murray, 1884], I, 94–95). The objection Croker raises in this letter to the 'two or three lines of prose' reflecting on the Bourbon family, almost certainly refers to B's original note to CHP III, 82, line 777, which note was omitted by JM – almost as certainly on account of Croker's objection (see CPW II, 310, and Letter 95 and n.2 thereto below).

My dear Murray –
I have read with great pleasure the poem you lent me; It is written with great vigor & all the descriptive part is peculiarly to

my taste, for I am fond of <u>realities</u>, even to the extent of being fond of <u>localities</u> – a spot of ground a yard square, a rock, or hillock, on which some great atchievement [*sic*] has been perform'd or to which any recollections of interest attach, incite my feelings more than all the monuments of art. Pictures fade & statues moulder & forests decay & cities perish, but the sod of Marathon is immortal & he who has had the good fortune to stand on that spot has identified himself with Athenian story in a way which all the historians – painters & poets of the world could not have accomplish'd for him. Shakespeare, whom nothing escaped, very justly hints that one the highest offices of good poetry is to connect our ideas with some "local habitation." [*A Midsummer Night's Dream*, V, I, 17] It is an old & mighty absurd phrase to say that poetry deals in fiction; alas, <u>history</u> I fear, deals in fiction; but good poetry is concern'd only with <u>realities</u> either of visible or moral nature – and so much for local poetry – but I did not read with equal pleasure a note or two which reflects on the Bourbon family; what has a poet who writes for immortality to do with the little temporary passions of political parties? such notes are like Pope's "flies in amber" [*Epistle to Dr. Arbuthnot*, 169–70]. I wish you could persuade Lord Byron to leave out these two or three lines of prose which will make thousands dissatisfied with his glorious poetry. for my own part, I am not a man of <tit> rank & family & have not therefore such motives for respecting rank & family, as Lord Byron has, yet I own (however I may disapprove & lament much of what is going on in France) that I could not bring myself to speak irreverently of the Children of St Louis, of, assuredly the most ancient and Splendid family of the Civilised world, of a house which is connected with the whole system of European policy, European literature, European refine-ment & I will add, European Glory. My love of realities comes in here again & I say to myself when I see Louis the 18th overlooking all his personal qualities here is the lineal descendant of fifty Kings; all famous, many illustrious; men who have held in their hands from <father to son> age to age, the destinies of millions; some of whom have been the benefactors of mankind, & others (& this part of the recollection is not the least <u>interesting</u>) who have astonished & afflicted the world by their crimes. No; Pray, use your influence, on this point – as to the poem itself, except a word or two suggested by Mr Gifford, I do not think any thing can be alter'd for the better –
    Yours faithfully
    JW Croker

  1. Writing to B on Friday 13 September, Kinnaird told him: 'Gifford has read & pronounc'd your new canto to be better than any thing you have yet written – Murray proposes 1500 guineas for the two Poems – Shall I say satis [i.e.,

enough]? He will pay the money down' (MA). On Sunday 29 September, however, Shelley wrote with superb sangfroid: 'You are to receive 2,000 guineas. There was no objection made on Murray's [*sic*], though there was a trifling mistake arising from his believing that he could get it for 1,200, which was no sooner made than obviated' (Shelley, *Letters*, I, 506). See also, Letter 89, nn. 4 and 6 above.

2. JM echoes the general Confession and the responses in the Communion service ('Lord, have mercy upon us'). In his reply of Sunday 29 September, B told JM he agreed with Kinnaird 'perfectly that the concluding *five hundred* should be only *conditional*' (on how well sales prospered), and reiterated this the same day in his letter to Kinnaird (*BLJ* V, 106).

3. In his reply of Monday 30 September, B said: 'You want the original M.S.S – Mr. Davies has the first fair copy in my own hand – & I have the rough composition here – and will send or save it for you since you wish it' (*BLJ* V, 108). This lost 'first fair copy' first came to light in 1976, discovered in an old trunk of Scrope Davies in the vaults of Barclays Bank, Pall Mall. For a facsimile edition of it, see *The Manuscripts of the Younger Romantics: Lord Byron. Vol. VII: Childe Harold's Pilgrimage, Canto III. A Facsimile of the Autograph Fair Copy Found in the 'Scrope Davies' Notebook*, ed. T. A. J. Burnett (New York & London: Garland Publishing, 1988); for a facsimile of the 'rough composition', see Erdman and Worrall, *The Manuscripts of the Younger Romantics*, 163–287. See also, Letter 92, n. 22 below)

4. JM had, in fact, been eager to establish such a monthly literary journal as early as 1806 with the poet Thomas Campbell as editor, but it came to nothing then or now – nor a year later (see Smiles, I, 323–25 and 475, and II, 64–68). None the less, in his reply of Monday 30 September, B promised to send JM anything he thought suitable (*BLJ* V, 108).

5. Writing to JM on Saturday 5 October, B told him: 'I do not want to see proofs – if Mr. G[ifford] will have the goodness to look over them' (*BLJ* V, 111).

6. Scrope had set out for England again on Thursday 5 September, carrying among other valuable items the 'fair copy' MS of *CHP* III (see n. 3 above). In his letter of Saturday 5 October, B told JM he was 'a good deal surprized that Mr. Davies has not arrived'; but by Wednesday 9 October he had heard he had, and instructed JM: 'he brings the original M.S. which you wished to see. – Recollect that the printing is to be from that which Mr. Shelley brought' (*BLJ* V, 110 and 113). Scrope duly showed the 'fair copy' to JM, but by then the Canto had been set up in type and JM returned it to him. For further details, see *CPW* II, 297–99, and T. A. J. Burnett, *The Rise and Fall of a Regency Dandy: The Life and Times of Scrope Berdmore Davies* (London: John Murray, 1981), 125–31 and 202–03.

Letter 91)   [Friday] 13 December 1816

London 13th. Decr. 1816

My Lord

I do believe that if all the instances of your indulgent kindness were put together they could not excite in me a greater obligation than I feel for the extreme forbearance exhibited in your Letter of the 25th ult. received this day – I expected a Shot from you that would have shivered all my nerves in return for my baseness in not answering your many most obliging and delightful Letters.[1] And instead of it you have amused me beyond measure with the Account of Venice, Juliet – the Capulets and the Bust[2] – but what is even this – the Marble Helen to the One capable of "Discernment" through animated "Oriental Eyes"[3] – By Heavens – if it be not profane to use the word – thou art squeesing [sic] out the very Life of Life – and wouldst make <we> us inferior <men> petty men believe that there never was any thing in the Rhind [sic] which you describe & fling to us[4] – Who would not endure thy fancied Pains for all thy delicious enjoyments – you who do what all so wish – but<t> want the power to do – We wonder & wonder & wonder but we have not the same creative powers of enjoyment which you possess – & our case is hopeless – even if the means of applying them were before us – here ends my phylosophy [sic] – but I admire, & delight in your genius for Pleasure in every shape and wish you the perpetuity of St Leon – to pursue its operations.[5]

Well you are so much in Love – that you will not condesend [sic] to think of Poetry – merely because all the world here are thinking of nothing else (the Shadow for the Substance) – I did not care to write to you until I could ascertain the opinions of the knowing ones respecting a recent publication of mine – entitled C. H<ar>. Canto III which has drawn the leaders of all our literary forces together in Consultation and they have determined – that this, alone, must have ensured the Author preeminent fame (Poetical, I mean) which had already been assigned to him, and this being allowed, it follows that it is in fact superior to his other efforts, by which a writer is always sure to be tried.[6] It is allowed that there are Stanzas in it equal to any thing that has been written & Mr Frere, in a Letter to me adds "to any thing either Antient or Modern – as applied to the Stanzas on Waterloo[7] – The Dream is also considered of the same high class – the Dream has created a division but the ayes are the majority – Kinnaird has had the cruelty read [sic] Ladies into Hysterics by it – I hope he had not the wickedness to take any naughty advantage of his art. Chillon in parts very fine – the Incantation fine[8]

– but then to the Practical Proof of this Summary – I thy Most faithful
Publisher, gave his Bretheren [sic] 99 in it earlier a dinner at the
Albion & sold them after the first Pint Five Thousand Pounds Worth
of thy Poetry[9] including 1,500 of the Works now 5̲ Vols <(but not>
1,800 Vol 5 separate (not̲ containing Childe H Canto 3 &c)[10] and 7,000
of C. Harold Canto 3 – & 7,000 of Prisoner of Chillon &c – for your
Lordship must know & will I trust excuse, that the auri sacra Fames[11]
induced me to divide the Works you sent me into two brochures at 5/6
each – to ensure my Pelf – & thy popularity – and so my speculation
will not fail – although your Lordships kind anxiety shall be gratefully
remembered.[12] – I have had a tremendous fight with a dirty Villain who
availing himself of the announcement of some New Poems advertised
vehemently that he would Publish "Lord Byrons Pilgrimage to the Holy
Land" and the "Tempest" – to the which I ventured to announce the
falsity – that mine was the real Simon Pure – the very next day the
fellow inserted an advertisement, cautiously worded, but insinuating
stoutly – the [sic] He had received these Poems from the Noble Author
& had paid for them Five Hundred Pounds!!!![13] an inuendo [sic] which Job
never contemplated[14] – However with the asstance [sic] of Mr S. Davies's
Oath accompanied by one from myself I tried the Lord Chancellor &
aided by the Literary recollections of Sir S. Romilly respecting Pope
& his annoyer Curl [sic] – we succeeded in obtaining an injunction
– which has operated very favourably in putting an end to his trash – &
in making known my Poems[15] – We must now think of prosecuting him
for damages – as a punishment & if any be obtained it may be sent to the
Middlesex Lying-in-Hospital whose funds, in consequence of so many
Gentlemen having returned to [sic] the Wars, is [sic] nearly exhausted. At
any rate I will prepare a power of Attorney enabling some one whom
your Lordship may choose to deligate [sic] – this shall be sent instantly
now that I know where to direct my Arrow.[16]

    <I h>In Literary Affairs I have taken the field in great Force Opening
with The Third Canto & Chillon – and, following up my blow, I have
since published Tales of My Landlord another Novel I believe but I
really dont know by the Author of Waverley &c – but excepting the
Character of Meg Meriles [sic] – much superior – every One is in extacy
[sic] about it – & I would give a finger if I could send it to you – but
this I will "contrive"[17] – Conversations with your friend Buonaparte
at St Helena – amusing but scarce worth sending[18] – – Ld Holland has
just put forth a very improved Edit [sic] of the Life of Lope de Vega &
de Castro[19] – Giffords Ben Jonson has put to death all former Critics
& is very much liked – you would like it greatly – The Faro-Table of
Tobin has been acted & successfully but it is very paltry – made up of

the School for Scandal[20] – Mr Legh an MP's accnt [sic] of his Travels contains a very remarable [sic] & well told incident wch would amuse you[21] – We have Letters coming out from Hume – Chesterfield – & Franklin wch may produce some <un> information[22] – Moore's Poem – to be in the press in February – so tells me its author[23] – I have a Poem, or rather one is coming to me by an Obscure Author on Paris[24] – which I am assured contains some very powerful passages indeed – this <g>Gifford allows – who by the way wants very much that you would give him a Carte Blanche respecting the Siege of Corinth – parts of which he abuses vehemently[25] – though I assure you he speaks with admiration of its author everywhere – indeed you could not stand better in Literary Fame wch has extinguished every other feeling, but an anxious desire to read more of you – <Poo> Mr K. has been ejected from Drury Lane – to his no small annoyance – this comes of quarrelling with a Woman[26] – Poor Semple whom you knew a Little of – has been killed in an Affray in Hudsons Bay – of wch he went out Gouverner [sic].[27] I pray your Lordship to let me know if I can, in any way, be made useful to you here – & I entreat you to honour me with a Letter as often as you can – I beg you to observe that I calculate on Canto IV by September Next[28] – the Scrap of your Journal delighted me – there is a poem in it[29] – Scott is writing the Hist^y of Scotland[30] – I beg my best remembrance to Mr Hobhouse[31] – from whom I hope to get the Prose Cantos of your joint-progresses. I am ever My Lord
    Your faithfully attached
    Servt J. M.

[On outside back cover:] This moment received what I suppose to be a Copy of Lope de Vega – for you – from the Noble author[32]

Notes to Letter 91)

Cover: a My Lord/My Lord Byron/Poste restant/a Venise/En Italie

1. By this time B had left Diodati and, having travelled with Hobhouse via Milan, Verona and Vicenza, had arrived in Venice on Sunday 10 November, whence he wrote to JM on Monday 25 November saying that it was 'some months since I have heard from or of you – I think – *not* since I left Diodati' (*BLJ* V, 132). In fact JM's last letter was Letter 90 above, since receiving which B had written no less than eight times, and was to write another four times before receiving this letter (91) (see *BLJ* V, 105–53).

2. B related these details in his letter of Monday 25 November: the 'Bust' was the '*Helen* of Canova', which B had seen at Countess d'Albrizzi's and upon

which he had written his lines opening 'In this beloved marble view' (a copy of which he also enclosed to JM – hence his 'Marble Helen') (*BLJ* V, 132–33). B had sent an earlier copy of the lines to Hobhouse, who drafted a Latin translation of them on the back of B's letter enclosing them (*BLJ* V, 132, and BL Add. 42093, f. 4*v*; cf. *CPW* IV, 461).

3. In his letter, B informed JM that he had fallen in love 'with the wife of a "Merchant of Venice"', who had 'large black Oriental eyes', besides other 'graces – virtues and accomplishments', and whose 'great merit' was finding out his, adding: 'there is nothing so amiable as discernment' (*BLJ* V, 133–34). This was Marianna Segati whose husband was a draper.

4. JM's erasures here suggest he has in mind Cassius's lines: 'Why, man, he doth bestride the narrow world/Like a Colossus, and we petty men/Walk under his huge legs, and peep about/To find ourselves dishonourable graves' (*Julius Caesar*, I, ii, 135–38).

5. JM alludes (a little tactlessly) to Godwin's *St. Leon* (1799), the third edition of which was published in December 1816, whose eponymous hero, having ruined himself and his family, is introduced to the mysteries of the philosopher's stone and the *elixir vitae* and is gifted with inexhaustible wealth and eternal life at the expense of personal and domestic happiness.

6. In his letter, B had said rather casually: 'Of the M.S. sent you I know nothing except that you have received it – & are to publish it &c. &c. but when – where – & how – you leave me to guess' (*BLJ* V, 134). Although JM does not expressly say so, *CHP* III had been published on Monday 18 November, and *The Prisoner of Chillon and Other Poems* on Thursday 5 December 1816. In his reply, B was gravely concerned with whether JM had '*omitted* any passage or passages', and bade him tell him in his next 'whether or not the *whole* of the Canto (as sent to you) has been published' (*BLJ* V, 154; see Letter 92 below).

7. Specifically, *CHP* III, 17–31.

8. 'The Dream' was included in *The Prisoner of Chillon and Other Poems*, as was 'The Incantation', which was later incorporated into *Manfred* (see *CPW* VII, 90–92 and 155).

9. This was one of JM's sales to the trade dinners that he held at the Albion Tavern, No. 153 Aldersgate Street. On these occasions, 'books and copyrights, and especially shares in book publication, were sold to the trade, chiefly in London. The custom was introduced from the Continent in 1676. In 1872, Longmans held their last book sale, and John Murray held his last in 1887. The last of them was Bentley's, in 1898' (Septimus Rivington, *The Publishing Family of Rivington* [London, 1919], 20). The figures for both the sales and persons present are no exaggeration. On another occasion Joseph Farington records in his Diary for Friday 19 February 1819 that, 'at a late Book sale of His publications, Murray sold Books to the amount of £16,000.

– Rogers's new poem *"Human Life"* [1819] the whole *Edition* is sold, though only just published'; and in his Diary for Saturday 27 December 1817, that at a similar *'Book sale to the Trade'* given by Caddell and Davies at the London Coffee House, which lasted three days, and was 'an old custom with them & other wholesale Booksellers': 'On the first day more than 120 Booksellers sat down to dinner & on the following days more than 90 each day, an unusual day. – After dinner the sale takes place. Catalogues of the Books to be sold with prices affixed are circulated round the table & each person puts down His name for whatever number of each Author He chooses to purchase' (*The Diary of Joseph Farington*, ed. Kathryn Cave [1984], XIV, 5129 and XV, 5328). See also, Smiles, II, 516–17, F. Espinasse, 'The House of Murray', *Harper's New Monthly Magazine*, LXXI, ccccxxiv (September 1885), 518, and Henry B. Wheatley, *London Past and Present* 3 vols (London: John Murray, 1891), I, 19–20.

10. *The Works of The Right Honourable Lord Byron. In Five Volumes* (1817), vol. V of which contained *The Siege of Corinth, Parisina* and other poems and was published on Friday 6 December 1816. This edition did not include *CHP* III or any of the poems in *The Prisoner of Chillon and Other Poems*, which JM issued in two separate 'brochures' as he calls them.

11. *auri sacra fames*: 'the accursed lust of gold' (Virgil, *Aeneid*, III, 57).

12. B's 'kind anxiety' was his making 'the concluding *five hundred ... conditional'* upon the sale of the poems (*BLJ* V, 106; see Letter 90, n. 2 above).

13. The 'dirty Villain' was J. Johnston of Cheapside, who had advertised the forthcoming publication of *The Right Honourable Lord Byron's Pilgrimage to the Holy Land; to which is added, The Tempest*, and other works purporting to be by B in both the *Courier* and the *Morning Chronicle* for Friday 8 November 1816. A week later, in the *Morning Chronicle* for Friday 15 November, he announced that these would be ready the following Wednesday, adding that 'the Copyright of this Work was consigned to him by the Noble Author himself, and for which he gives FIVE HUNDRED GUINEAS.' Beneath this on the same day appeared JM's announcement that such poems were not written by B and that he was the 'only Bookseller at present authorized to print Lord Byron's Poems' (see n. 15 below). In fact B had heard about this earlier from Shelley and had already written to JM twice to urge 'the most public and unqualified contradiction' (*BLJ* V, 138–39 and 151; see also, Shelley, *Letters*, I, 513, and see n. 15 below).

14. JM refers wittily both to Job's proverbial patience and to his wish 'that mine adversary had written a book' (Job 31.35), to which B himself had alluded in his letter to him of Monday 22 July 1816 (*BLJ* V, 84–85).

15. The case of Lord Byron vs. James Johnston came before the Lord Chancellor (Lord Eldon) in the Court of Chancery on Thursday 28 November, when 'Sir Samuel Romilly moved for an Injunction on the part of the Noble

Plaintiff, to restrain the Defendant from publishing a spurious edition of his Works': the Injunction was granted (*Morning Chronicle*, Saturday 30 November 1816). Among other literary precedents to which Romilly referred was that of Pope and the bookseller Edmund Curll (1683–1747); he also produced Scrope Davies's affidavit in support of JM's claim. In a letter to Kinnaird of Sunday 12 January 1817, B wrote wryly that he 'would give a trifle to see Scrope's affidavit' (see *BLJ* V, 159).

16. B was to delegate such matters to Kinnaird (see *BLJ* V, 268, and Letter 107, n. 14 below). Without wishing to spoil JM's little joke here, the Middlesex Hospital, situated as now at the top of Berners Street, was, according to the London Medical Directory, 'second to none in the kingdom', and had 'no lack of any thing but plenteous funds'. But it was not a Lying-in hospital. There were four of these, the Queen's Lying-in Hospital in Lisson Green, founded in 1794, being the only one 'intended greatly for the reception of the wives of soldiers' (*Authentic Memoirs ... of the Most Eminent Physicians and Surgeons of Great Britain; with ... An Account of the Medical Charities of the Metropolis. Second Edition, Enlarged* [London, 1818], l and lvi; see also, B. Lambert, *The History and Survey of London and its Environs*, 4 vols [London, 1806], IV, 9–10).

17. The first of Scott's pseudonymous *Tales of My Landlord*, containing *The Black Dwarf* and *Old Mortality*, was published in 4 vols by JM and Blackwood in December 1816. JM did '"contrive"' to send them, but they did not reach B till May 1817 (see *post*, and *BLJ* V, 220). Meg Merrilies is the striking character in Scott's *Guy Mannering* (1815) (see Letters 64 and 65 above).

18. William Warden's *A Series of Letters, written on board his Majesty's ship the Northumberland, and at St. Helena; in which the Conduct and Conversations of Napoleon, and his Suite, during the Voyage, and the First Months of his Residence in that Island, are faithfully described and related* was published in November 1816. Evidently JM did think them 'worth sending', as B had a copy (see *CMP*, 253, lot 194; see also, 250, lot 124: *Letters from the Cape of Good Hope in Reply to Mr. Warden* [1817]).

19. Lord Holland's *Some Account of the Life and Writings of Lope Felix de Vega Carpio* had first appeared anonymously in 1807; his 'improved' edition was *Some Account of the Lives and Writings of Lope Felix de Vega Carpio, and Guillen de Castro*, 2 vols (1817), of which B possessed a presentation copy (*CMP*, 249, lot 93). See n. 32 below.

20. For 'Giffords Ben Jonson', see Letter 89, n. 11 above. John Tobin's *The Faro Table; or, The Guardians. A Comedy* was performed at the Drury Lane Theatre on Tuesday 5 November and published by JM the same month. *The Times* for Wednesday 6 November did not think the author 'drew upon his genius for much original matter'; many features 'were, if not borrowed, adapted from the pens of others'.

21. *Narrative of a Journey in Egypt and the Country Beyond the Cataracts*, by Thomas Legh, Esq. M.P., was published by JM in December 1816. JM probably refers to a grisly adventure recounted in chapter III (pp. 111–23) when some of the party were asphyxiated in the treacherous mummy pits at Amabdi.

22. *The Private Correspondence of David Hume with several distinguished persons between the years 1761 and 1776* (1820) (see *CMP*, 254, lot 213); *Letters Written by The Right Honorable Philip Dormer Stanhope, Earl of Chesterfield, to Arthur Charles Stanhope, Esq. relative to the Education of his Lordship's Godson, Philip, the Late Earl* (1817); W. T. Franklin, *The Private Correspondence of Benjamin Franklin*, 2 vols (1817).

23. Moore had written to JM on 21 November 1816 asking him to send B's new works and adding 'I shall go to Press, I think, about the end of February' (Moore, *Letters*, I, 406). Writing to Moore on Tuesday 28 January 1817, B said he rejoiced to hear 'of your forthcoming in February' (*BLJ* V, 165); but in fact *Lalla Rookh* was not published by Longman until the end of May 1817.

24. This was the Rev. George Croly (1780–1860), 'Cambyses Croly', as B was to dub him in *DJ* XI, 57, whose *Paris in 1815. A Poem* was published by JM in 1817 and favourably reviewed by Croker in the *Quarterly Review*, XVII, xxxiii (April 1817), 218–29. See also, Letter 140, n. 17 below.

25. B replied: 'If Mr. G[ifford] wants Carte blanche as to the "Siege of Corinth" – he has it – & may do as he likes with it' (*BLJ* V, 157–58; see also, *CPW* III, 479, 481 and 485–87).

26. Kinnaird had resigned from the Drury Lane Theatre Subcommittee, which B told him required 'no great sagacity to attribute to the illustrious Frances Kelly of comic memory' (*BLJ* V, 158).

27. Robert Semple (1766–1816), traveller and author, had been sent out under the auspices of the Hudson Bay Company as Governor of the Red River Colony in Canada and had been massacred with his party in a territorial dispute with the North-West Company in June 1816. B did know him slightly (see *BLJ* III, 195).

28. B replied: 'the truth is that you are *afraid* of having a *4th*. Canto *before* September – & of another copyright – but I have at present no thoughts of resuming that poem nor of beginning any other' (*BLJ* V, 157; see Letter 92 below).

29. B had sent Augusta the Alpine Journal he had kept for her in September, telling JM on Monday 30 September he had done so but that it was 'not at all for perusal – but if you like to hear about the romantic part – she will I dare say show you what touches upon the rocks &c.' (*BLJ* V, 108). There was indeed 'a poem in it': *Manfred*, but JM did not know that yet.

30. Scott's *The History of Scotland* was eventually published in 2 vols in 1829 and 1830.

31. By this time Hobhouse had left B for a tour of Italy from which he did not
    return to Venice until the end of July 1817.

32. This postscript is written on the outside back cover after sealing. See n. 19
    above; B still had not received this by 4 April when he asked Rogers to
    thank Lord Holland for it none the less (*BLJ* V, 206; see also, Letter 92).

Letter 92)   Wednesday 22 January 1817

London 22nd Jany. 1817
Wednesday

My Lord

This is your birth day[1] and it is with feelings of the most sincere
friendship rather than from motives of interest that I rejoice in the
renewal of an event which has so largely contributed to my own
happiness & honour <and> as well as worldly advantage. Upon
the present occasion I feel <u>most</u> particularly grateful for the marked
confidence which I have received from you in the many kind &
interesting Letters with which your Lordship has favoured me during
your absence notwithstanding my tardiness to acknowledge the pleasure
which they have invariably afforded me – <n>in no small degree
heightened by the opportunity which you have also afforded me of
reading them under your Lordships own Portrait. – May you see many
truly happy returns of this day.

I have received all your Lordships Letters – the last dated Jany 2^d. the
former one, respecting the rogue in Cheapside, my legal success against
him, had anticipated in a way that was I trust satisfactory.[2] I sent to you
through the Foreign Office a Copy of all your recent Poems – that your
Lordship might make any corrections for a new Edition – I left out <u>only</u>
a note in Lines 18 [*sic*] – & a line [*sic*] in Chillon – because as [*sic*] I had
a great stake in the <first> instant Popularity of their publication at my
paying this natural regard to my own interest – and they will be
restored in a new Edition[3] – abstractedly [*sic*] from this I can honestly
say that both Mr Gifford & myself were convinced that their omission
could not be felt: but as I have just observed I did this purely for my
own interest – these passages picked out by malicious people would have
damped my first sale – so I entreat your Lordship to consider your
publisher & to be pacified. – At the time I sent your Lordship the Copy
of your Poems – I added a Set of "<u>Tales of my Landlord</u>" which I think
I spoke to you about in my Last, as a production of the same author as
Waverley &c but infinitely surpassing either [*sic*][4] – indeed I continue to

consider this work as one of the most wonderful of my time – perfectly
Shakespearean – and I flatter myself that your delight at receiving it will
compleatly overbalance your momentary rage at omitting a line. – I
forgot to observe that the Poem which is left out was done so by your
Editor who did not think it worthy of the rest[5] – and I beg you to
confide honestly in M[r] G – who is really your faithful friend and honest
monitor – as well as your earliest and firmest admirer – therefore trust
boldly to us – I am sure that the person who was to have been your
supervisor is a perfect <wreth> wretch – without any homogenious [*sic*]
qualities to compensate.[6] – but I am running from my subject – which
was the Tales – and moreover their author – whom I have discovered to
be Thomas Scott – Walter Scotts brother – he was Bailiff to Lord
Somerville – formerly and could not make up his accounts – ever since
he has been confined to the Isle of Man – until lately that [*sic*] they
have transported him to America – Canada – Scott did much to
Waverly [*sic*] in adding Anecdotes &c which occasioned many who had
heard these told by Scott himself, perfectly certain that he was the
author – but – though I can not here <tell your Lord> detail all my
grounds of reason for determining the certainty of this I venture to
pledge myself that your Lordship may rely upon the fact.[7] We have had
little else in Literature of a value or interest that should occasion any
regret at your Lordships privation. I am continually harrassed [*sic*] by
Shoals of MSS Poems – Two three four a day – I require a Porter to
carry – an Author to read – and a secretary to write about – them –
Maturin you will have heard from M[r] Kinnaird – has written two acts
of a New Tragedy[8] – wch I think they are spoiling by sending him
criticisms in limine[9] – instead of encouraging the whole scope of his
mind to spread out to its compleation – & then introducing the pruning
knife – – Schill [*sic*] another Irishman the Author of Adelaide
exceedingly applauded in Dublin but "hastily damned in London –
which a favourable wind by detaining the author one day longer at sea,
prevented him from witnessing – for he arrived the night after – tells
me that he has another in rehearsal wch is to be produced a [*sic*] Covent
Garden in a Month – entitled the Apostate[10] – I <have> am just about
to publish a strange political Rhapsody – by Lord Erskine – entitled
Armata – describing our constitution under a feigned name[11] – "damn
them" (says the author [*sic*] I'll show the world that I am not in my
dotage yet – What the Devils all this cries Frere taking up some sheets
of the said – Oh something that Murray is publishing – says Gifford –
Not upon his own account replies Frere – By the way Frere, who
always remembers you with honour, (& I told you before what he wrote
about the 3[d] Canto) likes very much the Armenian Grammar[12] – though

he would – prefer the English part of it. He wishes me to send you Mitford on the harmony of Languages wch I will do[13] – he says that the Type is not so large as it ought to be for a language which is not to be whipped into one – but that we should be coaxed into by the most enticing appearances – I will most willingly take 50 Copies even upon my love of letters – so they may be sent as soon as compleated[14] – We are all much interested with "the very curious books and MSS <u>chiefly translations from Greek originals now lost</u>" and I am desired to entreat that your Lordship will gain every particular respecting their history & Contents together with the best account of the Armenian Language which may form a very interesting introduction to the Copies which you send here – and which preface I will print myself – unless as a curiosity you print this there also – or if you would review the Grammar for me and insert all this knowledge in the article – which would certainly be the very best way of making the grammar known to the public. I wish besides obliging me with such a curious and interesting critique – that your Lordship would unknown even to thy bosom friend Hobhouse (to whom I beg to repeat my kindest remembrances [sic], attempt some work in prose, which I will engage to keep sacredly secret, and publish anonymously. I beg your Lordship to be perfectly assured that I am perfectly ready to undergo the Copyright of as many Cantos of Childe Harold – or any other Poem – as fast as they are compleated to your own entire satisfaction – but remember we have got to heap Ossa on Pelion – the higher the pile already – the far greater our future labour.[15] – I forgot to mention above that I have as yet ascertained only that there are no Armenian Types at Cambridge – in my next I will know with regard to this matter at Oxford – – If you can pick up at Venice a 4to entitled L' Istoria di Verona del Sig. Girolamo" [sic] – Verona 1594 you will find at page 589 – the Story of the Montagues & Capulets given historically – and related with great beauty & interest – Mr Kinnaird lent me the Volume to copy this for you but I have no amanuensis sufficiently literary & I think it likely that you may pick up the book at Venice[16] – pray keep an exact Journal of all you see or write me faithful accounts of sights, curiosities, Shows Manners &c – I will use nothing without your positive permission. – We had a quizzing Article on Wed. Webster – who has replied through the M. Chronicle in a Letter to Mr Gifford which he concludes by leaving him with "<u>feelings</u> of contempt and <u>Oblivion</u>"[17] – I am sorry that Mr Hobhouse is answering also – a man has no chance against an Army – & he should have laughed – he who quizzes others must calculate upon being quizzed himself – and I really esteem Mr Hobhouse & wish he had not done this.[18] I would <u>pay</u> any one to write

against me – In a few days I shall send you our Article on the Third
Canto – you will not have occasion to answer that[19] – <The> An
Edinburgh has not come out since the publication of your Poems – their
article on Coleridge was <u>base</u> – after what had passed between you &
the Editor[20] – Mr Gordon has carefully deposited your Spoils of
Waterloo – which ornament my Room – as the best & indeed only
means I have of preserving them for you – G – is a good creature but
his deafness is a most cruel & annoying drawback[21] – The MSS &
Bones have not appeared[22] – and I will write about them – I forward
your Letters carefully to Moore & to Mrs Leigh for whom I forwarded
one to you yesterday[23] – she is to be in town next week – Sir John
Malcolm is almost at Madras by this time[24] – he left <t>his sincere
good wishes for you – I let him read the MSS and he was in extacy [sic]
– All your old friends chez moi remember you & you are often the
subject of their conversation – as their eye catches yours in the Portrait
– which I am now facing & which is I assure you no small happiness to
me to possess – as it eternally renews the association of your <u>constancy</u>
to me – Lady — taking up the Waterloo Sword[25] – Oh – I wish I could
run it through his body – He is even yet I hope much more likely to
run your Ladyship through the body – <u>said</u> I. – You know that B— is
mad for love of M^rs L whom he has been pursuing through Italy[26] – I
am <sur>assured – without success – it has hurt his name, business – &
Character in Parliament. Sir Ja^s Mackintosh remembers you – I had a
Letter from Mr Ward to whom, at Paris, I sent the Poems & he is
delighted – and Mr Canning most particularly so with the 3rd Canto – I
now, this time print 10,000 of my Review – and you are in it.[27] – I
have the translation of a Chinese Comedy in the Press[28] – and of some
Tales by Antara – an hundred years previous to the conversion of the
Arabians to Mohamedanism [sic][29] – The Journal of Capt Tucker [sic]
who commanded the unfortunate expedition to Africa by the Congo –
<an>He & his officers died of fatigue & overexertion – but in all other
respect [sic] nothing could have been better planned or executed – and
the Journal is very interesting – this I will contrive to send you[30] – and
tho – not quite apropos – I may here say that I have procured the Tooth
Powder[31] – I think you should write me a <u>note</u> of thanks for Lord
Holland[32] – Your friend Sir James Burgess[33] with whom I dined
yesterday at Mr Crokers, often calls & talks to me about you – Walter
Scott always mentions you with kindness in his Letters – & he thinks
nothing better than Canto III[34] – – Give me a poem a good Venetian
Tale describing Manners formerly – from the Story itself – & now from
your own observations & call it – <u>Marianna</u>[35] – – I have ever loved –
upon my soul I believe so – by <u>Sympathy</u> all whom you have loved (in

<u>my</u> time) & so I venture to offer my Love to Marianna – can I give a
stronger assurance of my devotion to you My dear Lord whose faithful
servant I am <u>ever</u>

John Murray

Notes to Letter 92)

1. B was 29: I know of no other correspondent who thus touchingly remembered B's birthday.

2. For B's last letter of Thursday 2 January 1817, see *BLJ* V, 154–58; see also, Letter 91, nn. 13 and 15 above.

3. The parcel containing the poems had not arrived when B replied to this letter on Saturday 15 February 1817, so he did not 'exactly understand' what had been omitted and awaited clarification (*BLJ* V, 169; see Letter 95 below).

4. See Letter 91 above; strictly, 'all': *Waverley* (1814), *Guy Mannering* (1815) and *The Antiquary* (May, 1816).

5. See Letter 95 below.

6. This was Shelley, of whom JM seems to use the word 'homogenious' (homogeneous) in the unusual sense of 'befitting' or 'congruous'; 'sympathetic' or 'social' is perhaps what he means. (In the right-hand margin of the MS of this letter, interpolated between 'person' and 'who', someone – other than JM – has written an 'S'.)

7. JM told the same story to Blackwood (Smiles, I, 473–74), the only true part of which is that Scott's brother, Thomas, a solicitor and the steward of the Marquis of Abercorn (not Lord Somerville), had been found guilty of embezzlement, disqualified from practising, and had taken refuge from his creditors first in the Isle of Man and then in Canada.

8. Charles Robert Maturin's second play *Manuel; A Tragedy, In Five Acts*, a Gothic drama set in Spain, commissioned by Kean who acted the title-role, was first performed at Drury Lane Theatre on Saturday 8 March 1817 and ran for a further six nights. It was published by JM in 1817.

9. *in limine* = at the outset, on the threshold.

10. Richard Lalor Sheil's *Adelaide; or, The Emigrants: A Tragedy* was performed at Covent Garden on Thursday 23 May 1816 and was immediately withdrawn; his new play, *The Apostate, A Tragedy, In Five Acts*, was first performed at Covent Garden on Saturday 3 May 1817 and ran for a further six nights. It was published by JM in 1817. See also, Letter 103, n. 4 below.

11. Lord Erskine's *Armata: A Fragment*, an allegorical tale along the lines of *Gulliver's Travels*, was published by JM in February 1817.

12. See Letter 91 above, and n. 14 below.

13. William Mitford's *An Essay upon the Harmony of Language* (1774; 2nd enl. edn, 1804).

14. In his letter of Thursday 2 January, B sent JM 'some sheets of a grammar English & Armenian for the use of the Armenians' asking him whether he would take '40 or fifty copies' when it was printed. He also informed him of a forthcoming 'grammar for the *English* acquisition of Armenian' and enquired whether there were any '*Armenian types* or letter-press in England – at Oxford – Cambridge or elsewhere', adding: 'I can assure you that they have some very curious books & M.S. chiefly translations from Greek originals now lost' (*BLJ* V, 156–57). Although B did write a preface, it was not published during his lifetime. For further details, see *CMP*, 64–76 and 334–46 (esp. 338–39).

15. JM refutes B's charge of being '*afraid*' of another copyright (see Letter 91, n. 28 above); 'to heap (or pile) Ossa on Pelion' is proverbial from Virgil's account of the giants' attempt to scale the heavens (*Georgics*, I, 281: 'imponere Pelio Ossam').

16. In his letter of Monday 25 November 1816, B had expressed his surprise at the Veronese insistence on the historical truth of the story of Romeo and Juliet (*BLJ* V, 132). The events, described as having taken place in 1303, are related in *L'Istoria di Verona del Sig. Girolamo dalla Corte gentil' huomo Veronese, divisa in due parti, et in XXII Libri* (Verona, 1594), 589–95.

17. James Wedderburn Webster (B's friend and the husband of Lady Frances Webster), whose *Waterloo and Other Poems* (Paris, 1816) had been reviewed derisively by John Wilson Croker in the *Quarterly Review*, XV, xxx (July [pub. November] 1816), 345–50, replied with a long and angry letter to Gifford in the *Morning Chronicle* for Thursday 19 December 1816, in the course of which he stated that the article 'can create no feeling but disgust – and leave none but oblivion'.

18. Hobhouse's *The Substance of Some Letters Written by an Englishman Resident at Paris during the Last Reign of the Emperor Napoleon* was published anonymously in 2 vols in 1816, and was adversely reviewed by John Wilson Croker in the *Quarterly Review*, XIV, xxviii (January [pub. May] 1816), 443–52. Republishing the work as *The Substance of Some Letters Written from Paris during the Last Reign of the Emperor Napoleon; and addressed principally to The Right Hon. Lord Byron. By J. Hobhouse ... Second Edition, With Additional Notes, and a Prefatory Address* (1817), Hobhouse explained in his 'Prefatory Address', which is dated July 1816 and addressed to B, the significance of the altered the title and attacked with some venom the periodical and political principles of Gifford whom he mistakenly believed to be his reviewer. In his reply of Saturday 15 February 1817, B told JM that he knew little about the quarrel, though he had felt 'uneasy' and agreed that 'it would have been

better not to answer – particularly after Mr. W. W. who never more will trouble you – trouble you' (*BLJ* V, 169).

19. *CHP* III was very favourably reviewed by Scott in the *Quarterly Review*, XVI, xxxii (October 1816), 172–208. When B received it on Saturday 1 March 1817, he was overwhelmed by its 'generosity' (*BLJ* V, 178; see also, Letter 93 below).

20. Coleridge's *Christabel* and *Kubla Khan* were disgracefully reviewed in the *Edinburgh Review*, XXVII, liii (September 1816), 58–67, in the course of which the reviewer gibed twice at B for commending the poems (pp. 59 and 64). Shelley had already told B about this review when writing to him on 20 November 1816, but B himself had not yet seen it (Shelley, *Letters*, I, 514; see also, *BLJ* V, 150, 170 and 177). He had, however, as early as 28 October 1815, asked Moore to review the poems 'favourably' in the *Edinburgh Review*, as Coleridge was 'in distress' and praise would 'be the making of him' (*BLJ* IV, 324). But Moore did *not* write the review, though it continues to be ascribed to him despite all evidence to the contrary (see, for example, J. R. de J. Jackson, ed., *Coleridge: The Critical Heritage* [London: Routledge & Kegan Paul, 1970], 226–36; Rosemary Ashton, *The Life of Samuel Taylor Coleridge* [Oxford: Blackwell, 1996], 186 and 295; and Richard Holmes, *Coleridge: Darker Reflections* [London: Harper Collins, 1998], 438–40). Writing to Jeffrey on 23 May 1816, Moore told him: 'I had some idea of offering myself to you to quiz Christabel … but I have been lately told that Coleridge is poor – so poor as to be obliged to apply to the Literary Fund – and as this is no laughing matter – why – I shall let him alone'. Moore's informant was JM to whom he wrote on 24 December 1816: 'The article upon Coleridge in the Ed. Rev. was altogether disgraceful both from its dulness & illiberality – You know I had some idea of laughing at Christabel myself – but when you told me that Coleridge was very poor and had been to the Literary Fund, I thought this no laughing matter, and gave up my intention – I wonder much at Jeffrey letting that passage about Lord Byron appear' (Moore, *Letters*, I, 394–95 and n., and 407). The review is utterly humourless and almost gratuitously abusive, if not cruel, and it certainly does not smack of Moore's style: Moore would have laughed at the poem pleasantly and playfully, and the final paragraph in particular he would never have written (see also, Jeffery W. Vail, *The Literary Relationship of Lord Byron & Thomas Moore* [Baltimore and London: John Hopkins University Press, 2001], 192 and 230, n. 7).

21. After visiting Waterloo in May 1816 with Pryse Lockhart Gordon (1762–1845), an old friend of the Byron family living in Brussels, B wrote to Hobhouse that he had 'purchased a quantity of helmets sabres &c.' which Gordon would forward to JM for safe keeping (*BLJ* V, 76; see also, to JM, Thursday 27 June 1816, ibid., 82). In the event, it was his son, George Huntly Gordon (1796–1868), whose 'deafness' was a severe handicap, who undertook the consignment on his return from Brussels to Scotland where

he later became Scott's amanuensis (see Lockhart, *Life of Scott*, 675–78). In his reply to JM of Saturday 15 February 1817, B made him a present of the 'Waterloo spoils' (*BLJ* V, 169; see also, Letter 94 below, and Plate 11).

22. In his letter of Saturday 5 October 1816, B had informed JM that he had sent the 'rough original' MS of *CHP* III in a box addressed to Augusta, and a 'parcel containing the *Morat Bones* ... addressed to you' to his Swiss banker for Mr St Aubyn to forward to England (*BLJ* V, 110–11). Evidently concerned that they had not arrived, B replied on Friday 24 January 1817 instructing JM to enquire for St Aubyn who was 'of the university of Oxford, Son of Sir John St. Aubyn & lately travelling in Switzerland' (*BLJ* V, 163). James St Aubyn (1783–1862) was the eldest son of Sir John St Aubyn (1758–1839), MP and Sheriff of Cornwall who let Alfoxden to Wordsworth in 1797.

23. JM was the postman between B and many of his correspondents in England. B seems to have received Augusta's letter by Wednesday 19 February 1817 (see *BLJ* V, 170 and 175).

24. Sir John Malcolm set out reluctantly for Madras in October 1816 and did not in fact arrive until mid-March 1817 when he was appointed Brigadier in the army of the Deccan and took part in the Mahratta war of 1817–18.

25. This would have been Lady Caroline Lamb taking up one of the 'sabres' Gordon had deposited with JM (see n. 21 above).

26. Brougham and Mrs George Lamb (see Letter 89, n. 10 above).

27. See n. 19 above.

28. This was a comedy of domestic life entitled *Laou-Seng-Urh, or, "An Heir in his Old Age." A Chinese Drama* (by Hanchen Wu), prefaced by 'A Brief View of the Chinese Drama, and of their Theatrical Exhibitions', which JM published in 1817. It was translated by John Francis (later Sir John Francis) Davis (1795–1890), Chinese scholar of the East India Company in Canton, and was very favourably reviewed in the *Quarterly Review*, XVI, xxxii (January 1817), 396–416. JM was later to publish his *Chinese Novels, translated from the Originals: to which are added Proverbs and Moral Maxims, collected from their Classical Books and Other Sources. The Whole prefaced by Observations on the Language and Literature of China* (1822) and *Hien Wun Shoo. Chinese Moral Maxims* (1823).

29. *Antar, A Bedoueen Romance*, translated from the Arabic by Terrick Hamilton and published in 4 vols by JM in 1819–20, was a pre-Islamic chivalric epic narrating the deeds of the real poet-warrior Ali Absi Antarah ibn Shaddad (*fl.* 7th century). JM must have sent B a copy (see *CMP*, 246, lot 11).

30. *Narrative of an Expedition to explore the River Zaire, usually called the Congo, in South Africa, in 1816, under the direction of Captain J. K. Tuckey, R.N.*, edited by Sir John Barrow, was published by JM in 1818. Apparently JM did not 'contrive' to send it; it does not appear among B's books.

31. B does not appear to have asked JM to send him tooth powder (yet), but he had asked Hobhouse to bring with him 'some of Waite's *red* tooth-powder – & tooth-brushes' with him as early as June 1816 (*BLJ* V, 80).

32. B wrote via Rogers instead (see Letter 91, nn. 19 and 32 above).

33. Sir James Bland Burges (1752–1824), barrister and politician, was a friend of B's.

34. Scott had written to JM on 18 December 1816 saying: 'I have much to ask about Lord Byron if I had time. His third canto is inimitable ... I declare my heart bleeds when I think of him, self-banished from the country to which he is an honour'; and when sending his review on 10 January 1817 he said: 'If you think it like to hurt him either in his feelings or with the public in Gods name fling the sheets in the fire & let them be as *not written*. But if it appears I should wish him to get an early copy and that you would at the same time say I am the author at your importunity. No one can honor Lord Byrons poems more than I do and no one had so great a wish to love him personally though personally we had not the means of becoming very intimate' (Scott, *Letters*, IV, 319 and 365).

35. Upon this hint B spake: the result would be *Beppo*, composed in October 1817.

Letter 93)   [Friday] 7 February 1817

Albemarle tr [*sic*]
Feb. 7. 1817

My Lord

I have time only to write a few Lines with the inclosed Sheets wch may I not not [*sic*] dis-please you.[1] Mr Kinnaird has this moment popped in & tells me that you had not heard of the Poems wch vexes me much as I thought we had both told you of their Success – did I not give you the best practical critic<of>ism upon them – in the Account of my Sale[2] – no Review worth noticing has yet touched upon them[3] – Mrs Leigh is in town for the Drawing Room & I am to see her tomorrow.[4]

I hope your Lordship has received Tales of My Landlord – nothing but this & My Poems – have appeared this Season.

With best Compliments I am faithfully your Lordship's Servant.

Jno. Murray

Lords Grenville & Grey & the Whigs generally are differing[5]

Notes to Letter 93)

1. These were the 'Sheets' of Scott's review, which B received with the greatest 'gratification' on Saturday 1 March (*BLJ* V, 178; see also, Letter 92, n. 19 above, and Letter 94, n. 1 below).

2. Kinnaird would have received B's letter of Monday 20 January when B still knew nothing about the success or failure of his poems (*BLJ* V, 161). For the account of JM's '<u>Sale</u>', see Letter 91 above.

3. That is, neither the *Quarterly Review* (published Tuesday 11 February) nor the *Edinburgh Review* (published Friday 28 February) was yet out.

4. As one of Queen Charlotte's Ladies-in-Waiting, Augusta was in London to attend the 'Drawing Room' (formal reception) at St James's Palace to celebrate the Queen's official birthday (see Letter 94, n. 20 below).

5. It is rather extraordinary that JM should not have said what they were differing over: the Tory government's Bill to suspend Habeas Corpus currently under debate in Parliament with the Whig Lords divided – Lord Grenville supporting the measure, Lords Grey and Holland opposing it. The Bill was passed on Monday 3 March 1817, renewed on Friday 27 June 1817, and remained in effect until March 1818 (see *The Statutes at Large* [1817], 57 Geo. III, chs 3 and 55).

Letter 94)   [Tuesday] 18 February 1817

London Feb. 18 – 1817

My Lord

I inclose the Sheets of an Article on Childe Harold torn from my "<u>Mail Coach</u>" Copy of the Edinburgh Review – I hope you received some ten days since the pages on the same subject in the Quarterly and then I think you ought to feel compleatly satisfied[1] – as <u>I</u> am – like Mahomed [*sic*] your fame is suspended between these two literary attractives.[2] – Jeffery [*sic*] & Walter Scott are the authors of these critiques – and so you may be satisfied that I am ready for another <u>Copy</u> right whenever you are. – I received your Lordships Letter respecting Polidori whom I think I can assist with the very best recommendations[3] – I regretted that you do not in that Letter acknowledge a very long one which I wrote a month ago[4] – or the Tales of my Landlord & Copies of the late Poems which I sent to the under Secretary of State to be forwarded to you – two months ago – of the Tales I am eager to learn – your delight rather than opinion – M^{rs} L – will not be

convinced but that you are the author of them[5] – she is very well & in
very Good spirits – I will contrive to send you a copy of The Works[6]
by the Messenger Who goes tomorrow – though I regret that I must
send it without plates or Portrait.

I have just read the New Tragedy of Maturin entitled Manuel – the
first act of which is magnificent in all respects – but it appears to Mr G
& myself that the whole interest terminates with it – & the denuement
[sic] is terribly bad – The Style is much improved – it is repleat [sic]
with imagination – but there is a total want of judgment – Holland is
a monk again & there are Trials, processions, & Tournaments – they
proposed it to me at £500 – but I declined it.[7]

Your young friend Mr Gordon – is always most anxiously enquiring
after you & is sitting before me copying out a paragraph from a Letter
of Walter Scott to him & which I begged him to do,[8] as it shews that
privately as well as publicly, he is equally your friend – Mr Gordon
sends his most particular compliments to you.

A paragraph was inserted in the Morning Chronicle of last week
headed Mr Croker & Lord B – & saying you had written his character,
which they would give in a few days[9] – This was taking so shameful
a liberty with your name during your absence – that I called upon Mr
Davies respecting it & he obligly [sic] went to Perry – who confessed
that he had not seen the Lines – I suspect that it was your incessant
persecuter [sic] B – who was the source of all affected public opinion
respecting you[10] – but it would be as well perhaps to tell Kinnaird to
desire Perry not to use your name without your authority again – – I
gave Mr Davies the Article in the Ed. Rev. to read & he is delighted
with it – I have sent it also to Mrs Leigh – who was compleatly satisfied
with that in the Quarterly –

I hope your next will tell me that you have something nearly ready
for me in prose or verse or both – bene mixtura[11] – I have done
exceedingly well with the two last Poems & the works continue in
equal demand – indeed by the blessing of God on my honest labours
– all my publications appear to prosper – except Margaret of Anjou &
Ilderim – <Bo> The Missionary sold very well until the Author put his
name to it – & then it stopped[12] – I have just Published & nearly sold
the edition of Armata a political Romance by your friend Lord Erskine
– who was very much delighted by the note you had written in his
Pamphlet & he loves you staunchly[13] – I have many interesting Voyages
& adventures in the press & I wish I could amuse your Lordship with
some of them – They have a Tragedy coming forth at Covent Garden
by the Author of Adelaide – wch was damned last year.[14] Gifford sends
his best compliments to you & Mr Frere, Heber, Hallam,[15] & many

others always talk to me of you with delight – you and the Author of Tales of my Landlord – are said to be the only persons worth talking about now a days[16] – I hope to learn in your next that your Lordship is to return this spring, (by the way we have had nothing but Spring & summer, all this winter – this day is perfectly Summer – to make up for giving us Winter last Summer) but you must not return without visiting Rome[17] – You may expect to see Mr Sotheby at Venice he would be there this Month & he is always your friend – I will write & enquire after Mr St Aubin for no bones have yet appeared[18] – I always forgot, to assure your Lordship how much I felt obliged by your kind attention to my friend Mr Brown – when at Diodati[19] – There is a drawingroom tomorrow so that M^{rs} L will be fully occupied.[20] Pray favour me with an early Letter & tell me if I may expect a Copyright this Spring. I beg your Lordship to accept my hearty wishes for your happiness & to renew the assurance of remaining most faithfully

My Lord
Your obliged Servant
John Murray

Notes to Letter 94)

1. CHP III and *The Prisoner of Chillon and Other Poems* were very favourably reviewed by Jeffrey in the *Edinburgh Review*, XXVII, liv (December 1816), 278–310, published on Friday 28 February 1817. See also, Letter 92, n. 19 and Letter 93, nn. 1 and 3 above.

2. The coffin of Mahomet was supposed to be suspended miraculously in mid-air in the sacred enclosure at Medina until Burckhardt entered it in 1815 and discovered the truth: 'The stories once prevalent in Europe, of the prophet's tomb being suspended in the air, are unknown in the Hedjaz; nor have I ever heard them in other parts of the East, though the most exaggerated accounts of the wonders and riches of this tomb are propagated by those who have visited Medina, and wish to add to their own importance by relating fabulous stories of what they pretend to have seen. Round these tombs the treasures of the Hedjaz were formerly kept, either suspended on silken ropes, drawn across the interior of the building, or placed in chests on the ground.' When Sa'ud I (King of the First Saudi Empire, 1803–14) conquered Medina in 1804: 'Among the precious articles which he took, the most valuable is said to have been a brilliant star set in diamonds and pearls, which was suspended directly over the Prophet's tomb' (John Lewis Burckhardt, *Travels in Arabia*, ed. William Ouseley [London: Henry Colburn, 1829], 333–34). In fact, the fable had been dismissed more than a century earlier by William Daniel, who reached Medina in 1700 and reported: 'The chief *Mosque* is call'd *Mosque Akiba*, which signifies

most Holy; it is supported by four Hundred Pillars, and adorned with three Thousand Silver Lamps; and there is within this *Mosque*, at the *East-End*, a small Chappel, glittering, with Plates of Silver, in which stands *Mahomets-Coffin*, covered with Cloath of Gold, under a very rich Canopy, which the *Bashaw* of *Egypt* renews Yearly by the *Grand Seignours* Ordres. 'Tis commonly reported, that his *Coffin* was *Iron*, and it hung suspended in the Air by two Load-Stones, being Fabulous, and of no Credit, the ridiculous Assertion only of such who would impose on the Ignorant with their travelling Authority; for it is supported by two black Marble Pillars, of fifteen Foot high, which is surrounded with a *Ballester* of Silver, on which hang a great Number of Silver Lamps, whose Smoak and Heighth, being very high, render the Place obscure, and the black Marble Pillars invisible' (*A Journal or Account of William Daniel, His late Expedition or Undertaking to go from London to Surrat in India* [London, 1702], 67–68; this *Journal*, which Daniel had printed for the Directors of the East India Company at whose expense he had travelled and to whom it is dedicated, was serialized in an abridged form in *The Gentleman's Magazine*, LXXXII, Pt II [July–September 1812], 19–23, 124–27 and 225–28, see esp. 227).

3. JM had received B's letter of Friday 24 January in which he told him that Polidori, to whom he had given 'his congé', was returning to England and wished 'to go to the Brazils on a medical Speculation with the Danish Consul', and asked him: 'as you are in the favour of the powers that be – could you not get him some letters of recommendation from some of your Government friends' (*BLJ* V, 163).

4. That is, Letter 92 above, to which B had in fact replied, but which reply JM had not yet received.

5. See Letter 91, n. 17 above. Augusta had written to JM on Tuesday 10 December 1816 thanking him for sending *Tales of My Landlord* and asking suggestively, 'pray who is the Author of the first!!! which I am reading' (MA). The 'first' was *The Black Dwarf*, whose hero, outcast from society for his deformity, becomes a misanthropical recluse. Although B denied his authorship thrice to Augusta, once he had read them he understood why she had been so 'positive' in her 'erroneous persuasion' (*BLJ* V, 171, 175, 191 and 220).

6. That is, the collected edition of B's works (see Letter 91, n. 10 above).

7. See Letter 92, n. 8 above. In Maturin's first Gothic drama *Bertram; or, The Castle of St. Aldobrand*, published by JM and first performed at Drury Lane Theatre on Thursday 9 May 1816, Mr Holland took the part of the Prior of St Anselm; in *Manuel* he was Mendizabel, the Chief Justice of the Court of Cordova; it was Mr Bengough who took the part of Moncalde, a Monk. JM did publish *Manuel* (on Tuesday 11 March 1817).

8. See Letter 92, n. 21 above. There is no such letter from Scott to Gordon of this date extant.

9. In the *Morning Chronicle* for Tuesday 11 February 1817 appeared an unsigned article entitled 'THE ADMIRALTY SCRIBE *and* LORD B—.', attacking the 'Secretary', his '*spaiches* in the House' and his 'perishable' writings, adding: 'A very great Poet of our own day ... has, we find, taken pretty effectual steps for handing him down to posterity, by embodying *some particulars* respecting him in certain verses, of great merit and no little force. We shall probably have an early occasion of allowing our readers to judge how far our opinion is well founded as to the immortality that awaits this great man.' B thought this was some 'rhymes' that he had destroyed in JM's presence in 1814 (*BLJ* V, 184).

10. That is, Brougham, who had not only been instrumental in the publication of B's separation poems in *The Champion*, but soon after his departure from England had 'attacked Byron at Brooks's for his *deformity*' (Hobhouse, *Recollections*, I, 336) and spread the 'league of incest' story about B and Shelley in Switzerland (*CMP*, 375).

11. *bene mixtura* = well-blended.

12. Margaret Holford's *Margaret of Anjou, A Poem in Ten Cantos* (1816), Henry Gally Knight's *Ilderim. A Syrian Tale* (1816), and W. L. Bowles' *The Missionary: A Poem* (1813; 2nd edn, 1815; 3rd edn, 1816). B extemporized some jocular lines on these publications, which he repeated to JM, Moore and Hobhouse, but he also told JM he would 'have thought the Assyrian tale very succeedable' (*BLJ* V, 185, 187, 193 and 199).

13. See Letter 92, n. 11 above. B recorded in his Journal for Sunday 8 March 1814: 'Lord Erskine called, and gave me his famous pamphlet, with a marginal note and corrections in his handwriting. Sent it to be bound superbly, and shall treasure it' (*BLJ* III, 248). This was Erskine's *On the Causes and Consequences of the War with France* (1797), which went through 35 editions within the year. B's copy with his own marginal 'notes' in it was sold at his book sale in 1816 and bought by JM who showed it to Erskine (*CMP* 243, lot 326; and see Letter 95, n. 11 below).

14. See Letter 92, n. 10 above.

15. Henry Hallam (1777–1859), the historian, whose *View of the State of Europe during the Middle Ages* JM was to publish in 1818 (see Letter 107, n. 9 below).

16. Writing to Scott on Saturday 14 December 1816, JM told him: 'Heber says there are only two men in the world – Walter Scott and Lord Byron' (Lockhart, *Life of Scott*, 338).

17. After the notorious 'Darkness' of 1816, the succeeding Winter and Spring were remarkably mild. *Blackwood's Edinburgh Magazine*, I, ii (May 1817) commented: 'It may not ... be uninteresting to our readers to state, that the mean temperature of the four months of this year that have just elapsed,

considerably exceeds the mean temperature of the corresponding months of last year ... The effects of this difference are quite obvious in the unusually forward state of vegetation in gardens and orchards, and would have been equally conspicuous in the corn-fields, but for the severe and long-continued drought' (p. 226); and later: 'Nothing is to be heard in the country but comparisons between June 1817 and June 1816, and congratulations on the supposed return of summer to these northern regions, which appeared at one time to be threatened with perpetual winter' (ibid., I, iv [July 1817], 448–49). Although there was cloud over London on the day of JM's writing (18 February), the temperature at noon stood at 54° Fahrenheit; and a month later, on 18 March (see Letter 97 below), the day was fair with the temperature at 55° (*The Gentleman's Magazine*, LXXXVII, Pt I [January–June 1817], 190 and 286). In his reply of Sunday 9 March, B said he intended 'for England this spring ... without going to Rome'; but he changed his plans and went to Rome where he met 'that old Blue-*bore* Sotheby' (*BLJ* V, 184–85 and 229).

18. See Letter 92, n. 22 above.

19. See Letter 88 above.

20. See Letter 93, n. 4 above. The Drawing Room had originally been set for Thursday 6 February but was postponed on account of the King's health to Thursday 20 February (see the *Morning Chronicle* for Friday 21 February 1817 which also gives a detailed description of Augusta's attire on the occasion: 'A white petticoat, with a beautiful silver lama drapery, on British blond net, tastefully arranged and confined by bunches of violets and silver tassels, violet satin, elegantly trimmed with silver to correspond, and Brussels lace; head dress, plume of ostrich feathers, and a bandeau of pearls').

Letter 95)   Thursday 6 March 1817

London March 6 – 1817
Thursday

My Lord

I can not allow a moment to pass without acknowledging the receipt of your obliging Letter of the <15th> 15th Feb. which <I have jus> has just arrived[1] – I have been most anxiously looking for it fearful that mine might have miscarried & if so fearing that you must consider me strangely ungrateful for the favour of your obliging communications. I am sadly vexed to find that you<r> have not received the Copies of the Poems & of Tales of My Landlord which were sent by me <three> Two months ago, nearly. I have now put up other Copies of each which I will again send to the Secretary of States office & I will hope

for <be>their better fate. Your Lordship I rejoice to say will find the
[sic] my errors of omission come within the Pale of your forgiveness
– The Poem that was omitted is entitled "Extract from an unpublished
Poem" – there is no politics in this & it was omitted because Mr G
– thought it was so much eclipsed by the others – & the lines omitted
in Chillon are

     Nor slew I of my subjects one
     What Sovereign hath so little done

because they abruptly unhinged the pleasing associations arising from
the rest of the poem – The Note omitted was I think some personal
allusion to poor Louis XVIII – & this I desired lest it might in any way
interfere with the popularity of my book – I trust that your Lordships
usual indulgence will pardon this – and when we reprint either in 8vo or
when the small edition is printing the whole can be restored or not as
you, in your next shall do me the favour to desire.[2] – The sale of these
poems have [sic] equalled, which is more complimentary than if I said,
they had surpassed, my expectations – these I shall next winter publish
in the small size & they will form a Sixth Volume[3] – the Fifth Volume,
as I believe I have already informed your Lordship I have already
published, & what is better, nearly sold – consists of Siege of Corinth
Parisina <&> Monody – & the smaller Poems. I have paid Mr Kinnaird
£1000 – £500 I shall send him next week – and the fourth £500 I
shall give, with great convenience & with no less satisfaction to myself,
in a month or two. If it were perfectly agreeable to your Lordship to
sign your name to the inclosed paper – in the presence of some English
Gentleman, you can inclose it to Mr Kinnaird who will give it to me,
when my part is fulfilled[4] – there are all the smaller poems inserted
upon my presumption respecting your Lordships kindness.

     And now having nearly settled one account – I am perfectly ready
to open a new one – I always thought the "Incantation" exceedingly
wilde [sic] & beautiful – though I smiled at its being an extract from
"An Unfinished Witch Drama" – which I now Smile more heartily to
find to be a true bill – I shall send the interesting extracts with which
you have favoured me[5] – to Mr Gifford & faithfully detail to you his
opinion – in the mean time I hope you will spare a little time to the
writing of it out – I am much gratified by your Lordships expressions
respecting Mr Gifford – which the last Number of the Quarterly will
give you ample reason to be satisfied [sic] – he behaved with most
particular kindness on this occasion – I induced Mr S to write it – from
an expression of kindness regarding you in One of his letters – <& it
was thre> I thought his mind was full of the subject – & it was out in
three days.[6] I hope this has reached you safely & the Critique in the Ed.

Rev. both of wch I <had> tore out the moment I got them & inclosed
in Letters to you – <B> – If your Lordship have occasion to send any
MSS to me do me the favour to address it, under cover, to John Barrow
Esqr Sec^y Admiralty London[7] – as it is more likely to proceed in safety
– Moore has announced his poem Lallah [sic] Rookh – a Persian Tale –
not a very happy title – I think – he has taken a Cottage at Hornsey &
is gone down to bring his wife & family[8] – I shall put it under Covers
& send in that way if I do not find a better. – Poor Horners death at
Pisa has given universal regret no man was so thoroughly respected
by all parties – his fate was hard indeed[9] – he called upon me the last
four days he was in England – & solicited as a very great favour that
I would allow him to read your new Poems – a Pleasure which I was
most happy to grant – & so thank God we parted in great friendship.
– Manuel Maturins New Tragedy is to Come out on <u>Saturday</u> I have
not ventured upon it before its trial – as I did upon the last of which I
had the extraordinary good fortune to sell betwixt 6 & 7000[10] – Lord
<u>Erskine</u> has just interrupted me I believe I told your Lordship that I had
published a sort of political Romance – describing our own political
History under the name of <u>Armata</u>[11] – I have sold the best part of a
Second Edition – he is a staunch friend of yours – I told him I had
just heard from you, holding up your Letter "He is an excellent fellow"
– says he – "the best friend I have in the World" – He was quite
delighted by your Lordships notes in his pamphlet which I lent him
to quote from – As you have not received Tales of My Landlord you
will not comprehend Mrs Leigh's allusion to your <u>Prose</u>[12] – in which
<u>Language</u> I hope yet to have something – Not one word about your
Armenian Grammar – do write me a review of it & put in it all your
observations upon Italy &c &c – no matter how irrellevant [sic] – – I
trust from your not mentioning your health that you continue well[13] – I
am sorry you do not appear to think of visiting Rome during Easter
– Pray if your Lordship stumble upon any curious MSS &c – think of
me – I offer your Lordship my best thanks for your present of the Spoils
of Waterloo which I gladly accept & shall preserve – from the double
association[14] – Does your Lordship know of any Conveyance by wch I
could send you curious things[15] –

I am well & flourishing I printed 10,000 of the last Q. Rev & the
Number of the next is 12,000[16] – it is a great happiness to [sic] true to
be allowed the Pleasure of writing to you & of being honoured by your
Lordships interesting & always lively Letters – With most affectionate
regards I have the honour to remain My Lord
    Your faithful Servant
    John Murray

Notes to Letter 95)

Cover: My Lord/My Lord Byron/Poste Restant/Venetia/en Italie <u>received</u>: 24 March

1. See Letter 92 above. In his letter of Saturday 15 February, B told JM he had received his two letters but not the parcel he mentioned, adding that he expected JM would tell him exactly what had been omitted from the publications in his next (*BLJ* V, 169).

2. 'Extract from an Unpublished Poem' ('Could I remount the river of my years'), written in July 1816, was first published posthumously with this title by Moore in 1830. It is entitled '[A Fragment]' by McGann, who suggests (correctly it would seem in the light of this letter) that Moore may have 'had access to a different MS., now not forthcoming' (*CPW* IV, 29–30 and 456). The lines omitted from *The Prisoner of Chillon* (lines 389–90) were never restored by JM but were first incorporated in the poem by McGann (*CPW* IV, 16). The 'Note' on Louis XVIII would have been that appended to *CHP* III, 82, to which Croker objected in his letter to JM of 18 September 1816 (see headnote to Letter 90 above). It was first printed by McGann in *CPW* II, 310. B did not raise any objections to either of these omissions.

3. That is, Vol. VI of the collected works, published by JM in 1818 containing *The Prisoner of Chillon and Other Poems*, *Manfred* and *The Lament of Tasso*.

4. This was a copyright agreement. B replied on Tuesday 25 March saying that apart from the Consul and vice-Consul with whom he had not 'the slightest acquaintance', '"English gentlemen"' were 'very rare – at least in Venice'; on 12 October, however, he told him he had '*signed* and sent' the '*former copyrights* by Mr. Kinnaird' (*BLJ* V, 191 and 268; see also, Letter 107, n. 14 below).

5. 'The Incantation', with a note explaining that it was 'a Chorus from an unfinished Witch Drama', was published with *The Prisoner of Chillon and Other Poems* in 1816 (see Letter 91, n. 8 above). The 'Drama' was *Manfred*, which B told JM in his letter of Saturday 15 February 1817 was 'of a very wild – metaphysical – & inexplicable kind' and was now finished, though he had not 'copied it off' (*BLJ* V, 170). He enclosed three extracts selected 'at random ... but whether good bad or indifferent' he did not know (*The Newstead Byron Society Review* [July 2000], 7–8). In his reply to this letter (95), B said he had sent all three Acts of 'the "witch drama"' within the last month and valued it 'at *three hundred* guineas – or less if you like it' (*BLJ* V, 192).

6. In his letter of 15 February, B had spoken very kindly of Gifford (*BLJ* V, 169). For Scott, whom JM had 'induced' to write the review of B in the *Quarterly*, see Letters 92, nn. 19 and 34, and 94, n. 1 above.

7. John (later Sir John) Barrow (1764–1848), Secretary of the Admiralty, author and contributor to *Quarterly Review*.

8. Moore's poem was entitled *Lalla Rookh, An Oriental Romance*, not 'a Persian Tale'. This misinformation gave rise to B's blunder when writing to Moore on Tuesday 25 March, and to a disquisition on titles when replying to JM that day (*BLJ* V, 186 and 192). In mid-March 1817 Moore moved from Mayfield Cottage in Derbyshire to a cottage below Muswell Hill in Hornsey, Middlesex, six miles from London. He took his wife, Bessy, to see it on Friday 13 March who liked it 'exceedingly' (Moore, *Letters*, I, 413).

9. Francis Horner (1778–1817), barrister, co-founder of the *Edinburgh Review*, and MP for St Mawes, highly respected on both sides of the House, had died of ill-health at Pisa on 8 February. His death was first reported, 'with great pain', in *The Times* for Thursday 27 February 1817, and a fine 'Memoir' (compiled from numerous tributes to him) appeared in *Blackwood's Edinburgh Magazine*, I, i (April 1817), 3–8. B was sorry to receive this news, which he later rather irreverently attributed to the professional attentions of Polidori (*BLJ* V, 192, 211, 215 and 241, and XI, 164).

10. See Letters 92, n. 8, and 94, n. 7 above.

11. See Letter 92, n. 11 and 94, n. 13 above.

12. See Letter 94, n. 5 above.

13. See Letter 92, n. 14 above. B replied on Tuesday 25 March that one of the Armenian Grammars was published but 'the other is still in M.S.': 'My illness has prevented me from moving this month past – & I have done nothing more with the Armenian. – Of Italian or rather Lombard Manners – I could tell you little or nothing ... I have seen all their spectacles & sights – but I do not know anything very worthy of observation' (*BLJ* V, 193).

14. See Letter 92, n. 21 above.

15. B replied that it was 'useless to send to the *Foreign Office* nothing arrives to me by that conveyance – I suppose some zealous Clerk thinks it a Tory duty to prevent it' (*BLJ* V, 205).

16. B said he joyed in the success of the *Quarterly*, 'but I must still stick by the *Edinburgh* – Jeffrey has done so by me' (*BLJ* V, 204).

Letter 96)   Saturday 15 March 1817

London 15th. March. 1817
Saturday

My Lord

I had the pleasure of receiving your Letter of the 25th Feby the day before yesterday, Thursday 13th – I could not see Mr Love yesterday but this day I with a friend, found him at home & the result of opinion is that he may have been deceived by his workmen. – he will take the snuff boxes back & return either gold or goods for them – he is sorry for what has happed [*sic*] from its inconvenience to you – but his conscience – whatever his box has proved appears to be Sterling – & does not swerve at the touch of enquiry – he is anxious to see the box.[1]

I inclose a transcription of the passage from Moore's Italy in which by the way yr Lordship will observe that Moore has given the Name nearly right <u>Falliero</u>[2] – the Subject is a mighty one & with it you must spring over the head of Otway.[3] I have very strong and peculiar confidence in the success of your Lordships efforts in this department. – Confoundedly am I vexed at your not getting the books which I sent you – but I trust that the second Copy will not miss – & every day I look for your Lordships notice of the two Articles in the Quarterly & Edinburgh Reviews which I sent more than a month ago, under two covers & which with Mr Giffords very favourable opinion of the Specimens of the Witch Drama, which I have now authority for reporting to your Lordship, will <stimu> have stimulated you to compleat it & to the yet greater effort – the copying of it out – – Mr Gifford trusts that you will <u>finish</u> it[4] – Well Maturins new Tragedy appeared on Saturday last, and I am sorry to say that the opinion of my friend M^r G[5] – was establied [*sic*] by the impression made on the audience – The first Act very fine – the rest exhibiting a want of judgment not to be endured – it was brought out with uncommon splendour & was well acted Keans character as an Old Man a Warrior – was new and well sustained – for he had, of course selected it, and professed to be and he acted as if he were really pleased with it – but this feeling changed to dislike, after the first night for he then abused it & has actually walked through the part ever since – that is to say for the other three nights of performance – for they <th> do not act on Wednesdays, or Fridays & this night the performance is changed to <u>Lovers' Vows</u>[6] – I met Geo Lamb on <t> Tuesday[7] & he complained bitterly of Keans conduct, said that he had ruined the success of the Tragedy & that in consequence he feared,

Maturin would receive nothing − The expense to the managers must
have been very great − & it will compleat I suspect the ruin of Drury
under its present directorship − & so I rejoice that your name appears
not amongst them. − I send you the first Act − that you may read the
best of it. I have undertaken to print the Tragedy at my own expense &
to give the poor Author the whole of the Profit.

Still no word of the Armenian Grammar I have just published
a Drama translated direct from the Chinese, which is curious &
rather interesting for its view of Manners[8] − I wish I could shew you
extracts from the Pekin Gazettes in which the Chinese speak of our
Embassy − such contempt − we have got near to them by means of
Nepaul [sic] & before I die I hope we shall have a war with them[9]
− our expedition up the Congo too has proved unsuccessful − but
<I> it will be productive of two Works for me[10] − I have just received
in a way perfectly unaccountable a MSS from S[t] Helena − with not
one word − I suppose it to be originally written by Buonaparte or
his agents − it is very curious his Life − in which <all the> each
event<s are> is given in almost a word − a battle described in a short
sentence − I call it therefore simply Manuscrit venu de S[t] Helene d'une
maniere inconnue[11] Lord Holland has a motion on our treatment of
Buonaparte <in> at S[t] Helena for Wednesday next − & on Monday I
shall publish [sic] − You will have seen Buonapartes Memorial on this
Subject, complaining bitterly of all − pungent but very injudicious,
as it must offend all the other allied powers to be reminded of their
former prostration.[12] − − The report is strong that Miss Mercer − Lord
Keiths Daughter − is about to bestow − throw away − her hand
on Flah<o>t − do I spell him rightly − the french General − a fit
punishment for having made a fool of so many Englishmen − to be
at length made a fool of herself.[13] − I have a long & amusing Letter
from Sir Jno Malcolm from the Cape − in which he remembers you
− Lady Davy has the reputation of giving the most agreeable parties
in London just now − Walter Scott has had a most severe spasmodic
attack − from which he is recovering however − he always mentions
you in his letters[14] − M[r] Frere still enquires after you − & I have many
visitors to my Portraits − I now print 12.000 Copies of the Quarterly
Review which I believe exceeds the Editions of the Edinburgh − Veritas
− prevalebit!![15]

I hope to have occasion to write again, in a few days in answer to
Letters which I then hope to have received from you − in the mean
time I shall anxiously hope that you have perfectly recovered & that
you propose to be a little careful of yourself[16] − I hope you will give a
poetical description of Venice − its Carnival − &c &c &c

Mr Gifford ever desires me to present his Kind remembrances to you
– I remain
My Lord
Your faithful Servant
John Murray
I have sent the Whole of the Tragedy[17]
Mad. de Stael will not accept of my Offer 1000G^s – for 1500 Cop^s
& £500 – for each 1000 Cop^s after – & she can not yet get a purchaser[18]
Upon Consideration I have sent the Play & the Extract to the Foreign
Office

Notes to Letter 96)

Cover: My Lord/My Lord Byron/Poste restante/a Venise/en Italie

1. In his letter of Tuesday 25 February, B had asked JM to apprise Mr Love,
   a jeweller of Old Bond Street, that one of the snuffboxes he had purchased
   from him in 1813 had recently 'turned out to be *silver-gilt* instead of *Gold*
   – for which last it was sold & paid for', telling JM to 'state the matter to him
   with due ferocity' (*BLJ* V, 173). Replying to this on 2 April, B exclaimed:
   'So Love has a conscience – by Diana! – I shall make him take back the
   box though it were Pandora's' (*BLJ* V, 203).

2. B had asked JM to get transcribed from John Moore's *View of Society and
   Manners in Italy; with Anecdotes relating to Some Eminent Characters* (1781), the
   'account of the *Doge Valiere* (it ought to be Falieri) and his conspiracy' as he
   meant to write a tragedy on the subject (*BLJ* V, 174). This was to be *Marino
   Faliero, Doge of Venice*, which he did not begin until April 1820, and in one
   of the notes to which he was to call John Moore's a 'paltry and ignorant
   account' (*CPW* IV, 539).

3. Thomas Otway (1652–85), the dramatist; JM has in mind specifically his *Venice
   Preserved; or, A Plot Discovered* (1682), one of B's favourite plays. Replying on
   2 April, B granted what JM said but added: 'the story of Marino Falieri – is
   different & I think so much finer – that I wish Otway had taken it instead'
   (*BLJ* V, 203).

4. As he reiterated in his reply, B had sent the whole of *Manfred* by the time
   he received this letter (*BLJ* V, 203).

5. That is, Gifford.

6. The eponymous hero of *Manuel*, Manuel Count Valdi, is an old and infirm
   warrior who eventually goes mad with grief. There were no performances
   at Drury Lane Theatre on Wednesday and Friday, and on Saturday 15 March
   Elizabeth Inchbald's *Lovers' Vows*, an old favourite first performed in 1798,
   was acted. *Manuel* returned the following Monday.

7. George Lamb (he whom Brougham was cuckolding; see Letter 89, n. 10 above) was a member of the Drury Lane Theatre Subcommittee. See also, Letter 97, n. 5 below.

8. See Letter 92, n. 28 above.

9. In February 1816, Lord Amherst set out from England on an embassy to China with the object of improving diplomatic and trade relations between the two countries and of ameliorating the condition of British subjects living in China. Reports of the failure of the mission, and of a hostile engagement between the British frigate *Alceste*, which had conveyed the party, and a Chinese fort, were first announced in the papers on Monday 10 March 1817. JM's strong expressions in fact reflect the prevailing spirit of animosity towards China with whom British relations at the time were at their nadir; *The Times* for Monday 17 March commented: 'Many people suspect that, our conquests on the side of Nepaul are the latent cause of all the jealousies and unfriendly indications of the Chinese Government. If the difference be not soon adjusted, we have much underrated the evils of which the nation will be made sensible.'

10. In fact more than 'two'. For Captain Tuckey's *Narrative* of the Congo expedition, see Letter 92, n. 30 above; the embassy to China produced Third Commissioner Henry Ellis's *Journal of the Proceedings of the Late Embassy to China* (1817), Surgeon John M'Leod's *Narrative of a Voyage, in His Majesty's late Ship Alceste to the Yellow Sea, ... and ... to the Island of Lewchew; with an Account of her Shipwreck in the Straits of Gaspar* (1817), and Captain Basil Hall's *Account of a Voyage of Discovery to the West Coast of Corea, and the Great Loo-Choo Island* (1818).

11. *Manuscrit venu de St. Hélène, d'une Manière Inconnue* and its translation, *Manuscript transmitted from St. Helena by An Unknown Channel*, were both published by JM in March 1817. In fact the work, a political testament and apologia supposedly written by Napoleon himself and convincing many, was not by him at all but by Jacob-Frédéric Lullin de Châteauvieux (1772–1842), one of the Coppet set, who had sent the MS incognito by post to JM. Hobhouse read it in August and thought it a 'singular performance' (see *Recollections*, II, 77, 79, 87 and 93). B's copy forms part of lot 147 in his Sale Catalogue (1827) (*CMP*, 251).

12. For some months, rumours had been circulating in England about the treatment of Napoleon at St Helena. On Monday 10 March, Lord Holland gave notice of his intention to introduce a motion on the subject the following week (*The Times*, Tuesday 11 March 1817; see Letter 97, n. 3 below). 'Buonapartes Memorial', complaining of the strict conditions under which he was being held, was entitled 'Letter, by Order of Buonaparte, Addressed by General Count Montholon, to Sir Hudson Lowe, British Governor of the Island of St. Helena', and was printed in, for example, *The Times* for Friday 14 March 1817.

13. Dubbed by Hobhouse 'the fops despair' in 1814 (*Recollections*, I, 88), the Hon. Margaret Mercer Elphinstone (1788–1867), daughter of Admiral Lord Keith and wealthy heiress in her own right, companion of Princess Charlotte and friend of B's, married (to the disgust of her own family and the Tory establishment) Auguste, Comte de Flahaut (1785–1870), Napoleon's aide-de-camp at Waterloo, in Edinburgh on 20 June 1817 and remained with him till her death. B replied: 'You talk of "marriage" – ever since my own funeral – the word makes me giddy – & throws me into a cold sweat – pray don't repeat it' (*BLJ* V, 204). In fact Kinnaird had already told B as early as 13 September 1816 that 'Miss Mercer is to marry Gen¹. Flahaut' (MA). See also Letter 97, n. 7 below.

14. Sir John Malcolm was taking his time at the Cape of Good Hope on his way to Madras. Lady Jane Davy (1780–1855), the wife of Sir Humphry, was a leading London hostess whose parties B had frequented. Scott's two most recent and most kind-hearted letters concerning B are dated 10 and 22 January 1817 (Scott, *Letters*, IV, 363–66 and 377; see also, Letter 92, n. 34 above). His attack had taken place at a dinner party on 5 March 1817 when he was suddenly seized with cramp in the stomach and left the room 'with a scream of agony which electrified his guests' (Lockhart, *Life of Scott*, 343). B replied: 'Tell me that Walter Scott is better – I would not have him ill for the world – I suppose it was by sympathy that I had my fever at the same time' (*BLJ* V, 204).

15. *magna est veritas et praevalet*: Great is Truth and mighty above all things (*Apocrypha*, I Esdras 4.41; 'praevalebit', 'shall prevail', is an unauthorized though common reading).

16. B had told JM somewhat euphemistically that he was 'a little unwell – sitting up too late', and that 'some subsidiary dissipations' had lowered his blood a good deal, in his letter of 25 February (*BLJ* V, 174).

17. That is, *Manuel* (as are also 'the Play & the Extract' in the final line of this postcript).

18. B replied on Wednesday 2 April: 'You should close with Madame de Stael – this will be her best work', though he had not seen it himself (*BLJ* V, 204–05). *Considérations sur les Principaux Evénémens de la Révolution Françoise* was Madame de Staël's last work for which, as Baron de Staël wrote to JM on 28 June 1816, she insisted 'upon £4000, besides a credit in books for every new edition' (Smiles, I, 316). Although JM conferred with Longman as a potential joint-publisher, neither was willing to accept such terms and negotiations remained inconclusive until her death on 14 July 1817. The work was published posthumously in 3 vols by Baldwin, Cradock and Joy in 1818.

Letter 97) Tuesday 18 March 1817

London 18 March. 1817
Tuesday

My Lord

I hasten to acquaint you with the safe receipt of your short letter
of the 28th Feby with another Cover inclosing together the first act
of Man<uel>fred it came 5 minutes ago.[1] I have sent it to M^r G – &
tomorrow I will give it to the printer, intending to send the proofs
to your Lordship, as quickly as possible, with any remarks that M^r G
– make [sic] think proper to make, upon them. – Your Letter to M^r
Moore, arriving at the same time, I have forwarded to him – he has
taken a house at Hornsey as I hinted in my last. Surely you ought to
have received my packet containing the Q. Review which was sent away
on the 10th – – but upon calculating, I find to my consolation, that your
present letter has been 18 Days on its passage & so I hope mine will
have reached its destination in due course.

In my last, written on the 14th, I gave you my opinion of Love[2]
– he has called since, & told me that there was <u>one</u> box silver plated &
which he thinks you will recollect, that he induced you to include in
the bargain, you bought them in the lump & this was one which he was
anxious to get quit of – He speaks in the warmest terms of gratitude
<for> of your Lordships continual kindness to him and I can not but
believe his story – so pray, at any rate, open another Lid & try – I have
given the Man some orders in consequence of the fervour with which
he spoke of you – & made him a present of your Portrait!!! – So I
suppose you wont employ me in this way again –

I have published this hour my <u>Manuscrit venu de St Heléne d'une
maniere <an> inconnu</u> – & am now 3p.m setting off to the Lords to
hear Lord Hollands Motion – on the Illtreatment of Buonaparte – of
wch his valet de Cham. has published a grotesque Account.[3] Mr Ward is
here & asks about you – He is in great feather & in a debate with Sir Ja^s
Mackintosh, Rose, Hallam &c – he was decreed to be the <m> wittiest
Man in the Country –

We have had the mildest & most delightful weather throughout the
whole of the winter – which has passed without Snow or Cold & now
the Spring appears compleatly set in – – Pray tell me of your proposed
movements – the Chronicle of yesterday congratulated the world
– on Lord Byron's return in a few weeks – from Switzerland.[4] – Poor
Maturin's Play will not live Eight Nights & the expense of it – will
ruin the house – there is a Meeting of Proprietors on Thursday next

to determine on the propriety of letting the Theatre at the end of the Season[5] – After the Play on its first representation – the Green Room possessed all the long faces of a funeral no one spoke – for some time – at length Perry walked up to Ray [*sic*] & whispers [*sic*] – it wont do by G—d" [*sic*][6] – The Grand Duke Nicholas has enchanted every one – & has just gone carrying with him the Duke of Devonshire – to great grief [*sic*] of Miss Mercer – who has never smiled since[7] – Ward says that Coleridge is Summum Borium[8] – he has cheated me out of a Tragedy for wch I gave him £100 – I set up part of it – he took it away & I have not heard of it since – He says he will either return me my money – if he can get it – or write it out in some other way – but he is very welcome to the said sum.

I would not buy "My dear Lord" – Hunt's Rimini – & he abuses me like a pickpocket.[9] –

I hope soon to hear again from Your Lordship & offering every good wish I beg leave to be considered as remaining. My Lord
    Your faithful Servant
    John Murray

Notes to Letter 97)

Cover: My Lord/My Lord Byron/Poste restante/a Venise/en Italie arrived Venice 7 April

1. B's 'short letter' of Friday 28 February merely informed JM that in that '& another cover' was the first Act of *Manfred*; on the same day B had also written to Moore (*BLJ* V, 176–78; see also, Letter 95, n. 8 above).

2. In fact the 15th (see Letter 96 above). For Love, see Letter 96, n. 1 above. B did not reply to this directly, but on Monday 14 April he told JM that Polidori was returning with '*two Miniatures*' which he asked JM to forward to Augusta having first desired 'Mr. Love (as a peace offering between him & me) to set them in plain gold – with my arms complete – and "Painted by Prepiani – Venice – 1817" – on the back' (*BLJ* V, 212; see also, Letter 104, nn. 1 and 9 below).

3. See Letter 96, nn. 11 and 12 above. Lord Holland's motion on the personal treatment of Napoleon at St Helena came before the Lords on Tuesday 18 March and was negatived without a division (*Parliamentary Debates*, XXXV [January–April 1817], 1137–66; see also, *The Times*, Wednesday 19 March 1817). The 'grotesque Account' was a pamphlet entitled *An Appeal to the British Nation on the Treatment Experienced by Napoleon Buonaparte in The Island of St. Helena … With An Authentic Copy of the Official Memoir, Dictated by Napoleon, and Delivered to Sir Hudson Lowe*, which had been smuggled out of St Helena by Natale Santini, Napoleon's general factotum (or 'Huissier

du Cabinet de l'Empéreur', as he called himself), and published in English and French by Ridgways in March 1817. Its genuineness was, and still is, disputed (see Gilbert Martineau, *Madame Mère. Napoleon's Mother* [London: John Murray, 1978], 147–79, and Frank Giles, *Napoleon Bonaparte: England's Prisoner* [London: Constable & Robinson, 2001], 52–55; see also, the Earl of Ilchester, *The Home of the Hollands 1605–1820* [London: John Murray, 1937], 322–24).

4. 'The public will hear with pleasure, that Lord BYRON is expected in England within a few weeks, from Switzerland' (*Morning Chronicle*, Monday 17 March 1817).

5. This had been announced on Monday 17 March to take place the following Thursday (20 March) when various financial issues were discussed, the reletting of the theatre was approved and Lord Holland's resolution expressing 'full confidence' in the Management Committee was passed (see *The Times*, Monday 17 and Friday 21 March 1817).

6. Alexander Rae (1782–1820), actor and manager of Drury Lane Theatre. James Perry, the Editor of the *Morning Chronicle*, was also a member of the Drury Lane Committee.

7. The Grand Duke Nicholas (1796–1855), brother and successor of Alexander I, Tsar of Russia, had been touring England and had returned to London before embarking for the Continent on Saturday 15 March. During his final week, he was entertained lavishly by the Prince Regent and others where he was accompanied by William George Spencer Cavendish, 6th Duke of Devonshire (1790–1858) who was to travel with his Suite. The Duke's name had long been linked with that of Miss Mercer Elphinstone. Hobhouse, for instance, being in her box at the opera in 1814 noted: 'The Duke of Devonshire came in, and led Miss Mercer to the opposite box ... I should not wonder if it was a match' (*Recollections*, I, 142; see also, Letter 96, n. 13 above).

8. Ward's dog Latin for the 'greatest bore' (punning on *summum bonum*, 'the highest good'; Cicero, *De Officiis*, I, ii, 5). In 1816, JM had paid Coleridge £50 for his drama *Zapolya* and advanced him another £50 for 'some other Play, or Publication'. Subsequently, Coleridge had withdrawn the MS, explaining his reasons for so doing in a letter to JM of February 1817, but he did repay the £50 on *Zapolya* before the end of March, promising the other £50 when possible (see *Letters*, IV, 644, 703–07 and 716–18).

9. JM glances at Hunt's notorious Dedication to B of *The Story of Rimini* (1816), which opens familiarly: 'My Dear Byron' (p. v). In fact it was Hazlitt and not Hunt who had abused JM in a notice comparing Southey's *Wat Tyler* (1817) with his recent *Quarterly Review* article on Parliamentary Reform, in *The Examiner*, No. 480 (Sunday 9 March 1817) in which, having exposed Southey's hypocrisy to the satisfaction of the 'Old Times', he concludes:

'Before we have done, we shall perhaps do the same thing to the satisfaction of the publisher of the *Quarterly Review*; for these sort of persons, the patrons and paymasters of the band of gentlemen pensioners and servile authors, have "a sort of squint" in their understanding, and look less to the dirty sacrifices of their drudges or the dirtier they are ready to make, than to their standing well with that great keeper, the public, for purity and innocence' (p. 158, retorting Southey's own words in his article on Parliamentary Reform in the *Quarterly Review*, XVI, xxxxi [October 1816], p. 226: 'there is a kind of half knowledge which seems to disable men even from forming a just opinion of the facts before them – a sort of squint in the understanding which prevents it from seeing straightforward, and by which all objects are distorted'). To these two items of news B responded despairing on Wednesday 9 April: 'You & L[eig]h Hunt have quarrelled then it seems; I introduce him & his poem to you ... and the end is eternal enmity ... I introduce Coleridge & Christabel & Coleridge runs away with your money ... and ... I am the innocent Istmhus (damn the word I can't spell it ...) of these enmities' (*BLJ* V, 208).

Letter 98) Thursday 20 March 1817

London 20ᵗʰ March. 1817
Thursday

My Lord

I have to acknowled [*sic*] your Lordships kind Letter dated the 3ʳᵈ received this hour – but I am sorry to say that it has occasioned me great anxiety about your health – You are not wont to cry before you are hurt – & I am apprehensive that you are worse even than you allow – pray keep quiet & take care of yourself – My Review shews you that you are worth preserving and that the world yet loves you – If you become seriously worse – <pray> I entreat you to let me know it and I will fly to you with a Physician – an Italian one is only a preparation for the Anatomist – I will not tell your Sister of this – if you will tell me true[1] – I had hopes that this Letter would have confirmed my expectations of your speedy return – which has been stated by Mr Kinnaird & repeated to me by Mr Davies – whom I saw yesterday & who threatens to write[2] – We often indulge our recollections of you & he allows me to believe that I am one of the few who really know you.

Gifford gave me yesterday the first Act of Manfred with a delighted countenance – telling me it was wonderfully poetical & desiring me to assure that [*sic*] it well merits publication – I shall send proofs to your

Lordship with his remarks – if he have any – it is a wild and delightful
thing & I like it myself – <u>hugely</u>.

I had a Letter from Mrs Leigh yesterday, inclosing one for your
Lordship[3] – Mrs Leigh promises me a visit by the end of the Month.

The public very generally accord with your opinion of the Critique
in the Quarterly & it has actually as your friend Heber said produced
a sensation – it is equally honourable to Scotts head & Heart and I
rejoice much in my sagacity in selecting him to write it – Gifford said
to me – Lord Byron is much obliged to you – Scott was much satisfied
with it himself & still more by the praise which has followed it – &
this will be raised & confirmed by your Lordships approbation wch, in
substance, I shall venture to communicate.[4] – <Of> The Article is likely
to have proved the more efficacious <for>from the good fortune of its
having appeared in our perhaps very best Number – of which I have
sold already almost 10,000 Copies – of the Next Number I am printing
12.000 – the sale is not exceeded by the Edinb. Rev – The Article in
that Journal wch I also sent your Lordship is very good & satisfactory
– but ours is peculiar – and therefore the more attractive.

Mr Gifford who is at my Elbow & <who has> to whom I have just
read your letter at least that part of it referring to the Review – &
to the Procession[5] – desires me to present his sincere regards to you
& to assure you how much he joins in my anxieties & regret at your
Lordships illness – which however I will flatter myself with hoping that
your next will tell us <have> has very materially abated.

I long to be admitted to a sight of the <u>Miniature</u> – how many have I
seen?[6]

Wedderburn Webster is again at work he is composing a pamphlet on
the Subject of the recent Suspension of the Habeás [sic] Corpus Act.[7]

With the most sincere and anxious wishes for your Lordships Speedy
recovery

    I remain

    My Lord

    Your Lordships

    attached & faithful Servant

    John Murray

If any thing the least Curious or interesting happen to be published or
printed in the Course of your Travels – allow me to request that your
Lordship would send it to our Ambassadors Envoys or Consuls at the
place directed to J. W. Croker Esqr Admiralty under Cover – to Me[8]

Notes to Letter 98)

<u>Cover</u>: My Lord/My Lord Byron/Poste restante/a Venise/en Italie

1. See Letter 96, n. 16 above. By Monday 3 March B's illness ('a sort of lowish fever') had grown considerably worse, though he told JM 'not to mention this on any account to Augusta', adding with wonderful logic: 'I don't want a Physician & if I did – very luckily those of Italy are the worst in the world – so that I should still have a chance' (*BLJ* V, 178–79). Replying to this letter (98) on Wednesday 9 April, he remarked: 'You tell me to "take care of myself – " faith and I will – I won't be posthumous yet if I can help it', and comforted JM with the news that his 'recent malady ... is *gone* to the Devil' (*BLJ* V, 207–08).

2. B had rebuked Scrope for not writing in his letter to him of Friday 7 March; and though he wrote to him again on Thursday 10 April, Scrope himself did not carry out his threat to write until May (*BLJ* XI, 163–66, and see Letter 99, n. 3 below).

3. B does not appear to allude to this letter; he next wrote to Augusta on Saturday 10 and Sunday 11 May from Rome (*BLJ* V, 223–25).

4. Still unaware that Scott was the author of the review in the *Quarterly*, B had written to JM on Monday 3 March saying he thought it '*very well* written as a composition', and that it would 'do the journal no discredit'. Of the reviewer, he continued: 'he must be a gallant as well as a good man ... to write such an article even anonymously ... I even flatter myself that the writer whosoever he may be (and I have no guess) will not regret that the perusal of this has given me as much gratification – as any composition of that nature could give – & more than any other ever has given ... It is not the mere praise, but there is a *tact* & a *delicacy* throughout not only with regard to me – but to *others* – which as it had not been observed *elsewhere* – I had till now doubted – whether it could be preserved *any where*. – – Perhaps some day or other you will know or tell me the writer's name – be assured – had the article been a harsh one – I should not have asked it' (*BLJ* V, 178). Perhaps JM communicated something of this nature to Scott.

5. This was 'the new Patriarch's procession to St. Mark's', which B had 'missed seeing' but of which he nonetheless gave a very amusing account (*BLJ* V, 179).

6. See Letter 97, n. 2 above.

7. See Letters 92, n. 17, and 93, n. 5 above. B replied: 'So – Webster is writing again – is there no Bedlam in Scotland? – nor thumb-screw? – nor Gag? – nor handcuff?' (*BLJ* V, 208); perhaps there was, for Webster's pamphlet on Habeas Corpus, if ever written, does not appear to have been published.

8. Besides being a *Quarterly* reviewer, John Wilson Croker was Secretary to the Admiralty.

Letter 99)   Tuesday 25 March 1817

Albemarle Street
1817 Tuesday 25 Mar.

My Lord

Three Packets and not one Letter or line[1] – is sufficiently tantalyzing [*sic*] – but I console myself with the belief that if you had not been much better you would not have transcribed so much – and moreover Mr Davies came in soon after the arrival of the Second Act and read me a portion a [*sic*] Letter to himself written in spirits sufficient to satisfy me that you were better – By the way I do seriously aver that the Letter of J. H. is inferior in spirit & sagacity to that of W. W. – who yields to the other in <u>length</u> only[2] – M^r D has borrowed the 1st & 2nd Act [*sic*] for three hours[3] – in the mean time I inclose a proof of the first – & <to>by tomorrow I shall be able to send a duplicate with the remarks of M^r G – the others shall follow in the same way – in the little extract – from the extract – from your Journal wch I <was much> saw I was much struck with your description of pastoral life in the Alps[4] – wch I hope you do not omit & indeed as much of the first impressions made by this Scenery will be given as you can – all the world has been there & will be delighted to tread the Air again in imagination –

I shall have occasion to write again tomorrow – in the mean while I remain My Lord

Your faithful Servant

Jno. Murray

Capt. Byrons Lady – has a <u>Son</u>[5]

Mr Gifford has this moment brought me his Copy – he is truly delighted with it – & repeats that it is <u>exceedingly</u> good – he is only anxious lest you will not take the pains to bring it to a good conclusion which I really hope you will be able to do – make it compleat – for thine honour & reputation – I will send other proofs in a day or three – I send a duplicate of this in another Cover[6]

Notes to Letter 99)

1. JM had by now received the three several packets containing the first and second Acts of *Manfred*, the first Act of which was sent in two covers on Friday 28 February (*BLJ* V, 177–78 and 183).

2. See Letter 92, nn. 17 and 18 above. Writing cheerfully to Scrope Davies on Friday 7 March, B asked him his opinion of Webster's and Hobhouse's answers to the *Quarterly Review*, adding: 'I have yet seen neither – but my friendship for Hobhouse would naturally balance in his favour – now you are impartial – or I fear rather inclining to Webster – but pray let me know' (*BLJ* XI, 163). JM writes to put him right.

3. Writing to Scrope again on Thursday 10 April, B said: 'Murray tells me that you carried off two acts of "Manfred" which I think would suit you admirably' (*BLJ* XI, 165), to which Scrope replied some time in May: 'Your Witch Drama is in some parts divine', quoting especially *Manfred* II, i, 29 and II, ii, 18–19 (MA).

4. See Letter 91, n. 29 above. It is quite evident that JM had not only read the whole of B's Alpine Journal but had lent it to others: Maria Graham, for instance (a great admirer of B), 'perused [it] with the greatest interest', and returned it to JM in March 1817 with some warm-hearted remarks about B (Smiles, I, 381).

5. George Anson Byron (1789–1868), B's cousin and successor to the title, married Elizabeth Mary Chandos Pole in March 1816. Replying on Monday 5 May, B said: 'You tell me George B[yron] has got a son – and Augusta says – a daughter – which is it?' (*BLJ* V, 222). It was a daughter, Mary-Anne.

6. This 'duplicate' does not appear to be extant.

Letter 100)   [Friday] 28 March 1817

Albemarle St London

March 28 – 1817

My Lord

I received the last Act with yr favour of the 9th yesterday & now I inclose a proof both of the Second and Third Acts – with Title Dram Pers – &c – all for correction & emendation – by the way there are several errors wch may affront you as not existing in the Original – wch are owing to the haste with wch my family transcribed them – as I am anxious to preserve the original with wch I had not time to compare it – & having at first, after transcribing sent it to M^r G¹ –

For the Drama Do me the favour to draw upon me for 300 Gs
when[+] you please – & I hope to make a living profit upon it –

<No> I told you in my last that M[r] G was very much pleased with
Act 2 – & as you know he takes a paternal interest in your literary
well being – he does not by any Means like the Conclusion – now I
am venturing upon the confidence with wch your Lordship has ever
honoured me in sending the inclosed – I fear I am not doing right
– I am not satisfied – but I venture – & I entreat that you will make
a point of returning them.[2] I have told him that I have made a Letter
from them – but there is so much friendly good sense in them that I
<d> can not refrain – I am sure you can – & I am almost sure that you
will improve what begins & continues so beautifully in a <J> Drama of
any Kind – the last Act is the Difficulty & this you must surmount –

I very much fear that Mad de Stael is on the point of death – She is
very ill & has been so for some time[3]

I thank you for your reply about Croker[4] – I am going to a great
party at Perrys tonight to meet Mes[d] Fodor – Camperesi [sic] &c &c
&c & I shall say a word to him – I expect to meet M[r] Moore & Lady
– I sent him yr Letter received with mine yesterday – The Prince is
now enchanted by Mad. Fodor – goes no where where she is no [sic]
& sits 3 hours at the Piano with her[5] – – He has at length visited the
Duchess of Cumberland – with all his Courtiers – who had before
abused her – She is now a Marvelously [sic] ill used woman.[6] – Poor
Maturin will get little or nothing from the Theatre – Kean was
disgusted with his Character & ruined the Play – he has in this respect
behaved basely.

Scott is very much pleased that you like the Article in the Q. Rev. &
has told me I may now mention the Author[7] –

I am most happy to hear that you will return in May – I am
flattering myself that you are much better[8] –

Pray give us more of The Pastorals & Scenery of The Alps – & a
Close working of the Whole – do it will be the best announcement of
your Return – M[r] G – is equally firm & Sincere in his admiration of
Act 1 (most particularly) & of Act 2 – as poetry – wch he says can not
go far beyon [sic] it –

 Ever My Lord
 Most faithfully
 Your Servant
 Jno Murray

I beg you to offer my particular Compliments to M[r] Hobhouse – <for>
to whose Elephantine 4[to] I earnestly aspire[9]

———

⁺or I will pay it into Kinnairds

———

I shall pay the 3ʳᵈ £500 – tomorrow[10]

Notes to Letter 100)

1. B had sent the third Act of *Manfred* in his letter to JM of Sunday 9 March telling him to submit it to Gifford, and suggesting '*three hundred* guineas' for the copyright should it be published (*BLJ* V, 183). This 'family' transcription appears to have been printer's copy for the first edition (cf. *CPW* IV, 462).

2. Replying to JM on Monday 14 April, B agreed that the 'third act is certainly d–d bad', and that he would 'try at it again'; but he was 'very glad indeed' that JM had sent Gifford's opinion 'without *deduction*' (*BLJ* V, 211–12). Gifford's note is undated and reads as follows: 'I have marked a passage or two which might be omitted with advantage: but the Act requires strengthening. There is nothing to bear it out but one speech. The Friar is despicable, & the servants uninteresting. The scene with the Friar ought to be imposing, & for that purpose the Friar should be a real good man – not an idiot. – More dignity should be lent to the catastrophe. See how beautifully our old poet Marlow [*sic*] has wrought up the death of Faustus – Several of our old plays have scenes of this kind – but they strive to make them impressive. Manfred should not end in this feeble way – after beginning with such magnificence & promise – & the demons should have something to do in the scene. Do not send my words to Lord B. but you may take a hint from them – Say too that the last Act bears no proportion in length to the two former' (MA). In remitting the new third Act from Rome at the beginning of May, B said: 'The Abbot is become a good man – & the Spirits are brought in at the death' (*BLJ* V, 219; see also, V, 268). For the original version of Act III, see *CPW* IV, 467–71.

3. *The Times* first reported that Madame de Staël was 'dangerously ill of a bilious fever' on Monday 3 March 1817 and reiterated that she was still ill on Monday 17 March. She died on 14 July 1817.

4. See Letter 94, n. 9 above. In his letter of Sunday 9 March, B had expressed his indignation at these '*fabrications*', and asked JM to 'inform Mr. Perry from me that I wonder he should permit such an abuse of my name & his paper' (*BLJ* V, 184).

5. Violante Camporese (1785–1839), soprano, made her first English appearance in Cimarosa's opera *Penelope* at the King's Theatre on Saturday 11 January 1817, upon which *The Times* for Monday 13 January 1817 reported very favourably, adding: 'We anticipate no small pleasure from the united powers of Mesdames FODOR and CAMPORESI [*sic*], exerted throughout

the season in aid of each other.' It was to have that pleasure when she joined Joséphine Fodor-Mainvielle (1789–1870), soprano, who also played the harp and piano, in the English première of *Don Giovanni* on Saturday 12 April 1817 (see *The Times* for Monday 14 and Wednesday 16 April 1817). Shelley saw Camporese in Milan in April 1818 and thought her 'a cold and unfeeling singer and a bad actress' (Shelley, *Letters*, II, 14).

6. The Duchess of Cumberland, Princess Frederica of Solms-Braunfels, was the wife of Ernest Augustus, Duke of Cumberland (1771–1851), the younger brother of the Prince Regent, whom she had married in 1815. Having been twice married, once divorced and earlier engaged to the Duke of Cambridge, she was not received at Court. *The Times* for Thursday 27 March 1817, however, reported: 'The Duke and Duchess of CUMBERLAND opened their rooms for a grand concert on Tuesday evening. The company was numerous: the PRINCE REGENT was there.'

7. Scott had in fact asked JM to send B 'an early copy' of his review and 'at the same time say I am the author at your importunity' in his letter of 10 January 1817 (see Letter 92, n. 34 above).

8. In his letter of Sunday 9 March, B said he was 'getting better – and thinking of moving homewards towards May' (*BLJ* V, 185).

9. JM borrows 'Elephantine 4to' from B's letter to Scrope Davies of Friday 7 March, in which he refers to 'H[obhouse]'s future Elephantine quarto' (*BLJ* XI, 164). Writing to Hobhouse at Rome on Monday 14 April, B told him: 'Murray begs to have the refusal of your next quarto – & presents his compliments – though he is very much displeased with your preface' (*BLJ* V, 216; see also, Letter 92, n. 18, and Letter 99 above). Hobhouse's work was to be *Historical Illustrations of the Fourth Canto of Childe Harold*, which was published by JM in 1818.

10. That is, Morland and Ransom in which Kinnaird was a partner, and the third instalment for *CHP* III (see Letters 89, 90 and 95 above, and Letter 107, n. 13 below).

Letter 101)   [Tuesday] 8 April 1817

London 8 April
1817

My Lord

As the interval of hearing from you was much longer than I have lately been accustomed to calculate upon – I had begun to feel rather uneasy lest the cause should have been – an increase of your <un> fever – I am sorry that you have been so severely indisposed – but I trust that the worst is passed & that you have only to acquire strength to be perfectly restored – As I have now sent your Lordship a proof of the whole of the Drama – I shall presume upon your Placing all additions upon it & shall therefore retain the one you have now sent me until I hear from you again.[1] – It is very singular that you should not have received even the Second Copy wch I sent you of your last poems & of Tales of My Landlor [*sic*] I would have given much that you had received them during your illness[2] – I have just got a Letter from Augustus de Stael in which he tells me that his mother is out of danger – though there are yet very great apprehensions entertained by her friends.[3] – I have just been called away by a visit from Captain Byron – who has had a most dreadful attack of Rheumatic Fever – for a whole fortnight he did not know what it was to be free from the most acute pain – his wife has brought him a Son – as I think I told your Lordship[4] – I hope soon to hear that your Lordship is much better –

Is there no original Venetian Story that you can make use of to give us another Tale?

I am <Dear Sir>
your Lordships
faithful Servant
John Murray

I offer best Comps. to Mr Hobhouse – his Cambridge Adversary the son of Lord Townsend is dead[5] –

Notes to Letter 101)

Cover: My Lord/My Lord Byron/Poste restante/a Venise/en Italie <u>arrived</u>: 23 April <u>forwarded to</u>: Messrs Torlonia/a Rome thence to: No 66. <u>Piazza di Spagna</u>

B had left Venice on Thursday 17 April and, travelling via Ferrara, Bologna, Florence and Foligno, arrived in Rome 12 days later (Tuesday 29 April), where he evidently stayed at No. 66, Piazza di Spagna. Giovanni-Raimondo Torlonia, Duke of Bracciano (1755–1829), was the leading banker in Rome, at whose premises at No. 173 via del Corso he also entertained foreign visitors and the Roman elite.

1. The last letter JM had received from B was that of Sunday 9 March enclosing the Third Act of *Manfred*, to which JM's reply was Letter 100 above (see also, *BLJ* V, 183–85).

2. *Tales of My Landlord* reached B at Rome; he had read them by Friday 9 May (*BLJ* V, 220 and 229).

3. See Letter 100, n. 3 above.

4. See Letter 99, n. 5 above.

5. Charles Fox Townshend (1795–1817), founder of the Eton Society in 1811, had died on Wednesday 2 April 1817. He was the son of Lord John Townshend (1759–1833), MP for Cambridge University, with whom Hobhouse had had a misunderstanding over the Cambridge candidacy in 1814 (see *BB*, 130–31 and 179–80). See also B's letter to Hobhouse of Friday 3 March 1815 in which he asks: 'What has happed between you and Lord J. T. – I hear he has "lampooned you & your friends" – so says Kinnaird' (*BLJ* IV, 278 and XI, 226). What Kinnaird had actually said when writing to B on 17 February 1815 was: 'Hobhouse is in hot water about a letter of Lᵈ J. Townshend's – He swears he will have an interview with the said Lord – I have offer'd to be his second, seeing that you are married' (MA).

Letter 102)   Saturday 12 April 1817

Albemarle Street. 1817
Apˡ. 12. Saturday

My Lord

I was very much delighted by your amusing Letter of the 25ᵗʰ. received on Thursday – I forwarded the Letter to Mʳ Moore – & delivered that for Mʳˢ Leigh[1] – who came to town the day it arrived – on the Same day I sent sundry Packets – I Tooth Powder II – your Works 5 V – III Two Copˢ each of Harold & Chillon IV sundry Letters for you, accumulated during your absence – All of which Mʳ Croker very obligingly took charge off [*sic*], & has sent to you <u>via</u> Paris – with orders to Sir Chaˢ Stewart to forward them instantly.[2] Mʳ Croker has sent them by this Channel finding that the things I twice sent you by Messenger direct to Italy – from the foreign Office had never reached you – I <wri> send this by Post & I will be glad to learn the dates of the Arrival of the Parcel & this Epistle –

I lent Mʳ Croker – in reward the two first Acts of the Drama to read and I think there is so much justice in his mode of liking them – that I venture to inclose his letter to me[3] – I shew the Third Act to no one hoping that you will insist upon your Genius's making it what it ought to be – Gifford was very much amused with your Letter – but fears that you are determined – by your remarks up [*sic*] Kissing – you see a great deal more before you subside into habits of discretion.[4] – We admire the justice of your poetical criticism – as much as we laugh at your mode of expressing it – I fear you must yet make allowances for the tardy correspondence of Moore – who is in bed with the Muses[5] – what will come of it we are yet to learn –

Our friend Southey has got into a confounded Scrape – Some Twenty

years ago, when he knew no better, & was a republican he wrote a
certain Drama entitled Wat Tyler in order to disseminate wholesome
doctrine amongst the <u>lower</u> orders – this he presented to a friend,
with a fraternal embrace, who was at that time enjoying the cool
reflection generated by his residence in Newgate – His friend however
either thinking its publication might prolong his durance or fancying
that it would not become profitable – as a speculation – quietly put
it into his pocket – & now that the Author has most manfully laid
about him Slaying Whigs & Republicans by the Million – this Cursed
friend publishes – but what is yet Worse the Author upon suing for an
injunction – to proceed in which he is obliged to <u>swear</u> that h<is>e is
the <u>Author</u> – is informed by the Chancellor that it is <u>seditious</u> – & that
for sedition there is no Copyright – I will inclose either now or in my
next a 2^{dy} Copy – for as there is no Copyright everyone has printed it
– wch will amuse you.[6]

I am not surprised at your unacquaintance with the Vice-Consul
– because he is your <u>intimate</u> friend Mr Scott – <whom you> whose
Nephews & Nieces you made such fair efforts to increase – but the
Consul – my friend Mr Hoppner has the most charming wife a Swiss
that you have seen[7] – Mr Ward told me yesterday that She was just
one of the most accomplished & delightful Women he ever met with
– – Lord March married yesterday the Eldest daughter of the Earl of
Anglesea[8] –

I have got the Wat Tyler wch I inclose with a Letter from Mrs Leigh[9]
– who has been much distressed at your Lordships illness – I hope this
will find you recovered – Pray Work up the last Act of the Drama You
must not publish any thing that will not set the town in flames now
– after the good account we have given of you –

I send my most hearty good wishes to your Lordship & remain
My Lord
Your faithful Servant
John Murray

Notes to Letter 102)

<u>Cover</u>: My Lord Byron/a Venise

B received this letter in Rome on Friday 9 May and replied to it the same day
(*BLJ* V, 220–22).

1. B's letter of Tuesday 25 March enclosing those to Augusta and to Moore of
   the same date (*BLJ* V, 186–89 and 190–94).

2. Sir Charles Stuart (1779–1845), the English Ambassador at Paris (for a recent

biography of whom, see Robert Franklin, *Private and Secret: The Clandestine Activities of a Nineteenth-century Diplomat* [Lewes, England: Book Guild Publishing, 2005], esp. chs 6–10). Evidently finding JM's hand difficult to read, B replied from Venice on 30 May (whence he had returned two days earlier) saying that although he had received this letter (102) there was 'no sign nor tidings of the parcel sent through Sir – – Stuart', nor does it seem to have arrived until 7 August (*BLJ* V, 229 and 254).

3.   B replied on Friday 9 May: 'Croker's letter to you is a very great compliment – I shall return it to you in my next' (*BLJ* V, 220). The letter, dated 12 April 1817 from the Admiralty, is in MA and runs as follows:

Dear Murray

   For honour's sake do all you can to induce Lord Byron to go on with his tragedy – for such I suppose it is to be. Its wildness or, if you will, its extravagance, is to me its first recommendation – Our stage is grown so servile & tame that nothing but a bold stroke can redeem it – Voltaire calls Hamlet a "triste extravagance" & Fréron calld [*sic*] Voltaires Semiramis, in which he borrow'd so largely from Hamlet, by the same name; and you may be sure that nothing very good in literature (or perhaps even in the Arts) was ever done which did not at first startle the vulgar as extravagant – the very word indeed explains itself he is extravagant Who wanders beyond the beaten track & it is in this sense & with this hope that I entreat you to try to get Lord B— to go on with his extravagance. I will keep the proofs you sent me in order that when you let me see the rest, I may judge of the whole at present I <am> shd. be obliged to judge of the house <by> in the inspection of one of the bricks. I think however I may venture to say that you shd endeavour to hint to Lord Byron that a play is essentially intended to be played & that therefore care should be taken that its acts contain nothing which cannot be acted – I mention this because in the few pages you have sent me, I observe that there are the Voices of two Spirits, & the forms (I therefore, presume) of 4 others; the latter might be easily & <splendidly> impressively managed by gauze=clouds &c but I know not how the Spirit of the Mountains & the Spirit of the Waters could be sufficiently distinguish'd by their voices. After all it is possible that from its original conception, this drama may be "unactable" but Lord Byron must have (or at least have had) a thousand fancies in his mind capable of being reduced to action, & if he finds that you (who speak with the voice of the public) are very desirous of having a play of his writing, he may perhaps turn his thoughts that way – he has an art of painting from nature & yet producing results higher & more sublime & more terrific than nature, which I should call the first requisite of a tragedian & which as far as I know Shakespeare, alone of the Moderns, possessed

– Yours faithfully.

JW Croker

I have sent all your parcels carefully done up like official dispatches in a leathern bag & I have taken precautions to have the said bag dispatch'd – it will pass thro' Sir C. Stuarts hands at Paris; <two besides yours were> & perhaps thro' the french post office; but it is well sealed.

This letter, despite one or two inaccuracies and notwithstanding its relevance to *Manfred*, may well have had a more significant bearing on B's later composition, *Sardanapalus* (1821). In his *Dissertation sur la tragédie ancienne et moderne*, prefixed to *Sémiramis* (1749), Voltaire, who elsewhere condemns Shakespeare as 'un composé de grandeur et d'extravagance' (a compound of grandeur and extravagance), writes of *Hamlet*: 'parmi les beautés qui étincellent au milieu de ces terribles extravagances, l'ombre du père d'Hamlet est un des coups de théâtre les plus frappants' (amongst the beauties that sparkle in the midst of these terrible extravagances the ghost of Hamlet's father is one of the most striking pieces of theatre) (see *Voltaire on Shakespeare*, ed. Theodore Bestermann, in *Studies on Voltaire and the Eighteenth Century*, 54 [Geneva, 1967], 58 and 202). Élie-Catherine Fréron (1718–76), journalist and critic, author of *Lettres sur quelques écrits de ce temps* (1752–54) which developed into *L'Année Littéraire* (1754–90), was Voltaire's Zoilus. But it was not of *Sémiramis* itself, but of Voltaire's disparagement of past and present dramatists in both his *Dissertation* and his *Mensonges imprimés* (also published with *Sémiramis*), to which he applied the word 'extravagance'. Alluding covertly to Voltaire in a review of the works of Rémond de Saint-Mard, he said: 'Il n'appartient qu'à un petit esprit, enflé de présomption, de prétendre rabaisser les devanciers illustres et les célèbres contemporains, & d'imiter l'Empereur Commode, qui saisoit abattre toutes les têtes des statues d'Hercule, pour mettre la sienne à leur place. Il étoit reservé à notre siècle de voir renouveller une pareille extravagance' (It belongs only to a petty mind, puffed up with its own self-importance, to seek to depreciate his illustrious predecessors and celebrated contemporaries, and like the Roman Emperor Commodus [161–92 AD] tear down the statues of Hercules in order to set up his own in their place. It was reserved for our century to witness the renewal of a similar extravagance) (*Lettres sur quelques écrits de ce temps*, 13 vols [Londres: Duchesne, 1752–54], II, 39–40, Lettre II, 15 September 1749; see also, III, 43–66, esp. 61, Lettre III, 15 January 1750). What Fréron did deplore in *Sémiramis*, however, was the weak effect of the Ghost of Ninus, which appears at the end of Act III to warn Arzace, who is in fact Ninias, the son of Ninus and Sémiramis, that he is about to commit incest with his mother (Sémiramis) whom he eventually kills in Act V (cf. *Sardanapalus*, IV, i, 78–165, esp. 158). In a review of *Hamlet, Tragédie imitée de l'Anglois: par M. Ducis* in *L'Année Littéraire* (1770), II, 289–320, Fréron criticized Ducis for suppressing the appearance of the Ghost, 'le ressort employé par *Shakespeare* & par M. *de Voltaire*. Il falloit que l'Ombre parût; il falloit qu'elle fût sensible aux yeux du spectateur' (the resource employed by Shakespeare and Voltaire. The Ghost must be seen; it must be made palpable to the eyes of the audience) (296). But, he continues: 'L'Ombre de *Ninus* dans Sémiramis, quoiqu'elle produise peu d'effet, justifioit celle du père de *Hamlet*. L'Ombre dans *Shakespeare* laisse une impression forte & terrible; je viens de dire qu'elle produisoit peu d'effet dans M. *de Voltaire*; j'ajoûte qu'elle fait presque rire, parce que ce qui en résulte n'est point assez frappant. Elle devoit rendre tous les spectateurs immobiles d'effroi' (Although the Ghost of Ninus in *Sémiramis* produces little effect, it vindicates that of Hamlet's father. The Ghost in Shakespeare leaves a strong and terrible impression. I say that it produces little effect in Voltaire; I will add that it almost makes one laugh because it is not frightening enough: it should petrify the audience) (297). Hence, however pertinent Croker's etymological disquisition on 'extravagance' and his concern about the practicalities of staging the voices and spirits in *Manfred* may be, his allusion to Voltaire's *Sémiramis* and the implications that arise therefrom may well have prompted B to consult the play when writing *Sardanapalus*, which in turn would lend considerable weight to Weller's suggestion in his note to *Sardanapalus*, IV, i, 158 (see *CPW* VI, 621–22).

4. In his letter of 25 March, B had discussed the relative merits of entitling a poem a '*tale*', a '*fable*', a '*story*' or a '*romance*', had observed that the Italian women '*kiss*' better than those of any other nation' which was 'attributed to the worship of images and the early habit of osculation induced thereby', and concluded with a poetical postscript containing what McGann has entitled '[Versicles]' and '[To Mr. Murray]' (*BLJ* V, 192–94; *CPW* IV, 114–15).

5. *Lalla Rookh*'s birthday was overdue (see Letter 91, n. 23 above).

6. Southey's youthful Revolutionary dramatic poem *Wat Tyler*, written in 1794, had been piratically published on Friday 14 February 1817 only three days after his reactionary article on Parliamentary Reform had appeared in the *Quarterly Review*, XVI, xxxi (October 1816; pub. 11 February 1817), 225–79. Hazlitt had vilified Southey for his hypocrisy in *The Examiner* on Sunday 9 March (see Letter 97, n. 9 above); and William Smith, MP, in the debate on the Seditious Meetings Bill on Friday 14 March, had claimed that the poem was seditious and enquired why no proceedings had been instituted against its author (*Parliamentary Debates*, XXXV [1817], 1090–92). Southey sought an injunction against its publication, which was refused by Lord Chancellor Eldon on Wednesday 19 March on precisely the grounds JM here describes. B replied at some length, regretting most 'the intolerance of Apostacy' and wishing Southey 'damned – not as a poet – but as a politician' (*BLJ* V, 220–21; see also, *CMP*, 376–77). Southey was to answer Smith with *A Letter to William Smith, Esq. M.P. from Robert Southey, Esq.*, which was published by JM at the end of April (see Letter 103, n. 6 below).

7. In his letter of Tuesday 25 March, B had said he knew neither the Consul nor the Vice-Consul at Venice (*BLJ* V, 191). The Consul was Richard Belgrave

Hoppner (1786–1872), son of the portrait painter John Hoppner, RA (1758–1810), whom B eventually met in October 1817 and with whom he became very friendly. His wife, Isabelle, was Swiss; Hobhouse also found her 'charming' – as did Shelley, though he did not find her 'very accomplish[hed]' or 'very wise', and Henry Salt, though she could not speak 'a hundred words of English' (Hobhouse, *Recollections*, II, 86; Shelley, *Letters*, II, 36–38 and 42; and J.J. Halls, *The Life and Correspondence of Henry Salt*, 2 vols [London: Richard Bentley, 1834], I, 430, 432–33 and 440). There is no record of any Vice-Consul at Venice at the time, let alone one named Scott, and by June 1819 Henry Dorville was filling that office (see, for example, *BLJ* VI, 174n.); nor can he have been Alexander Scott whom B distinctly told Hobhouse twice was '*not* the Vice Consul', 'not the vice-Consul – but a traveller – who lives much at Venice – like My*sen*' (*BLJ* VI, 51 and 55). In view of JM's cryptic and evidently ironical references to 'intimate friend' and 'Nephews & Nieces', he must therefore have been William Scott (b. 1773), a disreputable lawyer and the brother and blackmailer of Lady Oxford (née Jane Elizabeth Scott, mother of the 'Harleian Miscellany' on which JM would therefore seem to be playing), on account of whose swindling activities the Oxfords had been obliged to leave England in 1813, and who himself seems to have led a nomadic existence escaping creditors. One way or the other, however, B does not appear to have known him.

8. In fact not 'yesterday' but the day before (Thursday 10 April), Charles, Earl of March (1791–1860), eldest son of the Duke of Richmond (whose wife gave the famous Ball before Waterloo), married Lady Caroline Paget (1796–1874), eldest daughter of Sir Henry William Paget, second Earl of Uxbridge (1768–1854), 'One Leg', created first Marquess of Anglesey in 1815 after Waterloo at which he commanded the cavalry and lost a leg. He was not in fact present at the ceremony, and the bride was given away by her brother (*The Times*, Friday 11 April 1817).

9. Perhaps a letter of November 1816 which B mentions when writing to Augusta on Saturday 10 May, the day after receiving this letter of JM's (*BLJ* V, 223–24).

Letter 103)   [Tuesday] 13 May 1817

London May 13. 1817

My Lord
    I have received safely your obliging Letters of the 14th. 2nd and 23rd April inclosing proofs returned of the Drama & many interesting observations on Men & Things[1] – Your favour of the 23rd arrived yesterday & I instantly sent the Lines upon Tasso <of> to Mr G – who

called with them Soon afterwards and assured me that they were
exceedingly good & that there was besides a difference in the style
which would by being novel prove additionally interesting – He thinks
they should should not be published separately but remain until we form
another pamphlet, probably with the Drama – & will you not finish
one of the many <u>Fables</u> (I think is your new name)[2] which you have
sketched out & then our Coach is full – I rejoice to find you so much
recovered for I suspect that you have been very ill indeed –

Moores Poem is to appear on the 22nd inst & I will try to send
it[3] – Mr Sheil the Author of Adelaide – has had most extraordinary
Success on the <u>Stage</u> with a Tragedy called the <u>Apostate</u> – merely from
forming a Series of interesting Situations – I read it with M^r G in
MSS & we both thought it impossible that it could succeed – & I went
fully convinced that it would be d—d – but nothing could exceed the
applause which it drew throughout – it had the advantage of giving
four exceedingly appropriate Characters to C. Kemble – McCreedy
[sic] Young & Miss O Neil [sic] – neither [sic] of whom ever had an
opportunity of acting better – its Success has been compleat & it must
be Acted as long as four good Actors can be brought together[4] –

Pray have you not received the Copy of Manuel by Maturin[5] wch
I sent you nor yet the Copies of your Own Poems? nor Tales of My
Landlord? Do you think that merely addressing you Poste Restante
– could have occasioned the failure?

Your friend Hunt, because I could not give him £500 for his Rimini
– has had the baseness to enter upon a Series of Abuse of me[6] – which
I really regard no further than that I never did give my name to the
Public, except in a business advertisement –

I breakfasted yesterday with your friend Mr Davies who is in health &
usual Spirits – I wish very much that he would marry Miss M— – <y>
whose Affections he gains by reading to her your
   "I should but teach him how to read
   Byrons Verses & that would woo her"[7] –
I received a letter from you yesterday containing the additional line – &
Some Tooth Powder [sic][8] – – I sent five Boxes to you via Paris & <Sir>
Sir Charles Stewart wch I hope you have got – & I will repeat the dose
with the addition of Magnesia in a day or two – Sir Ja^s Mackintosh is
in a corner reading with expressions of high commendation yr Lines of
Tasso – & he sends his Comps –

I shall write again on Tuesday in the mean time I remain, devotedly
My Lord
 Your Lordships faithful Servant
 Jno. Murray

Notes to Letter 103)

<u>Cover</u>: My Lord/My Lord Byron/Poste restante/a Venise/en Italie

1. B's letters of Wednesday 2 April (replying to Letter 97 above), two of Monday 14 April returning proofs of *Manfred*, and one from Florence of Wednesday 23 April enclosing the MS of *The Lament of Tasso* (*BLJ* V, 203–05 and 211–12 and 214, and XI, 190). JM had not received B's third letter of Monday 14 April sent via Polidori (*BLJ* V, 212–14).

2. B had expressed his preference for 'fable' as against '*tale*' in his letter of Tuesday 25 March (*BLJ* V, 192; see also, Letter 102, n. 4 above). *The Prisoner of Chillon* (1816) was the first of B's poems to be subtitled 'A Fable' (see *CPW* IV, 4).

3. *Lalla Rookh* was in fact published on 27 May 1817.

4. See Letter 92, n. 10 above. The play is set in Granada during the Spanish Inquisition: Charles Kemble (1775–1854) played Hemeya, a descendant of the Moorish kings; William Charles Macready (1793–1873), Malec, an old Moor; Charles Mayne Young (1777–1856), Pescara, the Governor of Granada; and Eliza O'Neill, later Lady Becher (1791–1872), Florinda, the only female part. As JM implies, this was a strong cast.

5. See Letter 102, n. 2 above. JM's 'dispatch' containing 'the extract from Moore's Italy – & Mr. Maturin's bankrupt tragedy' eventually arrived on Saturday 14 June (*BLJ* V, 237).

6. See Letters 97, n. 9, and 102, n. 6 above. This time JM was right: Hunt had attacked him as the publisher of Southey's *Quarterly Review* article and *A Letter to William Smith, Esq. M.P.*, in two satirical articles in *The Examiner*, entitled respectively 'Death and Funeral of of the Late Mr. Southey' (No. 485 [Sunday 13 April 1817], 236–37) and 'Extraordinary Case of the Late Mr. Southey' (No. 489 [Sunday 11 May 1817], 300–04), in the latter of which JM is cruelly caricatured and denominated 'Murrain' throughout.

7. JM adapts Othello's way of winning Desdemona's heart: 'And bade me, if I had a friend that lov'd her,/I should but teach him how to tell my story,/And that would woo her. Upon this hint I spake' (*Othello*, I, iii, 164–66). That Scrope was a great comfort to Miss Mercer Elphinstone at this time and was indeed dosing her with B is evident from her letter to him, dated simply 'Wednesday' (almost certainly of May 1817), returning a letter of B's he had lent her, and thanking him for his '<u>kindness</u>', 'good opinion' and 'friendship', and asking him to send her any new work by B (Scrope Davies Papers: BL Loan 70, Vol. I, ff. 62–64; B's letter would have been that to Scrope of Thursday 10 April; *BLJ* XI, 164–66). However, Scrope did not encumber her with nuptial overtures. On later occasions, and with different victims, Hobhouse told B that Scrope 'makes your poeshies pimp for him' (*BB*, 246; see also, Letter 112, n. 11 below).

8. B's letter of Saturday 26 April sending line 217 of *The Lament of Tasso* ('And woo compassion to a blighted name'), which he had omitted from his MS sent from Florence, and urgently requesting JM to send him '*Waite's tooth powder – red* a quantity – *Calcined Magnesia* of the best quality – a quantity – and all this by safe sure & speedy means' (*BLJ* V, 217–19; see also, *CPW* IV, 123).

Letter 104)   [Friday] 30 May 1817

London 30th May 1817.

My Lord

I have to acknowledge the arrival of your Letter by Mr Polidori & of two subsequently, from Rome, dated the 5th & 9th inst – of a short one also of corrigenda – – for all which I am grateful –

Now of their principal Topic – the Drama and Poem on Tasso – The Third Act is not only infinitely improved – but contains some of the finest passages in the Drama – most particularly am I delighted, and supported in it by Mr G, with your exquisite view of Rome struck off in the heat & in Your best manner – so that we shall do[1] –

Now respecting price I shall give the sum which you desire – but then I must publish in my own way – the Drama makes the same quantity as the third Canto or as any of the other publications – & therefore you must understand – as I <u>can</u> not put a larger price upon it – all that I give more is so much Money (expense) thrown away – & I mus [*sic*] therefore be allowed to print the Lament of Tasso Separately[2] – I will Say more about this in my next –

Mr G – has corrected the Proofs & I have just sent them to press, hoping to publish next week[3] –

I am glad that you have received the Parcel containing the Tales at last wch must have been a <u>particular</u> gratification to you from what you tell me[4] – – I must contrive to send you Moores Poem wch is very good but not within 50 Miles of you – I can assure you – I am doing all I can for him – & he tells me he has got the 3,000Gs. the price of his Volume is £2. 2. 0[5]

I suspect you are preparing a magnificent Third [*sic*] Canto – which I shall be most glad to receive in <u>October</u> next[6]

Upon my word I think you ought to be satisfied at our having printed your poems with no more than three very unimportant, & one self correcting error "lore" – "more"[7] – I pray you send me the Italian Copy of Chillon[8] & if any new & Curious Book or pamphlet spring under your way, pray do me the favour to dash it off to me

I am sorry to say that we do not like either of the Portraits[9] –

I hope you have received the Second Parcel with a Copy of the Poems in 5 Vols – pray did you get the Tooth Powder – & Letter?[10]

With best Compliments

I remain My Lord

Your faithful Servant

John Murray

I fear it is impossible for Mad. de Stael to recover[11]

Notes to Letter 104)

Cover: My Lord/Lord Byron/Poste restante/a Venise/en Italie <u>arrived</u>: 16 June

1. B's letter of Monday 14 April, conveyed 'By the favour of Dr. Polidori' and containing the '*two Miniatures*'; his letter of Monday 5 May, sending the new third Act of *Manfred*; and two letters of Friday 9 May, one containing his 'exquisite view of Rome', the other being '*Corrections* Canto 3d.' (*BLJ* V, 212–14 and 219–22, and XI, 190–91).

2. In his letter of 5 May. B demanded '*Six* hundred guineas' for *Manfred* and *The Lament of Tasso*: 'I won't take less than three hundred g[uinea]s for anything. – The two together will make *you* a larger publication than the "Siege & Parisina" – so you may think yourself let off very easy' (*BLJ* V, 219). In his reply to this letter (104) of Tuesday 17 June, B told JM: 'You are to print in what form you please – that is your concern', but warned him sharply he would 'desert at once to the "*Row*" – if you come over me with your pitiful-hearted speeches – about "can" & "*not*"' (*BLJ* V, 239–40).

3. *Manfred* was published on Monday 16 June, and *The Lament of Tasso* a month later on 17 July 1817.

4. B told JM he had at last received *Tales of My Landlord* in his letter of Friday 9 May (*BLJ* V, 220).

5. Moore received 3,000 guineas (a vast sum) for the copyright of *Lalla Rookh*, the Quarto of which sold at 2 guineas. B replied on 17 June: 'It gives me great pleasure to hear of Moore's success ... whatever good you can tell me of him & his poem will be most acceptable' (*BLJ* V, 239).

6. JM means a 'Fourth' Canto; this error accounts for B's reply: 'You are out about the third [*sic*] Canto – I have not done – nor designed a line of continuation to that poem' (*BLJ* V, 240). He was to begin the Fourth Canto of *CHP* on 26 June 1817.

7. In fact only two errors – 'love' for 'lore', and 'wide' for 'wild' (*CHP* III,

lines 798 and 959) – which B had indicated in his '*Corrections*' sent on Friday
9 May (*BLJ* XI, 190–91; see also, *CPW* II, 108 and 114).

8. In his letter of Friday 9 May, B told JM provocatively: 'the Italians have
   printed Chillon &c. a *piracy* a pretty little edition prettier than yours', and
   promised to send him a copy (*BLJ* V, 222). I have been unable to find a copy
   of this.

9. These were the '*two Miniatures*', painted by Prepiani, which B had sent via
   Polidori (see n. 1 above, and Letter 97, n. 2 above). JM's 'we' includes Scrope
   and Augusta, both of whom, Scrope told B, thought the miniatures 'hideous
   – have you had a paralytic stroke? or are you represented as being in the
   House of Lords? with the mouth on one side? They are positively hideous
   – and I need not add, very unlike the Original' (MA). B replied somewhat
   forlornly to Augusta on Thursday 19 June (*BLJ* V, 242). See also, Peach,
   Portraits of Byron, 87–91, Figs 51 and 52.

10. B answered this on Wednesday 18 June, saying: 'I got Maturin's Bedlam
    at last – but no other parcel – I am in fits for the tooth powder – & the
    Magnesia', adding 'I want some of Burkitt's *Soda* powders' (*BLJ* V, 242).

11. B made no allusion to this news; but see Letter 105 below.

Letter 105)   Tuesday 5 August 1817

London August 5. 1817
Tuesday

My Lord
    This day has brought me your Letter of the 15th July adding another
to the many instances of your truly kind indulgence to my unpardonable
indolence[1] – I am very sorry indeed to find that there is so little chance
of seeing you soon in England and I fancy you will suffer equal grief
when you learn that next year <I am> you will certainly have a visit
from me[2] – In the mean time if you will forgive me I will send you
a regular journal of news literary & domestic. – I perceive by your
Lordships reconing [*sic*] by stanzas that you are within Fourteen Stanzas
of compleating your <u>Opus Magnum</u> – for such I think it is your
determination to make Childe Harold[3] – The first Stanza Mr Gifford
thinks very highly of – as does Mr Frere & many more to whom I have
ventured to shew it[4] – Your Lordship need not be assured how much
I am rejoiced at the Prospect of again opening my Literary Campaign
<with> under such brilliant auspices – I should like to have time to
send the Proofs Sheets [*sic*] out for your Lordships inspection and this I

could easily do if I received the MSS next month.

I am sorry that you do not yet acknowledge the receipt of a Parcel containing Moores Poem &c & packages of Magnesia − Tooth Powder − wch I send [sic] under the care of Mr Rose[5] − who I think was to forward them to you from Padua − However as I have repeated with increase all that I sent by him in the packets which you will certainly have received before this from the kindness of Mr Kinnaird[6] − the loss is of less consequence − No word yet of the Parcel via Sir Chas Stewart? I can not find even a clue to <Sir Jno St Aubin> Mr St John I mean − can you tell me any place to apply?[7]

I am sorry that Mr S − has so unwittingly incurred your anger[8] − he always continues to speak of you with the most unfeigned kindness − I had wondered at the recent asperity of your remarks upon him − he is on his return freighted I fancy with <a> the Translation & A Tour − of the latter − I have already engaged for two One by Mr Rose who possesses an intimate knowledge of the People of Italy & their Language − and another by a Person perhaps even better informed − well known to poor Horner − a Mr Gaeliffe [sic] − Professor Playfair too is reported to have written one[9] − By the way − & if it be no sin − by the Lord − Polidori has sent me his Tragedy!!! do me the kindness to send me by return of Post a delicate declention [sic] of it − which I engage faithfully to copy[10] − I am truly sorry that he will employ himself in a way so ill suited to his genius − he is not without literary talents −

I sent yr Lordship Copies of Manfred & of Tasso which are I trust printed correctly[11] − they are both but particularly the former greatly admired by the best Critics − but they soar above the Million − Mr Frere, I think I told you, says that it and the Third Canto − place you in a higher Class of Poets − that is the very highest − − Amongst the Books I intruded upon Mr Kinnaird − was Coleridges Life & Opinions − wch will I think interest you[12] − you will pardon the occasional obscurities − & I fear absurdities − for its power in most parts − I think you will like my MSS de St Helena − Talma[13] said when he read it he conversed with Buonaparte − I sent him one splendidly bound − & he wrote me a Letter expressing his delight at what reminded him of past Glory

Your Lordship will have heard, not without regret, of the premature (for her age) death of Mad. de Stael who with all her faults was an excellent person[14] − I think she had a good heart − and I know that she was very kind to me − − I had a letter from the Hon. J. W. Ward dated Paris July 17 − in wch he tells me "I saw poor Mme de Stael four days before She died. She was looking wretchedly ill, and shewed marks of great langour & weakness. But her understanding was unimpaired. She evidently thought very ill of her own situation, tho' at the same time, she had no notion how near she was to her end. – There is a story here that just at last she was reconciled to the Church of Rome – chiefly it is said by the persuasion of the Viscount Montmorency. – Perhaps too Mr Schlegel contributed his influence to this event. He had already set the example. I do not know the fact for certain, but I think it not improbable. I also understand that it now appears she had been for some time married to Mr Rocca. I do not hear in what state of forwardness her book was – but I should hope that a part of it at least was fit for publi[cation."][15]

– She confessed her Marriage & acknowledged [a] Child a Son – born when she was 49 [sic] –

I inclose the Edinb. Criticism compleat it is written by Wilson (Isle of Palms) – and add two others from the British Rev.[16] – you will not be in the forthcoming No of the Q. R. – Mr Scrope Davis [sic] <offt> often does me the favour to call & we discuss your Letters Poetry &c &c – I saw Mrs Leigh three days ago in some trouble at the entrance of the Hooping Cough [sic] but otherwise well[17] – Mr Moore I believe I told you is gone to Paris with Mr Roges [sic] – who dedicates all his time to him[18]

Whilst Mr Kinnaird is with you I trust that you will do me the favour to confide any Commissions, particularly of cutting off M^r H—ns head heart or bowels he hath not – & any thing else[19] –

I beg the favour of you to offer my most particular remembrances & compliments to Mr Kinnaird – and to believe that I ever remain
My Lord
Your obliged & faithful Servant
John Murray

Mr Gifford always remembers you – he is now at Ramsgate after being very ill

[On back cover after sealing]

Your Armenian Friends have this Moment presented themselves with your Letter – I will take all their Grammars & do all otherwise to serve & assist them – I will recommend them to Sir John M – at Madras – I am very sorry they miss the value of M^r K's more powerful aid. 4 o Clock[20]

Notes to Letter 105)

Cover: My Lord/My Lord Byron/poste restante/a Venise/en Italie <u>arrived</u>: 20 August

1. Since replying to JM's last letter of 30 May (Letter 104 above), B had written four times (1, 8, 9 and 15 July), informing him of the commencement and progress of the Fourth Canto of CHP (*BLJ* V, 244–45, 247–48, 249 and 251–53).

2. In the event, this visit did not take place, though B told JM on 12 October: 'if you come out next Summer – let me know in time' (*BLJ* V, 269).

3. In his most recent letter of 15 July, B had told JM he had finished 'ninety & eight stanzas of the 4th. Canto', which would 'probably be about the same length as the *third*'; by the end of the letter, they had 'jumped to *104.* – & *Such stanzas*! by St. Anthony! ... some of them are the right thing' (*BLJ* V, 251–53). Both JM and B were a little out in their calculations: by the time it was published the Canto had 'jumped' to 184 stanzas.

4. In his letter of 1 July, B had written out the first stanza and a line or two of the second of the Canto and asked: 'now, Sirrah! – what say you to the sample?' (*BLJ* V, 244–45).

5. B had received this parcel through William Stewart Rose (1775–1843), the translator, by 4 September 1817 (*BLJ* V, 262; see also, n. 9 below).

6. This consignment suffered sadly in transit. Writing to JM on 13 August from Spa on his way out to join B in Venice, Kinnaird told him: 'The Packages & books which you confided to me for Lord Byron have reached this place in good condition save & except the damage they have sustain'd from being well powder'd with the red dust which you had intended for his Lordship's teeth – I am sorry to say that the boxes allowed the whole powder to escape, & I write this to apprize you of the circumstance & that you may further a second supply' (MA). Kinnaird also informed B, who in turn told JM (*BLJ* V, 262).

7. Correcting JM in his reply of Thursday 21 August, B said: 'It is not Mr. St. John – but *Mr. St. Aubyn*, Son of Sir John Aubyn', adding, '*Polidori* knows him – & introduced him to me ... the Doctor will ferret him out' (*BLJ* V, 258; see also, Letter 92, n. 22 above).

8. This was Sotheby of whom B had 'more than once' made 'dishonorable mention' in his letters to JM and which he explained in his letter of 15 July was because Sotheby had sent him 'an *anonymous* note containing some gratuitously impertinent remarks' (*BLJ* V, 252–53). When he learnt of these charges through a Mr Bedingfield and Hobhouse, Sotheby was 'Justly hurt' and wrote a vehement denial, dated 3 April 1818 and written in the third person, 'asserting, that, till yesterday, He was wholly ignorant of all or any of

the circumstances, directly or indirectly, connected with either imputation' (MA). JM enclosed this letter in one of his own, which is not extant but which B received on 23 April 1818 (*BLJ* VI, 34–36). Sotheby's *Farewell to Italy, and Occasional Poems* was published by JM in 1818 (see also, *CMP*, 85–87 and 355–58).

9. See also n. 5 above. William Stewart Rose's *The Court of Beasts: translated from the Animali Parlanti of Giambattista Casti: A Poem in Seven Cantos*, and *Letters from the North of Italy*, 2 vols, were both published by JM in 1819. For Francis Horner, see Letter 95, n. 9 above. Jacques Augustin Galiffe's *Italy and its Inhabitants; An Account of a Tour in that Country in 1816 and 1817*, 2 vols, was published in 1820; William Playfair's *France As It Is, Not Lady Morgan's France*, 2 vols, in 1819 and 1820 (see also, *CMP*, 85–87 and 355–58).

10. This elicited B's marvellous lines beginning 'Dear Doctor – I have read your play/Which is a good one in it's way' (*BLJ* V, 258–60; see also, *CPW* IV, 126–28, '[Epistle from Mr. Murray to Dr. Polidori]'). Although B had not read the tragedy himself, he had alerted JM to it and had asked him to assist Polidori as best he could in that and other matters in his letter of 24 January 1817 (*BLJ* V, 163–64; see also Letter 94, above). Polidori's letter accompanying his tragedy is in MA. Dated merely 'Wednesday Night' (probably, Wednesday 30 July 1817) and addressed 'for/— Murray Esqʳᵉ/ Albemarle Street', it runs as follows:

> My dear Sir
>   Accompanying this I send you a tragedy which I should wish to publish – I wish you would either peruse or get it perused so as to judge of its fitness – I should like to call it Count Orlando or the Modern Abraham but as the latter title may be objectionable as you like in case you publish it – It is improper for the stage because it works by religion & for this reason I have taken the liberty of introducing more imagery – if you would grant me the favour of forming a judgement upon it & increase that favour by doing it quickly & sending your answer to Norwich you would oblidge [*sic*] much your
> obed & hum. Serv
> J Polidori
> Direct merely
> Dʳ Polidori
> Norwich

The play was eventually published by Longmans in 1819 as *Ximenes, A Dramatic Action* in *Ximenes, The Wreath, and other Poems*. By J. W. Polidori, M.D. (pp. 1–103), in the preface to which he states that it was 'written in my eighteenth year', and though described as a 'dramatic action ... to all intents and purposes it is a tragedy'; and he reiterates that it was not fitted for the stage, the subject being religious (p. ix). Ximenes is Count Orlando's adopted pseudonym.

11. Acknowledging the arrival of *Manfred* and *The Lament of Tasso* on Tuesday 12 August, 'thanks to Mr. Croker's cover', B wrote indignantly: 'You have destroyed the whole effect & moral of the poem by omitting the last line of Manfred's speaking – & why this was done I know not' (*BLJ* V, 256–57; see Letter 107 below).

12. Coleridge's *Biographia Literaria* was published by Rest Fenner in 2 vols in 1817. B had read it by 12 October, on which date he told JM he thought Coleridge's 'attack upon the then Committee of D[rury] L[ane] Theatre – for acting Bertram', and 'attack upon Mathurin's Bertram for being acted', were 'not very grateful nor graceful on the part of the worthy auto-biographer'; and he added: 'He is a shabby fellow – and I wash my hands of, and after him' (*BLJ* V, 267; cf., however, Medwin, *Conversations*, 178–79).

13. François-Joseph Talma (1763–1826), the leading tragic actor at the Comédie-Française and an intimate of Napoleon's, had recently been in England to celebrate John Philip Kemble's retirement from the stage at a dinner at Freemasons' Tavern on Friday 27 June (*The Gentleman's Magazine*, LXXXVII, Pt II [July 1817], 79–80).

14. Madame de Staël had died on 14 July (Bastille day) 1817, aged 51. B told JM on Tuesday 12 August that he was 'very sorry' to hear of her death, 'not only because she had been very kind to me at Coppet – but because now I can never requite her. – In a general point of view she will leave a great gap in society & literature' (*BLJ* V, 256). He was to write her epitaph more at large in his generous note to *CHP* IV, 478 (*CPW* II, 235–36).

15. Square brackets indicate words torn off with seal. With the omission only of '(Matthew)' after 'Montmorency', and adding his own emphasis to '<u>part of it</u>', JM quotes verbatim from Ward's letter to him of 17 July from Paris in MA. Mathieu, Vicomte de Montmorency-Laval (1766–1826) was a former lover of Madame de Staël who did not share his reactionary and ultramontane views; August Wilhelm von Schlegel (1767–1845), the German scholar, was tutor of her children and one of the Coppet circle; the story of her being 'reconciled to the Church of Rome' through their 'persuasion' or 'influence' was unfounded (see also, Letter 106 below); in 1816 she had secretly married John Rocca (1788–1817), who had been her lover since 1811 and by whom she had had a son in April 1812 at the age of 46.

16. In his letter of Wednesday 9 July, B had complained that JM had only sent him half of the 'critique' on *Manfred*, which had appeared in *Blackwood's Edinburgh Magazine*, I, iii (June 1817), 289–95, and told him to send him the rest (*BLJ* V, 249). The review was by John Wilson (1785–1854), 'Christopher North', poet and editor of *Blackwood's*, author of *The Isle of Palms* (1812) and *The City of the Plague* (1816); B told JM 'it had all the air of being a poet's, & was a very good one' (*BLJ* V, 269). *The British Review*, IX, xvii (February 1817), 1–23, contained a not very favourable review of *CHP* III; and *The*

British Review, X, xix (August 1817), 82–94, a not very favourable review of *Manfred*. However, as B does not mention receiving any *British Review*, JM may have meant the *Edinburgh Review*, XXVIII, lvi (August 1817), in pp. 418–31 of which was a review of *Manfred* which B correctly took 'to be Jeffrey's own by it's friendliness' (*BLJ* V, 269).

17. Smiles adds 'into her family' after 'whooping cough' and misreads 'trouble' as 'tremble' (Smiles, I, 386). Augusta does not appear to have expressed such fears elsewhere, nor does there seem to have been the threat of such an outbreak at the time. *Blackwood's Edinburgh Magazine*, I, iv (July 1817), for example, reported: 'Hooping cough, which prevailed very generally during the last summer and winter, has now almost entirely disappeared; and there can be little doubt, that the dry and steady spring has contributed to its removal' (398).

18. JM had not in fact told B this. Moore and Rogers were in Paris together from 12 July to 20 August 1817. *Lalla Rookh* is dedicated to Rogers; hence JM's ironical emphasis.

19. B was extremely grateful for this offer, and replied on Thursday 21 August asking JM to visit Hanson and urge him 'to accelerate and promote the sales of Newstead and Rochdale', adding: 'I do not know a greater obligation that can be conferred upon me than the pressing these things upon Hanson – & making him act according to my wishes' (*BLJ* V, 257).

20. B's letter of Sunday 8 June 1817 stated it would be delivered by 'two Armenian Friars – on their way by England to Madras', who would 'also convey some copies of the Grammar' JM had agreed to take, and whom B asked JM to assist in any way he could (*BLJ* V, 235). There is no indication that they ever reached Sir John Malcolm who was by now involved in the Mahratta War; Kinnaird was on his way to B.

Letter 106)   [Friday] 15 August 1817

London 15 August
1817

My Lord

By this time Mr Kinnaird has I hope, reached you in safety and presented all my packets of poetry & toothpowder – and hereafter I hope to receive your comments on the one portion & your thanks for the other[1] –

Your Lordship will readily believe how much I am delighted to learn that [*sic*] the Fourth Canto of Childe Harold [*sic*] and if so please your Lordship to accept the exchange I shall readily present Fifteen Hundred

Guineas for the Copyright. (Mem. I entreat you to let me have the original MSS)[2]

M[r] Moore & M[r] Rogers have not yet returned from Paris – I have a Letter from M[r] Whishaw dated Paris Aug 10 in wch he begs me to contradict the Report of Mad de Stael having become Catholic – which he assures me from good authority was not the case[3] –

M[r] Davis [*sic*] was with me yesterday (wch I shall not forget as he promised me a Dozen of extraordinary Burgundy) & swore that he would bring me a long Letter for your Lordship tomorrow[4] – he is not very well – but in no worse spirits –

I hope soon to have the pleasure of hearing from your Lordship –
I beg the favor of you to present my Compliments to M[r] Kinnaird –
I remain My Lord
Your obliged & faithful Servant
John Murray

yr Lordships last Letter is dated July 20[5]

Notes to Letter 106)

Cover: My Lord/My Lord Byron/poste restante/a Venise/en Italie

The seal JM has used for this letter is of black wax and depicts B's head; hence B's opening play in his reply of 4 September: 'I knew that Calumny had sufficiently *blackened* me of later days – but not that it had given the features as well as complexion of a Negro ... Pray don't seal (at least to me) with such a Caricature of the human numskull altogether – & if you don't break the Seal-cutter's head – at least crack his libel (or likeness, if it should be a likeness) of mine' (*BLJ* V, 262). See Plate 13.

1. In his reply of 4 September, B told JM that Kinnaird had not yet arrived, but that by Rose he had 'received safely though tardily – Magnesia – and Tooth-powder' and Gally Knight's poems, and would 'clean my teeth with one – and wipe my – – not shoes with the other.' He did, however, thank him for *Lalla Rookh*, 'which is good' (though cf. *BLJ* V, 265), and for 'the Edin[burg]h and Quarterly – both very amusing and well-written' (*BLJ* V, 262; see also, Letter 108, n. 11 below).

2. JM seems to have lost his way halfway through this sentence; 'is completed' supplies the sense from B's letter of 20 July (*BLJ* V, 253; see n. 5 below). B replied on 4 September: 'You offer 1500 guineas for the new Canto – I won't take it. – I ask two thousand five hundred guineas for it' (*BLJ* V, 263). He got it; but JM got *Beppo* thrown into the bargain.

3. For Moore and Rogers, see Letter 105, n. 18 above. John Whishaw (1766–

1842), of Lincoln's Inn, Commissioner for Auditing Public Accounts, and
Secretary to the African Association; his letter is not forthcoming (see also,
Letter 105, n. 15 above).

4. Scrope seems to have fulfilled the latter promise (see Letter 107, n. 10
below).

5. B's letter of 20 July announcing he had 'completed the *4th.* and *ultimate*
Canto of Childe Harold' (*BLJ* V, 253–54; see n. 2 above).

Letter 107) [Friday] 29 August 1817

Broadstairs 29th August
1817

My Lord

I have received your Letter of the 12th this day and just as I left
London I had the pleasure of receiving that dated the 7th.[1] – I am glad
that you received even – <u>longo post tempore</u>[2] – the packet forwarded
to Paris by Mr Croker & am no less so that the Copies of Manfred &
Tasso have reached you – – Your Lordship will allow that Persons at a
distance from the means of rectifying an error are very apt to magnify
it & to misconceive its cause – I do assure you that in the present
instance as in any preceeding [*sic*] one you will find that I am absolutely
incapable of doing any thing which I did not think you would approve
– or at any rate that concealment – is totally out of the question – M^r
Gifford after consulting me omitted your close of the Drama from no
other motive than because he thought that the words you allude too
[*sic*] – lessened the effect – & I was convinced of this myself – and the
omission to send a Copy to you earlier was merely that having no direct
opportunity it did not, before, occur to me to send it by post – & upon
my honour the alteration was so trivial in my mind that I forgot the
imortance [*sic*] which it might have in the <finelier> eye of an author
– I have written up this day to have the page cancelled & your reading
restored – In future I propose to send you every proof by post – with
any suggestions of Mr G. upon them for your approbation – the slight
errors of the press wch you point out in the Fifth Volume have been
corrected against a new edition – I assure your Lordship that I take
no umbrage at <the spirit of> irritability which will occasionally burst
from a mind like yours[3] but I sometimes feel a deep regret that in our
pretty long intercourse I appear to have failed to shew, that a man in
my situation, may <be> possess the feelings & principles of a Gentleman

– most certainly I do think that from personal attachment, I could venture as much in any shape for your service as any of those who have the good fortune to be ranked amongst your Lordships friends – & therefore do [*sic*] cut me up at word as if I were your Taylor

How I have omitted to tell you what I have heard of Manfred – I can not conceive – but so it appears to be[4] – – All the higher critics such as Frere are in extacy [*sic*] with it averring that it places you far above all your former efforts – but it is not so popular with the general reader because the [*sic*] go through it at once expecting to find their pleasure in the intricacy & interest of the plot – & being therein disappointed – they do not recur to the beauties which they had hastily passed over – to conclude it is less popular but more praise [*sic*] – and this is the truth – Mr Crabbe did not think Tasso equal to yourself – but he added – who could <write> have written it but Lord Byron?

By the way I asked Gifford & some others how Scott would like to be called the Scotch Ariosto & no one can tell why you should call him so – except perhaps on account of his adopting the same measure[5]

I gave your message to a certain person respecting your kind license [*sic*] to the publication of the Italian translation of Glenarvon – & behold an answer[6] – Polidoris Father has sent me an Italian Translation of the Lament of Tasso wch I will forward to you[7]

I much regret that your Letters contain no word of civility to me from Mr Hobhouse[8] – from whom I had flattered myself with the hope of the offer of his Travels – I have nearly ready for publication – Our Mission to Africa by the Congo – & Lord Amhersts to China – also Two 4to Vols by Mr Hallam &c &c[9]

I directed a Letter to you from Mr S. Davies a few days ago – he would tell you about the Affairs of Col^l. L – wch as I before hinted are I fear deranged[10] – I see Newstead advertised for Sale this month & I trust that it may meet with a purchaser[11] – I wrote to your Lordship on the 16th proposing 1500G^s for Canto 4[12] – – it was a mistake only my mentioning Pounds for Gs – on the former things[13] – Send me the Assignment by Mr Lewis or some other friend & I will pay the balance to Mr Kinnaird[14] – who carries me also for Manfred & Tasso for wch the Amn^t is forthcoming on his return – this will I hope be in time – I hope the Daughters of the Physician at La Mira – are well[15] –

I beg you to offer my remembrances to Mr Hobhouse With unabated regard I have the honour to remain your Lordships

  obliged & faithful Servant
  John Murray

Notes to Letter 107)

Cover: Mylord/Mylord Byron/Poste Restante/a Venise/en Italie pm: Ramsgate 30 August arrived: Venice 17 September

JM had probably gone to Broadstairs in Kent to be near Gifford at Ramsgate (see Letter 105 above).

1. B's letters of Thursday 7 and Tuesday 12 August, announcing the arrival of the Paris packet by the 'abetment of Mr. Croker', complaining of some 'sad errors' in the fifth volume of JM's collected edition of B's works, and of the omission of 'the last line of Manfred's speaking' from the first edition of *Manfred* ('Old man! 'tis not so difficult to die'; *Manfred*, III, iv, 151), which was restored in the second (*BLJ* V, 254–55 and 256–57, and *CPW* IV, 102).

2. *longo post tempore*: after a long time (Virgil, *Eclogue*, I, 29).

3. In his letter of 12 August, B thought JM might have been 'out of humour because I wrote you a sharp letter' (that of Tuesday 17 June) (*BLJ* V, 257 and 239–40).

4. B had complained of JM's silence about the success or failure of *Manfred* in both his letters (*BLJ* V, 254 and 257). The poet George Crabbe (1754–1832) met JM for the first time on 30 June 1817; two days earlier, after visiting Rogers, he recorded in his Journal that *Manfred* was 'very fine – but very obscure in places. The Lament more perspicuous, and more feeble' (Faulkner, *Selected Letters and Journals*, 210 and 211).

5. In his letter of 7 August, B had said: 'I do not know whether Scott will like it – but I have called him the "Ariosto of the North," in my *text* [*CHP* IV, 40]. If he *should not – say so in time*' (*BLJ* V, 255; see also, *CPW* II, 137). In replying to this comment of JM's on Wednesday 17 September, B said 'surely their themes ... were as like as can be', but 'as to their "measures," you forget that Ariosto's is an octave stanza – and Scott's anything but a Stanza', adding: 'I do not call him the "*Scotch* Ariosto" which would be sad *provincial* eulogy – but the "Ariosto of the *North*" – meaning of *all countries* that are *not* the *South*' (*BLJ* V, 266).

6. B had told JM that the Venetian censor, '(Sr. Petrotini)', had refused to sanction the publication of an Italian translation of Lady Caroline Lamb's *Glenarvon* without B's consent; but that far from objecting, B had even 'desired him (against his inclination) to permit the poor translator to publish his labours'; and he added: 'You may say this with my compliments to the Author' (*BLJ* V, 255; Hobhouse spells the Venetian censor's name 'Petritini', and tells us that he was a Greek from Corfu [BL Add. 47234, ff. 17, 22–23, 27*v* and 33*v*, and cf. *BLJ* VI, 8, 14 and 19; see also, Letter 111, n. 9 below]). Acknowledging JM's enclosure of Caro Lamb's 'answer' (which is not forth-

coming), B said he was 'truly sorry (as she will one day be) that she is capable of writing such a letter – poor thing – it is a great pity' (*BLJ* V, 266).

7. A translation of B's *Lament of Tasso* into Italian *terza rima* by Polidori's father, Gaetano Polidori, first published in *La Magion del Terrore ... La Fantasia e il Disinganno ed altri metrici componimenti di Gaetano Polidori, colle sue traduzioni del Lamento del Tasso di Lord Byron* (Londra: Wilson and Ward, 1843), 111–24; this is followed by Gaetano Polidori's own 'Leonora al Tasso' (125–33).

8. Although Hobhouse had returned from Rome on 31 July, he had sent 'no word of civility' to JM through B.

9. For Captain Tuckey's *Narrative* and the publications consequent upon Lord Amherst's Embassy to China, see Letters 92, n. 30, and 96, n. 10 above. Henry Hallam's *View of the State of Europe during The Middle Ages* was published by JM in 2 vols, quarto, in 1818 (see also, Letter 94, n. 15 above).

10. This must be the letter that JM had told B in his previous letter Scrope 'swore' he would write him (see Letter 106 above); but in that letter Scrope does not mention the affairs of Colonel Leigh, Augusta's husband, though they were indeed 'deranged' (see *The Rise and Fall of a Regency Dandy*, 140–42).

11. *The Times* for Friday 8 August 1817 carried an advertisement for the sale of Newstead by Mr Farebrother at Garraway's on Tuesday 26 August at 12 noon. See also, Letter 108, n. 2 below.

12. In fact the 15th (see Letter 106 above).

13. In his letter of 7 August, B had queried JM's reference (in a letter which is not extant, though cf. JM's own note to Letter 100 above) to a payment in '*pounds*' rather than '*Guineas*' (*BLJ* V, 254). Replying to JM's present correction on Wednesday 17 September, B told him 'your rectification of guineas does not bring you quite right yet', and proceeded to explain why (*BLJ* V, 266).

14. B replied on 17 September saying he would 'send the assignment by Mr. Kinnaird' (*BLJ* V, 266). In his next letter of 12 October, written just after the Kinnairds' departure, B told him: 'I have *signed* and sent your former *copyrights* by Mr. Kinnaird – but *not* the *receipt* – because the money is not yet paid – Mr. K[innaird] has a power of Attorney to sign for me – and will when necessary' (*BLJ* V, 268; see Letter 91, n. 16, and 95, n. 4 above).

15. At the close of his letter from La Mira of Saturday 14 June, B told JM he was just going out for his evening ride, '& a visit to a Physician who has an agreeable family of a wife & four unmarried daughters – all under eighteen' (*BLJ* V, 238).

Letter 108)   [Tuesday] 9 September 1817

London Sep^t. 9th. 1817

My Lord

I thank you for your epistle poetical & prose which I had the pleasure of receiving this day[1] – I was very much rejoiced to perceive by the papers, in the Country, that Newstead had been knocked down at £95,000 odd – & both Surprised & disappointed to learn subsequently that it had not been bona fide sold[2] – as this sum had exceeded your expectations & limits as to positive sale my only hope is that you have received reasons for the reiterated non-execution of your positive injunction that satisfy you – One thing is certainly favourable that the price of land is every where rising, but yours has been suffered I hear from all hands to go into such careless waste that would [sic] have been better to have taken this fair sum, & thus have relieved you from an anxiety, & placed yourself in comfort or at least certainty as to the future, for the omission of which £10,000 <po> more or less can not afford I fear an<d> adequate compensation – As soon as I received your Lordships Letter I wrote [sic] Mr Davies to favour me with a call & he agrees in the sentiments which I have just expressed, and has undertaken to go tomorrow to Mr Hanson & obtain a thorough explanation of his conduct upon this point and to write you [sic] or to give me the means of writing to you on Friday – I have been most happy to learn that Rochdale is likely – certain of proving a property of infinitely more value than you have ever been allowed to suppose and this must very much increase if the present universal aspect of things maintain their [sic] improved estimate – What can be any satisfactory reason why M^r H—n – after repeated applications from M^r K & others – should persist in withholding a proper Statement of your account with him & thus keeping over your head a Cloud incessantly lowering & threatening with any thing & every thing – there must be some motive for these uncertainties & if this were once sent to you & the estate sold you would be perfectly free – he absolutely manacles you & two thirds of any uneasiness which you suffer arises from this source not always admitted – but still at the bottom of all – & you should insist upon having the veil drawn up –

I have just come to town for a few days & have my hands quite full[3] – I am preparing two accounts of the unfortunate China Expedition of which I know of no less than Eight have been written by Lord Amherst, Sir Geo Staunton – Mr Davies [sic] (an able young Man who understands the Language) Capt Hall – Mr Morrison the Interpreter

– Mr Abel – Naturalist – Mr McCleod – Surgeon & last <no> but
not least Mr Ellis (Ld Buckinghamshires Son – who was second in the
Embassy [sic] – the two last I am publishing & one other is announced
– – I have Capt Tuckeys Journal a very interesting one of the <Embass>
Mission to Africa Kept to the day of his death[4] – All Burkhardts [sic]
Papers (the Sikh Ibrim)[5] Two new Novels left by Miss Austen[6] – the
ingenious Author of Pride & Prejudice – who I am sorry to say died
about 6 weeks ago I am printing "A View of the Gouvernments [sic] &
History of the Middle Ages 2 Vols 4to – by Mr Hallam"[7] – And a Work
2 Vols 8vo by Mr Bankes the Member[8] – cum multis aliis[9] – I hope to
be allowed to place at the Head of this List Childe Harold Canto IV
and then I can leave the remainder of the Season to Chance do you
think 1500 Guineas enough? and has my proposal found favour in your
Lordships Sight?[10] – If so let me have it immediately that I may send
you the proofs before its publication.

You dont say a word about the books which I sent you, I mean in
the way of criticism & perhaps I had as well not ask it unless your prose
be less caustic than your poetry – Is Paris pretty good & Modern Greece
– & the MSS de St Helene? which I published to shew my independence
– I have sent you Coleridges Life – by Mr Kinnaird with other things
which will I trust arrive safe[11] –

Mr Ticknor the American has written to me from Paris to say that
hed [sic] did not go to Albania & wishing to know "what disposition he
is to make of a Present your Lordship gave him for Ali Pacha" in the
mean time he has deposited it, for your order, in the hands of Messrs
Wells & Williams Bankers, Rue Faubourg Poissonniere No 26 – Paris[12]
– I can not even hear of this Son of a — Sir Jno St Aubyn[13] – but the
winter shall not commence its darkness before I discover him & get
account of your Box – I admire your Poetical Epistle wch has too much
prose – not prosing good sense in it. J Murray[14]
Mr Hobhouse is marvelously [sic] ill used in the Quarterly just published
– where he is called a Bone-grubber to the no small entertainment of
that wicked wight S. B. Davies Esq[15]

I remain in Duty & faith
My Lord
Your affectionate Servant   Jno Murray

Notes to Letter 108)

Cover: Mylord/Mylord Byron/poste restante/Venise/en Italie arrived: Venice 24
September

The Kinnairds had arrived in Venice on Friday 19 September, and B remained with them until 27 September when he returned to La Mira. During that period and the following fortnight he appears to have written no letters whatsoever: his last was dated 17 September, his next 12 October – both to JM (*BLJ* V, 266 and 267–69; see also, Hobhouse, *Recollections*, II, 79–81).

1. JM had received B's letter of Thursday 21 August containing the 'delicate declention' he had requested in Letter 105 above (*BLJ* V, 257–61; see Letter 105, n. 10 above).

2. See Letter 107, n. 11 above. JM may have seen the advertisement in *The Times* for Friday 5 September 1817 announcing that Newstead would be offered for sale 'in sundry lots, in the month of October next, unless the whole should be previously disposed of by private contract'. It was; though B was not to learn until Wednesday 10 December that it had been bought for £94,500 by Thomas Wildman – 'my old schoolfellow and a man of honour', as he called him the following day when he wrote with evident relief and satisfaction to thank Hanson for his 'exertions' (*BLJ* V, 277–79; see also, Hobhouse, *Diary*, BL Add. 47234, f. 38).

3. Perhaps he had 'come to town for a few days' from Broadstairs (see Letter 107 above). For JM's publications on Lord Amherst's Embassy to China, see Letter 96, n. 10 above (Henry Ellis was in fact the *third* Commissioner); the other publications he refers to were: Sir George Staunton, *Notes of Proceedings and Occurrences, during the British Embassy to Pekin*, in 1816 (printed for private circulation in 1824); Robert Morrison, D.D., *A Memoir of the Principal Occurrences during an Embassy from the British Government to the Court of China in ... 1816* (1819); Clarke Abel, *Narrative of a Journey in the Interior of China, and of a Voyage to and from that Country, in the Years 1816 and 1817; Containing an Account of the most interesting transactions of Lord Amherst's Embassy to the Court of Pekin* (1818); and [Lord Amherst], *Scenes in China, exhibiting the Manners, Customs, Diversions and Singular Peculiarities of the Chinese ... Including the most interesting particulars in Lord Amherst's recent Embassy* (1820). For John Francis Davis, who was also attached to Lord Amherst's Embassy and whose name JM misspells here, see Letter 92, n. 28 above.

4. For Captain Tuckey's *Narrative*, see Letter 92, n. 30 above.

5. John Lewis Burckhardt (Sheik Ibrahim) (1784–1817), Swiss traveller in the East, discoverer of Petra and the tomb of Rameses II at Abu Simbel, and the first European and Christian to make the pilgrimage to Mecca, had died of dysentery at Cairo on 15 October 1817. He had studied at Cambridge and was an agent of the African Association. JM published his *Travels in Nubia* in 1819, and his *Travels in Syria and the Holy Land*, edited by William Martin Leake, in 1822 (B had both; see *CMP*, 253, lots 200 and 201). For a recent biography of Burckhardt, see Katharine Sim, *Desert Traveller: The Life of Jean Louis Burckhardt* (London: Gollancz, 1969).

6. Jane Austen had died on Friday 18 July 1817, leaving behind *Northanger Abbey* and *Persuasion*, which JM published together in 4 vols in 1818.

7. See Letter 107, n. 9 above.

8. *The Civil and Constitutional History of Rome from its Foundation to the Age of Augustus*, by Henry Bankes (1757–1834), MP for Corfe Castle and father of William Bankes, was published by JM in 2 vols, quarto, in 1818.

9. *cum multis aliis*: and many others (proverbial).

10. JM's proposal had not 'found favour in [his] Lordships Sight' (Genesis 18.3), as B reiterated in his reply of 12 October: 'My answer to your proposition – about the 4th Canto you will have received – and I await yours – perhaps we may not agree' (*BLJ* V, 267; see also, Letter 106, n. 2 above).

11. B had answered these queries in his letter of 4 September: 'Paris in 1815 &c. good. – Modern Greece Good for nothing' (*BLJ* V, 262). For George Croly's *Paris in 1815. A Poem*, see Letter 91, n. 24 above; *Modern Greece. A Poem*, by Felicia Hemans, was published anonymously by JM in 1817. B never seems to have acknowledged *Manuscrit venu de St. Hélène*, though he certainly received it (see Letter 96, n. 11 above). For 'Coleridges Life', see Letter 105, n. 12 above.

12. On his way to Europe in 1815, George Ticknor (1791–1871), Professor of French and Spanish Literature at Harvard from 1817 to 1835, had visited B who had entrusted him with a letter and 'a curious pistol' for Ali Pasha (*BLJ* IV, 299). Writing to JM from Paris on 28 August 1817, Ticknor said that having received 'no answer' to a letter written three months earlier enclosing one to B, 'the object of which was to learn what disposition I should make of a Present he gave me two years since for Ali Pacha, & which I shall not be able to deliver', he had deposited it as JM here directs to B (MA; his earlier letter and enclosure are not extant and were probably lost in the post). This was unfortunate as he could have returned it to B in person when he arrived in Venice in October 1817, where he told Hobhouse 'that Manfred was taken from *Goethe's Faust*' (*BLJ* V, 270; see also, Hobhouse, *Recollections*, II, 82–83). B does not appear to have attempted to retrieve the Parisian deposit.

13. For St Aubyn, see Letter 92, n. 22 above.

14. See n. 1 above; JM's signature here is squeezed in at the bottom of the page concluding the internal body of the letter. The remainder ('Mr Hobhouse ... Jno Murray') is written on the tucks of the cover.

15. Reviewing Lady Morgan's *France* (1817) in the *Quarterly Review*, XVII, xxxiii (April 1817), John Wilson Croker said that the reader would be struck by the 'similarity of its sentiments and language to those of [Hobhouse's] *Letters from Paris*, reviewed in a former Number', but that Lady Morgan had one advantage over Hobhouse: 'She insults and vilifies the royal family of France,

it is true, but she does not outrage humanity so far as to term them "bone-grubbers," because they piously sought to give the remains of their sovereign and father, a decent burial' (285 and 286). The review 'in a former Number' was by Croker himself, who had there made the same objections (see Letter 92, n. 18 above). For JM's 'wicked wight', cf. *The Faerie Queene*, I, i, 31, and I, ix, 33.

Interim Note

There is now a lacuna of some eight months in JM's surviving letters to B. From B's correspondence, however, we can deduce that between Letters 108 and 109 JM wrote at least seven more, three in 1817, and four in the early months of 1818. During this period JM had accepted B's revised figure of £2,500 for *CHP* IV (23 October 1817), B had sent him the MS of *Beppo* (19 January 1818), and Hobhouse had returned to England with the MS of *CHP* IV, which he delivered on Wednesday 4 February (*BLJ* V, 269, and VI, 7–8; and Hobhouse, *Recollections*, II, 92). Moreover, both poems had also been published: *Beppo* on 24 February, and *CHP* IV on 28 April 1818.

One of JM's missing letters evidently contained a phrase that B purloined in stanza 9 of his verse epistle to him of Thursday 8 January 1818 ('For the man "*poor and shrewd*"★ ... ★(Vide your letter)'; and either the same or another letter, the phrase 'amiable man', which B quotes in his replies to him of 25 March and 23 April and which clearly refers to Sotheby (*BLJ* VI, 5, 24 and 36). Fortunately, two others contained enclosures that have survived. The first of these is a note from Gifford to JM after reading the MS of *CHP* IV. It is dated simply 'Thursday morning', which we can gather from Hobhouse was clearly Thursday 5 February 1818 (*Recollections*, II, 92–93), and reads: 'I read it last night to the great damage of my eyes. It is beyond question, the <u>first</u> of his efforts. There are beauties in it which cannot be surpassed. It is desultory from its nature, and there are many prosaic words or passages, some of which the author may be induced, perhaps, to reconsider; for I suppose he will be desirous of seeing it in the proofs – but there is deep interest in it, and what will make for you & for him too, I suppose – there will be much contest about it – much applause and reproof, and wonder & pity. The conclusion of the address to Mr Hobhouse is bad, but tis no more than the usual story – the rest good and to the purpose. I have not of course opened the notes yet' (MA). B found this note 'highly gratifying' and returned it to JM on Wednesday 25 February 1818 (*BLJ* VI, 15). The second enclosure was Sotheby's refutation of B's charges against him, which B received on Thursday 23 April 1818 (*BLJ* VI, 34–36; see Letter 105, n. 8 above).

In addition, Shelley, who had written to JM on 7 March offering to take out any 'books or letters' to B, confessed when writing to B from Milan on 28 April that 'by an unfortunate mistake' he had left behind a volume of travels 'and a poem called "Beppo", which Murray sent to me for you', which would now come in a parcel he was expecting from Peacock and which Peacock eventually sent on 5 July (Shelley, *Letters*, I, 598 and II 13 and 24n.; Shelley was clearly unaware that B was the author of the poem).

On Tuesday 16 June 1818, B told JM that the last letter he had received from him 'was dated the 28 of April' (*BLJ* VI, 52). Over the next fortnight he wrote three more times with increasing impatience and threatening to withdraw to Longman, until on Tuesday 30 June he finally broke out: 'I will wait ten days longer – if by that time I do not hear from you – you will then receive the last letter to be addressed to you from me' (*BLJ* VI, 53–55 and 57). By some extraordinary blessing of Providence, JM's next letter (Letter 109) arrived before ten days had elapsed, and accordingly this volume may proceed.

Letter 109)   [Tuesday] 16 June 1818

Mr Gifford, whom I never recollect to be so well, always enquires after & remembers himself to you – cum multis Aliis

London 16 June 1818

My Lord

Having waited from day to day in the incessant expectation of the opportunity of sending my Letters and various packages by Hansons Clerk[1] – I gathered from Mr Hobhouse yesterday the continued uncertainty of his setting out and I can therefore delay no longer to thank your Lordship, in the first instance, for your several kind as well as entertaining Letters – Mr Hobhouse told me yesterday that Hanson had not yet paid any sums upon your account, to your bankers – and I have therefore sent this morning to Messrs Ransom Morland & Co a Thousand Guineas desiring them to remit it to your Lordship by this evenings Post[+] – with the remaining 1,500G^s I shall be prepared against your Lordships order, indeed if your Lordship drew upon me for this Sum at Sixty days Sight, it would settle this matter at once – but this as your Lordship may find most convenient ([+]they have since sent word that they will remit to <at>you this Ev^g)[2]

I have been collecting Soda Powder – &c &c &c to send by Hansons
Clerk which I have this day cause [sic] to be put up in small packages &
I will try to despatch them by my friends in Office –

I received very safely a few days ago by the care of Sgnor Gio^i. Bat^a
Missiaglia^++ – the curious collection of Letters belonging to the D^r
Aglietti^3 – and wch I gave in the first instance to Mr Gifford to read
– he thinks them very interesting as Autograph – but with the exception
of those pointed out by your Lordship – there are few others that would
afford more than extracts to be selected by a judicious Editor – I think
D Israeli from the nature of his Studies might be trusted with their
selection and I shall be able to send them to him tomorrow & by this
day week I will propose a sum for them to your friend the proprietor
– – Pope, whose unmanly persecution of Lady M. Montague & of her
friend Harvey [sic], arose from disappointed love,^4 is you see no less
insidiously spoken of by Ld Harvey – whose letters some three & some
bits are good but not of the first water – Lord Orford beats them all^5
– Grays Letter excellent – & Ldy Montagues Ideas equal to her literary
Character – I have been lately reading again her Letters particularly her
latest ones in her old age to her Daughter which are as full of wisdom
almost proverbial, as of beauty – I should think your Lordship may
stumble upon a letter full of anecdotes of her which I beg of you to
hoard up as I am the proprietor of her Works & would like to introduce
a new Edition with any variety of this kind.

Mr Frere is at length satisfied that your Lordship is the Author of
Beppo, he had no conception that you possessed the protean talent of
Shakespeare – thus to assume at will so different a character^6 – he and
every one continues in the same very high opinion of its great beauties
– I am glad to find that your Lordship is disposed to persue [sic] this
strain which has occasioned so much delight^7 – Does your Lordship
never think of Prose – though like Lord Harvey I suspect yr Lordships
thoughts fall so naturally in Rhyme that you are obliged to think twice
to put them in prose – yet the specimen of Prose in the dedication to
Hobhouse is so much admired and talked of that I should much like to
surprise the world with a more compleat <specimen> sample of it – to
be given at first anonymously^8 – none of the Dons in criticism have
yet taken the field for Canto IV but the next No^s of the Edinbro &
Quarterly will certainly contain papers upon it – wch I shall put into a
Cover & send to you at once^9 – the whole Canto has been quoted ten
times over in the different scraps wch diversity of Taste has selected in
the Monthly, Weekly, & daily, Journals of the Metropolis & Country^10
– so that some individual – or We^11 – have [sic] selected each part as the
best. – and in conclusion the public will be as eager to receive any thing

from your Lordships pen – as ever they were – I am now meditating or rather have made preparation to print a uniform edition of your Lordships poems in 3 Octavo Volumes – Childe Harold, <with>the four Cantos with your Lordships own notes, will form the <V>first Volume – All the Tales, including Beppo will constitute the Second – And the Miscellaneous Poems, Manfred &c will fill a Third – these I intend to print very handsomely & to sell very cheap – so that every facility shall be given to their popularity[12] – I propose to print at the same time the whole works in 5 Small Volumes – in which size when I print the 3rd & 4th Canto [sic] & Beppo – they will occupy 7 – which is too many – and they are printed loosely.[13] Westall has nearly compleated 25 beautiful designs to accompany these Editions[14] and I trust that your Lordship will have no objection to my engraving again Phillips's Portrait[15] – which every indifferent person thinks yet, by far the finest. I will be glad to be favoured with your Lordships early commands respecting Any alterations in the works and to know if my plan obtain your Lordships approbation – I mean that they shall both be ready in November[16] –

I have just put forth two more Cantos of Whistlecraft – which the knowing ones think excellent and of wch the public think nothing – for they can not see the drift of it – I have not sold 500 Copies of the first parts yet[17] – and of Beppo I have sold Six times that quantity in a Sixth part of the time & before indeed it is generally known to be yours – – I have heard no word more from Mr Sotheby – & as to my having ventured upon any alteration – or omission – I should as soon have scooped one of my eyes out.[18] – I am anxious to know if your Lordship is satisfied with Mr Hobhouses Notes – the part [sic] he thinks best of are those upon the Antiquities – but we feel very little interest for these & much prefer the Essay on Italian Literature wch if enlarged with yr Lordships assistance & with the addition of translations <f>, would become a popular Work – & one much wanted.[19] – Hobhouse set out last night for Dorchester (worn absolutely to Skin & bone in a vexatious & hopeless canvass of Westminster for Mr Kinnaird) – in the neighbourhood of wch he has some prospect of parliamentary success[20] – I am glad he avoided Westminster for after swallowing Annual Parliaments, & universal suffrage by Ballot – what Scope can a man have left himself – I <ho>Will do myself the pleasure of writing to your Lordship again in a few days in the mean time I beg your Lordship to be assured of the affectionate faithful & unabated devotion of yr Lordships

  obliged Servant

  J Murray

++I was <u>very much obliged indeed</u> by the Books & Periodicals wch your Lordship was so good as to send me

Notes to Letter 109)

Cover: <Thomas Moore Esq.> Lord Byron/Venice <u>arrived</u>: 7 July Venice

1. Hanson's clerk with legal documents relating to the sale of Newstead, whom B had been expecting in Venice since April, had not even left England; nor was he to do so. It was Hanson himself, his son and Wildman's representative who eventually came, and they did not arrive until November 1818 (*BLJ* VI, 31 and 74).

2. JM's asterisked note here appears exactly thus at the end of the paragraph in the MS. In his reply of Friday 10 July, B said he had received 'the credit from Morland's &c.', and had drawn on JM 'at sixty days sight for the remainder' (*BLJ* VI, 58).

3. B's letter of Sunday 12 April informed JM that it would be delivered by Giorgione Battista Missiaglia, 'proprietor of the Apollo library – and ye. principal publisher & bookseller now in Venice', to whom he had entrusted a quantity of MS letters belonging to his friend Dr Francesco Aglietti (1757–1836), written by various 18th century English residents in Italy to Count Francesco Algarotti (1712–64), poet, librettist, friend of Frederick the Great and author of the highly influential *Saggio sopra l'opera in musica* (1755; translated into English as *An Essay on the Opera* [1767]), which he suggested might make an 'amusing Miscellaneous vol.' edited by D'Israeli 'or some other good *Editor*' (*BLJ* VI, 30–31). Among those he singled out for special attention were the letters of Lord Hervey (1696–1743), whose name JM misspells, Lady Mary Wortley Montagu (1689–1762), and the poet Thomas Gray (1716–71). These letters are now in MA – except for one: Gray's letter to Algarotti of 9 September 1763, concerning the unity of the Arts, which was published in *Blackwood's Edinburgh Magazine*, IV, xix (October 1818), 38–40, under the rubric: 'Letter from Gray the Poet to Count Algarotti (This Letter is taken from the Correspondence in the possession of Mr Murray.)'. Unfortunately D'Israeli sent the original MS, which was not returned and is no longer forthcoming (see *Correspondence of Thomas Gray*, ed. Paget Toynbee and Leonard Whibley, corr. H. W. Starr, 3 vols [Oxford: Clarendon Press, 1971], II, 809–13, and III, Appendix O, 1235–36). Lady Mary's letters have been edited by Robert Halsband, who pays a gracious tribute to B: 'through the good offices of Byron, a collection of Algarotti's letters including six of Lady Mary's was bought by John Murray, the publisher' (*The Complete Letters of Lady Mary Wortley Montagu*, ed. Robert Halsband, 3 vols [Oxford: Clarendon Press, 1966], II, xi; the letters appear in II, 119, 129, 134–35 and 198–99, and III, 117–18 and 149–50). Halsband also quotes extensively from those of Lord Hervey

in his *Lord Hervey: Eighteenth-Century Courtier* (Oxford: Clarendon Press, 1973), 199–278.

4. Perhaps the best-known lines of Pope's 'unmanly' treatment of Lady Mary are: 'From furious Sappho scarce a milder fate,/Pox'd by her love, or libell'd by her hate' (*The First Satire of the Second Book of Horace*, 83–84); and of Lord Hervey, the lines on '*Sporus*' in *Epistle to Dr. Arbuthnot*, 305–33. In his letter, B had said that he himself had 'thought of a preface – defending Ld. Hervey against Pope's attack – but Pope quoad Pope the poet against the world' – which latter he was indeed to do in *Some Observations* (1820) and his contributions to the Bowles/Pope controversy (1821) (*BLJ* VI, 31; see also, *CMP*, 88–183).

5. Horace Walpole, fourth Earl of Orford (1717–97), the author and voluminous letter-writer whose *Private Correspondence of Horace Walpole, Earl of Orford. Now First Collected* was published by Rodwell and Martin in 4 vols in 1820. B does not mention any Walpole's letters amongst those he sent.

6. *Beppo* had been published anonymously on 24 February 1818; B's name first appeared on the title-page of the 5th edition published at the end of April (*CPW* VI, 483–84). In a letter to JM of 27 April, Frere had expressed his disbelief that B was the author; seven days later on 4 May, however, he acknowledged his error, adding: 'By-the-bye, that Shakespearian faculty of transforming himself was a quality which I did not think belonged to Byron in so high a degree as "Beppo" has shown that it does' (Smiles, II, 23–24).

7. At the close of his letter of 23 April, B had said: 'If Beppo pleases you shall have more in a year or two in the same mood' (*BLJ* VI, 36). Replying to this letter (109) on 10 July, he told JM he had 'two stories – one serious & one ludicrous (a la Beppo) not yet finished – & in no hurry to be so' (*BLJ* VI, 58–59; the one was *Mazeppa*, the other *Don Juan*).

8. That is, the dedication to Hobhouse of *CHP* IV (*CPW* II, 120–24). B replied on Friday 10 July: 'You talk of the letter to Hobhouse being much admired – & speak of prose – I think of writing (for your full edition) some memoirs of my life to prefix to them' (*BLJ* VI, 59; see also, nn. 13 and 16 below). These were the famous Memoirs which by the end of August were 'too long' and inappropriate for such a publication, and which he gave to Moore to publish when he was 'cold', but which found a rather warmer fate once he was – in a certain fireplace (*BLJ* VI, 63 and 235).

9. *CHP* IV had been published on 28 April 1818. Of the 'Dons in criticism', Scott reviewed the poem most favourably in the *Quarterly Review*, XIX, xxxvii (April 1818; pub. September), 215–32, while John Wilson reviewed it as favourably in both *Blackwood's Edinburgh Magazine* (see n. 10 below) and the *Edinburgh Review* (see Letter 111, n. 11, and Letter 112, n. 3 below).

10. To take an sample of each: in his review of *CHP* IV in *Blackwood's Edinburgh Magazine*, III, xiv (May 1818), 216–24 and *217-*220, John Wilson declared it

was 'the finest canto of Childe Harold, the finest, beyond all comparison, of Byron's poems', and quoted 63 stanzas from it; *London Chronicle*, Vol. CXXIII, No. 9265 (Tuesday 5-Wednesday 6 May 1818), 426, thought it 'equal to the ablest of his works', displaying 'his full mastery of metaphysic conception and impressive language', and quoted seven stanzas representing an Italian evening (stanzas 27–29 and 62–65); and *The Times* for Thursday 30 April 1818 extracted for the sake of their subject only the six stanzas on the death of Princess Charlotte (stanzas 167–72), the poem itself having, in its view, 'neither the facility of versification, nor the power of language, nor the energy of thinking which generally characterize Lord Byron's poetry'.

11. For JM's wry glance at the use of the critical 'We' here, cf. B's 'An Italian Carnival' (1823): 'In England – I – that is We – (for the anonymous – like Sovereigns multiply their Egotism into the plural number) have seen many a splendid and dull Masquerade' (*CMP*, 192).

12. This was *The Works of Lord Byron*, 3 vols (1819), printed exactly as JM here describes and sold at 2 guineas.

13. This is the continuation of *The Works of the Right Honourable Lord Byron* (the 'full edition', as B calls it; see n. 8 above), which eventually reached eight volumes, Vol. VI (1818) containing *The Prisoner of Chillon and Other Poems*, *Manfred* and *The Lament of Tasso*; Vol. VII (1819), *CHP* III and IV; *Beppo* found himself in Vol. VIII (1820).

14. Richard Westall (1765–1836), whose portrait of B painted in 1813 now hangs in the National Portrait Gallery, made 21 drawings to illustrate B's works, which were engraved by Charles Heath (1785–1848) and published by JM in 1820 (see Letter 133, n. 13 below).

15. An engraving of Thomas Phillips' portrait of B was made by Cosmo Armstrong (*fl.* 1781–1836), governor of the Society of Engravers, and published by JM with Heath's engravings in 1820 (see n. 14 above, and Letter 133, n. 13 below).

16. In his reply of 10 July, B told JM that his 'projected editions for November had better be postponed' as he had other things 'in project or preparation'; on 26 August, however, he said JM could go on with his edition, 'without calculating on the Memoir – which I shall not publish at present' (*BLJ* VI, 58 and 63; see also, n. 8 above).

17. The first two Cantos of John Hookham Frere's *Prospectus and Specimen of an intended National Work by William and Robert Whistlecraft*, 'in or after the excellent manner' of which B joyfully acknowledged *Beppo* was written (*BLJ* V, 267), were published by JM in 1817; Cantos III and IV in 1818. Writing on 17 July, B said he would 'be glad of Whistlecraft' (*BLJ* VI, 61). Frere later told Hobhouse 'he did not care about the failure of Whistlecraft – he knew that only 700 copies had been sold but he knew it to be damned good' (BL Add. 56540, f. 40*v*).

18. A curious remark to come from a man who has lost one eye already. In stanza 72 of *Beppo*, B refers to Sotheby as 'bustling Botherby'. Writing to JM on 23 April, B told him he could suppress the poem 'entirely at Mr. Sotheby's suggestion', but it was 'not to be published in a *garbled* or *mutilated state*': 'I will not alter or suppress a syllable for any man's pleasure but my own' (*BLJ* VI, 35).

19. The 'Notes' to *CHP* IV were written by Hobhouse. His *Historical Illustrations of the Fourth Canto of Childe Harold*, published separately at the same time by JM, was an augmented version of these and included an 'Essay on the Present Literature of Italy' (pp. 347–485). Much to his chagrin, the most popular part of the volume was the 'Essay', which was almost entirely the work of Ugo Foscolo (1778–1827), the author of *Ultime Lettere di Jacopo Ortis* (1802) which B much admired, who had fled to England in 1816. B does not appear to have replied to JM's enquiry, but he told Hobhouse in September he thought the Essay '*perfect*' (*BLJ* VI, 72). See also, E. R. Vincent, *Byron, Hobhouse, and Foscolo* (Cambridge: Cambridge University Press, 1949).

20. A General Election took place during June and July 1818. Having canvassed unsuccessfully for Kinnaird's nomination for Westminster, Hobhouse had set off for Dorchester to try 'another borough scheme' on Monday 15 June (BL Add. 47235, f. 24; see also, *BB*, 231–32; and also 235–41).

Letter 110)   Tuesday 7 July 1818

London July 7th. 1818
Tuesday

My Lord

Your Letters dated the 16th & 18th. June arrived both on Saturday last and I confess to you that my consciousness of merited rebuke made me very fearful of opening them[1] – but as usual you are very lenient with my sins of remissness in writing which arises from a love of indolence which is suffered too much to encrease – I do assure you I have rarely greater pleasure than when I am addressing you – unless it be when I am honoured by the favour of a Letter from your Lordship – Latterly I conceived that M[r] Hobhouse had been so constantly in communication with yr Lordship that my omissions would not have been heeded – but I implore forgiveness & will be less remiss in future. – I wrote to yr Lordship about three weeks ago advising that I had paid into Morlands upon your Account One Thousand Guineas which they engaged to remit by that days post & which has I hope been safely & opportunely received – I have this day paid in the further sum of One Thousand

Five Hundred Guineas – which yr bankers also promise to remit by this
nights post and I shall rejoice if it anticipate any inconvenience – I had
been incessantly expecting the Messenger of M^r [sic] your Solicitor
until Month melted into month without my being sufficiently aware of
the delay[2] – I have shipped for your Lordship – besides all the literary
Novelties wch I thought interesting to you – Soda Powders – Tooth
Powders – Tooth Brushes – Magnesia – Myrrh – Bark – 4 Cop^s Portrait
&c &c which you will hear of at M. Missiaglias – and I shall take every
other occasion of renewing the supply[3] –

I beg leave to assure your Lordship that the Success of the fourth
Canto has been equal to either of the former,[4] it is more desultory
as Gifford said at first but the parts taken separately are each & all
considered equal & in some instances surpassing any thing preceeding
them. No Critique of note has yet appeared upon it but if any thing
able on the subject appear I shall instantly send it to you[5] –

Your Lordship will have read with surprise & regret an account of
the death of yr friend Monk Lewis on his return from a second voyage
to the West Indies – he sent me his MSS notes upon this Place to read
and very curious indeed they were & I hope they will not be lost[6]
– Wilmot has positively succeeded at Newcastle under lyme – & is
returned MP.[7] – your Cousin George has another daughter lately – &
your friend Lady William Russell has just lost one[8] – I fancy that the
chief reason for your not hearing from either Hobhouse or Kinnaird
is that for the last four Months they have been compleatly absorbed in
Politics – though neither have [sic] got into parliament – they appear to
have cut the Whigs & to have plunged head over ears into Burdettism
– Annual Parliaments – & Universal Suffrage by Ballott [sic]!!!![9] –
Brougham has lost his election for Westmorland.[10]

May I hope that yr Lordship will favour me with some work to open
my Campaign in November with[11] – have you not another lively Tale
like Beppo – or will you not give me some prose in three Volumes – all
the adventures that you have undergone, seen, heard of or imagined
with your reflections on life & Manners – do tell me that I may at any
rate expect something by the end of September – – There will be three
more Vols of Tales of My Landlord – this Month wch I will convey
to you as speedily as possible[12] – with Mad de Staels new work which
has fallen almost still born from the press – it is by no means good[13]
– I called today upon Mr Hobhouse before he came to town & he has
just returned my visit – he declares that he always answers your Letters
by return of post, does every thing that you desire him to do – that
Kinnaird sent you £2000 – three weeks ago – and that he As well as I
(I declare) has repeatedly told you that the success of Canto IV has been

compleat – He promises to call again upon your friend Mr Hanson &
to accelerate his motions towards you – & I trust that his Clerk will set
out immediately[14] –

I saw young Mr Hammond yesterday who told me that he had left
your Lordship in good health & he appears much delighted by your
attention to him[15] – he said he could stay all his life at Venice

I am proceeding with an edition of your Lordships Works printing
them uniformly in 3 Vols 8vo & they are to be ready about November
next.[16]

I hope soon to be gratified by a Letter from your Lordship of a more
favourable aspect

In the mean time I remain
My Lord
Your Lordships
obliged & faithful Servt
John Murray

Notes to Letter 110)

Cover: Lord Byron/Venice arrived: 2 August

1. B's two letters of these dates expressing considerable anxiety about not only
   JM's 'inexplicable silence' but also that of Hobhouse, Kinnaird and Hanson
   which JM would have received on Saturday 4 July (*BLJ* VI, 52–54).

2. See Letter 109 above; B told Hobhouse his 'Monies' had come on 3 August
   (*BLJ* VI, 63; see also, *BB*, 237). The blank space here (for Hanson) is deliberate,
   rather than JM's temporarily forgetting the name.

3. B had asked for 'half a dozen of the coloured prints from Holmes's Miniature',
   and barring the 'Soda Powders' (a standing order), all the other items JM lists
   here in his letter of 11 April (*BLJ* VI, 26 and 29; see also, Peach, *Portraits of
   Byron*, 72–79, esp. Fig. 47). As Missiaglia was still in England at the end of
   September, JM must have 'shipped' these goods to his library rather than
   sent them via him (see also, *BB*, 245 and 249).

4. That is, *CHP* I and II, and *CHP* III, as publications not as Cantos.

5. For Gifford's remarks, see interim note above; the *Edinburgh Review* and the
   Quarterly Review were not yet out (see Letter 109, n. 9 above, and Letter 112,
   n. 3 below).

6. 'Monk' Lewis had died of fever aboard ship on his return from his estates
   in Jamaica on 14 May 1818. His 'MSS notes' were posthumously published
   as *Journal of a West Indian Proprietor* (1834). See also, Hobhouse, *Recollections*,
   II, 100, and *BB*, 238.

7. Robert Wilmot was elected Whig MP for Newcastle-under-Lyme (just south of Stoke-on-Trent) in late June (*The Times*, Thursday 25 June 1818). Curiously enough, JM pre-empts B's query in his letter of 17 July: 'Does the Coxcomb Wilmot get into parliament?' (*BLJ* VI, 61).

8. 'Cousin George' had not had 'another daughter' (see Letter 99, n. 5 above) but a son, George Anson, the future 8th baron, born at Cheltenham on 30 June 1818 (d. 1870); Lady George William Russell (formerly Bessy Rawdon) had given birth to a daughter at Paris on Thursday 9 April 1818 (*The Times*, Thursday 16 April 1818).

9. Hobhouse and Kinnaird had been campaigning (on a Reform ticket in a particularly ugly election campaign) in support of Sir Francis Burdett's candidacy for Westminster for which he was returned on Monday 13 July 1818 (*The Times*, Tuesday 14 July 1818). Hobhouse rehearsed the details for B in his letters to him of June and July 1818 (*BB*, 231–41).

10. Against all expectations, Brougham lost the Westmorland election to Lord Lowther and the Hon. Col. Lowther (*The Times*, Tuesday 7 July 1818). One person whose activities led to his defeat was Wordsworth, who attacked him and urged the support of the Lowthers in his highly reactionary *Two Addresses to the Freeholders of Westmorland*, which was printed at Kendal during February, March and April 1818 (see esp. his 'Second Address', pp. 19–74). When Shelley heard of this he was indignant (see Shelley, *Letters*, II, 24n. and 26).

11. B merely replied on 3 August that it was 'too hot and a Sirocco' to write at length but that he might perhaps have something for JM's 'November edition' (*BLJ* VI, 62).

12. *The Heart of Midlothian*, the second series of Scott's pseudonymous *Tales of My Landlord*, was published by Constable in 4 vols at the end of July 1818.

13. JM's opinion of Madame de Staël's posthumous work, *Considérations* (see Letter 96, n. 18 above), was not entirely shared by others. It received no notice in the *Quarterly Review* but was, with certain reservations, favourably reviewed in the *Edinburgh Review*, XXX, lx (September 1818), 275–317, and by J. G. Lockhart in *Blackwood's Edinburgh Magazine*, III, xviii (September 1818), 633–48, who exclaimed, 'what a present to posterity!' (636).

14. See n. 1 above. Hobhouse had in fact written to B on 5 June telling him that *CHP* IV 'sells prodigiously', that *Beppo* was in 'a fifth edition' and that B had 'made the man's [JM's] fortune', and promising that 'When Spooney's [Hanson's] man sets off you shall know', but B did not receive this till 25 June (*BB*, 231–32, and *BLJ* VI, 54).

15. This must have been the son of George Hammond, Edmund Hammond (1802–90), ex-Harrovian and later diplomat like his father, who evidently visited B in Venice in 1818. In his short reply of 3 August, B told JM to pass

on to 'young Hammond' some delicacies concerning the intrigues of 'his Dama' after his departure, which JM wouldn't understand but Hammond would (*BLJ* VI, 62).

16. See Letter 109, n. 12 above.

Letter 111)   [Tuesday] 22 September 1818

London Sepr. 22. 1818

My Lord

I was much pleased to find on my arrival from Edinburgh on Saturday night your Lordships Letter of the 26th August – the former one of the 21st. I received whilst in Scotland[1] – the Saturday & Sunday previous I passed most delightfully with Walter Scott who was incessant in his enquiries after your welfare[2] – he entertains the noblest sentiments of regard towards your Lordship & speaks of you with the best feelings – I walked ten Miles with him I believe round a very beautiful estate which he has by degrees purchased within two Miles of <Abbots> his favourite Melrose – & he has compleated nearly – the Centre & One Wing of a Castle on the banks of the Tweed where he is the happiness as well as pride of the whole neighbourhood & he is one of the most hospitable merry & entertaining of Mortals – he would I am confident do any thing to serve your Lordship and as the paper which I now inclose is a second substantial <int> proof of the interest he takes in your Literary Character perhaps it may naturally enough afford occasion for a Letter from your Lordship to him[3] – I sent you by Mr Hanson 4 Vols of a Second Series of Tales of My Landlord[4] and four others are actually in the press[5] – he does not yet avow them – but no one doubts his being their author – I should have much liked to see how you look in a full suit of Prose – for the slight drapery wch you have occasionally put on – affords a very promising specimen. I regret, of course your procrastination of the Memoir but this is a subject of delicacy wch should be regulated entirely by your own feelings – but the Tales I yet hope the Spirit may move you to compleat.[6] I return your Lordship my best thanks for the Italian books wch you were so kind as to send me by Mr Holworthy & which will prove a great literary service to me.[7] – I have already actually sent off, with several novelties for your Lordship, all the books which Mr Aglietti ordered except one Vol of the Transact^s of the Royal Society wch is out of print – but which I will try hereafter to pick up – they are sent to Mr Missiaglia who has a friend just setting out, as soon as I know their Amo^t I will Pay the Balance into Messrs

Morlands hands for I have transferred my Account for Books to my
present of Beppo – & it shall be made out & sent to your Lordship with
my receipt – I hope in the Search for Lady Montagues most interesting
Letters the D^r may stumble upon some others of Value[8] – Your Lordship
told me some time ago that a Lady was writing the Life of Lady
Montague as there may probably be some original anecdotes of that part
of it which was passed in Italy I should be glad to be favoured with
a Copy of it as soon as possible[9] – – I sent by Mr Hanson a number
or two of Blackwoods Edinburgh Magazine – & I have in a recent
parcel, sent the whole – I think that you will find in it a very great
Share of talent & some most incomparable fun & as I have purchased
half the Copy right of it I shall feel very much obliged if you would
occasionally send me some anonymous (if you please) fun to add to it[10]
– & Any news literary or Scientific that may fall in your way – if any
of your literary acquaintances are disposed to communicate interesting
Articles you may insure to them Ten Guineas a Sheet & if there be any
poor fellows to whom [sic] you would like to bestow such a trifle upon,
you can direct me accordingly. John Wilson who wrote the Article on
Canto IV on [sic] Harold (of which by the way I am anxious to know
your Opinion) has very much interested himself in the Journal & has
communicated some most admirable Papers – indeed he possesses very
great Talents – & various[11] – –

I sent you a very well constructed Kaleidoscope – a<n> newly
invented Toy wch if not yet seen in Venice will I trust amuse some of
your female friends[12] – – In the recent parcel I have again inclosed Soda
Powder & Magnetia [sic][13] – With unabated affection I remain My Lord
     Your obliged & faithful Servan [sic]
     Jno. Murray

Notes to Letter III)

Cover: Milord/Milord Byron/poste restante/Venise/Italie

1. JM had been in Edinburgh negotiating business with William Blackwood
   (see n. 10 below). He would have found B's letter of 26 August awaiting him
   on his return to London on Saturday 19 September (see *BLJ* VI, 63–64; B's
   letter of 21 August is not extant).

2. This would have been Saturday 12 and Sunday 13 September. Scott continued
   to expand and improve Abbotsford until 1824. From its upper windows he
   had a 'distant view of Eildon and Melrose', the ruined Abbey of which was
   his favourite spot to take visitors (Scott, *Letters*, III, 284; see also, Lockhart,
   Life of Scott, 381–82).

3. This was Scott's review of *CHP* IV in the *Quarterly Review* (see Letter 109, n. 9 above). There is no indication that B followed up JM's suggestion and wrote to Scott at this time.

4. *The Heart of Midlothian* (see Letter 110, n. 12 above). To B's fury, Hanson left these behind (*BLJ* VI, 77 and 82).

5. This was the third series of *Tales of My Landlord*, *The Bride of Lammermoor*, which far from being 'actually in the press' was not completed until May 1819. It was published with *A Legend of Montrose* in 4 vols by Constable in June 1819.

6. B had told JM of his two 'Tales' (*Mazeppa* and *Don Juan*, though not by name) in his letter of 10 July, and that he would not publish 'the Memoir' at present in that of 26 August (*BLJ* VI, 58–59 and 63; see also, Letter 109, n. 7 above).

7. This may have been James Holworthy (1781–1841), watercolour painter and close friend of Turner, who was also a friend of Henry Gally Knight; otherwise there is no further reference to him, and no indication as to what Italian books B had consigned to his care.

8. B had sent JM 'a list of books' which Dr Aglietti said he would be happy to take in part exchange for his manuscript letters, and proposed that the outstanding sum be settled between JM and himself in a manner to which JM here responds; he also said that Aglietti and he were 'going to hunt for more Lady Montague letters' (*BLJ* VI, 64; see also, Letter 109, n. 3 above). B told JM he would throw *Beppo* 'into the balance' of *CHP* IV in his letter of 23 October 1817 (*BLJ* V, 269).

9. As long ago as 3 December 1817, B had told JM that a 'Venetian lady' was intending to write a life of Lady Mary Wortley Montagu, though she knew nothing about her; he therefore asked JM to send him an edition of Lady Mary's works and any information about her, which he would then 'transfer & translate ... to the "Dama" in question' (*BLJ* V, 275–76). According to Hobhouse the '"Dama" in question' was Madame Petritini, who does not seem to have fulfilled her ambition (cf. *BLJ* V, 275n, and Hobhouse, *Recollections*, II, 85. Hobhouse does not say whether Madame Petritini was connected with Petritini, the Venetian censor, but the likelihood seems strong, and if so her name should be Petrotini; see also, Letter 107, n. 6 above). B does not appear to have alluded to this matter again.

10. In August 1818, JM had taken a half share of £1,000 in *Blackwood's Edinburgh Magazine*. B made no contribution to it, though he certainly made 'Some Observations' upon one article of it in 1820 (see Letter 127, nn. 7 and 8 below).

11. See Letter 109, n. 9 above, and Letter 112, n. 3 below.

12. When Hanson arrived on 11 November, the only things he had bothered to

bring out with him were 'his papers, some corn-rubbers, and a kaleidoscope', the last of which did not 'amuse' any of B's 'female friends' as he 'broke the glass & cut a finger in ramming it together' (*BLJ* VI, 77 and 82). He was not alone in finding the instrument difficult to assemble. Writing to Mary Shelley from Leghorn on 21 June 1818, Maria Gisborne told her: 'Kaleidoscopism is at this moment with us in a most triumphant state, though, owing to a *flaw* in the description your friend [Thomas Jefferson Hogg], Henry [Reveley] has had some trouble with the instrument. It is now complete; but we are not *eagle-eyed*, our initiation into this delightful science has occasioned us many a headache. But what ache would one not endure for so captivating an enjoyment!' (Frederick L. Jones, ed., *Maria Gisborne & Edward E. Williams, Shelley's Friends: Their Journals and Letters* [Norman: University of Oklahoma Press, 1951], 51–52; see also, Shelley, *Letters*, II, 69). The kaleidoscope was invented by the scientist David (later Sir David) Brewster (1781–1868) in 1816 and patented in 1817, but was soon pirated and manufactured as a toy (and exploited by B in *Don Juan* II, 93).

13. See Letter 110, n. 3 above.

Letter 112)   [Tuesday] 13 October 1818

London Oct[r]. 13. 1818

My Lord

Your Letter of the 24th Sep. wch I have this instant received – has compleatly baffled all my faculties of decovering [*sic*] – I perceive that the sudden discovery of some error of the press annoys you – and that you are outrageous [*sic*][1] – – I shall try to make out the emendation – and will endeavour to avoid – Error – (particularly of the press) in future – presuming that you<r> are hereby pacified – I proceed to thank you for the cheering notice – of the first Canto of a Poem in the Style of Beppo – and of something else which you – have nearly finished – about which I entreat your Lordship to be more particular[2] – & to tell me moreover if I may hope for a Volume this winter – which would give me great intermediate spirits. I wrote to yr Lordship on my return from visiting Walter Scott – in whose attachment you may confide – I am anxious to learn your real opinion of the <u>Edinburgh</u> Review of Canto IV – about which the [*sic*] is some division of opinion – the <g> more prevalent one being however that it is confused & unintelligible – though driving at some great object. John Wilson who wrote it is a man of powerful talents and very heartily your admirer – I think he told me he had the pleasure of knowing your Lordship formerly.[3]

I was surprised to learn by the outside note of yr Lordships letter to Mrs Leigh – that Mr Hanson has not yet arrived[4] – I have sent you some books wch I think must amuse you particularly Evelyns Diary[5] – I lay aside any thing good & will send it by first occasion – – I am really astonished to find that to this day Mrs Leigh believes you to be the Author of the Tales of my Landlord – & I still more wonder that she is equally confident that you are the writer of the New Series also – and that your aunt Miss Byron believes this no less – they tell me I keep the secret well!![6]

I am now preparing a compleat Edition of Sheridan's Works & Moore is busy in writing his life – as you once thought of assisting with Mr Rogers in this office perhaps you will convey any ideas of his character to Mr Moore[7] – Mr Moore told me had [sic] suggested to you the joining with him in the composition of a little volume of poetry, for the Winter – have you acceeded?[8] – I am proceeding with the New Edition of your Lordships Works in 3 Vols 8vo – wch I will print beautifully & sell very cheap – & you shall be universally read – if any correction or other emendation occur to your Lordship perhaps you will do me the favour to write me [sic] immediately.[9] I beg your Lordship to do me the favour to offer my remembrance to Mr Hoppner – whom you have enchanted as well as young Hammond – but there is no enjoyment in life they say after quitting your Society.[10]

With best wishes for your happiness
I remain
My Lord
Your Lordships
obliged & faithful Servt
John Murray

I saw Mr S. Davies – who brought Lady Frances Webster to see me – that is – my Portrait[11] – Mr Hobhouse in the Country[12] Mr Kinnaird – arranging for a New Banking House[13] – Gifford always asks for you as do a Billion of others – from friendship or wonder
We hear of the Rumpus with Countess Albrizzi[14]
Swimming Match[15]

Notes to Letter 112)

Cover: Pour/Le tres Honorable/Milord Byron/Paire d'Angleterre/a Venise/Italie
arrived: 28 October

   1. B's short and cross letter of 24 September complaining of misprints in *CHP*

IV, 132 ('Lost' for 'Left', line 1181), and 182 ('wasted them' for 'washed them power', line 1632), and telling JM to 'alter "In increasing Squadrons flew" to "To a mighty Squadron grew"' in line 6 of 'A Very Mournful Ballad on the Siege and Conquest of Alhama' (*BLJ* VI, 70–71; see also, *CPW* II, 168 and 185, and IV, 104). Of these, the second misprint ('wasted them') remained uncorrected in all editions of *CHP* until 1853, when JM's son published *Childe Harold's Pilgrimage. A Romaunt. By Lord Byron*; and the first time it was corrected in any collected edition was in 1855, when he published *The Poetical Works of Lord Byron. A New Edition. In Six Volumes* (1855–56). This corrects the apparatus to line 1632 of *CHP* IV in *CPW* II, 185 (see also, Andrew Nicholson, 'Byron's Copy of *Childe Harold* IV: emendations and annotations', *The Byron Journal*, forthcoming).

2. B said he had 'written the first Canto (180 octave stanzas) of a poem in the Style of Beppo – and have Mazeppa to finish besides' (*BLJ* VI, 71). As this was the first time B had mentioned *Mazeppa* by name, JM was understandably disconcerted, or perhaps could not decypher the title. By the time B received this letter (112) both poems, 'all spick and span, and in MS', had been 12 days en route to Hobhouse with Lord Lauderdale (*BLJ* VI, 82; see also, headnote to Letter 113 below).

3. See Letter 109, n. 9, and Letter 111, n. 11 above. JM refers specifically to John Wilson's review in the *Edinburgh Review*, XXX, lix (June 1818; pub. September), 87–120, which opens with the famous comparison between B and Rousseau as writers 'whose extraordinary power over the minds of men, ... has existed less in their works than in themselves' (87–88). In his reply of 24 November. B told JM: 'Scott's is the review of one poet on another – his friend; and Wilson's the review of a poet, too, on another – his *idol*; for he likes me better than he chooses to avow to the public, with all his eulogy. I speak, judging only from the article, for I don't know him personally' (*BLJ* VI, 84).

4. B had written to Augusta on Monday 21 September but this 'outside note' (i.e., on the cover) is not recorded (see *BLJ* VI, 69–70).

5. This was *Memoirs, illustrative of the Life and Writings of John Evelyn*, ed. William Bray, 2 vols, published by Henry Colburn in 1818, which was very favourably reviewed by Southey in the *Quarterly Review*, XIX, xxxvii (April 1818), 1–54.

6. See Letter 94, n. 5 above. JM refers to Sophia Maria Byron (1757–1821), B's maiden Aunt Sophy. B made no comment on this in his reply.

7. Moore had written to JM on 26 June telling him he had 'begun with Sheridan – taken to it *con amore*, and can promise it to you as a Christmas dish, without fail' (Moore, *Letters*, I, 455). This was a little premature: his *Memoirs of the Life of the Right Honourable Richard Brinsley Sheridan* was published in 2 vols by Longman in 1825. B had known of Moore's undertaking since 1 June

1818, when Moore had obviously asked him to recommend a 'good model' for it, and B had suggested Johnson's Life of Savage (*BLJ* VI, 47); but there is no evidence that B 'once thought of assisting Mr Rogers in this office'.

8. B had promised Moore to 'write again about your *plan* for a publication' at the close of his letter of 1 June 1818 (*BLJ* VI, 48), but nothing seems to have come of it, and Moore is not helpful here.

9. See Letter 109, n. 12 above; JM repeats himself almost verbatim. B seems to have offered no further 'correction or other emendation' than those in his letter of 24 September (*BLJ* VI, 71).

10. For Hammond, see Letter 110, n. 15 above. By this time, B had become very friendly with Hoppner, who later gave Moore an account of their relationship (*Byron's Life and Works*, IV, 82–84 and 225–31).

11. Writing to B on 4 November, Hobhouse told him that Scrope was 'deep in with' Lady Frances Webster to whom, he supposed, 'he makes love ... with your poetry' (*BB*, 250; see also, Letter 103, n. 7 above). Perhaps Scrope was testing the powers of B's portrait as well; for Lady Frances became besotted with him (see *The Rise and Fall of a Regency Dandy*, 230–33).

12. Since the beginning of August, Hobhouse had been living at Westcliff Lodge, Brighton.

13. This is obscure; Kinnaird remained with Morland and Ransom, although according to Hobhouse he consulted Sir Benjamin about his being a partner in the bank in April 1819 (BL Add. 56540, f. 71*v*).

14. The 'Rumpus' concerned various objections to Hobhouse's *Historical Illustrations* raised by Luigi di Breme in a letter (not extant), which B had forwarded to Hobhouse on 3 August, and in which di Breme had apparently spoken unhandsomely of the Countess Albrizzi (*BLJ* VI, 63). Hobhouse 'made a reply', which he sent to B asking him to send it to the Countess, 'or to any one who will make it public' (*BB*, 245 and 247). B duly forwarded it on Tuesday 5 January 1819 to the Countess's son, Count Giuseppino Albrizzi, who replied the following day that they had read it 'with the utmost pleasure and satisfaction', and that as Hobhouse wished to make it as public as possible, begged leave 'to keep it ... for some days, that I might procure to some friends the pleasure of reading it' (BL Add. 42093, f. 137; see also, *BLJ* VI, 90). A fortnight later, B told Kinnaird to tell Hobhouse that his letter 'has made a great Sensation – and is to be published in the Tuscan & other Gazettes'; and on the same day told Hobhouse himself that it had 'greatly pleased here', but that 'some expressions' were 'too strong for the Censure – & must be softened' (*BLJ* VI, 91–92 and 93–94; see also, *BB*, 263 and 264, and Vincent, *Byron, Hobhouse, and Foscolo*, 90–96 and 131–32, and E. R. Vincent, *Ugo Foscolo: An Italian in Regency England*, [Cambridge: Cambridge University Press, 1953], 87–94).

15. B had given Hobhouse a proud account of his latest swimming match with Alexander Scott and Cavalier Mengaldo in his letter of 25 June. He had swum 'from Lido right to the end of the Grand Canal', a distance of some 'four and a half of Italian miles', and 'was in the sea from half past 4 – till a quarter past 8 – without touching or resting': 'I could not be much fatigued having had a *piece* in the forenoon – & taking another in the evening at ten of the Clock' (*BLJ* VI, 54–55).

Letter 113)   [Friday] 19 March 1819

Albemarle Street
March 19 – 1819

My Lord
I am very much afraid that you will be sadly out of humour with all your advising friends here – Mr Hobhouse – Mr Kinnaird & I have consulted & unite in entreaties that you will let us publish one magnificent Canto of Don Juan – about which the greatest expectations prevail & which I long to realize – further it is decreed that Hazlitt's – should not be associated with your Lordships name – & if <it> the note upon him be printed perhaps you will call him a certain lecturer[1] – I shall have compleated this month a most beautiful edition of your works[2] and the appearance at this time of a popular original work from you would render me the greatest possible service – & as I say every one is expecting & asking for something from you – here is <u>Foscolo</u> at my side – deploring that a Man of your genius will not occupy some Six or Eight years in the Composition of a Work & Subject worthy of you[3] – & this you have promised to Gifford long ago & to Hobhouse & Kinnaird – since – Believe me there is no Character talked of in this Country as yours is – it is the constant theme of all classes & your portrait is engraved & painted & sold in every town troughout [*sic*] the Kingdom – I wish you would suffer Yourself to be fully aware of this high estimation of your Countrymen & not to run even a Slight or doubtful chance of risquing what is to be the noblest inheritance of a decendant [*sic*] who promisses to be so attractive[4] – Let me have the Second Canto of Don Juan & suffer Gifford who never swerves in his admiration of your talents – to prepare what he thinks worthy of you[5] – This I will instantly Set up in Proof & send out for your final alteration & compleation & there will yet be time to bring it out in May –
Mr Hobhouse promisses to write by this Nights Post[6]

With the sincerest attachmement [*sic*]
I remain My Lord
your grateful &
faithful Servant
Jno Murray

Notes to Letter 113)

Cover: Milord/Milord Byron/Poste Restante/a Venise/en Italie

The reason for the hiatus of some five months or so between JM's last letter
(Letter 112 above) and the present one is as follows. The 'cargo of poesy',
consigned to Lord Lauderdale and containing the MSS of *Don Juan*, *Mazeppa*
and *Venice. An Ode*, arrived at JM's on Saturday 26 December 1818 (Hobhouse,
Recollections, II, 107). It was directed to Hobhouse to whom B had unfortunately
delegated the publishing arrangements. Regarding *Don Juan* he had told him to
consult with Frere, William Rose, Moore, and any one else he pleased, and
fearing that 'the damned Cant and Toryism of the day' might 'make Murray
pause', instructed him to 'take any Bookseller who bids best' (*BLJ* VI, 76–78).
JM, however, was eager to advertise at once; the 'Hitch', as Hobhouse told B
in his letter of 29 December, would 'not come thence' (*BB*, 256). Quite right:
it came from Hobhouse himself, Scrope Davies, and most of all Frere, whose
'excellent reasons' against publication convinced Hobhouse (despite his sensing in
Frere 'a rival of "Don Juan's" style'), 'converted' Kinnaird, and eventually (though
only after Frere's saying 'stronger things' to him) persuaded JM (*Recollections*, II,
107–10). All this Hobhouse rehearsed with considerable delicacy and tact in his
long letter to B of 5 January 1819, 'advising a total suppression' but awaiting B's
'answer and decision'; he added that JM 'will publish but has, on my representation,
the same sentiments as myself' (*BB*, 256–62). B acquiesced 'in the *non*-publication',
but instructed JM on 25 January 1819 'to print privately – (for private distribution
–) fifty copies of Don Juan' (*BLJ* VI, 94 and 95, and XIII, 230 for correction ['*nan*'
to '*non*']). On 6 March, however, he wrote to Kinnaird saying he had 'determined
to have Don Juan published (*anonymously*)', and requested him to 'bargain with Mr.
Murray for that – for Mazeppa – & for the Ode – & also for a *second* Canto' of *Don
Juan*, which he had completed but not yet fair-copied (*BLJ* VI, 101). Negotiations
therefore resumed and JM now returns to centre stage.

1. In his *Lectures on the English Poets* (1818) Hazlitt had accused B of inconsist-
   ency in his treatment of Napoleon. B had replied in a note to be appended
   either to *DJ* I or to *Mazeppa*, but which in the event was printed with neither
   and was first published as a note to *DJ* I, stanza 2 in 1833 (*Byron's Life and
   Works*, XV, 111; see *CPW* IV, 493, and V, 682–83, and *BLJ* VI, 100).

2. JM refers to *The Works of Lord Byron*, 3 vols (1819) (see Letter 109, n. 12
   above).

3. For Ugo Foscolo, see Letter 109, n. 19 above. In what Hobhouse called 'a monstrous strange letter' (*BB*, 265), B replied to JM on Tuesday 6 April: 'So you and Mr. Foscolo &c. want me to undertake what you call a "great work" an Epic poem I suppose or some such pyramid – I'll try no such thing – I hate tasks – and then "seven or eight years!" God send us all well this day three months ... is Childe Harold nothing? you have so many "*divine*" poems, is it nothing to have written a *Human* one? ... since you want *length* you shall have enough of *Juan* for I'll make 50 cantos' (*BLJ* VI, 105).

4. 'As to the Estimation of the English which you talk of, let them calculate what it is worth – before they insult me with their insolent condescension. – I have not written for their pleasure' (*BLJ* VI, 105–06).

5. B sent the second Canto of *DJ* on Saturday 3 April, but insisted on 'no curtailments' other than those already agreed to: 'You shan't make *Canticles* of my Cantos ... I will have none of your damned cutting & slashing' (*BLJ* 104 and 105; for 'cutting & slashing', which B ascribes to Perry [*BLJ* VI, 91], see Sheridan, *The Critic*, II, ii, 364: 'Here has been such cutting and slashing, I don't know where they have got to myself' [Puff to Sneer]).

6. No such letter survives between Hobhouse's letters to B of 5 February and 27 April 1819 (*BB*, 263–69).

Letter 114) [Tuesday] 27 April 1819

London April 27 – 1819

My Lord

I have now the pleasure of inclosing the first proof of a certain poem, the remainder of which will follow in one or two posts – it is printed literatim for your own free determination[1] –

Amongst an assortment of new books which I forwarded to your Lordship through the kindness of Mr Hamilton of the Foreign Office,[2] was a Copy of a thing called the Vampire which Mr Colburn has had the temerity to publish with your Lordships name as its author – it was first printed in the New Monthly Magazine, from which I have taken the Copy wch I now inclose.[3] The Editor of that Journal has quarrelled with the publisher & has called this morning to exculpate himself from the baseness of the transaction – He says that he received it from – Dr Polidori – for a small sum – Polidori averring that the whole plan of it was your Lordships & merely written out by him – the Editor inserted it with a short statement to this effect – but to his astonishment Colburn cancelled the leafs [*sic*] on the day previous to its publication; & contrarety [*sic*] to & direct hostility [*sic*] to his positive order, fearing that this statement would prevent the sale of this work in a separate form which was subsequently done – He informs me that Polidori finding that the Sale exceeded his expectation and that he had sold it too cheap went to the Editor and declared that he would deny it – he wrote to Perry to say that it was <u>not</u> written by your Lordship – & the next day told him to suppress the Letter – he is now preparing a sort of Boswell diary of your Lordships Life[4] – I have now before me a long letter from the said Editor which I shall inclose to M[r] Hobhouse – who will probably see the said Doctor & then forward the Letter to your Lordship[5] – – I am glad to find that your Lordship is well. Your Stomach may be weak but upon my soul the Intellects are in full vigour – for I never read a more powerful Letter in my life than the last with which your Lordship so obligingly favoured me[6] – I wish you would send me One A Week & make the fortune at once of your Lordships poor servant ever[7]

Jno Murray

Notes to Letter 114)

<u>Cover</u>: Milord/Milord Byron/Poste restante/a Venise/en Italie <u>arrived</u>: 13 May

Between this Letter (114) and the preceding Letter (113) JM had evidently written two letters (not extant), dated 17 and 20 April respectively, to which B replied on Thursday 6 May (see *BLJ* VI, 122–23).

1. B returned the first proof on Saturday 15 May (*BLJ* VI, 125; see also, *CPW* V, 664).

2. William Richard Hamilton (1777–1859), antiquary and diplomat, formerly secretary to Lord Elgin in Constantinople and under-secretary for foreign affairs (1809–22). He appears in B's '[Epistle from Mr. Murray to Dr. Polidori]', 63 (*CPW* IV, 128; see also, *BLJ* V, 260 and 269).

3. *The Vampyre; A Tale, By the Right Honourable Lord Byron*, containing 'Extract of a Letter from Geneva', the title story, and 'Extract of a Letter containing an account of Lord Byron's Residence in the Island of Mitylene', was published by Sherwood, Neely and Jones in 1819. The first 'Extract' and the *Tale* were first printed in Henry Colburn's *New Monthly Magazine*, XI, 63 (1 April 1819), 193–206, and the whole was advertised in 'various numbers' of Galignani's *Messenger*, which is where B first saw the attribution to himself (*BLJ* VI, 118–19). The entire work, however – which purported to be B's contribution to the ghost-story agreement with the Shelleys at Diodati in 1816 – was that of Polidori, who later acknowledged his authorship and somewhat disingenuously attempted to vindicate himself in a letter to the *Courier* of Wednesday 5 May 1819, and in the preface to his novel *Ernestus*

Berchtold; or, The Modern Œdipus (1819), vn-vin. In his reply of 15 May, B vigorously denied being the author, and sent JM the beginning of his own ghost story saying JM might publish it, if he wished, in *Blackwood's Edinburgh Magazine*, '*stating why*, & with such explanatory proem as you please' (*BLJ* VI, 125–26). Much to his displeasure, however, JM chose to publish it as 'A Fragment' at the end of the volume of *Mazeppa* (1819) (*BLJ* VII, 58). For further details, see *CMP*, 329–31.

4. B asked: 'What do you mean by Polidori's *diary*? – why – I defy him to say any thing about me' (*BLJ* VI, 127). He did, but not during B's lifetime: *The Diary of John William Polidori*, edited by William Michael Rossetti, was not published until 1911.

5. Hobhouse wrote on 3 May merely repeating much of what JM here tells B (*BB*, 270–71).

6. In his 'powerful Letter' of Tuesday 6 April, B had said that at the beginning of the year he had been 'in a state of great exhaustion – attended by such debility of Stomach – that nothing remained upon it' (*BLJ* VI, 106).

7. JM is in his Horatio role again (see Letters 49 and 65 above).

Letter 115)   [Thursday] 29 April 1819

My Lord

I inclose another Proof[1] – Mr Hobhouse tells me that he has written to your Lordship fully – and he has taken Polidori in hand, with equal propriety & Judgment.[2]

Missiaglia has sent me another Cargo of Books – many of old date, of no value – I merely want any thing very new and attractive[3] –

With best Compliments I remain
My Lord
most faithfully yrs
Jno Murray

London
April 29 – 1819

Notes to Letter 115)

<u>Cover</u>: Milord/Milord Byron/Poste restante/a Venise/en Italie

1. B returned these 'second proofs' on 17 May and told JM he had done so the following day (*BLJ* VI, 130 and 133; see also, *CPW* V, 664).

2. See Letter 114, n. 3 above.

3. For Missiaglia, see Letter 109, n. 3 above. B made no allusion to this information.

Letter 116)   [Monday] 3 May [1819]

London May 3

My Lord

I find that Julias Letter has been safely received − & is with the printer[1] − the whole remainder of the Second Canto will be sent by Fridays Post[2] − the enquiries after its appearance are not a few − pray use your most tasteful discression [sic] <in>an [sic] wrap up or leave out certain approximations to indelicacy.[3]

I am My Lord
Yr faithful Serv[t]
Jno Murray

Notes to Letter 116)

1. B had sent 'Julia's Letter' (*DJ* I, 190−98) on 7 December 1818; but by JM's account in one of his missing letters it evidently 'miscarried'. B therefore made a second copy, which he sent to JM on 6 May, by which time the first copy had, as JM here states, 'been safely received' (see headnote to Letter 114 above, *BLJ* VI, 104, 122 and 125, and *CPW* V, 665 and esp. 666).

2. B had sent the MS of the second Canto of *DJ* on 3 April 1819 (see Letter 113, n. 5 above). As he had received no proof prior to his leaving Venice on 1 June to join the Guicciolis in Ravenna, he told JM it would be 'idle to wait for further answers', and directed both him and Hobhouse to publish without delay (*BLJ* VI, 139, 142, 145 and 148).

3. This prompted B's delightful repartee: 'You talk of "approximations to indelicacy" − this reminds me of George Lamb's quarrel at Cambridge with Scrope Davies − "Sir − said George − he *hinted at my illegitimacy.*" "Yes," said Scrope − "I called him a damned adulterous bastard" − the approximation and the hint are not unlike' (*BLJ* VI, 138).

Letter 117)   [Friday] 28 May 1819

London May 28 – 1819

My Lord

The best acknowledgment of the Agreeable letter and lines which I had the pleasure of receiving on Saturday last, is the inclosing of the verses in print.[1] I think you may modify or substitute others for, the lines on Romilly whose death should save him[2] – – the verse in the Shipwreck – LXXXI the Masters Mates disease – I pray you oblitterate [sic] – as well as the suppression of Urine – these Ladies may not read – the Shipwreck is a little too particular & out of proportion to the rest of the picture – but if you do any thing it must be with extreme caution – for it is exceedingly good – & the power with which you alternately make ones blood thrill & our Sides Shake is very great[3] – nothing in all poetry is finer than your description of the two females in Canto II – it is nature speaking in the most exquisite poetry – but think of the <u>effects</u> of such seductive poetry? [sic][4] – It probably surpasses in talent any thing that you ever wrote – – Tell me if you think seriously of compleating this work & if you have sketched the Story[5] – I am very sorry to have occasioned you the trouble of writing again the Letter of Julia – but your Lordship is always very forgiving in such cases[6] – I do assure you I was exceedingly gratified by the kindness of your Lordships last letter[7] and I have had no greater pleasure than it afforded me since you<r> went abroad – I beg you to do me the favour to believe that I remain

My Lord

Your faithfully attached Serv[t]

Jno. Murray

Notes to Letter 117)

Cover: <Milord> May Twenty Eight 1819/Milord Byron/Poste restante/a Venise/ en Italie arrived: 16 June Venice

This letter was forwarded from Venice to Ravenna and arrived on 29 June (*BLJ* VI, 167).

1. 'Saturday last' would have been 22 May when JM would have received B's letter of Thursday 6 May enclosing his second copy of 'Julia's Letter' (see Letter 116, n. 1 above). 'Agreeable' it certainly was: 'I have a great respect for your good & gentlemanly qualities – & return your personal friendship towards me – and although I think you a little spoilt by "villainous company" – Wits – persons of honour about town – authors – and fash-

ionables – together with your "I am just going to call at Carlton House[;] are you walking that way?" I say notwithstanding your "pictures – taste – Shakespeare – and the musical glasses" – you deserve and possess the esteem of those whose esteem is worth having – and none more (however useless it may be) than yrs. very truly B' (*BLJ* VI, 123 and n., quoting also *I Henry IV*, III, iii, 10).

2. The lines on Sir Samuel Romilly occur in *DJ* I, 15, and were omitted in the 1st edn, despite B's directions to the contrary in his reply of 29 June, which arrived too late (*BLJ* VI, 167; see also, *BB*, 275). The stanza was restored in 1833 (*Byron's Life and Works*, XV [1833], 118).

3. The Shipwreck episode takes place in *DJ* II, and forms about 80 stanzas of the 216; the interesting disease of the fat 'master's mate' saves him from being eaten by his fellows in *DJ* II, 81, which stanza was not removed from the 1st edn; the 'suppression of Urine' originally formed part of Donna Inez's syllabus at Sunday School in *DJ* II, 10 ('Their manners mending, and their morals curing,/She taught them to suppress their vice and urine'); but at Hobhouse's insistence B altered the lines to their present reading (*CPW* V, 92 and apparatus, and 688; see also, *BB*, 272).

4. The 'two females' are Haidee and Zoe on whom Juan first opens his eyes after the shipwreck in *DJ* II, 112. B replied: 'as to "thinking of the effect" – think *you* of the sale – and leave me to pluck the Porcupines who may point their quills at you' (*BLJ* VI, 167, alluding to Goldsmith, *The Vicar of Wakefield*, ch. 20: 'The whole learned world, I made no doubt, would rise to oppose my systems; but then I was prepared to oppose the whole learned world. Like the porcupine I sate self collected, with a quill pointed against every opposer'; cf. also, *BLJ* VI, 105).

5. To this enquiry B replied: 'You ask me if I mean to continue D[on] J[uan] &c. how should I know? what encouragement do you give me – all of you with your nonsensical prudery? – publish the two Cantos – and then you will see' (*BLJ* VI, 168).

6. See Letter 116, n. 1 above.

7. See n. 1 above.

Letter 118)   [Friday] 16 July 1819

Wimbledon Common
July 16. 1819

My Lord

La Sort est jetté[1] – Don Juan was published yesterday, and having
fired the Bomb – here I am out of the way of its explosion – its
publication has excited a very very great degree of interest[2] – public
<opinion ha> expectation having risen up like the surrounding boats
on the Thames when a first rate is struck from its Stocks[3] – As yet
my Scouts & dispatches afford little clue to public opinion, it certainly
does not appear to be what they had chosen to anticipate a work of
Satyre [sic] in which every man of note – it was hoped – would be
abused – fathers forbid it their families[4] – and its beauties may not be
talked about – but as soon as these beratings find their way in words
& vent in newspapers & reviews – by the Lord you shall have them
all – that you may repel them & those who are calling every half
hour, I understand – sorry that Mr Murray has "had any thing to do
with it" – To you I look for protection against all this & for a Mighty
effort – and an early one too, that shall burst the fences of present
disapprobation – and carry again the Castle of Admiration in which
you have stood so long preeminent & alone – Gifford who never ceases
his fatherly estimation of your Genius says that he has lived to see
three Men equally great <in thei> and unequalled in their line – Pitt
– Nelson – Wellington – & that You Are – or were – or may yet be
the fourth[5] – if you will not entirely break the feelings of a nation
which are yet entirely with you – as to poor me though the most
minute particle of the Comets Tale [sic] – yet I rise & fall with it – &
my interest in your soaring above the other Stars – & continuing to
create wonder even in your aberrations – is past calculation[6] – I wish
you would let the proofs of your next poem go out to you with Mr
G's confidential remarks – think of what he says of the Moral part
– attend with liberality to his remarks upon the poetry – in many
parts of Don Juan there is much that is prosaic & long – & the hint of
such a critical friend would enable you to make it perfect. The parts of
Juan which are Masterly appear to me to be is [sic] the Scene in wch
Don Alfonso <discovers> surprises the Lovers until to [sic] Juans escape
– in Canto 2 – the Shipwreck though of an unproportioned length
– And lastly the Description of the two Women until it rises <it>
into the most surpassing exquisiteness of beauty of Haidees seduction[7]
– this has probably never been surpassed – But as soon as I can gather

opinions worth detailing I will send them – Your Lordships unvarying confidence induces me to be thus bold.

I sent you about three weeks ago by Sea a large Assortment – of Macassar Oil – Tooth Powder – Magnesia Soda & the like – with All our best New Publications – they go to the Apollo Library & Missiaglia will advise you of their Shipment & probable arrival[8]

Mr Kinnaird will I trust have advised your Lordship of my Arrangements with him & Mr Hobhouse for the Copyright of Mazeppa & Don Juan Cantos 1 & 2 – and as my proposal met with their approbation I shall be happy if it receives yours[9]

There has been an Exhibition of Harlows Pictures & Drawings amongst them the small portrait wch he made of yr Lordship and Another of a Certain Lady – with your Autograph on both – – for others of the same size they asked Ten Guineas a piece but for these – they made me pay Forty Guineas each – but I would not part with them for ten times this sum[10] – – The Marquis of Lansdowne wanted me very much to spare him the Lady – but I told him it was a family portrait & I could not – but any others he might have – & he took Mrs Siddons – will you give me some little Account of the Said Lady that I make [sic] append it.

I send you a very fair Account of Don Juan wch I received whilst writing this Letter – it is from a very Sensible Man of Great Genius a friend of Jeffray [sic] & the Author of several papers in the Edinburgh Review.[11]

You gave me a most delightful Epistle from Bolognia [sic] as it contained an account of your Travels & yr Remarks on what you saw[12] – that dated Ravenna arrived yesterday – I hope the catastrophe which you anticipate may not happen to the Countess and that your active attentions will be productive of Life.[13]

Adieu <I> expect all the Abuse & all the Commendation of Juan – which I can gather – I am very grateful for your Lordships kind Letters & you may rely upon my remaining

My Lord
Your much obliged – & tolerably
+old – & faithful friend & Servant
John Murray

+ With very near Six Children[14]

Notes to Letter 118)

<u>Cover</u>: Lord Byron/poste restante/Venise/Italie <u>arrived</u>: 29 July Venice

1. 'The die is cast'; *DJ* I and II were published together in a single volume quarto on Thursday 15 July 1819, priced at £1 1s 6d. The title-page bore neither the author's nor publisher's name. JM had escaped to Wimbledon where he had bought 'a little place ... lately', as he told Blackwood on 22 May 1819 (Smiles, II, 82). B first replied to this letter on 1 August telling JM that he seemed 'in a fright' and not to be alarmed (*BLJ* VI, 192).

2. JM had certainly done his best to vamp the sales. Over the three days prior to publication tantalizing advertisements had appeared in, for instance, *The Times*, front page, centre column, top, announcing successively: 'ON THURSDAY, DON JUAN. – Sold by all Booksellers' (Monday 12 July); 'DON JUAN, the day after To-morrow' (Tuesday 13 July); 'TO-MORROW, DON JUAN. – To be had of all Booksellers' (Wednesday 14 July); and on the day itself, 'THIS DAY, DON JUAN' (Thursday 15 July). Moreover, as Hobhouse told B, JM had 'managed so well that Mazeppa was taken for Don Juan and greadily bought up' (*BB*, 275–76; see also, Moore, *Journal*, I, 189–90). *Mazeppa*, containing the title poem, 'Venice. An Ode' and the ghost story 'Fragment', was published on 28 June 1819.

3. That is, the launching of a Ship. JM may have borrowed this image from Campbell, whose polemical deployment of which in *Specimens of the British Poets* (7 vols [1819], I, 265–66), published by JM in February 1819, was to become a crux in the Bowles/Pope Controversy (see *CMP*, esp. 129–32 and 424–25). Replying to Hobhouse on 4 August, B himself seems to have picked up JM's usage, telling him that JM seemed 'in a state of perturbation', and had 'taken refuge at Wimbledon from the torrent which was in all its foam against "his little bark" [Pope, *Essay on Man*, IV, 385] and the larger vessel also – To be sure – his (Murray's) is no *Steam-boat*, it won't work against the stream' (*BLJ* VI, 200).

4. B was to exploit this prohibition in *DJ* IV, 97: 'the publisher declares, in sooth,/Through needles' eyes it easier for a camel is/To pass, than those two cantos into families' (*CPW* V, 234).

5. Writing to JM from Ryde in the Isle of Wight on 1 July 1819, Gifford remarked: 'Lord B's letter is shockingly amusing. He must be mad; but then there's method in his madness – I dread however, the end. He is or rather might be the most extraordinary character of his age. I have lived to see three great men – men to whom <u>none came near</u> in their respective provinces Pitt, Nelson, Wellington – morality & religion would have placed our friend among them, as the fourth boast of the time, even a decent respect for the good opinion of mankind might have done much now – all is tending to displease him' (MA; see also, Letter 119 below). The 'letter'

to which Gifford here refers was almost certainly that of Tuesday 18 May in which B describes in lively detail a somewhat waterlogged 'rendezvous' with Angelina to whom he 'went dripping like a Triton to my Sea-nymph' having 'tumbled into the Grand Canal' en route (*BLJ* VI, 133–34). JM also showed this letter to Moore, whose moral indignation was roused not only by the story itself but also by B's having told it to JM, 'to *him* (Murray, the bookseller – a person so out of his caste & to whom he writes formally, beginning "Dear Sir")' (see Moore, *Journal*, I, 187 and 225).

6. JM applies an appropriately topical image (the very phraseology of which bears an uncannily close comparison to that later employed by Shelley in his 'Sonnet to Byron' [January 22 1822]): the Comet visited Earth in the summer of 1819 and was seen over England and Europe in July. *The Times* of Monday 5 July, for instance, reported a sighting the previous Saturday evening, and observed: 'the nucleus is very bright, and the tail well defined'; and on Thursday 8 July, of the same sighting from Paris: 'The luminous point is not very distinct, but its train is long'. Cf. also, B's use of the image in his letter to JM of 25 January 1819 (*BLJ* VI, 95).

7. See Letter 117, nn. 3 and 4 above; for Don Alfonso's disturbance of Julia and Juan and the latter's flight, see *DJ* I, 136–86 (*CPW* V, 52–68).

8. B does not seem to allude to this consignment.

9. Kinnaird had written to B on 15 June telling him he would receive 'two thousand guineas for your M.S.S.', and that the offer had been made by JM and 'accepted by Hobhouse & myself' (MA). The following day Hobhouse also told B who replied on 30 July: 'if *it* (i.e. D.J. fails) the Sum is too much, if it succeeds it is too little by five hundred guineas in coin or ingots' (*BLJ* VI, 187; see also, *BB*, 272). Nevertheless, the original figure stood (£1,575 for *DJ* I and II, and £525 for *Mazeppa*).

10. George Henry Harlow (1787–1819), the portrait and historical painter, had recently returned from Italy and died in poverty of a throat infection on 4 February. His collection of paintings was sold in June 1819 and his works were exhibited at 87 Pall Mall on Tuesday 13 July (*The Times*, Tuesday 13 July 1819). His portrait of Mrs Siddons as Queen Katharine in the *Trial scene* from *Henry VIII* was first exhibited at the Royal Academy in 1817; his drawings of B and Margarita Cogni, both autographed by B, were made in late 1818. Moore also saw the latter at the Exhibition, but none of the three appears in the Exhibition Catalogue (*Exhibition of Paintings and Drawings of The late Mr. G. H. Harlow, at No. 87, Pall Mall* [1819]; and Moore, *Journal*, I, 187–88). In his reply of 1 August, B said he thought JM had bought the drawings 'rather dear methinks', but obliged him with an 'Account of the Said Lady' in what is, I believe, the longest letter he ever wrote (*BLJ* VI, 192–98; see also, Peach, *Portraits of Byron*, 91–93, Fig. 65).

11. This was Francis Cohen, later Sir Francis Palgrave (1788–1861), historian

and barrister who adopted the name Palgrave on embracing both a wife
and Christianity in 1823. He was a friend of Jeffrey and contributed to the
Edinburgh and *Quarterly* reviews. His letter, dated simply 'Thursday ev^g.',
but posted to JM at Wimbledon at 10 p.m. on 16 July, is in MA. Except
for the opening paragraph (for which see n. 14 below) and closing address,
I transcribe it verbatim:

> Don Juan is an extraordinary performance indeed. I am sorry that
> Lord B. has published it. Not that I have any right to care about
> principles & morality, but as an admirer of his transcendent genius I
> fear it will do him a mischief. Don Juan won't do any mischief, no,
> no mischief at all; it is a miserable piece of mock modesty to cry out
> against such things. If a woman is inclined to be kissed otherwise
> than as the law directs, the devil cannot teach her more than she
> does know, nor can all the angels in heaven cause her to unlearn
> her lesson. – The sins which will be imputed to the Don are less
> than venial, as far as regards the effect & tendency of the work.
> That Lord Byron is guilty towards <himself> himself, the abuse
> of his wife is cruel & unmanly. The bursts & touches of poetry of
> a higher order are exquisite. his wit is graceful, elastic, nervous &
> supple. – like Shakespeare he shews that his soul can soar even into
> the seventh heaven, & that when she returns into the body she can
> be as merry as if sublimity ne'er was known. – but Lord B. should
> have been grave & gay by turns; grave in one page & gay in the
> next; grave in one stanza, & gay in the next; grave in one line, &
> gay in the next. And not grave & gay in the same page, or in the
> Same stanza, or in the Same line. – If he had followed <Pulci more
> closely> Ariosto more closely, he would have produced a masterpiece
> & not a sport of fancy. Nothing can be better calculated to display
> the talent of a great poet, than a composition admitting of a ready
> transition from fun & drollery to sublimity & pathos, but then they
> must be interchanged. they must not be mixed up together. they
> must be kept distinct though contemplated jointly. If we stand on a
> mountain we gladly view a storm beating on one side of the horizon
> & dark clouds impending & the sun shining bright & calm in the
> other quarter of the heavens. but we are never drenched & scorched
> at the same instant whilst standing in one spot.
>   Don Juan must sell; Grave good people, pious people, regular
> people, all like to read about naughty people, & even wicked words,
> such as I must not write, do not really offend many very modest
> eyes. Even D'Israeli has no objection. to a little innocent bawdry.
> Shag is a main article in the tobacconist's shop: it sells better than
> pig tail. –
>   Let me have Casti by all manner of means.
>   Yours truly
>   F. C.

['Shag' = strong, coarse tobacco cut into fine shreds; 'Pigtail' = tobacco twisted into a thin rope; Cohen was helping Gifford edit Foscolo's formidable essay on Italian Poetry (ostensibly a review of Frere's 'Whistlecraft' and Rose's translation of Casti's *Animali Parlanti*), which appeared under the general rubric of 'Narrative and Romantic Poems of the Italians' in the *Quarterly Review*, XI, xlii (April [pub. September] 1819), 486–556.]

B answered these comments at some length and with considerable verve (particularly the '"scorching and drenching"') in his letter to JM of 12 August (*BLJ* VI, 207–08): the reason why he there refers to 'C. V.' rather than 'F. C.' is because, on holding Cohen's letter up to the light, heavy show-through of an ornate postal '3' on the verso makes the closing signature look like 'F. C. V' (the 'V' having curling risers).

12. B's letter of 7 June from Bologna, written after 'picture-gazing' and visiting 'the beautiful Cimetery of Bologna', and remarking on the epitaphs he had seen at Ferrara (*BLJ* VI, 148–50).

13. B's letter of 29 June from Ravenna (his reply to Letter 117 above), in which he told JM that he had come to Ravenna to see his '"amica" the Countess Guiccioli' (the first time he had mentioned her to JM), who was still very unwell after miscarrying in May and for whom, he said, neither medical remedies, 'nor some recent steps of our own to repair at least the miscarriage' had done any good; nevertheless, he added, she 'bears up most *gallantly* in every sense of the word' (*BLJ* VI, 167–68; see also, *LBLI*, 142–54).

14. JM and Annie were expecting their sixth child. Cohen had opened his letter to JM (see n. 11 above) with the injunction: 'Tell M^rs. Murray that if she presents you with a boy, you must christen him Don Juan, & if it is a girl; why then you must call her Mazeppa' (which seems rather hard on the girl). It was obviously reading this, together with JM's comment here, that prompted B to close his letter of 9 August: 'I hope Mrs. M. has accouched' (*BLJ* VI, 206). Unfortunately, Annie was to miscarry (see Letter 121 below).

Letter 119)   [Friday] 23 July 1819

London July 23 – 1819

My Lord

I was so much frightened at the two or three Stanzas in Don Juan, which if omitted would have made the poem imaculate [*sic*] that I did not in my last dwell sufficiently on its unrivalled beauties. There appears to me no doubt but that you have infinitely surpassed all your former efforts and that <y> this poem isolates you compleatly from any thing that the age has produced – the plan of the poem is in itself

an entire novelty in our language and if you Do but compleat it in
the way you have began [sic] – you need attempt nothing further for
immortality – Since its publication I have read it Six times and always
discover some new excellence. Every one laments therefore in a tenfold
degree the few passages which merely in kindness to your friends it
was hoped you would have suffered to be replaced by others in which
you would have excited delight only – do I beseach you as the greatest
mark of your Lordships continued favour to us – make the few slight
alterations which we so anxiously wish and you will confer upon me
most particularly the greatest – of very many of my – innumerable
and delightful obligations to you[1] – Gifford who admires even in his
tears this splendid effort of Genius – says in a Letter "I read again this
morning the Second Canto of Don Juan & lost all patience at seeing
so much beauty, so wantonly & perversely disfigured. A little care
& a little wish to do right would have made this a superlative thing
– As it is it better [sic] than any other could have written – but this
is poor praise for Lord Byron" – "I never much admired the vaunt of
Drawcansir
        "'And all this I dare do, because I dare'"
Yet what but this is Lord Byrons plea"[2]
Crabbe says – "I thank you for a very handsome & indeed splendid
Work – which probably only one Man could write – but certainly only
that one would be both able & willing – I know not which most to
admire or regret [sic] these are both men who admire you & whose
admiration is not undeserving of you – by no means fastidious – & who
are steady in their regard for you – recall Giffords fatherly Letter to
you & oblige his feelings[3] – Stanza 129 – "What opposite discoveries"
the two last lines & the continuation of the allusion in 130 – 131 in
the Shipwreck – the contribution of the Ladies – the Parody on the
Ten Commandments[4] – fill up these & with something better & let us
put forth the New Edition with your Lordships name – and proceed
I entreat you we never can have enough of such delicious Stuff as this
– it <is> resembles Child [sic] Harold – as Comedy does Tragedy – such
prodigious power of Versification there is too and so much wit and
excellent pleasantry – with some most magnificent Poetry[5] – I declare
to God I never felt so much delight as in the Second Canto – never – it
is the very Soul of Poetry – tell me how long you were in framing this
Second Canto – and will you let me have Any fragments of your first
design which I should like amazingly to see & keep.
    Depend upon this – the Public are astonished – & the Wonderful
powers displayed in this Poem – they are yet unable sufficiently to
estimate – but you never did any thing greater.

I trust that your Lordship will not be offended at the remarks which I have made – for believe me I never felt more proud of any former Work even of yours – bating the few defects –

– Have you any Settled Plan for the continuation of this immortal work[6] – which is so fully entitled to all your care – Pray live to finish it – it is the Battle of Waterloo.[7] I hope you will have made a pleasant tour & that you will return in renovated health – Pitt – Nelson – Wellington – Byron[8] –

Most faithfully & gratefully
Your Lordships Servant
John Murray

Notes to Letter 119)

Cover: Mylord/Mylord Byron/poste restante/Venise/en Italie arrived: Venice 9 August

1. In his letter of 12 August from Bologna, B replied: 'You are right – Gifford is right – Crabbe is right – Hobhouse is right – you are all right – and I am wrong – but do pray let me have that pleasure. – Cut me up root and branch ... but don't ask me to alter for I can't – I am obstinate and lazy' (BLJ VI, 206–07).

2. Writing from Ryde on 19 July, Gifford had actually said: 'I read the second Canto this morning, & lost all patience at seeing so much beauty so wantonly & perversely disfigured. A little care, & a little wish to do right, would have made this a superlative thing – As it is, it is better than any other could have written – but this is poor praise for Lord Byron. What a store of shame & sorrow is he laying up for himself? [sic] – I never much admired the vaunt of Drawcansir "And all this I dare do, because I dare" – yet what but this is Lord Byron's plea?' (MA). For Drawcansir's boast, see George Villiers, Duke of Buckingham, The Rehearsal, IV, i, 213–14: 'I drink I huff, I strut, look big and stare;/And all this I can do, because I dare.' (Burlesque Plays of the Eighteenth Century, ed. Simon Trussler [Oxford, 1995], 41). For B's advice on how to draw 'some Drawcansir', see Hints from Horace, 171–72; to his credit Juan proves to be 'not in literature a great Drawcansir' in DJ XI, 51 (see CPW I, 295, and V, 480 respectively).

3. For Gifford's 'fatherly Letter' (of 15 June 1813), see Letter 10 above. Crabbe had written from Trowbridge on 20 July 1819, 'in the midst of Election – Strife & Tumult': 'I have the Pleasure of returning Thanks for a very handsome & indeed Splendid Work, which probably only One Man could write, but certainly only that one would be both able & willing. I know not which most to admire or regret'. On re-perusing this letter some years later, JM added an asterisk to 'Work' and incorrectly noted: 'Lord Byrons "Cain"/J.M' (MA).

4. That is, B's allusions to the 'pox' in *DJ* I, 129–31 and II, 81 (the latter being a 'contribution' made to the master's mate by the ladies of Cadiz), and his parody of the Ten Commandments (being his poetical prescriptions and proscriptions) in *DJ* I, 205–06 (*CPW* V, 49–50, 114, and 74–75).

5. JM seems to have been encouraged in his expressions here by Croker's letter of 18 July, written from Ryde: 'I am agreeably disappointed at finding "Don Juan" very little offensive. It is by no means worse than "Childe Harold," which it resembles as comedy does tragedy. There is a prodigious power of versification in it, and a great deal of very good pleasantry. There is also some magnificent poetry, and the shipwreck, though too long, and in parts very disgusting, is on the whole finely described. In short, I think it will not lose him any character as a poet, and, on the score of morality, I confess it seems to me a more innocent production than "Childe Harold." What "Don Juan" may become by-and-bye I cannot foresee, but at present I had rather a son of mine were Don Juan than, I think, any other of Lord Byron's heroes. Heaven grant he may never resemble any of them' (Jennings, *The Croker Papers*, I, 145–46).

6. B replied that he '*had* no plan', nor did he '*have*' any plan, but that he did have 'materials'; that 'the Soul of such writing' was its 'licence ... at least the *liberty* of that *licence*; and, dismissing the accusation of 'indecency', insisted that his only intention was 'to giggle and make giggle' (*BLJ* VI, 207–08).

7. B may have had this in mind when he reached *DJ* XI, 56: 'But Juan was my Moscow ... / ... my Mont Saint Jean seems Cain' (*CPW* V, 482).

8. See Letter 118, n. 5 above.

Letter 120)   [Friday] 6 August 1819

My Lord

I send you the inclosed cut out of "<u>My Grandmothers Review the British</u>" N⁰ XXVII published on the 2ⁿᵈ of August – <it> nothing can be more absurd & a better subject for fun you can not have – <it> it is written by the Editor Roberts himself – I will send more in a day or two

most truly yours

J Murray

Aug 6 – 1819

Notes to Letter 120)

<u>Cover</u>: M<y>ilord/Milord Byron/Poste restante/a Venise/en Italie <u>arrived</u>: Venise
19 August <u>redirected to</u>: Sig^r. Cro Insom/Bologna <u>arrived</u>: Bologna 22 August

Signor Christoforo Insom (whose name B misspells Imsom) was B's banker at
Bologna to whom B had directed his post to be sent or forwarded from Venice
(see, for example, *BLJ* VI, 200 and 205). This letter (120) was merely a covering
note to accompany the enclosure. In *DJ* I, 209–10, B had facetiously accused the
editor of his 'grandmother's review – the British' of accepting his bribe to puff
the poem. The editor of the *British Review*, William Roberts (see Letter 122,
n. 10 below), was unwise enough to take the accusation seriously and indignantly
denied the charge in the *British Review*, XIV, xxvii (August 1819), 266–68. On
receiving this, B immediately wrote his wonderfully witty reply, 'To the Editor
of the *British Review*', which he sent by return to JM on 23 August telling him
to publish it in what form he pleased: 'I have had many proofs of man's absurdity
but he [Roberts] beats all, in folly' (*BLJ* VI, 215). See Letter 122, nn. 7, 8 and
10 below; and for fuller details and B's reply to Roberts, see *CMP*, 78–85 and
348–55.

Letter 121)   [Friday] 3 September 1819

London Septr. 3. 1819

My Lord

I have been this moment favoured with your most obliging Letters –
Ravenna Aug 9 – Bologna Aug. 12 – & last week I had the gratification
of getting another entertaining Letter with the history of my portrait[1]
– I should have acknoweldged [*sic*] this much sooner but it arrived at a
time when I was in misery at the almost certain prospect of losing my
wife – which with five young children would have been irreparable
– She is now thank God out of danger.[2]

I will apply instantly for the appointment which you desire for your
noble friend.[3]

Upon my word I can not help acknowledging again your extensive
patience of me in all that I have ventured to say & suffer to be done
about Don Juan – I now inclose the leaves which have the Asterisks &
beg you to fill them up as you list – all I petition for is the removal of
allusions to a certain disease[4] – Send me any preface or any thing else
and the second edition which shall wait for your commands shall be
published as you wish – but I wish you would revise for some parts are
really heavy – Mr G. was speaking of this again yesterday & it requires

only a few of your promethean touches to brighten all into flame again
– there is a great outcry – but every body reads – I have 300 left out
of 1,500 printed – it was published late in the season – pray set to work
and let me have too [*sic*] more Cantos – to publish about February –

However much you may <be> regret the occasion yet I know that
you will rejoice in the news that <u>Moore</u> sets out on his way to Venice
tomorrow[5] – he has just been here & entreats you to give him the
meeting or he shall lose the greatest Lion in Italy – respecting his case
it is this – He forgot that he was in office – & allowed a cursed deputy
to play the rogue – there is a defalcation of 6,000£ & he is obliged to
fly – his friends think however that when the Creditors find that they
are likely to get nothing otherwise they will be glad to compromise &
will take a Third of that sum – which his friends will with ease advance
– he travels with Lord John Russell whom he is to leave at Paris – but
whom he thinks will easily be persuaded to accompany him to Venice.[6]

I am sending Gun Powder & sundries by Mr Knowles who will start
for Italy next week[7] – I sent you a Snuff-box by a friend of mine M^r
Allan who deposited it with Mr Hopp<en>ner[8] – Did you ever receive
a parcel of Books & Magnesia &c &c &c wch I sent out by some Ship
about 2 Months ago to the care of Missiaglia?[9]

Do me the favour to make every improvement that you can upon
the two first Cantos of Don Juan & let me bring out the new Edition
in great force in the winter – In the opinion of the best Critics the
larger portion of them surpass [*sic*] all that you have written & the rest
is deserving therefore of re-casting or at least of re-consideration – Pray
tell me if you see any Newspaper published in England – for I would
occasionally send them to you[10] – Take care of your health

I remain My Lord
your faithful & attached friend
& Servant
John Murray

Notes to Letter 121)

<u>Cover</u>: Milord/Milord Byron/Poste restante/Venise/en Italie <u>arrived</u>: Venice 16
September

1. B's three letters of 1, 9 and 12 August replying to JM's Letters 118 and 119
   above (see *BLJ* 192–98, 205–06 and 206–10).

2. See Letter 118, n. 14 above. Annie had suffered a miscarriage and was severely
   ill. She seems to have improved by 4 October when JM's stepfather wrote
   to congratulate him 'on the recovery of M^{rs}. Murray' (MA).

3. In his letter of 12 August, B had asked JM to ask one of his 'Government friends' to appoint 'a noble Italian' (Teresa's husband, Count Alessandro Guiccioli) 'Consul or Vice Consul for Ravenna' (*BLJ* VI, 208–09; see also, *LBLI*, 170–71). JM applied to Croker, who replied from the Admiralty on 15 September saying that a Consulship, being a Government appointment, was 'out of the question', but that Vice-Consuls were nominated 'by the Consuls & only approved (generally as a matter of course) at the Foreign office', and suggested B should approach Hoppner directly (MA; see also, Jennings, *The Croker Papers*, I, 145). Curiously enough, B had already asked Hoppner in a letter to him of 22 June, but nothing seems to have come of it (*BLJ* VI, 164–65; see also, Letter 126 below).

4. For the 'certain disease', see Letter 117, n. 3, and Letter 119, n. 4 above. In his letter of 9 August, B had said that he had heard nothing from JM about *DJ*, but that from extracts he had seen in Galignani's *Messenger* he saw there 'hath been asterisks' and 'pains taken to exculpate the modest publisher – he had remonstrated forsooth!', and added: 'I will write a preface that *shall* exculpate *you* and Hobhouse &c. *completely* – on that point – but at the same time I will cut you all up (& *you* in particular) like Gourds' (*BLJ* VI, 205–06).

5. Since 1803, Moore had held the sinecure of Admiralty Registrar at Bermuda. In early July 1819, it was discovered that his deputy had embezzled funds to the tune of £6,000 for which Moore was responsible and he was advised to leave the country (see Moore, *Journal*, I, 195–96). B had already read something of the matter in Galignani's *Messenger*, and had asked JM on 9 August whether it was 'anything in which his friends can be of use to him?' (*BLJ* VI, 205).

6. Moore set out from London on Sunday 5 September accompanied by Lord John Russell, first Earl Russell (1792–1878), MP for Tavistock, future statesman and biographer of Moore. They travelled leisurely via Paris, Geneva and Milan, where they parted, Moore continuing to La Mira where he arrived at 2 p.m. on Thursday 7 October 1819 and found B 'but just up & in his bath'. Four days later, on Monday 11 October, Moore left for Rome with a new travelling companion – B's Memoirs (Moore, *Journal*, I, 211–27, esp. 211, 223 and 227; see also, *BLJ* VI, 232 and 235–36).

7. In an undated 'Memorandum for Mr. Knowles' (which should almost certainly be dated July–August 1819), B had requested JM 'to commit ... to the care of the bearer', 'Some Gunpowder from Manton's', 'Military Sashes', and the usual assortment of ablutionary articles (*BLJ* VI, 90). The 'bearer' was very probably John Knowles (1781–1841), chief clerk in the Surveyor's Department at the Navy Office, author of a number of works on naval architecture, and the friend, executor and biographer of Fuseli.

8. B had already received this snuffbox by the time this letter of JM's arrived and had written him the following letter, the original of which is no longer extant. It is misprinted in *BLJ* VI, 223–24 (see also, *BLJ* XI, 192, and the

present text is taken from the facsimile of it, which is tipped in at page 1 of *The Complete Works of Lord Byron* (Brussels: Librairie Lecharlier, 1830), a single copy of which is in the BL (press-mark: RB.23.b.1942):

Bologna. Sep^{tr}. 7th. 1819

Dear Sir –

I have received a snuff box consigned by you to a M^r. Allan – with three portraits in it – Whom am I to thank for this? You never alluded to it in any of your letters. I enclose you an advertisement of Cognac Brandy – from Galignani's Messenger – it <is> runs "in order to facilitate the consumption of <u>that truly wholesome</u> and agreeable article." Is not this delightful? the gravity of the author – and the "<u>truly</u> wholesome?" –

y^{rs}
[scrawl]

A printed copy of the advertisement is pasted onto the facsimile and runs as follows:

Cognac Brandy in Bottles. – W. Coates, Jun. Brandy merchant at Cognac, begs leave to inform the Public that in order to facilitate the consumption of the truly wholesome and agreeable article, and to prevent the adulteration of it, which takes place in the retail, he has adopted the plan of making it up into small cases of 25 bottles which he forwards to any part of France, by the Diligence or Waggon. Price of each Case of 25 bottles, new Brandy, 50 francs. – old ditto, 75 francs. – The strictest attention will be paid to any order accompanied by a receipt of the price of the Goods from the Post-Office, if it is a Provincial Town, or from Mr. Galignani, 18, Rue Vivienne, Paris.

N.B. English understood.

Mr. Allan is unidentified. Regarding the snuffbox, Teresa describes it as having a portrait of the Empress Marie Louise on its lid, and inside, operated by a secret spring, two miniatures – one of Napoleon and one of the King of Rome. She thought it was obviously 'a present from <the Austrian Princess> the *ex-Empress*, who had already let Lord Byron know in Venice of her desire to make his acquaintance' (*LBLI*, 525; see also, *BLJ* VI, 178 and 220–21, and Letter 124 below).

9. See Letter 118, n. 8 above.

10. B does not appear to have replied to this offer.

Letter 122)   [Tuesday] 14 September 1819

London Sepr. 14 – 1819

My dear friend

Your Letters of the 24 & 29th Aug. received this moment have excited
in me an alarm & uneasiness which I would I were within a moderate
distance <so>that I might fly to you for their explanation[1] – But you
have just sufferered [sic] some vexation which your <as> warm blood
has occasioned you to feel with too great exasperation and I hope you
will just take care of yourself for a few days and it will subside – Do
consider that your mode of life requires occasional pauses and you
should submit now & then to diet & medicine yourself, & if this were
done rather in periodical anticipation of indisposition than when its
accumulation renders it necessary, you would keep in very fair trim.
– Mr Hobhouse <which> has received Letters from you last week, wch
have made him very apprehensive that you are seriously ill & unless
he has his doubts relieved he will I fancy set out for Italy[2] – I wish if
he did that you would think of returning to England with him, where
your Lordships arrival would give a pleasure of an extent to which you
will not allow yourself to believe – for your name is in the mouth of
every School Boy – My eldest Son[3] was lately at a Great School D^r
Pearsons East Sheen – & now at the Charterhouse & at both the first
enquiry was if his father was publisher to Lord Byron & he footed up
to the first rank of estimation immediately – I declare upon my honour
that your Lordship is the subject of conversation & your works also of
admiration in every party that I am present at or hear of and if you
would only condescend to keep in the line – every one will gladly
yield to you the head of it – come I pray you & <u>tantum patiatur amari</u>[4]
– come & visit us – merely to have the means of taking your or rather
of leaving your Proxy[5] – I have written to an Official friend, who is
now out of town, in favour of your Italian one & if it is to be done I
have no doubt but that it will be done – & on friday I shall be able to
tell you[6] – I received the Epistle and think it very good farce – as there
is not a Soul in town at this time I propose to send it for your revision
– in case Mr Hobhouse thinks it worth while – but at any rate I will
send you a Copy of the Proof – if possible this night – too [sic] be sure
it was the very thing one could have desired the Editor to fall into "If
any <pers> one has personated the Editor of this Review"? An Ass[7]
– & then for his principles – why the <R> Losses of <the> his Review
are paid by the Saints[8] – Every One continues in the Same Mind as to
the lavish display of talent in Don Juan – & its sale would have been

universal if some 20 Stanzas had been altered & wch by preventing the book from being shewn at a Ladys work table – have cut up my Sale – As to any fears for myself – I have neverer [*sic*] had the slightest – I did not want unnecessarily to give my name to a publication that I knew would be liable to such an outcry – but it does not follow but that I should have done so had you given yours & had your Lordship desired it – but it was not necessary – – I have just received the Letter wch I inclose[9] – observe Roberts is not a +Clergyman but a Barrister – without business – a Commissioner of Bankrupts – nephew of D[r] Roberts of S[t] Pauls School – a very respectable Man – but having too great an estimation of <p> the powers of his own talents – He was the writer of the Looker-on – +Perhaps you can notice this error in some drole way, in the postscript[10]

I entreat you to let me hear from you by return of post – if you are ill seriously [I] will instantly set out & give you [all] the personal care that I can – if [there] is an English Physician pray induce him to remain with you night & day & administer & see the effect of his prescriptions – I owe my wifes life entirely to attention of this kind[11] – I will write again on friday – In the mean time I will hope for an early letter in better Spirits – Pray rely upon my utmost attention to all your wishes & of my remaining ever My Lord

your grateful & faithful friend

John Murray

Kind Comp[s] to M[r] Moore if he has arrived[12]

Notes to Letter 122)

Cover: Milord/Milord Byron/Poste restante/a Venise/en Italie arrived: Venice 27 September

1. In his letter of 24 August, B had written from Bologna in very low spirits indeed (Teresa had gone to the country for a few days), saying 'I am out of sorts. – out of nerves – and now and then – (I begin to fear) out of my senses'; in his letter of 29 August, he had written 'in a rage' at a difference he had had with a Hanoverian officer, Lieutenant Rossi, who had swindled him over a horse, and which nearly resulted in a duel (*BLJ* VI, 216–17 and 218–20; see also, *LBLI*, 172). Replying to JM on 27 September from Venice, whence he had by now returned, B told him: 'You must not mind me when I say I am ill; it merely means low spirits – and folly', but he was 'not the less obliged' by JM's 'good-nature' (*BLJ* VI, 224).

2. B had written in as miserable a vein to Hobhouse on 20 and 23 August, to which Hobhouse replied on 10 September saying he was 'distressed beyond

measure' at B's account of himself, and begged him to 'come home' (*BLJ* VI, 211–12 and 213–15, and *BB*, 278).

3. This was the future John Murray III (1808–92), who was first educated at Temple Grove, East Sheen, whose founder and first headmaster (1811–17) was the astronomer, the Rev. Dr William Pearson, FRS (1767–1847), who also founded the Royal Astronomical Society in 1820. The school was named after Sir William Temple whose residence it had formerly been, and was described as 'a preparatory establishment of eminence for the education of Gentlemen' (John Evans, *Richmond and its Vicinity*, 2nd edn corr. [Richmond: James Darnill, 1825], 34–35; see also, C. Marshall Rose, *Nineteenth Century Mortlake and East Sheen* [privately printed, Albert Clark, 1961], 52–56). Pearson sold it in 1821, and it has since moved to Uckfield, Sussex. He proceeded to Charterhouse (the London Charterhouse as it was then known) in Charterhouse Square, whose progressive headmaster, John Russell (1786–1863), gained it a high reputation. The school moved to its present location in Godalming, Surrey, in 1872.

4. *tantum patiatur amari*: and bear being loved so much (adapted from Ovid, *Amores*, III, ii, 56–57: 'inceptis adnue, diva, meis/daque novae mentem dominae! patiatur amari!' [smile kindly on my undertakings, O goddess, and put the right mind in my heart's new mistress! Let her bear to be loved!]).

5. B *had* left his 'Proxy'; in April 1816 it was entered to Lord Essex (see Jane Stabler, *Byron, Poetics and History* [Cambridge: Cambridge University Press, 2002], 1 and 198). When B was planning to leave England in 1813, Lord Holland wrote to him in May saying how 'gratified & flattered' he would be to hold his proxy during his absence, though requesting 'the discretion of entering it to my own or one or two other names'. A few days later he sent it to B to sign and seal with his 'arms' (BL Add. 51639, ff. 135–39). But with the closing of the Session in 1817 the proxy became extinct; and in March 1818 Holland sent a new one for B to sign and seal (MA; see also, B to Hobhouse, 25 March 1818 [*BLJ* VI, 25–26]). However, this was not adequate enough to satisfy parliamentary requirements, and on 8 January 1819 Holland wrote again, saying: 'You cannot vote by proxy in a new Parliament till you have taken your seat & though through the means of the post or Lauderdale you may delight the English world with <your> a poem & your bookseller with the profits of it, we cannot allow you to give your opinion on the state of affairs in our house till we have the pleasure of seeing you & learning from your own mouth that you do not invoke a Virgin or devour a God at Venice' (MA).

6. See Letter 121, n. 3 above; 'friday' would have been Friday 17 September, but JM did not fulfil his promise to write, reiterated at the close of his letter.

7. See Letter 120 above. In his article Roberts had indeed made an 'Ass' of himself: 'If somebody personating the Editor of the British Review has received money from Lord Byron, or from any other person, by way of a

bribe to praise his compositions, the fraud might be traced by the production of the letter which the author states himself to have received in return' (see *CMP*, 350).

8. JM glances at 'the Clapham Sect', a group of evangelical philanthropists (including William Wilberforce and Zachary Macaulay but not Roberts) nicknamed 'the Saints' (see Ernest Marshall Howse, *Saints in Politics: The "Clapham Sect" and the Growth of Freedom* [London: George Allen & Unwin, 1952). B exploited this in revising the proof of his reply to Roberts: 'Is it true that the Saints make up the losses of the review?' (*CMP*, 85; see n. 10 below). See also, *EBSR*, 632–33: 'Raise not your scythe, Suppressors of our vice!/Reforming Saints! too delicately nice!' In his Journal for Wednesday 11 November 1829 Moore noted: 'Clapham Common, from being a great abode of the Saints, called "Campo Santo"' (Moore, *Journal*, III, 1260).

9. That is, the proof of B's 'Letter to the Editor of the *British Review*', which JM had obviously 'just received' in the course of writing this letter.

10. JM's asterisked note here appears exactly thus in the MS. William Roberts (1767–1849), nephew of Dr Richard Roberts (d. 1823), High Master of St Paul's School (1769–1814), was a barrister, a Commissioner of Bankrupts and a Charity Commissioner, and later author of *The Portraiture of a Christian Gentleman* (1829) and *Memoirs of the Life and Correspondence of Mrs. Hannah More*, 4 vols (1834). Between 1792 and 1793 he had edited his own journal called *The Looker-on* under the pseudonym of 'the Rev. Simeon Olivebranch'. This, and the tone of his article in the *British Review*, which was an evangelical periodical, may have led B to think he was a clergyman and to have addressed him as such throughout his reply (see *CMP*, 78–85). In the light of JM's present information, however, B obviously altered his references to Roberts and concomitant vocabulary from the clerical to the legal when correcting the proof, which is not extant but which he returned on 27 September (*BLJ* VI, 224). At the same time he must also have added in proof the entire 'P.S. 2nd.', which is not in the MS, and whose opening line is borrowed from this letter of JM's (see n. 8 above). (This corrects some of my misstatements in the commentary and notes in *CMP*, 351–55.)

11. The words in square brackets here have been torn off with the seal. For Annie's illness, see Letter 121, n. 2 above.

12. Moore had not yet arrived (see Letter 121, n. 6 above).

Letter 123)   [Friday] 15 October 1819

London Octr. 15 – 1819

My Lord

I have been very greatly relieved by the Letter dated Sep 27 – Venice wch I have just had the satisfaction of receiving[1] – your former ones had left me in alarm & suspense – I am truly happy that your Lordship has recovered – and I hope you have determined to take some little care of yourself for the future – I wish I had found in this Letter the further pleasure of a hint even that your Lordship <pro> meditated a visit to England at the beginning of the year & I will yet hope that the notice of such an intention was rather an omission than a total want of <such> it – I have received Roberts wch is very good & will annoy the party sufficiently – I hope b<y>efore you receive this that your Lordship will have been cheered by a visit from Mr Moore & I wish he may assist in seducing you home[2] –

May I expect something from you to open the Ball with?[3]

With Compliments I remain My Lord

your faithful Servant

John Murray

No less than <u>two</u> – <u>Third</u> Cantos of Don Juan have been advertised[4]

Notes to Letter 123)

<u>Cover</u>: Milord/Milord Byron/Venise/Italie <u>arrived</u>: Venice 28 October

1. B's letter of 27 September from Venice returning the proof of 'Letter to the Editor' and telling JM he was well (*BLJ* VI, 224; see Letter 122 above).

2. By this time Moore had come and gone (see Letter 121, n. 6 above). Replying on 29 October, B said they had 'passed some merry days together' and 'did nothing but laugh': 'but so far from "seducing me to England" as you suppose – the account he gave of me and mine – was of any thing but a nature to make me wish to return' (*BLJ* VI, 236).

3. B replied on 29 October that he had written 'about a hundred stanzas of a *third* Canto to Don Juan', and 'about 600 lines of a poem – the Vision (or Prophecy) of Dante', but that they were 'both at a standstill – for the present' (*BLJ* VI, 235).

4. These were William Hone's *Don Juan, Canto the Third* (1819), and William Wright's *Don Juan: with a Biographical Account of Lord Byron and His Family; Anecdotes of His Lordship's Travels and Residence in Greece, at Geneva, &c.*

including, also, a Sketch of the Vampyre Family ... Canto III (1819). In his reply, B remarked: 'You should not let those fellows publish false "Don Juans"' (BLJ VI, 236).

Letter 124)   [Tuesday] 9 November 1819

Wimbledon Commⁿ
Novr. 9 – 1819

My Lord
   As Mr Hobhouse was wandering about in search of perpetual
(com)motion & in uncertainty of his address I ventured according to
your instruction to open your Letter addressed to him.[1] There I found
you [sic] plan of South America[2] – but if you will reflect upon all that
has yet transpired – you will be assured I think that there can be no
security for property in that Country for this half Century to come
– every account and the decided opinion of every <well> man well
informed upon that subject here testifieth unto the truth of this – at
[sic] to the ultimate result it is not the present question but for security
of property there is not & can not be the least – With respect to this
Country – you will never find another – for the thing is impossible
– where you can be so enthusiastically admired – where so much
regret is felt at the idea of your expatriation – or where your Lordships
return would give so much universal Satisfaction – I had the pleasure
of seeing your Lordships daughter Ada yesterday & it is impossible to
speak in adequate terms of her promise in every respect intellectual
& personal[3] – She would interest all your feelings and deserve all
your care – and I earnestly hope that you will yet see her in the
Spring – but do not listen to the opinion of foreigners, who know
nothing of the elasticity of the british constitution & its regenerating
faculties – who would make you believe that we are upon the eve of
revolution[4] – it is much more probable that Italy will be overwhelmed
with Lava – than that we shall have a revolution here – I only wish
the funds were down below Zero – & I would sell every thing that
I have & buy them up[5] – the business was at first neglected & then
Stupidly mismanaged by the Ministers in the first instance[6] – or it
would have ended in ridicule – wch will speedily absorb it – nor can
I flatter you with the Chance of a <ch> total Change of Ministers
– the Whigs with their inherent want of tact have again taken a part
against the <u>Country</u> – instead of the Ministers – & the latter will be
more strengthened than ever by the division of their Adversaries – I

<am as ce> wish I were as sure of receiving two Cantos more of Don Juan from yr Lordship this month as I am of the truth of what I have ventured to assure you on the political State of the Country – which I entreat your Lordship to come over & verify

But to my Leather [*sic*]

A Villain has had the Audacity to print the Whole of my Don Juan[7] – literatim – selling it publicly at 4/6 & this he has done conceiving that the Lord Chancellor would decide as he did most absurdly & unjustly in the Case of Southeys Wat Tyler[8] – that is to say on my application for an injunction he grants it – the next day the other party get up & read certain passages wch his Lordship chooses to denominate – indelicate – or blastphefous [*sic*] & he instantly tells me there can be no Copyright in Such things – I have got the opinion of two Counsellors – & they both tell me that Lord E. will decide in this way & I am afraid to mute [*sic*] the Question – this however I shall do if I can do it in any way likely to be successful – In the mean time I wish to solicit as a favour that your Lordship would give me some dozen new Stanzas wch will be enough to render my Edition the best – & will thus Secure to me in a certain degree the Copyright – I have published an Octavo Edition.[9] There is no division of opinion as to the talent of this Poem – surpassing yourself and every other poet – I wish therefore you would make some few alterations because <it> the circulation is stopped by certain passages of no use to the Poem – wch keep it out of families & this you see reduces it to a matter of business <to> in wch I submit to you the interest of your [*sic*][10] – Will you revise it & send me another Canto & I will send your Lordship a Thousand Guineas – no [*sic*] is there not reason in this

Upon my honour nothing in all Poetry surpasses the fine things in this Poem – & it is cruel to cripple its circulation – & there is less occasion – <it>as it may be had as your Lordship originally wrote it –

Will you I entreat – b<g>eg Missiaglia to desist from sending me so much trash as he yet persists in doing –

It was from me that the Snuff Box was presented to yr Lordship[11] –

I remain My Lord
your grateful, attached, & faithful
friend & Servant
John Murray

If Mr Moore be with yr Lordship pray offer my kind regards to him
P. S.

Your Lordship will recollect that you anathematized my seal Head – are there not ingenious artists in this line in Venice – or if not – could you not reach them in other parts of Italy – if you could & would cause to be made for me an excellently cut portrait of yr Lordship, as a Seal not too large (because it becomes less useful) cut in the best pebble that can be obtained – you will very much oblige & gratify me – I paid £26 – for the stupid one wch I have – I would like also a <u>Camao</u> [*sic*] Ring of the <the> Same if you know a good Artist – & I dont mind the price[12] – Pray will yr Lordship tell me if the portrait of you by Hayter is considered by yr friends as a good likeness.[13]

   J. M.

Notes to Letter 124)

<u>Cover</u>: Milord/Milord Byron/poste restante/a Venise/en Italie <u>arrived</u>: Venice 26 November

1. B enclosed his letter to Hobhouse of 3 October in a short one to JM of the same date, telling him that if Hobhouse were not in London he could open and read it as JM might better be able to supply the information he therein requested (*BLJ* VI, 225–27). Hobhouse was then living in Ramsbury but was away immersed in provincial politics and unobtainable at the time. JM therefore opened the letter.

2. In his letter to Hobhouse, B asked for advice and information about settling in South America, an idea prompted by an advertisement which he enclosed, and suggested that James Perry or Edward Ellice (1781–1863), MP (whose father was Director of the Hudson Bay Company), 'or any other of our great merchants', should be approached. He wanted 'a country – and a home – and if possible – a free one': England was 'out of the question'; there was 'no freedom in Europe', which was 'a worn out portion of the globe' (*BLJ* VI, 226–27; see also, Prothero IV, 356n. for the advertisement).

3. JM employs a little emotional bribery to lure B home and to counter his stated intention to go to South America 'with my natural daughter Allegra' (*BLJ* VI, 226). JM would have seen Ada with her mother on their return from Tunbridge Wells to Kirkby (see Letter 126, n. 3 below).

4. Of England B had said he did not 'hate it enough to wish to take part in it's calamities', but added ominously and in the words of Chamfort: 'revolutions are not to be made with rose water' (*BLJ* VI, 226; see Jean-François Marmontel, *Mémoires d'un Père*, 4 vols [1804], iv, 84: 'Voulez-vous qu'on vous fasse des révolutions à l'eau rose?' ['Do you want revolutions made for you with rose water?']). He had also told Augusta on 15 October: 'To me it appears that you are on the eve of a revolution which won't be made with rose water however' (*BLJ* VI, 229). The picture JM paints of the political climate in England is far from the truth: events were already proving otherwise and were to deteriorate further (see n. 6 below).

5. And thus clear a good profit; a manoeuvre intended to convince B of his absolute faith in the stability and security of the country.

6. A somewhat abrupt and covert allusion to 'the Peterloo Massacre' of 16 August 1819 when some 60,000 perfectly peaceable people assembled at St Peter's Field, Manchester to hear Henry 'Orator' Hunt address them on parliamentary reform, and the local magistrates, panicking, ordered the yeomanry to arrest him and disperse the crowd, resulting in 11 killed and more than 400 wounded. The outcry was immense and national, but the Government and the Prince Regent gave their full support to the action, and when the next Parliamentary session opened on 23 November 1819 the repressive 'Six Acts' were passed in swift succession. Although the Whigs condemned 'Peterloo', they kept aloof from the Radical Reformers of whom Hobhouse and Sir Francis Burdett were the most active and vocal representatives in the metropolis.

7. The 'Villain' was J. Onwhyn who had published *Don Juan ... An Exact Copy from the Quarto Edition*, priced at 4s.

8. For Southey and *Wat Tyler*, see Letter 102, n. 6 above. JM approached his lawyer, the historian Sharon Turner (1768–1847), who took the advice of Mr Loraine and John Bell, both of whom doubted Lord Eldon would sustain an injunction or afford protection to the copyright (see Smiles, I, 405–06). Replying on 4 December, B told JM he could do as he pleased though he thought the case hopeless; and he warned him that if the poem were 'pronounced against on the grounds you mention as *indecent & blasphemous*', he would lose all paternal rights over Ada. He did not offer to alter or revise the poem in any way, but he did volunteer to refund the copyright as he thought it hard for JM to 'pay for a non-entity'. He added that the third Canto was completed, but thought it 'useless to discuss' until the property question were ascertained (*BLJ* VI, 252–53; see also, Letter 125 below).

9. JM printed a 'New Edition' of *Don Juan* in Octavo, priced at 9s 6d, still without the name of the author or the publisher.

10. Perhaps JM was distracted at this point, intending to add 'publisher'.

11. B made no reference to either of these two points; for the snuffbox, see Letter 121, n. 8 above. Unless B had genuinely forgotten that it was JM who gave him this snuffbox, four years later when writing to Charles Barry on 25 May 1823, he fibbed: 'it was sent to me at Bologna – some years ago – and I never knew by <u>whom</u> – nor from what quarter' (*BLJ* X, 185).

12. See headnote to Letter 106 above; B evidently made enquiries and later replied to this (see Letter 127, n. 18 below).

13. George (later Sir George) Hayter (1792–1871), historical and portrait painter, was appointed painter of miniatures to Princess Charlotte in 1815 and studied in Rome from 1816 to 1818. On his return to England he visited Venice

in the autumn of 1818 where B befriended him and introduced him, and his brother John (1800–95) who had come out to join him, to various *conversazioni*, and when he presumably made this (hitherto unknown and untraced) portrait of B. B did not reply to JM's query, but for his single letter to Hayter of 29 September 1818, see *BLJ* XIII, 49. There is no other record of his meeting with B and the portrait does not appear in any checklist of his works. For a reference to John Hayter, see Peach, *Portraits of Byron*, 96 and 97 n. 9.

Letter 125)   [Sunday] 14 November 1819

Wimbledon Commⁿ.
Novr. 14 – 1819

My Lord

I am very anxious for the favour of a Letter from you, as the success of my winter Campaign will depend upon any thing with which you may be disposed to favour me. In my last I mentioned my dilemma with regard to the Copyright of Don Juan which a villain had invaded and as I fear, with the prejudices of the Chancellor, successfully, I am not however disposed to yield without a struggle.[1] The opinion of one Counsellor is "considering the general nature of the subject the warmth of description in some parts & the scriptural allusions in others I think in the present temper of the times a court will not afford its protection to this book" so sayeth John Bell[2] – the leading man at the Chancery Bar. But another – Shadwell[3] has discovered "that one great tendency of the book is not an unfair one – it is to shew in Don Juans ultimate (mark that) Character, the ill effect of that injudicious maternal education which Don Juan is represented as having received & wch had operated injuriously upon his mind"[4] – Here is an excellent moral and I hope you will avail yourself of it – and send me over two other Cantos in wch the first approximation may be seen – If you would seriously send me some thing in this way your admirers here would become your adorers & if added to this it be possible for you to sustain the same flight to wch the first & Second Cantos have carried you – your Immortality is fixed for ever. It is really a vexation – to me particularly that any thing should have appeared in the first part to restrain its circulation – wch would have been otherwise unbounded – I do not in any was [sic] affect to be squeamish – but the character of the Middling Classes in the country – is certainly highly moral – and we should not offend them – as you curtail the number of your readers – and for the rest the subject of Don Juan is an excellent one – and nothing can surpass the exquisite beauties scattered so lavishly through the first two Cantos – Go on in equal spirit and I shall be able to offer yr Lordship a Thousand Guineas for each Canto until your plan is sublimely compleated. Do me the favour to condescend (as the Scotch say)[5] upon this subject & let me know yr Lordships intentions.

You have never told me if you received a Copy of Crabbes Tales of the Hall & what you thought of them, certainly there is in quantity one half that is admirable but as I know you to be an admirer of Crabbe I am anxious for your Lordships opinion[6] – I have purchased With the Tales of the Hall – the Copyright of all his former works of wch I am preparing a uniform edition[7]

Scott still goes on indefatigably two works by the author of Waverley are announced <u>Ivanhoe</u> a Romance & some other whose name I forget[8] – nothing will persuade M[rs] Leigh that you are not the Author of every series of Tales of My Landlord –

M[r] Hobhouse promised me a Copy of your Lordships Bust by Torwalsten [sic] but none have [sic] yet arrived – could your Lordship obtain one for me[9]

I hope to find by your next that your Lordship has finally determined to visit England in the Spring

With most unfeigned affection I remain

My Lord

your obliged & faithful Servant

John Murray

Best Comps to M[r] Moore[10]

Notes to Letter 125)

This Letter and Letter 126 below were sent under the same cover, the latter following on contiguously from the former. Together they comprise one bifolium and a single leaf (six pages in all). Apart from the postscript (see n. 10 below), JM has written Letter 125 on the recto and verso of the first leaf of the bifolium, which he has addressed to B, 'Milord/Milord Byron/Poste restante/a Venise/en Italie', on the verso of the second leaf of the bifolium. He has then begun Letter 126 on the recto of the second leaf of the same bifolium, continued it on the verso (writing around the address originally intended for Letter 125 which he has not erased), and concluded on the recto of a new single leaf, on the verso of which he has written the covering address of the whole (for which, see Letter 126 below).

1. See Letter 124, nn. 7 and 8 above.

2. John Bell, KC (1764–1836), barrister, who on his own admission had not

studied the poem with particular assiduity (Smiles, I, 406).

3. Lancelot (later Sir Lancelot) Shadwell, KC (1779–1850), barrister. In a letter to JM of 12 November 1819, Sharon Turner told him that he had seen Shadwell that day, who had gone through *DJ* 'with more attention than Mr. Bell had time to do' and did 'not think the Chancellor would refuse an injunction, or would overturn it if obtained' (Smiles, I, 407). Writing again the next or the following day, he told him that though Shadwell 'disapproves of the passages, he is remarkably sanguine that they do not furnish sufficient ground for the Chancellor to dissolve the injunction. He says the passages are not more amatory than those of many books of which the copyright was never doubted. He added that one great tendency of the book was not an unfair one. It was to show in Don Juan's ultimate character the ill effect of that injudicious maternal education which Don Juan is represented as having received, and which has operated injuriously upon his mind.' And in his postscript Turner added: 'Whatever becomes of this, I think your idea of getting Lord B. to prune and replace highly laudable, provided he will do it effectually' (Smiles, I, 407–08; for Juan's injurious education, see *DJ* I, 38–51).

4. B replied on 10 December: 'You may try the copy question – but you'll lose it – the cry is up – and cant is up', and again offered to return the price of the copyright, telling JM to speak to Kinnaird to whom he had written on the subject. In his letter to Kinnaird of the same date, he had stated clearly that he would prefer to return the money than have JM 'bring *in my* name' (*BLJ* VI, 256; see Letter 126 below).

5. To condescend upon = to deliberate or consider carefully (Scottish).

6. JM published Crabbe's *Tales of the Hall* in 2 vols in June 1819, and had probably sent them to B in one of his recent parcels. Although B never acknowledged receiving them, they form lot 41 in his Sale Catalogue (1827) (*CMP*, 247). JM would have known of B's admiration for Crabbe from *EBSR*, 855–58 (*CPW* I, 256), and more recently from his letters of 15 September 1817 and 25 January 1819, where he exempts Crabbe from the 'wrong revolutionary poetical system' he and other poets of the day were upon (*BLJ* V, 265–66, and VI, 95).

7. For the copyright of *Tales of the Hall* and all his former works, JM gave Crabbe £3,000, which Crabbe and Moore thought 'a good bargain' (see Moore, *Journal*, I, 98–99 and 190). JM published *The Poetical Works of the Rev. George Crabbe* in 5 vols in March 1820.

8. *Ivanhoe; a Romance*, By the Author of Waverley was published by Constable in 3 vols on 23 December 1819; *The Monastery; a Romance*, By the Author of Waverley was published by Constable in 3 vols in April 1820.

9. The Danish sculptor, Bertel Thorwaldsen (1770–1844), had made a bust of B at Rome in May 1817 at the request and expense of Hobhouse, who told

JM in a letter to him from Venice of 7 December 1817 that he was 'very welcome to a copy' (see Smiles, I, 391; see also, Peach, *Portraits of Byron*, 79–87, and Figs 49 and 55). B did not immediately reply to JM's request; but see Letter 127, n. 17 below.

10. This postscript is written on the recto of the second leaf of the bifolium, to the above left of the address and date of Letter 126, and from the ink and orthography seems to belong to Letter 125.

Letter 126)   Tuesday 16 November 1819

Albemarle Street
Tuesday Novr 16. 1819

My Lord
    \<I\>
I brought what I have written to town with me today when I had the satisfaction, as far as its usual confidence & kindness goes, to find your Letter of the 29th. Oct^r. – the deduction from my satisfaction is that you give up so compleatly the notion of visiting England which I had calculated upon[1] – Mr Moore must have very different notions of all affairs in this country touching your Lordship if he has given a representation that prevents you from visiting us[2] – – for your name is in every mouth – your writings in every hand and universal admiration is \<chel\> checked merely by your casting our grateful feelings from you – I am much ashamed at my negligence in not informing your Lordship of the safe arrival of your Letter to Lady Byron \<it\>& of her Ladyships receipt of it – the fact is that Lady B – was travelling at the time at [*sic*] it was a month before her Ladyship got it when she did me the favour to write & acknowledge it.[3] For the Vice Consulship Mr Croker instantly took it in hand but found that he is never appointed by the Gouvernment [*sic*] but by the <u>Consul</u> – Hopper [*sic*] is Consul General & if he will nominate your Lordships friend Mr Croker will undertake to have the appointment confirmed.[4] The cause of my not indulging myself in the favour of being allowed to write longer Letters to your Lordship whom I ever cherish as the most valuable & indulgent friend that I ever could venture to call so is – the distraction wch I \<now\>have for two years undergone from the numbers of people all of a certain name, but most of uncertain use to me, who have been introduced to my Drawing Room – until at length I can endure it no longer for it unhinges my mind so compleatly from all or any connected thought that I can not carry on my business and I have this moment refitted my house & shall

confine this meeting to some dozen persons with whom I have actual business – and your Lordship will find my first object will be to give you the largest portion of my mind & humble servises [sic].

It is really a mistaken notion that Don Juan has not been well received – the Sale has been lessened by an outrageous outcry against some parts of it but its estimation in point of Genius carries your Lordship higher than ever & its circulation will be every day increasing. I have this instant returned from a consultation with Shadwell & Horne[5] the two most eminent Counsel at the Chancery Bar to know if they think that the Chancellor will grant an injunction against the Villain who has printed my two first Cantos of Don Juan & they both agree that he will protect my property – & I am about to try it – but I am again in a Dilemma about yr Lordships name as my Solicitors say that I must name the Author in my Affidavit – at wch rate a man has only to pirate Waverley &c <&>to oblige the Author to declare himself – this I will try & if I must give up the Name I will not proceed further until I have your Lordships pleasure on this point.[6] I hope my recent letters may have had the effect of inducing yr Lordship to compleat the Third Canto and if that be compatible with your preparations a Fourth – but upon my Soul you have a superhuman task to make these equal the two first – which I tremble at but having done what you have done I might venture to feel confidence rather than apprehension – The Prophecy of Dante is a fine Subject[7] – from the Character of Dante & from a similarity illicited [sic] in parts of yr writings of your power compleatly to assume it – I burn to hear more of these things

I will send you immediately the various recently published works upon Spanish America that your Lordship may form your own estimate of the probability of there being within half a century any fixed Stable Gouvernment [sic] or any Chance of security for property[8] – The opinion wch is conveyed to yr Lordship by the Newspapers & particularly by those on the Continent of this Country is really erroneous – There is apprehension of Revolution I assure you – Reforms of various Kinds we ought & must have – & Ministers can not stand more in their own light than by opposing themselves to the March of the Intellect – the progress of Society.[9] – Hobhouse will make nothing of his politics I am afraid for he is a good hearted & able headed Man – & always so friendly to me that I am interested in what he undertakes – He wants to mount a Horse that will not carry double – & one wch the experience & Skill of Sir Francis Burdett – can scarcely manage[10] – He tells me he will make every enquiry about New Spain – but he thinks ill of it at present[11] – Well you will think me troublesome – I will write on friday ab^t Don Juan[12]

Believe that I ever am My Lord
your faithful Servant
John Murray

Notes to Letter 126)

Cover: Milord/Milord Byron/poste restante/a Venise/en Italie <u>arrived</u>: Venice 2
December

1. See headnote to Letter 125 above. B's letter of 29 October, in reply to Letter
   123 above, informing JM of his progress in the third Canto of *DJ*, of his
   having written *The Prophecy of Dante*, and of his intention not to come to
   England (*BLJ* VI, 235–36).

2. See Letter 123, n. 2 above.

3. In his letter of 29 October, B had expressed his concern that JM had not
   mentioned a letter to Annabella he had addressed to JM's care on 31 August
   with a note on the cover asking him to forward it (*BLJ* VI, 235, and 180–82
   for the letter to Annabella and cover note to JM). Annabella had taken Ada
   to Tunbridge Wells and the Isle of Wight over August and September and
   did not return to Kirkby (via London where she stayed a month) until mid-
   November (see also, Letter 124, n. 3 above).

4. See Letter 121, n. 3 above. In his letter of 29 October, B said that he inferred
   from JM's silence on the subject that 'the thing will not be done' (*BLJ* VI,
   235).

5. For Shadwell, see Letter 125, n. 3 above; William (later Sir William) Horne,
   KC (1774–1860), barrister, who was, in the words of Sharon Turner, 'our
   first man now before the Chancellor' (Smiles, I, 407).

6. For B's disinclination to have his name brought in, see Letter 125, n. 4 above.
   As this would have been required, JM did not pursue the matter further (see
   Letter 127 below; Smiles incorrectly asserts that an 'injunction to restrain
   the publication of "Don Juan" by piratical publishers was granted' [Smiles,
   I, 408]; this is not so).

7. See n. 1 above and Letter 123, n. 3 above.

8. See Letter 124, n. 2 above. In his letter to Hobhouse, B had not requested
   books about 'Spanish America', but '*information* as to the encouragement
   – the means required – and what is accorded & what would be my probable
   reception', as well as 'letters to Bolivar and his government' (*BLJ* VI, 225–27;
   Prothero, IV, 357 for correction of 'Boliver' to 'Bolivar'). Nevertheless, JM
   almost certainly sent B three pertinent works (for the first two of which,
   see *CMP*, 249, lots 87 and 92): Major Alexander Gillespie's *Gleanings and
   Remarks: collected during many months of residence at Buenos Ayres* (Leeds, 1818),
   James Hackett's *Narrative of the Expedition which sailed from England in 1817,*

to join the South American Patriots (1818) and Col. G. Hippisley, *A Narrative of the Expedition to the Rivers Orinoco and Apuré in South America, which sailed from England in November 1817, and joined the Patriotic Forces in Venezuela and Caraccas* (1819), which two last were both published by JM himself.

9. Catchphrases of the reform movement, the former more familiarly known perhaps from Keats' declaration to John Hamilton Reynolds in his famous 'Chamber of Maiden-Thought' letter of 3 May 1818, 'there is really a grand march of intellect', but in fact deriving from Burke ('The march of the human mind is slow') in his 'Speech on Conciliation with America' (1775), and echoed by Lord Erskine in his 'Speech on the Trial of Thomas Paine' (1792) (see Maurice Buxton Forman, ed., *The Letters of John Keats*, 3rd rev. edn [Oxford: Geoffrey Cumberlege, 1947], 144; Edmund Burke, *On Empire, Liberty, and Reform*, 104; and *The Speeches of the Right Hon. Lord Erskine ... Collected by the Late James Ridgway*, 4 vols [London, 1847], I, 423). Thomas Wooler announced somewhat boldly that the 'progress of public opinion is now unimpeded' in his article entitled 'March of the Public Mind' in the *Black Dwarf*, III, 22 (Wednesday 2 June 1819), 343; and the phrase was later the subject of a poem, *The March of Intellect*, by W. Hersee in *The Gentleman's Magazine*, XCVII, Pt II (July–December 1827), p. ii, and a leitmotiv of much mirth in Peacock's *Crotchet Castle* (1831). See also, Mrs Gordon, *'Christopher North'. A Memoir of John Wilson* (Edinburgh, 1879), 268, and R. J. White, *Waterloo to Peterloo* (London: Heinemann, 1957), 139.

10. See Letter 124, n. 6 above. The political division between the Whigs and the Radical Reformers had widened in the aftermath of 'Peterloo'. Hobhouse, who was certainly seen by some of his adversaries as playing second fiddle to Burdett, had just published his pamphlet *A Trifling Mistake in Thomas Lord Erskine's recent Preface* (November 1819), for which, on 13 December, he was to be committed to Newgate where he remained until 28 February 1820. (For further details, see Robert E. Zegger, *John Cam Hobhouse: A Political Life, 1819–1852* [Columbia: University of Missouri Press, 1973], ch. III; Malcolm Kelsall, ed., *John Cam Hobhouse: A Trifling Mistake and Reform of Parliament* [Cardiff: University College Cardiff Press, 1984].) In alluding to Hobhouse's wanting 'to mount a Horse that will not carry double' (that is, one in the saddle and one on the crupper), JM may have in mind the disastrous attempt so to mount the mule in *Don Quixote*, vol. I, bk. IV, chap. 2.

11. This is tactful of JM; Hobhouse had in fact written to him saying that B should not expect them to encourage him in 'this mad scheme' which was 'the wildest of all his meditations', and told JM to tell him so (Smiles, I, 409).

12. JM did not write again on 'friday', which would have been 19 November 1819.

Letter 127)   [Monday] 24 January 1820

London Jany. 24 – 1820

My Lord

As Mr Moore is still on the Continent, & uncertain if the Letter
might not demand an immediate answer I availed myself of your
direction to open it – and pounced at once on all its poetical opusculæ
– the epigrams are all good & I intend to avail myself of them without
hinting at their Author[1] – – I was much disappointed at the change of
your intention of visiting England, but I <have> am resolved to see you
before the year closes[2] – unless you migrate to South America whose
distance is to [sic] great for my pursuits [sic] –

I had a conversation with Mr Kinnaird upon the subject of your
liberal proposal respecting Don Juan but as this is almost the only
occasion on wch I have found it necessary to disobey your Lordships
wishes, I hope for your forgiveness. Re-funding is <a> dangerous as
a precedent.[3] I admire the poem beyond all measure & am supported
in this estimation by every man of judgment in the kingdom – who
wish [sic] for a few alterations merely to give wings to the rest & so far
am I indisposed to receive back the Copy Money – that I would not
take double the sum if it were offered to me – the pirate edition is not
countenanced by the booksellers & if it were or had any important sale
I would sell mine for nothing & give every purchaser a Glass of Gin
into the bargain. You will have done me the justice to believe that no
personal consideration would have induced me, under the circumstances,
to have gone into court, & my process was abandoned the moment I
found that the authors name must be given up[4] – wch is by the way
rather absurd for this puts an end to all anonymous writing – if a
rascal chooses to print Waverley for instance – the bookseller <ca> or
proprietor can have no redress unless he disclose the name of the Author
– I have printed Don [sic] in 8vo to match the other Poems & again in a
Smaller form – the latter not yet published[5] – of the Octavo I have sold
3.000 Copies so you see we have circulation in us – I want nothing so
much as a third & fourth Canto which I entreat you to compleat for me
as progressive to the remaining <u>Twelve</u>.[6] I am anxious to know more of
Dantes Prophecy wch is exactly suited to you.

You must know that Blackwoods – commonly called Blackguards
– Magazine is a scurrilous publication – I was smitten by some
cleverness in it & thought I could have regulated its judicious application
– but finding I could not I instantly cut the concern – although I had
paid £1,000 for a half share.[7] It is conducted by Wilson the Author of

the Isle of Palms – a man without principle & who reviewed Don Juan
merely to catch a penny & who is incessantly writing composing &
singing – bawdy & blastphemous [sic] paraphrases of the PSalms [sic] to
all the Young fellows of Scotland[8] – the publisher has been repeatedly
kicked – <wh> & scourged – & persecuted – but he is perfectly callous
– a base fellow <to> whom I once introduced to your Lordship[9] & who
has gained both honour & profit – as my agent by the sale & reputation
of your Lordships Poems – they are a most unprincipled set – To shew
how the public taste still obtains for our various writings – I printed a
very beautiful edition[10] of the Works 3 Vols 8vo for £2. 2. 0 No 3,500
Copies wch were brought out in April last & they are nea<l>rly all sold
– in less than 12 Months – – therefore More – I pray you More – it is
the universal decision that in beauties Don Juan surpasses all that has
preceeded it – Can you keep up to this?

Will you send me a series of Epistles Prose & poetry on Manners &c
of Italy? One Octavo Volume?[11] – Capt. Fyler[12] has been with me &
will positively fulfill your commission about Dogs – I bought a Capital
Bull Dog for you & after paying for his feed for 4 Monts [sic] I got the
Man to take him back thinking – as you never renewed your order
on this subject to me that you had mentioned it in Joke[13] – By the
same first conveyance I will send you a supply of all things including
Dentifrice Soda Books &c.

With regard to domestic politics I can assure you that all revolution
is compleatly overcome – the Whigs made compleat fools of themselves
& have lost all chance of getting into power on the backs of the
Radicals –

I am exceedingly vexed at the conduct of Mr Hobhouse for he
<is no> has not taken a line in wch there is even the possibility of
advantage to him[14] – Sir Francis stands & will stand alone – there is not
room for another on the same pedestal – & there he sits in Newgate
contenting himself for the loss of liberty by the comfortable reflection
"that the House of Comms have no <u>right</u> to send him there" – I have
often visited him since his confinement[15] & I do most sincerely regard
him as a very kind friend – but I am certain that he has no <u>tact</u> in
politics – no more than I have to be a <Sta> Sculptor –

Let me have the pleasure of hearing from you immediately telling
me of your health and <u>Spirits</u> and that you really meditate to oblige
me with some Work for the Spring. let me know to [sic] of the Sundry
domestic goods of wch you stand in need – that I may collect & send
them to you[16] –

What has become of the bust wch Torwalstein [sic] I think made
of you & of wch Mr Hobhouse kindly promised me a cast – can you

purchase & send me one[17] – & I entreat you not to omit any <u>very</u>
good occasion of letters wch have a ring & a seal – Camao [*sic*] &
intaglio – of your head or I shall <pes> haunt you with the Seal wch
Love cut in every Letter[18] – would you indulge me too with a portrait
of <u>Allegra?</u>[19]

Capt Fyler declares that Harlows little portrait of you is the only
likeness he had seen[20] –

May you live many happy 22^{nds} of January[21] in spite of your
perversity to the Honour & Glory of Your Country. – I entreat you to
believe that I continue with unabated devotion – My Lord

Your obliged Affectionate
and faithful friend
John Murray

The Duke of Kent died at Sydmouth [*sic*] on Saturday last after a Weeks
illness from Cold[22] – – the King is not expected to live a fortnight[23]
– this on ye best Autority [*sic*] – Also a Revolution of a very important
nature has taken place in Spain – & the Vile Ferdinand is I trust for
ever dethroned[24]

Notes to Letter 127)

<u>Cover</u>: Milord/Milord Byron/poste restante/a Venise/en Italie <u>arrived</u>: Venice 11
February <u>redirected to</u>: Ravenna

1. Moore was in Paris at the time; B's letter to him of 2 January 1820, written
   on the anniversary of his wedding day and containing two epigrams thereupon, and one each on Castlereagh, Pitt, and Cobbett digging up Paine's
   bones, was enclosed with a note to JM of the same date saying he could open
   it if Moore were not in England (*BLJ* VII, 14 and 16–18; see also, *CPW* IV,
   279–80). JM did not publish the epigrams but no doubt did 'avail' himself
   of them among his friends.

2. JM did not fulfil this resolution, nor did B refer to it in his reply.

3. See Letter 125, n. 4 above.

4. See Letter 126, n. 6 above.

5. The Octavo edition of *Don Juan* was uniform with *The Works of Lord Byron*,
   3 vols (1819) (see Letter 109, n. 12 above; see also, n. 10 below); the 'Smaller
   form' was uniform with *The Works of the Right Honourable Lord Byron*, 8 vols
   (1815–20) and was published in 1820 (see Letter 109, n. 13 above).

6. B replied on Monday 21 February saying he had sent off Cantos III and
   IV of *DJ* on Saturday (19 February). '<u>Twelve</u>' would be the traditional Epic

number of Cantos or Books B had promised the reader in *DJ* I, 200; but by
the time he got to Canto XII (1822; pub 1823) he thought he might 'canter
gently through a hundred' (*DJ* XII, 55).

7. See Letter 111, n. 10 above. On account of its scurrilous articles, JM had
pulled out of *Blackwood's Edinburgh Magazine* exactly six months after joining
it, his name having first appeared on the title-page of Vol. III, xvii (August
1818), and last on that for Vol. IV, xxii (January 1819). It was jointly edited
by John Gibson Lockhart (see Letter 128, n. 9 below) and John Wilson
(1785–1854), 'Christopher North', poet and author of *The Isle of Palms*
(1812) and *The City of the Plague* (1816). In his letter to JM of Wednesday
1 March, B asked him why he abused the magazine and Wilson: 'last year
you were loud & long in praise of both – and now damnify them. – You
are somewhat *capricious* – as we say here in Romagna – when a woman
has more than the usual Staff establishment of Aides de Cons.' (*BLJ* VII,
49).

8. In *Blackwood's Edinburgh Magazine*, V, xxix (August 1819), 512–18, there
appeared an article entitled 'Remarks on Don Juan' in which the author,
while praising B for having 'never written any thing more decisively and
triumphantly expressive of the greatness of his genius', viciously attacked
him on moral and religious grounds and for the 'elaborate satire on the
character and manners of his wife'. B was deeply hurt, and had written to JM
on 10 December 1819 saying: 'I like & admire Wilson – and *he* should not
have indulged himself in such outrageous license' (*BLJ* VI, 257). As JM does
not here deny that Wilson was the author, it may be that he was, though
Moore says it was not him, and more recently the article has been attributed
to John Gibson Lockhart. On the assumption that Wilson was the writer,
however, B replied with *Some Observations Upon an Article in Blackwood's
Edinburgh Magazine* (March 1820; pub. 1833), in which he jocularly exploited
JM's present remarks: 'did he [Wilson] never compose, recite, or sing, any
parody or parodies upon the Psalms, (of what nature this deponent saith not)
in certain jovial meetings of the youth of Edinburgh?' (see *CMP*, 88–119,
esp. 118–19, 360 and 396). Whether or not Wilson himself did so, certainly
his characters do in *The City of the Plague*, where, in answer to the admoni-
tions of the Priest in Act I, Scene iv, the Young Man turns to his fellow
revellers and irreverently suggests their singing the hundredth psalm (in its
metrical arrangement) – 'They have a design against the hundredth Psalm./
Oh! Walsingham will murder cruelly/"All people that on earth do dwell."/
Suppose we sing it here – I know the drawl' (*The City of the Plague and Other
Poems* [1816], 55) – to which B himself facetiously alludes in the concluding
line of *The Vision of Judgment*, where he leaves King George 'practising the
hundredth psalm' (*CPW* VI, 345).

9. JM had introduced Blackwood to B in August 1814 (see Letter 56 above).

10. That is, the first item noted in n. 5 above.

11. B replied on 21 February: 'You ask me for a volume of manners &c. – on Italy', and proceeded to give JM four paragraphs (*BLJ* VII, 42–44).

12. Captain Fyler was almost certainly James C. Fyler of Twickenham whose wife, née Mary Frederick of Burwood Park whom he had married on 19 June 1815, gave birth to a son at the baths of Lucca, Italy, on 13 August 1818 (see *The Gentleman's Magazine*, LXXXV, Pt I [January–June 1815], Supplement, 641, and LXXXVIII, Pt II [September 1818], 273). B told Hobhouse in July 1819 that he had 'bought an English horse of Capt. Fyler some time ago'; and at some point he gave Fyler his annotated copy of D'Israeli's *The Literary Character* (1818), which annotations D'Israeli reproduced in later editions of his work (*BLJ* VI, 188 and IX, 156 [where 'Tyler' should read 'Fyler'], and *CMP*, 219–21 and 546–49). Hobhouse records in his Journal for Wednesday 10 May 1820 that he 'went to smoke a Turkish pipe at Captain Fylers' (BL Add. 56541, f. 35r); and in Paris, on Thursday 1 February 1821, Moore 'went for about ten minutes in the evening to a Mrs. Fyler's, and saw a number of pretty English girls, as refreshing to the eyes in this country as a parterre would be in a desert' (Moore, *Journal*, II, 422–23).

13. B had first asked JM for 'a Bulldog – a terrier – and two Newfoundland dogs' in May 1819 (having asked Hobhouse for the same in different permutations four days earlier), but had not repeated his request since then (*BLJ* VI, 138 and 140). Replying to JM on 21 February, B told him that the bulldogs would be 'very agreeable' as those of Italy had not 'the tenacity of tooth and Stoicism in endurance' as those of his 'canine fellow citizens', and that Kinnaird would disburse for them 'on your application or on that of Captain Fyler' (*BLJ* VII, 41).

14. From B's letter to Moore, JM would have known that B knew that Hobhouse was threatened with (but not yet in) Newgate, to which he had in fact been committed on 13 December 1819 and where he was to remain until 28 February 1820. Hobhouse himself told B all the details in his one letter to him from Newgate of 18 January 1820, when he also gave him a warning: 'do not write any thing to Albemarle Street you do not wish to be seen by all the public offices – The man does not mean to do you a mischief – but he is vain, Sir damn'd vain – and for the sake of a paragraph with "my dear M" in it would betray Christ himself' (*BB*, 283).

15. In his Journal, Hobhouse certainly mentions receiving books from JM but no visits from him up to this time (but see Letter 128, n. 13 below).

16. B replied on 1 March: 'In your last you ask me after my articles of domestic wants – I believe they are as usual – the bulldogs – Magnesia – Soda powders – tooth-powder – brushes – and everything of the kind which are here unattainable ... You enquire after my health – and *Spirits* in large letters – my health can't be very bad – for I cured myself of a sharp Tertian Ague – in three weeks ... As to *Spirits* they are unequal – now high now low – like other people's I suppose' (*BLJ* VII, 48).

17. See Letter 125, n. 9 above. In his letter from Newgate, Hobhouse had also written saying that Thorwaldsen had not sent him B's bust yet, and asking him to write to him at Rome 'to transmit it immediately' (*BB*, 283). In his reply to JM of 21 February, B said that he knew nothing of the bust and that 'Hobhouse should himself write to Thorwalsen' (*BLJ* VII, 44; see also, Letter 128, n. 15 below).

18. See Letter 124, n. 12 above. Replying on 21 February, B said that 'no Cameos or Seals are to be cut here or elsewhere that I know of in any good style' (*BLJ* VII, 44); he did not, however, allude to the seal JM has used for this letter, which is the same as that to which he had earlier taken exception (and for which see headnote to Letter 106 above; for Mr Love, the jeweller, see Letters 96, n. 1, and 97, n. 2 above).

19. B did not reply to this request; he had sent Augusta a miniature of Allegra in October 1818 (*BLJ* VI, 74).

20. For Harlow's 'little portrait' of B, see Letter 118, n. 10 above.

21. JM affectionately remembers B's birthday (32 on 22 January 1820).

22. Edward Augustus, Duke of Kent (1767–1820), the fourth son of George III, died at Sidmouth of a pulmonary disorder on Sunday 23 January 1820. His only child, a daughter born at Kensington Palace on 24 May 1819, became Queen Victoria.

23. Not even that long: George III died on Saturday 29 January 1820, the Prince Regent thus becoming George IV.

24. On 1 January 1820 a Revolution led by Colonels Raphael del Riego and Antonio Quiroga broke out in Spain against the tyrannical administration of Ferdinand VII (1784–1833), who was forced on 7 March to swear to the Constitution of the Cortes of 1812, which he himself had abrogated on Napoleon's orders in 1814. The movement was not only connected with the struggle for independence in South America, in which B had interested himself, but was also shortly to spread to Italy where he became directly involved. These events occupied much of the attention of the press and are well documented in *The Annual Register ... For the Year 1820* (1822), chs XII and XIII.

Letter 128)   Tuesday 7 March 1820

London March 7 – 1820
Tuesday

My dear Lord (Hunt)[1]

Your most kind and valuable packets, which have put fresh vigour, if not new life into me, arrived (4 in number) very safely half an hour ago.[2] I am truly rejoiced in the receipt of them, these Cantos I shall announce instantly & publish fearlesly [sic]. My eyes have searced [sic] in <fi> vain for the pleasure of finding a Letter inclosed – but I shall look for this by the earliest post, in the mean time I shall send these two Cantos to the Printer. Probably you will tell me if we shall print the Translation from Pulci, with its facing Italian at the end of the Volume.+[3] With regard to what your Lordship says as to what was permitted in a Catholic & bigoted age to a Clergyman – I humbly conceive & am surprised that you do not perceive that – religion had nothing to do with it – It was <u>Manners</u> – and they have changed – A<s> man might as well appear without Cloaths – – and quote our Saxon Ancestors – The Comedies of Charles<s> Seconds days are not tolerated now – and even in my Own time I have gradually seen my favourite Love for Love[4] absolutely pushed by public feeling – from the stage – it is not affectation of morality but the real progress and result of refinement – and <we> our minds can no more undergo the moral & religious grossness of our predecessors that [sic] our bodies can sustain the heavy Armour which they wore[5] –

Have you seen or heard of Don Juan – your Don Juan in <u>Prose</u> – well I have now before me "Œuvres de Lord Byron, traduites de L Anglais en VI Volumes" Don Juan is the last of these – Canto for Canto[6] – They are printing the Works in English in Brussells [sic] – in Germany &c – so take care what you <say> write – for <u>All the World</u> will know it – Shall I send yr Lordship the French Version as a Curiosity – & I wish you would review it.[7]

Walter Scott after Ivanhoe – is again in the Field with the Monastry [sic] & whilst One half of the Empire is reading his Novels – the other half are [sic] seeing them Acted[8] – His Daughter – a fine Girl with a great deal of Character is on the point of marriage with a Mr Lockhart one of the Editors of Blackwoods Magazine wch I gave a Share – for wch I paid £1000 – on account of its Scurrility [sic][9]– Milman after the tediousness & bad Taste of Samor – has succeeded in writing a truly noble Dramatic Poem – a Tragedy – not for acting – – The Fall of Jerusalem nothing that ever I received – except from yr Lordship ever fascinated me so much[10] – – I took the MSS up to dinner – intending to thinking [sic] of nothing but what excuse I could make in rejecting it – opened one Page – & was riveted until 3 in the Mornᵍ – This would have been a fine Subject for you – but let me wait until I hear what you say of it.

No Magazine begins now without a Portrait of yr Lordship – & "a critique upon his writings"[11] –

I want to engrave my portrait of Margarita Cogni as the portrait of Donna Julia – may I – sans mot[12]

– I am about to send your Lordship a box of books Pʳ Land wch will be addressed to M. Missiaglia – will you have the goodness to tell him this & give directions for forwarding them to your Lordship.

I dined with Hobhouse – in Newgate & passed a pleasant day – Foscolo I took with me[13] – The Election has commenced with the Electors all in perfect Apathy & he & George Lamb will float on like two pieces of straw on a dull Stream no one knowing wch may reach the border first.[14] I am glad, really, that you did not happen to be in England, during our frustration – wch like the unpleasant expurgation wch takes place in confined Thames Water – results only in its purification – if let alone – We have a noble Session – for the Genius wch it elicited.

Hobhouse has never received from Thorwalstein either bust or Copy – Could your Lordship write to him – for I want one greatly – I have the portrait of your Lordships beautiful daughter Ada – wch I will convey by the first careful opportunity.[15]

Again I beg leave to thank your Lordship for the interesting MSS received this day – With unceasing regard

I ever remain
My Lord
your Lordships
faithfully devoted Servant
Jno Murray

+This would make a Volume of equal bulk with the former. The Prophecy is it compleated?

Notes to Letter 128)

<u>Cover</u>: Milord/Milord Byron/poste restante/a Venise/en Italie <u>arrived</u>: Venice 20 March

1. Another wry glance at Hunt's Dedication to B (see Letter 97, n. 9 above).

2. B had sent JM 'four packets', containing *DJ* III and IV but with no accompanying letter, on Saturday 19 February, telling him he had done so in his letter of 21 February, which JM had not yet received (*BLJ* VII, 42).

3. JM's asterisked note is written at the foot of the page; for *The Prophecy of Dante*, see Letter 129, n. 2 below. In his letter of Monday 7 February, B told JM he was translating the first Canto of Pulci's *Morgante Maggiore* and added: 'I think my translation ... will make you stare – it must be put by the original stanza for stanza and verse for verse – and you will see what was permitted in a Catholic country and a bigotted age to a Churchman on the score of religion; – and so tell those buffoons who accuse me of attacking the liturgy' (*BLJ* VII, 35; see n. 5 below).

4. William Congreve's comedy *Love for Love* first performed in 1695.

5. JM's allusion to 'Saxon Ancestors' may have been prompted by reading (or seeing) Scott's *Ivanhoe* (see Letter 125, n. 8 above, and n. 8 below). B replied on Wednesday 29 March: 'You have given me a screed of Metaphor and what not about *Pulci* – & manners, "and going *without clothes* like our Saxon ancestors" now the *Saxons did not go* without cloathes and in the next place they are *not* my ancestors, nor yours either, for mine were Norman, and yours I take it by your name were *Gael*. – – And in the next I differ from you about "refinement" which has banished the comedies of Congreve – are not the Comedies of *Sheridan* acted to the thinnest houses? ... Pulci is *not* an *indecent* writer ... You talk of *refinement*, are you all *more* moral? are you *so* moral? – No such thing' (*BLJ* VII, 61).

6. An advertisement for 'Œuvres de Lord Byron, traduites de l'Anglais, 6 vols. 12mo. £1, 4s.' appeared under 'New Foreign Works, imported by Treuttel and Würtz, Soho-Square, London' in *Blackwood's Edinburgh Magazine*, XXXVII, vi (March 1820), 717. This must correspond to the first six volumes (which B himself seems to have possessed; *CMP*, 246, lot 27) of *Oeuvres Complètes de Lord Byron*, traduites de l'Anglais Par MM. A[médée].-P[ichot]. et E[usèbe].-D[e]. S[alle].; Troisième Édition, entièrement revue et corrigée [15 vols., 12mo.] (1821–24), a copy of which the BL holds, and vol. 6 of which (1821) contains a prose translation of *DJ* I and II, and 'Le Vampire' (by Polidori).

7. These were *The Works, of The Right Honourable Lord Byron, In Seven Volumes* (Brussels: The English Repository of Arts, 1819), and *The Works of the Right Honourable Lord Byron*, 13 vols (Leipsick: Gerald Fleischer, 1818–22) (Vols 1–7,

1818–19; Vols 8–13, 1821–22). JM's '&c' perhaps also includes *The Works of the Right Honourable Lord Byron*, 6 vols (Paris: Galignani, 1819).

8. See Letter 125, n. 8 above. Since 1816, beginning with *Guy Mannering*, Scott's novels had been subject to what he jocularly called '"the art of *Terryfying*"' – that is, adapted for the stage by his friend the actor Daniel Terry (1780–1829) (see Lockhart, *Life of Scott*, 329, 366 and 389). In 1820, when the Nation came out of mourning after the King's death, the theatres reopened on Thursday 17 February with performances of *The Antiquary* at Covent Garden, *Ivanhoe; or, The Jew's Daughter* at the Surrey Theatre, and *Ivanhoe; or, The Saxon Chief* at the Adelphi. *Guy Mannering* returned to Drury Lane Theatre on Tuesday 29 February, and the first performance of *The Hebrew* (another adaptation from *Ivanhoe*) took place there on Thursday 2 March, on which date *Ivanhoe; or, The Knight-Templar* was first performed at Covent Garden.

9. JM means gave 'up' a share (see Letters 111, n. 10, and 127, n. 7 above). Scott's daughter, Sophia (b. 1799), married John Gibson Lockhart (1794–1854), author, joint-editor of *Blackwood's Edinburgh Magazine* and future biographer of Scott, in Edinburgh on 29 April 1820 (Lockhart, *Life of Scott*, 164n and 428).

10. The Rev. Henry Hart Milman (1791–1868), poet and later Dean of St Paul's, author of *Fazio. A Tragedy* (1815), of which JM published the 3rd, 4th and 5th edns in 1818, and whose *Samor, Lord of the Bright City. An Heroic Poem* he published in April 1818, and *The Fall of Jerusalem: A Dramatic Poem* in April 1820. See also, Letter 131 below.

11. A slight exaggeration. In *The Times* for Saturday 1 January 1820, Gold and Northhouse announced the publication of the first number of *The London Magazine and Monthly Critical and Dramatic Review*, 'embellished with a striking likeness of Lord Byron, and containing Original Memoirs of his Lordship, communicated by an early acquaintance'. The 'striking likeness' is a truly appalling engraving of B by Henry Meyer, after a drawing by Henry Whitaker (*fl.* 1825–50) (see Peach, *Portraits of Byron*, 37, no. 10.14).

12. For the portrait of Margarita Cogni by Harlow, see Letter 118, n. 10 above. Replying on Thursday 23 March, B said revealingly: 'If you choose to make a print from the Venetian you may – but she don't correspond at all to the character you mean her to represent – on the contrary the Contessa G[uiccioli] does (except that She is remarkably fair) and is much prettier than the Fornarina' (*BLJ* VII, 59; see also, Letter 154, n. 3 below).

13. JM and Ugo Foscolo dined with Hobhouse in Newgate on Thursday 15 February when Hobhouse recorded in his Diary: 'Murray was entertaining – but told all the secrets of all his friends – and abused them practically one after the other' (BL Add. 56541, f. 5).

14. With the dissolution of Parliament, Hobhouse was released from Newgate on Monday 28 February. In the ensuing election he consistently came second

after Burdett, with George Lamb third, and was eventually elected MP for Westminster on Saturday 25 March 1820 (BL Add. 56541, ff. 12v–20). He wrote to B on 31 March to tell him the news (*BB*, 286–88).

15. See Letters 125, n. 9, and 127, n. 17 above. B replied on Saturday 25 March that he had 'caused write to Thorwalsen', and anxiously requested JM to 'be careful in sending my daughter's picture – I mean that it be not hurt in the carriage – for it is a journey rather long and jolting' (*BLJ* VII, 60). B had written to Annabella on 20 February saying he would be 'very glad of Ada's picture whenever it can be forward[ed]' (*BLJ* VII, 41). See Letter 133 below.

Letter 129)   [Friday] 28 April 1820

London April 28 – 1820

My Lord

One of my letters must have miscarried[1] – I have received safely all your interesting packets – Pulci – Rimini – Blackwood – the whole of wch is <n> this day set up in Types [*sic*] & will be sent to M*r* Hobhouse for his correction – Dante is very grand and worthy of you – and Pulci excellent – Rimini – not so much admired & there are marks of hase [*sic*] in the repetition of the same word – Foscolo – Milman Gifford & Hallam are the critics in these cases[2]

– <The Lett> These Poems are not for the Million & we must not expect them to be popular – The Letter on Blackwoods Magazine is very curious & interesting – & must make a noise – I am sorry however that you touch upon the idle talk about Incest – & it is not well to let the world know – as a quoteable [*sic*] thing – your having had both those Ladies.[3] Pray absorb all your faculties in the Tragedy[4] – & you will do the greatest thing you have effected yet and again confound the world – who are all most anxious that you should do this –

We admire your powerful & acute defence of Pope[5] –

I am in haste for post

My Lord

Most truly yr*s*

Jno Murray

Notes to Letter 129)

Cover: Milord/Milord Byron/Poste restante/Ravenna/Italie arrived: Forli 18 May

1. Since receiving Letter 128 above, to which he had replied on 23, 25 and 29
   March, B had heard nothing from JM and had written rather sharply to say
   so on 9 and 16 April (*BLJ* VII, 73–74 and 76–77). On 23 April, however, he
   received a letter from JM (dated 7 April, but no longer extant), enclosing the
   proofs of *DJ* III and IV (and commenting that '*one half*' was 'very good'),
   acknowledging the receipt of the various compositions to which he here
   again refers, and informing B of Scott's knighthood (see *BLJ* VII, 82–83
   and 96). Scott's baronetcy was first announced in the *Gazette* on Saturday 1
   April 1820 and reported in the papers the following Monday (see *The Times*,
   Monday 3 April 1820, and the *London Chronicle*, CXXVII, 9563 [Saturday
   1-Monday 3 April 1820], 320). It is possible that in his letter which 'must
   have miscarried', or his letter of 7 April no longer extant, JM made some
   use of the following letter of Sunday 26 March from Croker concerning *DJ*
   III–IV which is in MA (cf. Smiles, I, 413–16):

   > Munster House
   > Mar 26th 1820
   > a <u>rainy Sunday</u>

   Dear Murray

   Many thanks for the print which arrived safe & which adorns
   my billiard room – with all its imperfections it is very interesting to
   me & with still greater defects it would be still interesting donatoris
   causâ [as a bequest].

   I am also to thank you for letting me see your two new cantos
   – which I return. What sublimity – what levity; what boldness what
   tenderness; what majesty what trifling; what variety, what <u>tedious-</u>
   <u>ness,</u> for tedious to a strange degree it must be confessed that whole
   passages are – particularly the earlier stanzas of the 4th Canto – I
   know no man of such general powers of intellect, as Brougham; yet
   I think <u>him</u> insufferably tedious, & I fancy the reason to be that he
   has such <u>facility</u> of expression, that he is never recalled to a <u>selec-</u>
   <u>tion</u> of his thoughts – a more costive orator would be obliged to
   choose & a man of his talents could not fail to choose the best; but
   the power of uttering all & every thing which passes across his mind
   tempts him to <do all> say all – he goes on without thought, I
   should rather say without pause – His speeches are poor from their
   richness, & dull from their infinite variety – an impediment in his
   speech would make him a perfect Demosthenes – Something of the
   same kind, & with something of the same effect, is Lord Byrons
   wonderful fertility of thought & facility of expression: & the Pulcian
   style of Don Juan, instead of checking (as the fetters of rythm [*sic*]
   generally do) his <gigantic> natural activity not only gives him
   wider limits to range in, but even generates a more roving disposition – I dare swear, if the truth were known, that his digressions &
   repetitions generate one another, & that the happy jingle of some of
   his comical rhymes has led him on to episodes of which he never

originally thought – & thus it is that, with the most extraordinary merit, <u>merit</u> of <u>all kinds</u>, these two cantos have been to <u>me</u>, in several points, tedious & even obscure.

As to the <u>principles</u>, all the world, & you, Mʳ Murray <u>first of all</u>, have done this poem great injustice, there are levities here & there – more than good taste approves – but nothing to make Such a terrible rout about; nothing so bad as Tom Jones, nor within an hundred degrees of Count Fathom – I know that it is no justification of one fault to produce a greater – neither am I justifying Lord Byron. I have acquaintance none or next to none with him & of course no interest beyond what we must all take in a poet who on the whole is one of the first, if not the very first, of our age; but I direct my observations against you & those whom you deferr'd to – If you print & sell Tom Jones & Peregrine Pickle why did you start at Don Juan? why smuggle it into the world &, as it were, pronounce it illegitimate in<s> its birth, & induce so many of the learned rabble, when they could find so little specific offence in it, to refer to its supposed original state, as one of original sin – If instead of this you had touch'd the right string & <addressed it> in the right place – Lord B's own good taste, & good nature would have revised & corrected some phrases in his poem which, in reality, disparage it more than its imputed looseness of principle; I mean some expressions of political & personal feelings which, I believe he in fact, never felt, & threw in wantonly & de gaieté de cœur & which he would have omitted, advisedly & de bonté de cœur, if he had not been goaded by indiscreet contradictions & unjust <u>criticisms</u>, which, in some cases, were dark enough to be called <u>calumnies</u>. but these are blowing over, if not blown over, & I cannot but think that if Mʳ Gifford, or some friend in whose taste & disinterestedness Lord B. could rely, were to point out to him the cruelty to individuals, the injury to the national character, the offence to public taste & the injury to his own reputation, of such passages as those <rel> about <Waterloo> Southey & Waterloo & the British Government & the head of that Government, I cannot but hope & believe that these blemishes in the past [*sic*] cantos would be wiped away in the next edition, & that some that occur in the two cantos (which you sent me) would never see the light – What interest can Lord Byron have in being the poet of a party in politics or of a party in morals or of a party in religion – why should he wish to throw away the suffrages (you see the times infect my dialect) of more than half the nation – He has no interest in that direction & I believe has no feeling of that kind. – In politics he cannot be what he appears, or rather what Meˢˢʳˢ. Hobhouse & Legh [*sic*] Hunt wish to make him appear. a man of his birth, a man of his taste, a man of his talents, a man of his habits can have nothing

in common with such miserable creatures as we now call <u>radicals</u>,
of whom I know not that I can better express the illiterate & blind
ignorance & vulgarity than by saying that the best inform'd of them
have probably never heard of Lord Byron – No no Lord Byron may
be indulgent to these Jackall [*sic*] followers of his; he may connive
at their use of his name, nay it is not to be denied that he has given
them too too much countenance, but he never can, I should think,
now that he sees not only the road, but the rate they are going,
continue to take a part so contrary to all his own interests & feelings & to the feelings & interests of all the respectable part of his
country – & yet it was only yesterday at dinner that somebody said
that he had read or seen a letter of Lord B's to somebody saying
that if the radicals only made a little progress & showed some real
force he would hasten over & get on horseback to head them – this
is evidently either a gross lie altogether, or a grosser misconstruc-
tion of some epistolary pleasantry; because if the proposition were
serious the letter never could have been shown – yet see how a
bad name is given – we were 12 at dinner – all (except myself)
people of note & yet (except Water [*sic*] Scott & myself again) every
human being will repeat this story to 12 others & so on <until
it> But what is to be the end of all this rigmarole of mine – To
conclude, this; to advise you, for your own sake as a tradesman for
Lord Byron's sake as a poet, for the sake of good literature & good
principles which ought to be united, to take such measures as you
may be able to venture upon, to get Lord Byron to revise these
two cantos & not to make another step in the odious path which
Hobhouse beckons him to pursue – there is little very little of this
offensive nature in these cantos the omission I think of 5 Stanzas
out of 215 would do all I should ask on this point; but I confess that
I think it would be much better for his fame & your profit if the
two stanzas [*sic*] were thrown into one & brought to a proper length
by the retrenchments of the many careless, obscure, & idle passages
which <u>incuria fudit</u> [show carelessness; Horace, *Ars Poetica*, 352] – I
think Tacitus says that the Germans formed their plans when drunk
& matured them when sober [Tacitus, *Germania*, 22] – I know not
how this might answer in public affairs, but in poetry I should think
it an excellent plan, to pour out, as Lord Byron does, his whole
mind in the intoxication of the moment, but to revise & condense
in the sobriety of the morrow. One word more; experience shows
that this Pulcian style is very easily written – Frere – Blackwood's
Magaziners – Rose – Cornwall, all write it with ease & success, it
therefore behoves Lord Byron to distinguish his use of this measure
by superior & peculiar beauties – he should refine & polish & by
the <u>limæ labor et mora</u> [the toil and tedium of the file; Horace, *Ars
Poetica*, 291] attain the perfection of ease – a vulgar epigram says

that "Easy writing's damned <u>hard reading</u>" ['You write with ease, to show your breeding,/But easy writing's vile hard reading'; Sheridan, 'Clio's Protest' (written 1771; pub. 1819)] & it is one of the eternal & general rules by which heaven <has> warns us, at every step & at every look, that this is a mere transitory life, that <nothing> what costs no trouble soon perishes – that what grows freely dies <soon> early – & that <the> nothing indures [*sic*], but in some degree of proportion with the time & labor it has cost to create. – Use these hints if you can but not my name – y^{rs} ever

JWC.

The only recent letters of B's expressing any such intention of coming over to England to be among the reformers were those to Kinnaird of 19 August 1819, '[August 27?]' (postmarked 7 September 1819), and 26 October 1819 (*BLJ* VI, 210–11, 217–18 and 232–33). Who the 'somebody' was who mentioned reading or seeing such a letter 'yesterday at dinner' is difficult to say. In his Diary for Saturday 25 March 1820, Croker records that 'Scott and his son dined at Munster House [Croker's house in Fulham] with Palmerston and Miss Temple, Mr. and Mrs. Arbuthnot, Yarmouth, Torrens, &c.' (Jennings, *The Croker Papers*, I, 169). The '&c.' is tantalizing. Scott does not mention this dinner-party, and Harriet Arbuthnot merely records that she 'Dined at Mr. Croker's & sat at dinner by Walter Scott' with whom she conversed (Francis Bamford and the Duke of Wellington, eds, *The Journal of Mrs. Arbuthnot 1820–1832*, 2 vols [London: Macmillan, 1950], I, 10–11).

2. B quoted these 'opinions ... from Murray and his Utican senate' in his letter to Moore of 25 May 1820 (*BLJ* VII, 106). He had sent JM his translation of the first Canto of Pulci's *Morgante Maggiore* on Monday 28 February, *The Prophecy of Dante* on Tuesday 14 March, his translation of 'Francesca of Rimini', from Dante's *Inferno*, Canto V on Monday 20 March, with further variants on Thursday 23 March, and *Some Observations upon an Article in Blackwood's Edinburgh Magazine* on Tuesday 28 March, with a further 'note ... on Pope' the following day (*BLJ* VII, 28–29, 57, 58–59 and 60–61; Marchand's note here [61n.] suggesting that this 'note' was 'probably an early form of Byron's reply to Bowles on the Pope controversy' is incorrect; see *CMP*, 359).

3. In *Some Observations* B dismisses what he thought was Southey's accusation that in 1816 he and Shelley had lived 'in promiscuous intercourse with two Sisters "having formed a league of Incest"'; in fact the rumour had been spread by Brougham (*CMP*, 100 and 375). Returning the proof of *Some Observations* on 20 May and telling JM he could publish it, B said: 'You are wrong – I never had those "*two* ladies" – upon my honour! never believe but *half* of such stories' (*BLJ* VII, 102).

4. In his letter of 9 April, B had informed JM that he had 'begun a tragedy on the subject of Marino Faliero, The Doge of Venice, but you shan't see

it these six years if you don't acknowledge my packets with more quickness and precision' (*BLJ* VII, 74).

5. A fair proportion of *Some Observations* consists of a vigorous defence of Pope (see *CMP*, 104–18).

Letter 130)   [Tuesday] 13 June 1820

London June 13. 1820

My Lord

I have delayed writing until I thought that you would have heard from Mr Hobhouse & Mr Kinnaird their opinions as to the propriety of publishing any of the poems and prose wch we have lately received – I saw Mr Hobhouse a day or two since and he perfectly agrees with me in recommending delay.[1] Let us wait until you send me something – better than any thing you have yet written, for this however arduous to effect and impertinent to ask, is indispensable in order to produce that sensation which has hitherto attended the publication of your works – I am confident that the Tragedy upon which you are now occupied will excite all your mind – let us put forth some thing of this Calibre <now> first & the other poems may follow – Upon my soul I never felt more at a loss to express myself – We all think Canto III by no means equal to the two first – Pulci very admirably executed as it is possible – but we are convinced that it will not be <liked> popular in England – Blackwood is not worth your notice – wch would be sure to raise the reputation of his Magazine – for [*sic*] wch I have withdrawn on account of its shameful personality – All that your Lordships [*sic*] says about Pope – is excellent indeed & I wish you could be induced to enlarge it & I would print it with any thing else in the Shape of Notes that you would make for me in an Edition of Popes Poetical Works wch I am very anxious to rescue from Mr Bowles[2] – The Dante is very good but perhaps not of sufficient importance for separate publication – But after venturing to obtrude my opinion I trust that you will do me the favour to understand that it is given with the utmost deference to your own – and most particularly as to the busi<siness>nes [*sic*] part of it I will subscribe to any thing that your Lordship may think proper to propose.[3]

I have just heard that Mr Moores new poems Rhymes on the Road" [*sic*] after printing Six Sheets are found so dull that they have been suppressed[4] – – I will write you a Letter of News on friday I confess to you this has been most confoundly against the grain[5] –

I remain My Lord

Your faithful friend & Servant
John Murray

Notes to Letter 130)

Cover: Milord/Milord Byron/poste restante/Ravenna/Italie arrived: Forli 6 July

1. Hobhouse had called on JM on Thursday 8 June '& told him my opinion about Byron's poems – in MSS' (BL Add. 56541, f. 41); he had evidently written to B prior to this (probably some time in May) advising him not to publish *Some Observations* but to salvage from it the portion on Pope (his letter is not extant, but see B's letter to him of 8 June 1820 [*BLJ* VII, 114–16]).

2. Coincidentally, in his reply to Hobhouse of 8 June B himself had proposed that the Pope part 'might be appended to that Popean Poem' *Hints from Horace* (*BLJ* VII, 114; see also, Letter 141, n. 8 below). JM was 'anxious to rescue' Pope from 'Mr Bowles' because Bowles had impugned Pope's reputation in his edition of Pope's works (see Letter 141, n. 8 below).

3. Replying on 6 July, B said he found no fault with JM's 'opinions' nor with his acting upon them, but protested against being kept '*four months in suspense* – without any answer at all'. He told him to 'keep back the remaining trash till I have woven the tragedy of which I am in the 4th act', and with regard to terms he 'named & *name* none' (*BLJ* VII, 124).

4. B did not allude to the precocious suppression of *Rhymes on the Road*, eventually published with *Fables for the Holy Alliance* (1823), though he did write to Moore on 13 July saying: 'Your publishers seem to have used you like mine' (*BLJ* VII, 127). In fact Moore himself was somewhat relieved by the suppression. Writing to JM from Paris on 14 April 1820, he told him: 'You see I announced a Fudge Family in Italy, but I have not been able to make it what I wished, and accordingly, for the present, it is laid up in ordinary. I shall, however, publish a few detached trifles in May, merely as a fly-catcher in the warm weather' (Moore, *Letters*, II, 484). However, on 17 July 1820 he wrote to Rogers: 'You have heard, I dare say, that the Longmans have suppressed my book, at which I am not at all sorry, for I can make a much better thing out of its materials at another time, and I have availed myself of their readiness to withhold the publication, though with very different views from those upon which they recommended it.' And he added a telling observation on his relations with Longmans which might be compared with those between JM and B: 'Nothing can be more liberal, considerate, and kind than the conduct of those men to me. It is really friendship, assuming the form of business, and making itself actively useful, upon a fair debtor and creditor account of obligations' (Moore, *Letters*, II, 485; see also, Moore, *Journal*, 1, 317 and 321).

5. JM did not fulfil his promise to write on 'friday' (16 June).

Letter 131)   [Thursday] 29 June 1820

London June 29th 1820

My dear Lord

You can not conceive how much my mind has been relieved your
[sic] most kind & liberal acceptation of our opinion of the propriety of
publishing any of the new Poems immediately[1] – but I do beseach you
not to conceive it possible the mere L. S. D have any thing to do with the
business for as I observed in my last I will most joyfully give whatever
estimation you or your friends may place upon them, soliciting only
a discretionary power as to the time of publication – in fact as I have
already ventured to state I wish previously to have the honour of putting
forth some very original & powerful poem by your Lordship – & then to
follow it by these which I now have – This I think the <u>Tragedy</u> will do.
In all this my own advantage is identified with your Lordships fame and
for the rest entirely upon the principles which have hitherto secured to
me the favour of your Lordships unvarying confidence.

I am glad that your Lordship appears by your just & pungent notice
of some of them to have received at least one of the packets of books
which I sent out to you by way of experiment[2] – you do not happen
however to notice <either> any one of those sent out by another
conveyance, <u>at the same time</u> – but this may arise from the accident
of your not having read any of them – other two parcels are on the
road – Today I have put up <f>a supply of tooth Powder Myrh [sic] &c
& some novelties,[3] and having discovered this safe & regular mode of
communication I will take care to supply you with all necessaries.

I dont know what to make of Goethes Rhapsody on Manfred[4]
I shewed to [sic] Mr Frere who said that he still continued to place
Manfred in thighest [sic] Class of Poetry – Whistlecraft is perfect
Caviere [sic] to the Million – and the author is very much in dudgeon
at this[5] – You do not say a word of three books of wch I much
desire your opinion Anastasius – long attributed to you – The Fall of
Jerusalem and The Diary of an Invalid.[6]

Sir Humphry Davy is returned and is to be the Successor of Sir
Joseph Banks at the Roy^l Society[7] A Literary Society composed of Buffs
& Blues[8] – meets on Tuesdays at Lydia Whites[9] – Lady Besboroughs
[sic] &c – One evening at Lydia Whites – Mr Rose said addressing
himself to Lady B – I tell you what Lady B – I propose – that no lady
of unimpeached [sic] shall be a member of this Society – (Lydia White
pummelled him with her fan) – but, continues Rose, – then they say
that this might exclude Lydia White (Lydia was pacified) – but then

they say – that there is a Story about Lydia White – at Bath –

We are in a pretty Scrape with the Queen[10] do you remember <the the adv> "L'avanture [*sic*] du pot de chambre"?[11]

I shall be anxious until I have the satisfaction of hearing from yr Lordship again – With Compliments I remain

My Lord

your obliged & faithful Servant

John Murray

Notes to Letter 131)

Cover: Milord/Milord Byron/Poste restante/Ravenna/Italie arrived: Forli 20 July

1. B had written on 8 June saying he had heard of JM's hesitancy 'to make propositions with regard to the M.S.S.' transmitted to him, and assuring him he was 'in no respect limited to any terms' and should not consider himself bound by any former propositions, 'particularly as your people may have a bad opinion of the production – the which I am by no means prepared to dispute' (*BLJ* VII, 114).

2. In his letter of 7 June, B told JM he had 'received *Ivanhoe*; – *good*', and proceeded to observe that '*Ricciardetto* should have been *translated literally or not at all*. – As to puffing *Whistlecraft* – *it won't do*' (*BLJ* VII, 113 and n.; Marchand's note, following Prothero's speculation [Prothero, V, 37n], is incorrect here). This almost certainly refers to John Herman Merivale's *The Two First Cantos of Richardetto, freely translated from the Original Burlesque Poem of Niccolo Fortiguerra, otherwise Carteromaco*, published anonymously by JM in January 1820, in which the translator, readily conceding in his Preface that those 'acquainted with Italian poetry, will easily discover where he has followed, and where deviated from his original' (p. xi), puffs *Whistlecraft* in stanzas 3 and 4 of his dedication and summarizes in prose the last 40 stanzas of the first Canto of Forteguerri's original. B also commented on Barry Cornwall, the pseudonym of his old schoolfellow, Bryan Waller Procter (1787–1874), whose recent publications included *Dramatic Scenes and Other Poems* (1819; 2nd edn, 1820), *A Sicilian Story, with Diego de Montilla and Other Poems* (1820) and *Marcian Colonna, An Italian Tale, With Three Dramatic Scenes and Other Poems* (1820), and on Felicia Hemans, whose *The Sceptic: A Poem*, published by JM in 1820, was 'too stiltified, & apostrophic – & quite wrong' (*BLJ* VII, 113; for Barry Cornwall, see also, *BLJ* VIII, 56). He concluded his remarks by asking: 'What does Helga Herbert mean by his *Stanza*? which is octave got drunk [or gone] mad' (*BLJ* VII, 114). For the Hon. William Herbert and his poem *Helga*, see Letter 70, n. 3 above; his *Hedin; or The Spectre of the Tomb: A Tale. From the Danish History*, published by JM in 1820, is written in what might best be described

as curtal Spenserians (Spenserian stanzas without the middle – the fifth – line).

3. B had asked JM for 'some tooth powder & *tincture* of Myrrh' in his letter of 7 June (*BLJ* VII, 113; gum myrrh was used in fragrances and tooth powder, and in tinctures – of myrrh and claret – for sore mouths and gums and preserving teeth in old age).

4. In his letter of 7 June, B had sent JM the German original, together with Hoppner's translation and an Italian one of 'the opinion of *the* Greatest man of Germany – perhaps of Europe – upon one of the great men of your advertisements ... in short – a critique of *Goethe's* upon *Manfred*', telling him to 'keep them all in your archives – for the opinions of such a man as Goethe whether favourable or not are always interesting – and this is moreover favourable' (*BLJ* VII, 113; for Goethe's original and Hoppner's translation, see Prothero, IV, Appendix II).

5. *Hamlet*, II, ii, 430–32: 'the play, I remember, pleas'd not the million; 'twas caviary to the general'. For Frere's reaction to the fate of *Whistlecraft*, see Letter 109, n. 17 above; for his opinion of *Manfred*, see Letter 107 above.

6. Thomas Hope's *Anastasius: or, Memoirs of a Greek; Written at the close of the Eighteenth Century*, published anonymously by JM in 3 vols in December 1819. JM had also sent a copy to Hobhouse in Newgate, who thought it 'a delightful book' and recorded in his Journal for Thursday 16 December 1819: 'I was sure at first reading that our good folks would think of Lord Byron in reading it – and I have since found that the work is attributed to him – neither He nor any Englishman could write a page of it I think' (BL Add. 56540, f. 125). For Milman's *The Fall of Jerusalem*, see Letter 128, n. 10 above. *The Diary of an Invalid; being The Journal of a Tour in pursuit of health; in Portugal, Italy, Switzerland, and France, in the years 1817, 1818, and 1819* (1820) was by Henry Matthews (1789–1828), barrister, the younger brother of B's and Hobhouse's friend, Charles Skinner Matthews (1785–1811), who drowned in the Cam in August 1811 (see also, Letter 138 below). Replying to JM on 22 July, B said he thought 'Jerusalem ... the best. – Anastasius good but no more written by a Greek – than by a Hebrew – the diary of an Invalid good and true bating a few mistakes about "Serventismo" which no foreigner can understand or really know – without residing in the country' (*BLJ* VII, 138).

7. Sir Joseph Banks (1743–1820), President of the Royal Society, had died on 19 June; Sir Humphry Davy was nominated for the Presidency and elected on 30 November 1820.

8. I.e., Whigs and Bluestockings (or Literary ladies) ('Buff and blue' were the colours of the Whig party; cf. *DJ*, Dedication, 17).

9. Lydia White, who died of dropsy in 1827, was a society hostess renowned for her bons mots and quickness of repartee. Henry Fox records one occasion

when, on entering a room and seeing Rogers and Foscolo together, she exclaimed: "'Good God, the day of judgment! The quick and the dead!'" (*The Journal of the Hon. Henry Edward Fox (afterwards fourth and last Lord Holland) 1818–1830*, ed. the Earl of Ilchester [London: Butterworth, 1923], 48; see also, 96–97 and 128). B and Annabella persuaded Miss Berry to accompany them and William Spencer to one of her soirées on Monday 8 May 1815 (*Extracts from the Journals and Correspondence of Miss Berry*, ed. Lady Theresa Lewis, 3 vols, 2nd edn [London, 1866], III, 49). B lent her his copy of Moore's *Lalla Rookh* when she came to Venice in 1818 (*BLJ* VI, 46), and three years later cast her as 'Miss Diddle' in *The Blues* (1821; pub. 1823) (see *CPW* VI, 665). Moore records that she was one of the 'blue Dragonesses' he saw at a Sotheby assembly in May 1819, and that at her own assembly on Monday 24 May 1819 'a little girl acted in a French proverb, who was found amidst the conflagration of Moscow – quite an infant – & not known whether French or Russian now 7 years old & acted very archly' (Moore, *Journal*, I, 175 and 180; perhaps he mentioned this to B when they met in Venice in October that year, and it later re-emerged in the Leila episode in *DJ* VIII, 91ff.) She was a great consolation to Lady Caroline Lamb who, in dedicating *Ada Reis* to her, expressed her 'grateful recollection of your kindness to me in the time of affliction', and paid her a warm and generous tribute for having 'succeeded in retaining around you, even when sickness has rendered you incapable of exertion, many who are distinguished by superiority of intellect and literary talents', adding: 'your society is eagerly sought by those anxious and affectionate friends, who find their pleasure in the enjoyment of your conversation, and in the contemplation of your fortitude and magnanimity' (*Ada Reis, A Tale*, 3 vols [London: John Murray, 1823], I, iii–v). One such friend was Hobhouse who, dining 'at poor Lydia White's' on Saturday 24 July 1824, found her 'a sad sight – she sat painted up to the eyes with a large belly of which she is dying – from a dropsy in the womb' (BL Add. 56549, f. 26). On hearing of her death, Scott paid her a fine tribute in his Journal for Friday 2 February 1827 (*The Journal of Sir Walter Scott*, ed. W. E. K. Anderson, rev. edn [Edinburgh: Canongate Books, 1998], 309–10). See also, *Lady Morgan's Memoirs*, 2 vols, 2nd rev. edn [London, 1863], II, 227–28 and 235–37; Lady Charlotte Bury, *The Diary of a Lady-in-Waiting*, ed. A. Francis Steuart, 2 vols [London, 1908], II, 199–200, 209–10, and 226–28); Thomas Constable, *Archibald Constable and His Literary Correspondents*, 3 vols [Edinburgh, 1873], II, 17–20; and especially, William Prideaux Courtney, *Eight Friends of The Great* [London, 1910], 149–71). Lady Bessborough was the mother of Caroline Lamb; for William Stewart Rose, see Letter 105, nn. 5 and 9 above.

10. With the death of George III, Queen Caroline returned to England after six years abroad to assume her role as the consort of the King. She had arrived in London on 6 June 1820 to great popular acclaim; but divorce proceedings were immediately instituted against her on the grounds of adultery, and on 5 July Lord Liverpool introduced a Bill of Pains and Penalties designed to

deprive her of all her regal rights and privileges and to dissolve her royal marriage. The second reading of the Bill was fixed for 17 August on which day her Trial began; but public feeling ran so high that the Bill was eventually withdrawn on 10 November and the case abandoned. (For two recent accounts of the whole affair, see E. A. Smith, *A Queen on Trial: The Affair of Queen Caroline* [Stroud: Alan Sutton, 1993], and Flora Fraser, *The Unruly Queen: The Life of Queen Caroline* [London and Basingstoke: Macmillan, 1996], esp. chs 15–17). JM refers to the subject on a number of later occasions; replying to his present allusion on 22 July, B told him he thought the Queen would win: 'I wish she may – she was always very civil to me' (*BLJ* VII, 139).

11. B replied on 22 July: 'I remember what you say of the Queen – it happened in Lady O[xford]'s boudoir or dressing room if I recollect rightly, but it was not her Majesty's fault – though very laughable at the time – a minute sooner she might have stumbled over something still more awkward. – How the *Porcelain* came there I cannot conceive – and remember asking Lady O[xford] afterwards – who laid the blame on the Servants' (*BLJ* VII, 139). It may be, however, that JM is referring to the 'celebrated *pot-de-chambre*' of Lady Holland's, with one of whose adventures Morritt entertains Scott in a letter of April 1812 and which Scott may well have recounted to B and JM in 1815 (see Wilfred Partington, ed., *The Private Letter-Books of Sir Walter Scott* [London: Hodder and Stoughton, 1930], 181, and Scott, *Letters*, III, 113–14).

Letter 132) [Friday] 14 July 1820

London July 14th
1820

My Lord

Mr Hobhouse has just called and with a kindness which makes me feel the more severely, has communicated your displeasure at my long & Stupid silence upon the subject of the Poems.[1] I assure you I am most sincerely grieved at this but I could not induce myself to write about any thing at once so delicate & disagreeable – & until I was assured of the concurrent opinion of Mr Hobhouse & Mr Kinnaird could I venture [*sic*] to state what had occurred to me – but this <rea> was I assure your Lordship the sole cause of my long silence and as it was constituted of respect & friendship I hope you will do me the favour to renew your wonted kindness & confidence – believing that I will do so no more I assure you if you knew the distress my silence occasioned me you would not compleatly anihylate [*sic*] me with your displeasure. I have already told your Lordship if you still desire to publish the poems &c I will do so – but I would recommend the previous publication of the Tragedy –

I see constantly your friend Mr Bankes who never fails to talk to me about you, I wish you had seen his drawings I am perfectly condfounded [*sic*] by his Stupendous labours & the novelties wch he has elaborated by his inconceivable industry[2] – if you had been the least aware of what was to have been done in Egypt I think you would have accompanied him – I have nearly finished a most interesting Work on the same Subject by Belzoni which I will send your Lordship[3] –

Pray tell me how you like the Fall of Jerusalem – Diary of an Invalid & Anastasius – all remarkable of their kind – & Ricciarda also by Foscolo[4] We neither speak nor hear anything here except about the Queen.[5]

Mrs Leigh who was with me just now is anxious to hear from you[6] – I entreat you to send me a Letter of forgiveness & to believe that I am

My Lord
Your grateful & truly faithful
friend & Servant
John Murray

Notes to Letter 132)

<u>Cover</u>: Milord/Milord Byron/Poste restante/Ravenna/Italie

1. Exasperated at not having heard from JM since April (Letter 129 above), B had written very stiffly to Hobhouse on 22 June telling him to withdraw the MSS in JM's hands and to put them into those of Longman or 'any respectable publisher who will undertake them': he said he had 'no *personal* difference' with JM, nor was it because JM declined to publish that B disapproved, 'but because he *hesitates* and *shuffles*' (*BLJ* VII, 121). Hobhouse received this letter in the very middle of writing to B on 14 July and replied: 'do not be angry with Murray until you hear finally from me' (*BB*, 296). He must have gone directly to JM and shown him B's letter, upon which JM then wrote the present letter received by B on 7 August (*BLJ* VII, 150).

2. William John Bankes (*c.*1786–1855), traveller and old Trinity friend of B's, had recently visited B on his return from Egypt where he had made important discoveries of Ptolemaic inscriptions and hieroglyphs (see *BLJ* VI, 243–44, and VII, 39–40 and 45; see also, for example, the *Quarterly Review*, XXII, xliv [January 1820], 454–56, and XXIV, xlviii [October 1820], 140 and 153–54). His *Geometrical Elevation of an Obelisk from the Island of Philæ* – comprising three superb plates of his drawings of an obelisk and its inscriptions, which he had discovered in 1815 and had subsequently had removed to England

under the supervision of Belzoni (see n. 3 below) – was published by JM on 27 November 1821. B replied: 'Bankes *has* done *miracles* of research and enterprize – salute him' (*BLJ* VII, 150). For a recent study of that 'research and enterprize', see Patricia Usick, *Adventures in Egypt and Nubia: The Travels of William John Bankes (1786–1855)* (London: British Museum Press, 2001). For a recent biography of Bankes, see Anne Sebba, *The Exiled Collector: William Bankes and the Making of an English Country House* (London: John Murray, 2004).

3. Giovanni Belzoni (1778–1823), actor, engineer and traveller, whose *Narrative of the Operations and Recent Discoveries within the Pyramids, Temples, Tombs, and Excavations, in Egypt and Nubia; and of a Journey to the Coast of the Red Sea, in search of the Ancient Berenice; and of another to the Oasis of Jupiter Ammon* was published by JM in December 1820. B's copy forms lot 199 in his Sale Catalogue (1827) (*CMP*, 253).

4. See Letter 128, n. 10, and Letter 131, n. 6 above. *Ricciarda, Tragedia di Ugo Foscolo* was published by JM in June 1820. B replied: 'I have sent you my Say upon yr. recent books – Ricciarda I have not yet read – having lent it to the natives – who will pronounce upon it' (*BLJ* VII, 150).

5. Indeed, writing to his brother, Archie, on 26 July, JM told him: 'It is astonishing how every kind of business has been ripped up by the affair of the Queen – which you are lucky in having escaped from' (MA); and JM was not the only publisher to suffer: James Hessey, of Taylor & Hessey, the publishers of Keats and Clare, wrote to Clare as late as November saying that 'the Queen's business' had 'almost put a stop to all other business' (see Tim Chilcott, *A Publisher and His Circle* [London: Routledge & Kegan Paul, 1972], 50–51).

6. B next wrote to Augusta on 10 August (*BLJ* VII, 155–56).

Letter 133)   [Saturday] 12 August 1820

London August 12. 1820

My Lord

You<r> will easily believe the gratification which I felt at the mark of your Lordships continued confidence which I received in the receipt yesterday, on my return from Ramsgate, of the First Act of The Tragedy – whi<t>ch I instantly sent to the printer & proofs of which I hope to send you on Tuesday next or at any rate by Friday.[1] I will send a proof also to Gifford & request any remarks that may occur to him – The Italian prose I have given to be translated & when set up I shall submit it to your Lordships correction. If you have put your soul into this Tragedy it will make a sensation which I long to report to you[2] – pray register carefully every improvement & every new beauty that may in the mean time suggest themselves to you; My heart is in the next work of yours –

I am much rejoiced to have discovered so certain a conveyance of parcels to you & I will take care to send anything of interest – I am much gratified to find that you think well of the Fall of Jerusalem – after Samor <I w> the expectations excited by Fazio – were sadly depressed – & when the MSS was sent me I shuddered – I took it up stairs with me at dinner intending to send it to Gifford entreating him to read a few pages – & to invent for me some new excuse for declining to print it – – in this process I accidentally wandered on the first page – I never quitted the MSS until I had finished it at 3 in the morning – I can not tell why you should be lugged in[3] – one way or other in every criticism upon Poetry – antient [sic] or modern of the present day, except that you are the Standard perpetually in mens thoughts & are spoken of in some shape or other – as envy disappointment or admiration direct – there is not a poem reviewed in the Million of Newspapers Magazines & the devil knows what – but what [sic] you are pecked at – and every new work of yours hitherto has just dashed to they [sic] primitive Mud – all the Statues of Clay wch stupidity has endeavoured to place by your Side.[4] – As to favouring the Author of Eastern Sketches[5] believe me there is no such feeling in my mind wch in matters of Literature is regulated by more other than my own reputation as a publisher – but you can not always resist the entreaties of friends – the Author is without drawback one of the most amiable of Men – & consequently has many friends at work for him – but trust me I will give up Nine thenths [sic] of the works wch one sort of persuasion or another induced me to print – for the honour alone of publishing one of yours & "si tu deseris me periam"[6] – I have subjected myself to such incessant interruption that my mind is dissipated in the day – and fatigued at night – & wishing to write fully to you & being unable to collect my thoughs [sic] I must I allow appear shamefully remis [sic] in not answering immediately your ever kind & interesting letters – but I declare to God I never have swerved one iota from my sincere & affectionate attachment & gratitude to you to whose fame & steady friendship I am so largely indebted.

I have sent to Moore your Letter to him of January, which I had mislaid – They tell me that his "Rhimes [sic] on the Road" were so dull that after setting up <6> Six Sheets they were obliged to distribute them & give up the publication.[7] I wish you would send me a very small

volume of facetious nonsense to be published Anonymously – & I
would print it in Edinburgh[8] – – "Advice to Julia" it is written by a M[r]
Luttrell[9] – <I am just now engaged in publishing an Account of> Send
me some half dozen Poetical Epistles in wch you may amongst other
topics notice all, or several<,> of, the new books Reviews &c – wch
<you> have struck you –

I am now printing Belzonis Acco[t] of his Excavations in Egypt – wch
is very interesting indeed – I wish you had been there in company with
your friend M[r] Bankes[10] – who has been indefatigable in his labours &
has brought home collections that will immortalize him – he is by far
the most Valuable traveller that ever existed – He speaks of you in the
highest terms of friendship & regrets that he could not shew you his
drawings – wch, after all that I had heard of them – very far indeed
surpassed all that I could conceive possible –

I have been most unlucky in not finding a confidential person to
whom I could confide the beautiful portrait of Ada!!! <w> I have
succeeded in getting it most exquisitely engraved & I now enclose two
Copies of it[11] – & One also of an Engraving from Haydons Portrait of
your self[12] – wch by the way I do not think like – I have inclosed four
Engravings for Don Juan – of all of wch I beg yr opinion[13] – I hope
you continue well – Accept my Kindest Compliments & believe that at
all times I remain
    My dear Lord
    your Lordships faithful
    & devoted Servant   Jno Murray

Notes to Letter 133)

Writing to Archie on 26 July 1820 JM told him: 'We have taken a house at
Ramsgate & the motive for selecting this place is that M[r] Gifford is there &
unwell & that it enabled me to prove my attention to him'; otherwise he would
have preferred Brighton and even more so Ryde (MA). He must have remained
at Ramsgate, with frequent visits to town on business, until mid-September (see
Letter 136 below).

1. B had written on 24 July enclosing Marin Sanuto's account of Faliero which
   he said must be translated and appended with the original to *Marino Faliero*,
   the first Act of which he sent the following day (*BLJ* VII, 141–42).

2. B replied on 31 August: 'I *have "put my Soul* into the tragedy" (as you *if* it)
   but you know that there are damned Souls as well as tragedies' (*BLJ* VII,
   168).

3. See Letter 128, n. 10 above. In his letter of 17 July, B had complained 'why

your Quarter*ing* Reviewers – at the Close of "the Fall of Jerusalem" accuse me of Manicheism? – a compliment to which the sweetener of "one of the mightiest Spirits" by no means reconciles me ... This is the second thing of the same sort – they could not even give a lift to that poor Creature Gally Knight – without a similar insinuation about "moody passions"' (*BLJ* VII, 132). Reviewing *The Fall of Jerusalem* in the *Quarterly Review*, XXIII, xlv (May 1820), 198–225, Reginald Heber declared that 'by a strange predilection for the worser half of manicheism, one of the mightiest spirits of the age has, apparently, devoted himself and his genius to the adornment and extension of evil' (225); while Stratford Canning, reviewing Gally Knight's *Eastern Sketches* in the *Quarterly Review*, XXII, xliii (July 1819), 146–58, stated that Knight's Muse gave 'no indications of a spirit disturbed by moody passions, or scarred and scathed by painful recollections' (150).

4. JM seems to glance at Pope's *The Dunciad*, II, esp. 269ff., as does B in his reply (see n. 5 below).

5. B had concluded his complaint in his letter of 17 July by supposing that JM was 'tender of' Gally Knight because he bought 'two thousand pounds' worth of books in a year'; to JM's present comment he replied on 31 August: 'pretty Galley! so "*amiable*"!! – you Goose you – such fellows should be flung into Fleet Ditch' (*BLJ* VII, 132–33 and 169; cf. also *The Dunciad*, II, 271, and n. 4 above). 6. 'if you desert me I shall perish' (perhaps adapting Catullus XXX, 5: 'quae tu neglegis, ac me miserum deseris in malis' [all this you disregard, and desert me in my sorrow and troubles]).

7. See Letter 127, n. 1 above. B had first asked JM to forward his letter to Moore on 20 May. Four days later he first told Moore he had written it, adding that JM should have forwarded it to him 'long ago'. As Moore had told B in early July that he had still not received it, B reiterated his request to JM in his letter of 17 July (*BLJ* VII, 102, 104, 127 and 131; Moore's letter to B is not extant; for his *Rhymes on the Road*, see Letter 130, n. 4 above; by 'distribute' here, JM means dismantling the forme and replacing the type in its correct box and case).

8. On 31 August B replied with some irony: 'I send you a tragedy and you ask for "facetious epistles"; and on 28 September responded in rhyme: 'You ask for a "*volume of Nonsense*" ...' (*BLJ* VII, 168 and 183).

9. *Advice to Julia, A Letter in Rhyme*, by the society poet, wit and conversationalist Henry Luttrell (1765?–1851), was published by JM in June 1820. B thought it was 'excellent in gay poetry – & must have been written by a Gentleman' (*BLJ* VII, 165).

10. See Letter 132, nn. 2 and 3 above.

11. B replied: 'Ada – all but the mouth – is the picture of her mother – and I am glad of it', adding, 'the mother made a good daughter' (*BLJ* VII, 165 and 168). For a reproduction of Ada's portrait, see Malcolm Elwin, *Lord*

Byron's Family: Annabella, Ada and Augusta 1816–1824 [London: John Murray, 1975], facing p. 118, and (in colour) Fiona MacCarthy, *Byron: Life and Legend* [London: John Murray, 2002], Plate 44; for an engraving of it, see Prothero, III, facing p. 252).

12. Benjamin Robert Haydon (1786–1846), portrait and historical painter and friend of Keats and Wordsworth, made no portrait of B nor did B ever sit to him. He began a sketch for 'Byron Musing on a Distant View of Harrow' in September 1845, but this remained unfinished (see Willard Bissell Pope, ed., *The Diary of Benjamin Robert Haydon*, 5 vols [Cambridge, MA: Harvard University Press, 1960–63], V, Appendix I, 600, item 179). His masterwork, *Christ's Entry into Jerusalem*, had been exhibiting at the Egyptian Hall, Piccadilly, since March 1820, so perhaps JM confused his name with Hayter's (for whom, see Letter 124, n. 13 above), or with Thomas Phillips', whose portrait of B engraved by Cosmo Armstrong he did 'not think like' (see n. 13 below).

13. These were four of *A New Series of Twenty-one Plates to Illustrate Lord Byron's Works. Engraved by Charles Heath, from Drawings by R. Westall, R. A. With a Portrait, engraved by Armstrong, from the original Picture, by T. Phillips, R. A.*, published by JM in quarto, octavo and foolscap octavo in May 1820 (see also, Letter 109, nn. 14 and 15 above). B replied: 'The drawings for Juan are superb – the brush has beat the poetry' (*BLJ* VII, 168; see also, VII, 165, though Marchand's note here, following Prothero's [Prothero, V, 68n.], is incorrect).

Letter 134)   [Tuesday] 15 August 1820

London Aug. 15th.
1820

My Lord

This very hour brought me the Second Act of the Tragedy[1] – I now inclose a proof of the first – which has just come in from the Printer & which I shall read this evening –

I have been sitting with Mrs Leigh this Morning She has had much anxiety about three of her children in the Hooping [*sic*] Cough[2] – I find that Sir Ralph & Lady Noel are both very ill indeed.[3] I have just had a visit from Lady <u>Webster</u>, who would be most happy to see you again She has lately been confined with a child who lives to encumber her[4] – She tells me that Scrope Davies is gone to South America – he was her great Admirer some time ago but I suspect not a <u>bonnes fortunes</u>[5] – I was very sorry to find that you should lose the Rochdale cause[6] – but a Short time will bring you the Wentworth property &

then you need not care[7] –

At a Masquerade last Week Lady Caroline personified Don Juan – & had the Devils from the Theatre to attend her – it is positively true[8] – Adieu – I shall write again on Friday with Act 2[9]

  I remain My Lord
  your faithful Serv[t]
  Jno Murray

I wrote last Friday[10]

Notes to Letter 134)

1. B had sent the second Act of *Marino Faliero* at the beginning of August (*BLJ* VII, 146).

2. Perhaps Augusta's children did have whooping cough at the time; at least Annabella used this as an excuse to try to avoid meeting her (see Michael & Melissa Bakewell, *Augusta Leigh: Byron's Half-Sister – A Biography* [London: Chatto & Windus, 2000], 269).

3. Sir Ralph Milbanke and Lady Noel, Annabella's parents. B replied on 7 September: 'You speak of Lady Noel's illness – she is not of those who die – the amiable only do; and they whose death would DO GOOD – live' (*BLJ* VII, 172; see also, n.7 below).

4. Lady Frances Wedderburn Webster (now Webster Wedderburne [*sic*]) had given birth to a son at her mother's, the Countess Dowager of Mountnorris's in Piccadilly, on Saturday 1 July 1820. During 1818 and 1819 she had been besotted with Scrope who had fled to the Continent (not to South America) to avoid creditors in January 1820 (see *The Rise and Fall of a Regency Dandy*, 191–92, *BB*, 283 and *BLJ* VII, 50; see also, Letter 112, n. 11 above).

5. That is, not a fortunate alliance (cf. *DJ* XIV, 64: "'Tis best to pause, and think, ere you rush on,/If that a *"bonne fortune"* be really "bonne."').

6. B had recently heard from Kinnaird that after 15 years of litigation over disputed mining rights at Rochdale he had lost the question; he told JM of this when returning the second Act of *Marino Faliero* (*BLJ* VII, 146).

7. The devolvement upon B of the property of Lord Wentworth, Annabella's uncle who had died in 1815, depended on the death of Lady Noel who still had two years to run (see n.3 above, and Letter 141, n. 15 below).

8. Describing a 'Masquerade at Almacks', held on Tuesday 1 August, the *Morning Chronicle* for Friday 4 August 1820 reported: 'Lady Caroline Lamb appeared, for the first time, in the character of *Don Giovanni*, but unfortunately there were too many *Devils* provided for the climax. There seemed to be a whole legion of them, principal and subordinate; and so little inclined were they

"to do their spiriting *gently*," [*The Tempest*, I, ii, 298] that (notwithstanding they had been repeatedly drilled by the *Don* in private), they appeared determined to carry the whole crowd off to Tartarus by a *coup de main*.' She had probably borrowed the outfit from the English Opera House where Thomas Dibdin's *Don Giovanni; or, a Spectre on Horseback* was performed as an afterpiece from Monday 17 July to Thursday 3 August 1820. Hobhouse noted in his Journal for Tuesday 25 July that she had tried to inveigle Madame Vestris to the masquerade but 'had frightened her with certain testimonies of personal admiration' (BL Add. 56541, f.54*v*). B replied pithily to JM on 31 August: 'What you say of Lady Caroline Lamb's at the Masquerade don't surprise me – I only wonder that She went so far as "the *Theatre*" for "*the Devils*" having them so much more natural at home – or if they were busy – she might have borrowed the bitch of her Mother's – Lady Bessborough to wit – – The hack whore of the last half century' (*BLJ* VII, 169).

9. See Letter 135 below.

10. In fact Saturday (see Letter 133 above).

Letter 135) [Friday] 18 August 1820

My Lord
  I now inclose act II – You will see by the inclosed what M^r G – thinks of Act I[1] – I long for the rest – – The Chronicles [*sic*] says that you arrived in London yesterday[2] –
  Ever yr Lordships
  faithful Servt
  Jno Murray

Aug. 18/20

Notes to Letter 135)

1. Gifford's comments must have been written on the proof itself, which is no longer extant (see *CPW* IV, 521–23). What he said, however, may be gleaned from B's reply to JM of 11 September: 'What Gifford says is very consolatory – (of the first act) "English sterling *genuine English*"' (*BLJ* VII, 175; see also, VII, 194).

2. The *Morning Chronicle* for Friday 18 August 1820 announced: 'We rejoice to learn that Lord BYRON yesterday arrived in town from Italy. The Noble Lord has finished a tragedy, which we should hope will be brought out before Mr. KEAN'S departure for America' (after 'out', Prothero [V, 72n.]

inadvertently adds 'at Drury Lane theatre,' which is not in the *Morning Chronicle*). B initially replied on 7 September: 'Pray do not let the papers paragraph me back to England – they may say what they please – any loathsome abuse – but that. – Contradict it'; but he was rather more fierce seven days later, as it was 'the cause of all my newspapers being stopped at Paris' (*BLJ* VII, 172 and 176). See also, Letter 136, n. 9 below.

Letter 136)   [Friday] 8 September 1820

Ramsgate
Sep[r]. 8. 1820

My dear friend

Do not I entreat your Lordship be offended at the reitterated [*sic*] arrival of more proofs of the Tragedy wch had been sent off before I was aware of your mighty dislike to the same[1] – and wch I sent from the fear that the printer might have made important errors – therefore receive them patiently I pray – I have received Act 5 – notes & Preface All of which we will print carefully – Gifford thinks the whole "fine writing but evidently intended for Study & not the Stage – the author will, however, lose no credit by it" This will be a good time as you say to put forth the Prophecy of dante [*sic*] – Pulci also & Don Juan shall also [*sic*] appear & the latter in the way your Lordship desires[2] – As soon as the public are in the humour to read any thing but about the Quean.[3] How this unhappy affair will terminate no one that I have seen, affects, yet, to prognosticate. – All Peers who were abroad previous to the origin of this trial were exempted from the penalties of non attendance[4] – With the Books lately sent, amongst them the earliest Copy of the Abbott [*sic*],[5] you will find the whole trial, wch I though [*sic*] you would be curious to see – I am sorry that your Lordship thinks so very meanly of M[rs] Hemans[6] – I send you all sorts of books that you may see what is doing here – <is> In the next or following Number of the Quarterly Review you will find a very curious Paper on Mitchell's Aristophanes – by Frere[7] – who has just saild [*sic*] to Malta as a last hope of saving Lady Errol – who will probably die on the passage.[8]

There are continued reports in the Papers of yr Lordships arrival in England – one recently is so circumstantial that I inclose it[9] – and can add that One person has had the temerity to wager an £100 that he saw you the week before last in the Streets of London – Do give me a paragraph on the more important of the books that I send you – I

am surprised & disappointed that you have not been more struck with
Anastasius – which it [sic] thought to display something like Genius
– for a long time it was believed to be yours – & few even now though
in the Second Edition he has put his name to it, will believe it to be
written by Mr Hope.[10] –

Rose is making progress in a translation of Ariosto three Cantos
of wch he has just printed to shew to his Critical friends[11] – Gifford
& others think very highly of it – His verses to you are very good
– When I return to town – on Monday – I will apply to Mr Kinnaird
for the Verses of [sic] the Po – wch he had long told me were in your
happiest Vein.[12]

The Times are sadly out of Joint[13] – By the way they have made one
of the most interesting little Melo Drams [sic] out of the Vampire that I
ever saw[14] Let me know how you like the Abbott [sic] – there are some
fine Parts in it[15] & <he is a> Sir Walter is a truly Noble fellow

With best compliments I remain Dearest Sir
Your Lordships
faithful friend & Servant
John Murray

Notes to Letter 136)

Cover: Milord/Milord Byron/Poste restante/Ravenna/Italie arrived: Forli 28
September

1. B had sent JM the fifth and final Act of *Marino Faliero,* together with some
    historical notes, on 17 August stipulating that he be sent *'no proofs',* which
    he reiterated rather more vehemently on 22 August (*BLJ* VII, 158 and 161).
    Gifford's remarks were probably made viva voce to JM who was still at
    Ramsgate. B replied somewhat impatiently on 28 September: 'I thought that
    I had told you long ago – that it *never* was intended nor written with any
    view to the Stage. – I have said so in the preface too' (*BLJ* VII, 182).

2. On 17 August B told JM that the 'time for the *Dante* would be now – (did
    not her Majesty occupy all nonsense) as Italy is on the Eve of great things';
    and on 24 August, enclosing 'an additional note' and the preface to *Marino
    Faliero,* that JM 'should not publish the new Cantos of *Juan separately* – but
    let them go in quietly with the first reprint of the others', and adding: 'The
    Pulci – the Dante – and the Drama – you are to publish as you like if at
    all' (*BLJ* VII, 158 and 162).

3. 'Quean' means a whore; JM echoes B's play on the word in the epigram he
    had sent him on 17 August: 'Why should *Queens not be whores?* every *Whore*
    is a *Quean*' (*BLJ* VII, 159).

4. B had asked JM whether it was true 'that absent peers are to be mulcted' and whether it included 'those who have not taken the oaths in the present parliament' (*BLJ* VII, 159).

5. Scott's *The Abbot* was published by Constable in 3 vols on 2 September 1820.

6. On 12 August B had told JM to send 'no *more modern* poesy': 'neither Mrs. Hewoman's – nor any female or male Tadpole of Poet Turdsworth's – nor any of his ragamuffins' (*BLJ* VII, 158). Replying on 28 September, B qualified his criticism: 'I do not despise Mrs. Heman[s] – but if [she] knit blue stockings instead of wearing them it would be better', adding in verse: 'Or if you prefer the bookmaking of women –/Take a spick and Span "Sketch" of your feminine *He-man*' (*BLJ* VII, 182; see also, Letter 131, n. 2 above).

7. JM published the first volume of Thomas Mitchell's *The Comedies of Aristophanes, translated from the Greek* in March 1820, which was reviewed in the *Quarterly Review*, XXIII, xlvi (July [pub. October] 1820), 474–505, with great erudition and not altogether favourably by John Hookham Frere, who was to publish his own metrical translations of four of Aristophanes' comedies in 1840. B replied on 29 September: 'Mitchell's Aristophanes is excellent – send me the rest of it' (*BLJ* VII, 184). JM did: two copies of the second volume, which he published in 1822, were sold at the sale of B's books in 1827 (*CMP*, 245–46, lots 3 and 12).

8. Frere sailed on board *The Sicily*, Captain Cupper commanding, at the beginning of September, bound for Malta where he remained with occasional visits home for the rest of his life. His wife, Lady Erroll, did not 'die on the passage', but recovered her health enough to survive until January 1831 (see Frere and Frere, *The Works of John Hookham Frere*, I, clxxv–clxxvi).

9. See also, Letter 135, n. 2 above. Certainly one such report appeared in the *London Chronicle*, CXXVIII, 9623 (Saturday 19–Monday 21 August 1820), 175: 'Just as the House of Lords rose on Thursday evening, and the QUEEN had taken her departure, Lord BYRON arrived in Palace-yard. His Lordship came in a curricle and pair. His Lordship had letters for her MAJESTY from abroad, and being informed that she was gone, he followed her to Lady FRANCIS'S house, in St. James's-square.' Leigh Hunt had also seen this report, and Shelley had read it in Galignani's *Messenger* (*The Correspondence of Leigh Hunt*, ed. His Eldest Son, 2 vols [London: Smith & Elder, 1862], I, 157, and Shelley, *Letters*, II, 236). Writing to JM on 21 September, B said: 'My Sister tells me that you sent to her to enquire where I was – believing in my arrival – "driving a curricle," &c. &c. into palace yard: do you think me a Coxcomb or a madman to be capable of such an exhibition?' (*BLJ* VII, 177). The person who made (and lost) the wager is not known; but B wrote again on 6 October saying that what JM had told him 'of the "Bet of 100 guineas"' reminded him of a similar incident that had happened to him in 1810, and duly rehearsed the story (*BLJ* VII, 191–92).

10. B replied on 28 September: 'I thought *Anastasius excellent* – did I not say so? – Matthews's Diary most excellent – it and Forsyth and parts of Hobhouse – are all we have of truth or sense upon Italy', adding on 29 September: '*Matthews* and *Forsyth* are your men of truth and tact' (*BLJ* VII, 182 and 183; see also, Letter 131, n. 6 above). The second edition of *Anastasius* was published by JM in March 1820, still without the author's name on the title-page but with the dedicatory preface signed 'Thos. Hope'.

11. This would have been a privately printed and circulated version by William Stewart Rose of what was eventually published by JM in 8 vols as *The Orlando Furioso. Translated into English Verse from the Italian of Ludovico Ariosto* (1823–31). B had sent JM 'some verses Rose sent me two years ago and more. – They are excellent description' on 7 August (*BLJ* VII, 150). The verses are in MA and run as follows (the text and asterisked notes are in Rose's hand; the date, place and endnote are in B's; an introductory note made by Hobhouse after B's death and merely repeating what B says has not been reproduced):

May 1818 – Venice – <May181<9>8>

1

Byron*, while you make gay what circle fits ye,
Bandy <v>Venetian slang with the Benzòn,
Or play at company with the Albrizzi,
The self-pleas'd pedant, & patrician crone,
Grinanis, Mocenigos, Balbis, Rizzi,
Compassionate our cruel case, – alone, –
Our pleasure an academy of frogs,
Who <all> nightly serenade us from the bogs

* I have <u>hunted</u> out a precedent for this unceremonious
address.[i]

2

'Twixt Adige & 'twixt Brenta, by those hills,
'Whose scenes the <exiled> wandering Trojan so delighted
'With their sulphureous veins & gentle rills,
'& meads, <with> & fields with fruitful furrows dighted,
'That he for these the pools which Zanthus fills,
'& Ida & the lov'd Ascanius slighted,' –*
E'en from this spot I date my sad advices,
But I can't sympathise with good Anchises;

* So says Ariosto[ii]

3.

So <th> take the picture from another hand,
& look at least for truth in my relation;
See a dull level for two miles expand,
Then hills, which break all healthy ventilation:

Hot ditches, & green pools, which stink & stand,
  & reek with a mephitick exhalation;
(Fenc'd to the North, expos'd to the Scirocco)
Add the congenial climate of Morocco.

4.

One glance at home! – We're chamber'd in a garret<;>,
  Because the other rooms were painted late;
Our sole resource the Poodle & the Parrot;
  But Buffo's cut his paw & 'keeps his state'iii
& Jacquot molts. – for food; there's not a carrot,
  Or pea within two miles; our <browze><sup><scoff> soup is
                                            late
& seedy Cabbage, <infus'd> mix'd in whats <the French> call'd
                                   rotten-pot.*
As for our wine; it might checkmate a Hottentot.

                                *pot pourri in French
                                  putrida in Venetian

5.

<Not that we've either>
  & yet we dine at half past one or two;
Not that we've either heart, or hope to eat,
  But that we do not know what else to do;
For when at that long wish'd for hour we meet,
  We gaze despondingly on roast & stew,
Exchange sad looks & curse the carrion-meat
The <The> stall which bred it & the grass which fill'd it
The slave who cook'd it, & the knave who kill'd it.

6.

We <gaze> look upon eternal flats of clover,
  Without variety of falls, or swells;
See nought that 's life beyond a beast or drover;
  & only change our frogs for chimes & bells.
We've read what books we brought at least twice over.
  But as I write, <the> my list of miseries swells.
A life <so> more melancholy never brèd ryme;
'Tis all we can to get it to be bed-time;

7.

For tis 'too [sic] broiling hot to rove & ramble,
  At least for one in my diseased condition. –
At length I have got thro' this long preàmble;
  Now <for> to the pith & pray'r of my petition!
Send me provision fresh from Murray's shamble
  & I shall hail you as my best physician.

Send it, I pray, by Padua's ill nam'd jockey*
'Recapito caffè di Pederocchi.' iv

*corriere di Padova.v

8.

But if you've had my pray'r in prose, by Bappi,
Forgive that I repeat things said before,
& lay to the account of our unhappy
Condition this unnecessary bore.
Think, we're reduc'd to play at <u>slipi</u>, <u>slapi</u>,
<u>Slorum</u>, & <u>cala braghe</u>, & <u>tre sette</u>vi
With <u>Santo</u> the old bathingman & Betty.

These verses were sent to me by W. S. Rose from Albaro in the Spring of 1818. – – – They are good and true – and Rose is a fine fellow – and one of the few English who understand <u>Italy</u>. – without which Italian is nothing. –

Notes to verse

i. Transposed from foot of page: Rose glances at Hunt's Dedication to B ('My Dear Byron'; cf. Letter 97, n. 9, and Letter 128, n. 1 above), and perhaps also at the opening line of Hunt's poem on B's departure from England, 'Since you resolve, dear Byron, once again' (*The Examiner*, No. 435 [Sunday, April 28, 1816], 266–67).

ii. *Orlando Furioso*, Canto 41, stanza 63.

iii. Biblical (e.g., Deuteronomy 6.2).

iv. 'Addressed to Café Pederocchi'.

v. The Courier or forwarding agent of Padua.

vi. *calabrache* and *trèsette*: Italian card games.

12. In his letter of 7 August, B had told JM to ask Kinnaird for a copy of his lines 'To the Po' (written in June 1819) saying, '"they be good rhymes" and will serve to swell your next volume'; he also asked Kinnaird to give JM the lines on 1 October, which Kinnaird said he had done in a letter to B of 14 November (*BLJ* VII, 150 and 191, and MA). He had originally sent them to Kinnaird on 14 April 1820 who had replied rather irreverently on 16 May: 'Your lines to the Lady on the <u>Pot</u> (q. de Chambre) are more exquisite than any you have written – I take the liberty to treat the Dilettanti with a <u>hearing</u> – but no <u>copies</u>' (*BLJ* VII, 76, and MA). They were not published in B's lifetime (see *CPW* IV, 496–97).

13. Echoing *Hamlet*, I, v, 189: 'The time is out of joint'.

14. *The Vampire; or, The Bride of the Isles*, 'a new romantic Melodrama, founded on the celebrated Tale,' opened at the English Opera House on Wednesday 9 August 1820, was well reviewed in *The Times* for Thursday 10 August, and ran until the end of September. It was a free translation by James Planché of *Le Vampire, mélodrame en trois actes* by Pierre Carmouche, Jean Nodier, and Achille de Jouffroy d'Abbans, first performed at the Théâtre de la Porte-Saint-Martin on 13 June 1820.

15. B thanked JM for *The Abbot* which had 'just arrived' on 16 October and told him it would have 'more than ordinary interest' for him for family reasons, though offering it to Hoppner a fortnight later he told him it was not Scott's best (*BLJ* VII, 204 and 214).

Letter 137)   [Friday] 15 September 1820

London Sepr. 15. 1820

My Lord

Preface – notes & all have now arrived safely & I send the first according to your desire – as the Subject of the Tragedy is so compleatly Venetian I was anxious to know what Foscolo would think of it – & I think there is no harm in sending your Lordship his account of his feelings on reading it.[1] – I hope you may be in the mind to revise & lop off any redundancies – for it is a great work & deserves your careful finish.

This I propose to print separately – and then shall I put Prophecy of Dante – Po<o> – Juan III & IV – Dante – Pulci – into another Volume – without the Authors name – & bring them out at the same time – adding Letter to My Grand Mothers Review – & Blackwoods Mag. – these will surely be variety enough.[2]

I have this day received some alterations of the Tragedy & the Curious Italian Letters from the Marquis wch I will send to Mr Hobhouse who will I dare say translate them for me[3] – it is prodigious fun – for you to have gained the cause against the Marquis –

I am anxious to hear from you again great events may have occurred – we are in a queer state here – but after all I apprehend that John Bulls good Sense will weather the Storm[4] –

I remain My Lord
your faithful Servant
John Murray

Notes to Letter 137)

Cover: Milord/Milord Byron/Poste restante/Ravenna/Italie arrived: Forli 5
October

1. See Letter 136, n. 1 above. B replied delightedly on 8 October: 'Foscolo's
   letter is exactly the thing wanted', and proceeded to discuss some of the
   issues it raised (*BLJ* VII, 194–96; see also, *CPW* IV, esp. 559). The letter,
   undated (though probably of 14 September 1820), is in MA and reads as
   follows (the closing 'H.' stands for Hugues, as Foscolo elsewhere signs his
   letters):

   Dear Mr. Murray
      The poem is full of grandeur and of that truth which spring [*sic*]
   out from the depths of the human heart. The tragedy, possibly, is
   too long: they act less than they talk – yet I would not expunge
   a singe [*sic*] a Line [*sic*]. The Doge is magnificent; and although I
   would not attempt to put in his mouth so long speeches nor make
   him repeat so often the same things, his eloquence however flow
   [*sic*] so warm [*sic*], is [*sic*] mind is so lofty, and the repetition, seem
   [*sic*] to be dictated by his actual circumstances and feelings and feelings [*sic*], so naturally that I am still forced to admire what, were
   I able, I would never venture to imitate. The other characters are
   admirably well drown [*sic*]; Israel is a true plebeian and Venitian [*sic*]
   Gracchus, and Angiolina is a model of female perfection without
   any of those attempts to Idealisme which is the favourite resource
   [*sic*] of those writters [*sic*], – and of some among your poets, who by
   their little knowledge of Nature endevour [*sic*] to copy the <imag-
   inar> visionary one which, I believe, was first born in Germany.
   The trial and the judges are exhibited with such an exactitude as
   to allow the historical picture of the age old manners; – and the
   last prophecy of Faliero, unhappily for my country is exactly true:
   Having lived long on the spot and among the inhabitants, the author
   contrived to exhibit at last a true Venitian [*sic*] tragedy; for in the
   others, although beautiful in themselvels [*sic*], I <never could find>
   <was> never was able to find any thing belonging to the history
   or manners of Venice, except the name of the City. The plot is
   continued with very great art; <and> it consists almost always of
   speeches, and yet I never felt the want of action and the interest is
   kept up to the very last line. I dislike the act of Calendaro when he
   spits on the face of Bertram; it is very natural, but it is not necessary
   to mark the utter contempt: besides a real contempt does not show
   itself by <injor> injurious acts. Such is my opinion of the general
   merit of this tragedy – and I admire it <the more than I> more and
   more, because when you told me the subject I could not conceive
   how it would be possible to make of it a good poem. – I hope you

understand my new, childish, Savage English gibberish – Accept my
thanks for the Loan of M^r. – I beg you pardon [*sic*] – of Sir Walter's
novel; and I will read it, being the first of his novels which I open:
I am ashamed of it; but I never did read one. – I am ashamed also,
but I am compelled unhappily for me, to beg you for fifty pounds,
for in this moment I am extremely poor – I should be very happy
if I could be always tollerably [*sic*] poor. I do not know, <and>
whether the Ricciarda had sale enough to authorize my application,
the less so as I do not hope a great relief from my dear Ricciarda
nor from any of my Dear Ladies. But whatever might be her gratitude towards me, I will meanwhile recieve [*sic*] the fifty pounds
from you as a Loan – [in JM's hand: Draft N° 374]

I send you the the [*sic*] good morning and many thanks for the
<u>Lecture</u> of the tragedy. I corrected in the notes some Italien [*sic*]
words. They ought to write <u>Mario Sanuto</u> Instead of <u>Maria Sanato</u>.
–

    Yours for ever
    H. Foscolo.

Foscolo's allusion to his straitened circumstances, and to his tragedy *Ricciarda*
which JM had published, prompted B not only to compassionate with him,
being reminded of his own circumstances in 1815 and of JM's kindness to him
at the time ('I have not forgotten it although you probably have'), but also to
offer to get *Ricciarda* reprinted in Italy if he found it took among his Italian
friends (*BLJ* VII, 195). This he must indeed have done; for the tragedy was
printed with exactly the same title-page, but without Davison's imprint, in
Turin on paper with an Italian watermark (seemingly, 'F^{ndo} A^{do}' [Fernando
Ado?]), a copy of which the BL possesses (press-mark: 1342.l.26(2)).

2. 'Dante' here means B's translation, 'Francesca of Rimini' (from Dante's
   Inferno), which JM sometimes calls 'Rimini' (see, for example, Letter 138
   below). In his letter of 12 October, B recommended '*not* publishing the
   prose – it is *too late* for the letter to Roberts and that to Blackwood – is too
   egoistical' (*BLJ* VII, 201). For the eventual publishing arrangements of the
   poetry, see Letter 138, n. 6, and Letter 142 below.

3. B had sent JM some alterations to *Marino Faliero* on 28 August, and on 29
   August had sent him for Hobhouse, but 'with liberty to read and translate or
   get translated – if you can', '*copies* of the letter of Cavalier Commendatore
   G[uiccioli] to his wife's brother at Rome – and other documents' explaining
   what he euphemistically referred to as 'this business which has put us all in
   hot water here' (i.e., the *ménage à trois* in the Guiccioli household) (*BLJ* VII,
   164–65).

4. JM alludes to the Queen's trial, which now occupied public attention to the
   exclusion of everything else, and to John Bull, the archetypal Englishman,
   who was stoutly behind the Queen.

Letter 138)   [Monday] 16 October 1820

Hereford Octr. 16. 1820

My Lord

I am sure when you hear the cause of my recent silence you will
with your accustomed clemency, forgive me – My wifes continued
illness,[1] escaping so recently from death, has induced me to aval
[*sic*] myself of the dullest season that I ever remember, to follow the
repeated injunctions of her Physician to try the effect of travelling in
incessant change of air & place and for a month I have passed in this
way – I arrived here yesterday & found six of your Lordships Letters.[2]
previous to my leaving home I gave directions that those letters wch
appeared to contain the returned proofs should be opened & their
contents to be immediately forwarded to Mr Gifford with whom
I had arranged that he would go over each act with care & make
his observations in writing so that they might be submitted to your
Lordship & he had preferred doing this after they had passed through
your hands, lest he should have been confused with printers errors
– on my return I shall find this done & they shall be immediately
sent to you. – The cause of the latter proofs being sent under blank
covers was that I had directed them to be forwarded by the printer,
to save time[3] – Mr Gifford had not written to me, his opinion on
the succeeding acts merely expressing his general approbation[4] & for
some time he was incapable from illness of attending to any thing.
I sent you Foscolos opinion. – Regarding the Prophecy of Dante I
will publish this, with the beautiful lines on the Po[5] – the very first
moment that I perceive the public inclined to attend to any subject
but the most injudicious trial of the Quean – sometime next month
– & I will be glad know [*sic*] immediately if your Lordship have any
alterations or additions – notes &c to add to it. The Tragedy shall be
announced at the end of it & be published in December[6] – and the
other Pulci – <Dan> Rimini – Juan – on which <G> Mr Gifford is
also making his remarks – at or about the same time – subject always
to your Lordships wishes & commands.[7] The moment I go to town I
will arrange with Mr Kinnaird & Mr Hobhouse the commercial part
<o>for these valuable commodities – If you would but yield to our
united wishes about the Don Juans I could sell millions of them – &
you would have the full enjoyment of fame arising from One of the
finest poems in any language – in mine & the opinion of Many of
the first critics – considering the variety of talent which it exhibits, it
surpasses all your works – by the way Manfred stands very near the

top – I am glad that your Lordship likes the plates for it, wch I really think most beautiful & managed with great Skill.[8]

There is one thing at which I am vexed to absolute <u>rage</u> – at the infamously impertinent lying passage in "<u>Sketches from Italy</u>"[9] – had I been aware of it – I would have cut my throat so help me God I would rather than have published the work wch contains it – & now to explain why I did <u>not</u> know of it – The Author is a Lady of fortune & very agreeable – whom I made acquaintance with in Scotland – where her father has a beautiful estate at Kelso – she told me of this work & judging of her book from herself I promised – without seeing the MSS – a thing I never do to publish it – she sent the MSS written in so cursed a hand that neither I nor any other person could decypher it – after making all sorts of excuses for Six months – I though [*sic*] myself bound – thick & thin to send it to the printers Devil – I wish it had gone to Hell – & he made it out – I read with Gifford the first quarter of the volume & we liked it – & let it go on without reading more – if we had I certainly should have stopped – I have ordered every other Copy & I have sold very few – remaining to be cancelled – What they choose to say of you in the Quarterly – I can not always prevent – but may the judgment of God fall upon me if I would publish any work containing a line against one for whom independent of my devoted affection for his persevering friendship – I am on so many accounts under everlasting obligation – allow me to add that your behaviour on all such points is truly noble – any other man would have done with his publisher for ever for apparently so willful an act of ingratitude – but I think you will confide in the truth of this explanation – I will at any rate send the note to you printed & then you will do as you please – it must have been said in the thoughtlessness of vanity. – I will send no more works about Italy – I was desirous of trying them upon you – Roses you will have liked – but the public does not – & I have not yet got through an edition[10] –

Lest I forget I will just say that your variations &c of lines in the Tragedy are all with Mr Gifford[11]

<I>You received did you the paragraph about your arrival – you think my believing in its <u>possibility</u> – as absurd as the report – but it my doubt [*sic*] – arose from Hobhouse having told me some time before that he had written earnestly soliciting your Lordships attendance in the Quean's trial[12] – a thing wch I though [*sic*] extremely injudicious – but as the trial was raising the Dead I did not know what effect it might have upon the fiery living.

Gifford, by the way, expresses his astonisment [*sic*] at the inconceivable

purity of the Style of the Tragedy[13] – wch is extraordinary – breathing
as you have done for so many years nothing but Italian.

Did you mean that I should print, with Rose's consent, his beautiful
lines to you? – he has made progress in <his> a translation of Ariosto
– he has set up, to shew to friends, two Cantos[14] – wch Gifford &
others very much like – he is getting in good health & was last winter
– in great spirits – I have the pleasure of seeing him continually – he
continues your fast admirer & friend

You are very liberal in your notice of Milman in the preface to the
Doge[15] – his stile [sic] in Jerusalem is very beautiful – but every line is
obviously laboured – whereas in your play – they flow on apparently
without effort. Your approbation of Matthews arrived most <u>apropos</u>
– for he was with me yesterday when I opened your Letter – are you
aware that he is the brother of your amiable promising lost friend
Charles – & he himself I think known to you[16] – his father one of
the most accomplished & most compleat<ly> <u>gentle</u> – man – I ever
met with has a beautiful estate in this neighbourhood – on the banks
of the enchanting Wye – he is the author of that unique effort of Wit
– the paraphrase of Popes Eloisa+ to Abelard[17] – wch Porson was so
fond of & wch your Lordship can not but have read or heard [sic] – if
not I will try & send it – he is the translator of Fontaine – reviewed,
without his most distant suspicion, in the Quarterly – They think of
drawing up a Memoir of Charles & Henry with compliments solicits
the favour of any recollections Letters &c that may suggest themselves
to you – Henry the author of the Tour – promises to make a figure at
the Bar.

I thought you might not get a full account of the trial of the Queen
and I therefore sent you the Queens Magazine & I am happy in having
done so. How it is to terminate the Devil alone who instigated it – <t>
can tell – Brougham h<is>as exhibited super human powers & deserves
to win – if the Queen succeed I think those ladies who have formerly
been divorced from their Lords – have been very ill used & ought to
move for new trials – shewing as cause that they had not Brougham &
Denman for their advocates – & the Mob – for their judge – it has just
occurred to me to get & send to you the Lords Copy of the Trial wch
contains diagrams of the Rooms &c[18]

I am printing a new Edition of your Lordships works compressed
into five small volumes[19] – very beautifully – & I have engraved 22 new
Plates[20] – from Westalls designs wch I will send in next [sic] parcel if
not already sent – I am by no means satisfied with the designs for each
of which I gave Twelve Guineas & for each engraving 25Gs – for the
engravings of Juan I gave 40Gs each –

I am most happy to find that you approve of the engraving of the beautiful [*sic*] – as I hope you will one day see the original – of Ada[21] – shall I send yr Lordship more Copies – & of Juan & for Works – to give in presents.

I confess I joins [*sic*] in all yr regrets that a certain very important Revolution has not taken Place[22] – for never was there more necessity for one – but a Revolution here were madness – it is utterly impossible in the nature of Mankind – that we could create a new one that has baffled ages & is yet the admiration of all Mankind.[23]

With the sincerest wishes for your Lordships health – I remain ever My Lord
    your Lordships
    grateful faithful & affectionate
    Servant & friend
    John Murray

entitled Eloisa en deshabille

Notes to Letter 138)

Cover: Milord/Milord Byron/Poste Restante/Ravenna/Italie arrived: Forli 9 November

1. Annie must have had a relapse; in his letter of 26 July to Archie, JM had said that she was 'if anything rather better but very far indeed from progressive health – getting little accession of strength & feeling as if she were worn out – but five weeks perseverance may still I hope effect the object of her visits' (MA). It seems a curious lapse on B's part that he nowhere offers JM his condolences or good wishes. By 'dullest season' JM almost certainly alludes to trade (see Letter 132, n. 5 above).

2. The last letter JM acknowledged having received from B was that of 29 August (*BLJ* VII, 165). Since then B had written at least ten letters that JM should have received (*BLJ* VII, 165–84).

3. On 21 September, B had complained of receiving yet a 'second packet … unaccompanied by a single line of good bad or indifferent', and said it was 'strange' JM had 'never forwarded any further observations of Gifford's' (*BLJ* VII, 176).

4. See Letter 137, n. 1 above.

5. For *The Prophecy of Dante*, see Letter 136, n. 2 above, and nn. 6 and 22 below; for the lines on the Po, see Letter 136, n. 12 above.

6. JM announced that 'Lord Byron has a tragedy nearly ready for publication,

entitled the Doge of Venice' in the *Monthly Literary Advertiser*, 188 (9 December 1820), 94. See Letter 145, n. 9 below.

7. See Letter 137, n. 2 above; for publication details, see Letter 142 below.

8. In his letter of 28 September, B had said he thought *Marino Faliero* 'equal to Manfred – though I know not what esteem is held of Manfred' (*BLJ* VII, 182). By 'plates for it', JM means those for *DJ*, not for *Manfred* (see Letter 133, n. 13 above). Concerning *DJ*, B replied: 'I don't feel inclined to care further about "Don Juan"' (BL Ashley 4745, f. 4r; *BLJ* VII, 202, but see n. 10 below).

9. On 8 September, B had written angrily to JM ordering him to publish 'the enclosed *note without* altering a word' at the end of *Marino Faliero*, and telling him 'to inform the author – that I will answer personally any offence to him' (*BLJ* VII, 173). His wrath had been prompted by reading *Sketches descriptive of Italy in the Years 1816 and 1817*, published anonymously by JM in 4 vols in 1820, in which the author, commenting on Giorgione's painting in the Palazzo Manfrini 'so admirably described in the witty "Beppo" of Lord Byron' (IV, 159; see *Beppo*, sts 11–15), appends the footnote: 'I cannot but be flattered by finding, in some cases, a similarity between my own ideas and those since so admirably expressed by his lordship in Childe Harolde [*sic*] and Beppo. Except the above, I have not altered a single sentence I wrote while at Venice, though sensible that by so doing I lay myself open to the charge of plagiarism – a charge I can solemnly, and with strictest truth, assert, would be wholly unfounded: nor can I have borrowed his ideas from conversation, since I repeatedly declined an introduction to him while in Italy' (IV, 159n.–60n.) The author was Jane Waldie (1793–1826), landscape painter, third daughter of George Waldie of Hendersyde Park, Kelso (see Letter 140, nn. 8 and 9 below: in all fairness to her, she does not say she declined a direct invitation from B to be introduced to him; an offer could have been made by a third party without B's knowledge).

10. In his letter of 7 September, B had complained: 'Why do you send me so much *trash* upon Italy – such tears – &c. which I know *must be false*' (*BLJ* VII, 172). William Stewart Rose's *Letters from the North of Italy. Addressed to Henry Hallam, Esq.* was published by JM in 2 vols in 1819 (see also, Letter 105, n. 9 above); but B told JM in his reply: 'Rose's work I never received – it was seized at Venice Such is the liberality of the Huns with their two hundred thousand men – that they dare not let such a volume as his circulate. –' (BL Ashley 4745, f. 4*v*; see also, n. 8 above and cf. *BLJ* VII, 202: the whole of the final paragraph of this letter ['I don't feel inclined ... circulate. –'] is written on a separate fragment from the letter with which it has been printed [12 October 1820]. The MS of this fragment has been dated at the foot of verso '12 oct^r. 1820', once in ink and once in pencil but neither in B's hand nor JM's; and from a number of indications very evidently belongs to a later letter, perhaps that of 9 November 1820; see also, Letter 140, n. 18 below).

11. See Letter 137, n. 3 above; B had sent JM two further alterations to *Marino Faliero* on 31 August (*BLJ* VII, 169–70).

12. See Letter 136, n. 9 above. Hobhouse had written urging B to return to support the Queen on 14 July, and again more resignedly on 31 August (*BB*, 295–96 and 298–99).

13. See Letter 135, n. 1, and Letter 136, n. 1 above.

14. See Letter 136, n. 11 above. B replied on 9 November: 'Rose's *lines* must be his own option – *I* can have no objection to their publication. – Pray salute him from me' (*BLJ* VII, 225). Rose never published his lines.

15. In his Preface to *Marino Faliero*, B writes: 'surely there is dramatic power somewhere, where Joanna Baillie, and Milman, and John Wilson exist. The "City of the Plague" and the "Fall of Jerusalem" are full of the best "matériel" for tragedy that has been seen since Horace Walpole' (*CPW* IV, 305).

16. For Matthews, see Letter 131, n. 6, and Letter 136, n. 10 above. B replied on 9 November that he did know him, 'he is the image to the very voice of his brother Charles only darker – his *laugh* his in particular', and proceeded to relate various memories and anecdotes which he elaborated at considerable length in his later letter of 19 November 'for the purposed Memoir of his brother' (see below in this Letter) (*BLJ* VII, 224–25 and 230–34). Henry was called to the Bar in 1821.

17. JM's asterisked note appears at the foot of the page (with no asterisk). John Matthews (1755–1826), poet and physician and the father of Charles and Henry, had bought the estate of Clehonger near Hereford in the 1780s where he built Belmont and laid out the grounds on the banks of the Wye. He was the author of *Eloisa en Déshabille*, a parody of Pope's *Eloisa to Abelard* (1717), first published in 1780 as being 'By a Lounger', the 6th edn (1819) as being 'By the Late Professor Porson'. JM had published his *Fables from La Fontaine, in English Verse* in May 1820, which was favourably reviewed by his son, Henry Matthews, in the *Quarterly Review*, XXIII, xlvi (July [pub. October] 1820), 455–65.

18. *The Queen's Magazine* was published in numbers by W. Wright of Fleet Street and contained a full account of each day's proceedings. In fact throughout the Trial verbatim reports appeared daily in the national press and were also issued weekly in sixpenny parts (by Fairburn, for instance); but B does not acknowledge receiving any particular one from JM. The 'diagrams' were sketches of the ship in which the Queen and her suite had sailed from Jaffa, showing the arrangement of the rooms they occupied, which had been drawn (from memory) by Gaetano Paturzo during his examination before the Lords on Wednesday 23 August (*Parliamentary Debates, New Series*, II [June–September 1820], 903 and 904; see also, *London Chronicle*, CXXVIII, 9625 [Saturday 26-Monday 28 August 1820], 199). The *London Chronicle*

(CXXVIII, 9646 [Saturday 14-Monday 16 October 1820], 361) also published a 'Plan of the Grotto at the Villa d'Este', which had been exhibited during the proceedings as material evidence. At the time of JM's writing this Letter, Henry Brougham and Thomas Denman (1779–1854) were halfway through their case for the defence (Tuesday 3 to Thursday 26 October) (*Parliamentary Debates, New Series*, III [September–November 1820], 112–1238).

19. *The Works of Lord Byron*, published by JM in 5 vols, small octavo, in 1821.

20. In fact 21 Plates and 1 Portrait; see Letter 133, n. 13 above.

21. See Letter 133, n. 11 above.

22. JM refers to the Neapolitan revolution, the progress of which was being followed in the English press, and of which B had written most recently at any length on 7 September: 'My last letters will have taught you to expect an explosion here – it was primed & loaded – but they hesitated to fire the train. – One of the Cities shirked from the league ... Bologna paused ... the Huns are on the Po – but if once they pass it on their march to Naples – all Italy will rise behind them ... If you want to publish the Prophecy of Dante – you will never have a better time' (*BLJ* VII, 172; see also, nn. 5 and 6 above).

23. JM refers to our 'Glorious Revolution' of 1688.

Letter 139)   [October 1820?]

My Lord
 I send you what will I think prove a treat in the originality of the humour of <u>Knickerbocher</u> [*sic*] – you will make allowances for its locality – I entreat you to keep the book to yourself as if I get the other I will publish this.[1] –
  M[r] Gifford & M[r] Rose are here
  ever Dear Sir[2]
  y[rs] J. M

After the other

Notes to Letter 139)

The dating of this letter is conjectured from Letters 140 and 141 below. The first volume of Washington Irving's *The Sketch Book of Geoffrey Crayon, Gent.* was published in February 1820 by John Miller of Burlington Arcade who shortly afterwards went bankrupt. JM published the second edition of this, together with the first edition of a second volume, in September 1820. At the same time he also published 'A New Edition' (that is, the English edition) of Irving's *A History of New York, from the Beginning of the World to the End of the Dutch Dynasty ... By Diedrich Knickerbocker*, originally published in America in 1809. Both were advertised in the new publications section of the *Quarterly Review*, XXIV, xlvii (October 1820), the first under 'Miscellaneous' (275), the second under 'History' (273). Washington Irving (1783–1859), the American author and traveller, had arrived in England in 1815 to visit his brother who ran the English end of the family import business which went bankrupt the following year. He remained in England, toured the country and soon became acquainted with the literary circle that gathered at JM's (see McClary, *Washington Irving and the House of Murray*).

1. A paraphrase of this might run: 'if I get the other [*Sketch Book*] I will publish this [*A History*] ... After the other [*Sketch Book*]', which is precisely what he did do; but in the case of the latter, he had to compete with a 'spurious edition', published (with exactly the same title except for the superfluous addition of 'Humourous' before 'History') by W. Wright of Fleet Street also in 1820. However, this does not account for the fact that JM had already secured the copyright for *The Sketch Book* on 16 August 1820 (see McClary, *Washington Irving and the House of Murray*, 25).

2. JM's closing address ('Dear Sir') suggests an increasing intimacy with B: cf. the close of Letter 140 below, and the more personal opening addresses of his succeeding letters; cf. also, B's frequent use of 'Dear Moray' and its cognates (borrowed from Scott) from 17 August 1820 onwards (*BLJ* VII, 158ff.)

Letter 140)   [Tuesday] 24 October 1820

London Octr. 24 – 1820

My dear Lord

Upon my return here on Saturday I found your Lordships most gratifying Letters[1] with inclosures of the 28th Sepr. and they were really cordials to me for I feard [*sic*] that my long silence from the causes stated in my last must have offended you. –

As to the Satire it is one of the most superlative things that ever was written[2] – I hastened with it the next morning to Mr Gifford I put it into his hand without saying a word – and I thought he would have died with extacy – he thinks that if it do not surpass it at least equals anything that you have written & that there is nothing more perfect of its kind in the language – he knew the Portrait as readily as if the Person had been before him – This is certainly your natural talent and you should improve it into a Classical Standard series of Satires – & be at once Persius – Juvenal – Boileau & our own Pope[3] – it betrays a knowledge

of human nature – as well as identity of character that is amazing – If
you could do this upon a plan not of selecting individuals but general
Character Manners &c – you would do a national Service – <it> this &
the purity of your language in the Tragedy shew you to be in the most
unabated & powerful command of intellect – I will give no one a Copy
of this upon any account not [sic] allow it to go out of my sight – once
or twice since when I have been alone with Gifford I have taken it out
& it operates like a cordial – Today I met Mr Kinnaird & I brought him
home to read it & he was as much astonished & delighted as we had
been – I conjured him not to speak of it – to Hobhouse I will also shew
it – & to one more – Ward – but he shall call <for it> to read it in his
chaise as he goes to the Continent[4] – for I will not trust him with such
a marketable commodity otherwise – in a word it is exquisite – – the
Person is behaving very well just now & I am under obligations for his
allowing me the honour of being his publisher[5] & I trust therefore you
will not allow another Copy to escape – for in all his conversations with
me of late he speaks with unfeigned honour of you[6] –

You are the Prince of all[7] – with all that has occurred since you
wrote – none has come half way up the hill to you –

You are very noble in your treatment of the poor Authoress[8] – I see
by this days paper that she was married at Kelso last week[9] –

I have sent you your own Lords Copy of the Queens trial with
one or two new things – "Essays on Men & Manners by a Gentleman
who has left his Lodgings" – is written by Lord John Russell[10] – Hope
was here today & is much gratified by y^r approbation of Anastasius[11]
– I am glad you like Mitchell[12] – do you like the Sketch Book – &
Knickerbockers New York[13] –

I inclose the first Sheet of the Tragedy with Mr Giffords remarks[14]
– & others will now follow regularly –

With Compliments I remain Most dear Sir[15] Your Lordships admiring
& faithful Servant

John Murray

Is there any thing but tinsel in Keates [sic][16] – Cornwall & Croly pray
tell me[17]

Have you no answer from Torwalstein [sic][18]

Notes to Letter 140)

Cover: Milord/Milord Byron/Poste restante/Ravenna/Italie <u>arrived</u>: Forli [date obscured]

1. 'Saturday' would have been 21 October, the date when JM would have received B's two letters of 28 September, the latter containing a long post-script dated 29 September (*BLJ* VII, 181 and 182–84).

2. This was B's biting satire on Rogers, 'Question and Answer' ('Nose and chin would shame a knocker'), which B had sent JM in his first letter of 28 September telling him to *'give no copies'* and 'to permit *no publication'*, but allowing him to *'show* it – to Gifford – Hobhouse – D. Kinnaird and any two or three of your own Admiralty favourites'; among other levities, he said that if JM thought it good he would send him others as he had 'a batch of them' (*BLJ* VII, 181; see also, *CPW* IV, 165–67).

3. The great satirists of the Classical and Augustan eras; Nicolas Boileau-Despréaux (1636–1711), satirist, critic and author of *Le Lutrin* (1674–83), whose works Dryden and Pope held in high esteem.

4. Ward did not go 'to the Continent' but remained in London until the following autumn (Romilly, *Letters to 'Ivy'*, 308–09).

5. JM had recently published Rogers' *Human Life, A Poem* (1819).

6. Echoing several of JM's phrases in this paragraph, B replied on 9 November: 'The talent you approve of is an amiable one and as you say might prove "a national Service" but unfortunately I must be angry with a man before I draw his real portrait – and I can't deal in *"generals"* so that I trust never to have provocation enough to make a *Gallery.* – If *"the* person" – had not by many little dirty sneaking traits provoked it – I should have been silent'; and he enclosed an alteration and some additional lines to his portrait (*BLJ* VII, 223).

7. Perhaps JM has in mind 'Prince of Poets', a title bestowed on only two other poets: Homer and Milton.

8. See Letter 138, n. 9 above. In his letter of 29 September, B had written: 'on reading more of the 4 volumes on Italy – where the Author says *"declined* an introduction" I perceive (horresco referens) that it is written by a WOMAN!!! In that case you must suppress my note and answer – and all I have said about the book and the writer … I can only say that I am sorry that a Lady should say anything of the kind. – What I would have said to a person with testicles – you already know' (*BLJ* VII, 183). So do we: when sending his note on 8 September, B had said the author was 'a cursed impudent liar'; and the note itself, which was printed at the end of the Notes to the first edition, still stands (*BLJ* VII, 174 and *CPW* IV, 543–44).

9. '[17 October 1820] At Hendersyde-park, Roxburghshire, by the Rev. William Kell, Captain George Edward Watts, Royal Navy, to Jane, youngest daughter of George Waldie, Esq., of Hendersyde' (*The Times*, Tuesday 24 October 1820).

10. See Letter 138, n. 18 above. For Lord John Russell, see Letter 121 above; his *Essays, and Sketches of Life and Character. By a Gentleman who has left his Lodgings*, with a Preface signed Joseph Skillett, was published by Longmans in 1820.

11. Thomas Hope (1770?–1831), the author of *Anastasius* (see Letter 131, n. 6 above).

12. See Letter 136, n. 7 above.

13. See Letter 139 above. B said 'Crayon is very good' in his letter of 12 October, which JM must have received the day after his present writing and there-upon immediately relayed B's opinion to Irving who replied from Paris on 31 October: 'I have just received your letter of the 25th which has almost overpowered me with the encomiums it contains ... Had any one told me a few years since in America, that any thing I could write would interest such men as Gifford and Byron I should have as readily believed a fairy tale' (McClary, *Washington Irving and the House of Murray*, 31, and *BLJ* VII, 200; see also, Letter 141, n. 18 below).

14. The 'first Sheet' comprised the Preface to *Marino Faliero*, of which JM sent a 'revise' in his next Letter (see Letter 141, n. 19 below).

15. Cf. the close of Letter 139 above.

16. B had expressed his instant distaste for 'Johnny Keats's *p-ss a bed* poetry' and 'the drivelling idiotism of the Mankin' in his letter of 12 October (*BLJ* VII, 200 and 202, echoing Lockhart's 'drivelling idiocy of "Endymion"' in *Blackwood's Edinburgh Magazine*, III, xvii [August 1818], 519). Replying to JM's present query, he was no less forthright: 'Mr. Keats whose poetry you enquire after – appears to me what I have already said; – such writing is a sort of mental masturbation – he is always f-gg-g his *Imagination*. – I don't mean that he is *indecent* but viciously soliciting his own ideas into a state which is neither poetry nor any thing else but a Bedlam vision produced by raw pork and opium' (*BLJ* VII, 225; see also, VII, 217 and 229). JM may have sent Keats' most recent volume, *Lamia, Isabella, The Eve of St Agnes, and other Poems*, published in July 1820; but B had certainly read and possessed his *Poems* (1817) and *Endymion* (1818) (see *CMP*, 113–17, 157, and 249, lot 109).

17. B replied: 'Barry Cornwall would write well if he would let himself. – – Croly is superior to many – but seems to think himself inferior to Nobody' (*BLJ* VII, 225). For Barry Cornwall, see Letter 131, n. 2 above. For George Croly, see Letter 91, n. 24 above: his *The Angel of the World; An Arabian Tale:*

> *Sebastian; A Spanish Tale: with Other Poems* was published by John Warren
> in 1820; perhaps B thought the Preface somewhat condescending and self-
> important; his copy forms part of lot 37 in his Sale Catalogue (1827) (*CMP*,
> 247).

18. B replied: 'Thorwaldsen is in Poland, I believe, the bust is at Rome still – as
    it has been <u>paid</u> for these 4. years. It should have been sent – but I know [*sic*]
    no remedy<. – –> till he returns' (BL Ashley 4745, f. 4*v*; cf. *BLJ* VII, 202,
    where this is mistranscribed; this is part of the same MS fragment referred
    to in Letter 138, n. 10 above).

Letter 141)   [Friday] 27 October 1820

London Octr. 27. 1820

Dear Lord Byron

You have made me compleatly happy in the receipt of your kind &
interesting Letters of Octr 6 & 8 which arrived yesterday & the day
before[1] –

What you say as to the want of selection in the books which I
send you is true – but it has not been occasioned by my bad taste[2]
– the Poems are all of them at least Keates [*sic*] Croly &c by a set
of fellows who are everlastingly blowing themselves into notoriety &
you will find in the last Edinb. Review that Jeffry [*sic*] has allowed
some of them to be praised there[3] – <and> the fact is I sent these to
you on purpose to provoke your contempt & give you memoranda
for a new Baviad[4] wch we very much need to flap away a nest of
pretenders[5] – – I have written to Mr Hobhouse for the "Hints from
Horace" which with the novelty which you will probably throw into
it will make a very servisable [*sic*] as well as a very interesting poem
– There is the English Bards printing over & over again in Dublin[6] &
circulating in a way by poor wretches in the Country that prevents the
law from stopping it – – I much approve of your intention to preserve
in notes to the Hints all that you have so manfully & judiciously said
about Pope[7] – it will come a propos for there is a great discussion
upon his merits going on now – & Bowles who in his own edition of
Pope so shamefully abused him is now furious at an article upon this
subject which appeared in the last Quarterly[8] – Gifford is very warmly
on your side – by way [*sic*] he a little resembles Pope in character[9] – I
wish you may have Bowless edition by you[10] that you may see fairly
what he there said & to prevent you <ju> from judging merely from
his pamphlet to Campbell –

Kinnaird has promissed to send me the beautiful lines on the Po.[11]

I am glad that my shewing the Tragedy to Foscolo has met with your approbation & I thought his opinion warm critical & just[12] – He is a fine fellow whom I am most anxious to serve – The Tragedy is now with Hobhouse & I have urged him for his opinion[13]

I should upon no account put the authors name to Don Juan for in this strange state of law & the abuse of human intellect – the result which you apprehend might be produced[14] – I saw Mrs Leigh yesterday who is pretty well – though much over occupied – with making Cloaths – nursing – educating & tending her numerous family[15] – She told me that both Sir Ralph & Lady Noel are exceedingly ill and that she apprehends a catastrophe in that quarter soon – Lady Byron has lately lost one of her Maidservants in Typhus fever – but her <&>Ladyship <had> and the little Girl had escaped it altogether[16] – I could not have supposed until you pointed it out, the frequent occurrence in the olden time of Ada – Capt Byron had before described to me your hunting it out on hands & knees – from your own Pedigree – – I am rather surprised that however contemptuously you may justly estimate the Sign Post Face of the Earl of Huntingdon[17] – that you have not been amused with the Book – which his [sic] thoughs [sic] remarkably interesting.

I am glad that you like the Sketch Book – it is the production of an American named Irving – the best specimen of American talents with manners that ha<ve>s yet floated to this Country – He is likewise the Author of Knickerbockers New York a work wch will be to America – what Don Quixote is to Spain & Hudibras to England – pray tell me if you like it[18] –

I inclose a revise of the preface[19] – wch I received from you the day before yesterday – I have added to it one or two notes received a little time ago – – I shall get another sheet of the Tragedy with Giffords remarks tomorrow.

The report of this day is that the House of Lords confident that the Bill of Pains &c will be rejected by the Commons are jealous of the honour of it & will therefore throw it out themselves – Lord Liverpool to resign – Lord Castlereagh!!!! to succeed him as prime Minister – the Duke of Wellington to be Secretary of State[20] –

a First Copy of the Monastery[21] was sent you Pr Coach June 2nd – with Egeworths [sic] Memoirs[22] – Forman (a wild) [sic] novel)[23] & the Life of Camoens[24] – have you received none of these? a Second Copy of the Monastery Sep 30 – the moment you said you had not got it – Poor Wait [sic] the Dentist died a few days ago[25] – I sent the Abbot Sep 4 – Kennelworth [sic] – by the same author is printing[26] –

<your> the persevering kindness of your interesting Letters render
[*sic*] me more than ever Dear Lord Byron

your grateful friend   Jno Murray

Notes to Letter 141)

Cover: Milord/Milord Byron/Poste restante/Ravenna/Italie <u>arrived</u>: Forli 16 November

1. JM must have received not only B's letters of 6 and 8 October but also that of 12 October (*BLJ* VII, 191–93, 194–96 and 200–02).

2. See Letter 140, nn. 16 and 17 above. In his letter of 12 October, B begged JM: 'Pray send me *no more* poetry but what is rare and decidedly good. – There is such a trash of Keats and the like upon my tables – that I am ashamed to look at them. – I say nothing against your parsons – your Smedleys – and your Crolys – it is all very fine – but pray dispense me from the pleasure, as also from Mrs. Hemans … You are *too liberal* in *quantity* and somewhat careless of the quality of your missives' (*BLJ* VII, 200–01).

3. Keats' poems were reviewed very favourably by Jeffrey in the *Edinburgh Review*, XXXIV, lxvii (August 1820), 203–13. On first reading this, B remarked to JM on 4 November: 'The Edinburgh praises Jack Keats or Ketch or whatever his names are; – why his is the *Onanism* of Poetry'; but replying to JM's present Letter on 18 November he exploded: 'Of the praises of that little dirty blackguard KEATES in the Edinburgh – I shall observe as Johnson did when Sheridan the actor got a *pension*. "What has *he* got a pension? then it is time that I should give up *mine*"' (*BLJ* VII, 217 and 229).

4. Gifford had satirized the poets of the day (principally the Della Cruscans) in his *Baviad* (1794) and *Maeviad* (1795), which B greatly admired (see esp. *EBSR*, 93–96, 741–830). B himself had written to JM on 11 September: 'Oh! if ever I *do* come amongst you again I will give you such a "Baviad and Mæviad" not as *good* as the old – but even *better merited* … what with the Cockneys and the Lakers – and the *followers* of Scott and Moore and Byron – you are in the very uttermost decline and degradation of Literature' (*BLJ* VII, 175).

5. Cf. 'Yet let me flap this Bug with gilded wings,/This painted Child of Dirt that stinks and stings' (Pope, *Epistle to Dr. Arbuthnot*, 309–10).

6. This may have been one of the spurious editions issued by Cawthorn – such as a 'Fourth Edition', 'Printed for James Cawthorn', bearing neither date nor printer's imprint, but the paper of which is watermarked 'C WILMOT 1819', which is in the BL (Ashley 318). For the entanglements of the spurious editions, see Coleridge, *Poetry*, VII, 305–07. See also, Richard Cargill Cole, *Irish Booksellers and English Writers, 1740–1800* (London: Mansell Publishing, 1986), esp. 55–56, 152 and 156.

7. In his letter of 23 September, B had told JM to get his *Hints from Horace* (written at Athens in 1811) from Hobhouse and to send him 'a proof (with the Latin)', as he thought that 'with some omissions of names and passages' he might publish it with his 'late observations *for* Pope [that is, those contained in *Some Observations*] among the notes with the date of 1820' (*BLJ* VII, 179; see also, Letter 130 nn. 1 and 2 above). However, replying to this present Letter on 23 November, B said that Hobhouse thought the poem would need 'a good deal of slashing – to suit the times', and that he did not feel 'at all laborious just now'; in the event, the poem was not published in his lifetime (*BLJ* VII, 238; see also, *BB*, 302, *CPW* I, 426, and *CMP*, 359).

8. The 'great discussion' was the Bowles/Pope controversy, into which B entered with furious energy. For full details, see *CMP*, 399–410. Briefly, the Rev. William Lisle Bowles (1762–1850), poet and critic had, as JM rightly says, 'shamefully abused' Pope in his own edition of Pope's works, *The Works of Alexander Pope, Esq. in Verse and Prose*, 10 vols (1806). Isaac D'Israeli had taken issue with him in the *Quarterly Review*, XXIII, xlvi (July 1820), esp. 407–34, when reviewing, along with Spence's *Anecdotes* (1820), Bowles' pamphlet *The Invariable Principles of Poetry: In a Letter addressed to Thomas Campbell, Esq.* (1819), which had itself been prompted by adverse observations on his edition of Pope by Campbell in his *Specimens of the British Poets* (1819). See also n. 10 below.

9. In poetical 'character' there certainly was a resemblance; but JM is also implying, though tactfully avoiding saying outright, that Gifford 'resembles Pope' in his unfortunate physical conformation.

10. See n. 8 above. Curiously enough, although Bowles' edition of Pope's *Works* appears in the Sale Catalogue of B's books in 1816, it does not do so in that of 1827, though Campbell's *Specimens of the British Poets*, which B had certainly received by 20 May 1820, does (*CMP*, 240, lot 257, and 247, lot 40; *BLJ* VII, 101–02).

11. See Letter 136, n. 12 above.

12. See Letter 137, n. 1 above.

13. JM did not have long to wait: on Saturday 28 October Hobhouse recorded in his Journal that he 'wrote a letter to Murray with opinion of the Tragedy'; and on 6 November he wrote to B praising it, and saying he thought it 'would succeed completely on the stage' (BL Add. 56541, f. 88*v*, and *BB*, 301–02).

14. In his letter of 8 October, B expressed his concern that if JM put his name to *DJ*, 'any lawyer might oppose my Guardian right of my daughter in Chancery – on the plea of it's containing the *parody*', and that the Noels would not let such an opportunity slip: 'Now I prefer my child to a poem at any time – and so should you as having half a dozen' (*BLJ* VII, 196).

15. In fact Augusta seemed far more concerned about the outcome of the Queen's trial, telling Annabella on 27 October that she was 'dreading next week' (Bakewell and Bakewell, *Augusta Leigh*, 269–70). However, writing to her on 18 November, B enquired: 'How is all your rabbit-warren of a family?', and on 30 November: 'Is it true or no that Lady N[oel] is ill, or *was* ill? – – Murray said so & quoted *you* as his authority' (*BLJ* VII, 227 and 239). Lady Noel was ill and remained so until her death on 28 January 1822. B did not comment on the loss of Annabella's maidservant.

16. In his letter of 8 October, B said that if JM were to turn over the earlier pages of *The Huntingdon Peerage* he would see 'how common a name *Ada* was in the early Plantagenet days' (*BLJ* VII, 196). In Henry Nugent Bell's *The Huntingdon Peerage* (1820), two thirteenth-century ancestresses of the Earl of Huntingdon bore the name Ada (pp. 4–5). See n. 17 below.

17. See n. 16 above. In his letter of 12 October, B remarked: 'Lord Huntingdon's blackguard portrait may serve for a sign for his "Ashby de la Zouche" Alehouse – is it to such a drunken half-pay looking raff – that the Chivalrous Moira is to yield a portion of his titles?' (*BLJ* VII, 200). *The Huntingdon Peerage* is an entertaining and anecdotal history of that earldom and an account of its restoration in 1818 after a dormancy of 30 years through the efforts of Henry Nugent Bell (1792–1822), the author of the work and 'Student of the Inner-Temple', as he describes himself on the title-page. The successful claimant was Hans Francis Hastings (1779–1828), a relative of Lord Moira's and now the eleventh Earl. B alludes to the very far from flattering engraving of the Earl which adorns the frontispiece, and to The White Hart at Ashby de la Zouch in Leicestershire where his seat lay, which had been renamed The Huntingdon Arms in his honour (p. 387).

18. See also Letter 140, n. 13 above. In an undated MS fragment, which almost certainly belongs to B's letter of 9 November 1820 and which, therefore, would have crossed with JM's present Letter and would not have been a reply to it, B told him: 'I prefer "New York" to the "Sketch Book" but the public won't. – – the humour is too good [*sic*] & too dry for them – it is like Hudibras in prose. – He must have meant to quiz the three presidents or at least two – Jefferson & Madison – one of them had a wooden leg like <Stu> Peter Stuyvesant' (MA; cf. *BLJ* VIII, 53, where this is mistranscribed. In *BLJ* V, 240–41, the recto of this fragment is misplaced as the postscript to B's letter to JM of 17 June 1817). B is mistaken: neither Jefferson nor Madison, nor their two predecessors Washington and Adams, had a wooden leg. Peter Stuyvesant, to whom and to whose formidable leg we are introduced in Book V of *A History*, finds his prototype in the real Peter Stuyvesant (1592–1672), Governor of New Amsterdam (New York City), who had a wooden leg. Nonetheless, B's and JM's joint comparison of *A History* to Samuel Butler's satirical mock-romance, *Hudibras* (1663–78), and JM's to *Don Quixote*, could not be more apt; but B's prediction as to its popularity was to prove correct. Although Lockhart had already praised it briefly as 'a singular production

of genius', in an article 'On the Writings of Charles Brockden Brown and Washington Irving' in *Blackwood's Edinburgh Magazine*, VI, xxxv (February 1820), 551–61, and promised to return to it in the next issue but did not do so, neither the *Edinburgh Review* nor the *Quarterly Review* deigned to notice it. *The Sketch Book*, however, was very favourably reviewed both by Jeffrey in the *Edinburgh Review*, XXXIV, lxvii (August 1820), 160–76, and by Henry Matthews in the *Quarterly Review*, XXV, xliv (April 1821), 50–67.

19. B returned the Preface on 18 November, reminding JM 'that the Italian extract from the Chronicle must *be translated*' (*BLJ* VII, 228; see also, Letter 133, n. 1 above, and Letter 142 below).

20. JM's four marks of appreciation suggest that this 'report' might be a joke, or that he himself regarded it as such; at all events, it was ill-founded: the Bill was withdrawn on 10 November; Liverpool did not resign, nor did Wellington become Secretary of State, and Castlereagh remained Foreign Secretary.

21. In his letter of 12 October, B had complained (in verse and prose) that he had still not received Scott's *Monastery* (*BLJ* VII, 200 and 201). It arrived while he was writing to JM on 4 November and was clearly the 'Second Copy' sent on 30 September; for replying to JM's present Letter on 18 November, B told him: 'The parcel of the *second* of June – with the late *Edgeworth* – & so forth – has *never* arrived – parcels of a later date have' (*BLJ* VII, 217 and 229).

22. See n. 21 above: the parcel containing *Memoirs of Richard Lovell Edgeworth, Esq. Begun by Himself and Concluded by His Daughter, Maria Edgeworth*, which was published by Baldwin, Cradock and Joy in 2 vols in May 1820, must have arrived by 19 January 1821 (see *BLJ* VIII, 29–30 and 42, and *CMP*, 248, lot 63).

23. *Forman: A Tale*, by Abel Moysey (1778–1839), barrister, was published anonymously in 3 vols by Ogle and Duncan in July 1819: its witchcraft and supernaturalism appealed to Scott, who did not, however, think that the author had treated 'the days of *Gentle King Jemmy* our Scottish Solomon' (James VI of Scotland, James I of England) 'with a strong hand', and proceeded to supply the deficiency with *The Fortunes of Nigel* (1822) (see Scott, *Letters*, V, 397–98, and VII, 16). B does not appear to have received or to have possessed *Forman*.

24. John Adamson's *Memoirs of the Life and Writings of Luis de Camoens* was published in 2 vols by Longmans in 1820, and appears in B's Sale Catalogue (1827) (see *CMP*, 245, lot 2).

25. John Waite (*fl.* 1803–20), Surgeon-Dentist, was B's dentist and the supplier of all those articles of oral hygiene he so frequently requested. He had told B in 1814 that his teeth were 'all right and white', but that he ground them in his sleep and chipped the edges (*BLJ* III, 245). His death was announced

at unusual length in the *Morning Chronicle* for Thursday 26 October 1820:
'At the Swan Inn, Mansfield, Notts, on the 23d instant, on his way to town,
John Waite, Esq. of Old Burlington-street; he was of great eminence in
his profession, and of strict integrity in his private character; his loss will
be long and deeply lamented by his numerous relatives and friends', and
no less so than by B, who replied to JM on 18 November: 'The death of
Waite is a shock to the – teeth as well as to the feelings of all who knew
him. – Good God! – he and *Blake* – both gone! – I left them both in the
most robust health'; and having delivered a panegyric on the preservative
powers of both, and anxiously enquiring where his supplies were to come
from now, concluded of Waite: 'he was such a delight – such a Coxcomb
– such a Jewel of a Man ... Do not neglect this commission – *who* or *what*
can replace him?', and wrote as urgently on the subject to Augusta the same
day (*BLJ* VII, 227 and 228; see also, Letter 144, n. 7 below).

26. *The Abbot* had arrived on 16 October (*BLJ* VII, 204); Scott's *Kenilworth* was
published in January 1821.

Letter 142)   [Friday] 3 November 1820

London Novr. 3. 1820

Dear Lord Byron
    I now inclose other sheets of the Tragedy wch Mr Gifford left with
me today – he told me besides particularly to say that his high opinion
of it is more than confirmed by a second & more attentive perusal[1] –
    Your Lordships Letter of the 16th October reached me the day before
yesterday in company with one for Hobhouse to whom I have written
to announce it <&> as his residence is uncertain. I am glad that you
have got the Abbot – but that you should not have received either of
the Copies of the Monastery is surprising & vexatious – being the only
parcels wch have miscarried – you shall have another copy with Soda
powders P^r next parcel[2] –
    I have not yet received the "Hints" from Mr Hobhouse who tells
me that he is radicalizing at Battle Abbey – but I sent him your Letter
yesterday and I fancy he will be in town in a day or two[3] – I begin to
think that it may be better when you finish the "Hints" to put forth
2 Vols 8vo at once wch will surprise by Variety as well as excellence
rather than make repeated calls upon public attention by reitterated [*sic*]
publications of each work separately The Volumes will then consist of

The Doge	Pulci
Dante	&

Po	Italian
Rimini	Hints from Horace

Will your Lordship approve of this? they will form a very interesting Work[4] –

I send in a Cover the translation of the Italian Prose which has been made with much care by a a [sic] gentleman in high esteem here for very great talents[5] & it is done by him con amore[6] proud of any thing that associates <wi>him with you.

Captain Parry,[7] from the Polar Expedition was with me hesterday [sic], he has been most fortunate in his Discoveries having saild [sic] compleatly through what was sworn to be Mountains by Capt Ross – but wch Parry found to be an open sea Forty Miles broad. They wintered Eleven Months in a newly discovered uninhabited Island where they amused themselves with acting Plays – writing periodical papers & were as happy as possible the Cold 74 degrees below our freezing point – In another year, by taking a different lattitude [sic], he thinks he might succeed in penetrating to Behrens Straits – I have got his Narrative wch is most uncommonly interesting[8]

Yesterday the Lords divided with the Small Majority of 28 in favour of the Second Reading – This day the Degradation part without alteration has compleatly passed Nem Con – She is going abroad again[9] –

I remain Dear Lord Byron
your Lordships
faithful Servt
Jno Murray

Notes to Letter 142)

Cover: Milord Byron/Poste Restante/Ravenna/Italie arrived: Forli 23 November

1. These sheets contained 'the preface – the translation' and various portions of the proof-pages of *Marino Faliero*, which B acknowledged and returned on 23 November (*BLJ* VII, 238).

2. B's letter of 16 October, thanking JM for *The Abbot* 'just arrived', and for *The Monastery* '*when you send it!!!*', which had itself 'just arrived' on 4 November (*BLJ* VII, 204 and 217; see also, Letter 141, n. 21 above). B had last asked for Soda powders ('Instead of poetry') in his letter of 12 October (*BLJ* VII, 201).

3. B had asked JM again for a proof of *Hints from Horace* in his letter of 6 October, and had written on other matters to Hobhouse, care of JM, on 17 October (*BLJ* VII, 192 and 204–06). In fact, by his own account in his reply to B of 6 November, Hobhouse had not exactly been 'radicalizing' at Battle Abbey (Sir Godfrey Webster's seat in Sussex), but had been to 'a jollification' there, where they 'drank like fishes, ate like wolves' (*BB*, 301–02, playing on *Henry V*, III, vii, 146–47: 'give them great meals of beef and iron and steel; they will eat like wolves and fight like devils').

4. B replied on 23 November: 'Your *two volume* won't do; – the first is very well – but the second must be *anonymous* – & the *first with* the *name* ... You had better put the Doge – Dante – &c. into *one* volume, – and bring out the other *soon* afterwards – but not on the same day'; the effect of *Hints from Horace* 'would perhaps be greater in a separate form, and *they* also [*sic*] must have my name to them'; but if they were published in the same volume with *DJ* they would 'identify Don Juan as mine – which I don't think worth a Chancery Suit about my daughter's guardianship' (*BLJ* VII, 238: 'all' corrected to 'also' from MS MA). In the event, JM's two-volume plan did not materialize: *Marino Faliero* and *The Prophecy of Dante* were published together in a single volume; the remainder, after B's death (for the publication details of which, see *CPW* I, 426–27, and IV, 496–97, 506–09 and 515–16).

5. See also, Letter 141, n. 19 above. Francis Cohen had translated Sanuto's account of Doge Faliero, which was published in the Appendix to *Marino Faliero* (see *CPW* IV, 532–37). B was very grateful: 'The translation is extremely well done and I beg to present my thanks & respects to Mr. Cohen for his time and trouble. – The old Chronicle Style is far better done – than I could have done it' (*BLJ* VII, 238; for Cohen, see also, Letter 118 above).

6. *con amore*: with devotion, wholeheartedly.

7. The spacing in the MS between the first four paragraphs of this letter and these last two indicates, as does the item of news in the final paragraph, that they were added on the day the letter was posted (Tuesday 7 or Wednesday 8 November; there is no visible postmark on the cover). See n. 9 below.

8. In 1818, under the auspices of the Admiralty, Captain John Ross, R.N. (1777–1856) had led an expedition to discover a North-West Passage from the Atlantic to the Pacific, his account of which, *A Voyage of Discovery, ... for the purpose of Exploring Baffin's Bay, and Inquiring into the probability of a North-West Passage*, was published by JM in quarto in 1819. The following year, Captain William Edward Parry, R.N. (1790–1850) led a similar expedition, his account of which, *Journal of a Voyage for the Discovery of a North-West Passage from the Atlantic to the Pacific; performed in the years 1819–20*, JM was also to publish in quarto in 1821. As JM rightly says (and as can best be seen by comparing the chart facing p. 1 in Parry's volume with those that form the

frontispiece and insertion between pp. 174–75 in Ross's volume), Parry had sailed right through Lancaster Sound (which Ross had thought to be blocked by mountains which he had called Croker Mountains in honour of John Wilson Croker, in his Admiralty rather than *Quarterly* capacity, who was now reduced to a Bay) and discovered a group of islands, which he called North Georgian Islands in honour of George III, on one of which, named by him and still so named Melville Island (after Lord Melville, the First Lord of the Admiralty), they wintered for ten months. They did indeed amuse themselves with acting plays: their first, Garrick's farce, *Miss in her Teens*, performed on Friday 5 November 1819, was so successful that they set up a regular theatre – Theatre Royal, North Georgia. They also established a weekly newspaper, the *North Georgia Gazette and Winter Chronicle* (Captain Sabine editor), which ran for 21 numbers and which JM published in 1821, and built an Observatory. But the lowest temperature they experienced (on Tuesday 15 February 1820) was minus 55; JM mistakes '74 degrees' for the latitude reckoning. Although Parry made later expeditions (his accounts of which JM also published), he never reached Bering Strait.

9. See n. 7 above. The Lords divided on the second reading of the Bill on Monday 6 November, with 123 voting in its favour, and 95 against – a majority of 28, which was tantamount to a defeat. Over the following two days (Tuesday 7 and Wednesday 8), the Lords debated whether the divorce clause (the inclusion of which would prevent the Bill's being passed in the Commons) should stand as part of the Bill. The division took place on Wednesday 8 when 129 voted for its retention, 62 against – a majority of 67 (hardly 'Nem Con' but again another defeat) (the *Morning Chronicle* for Tuesday 7, Wednesday 8, and Thursday 9 November 1820; see also, *Parliamentary Debates, New Series*, III [8 September–23 November 1820], 1698 and 1726). Replying on 23 November, B said he regretted 'to hear that the Queen has been so treated on the second reading of the bill' (*BLJ* VII, 238). She did not go abroad again except posthumously to be buried in her own country.

Letter 143)   [Tuesday] 19 December 1820

London Decr. 19 1820

Dear Lord Byron

I now inclose the Second & third Sheets of the Tragedy wch I sent three weeks ago & wch was returned to me on Saturdy [*sic*] from the accident of my man having neglected to pay the postage – I have waited for some time to send you the whole remainder (the intervening or fourth Sheet E – was sent before) Gifford has read all now with increased satisfaction & excepting a few scratches o<f>n Sheet C – he

had nothing <to re> otherwise to remark[1] – I perfectly agree with your
Lordships suggestion as to publishing the Tragedy with the Prophecy of
Dante it will make an appropriate volume <at> and it shall be published
as soon as you return the Sheets & I have arranged with Kinnaird[2]
– There is one circumstance of which you are probably not aware
that as the Copyright law now stands, the Theatres have a right to act
any play that is published – altering – adding to &c <&> without any
controul [sic] of the author – for their own emolument[3] – This is an
unfortunate oversight in the Law – Harris[4] has already sent a person
with his compliments & would be obliged if I would let him have a
copy of the Tragedy before it was published – Both Houses are in a
dreadful State both as to finances & Actors but at Drury Lane they have
none in Tragedy – Notwithstanding any thing that you can do they will
make the Doge an <u>acting</u> Tragedy & cutting & maiming – & then by
tacking together all the fine passages – "Thy very name is a Tower of
Strength"[5] & will bring Houses – They behaved in this way with Fazio
– & when the author remonstrated they sent him an impertinent answer[6]
– of the two it will be better acted at Covent Garden where they have
Chas Kemble – & Macready – the latter very much improved but let me
know your pleasure upon this[7] –

If you cant furbish – omit & very largely add to the Hints – wch is
mostly excellent[8] – I <shall> send it <next post> under another Cover
– as Gifford has made no remarks on any but the Sheet now sent (C)
I will not put you to the expense of the rest Pr post but send it by
Coach with some books – You would Cohen [sic] very happy & confer
a great favour upon him if you would mention him in the preface – he
is preparing a Work for press & a notice of him from you would much
serve him by bringing his name before the public[9] –

The Letter to Lay [sic] B – was safely received & sent[10] – & Mrs Leigh
tells me acknowledged – to her –

I will send Holmess Portrait in [a pa]rcel[11] –

I am My Lord
Your Lordships faithful Servt
Jno Murray

Notes to Letter 143)

Cover: Milord/Milord Byron/Poste Restante/Ravenna/Italie <u>arrived</u>: Forli 11
January 1821

1. B received and returned these proof 'Sheets' of *Marino Faliero* on 11 January
   1821 (*BLJ* VIII, 59; see also, *CPW* IV, 523); the 'intervening or fourth Sheet

E' must have been that received and returned by B on 23 November (*BLJ* VII, 238; see Letter 142, n. 1 above).

2. In his letter of 23 November, B had told JM that he 'had better put – the Doge – Dante – &c. into *one* volume' (*BLJ* VII, 238; see also, Letter 142, n. 4 above); he had also written to Kinnaird on 30 November telling him that 'Murray must come down [hand]somely' (*BLJ* VII, 239).

3. B had said all along that *Marino Faliero* was never intended for the stage and was not an acting play. Replying on 11 January 1821, he stated very firmly: 'I protest – and desire you to *protest* stoutly and *publicly* – (if it be necessary) against any attempt to bring the tragedy on *any* stage. – It was written solely for the reader ... I will not be exposed to the insolences of an audience – without a remonstrance', which he proceeded to supply (*BLJ* VIII, 59–60; see also, n. 7 below).

4. Henry Harris (d. 1839), manager of Covent Garden Theatre.

5. *Richard III*, V, iii, 12: 'Besides, the King's name is a tower of strength'.

6. Milman's *Fazio* was performed at Covent Garden on Thursday 5 February 1818 and was such a success that it was repeated on nine further nights until Monday 9 March. *The Times* for Friday 6 February 1818 deplored that it had been allowed to 'slumber unnoticed, except by magazines and reviews, for three years, and at last be called into notice by its performance on a provincial stage'. In fact such efforts to have it staged had been made by B, who wrote to Rogers on 3 March 1818: 'They have brought out Fazio with great & deserved success at Covent Garden – that's a good sign; I tried during the directory to have it done at D[rury] L[ane] but was overruled' (*BLJ* VI, 18).

7. Charles Kemble and William Macready were the two leading actors in comedy and tragedy respectively at Covent Garden Theatre. In his second letter of 11 January 1821, B replied: 'You say – speaking of acting – "let me know your pleasure in this" – I reply that there is no pleasure in it – the play is *not for acting* – Kemble or Kean could *read* it – but where are they? – Do not let me be sacrificed in such a manner – depend upon it – it is some party-work to run down you and yr. favourite horse' (*BLJ* VIII, 60; see also, n. 3 above).

8. In his letter of 18 November, B had said: 'With regard to what you say of retouching the Juans – and the Hints – it is all very well – but I can't *furbish*. – I am like the tyger (in poesy) if I miss my first Spring – I go growling back to my Jungle. – There is no second. – I can't correct – I can't – & I won't' (*BLJ* VII, 228–29). Nonetheless he told JM in his second letter of 11 January 1821 that he had read the proof 'with attention' and had made what corrections he would, but would 'omit nothing and alter little', reiterating this in his third letter of that date; see also, his Ravenna Journal for 11 January 1821 (*BLJ* VIII, 21, 60 and 61).

9. See Letter 142, n. 5 above. B opened his reply of 11 January 1821: 'Put this – "I am obliged for this excellent translation of the Old Chronicle to Mr. Cohen, to whom the reader will find himself indebted for a version which I could not myself (though after so many years intercourse with Italians) have given by any means so purely and so faithfully"' (*BLJ* VIII, 59; see also, *CPW* IV, 537). Francis Cohen published no work under his own name at this time, though he did review A. Pugin's *Specimens of Gothic Architecture* (1821) in the *Quarterly Review*, XXV, xlix (April 1821), 113–47; perhaps JM had in mind the report Cohen was preparing for negotiating the publication of the Public Records, of which he was soon to become the editor and later Deputy Keeper.

10. At the end of his letter of 23 November, B had asked whether JM had received and forwarded a letter to Annabella that B had enclosed to him 'some time ago' (*BLJ* VII, 239). The letter in question was that of 25 October, which B had enclosed with that to JM of the same date (*BLJ* VII, 210–12).

11. Square brackets indicate words torn off with seal. B had made no recent request for any portrait by Holmes.

Letter 144)   [Friday] 29 December 1820

London Decr. 29 – 1820

Dear Lord Byron

I have this instant received your very interesting Letter detailing the extraordinary death of the unhappy Commandant – your bold & prompt attendance upon him do honour to your feelings and it is to be lamented that they were not efficacious[1] – These are amongst the evils which reconcile an Englishman to taxation & gagging Bills[2] – At the same time I <have> got your Letter inclosing one to Lady Byron[3] for whose address I have just sent to enquire of Mrs Leigh & it shall be forwarded tonight.

Your Letters – your poetry the variety of their Subjects & the power with which they are all written assure me that you are in the full bloom of intellect – your mind takes in & reflects every thing that is passing in the world to which your remarkable good sense affixes their proper level & places – neither in politics nor Poetry are you – or in any thing else – to be hum-bugged – – I am very grateful & so is his brother for your long reminiscenses [*sic*] of poor Matthews which I have allowed him to copy & of which I presume your Lordship will not object to his making discreet use of it [*sic*] in any Memoir[4] – – I am glad to find so much "prudence" in what you say of the Austrian Gouvernment" [*sic*][5] – Poor

Waite[6] & Poor Blake[7] – but Waites Son (how valuable is Marriage) carries
on the Tooth Powder & Brush business & I have already sent you some –

A Fifth Canto of Don Juan[8] – if it be equal to the <u>Fourth</u> it will be
grand if you would but let us cut up the Third – for we all think it
<u>dull</u> [five times underlined] (hear, hear – hear)[9] – Kinnaird, Hobhouse,
Gifford – Upon my Soul this Variety by the same hand will astonish
the public – – As M[r] Gifford has attended to all your corrections
– alterations additions &c in the Tragedy & made no other remarks
himself than those which I have forwarded to you no more than the
four Sheets wch you have received & three of which I have received
back from you [sic][10] – when I receive the fourth from you I will
instantly publish – I have announced it – with a very extraordinary
collection a list of which I inclose a Copy[11] – The English Bards is
publicly sold on every <u>Stall</u>[12] – they have printed it in Ireland & we can
not get hold of them – I hope you have received & are interested with
Belzonis Work – the plates are curious but <u>Atlas Folio</u> & therefore I did
not send them[13] –

I have lately had the pleasure of being introduced to the acquaintance
of Lord Holland of whom I got the Waldegrave & Lord Orford papers
wch are very interesting[14] – he is a most delightful Man and very
obliging to me – he wants me to shew him the Cantos of Don Juan
wch I dare Say you will think it right for me to do –

Respecting the acting of the Doge at the Theatres I really would
recommend that it should be given to Covent Garden – for they have
not positively One Tragic Performer Male or Female – at Drury Lane
– I have no other reason for this preference[15]

Kean is gone you know[16]

I shall write again soon – pray take care of yourself –

I am ever Dearest Sir

Your Lordships

greatly obliged

& faithful Servant

John Murray

Notes to Letter 144)

<u>Cover</u>: Milord/Milord Byron/Poste restante/Ravenna/Italie <u>arrived</u>: Forli 18?
January 1821

1. B's letter of 9 December detailing the shooting of the Military Commandant
   of Ravenna in the street only a moment before, and his own humane and
   courageous action of taking him into his house where the man – 'a brave
   officer – but an unpopular man' – 'said nothing 'but "O Dio!" and "O Gesu"

two or three times' before dying (*BLJ* VII, 247–48; B was to exploit this episode in *DJ* V, 33–39, for an excellent discussion of which, see Bernard Beatty, *Byron's Don Juan* [London: Croom Helm, 1985], ch. 1).

2. JM refers to the most recent 'gagging Bills', the 'Six Acts' of 1819 (see Letter 124, n. 6 above).

3. B's letter to Annabella of 10 December concerning financial matters and telling her also of the shooting of the Military Commandant, which he sent to JM asking him to acknowledge and 'forward immediately' (*BLJ* VII, 248–49).

4. B's 'long reminiscences' of Charles Skinner Matthews, Henry's brother, contained in his letter of 19 November (*BLJ* VII, 230–34). The proposed 'Memoir' was never published; Hobhouse, who had also been solicited for a contribution, called at JM's on Saturday 10 March 1821 and 'saw Henry Matthews – the Invalid – reminded me very much of poor Charles Skinner – he appears to have given up his notion of publishing a memoir of Charles' (BL Add. 56542, ff. 8*v*–9*r*).

5. In his letter of 23 November, B had said: 'Of the state of things here – it would be difficult & not very prudent to speak at large – the Huns opening all letters'; nonetheless, he abused them heartily, calling them 'damned Scoundrels and Barbarians – their Emperor a fool – & themselves more fools than he', concluding defiantly: 'God is not an Austrian' (*BLJ* VII, 238–39).

6. See Letter 141, n. 24 above. JM's parenthetical '(how valuable is marriage)' glances wryly at B's remark in his letter of 18 November: 'I hear that Waite had married – but little thought that the other decease was so soon to overtake him' (*BLJ* VII, 228). John Waite was succeeded by his son, George Waite, Member of the Royal College of Surgeons and Lecturer on the Physiology of Teeth, who followed his father's enlightened practices and was the author of *The Surgeon-Dentist's Anatomical and Physiological Manual* (1826), which he dedicated to the memory of his father, and a number of other works, two of which earned the praise of *The American Journal and Library of Dental Science*, II, ii (December 1841), 206–07. See also, J. Menzies Campbell, 'An Exhibition of Early Dentistry', *British Dental Journal*, 99, 7 (October 4 1955), 239–43.

7. See Letter 141, n. 25 above. In his letter of 18 November, B had also deplored the death of Blake whose 'Independence' he celebrates in his note to *Hints from Horace*, 474 ('And keep your bushy locks a year from Blake') (*CPW* I, 306 and 437), and to whom he refers in a letter dated simply 'Monday. [1813]' to Lady Melbourne: 'Blake in the course of [a] month will perform the part of a Gnome better than even your dextrous La-ship' (*BLJ* III, 3 and n.; this letter should almost certainly be dated 'Monday 29 March 1813', and the reference, which Marchand says 'is not clear', is to Lady Caroline's request for a lock – or other – of B's hair, and to Pope's *The Rape of the Lock* where

the 'Gnome' is the mischief-maker in the machinery; see Lady Melbourne's letter to B of Thursday 25 March 1813, and B's to Lady Melbourne of Friday 26 March 1813 [*LLLM*, 140 and *BLJ* III, 31]). Coleridge tentatively suggests that Blake 'was, presumably, Benjamin Blake, a perfumer, who lived at 46, Park Street, Grosvenor Square' (*Poetry*, I, 422n.) which McGann seems to follow (*CPW* I, 437). In 1803, apparently, Benjamin Blake was at 55, Hans Square, Sloane Street, and John Waite at 2 Old Burlington Street (*Boyle's Fashionable Court and Country Guide, and Town Visiting Directory* [London, January 1803], Pt II, 29 and 295 respectively; in neither case is any profession given). However, in an undated and mutilated fragment of a reply to Augusta (postmark Sept. 23 [1819]), B writes with reference to Blake: 'Who would have thought it? a Stage Coach? – was it a long Coach? – was he inside or out?', adding: 'Pray tell Waite to take a post-chaise – for if our Dentist follows our barber – there will be ne'er a tooth or hair left ... I am truly sorry for Blake ... It were to be wished however that Coachmen did not help people over the Styx' (*BLJ* VI, 222–23). This suggests that Blake the barber was the same gentleman whose death was announced in *The Gentleman's Magazine*, LXXXIX, Pt II (August 1819): '[10 August 1819] Mr. Blake, of Burlington-gardens, London, and of How-green, near Hertford. His melancholy death was occasioned by the overturning of one of the Brighton coaches (of which he was a passenger) on the preceding day, at Cuckfield' (189; it also noted that this was the '*third* fatal accident recorded in this page, arising from want of due care in the driving stage-coaches' – a point also made by *The Times* for Thursday 12 August 1819 in its report of the same accident).

8. B told JM on 10 December that he had 'finished [a] fifth Canto of D[on] J[uan] 143 Stanzas – So prepare' (*BLJ* VII, 250).

9. JM's emphasis is a five-line squiggle. B replied on 19 January 1821: 'The *third* Canto of D. J. *is dull* – but you really must put up with it – if the two first – and the two following are tolerable – what can you object? ... If you publish the three new ones [i.e., *DJ* III–V] without ostentation – they may perhaps succeed'; and he told him to publish *The Prophecy of Dante* and his translation of Pulci, and 'bring them all out about the same time – otherwise "the variety" you wot of – will be less obvious' (*BLJ* VIII, 65). B must have spoken of this low opinion of the third Canto when Shelley visited him at Ravenna in August 1821, for writing to B on 21 October, thanking him for sending him *DJ* III–V, Shelley not only praised the volume as a whole but specifically: 'The character of Lambro – his return – the merriment of his daughters guests made as it were in celebration of his funeral – the meeting with the lovers – and the death of Haidée – are circumstances combined & developed in a manner that I seek elsewhere in vain. The fifth [*sic*] canto, which some of your pet Zoili in Albermarle St. said was *dull*, gathers instead of loses, splendour & energy' (Shelley, *Letters*, II, 358).

10. See Letter 143, n. 1 above.

11. JM may well have enclosed the list of books he advertised in the *Monthly Literary Advertiser*, 189 (10 January 1821), which extends to four columns, two full pages (pp. 6–7), and contains 45 publications, many of which he was to send to B.

12. See Letter 141, n. 6 above.

13. For Belzoni's work, see Letter 132, n. 3 above. At the same time JM issued 44 coloured Plates in Atlas folio to illustrate the work, which were sold separately at six guineas a set.

14. Lord Holland had written to JM in November saying he had 'two historical works' he was 'authorized to dispose of' and wished to offer JM first refusal, and suggested a meeting to discuss terms (Smiles, II, 88–90). The works were *Memoirs from 1754 to 1758, By James, Earl Waldegrave K. G.*, published by JM in April 1821, and Horace Walpole, Lord Orford, *Memoires [sic] of the Last Ten Years of the Reign of George the Second*, published by JM in 2 vols in March 1822. B possessed both (*CMP*, 254, lots 219 and 229).

15. See Letter 143, nn. 3 and 7 above. B replied very firmly on 19 January 1821: 'I must really and seriously request that you will beg of Messrs Harris or Elliston – to let the Doge alone – it is *not* an acting play; – it will not serve *their* purpose – it will destroy *yours* (the Sale) – and it will *distress* me'; and he added that if they persisted then JM must publish the protest B had sent him on 11 January 1821 in the newspapers (*BLJ* VIII, 59–60 and 64–65). The following day he wrote again enclosing a letter to the Lord Chamberlain, which he desired JM to '*present in person*' (*BLJ*, VIII, 30 and 66). Whether or not JM did so is not known: he does not allude to it and no such letter is extant.

16. Kean had given his farewell performance in the role of Richard III at Drury Lane Theatre on Saturday 16 September 1820 before sailing for America on 11 October 1820 whence he returned the following July.

Letter 145)   Friday 5 January 1821

London Jany. 5. 1821
Friday

Dear Lord Byron

I got your Letter of the 14th 10bre the day before yesterday, & previously I had acknowledged the favour of a very interesting one describing so truly the assassination of the Commandant[1] – Italy is in a Sad State but a foreigner never fares well in foreign troubles & it is a great comfort to your friends here to know that you are too wise to interfere. Every Letter that I receive and every poem that you compose, render [sic] your life more valuable to this country, and I trust that you will not put it to uncalled for or thankless hopeless hazard – – It is as you say a strange people[2] – most absurdly & barbarously gouverned [sic] – This Nation will take no part on either side –

I have sent your Lordship every Sheet upon which Mr Gifford had made his marks and as your corrections in all the others have been carefully attended to by him, I hope when I receive the last proof sent you back that we may instantly publish – The Tragedy is sufficient to fill the Public Mind & I would suffer them to ponder on it, without the addition of the Prophecy of Dante[3] – for which the Tragedy will have prepared them & which will follow well in the Volume with Pulci Dante[4] &c – You are up to the hight [sic] of anxiety as to the fate of Italy situate [sic] as you are – but here it is only began [sic] with Politicians & will just have descended to the Mark of popular feeling by the time, hearing from your Lordship the Tragedy may be brought out – My Plan <I> is I thing [sic] to publish this separately in the form & at the price 5/6 of the Corsair[5] &c & wch appears abstracted from higher merits, to have succeeded – at the end of it I can announce the Prophecy of Dante &c as in the press –

I am confident that an attempt will be made to act it if we make any arrangement with either house previously – then you can not complain and as I perceive clearly that your Lordship is disinclined to its appearance on the Stage as far as you can prevent it,[6] it will be better to forego the <lit> Trifle that they would offer for the preference, than to appear to court its representation. It is a vexatious thing & merits reprehension in the preface – Pray notice Cohen if you can[7] – he well de [sic] deserves the honour & the favour – I sent, the week before last a proof of the English Bards[8] – & if I send you more trashy Poetry you will know the kindness towards the public which it indicates –

"The Doge of Venice" simply, is a more captivating Title <than> without the pre addition of Marino [sic] & in my advertisements, at least, I have ventured to adopt it.[9] – The enquiry for it is now gathering to a great extent – Foscolo is always wondering how from such a Speck of Story you have depicted so much passion[10] – The Review of Ricciarda in the Quarterly is by Milman[11]

Many very happy returns of the Year – We have had very severly [sic] Cold windy Weather but dry this is the first day of Snow[12] – –

I remain ever My Lord
Your faithful Servant
John Murray

Notes to Letter 145)

<u>Cover</u>: Milord/Milord Byron/Poste Restante/Ravenna/Italie <u>arrived</u>: Forli 27? January

1. B's letters of 9 and 14 December 1820, to the first of which JM had already replied (Letter 144 above).

2. B had closed his letter of 9 December 1820: 'The Lieutenant who is watching the body is smoking with the greatest Sangfroid – a strange people'; but he had also said that he would 'never be deterred from a duty of humanity by all the assassins of Italy' (*BLJ* VII, 247–48).

3. B replied on 27 January 1821: 'I differ from you about the *Dante* – which I think should be published *with* the tragedy' (*BLJ* VIII, 69; see also, n. 9 below).

4. That is, B's translation from Dante, *Francesca of Rimini*.

5. *The Corsair* (1814) was published in octavo at five shillings and sixpence, and *Marino Faliero* at 12 shillings (see n. 9 below).

6. See Letter 143, nn. 3 and 7, and Letter 144, n. 15 above. Replying on 27 January, B said that JM would already have received several letters from him 'upon the subject of the *Managers*', and reiterated once again his strong resistance to the staging of the play (*BLJ* VIII, 69).

7. B replied that he had done so (*BLJ* VIII, 69; see Letter 143, n. 9 above).

8. JM means *Hints from Horace*, for the proofs of which B had again asked in his letter of 14 December 1820, but which JM had said he would send 'under another Cover' in his letter of 19 December (*BLJ* VII, 251; see also, Letter 143 above). In his reply of 27 January 1821, B asked for the 'remainder of the "Hints"', as JM had only sent 'about half of them' (*BLJ* VIII, 69).

9. See Letter 144, n. 11 above. In JM's list of new publications *Marino Faliero* was advertised as 'The Doge of Venice. An Historical Tragedy, in Five Acts. By the Rt. Hon. Lord Byron. 8vo.'; in the month of its publication it was advertised as 'The Doge of Venice, an Historical Tragedy, in Five Acts, with a Preface, Notes, and an Appendix of Original Documents; and the Prophecy of Dante. By the Rt. Hon. Lord Byron. 8vo, 12s.' (*Monthly Literary Advertiser*, 189 [10 January 1821], 6, and 192 [10 April 1821], 26). It was actually published, however, as *Marino Faliero, Doge of Venice. An Historical Tragedy, In Five Acts. With Notes. The Prophecy of Dante, A Poem*. By Lord Byron.

10. B replied that he was 'glad of Foscolo's approbation' (*BLJ* VIII, 69).

11. Foscolo's *Ricciarda* was very favourably reviewed by Milman in the *Quarterly Review*, XXIV, xlvii (October [pub. December] 1820), 72–102, in the course

of which he writes that 'What Lord Byron has said of Venice being endeared and hallowed to us, as it were, by Shakspeare and Otway, is not less true of Italy in general' (p. 74).

12. B thanked JM for his 'compliments of the year' and hoped it would be 'pleasanter than the last' (for reasons he adumbrated), adding, 'the winter is as cold here – as Parry's polarities' (*BLJ* VIII, 69–70, and 31; see also, Letter 142, n. 8 above). At the time of JM's writing, the strong winds had subsided, but the Thames was unnavigable for ice above Richmond Bridge; there was skating in St James's Park and on the Serpentine; and at Brighton they were ankle-deep in snow (*London Chronicle*, CXXVIII, 9679 [Saturday 30 December 1820–Monday 1 January 1821], 631, and CXXIX, 9681 [Thursday 4–Friday 5 January 1821], 11 and 16).

Letter 146)   [Tuesday] 16 January 1821

London Jany. 16th.
1821

Dear Lord Byron

I have this day received your Lordships Short Letter announcing the actual conveyance of the fifth Canto of Don Juan to Mr Kinnaird to whom I have already written – he is going to Paris immediately.[1] Expecting that Mr Gifford would have got better day after day slipped away till a mass of time accumulated <until> of which I was not aware – he made no marks upon any other proofs except the 4 or 5 which I have sent & as soon as I receive One more the only one you have – I shall push it out with the appendage of the Prophecy of Dante.

I wrote to Galignani[2] & told him that if he would send me any reasonable Sum – <he> I would transmit your Lordships Assignment to him – which I think tolerably fair[3] – I saw Mrs Leigh a few days since & heard your just complaints against my cursed silence & I have this moment received a summons to hear another Lecture just received – from the same quarter[4] – which I ought <to> to undergo – I am so broken in upon & my mind so distracted that I can not collect my thoughts to write – and I really wish you would do me the favour to return to London & come & talk all the day long – or send for me at night – as formerly – I have positively made my arrangements to go to Ravenna in the course of the present year[5] – Your Lordship will see by the list of Books wch I inclosed in my last, that I am not idle[6] –

I hope by Friday to have read the Fifth Canto when I shall have the pleasure of writing again[7] – With best compliments I remain Dear Lord

Byron
  Most truly yours
  John Murray

Notes to Letter 146)

1. B had sent the fifth Canto of *DJ* to Kinnaird on 28 December 1820, and had apprised JM of having done so on the same date (*BLJ* VII, 255 and 256). Unfortunately, Kinnaird had already left for Paris and did not return until late February, so JM had some time to wait before he read it (see Letter 150 below).

2. Jean Antoine Galignani (1796–1873), the Paris publisher and bookseller, had written to B on 17 October 1820 informing him that another Parisian bookseller (a Mr Louis) was publishing the whole of B's works 'wretchedly got up' at 10 francs. He enclosed a copy of the work saying that its sale would materially affect both JM's interest and his own, 'and could not be agreable [*sic*] to your Lordship'. He therefore asked B to copy out and sign the annexed 'Paper', which he had backdated to 20 April 1818 (being the date on which he first began to publish B's works), saying that he would, 'instantly on its receipt have Mr Louis [*sic*] edition suppressed', pledging his word that it would be used 'for no other purpose whatsoever but the one for which it is now most earnestly requested'. Two days later, on 19 October, he sent B a duplicate of both this letter and the 'Paper', with a covering note explaining that only B's authority and not JM's could have any effect, 'as in France the Author is the sole person whose interference in such matters is legally efficient' (MSS MA; the 'Paper', which B signed in October 1820, but which is dated 20 April 1818, appears in *BLJ* VI, 33). B replied to Galignani on 5 November 1820 saying that he had '*signed the permissions & sent them to London addressed to Mr. Murray*' (*BLJ* XIII, 57). This he had done the day before (4 November), telling JM: 'As the poems are your property by purchase, right, & justice, *all matters of publication &c. &c. are for you to decide upon*', and that he had signed them 'merely to enable you to exert the power you justly possess more properly'; but hearing nothing from JM, he wrote again on 28 December 1820 asking him whether he had received 'two letters &c. from Galignani to me – which I enclosed to you long ago?' (*BLJ* VII, 216 and 256). This clearly prompted both JM's present answer to B, and his letter to Galignani of the same date (16 January 1821) saying he would make over the assignment to him if Galignani sent him £250, asking him at the same time what he would offer him for the right to print *DJ* III–V and *Marino Faliero* in France (MS Pforzheimer Library).

3. 'I wrote … fair': B has drawn a line down the left margin of this passage and underlined 'tolerably fair', and may very well have enclosed (or initially intended to enclose) this Letter (146) to Kinnaird, to whom he sent his reply to JM of 2 February saying: 'Read the enclosed letter to Murray

– put a wafer in it – and either present – or forward it as you please' (*BLJ* VIII, 73).

4. B had written to Augusta on 21 December asking her to inform JM that he had had no letter from him 'for six weeks ... although for fifty reasons he ought to have written. – Either the Post plays false, or he is a shabby fellow' (this would account for the first 'Lecture'); on 29 December he had written again even more sharply: 'Ask Murray if he is mad? or drunk? or stupid? that he has not answered a letter of mine since the 2d. reading of the Queen's bill?' (this would be the second 'Lecture' for which JM was stiffening himself) (*BLJ* VII, 251 and 257).

5. B replied on 2 February: 'If you venture as you say – to Ravenna this year – through guns, which (like the Irishman's) "shoot round a corner" I will exercise the rites of hospitality while you live – and bury you handsomely (though not in holy-ground) if you get "shot or slashed in a creagh or Splore" which are rather frequent here of late among the native parties' (*BLJ* VIII, 74).

6. See Letter 144, n. 11 above.

7. Neither 'hope' nor 'pleasure' was fulfilled (see Letter 147 below).

Letter 147)   [Tuesday] 23 January 1821

London Jany 23. 1821

Dear Lord Byron

Yesterday was your Birth Day which I kept with a jovial party who drank your he<l>alth with heartfelt glee[1] – you have <g>yet gone so little way in life that you my [*sic*] return & start again – may all your plans involve your certain happiness of which I wish that England may form the future Theatre –

I have this instant received your Lordships Letter of the 4th inst[2] – every Letter increases my obligation to your magnanimous temper upon my Silence of which of late & I trust in future you will have no cause to complain of [*sic*] – All your late letters I have answered on the day –

Mr Kinnaird has not yet returned to England & consequently I have not seen the Fifth Canto.[3]

Barry Cornwall has been fortunate in the happy exertions of Kemble & Macready & his play goes on well – I sent it to you the day of its publication last week – There is much poetry and greater promise in it – I shall be happy to hear your opinion – I shall tell the Author

Procter of your generous feelings towards him[4] – here I am interrupted
by receiving from your Sister – your rebuke of me[5] – but I tell her that
my answers will now fall upon you like an <u>Avalanche</u> – when once My
<Silence> [sic] when once [sic] the thaw of my Silence reaches you –

The King opened the Session today in Person I mixed with the
Crowd – & certainly the Popular – the Mass of expressed feeling was in
his favour – I cut the Speech out of the Courier & inclose it[6] – Warm
debating & a protacted [sic] debate is expected – but Ld Grey & ye Duke
of Bedford met Foscolo at my door an hour ago – & say that Ministers
will stay in – Canning is gone to Paris where he is to remain until as
he told Gifford "We talk decent" – For <u>Once</u> – he <h> has acted with
discretion[7] –

I have told Kinnaird that I will give £1,000 for the Doge &
Prophecy – wch is upon my honour the Utmost that they can possibly
produce – according to any rational Speculation[8] – & then they will sell
with the Works afterwards – I will print & publish the two in the Same
Volume

You are most grateously [sic] remembered here by all yr forsaken
Admirers & are the incessant subject of Conversation & Enquiry – I am
going to Lady Davys tonight to whom Moore has, I understand, lent
your MSS Memoirs when at Paris – is this Right I have not seen them
yet[9] –

Many happy new Years to you
Your indulgence to my disease of Silence allows me to hope that you
yet believe me to be Dear Lord Byron
    your grateful & faithful Servant
    John Murray

Should I not send Parcels with Books &c to some friends at <Vienn>
Venice would it not be safer – to Hoppner[10]

Notes to Letter 147)

Cover: Milord/Milord Byron/Poste restante/Ravenna/Italie <u>arrived</u>: Forli 11?
February 1821

1. There is no indication as to who was present at this 'jovial party', but they
   were celebrating B's thirty-third birthday, the passing of which B himself
   had recorded with considerably less cheer in his Ravenna Journal (*BLJ* VIII,
   31–32).

2. B's letter of 4 January complaining yet again that he had still heard nothing
   from JM 'since the first days of November' (*BLJ* VIII, 12 and 56).

3. See Letter 146, n. 1 above.

4. In his letter of 4 January, B had said that he had seen that there was 'a new tragedy of great expectation by Barry Cornwall' (the pseudonym of Bryan Waller Procter, for whom see Letter 131, n. 2 above), and that as he was an old schoolfellow of his B took 'more than common interest in his success' and would be 'glad to hear of it speedily': 'I think him very likely to produce a good tragedy – if he keep to a natural style – and not play tricks to form Harlequinades for an audience' (*BLJ* VIII, 56; see also, B's letter to Procter dated 'Pisa 1822' [*BLJ* IX, 83–84]). Procter's *Mirandola*, with William Macready as John, Duke of Mirandola, and Charles Kemble as Guido, his son, was first performed at Covent Garden Theatre on Tuesday 9 January 1821 and ran for a further 14 nights until Wednesday 14 March. *The Times* for Wednesday 10 January 1821 commented that the play had, 'since its first announcement, ... excited a very lively interest in the public mind', and was performed 'with a degree of success that must justify high praise of the composition and offer flattering auspices to the interests united in its production'. In particular it noted that the 'natural dialogue' and 'colloquial ease' of its language brought serious drama down from its 'usual elevation' without 'endangering its dignity'. *Mirandola. A Tragedy*, By Barry Cornwall was published by John Warren in early January 1821. Although it does not appear in his Sale Catalogue (1827), B told Procter he had 'never received the copy from the author, but a single copy sent from the bookseller as his own' (*BLJ* IX, 83).

5. Presumably this was the impending (perhaps postponed) 'Lecture' JM had 'received a summons to hear' in his last Letter (see Letter 146, n. 3 above).

6. George IV opened the new Session of Parliament on Tuesday 23 January 1821 with a speech from the throne, which the *Courier* reported the same evening but which was hardly a specimen of eloquence to send all the way to B in Italy. As Hobhouse recorded in his Journal for that day: 'The Speech from the throne was mere milk & water – the Queen was mentioned & a suitable provision for her – nothing said of blasphemy & sedition – but the loyal addresses lauded' (BL Add. 56541, f. 137r).

7. On account of the government's treatment of the Queen, George Canning had resigned from his cabinet position as President of the Board of Control for India on Thursday 21 December 1820, and left for Paris on 17 January 1821 where Moore called on him on Sunday 28 January and dined with him the following Friday (Moore, *Journal*, II, 422 and 423).

8. After underlining 'upon my honour the Utmost', B sent this Letter (147) to Kinnaird on 12 February saying: 'By the enclosed paragraph you will perceive Mr. Murray's opinion of his own offer for the drama and P. – [*sic*]'; he could not understand how JM could offer 'a *thousand guineas* for every canto of a poem so decried and proscribed' as *DJ*, and then say 'he could not make more of the T. [*sic*] and P. – – at "any rate or [*sic*] speculation"'

(*BLJ* VIII, 76, corrected from MS MA: the 'T.' [not 'F'] stands for 'Tragedy' [*Marino Faliero*]; the 'P.', in both cases, for *The Prophecy of Dante* [not 'Pulci']; and 'rate of' corrected to 'rate or'). Replying to JM on the same date, he said: 'If the thing fails in the publication – you are *not pinned* even to your own terms – merely print and publish *what* I desire you – and if you don't succeed – I will abate whatever you please' (*BLJ* VIII, 77).

9. Moore had lent B's Memoirs to numerous people in Paris, but he does not specifically mention having lent them to Lady Davy, who had been in Paris since May 1820. Writing to B on 15 February 1821, Hobhouse also told him: 'Moore has lent your life & adventures to Lady Davy who enlivens, so I hear, her bluestocking circles with your commentaries. I think it right you should know this seeing that perhaps such communication was not i' the [*sic*] bond by which you originally imparted the treasure to Thomas Moore' (*BB*, 304, corrected from MS MA; punning very aptly on Shylock's 'Is it so nominated in the bond? ... 'tis not in the bond', *The Merchant of Venice*, IV, i, 254–57). But it was: B had not only granted 'such communication' but had told Moore that he had 'no objection, nay, ... would rather that *one* correct copy was taken and deposited in honourable hands' (*BLJ* VII, 125; see also, Moore, *Journal*, I, 334).

10. B does not appear to have replied to this question.

Letter 148)   Friday 26 January 1821

London Jany 26. 1821
Friday

Dear Lord Byron

Yesterday I received yours of the 8th Inst inclosing a note for the 5th Canto of Don Juan[1] – Mr Kinnaird is not yet come back from Paris. The Epigram on the Braziers may be published without any chance of the discovery of its author – there is no such extraordinary wit to betray itself[2] –

The Town is suddenly filled and all are impatient for the Doge, and I am very anxious to learn its effect upon the public – it will probably be more estimated by the Critics than popular with the Million[3] – I long to read Juan – I print it at once the Three Cantos in <u>Octavo</u> for if published as before in 4to some villain may again pirate it & leave no alternative for the preservation of the Copyright but the public legal discovery of the Author – I wish you would have allowed Gifford to advise as to omissions – for a poem of this nature should at least retain nothing that is dull – but Genius is obstinate & I do not expect you to do any thing – Respecting the purchase of these Cantos, considering the precarious tenure of the Copyright I think I may venture, upon the strength of all our transactions, to ask you to allow me to publish it first and to try what it will produce before I enter into any specific bargain at the same time if you do not approve of this I hold myself to giving for as 2 Cantos the sum which I have more than once offered[4] – You do not talk of having finished the Poem of Juan in the fifth Canto & I infer that you have not.[5]

Did you see in any of the papers that the King has been induced to place himself at the head of a new institution for the encouragement of Men of Letters & that each year three Prizes are to be given – the first, this year is for – the best Essay on the Writings of Homer &c £100 – Nº 2 – £50 for the best <u>POEM</u> – on on – on DARTMOOR!!!!. – will you try?[6]

This night there is to be a trial of strength with the Ministers & the — <would> Would-be-Ministers it is yet uncertain if the Motion of the Opposition is to be for a Vote of censure on the Ministers for having <u>Struck out</u> the Queen's name from the Liturgy – Or to propose its re-insertion[7] –

Here is Mʳ Lockhart, Sir W. Scotts newly made Son in Law – & quondam Co-Editor of Black – wood [sic] (Qʸ <u>guard's</u>) Magazine – has left the Arms of his Wife & come up to town to Challenge Scott[8] – the Author [sic] of the London Magazine but Scott – declines – Putting this Question – did you ever receive emolument in any way for writing in Blackwoods Magazine? – If you <u>wont</u> answer this question I shall not fight – and if you do – in the affirmative – I cant fight you – Pray think of a Baviad – I will send you Materials – by the Way Barry Cornwalls Printer sent to my fellow Type Founder to order a Letter <u>precisely</u> the same as that in wch Lord Byrons Poems were printed – <u>Ready Money</u>[9]

Gifford always speaks of you with admiration & nothing is so great a treat to him as your interesting letters – how little do <u>I deserve</u> them.?

Accept my most sincere regard & good wishes & believe me
Dearest Sir
your Lordships faithful Servant
John Murray

Have you received Belzoni? Is he not a fine fellow? the best travels we have had since Park?[10]

Notes to Letter 148)

<u>Cover</u>: Milord/Milord Byron/poste restante/Ravenna/Italie <u>arrived</u>: Forli 15 February

1. B's letter of 8 January 1821 enclosing a long note correcting 'blunders in *nine* [in fact, ten] apophthegms of Bacon', which was added to stanza 147 of *DJ* V (*BLJ* VIII, 14, 18 and 58; see also, *CPW* V, 711–13).

2. In his letter of 8 January, B had also enclosed his epigram 'On the "Braziers' Address to be presented in *Armour* by the Company &c. &c." as stated in the Newspapers' which was '*not* for publication' (*BLJ* VIII, 14, 18 and 58–59; see also, *CPW* VI, 1). JM's little joke (implying that the epigram was not clever enough to make anyone suspect B of having written it) elicited a delightful retort from B on 16 February: 'So – *you epigrammatize* upon *my epigram*. – – I will *pay you* for *that* – mind if I don't – some day. – I never let anyone off in the long run – (*who first begins*) – remember *Sam* – and see if I don't do you as good a turn. – You unnatural publisher! – what – quiz your own authors! – You are a paper Cannibal' (*BLJ* VIII, 78; 'Sam' refers to Rogers and B's lampoon, 'Question and Answer', for which see Letter 140, n. 2 above). JM honoured B's prohibition; but as Hobhouse told B on 19 June: 'John Murray shows about the epigram about the braziers, which I own I was sorry you had sent to him – he being totally unworthy of trust – he would sell you & all the world for a half farthing' (*BB*, 311).

3. JM glances at *Hamlet*, II, ii, 430–31: 'the play, I remember, pleas'd not the million'. B replied on 16 February: 'You say "the Doge" will not be popular – did I ever write for *popularity*? – – I defy you to show a work of mine (except a tale or two) of a popular style or complexion', and proceeded to discuss the sort of dramatic style he was aiming at (*BLJ* VIII, 78).

4. Replying on 16 February, B said: 'I agree to your request of leaving in abeyance the terms for the three D.J.s till you can ascertain the effect of publication. – If I refuse to alter – you have a claim to so much courtesy in return' (*BLJ* VIII, 77).

5. Quite right; B replied gloriously: 'The 5th. is so far from being the last of D. J. that it is hardly the beginning. – I meant to take him the tour of Europe – with a proper mixture of siege – battle – and adventure – and to make him finish as *Anacharsis Cloots* – in the French revolution. – To how many cantos this may extend – I know not – nor whether (even if I live) I shall complete it – but this was my notion. – I meant to have made him a Cavalier Servente in Italy and a cause for a divorce in England – and a Sentimental "Werther-faced man" in Germany – so as to show the different ridicules of the society in each of those countries – – and to have displayed him gradually gaté and blasé as he grew older – as is natural. – But I had not quite fixed whether to make him end in Hell – or in an unhappy marriage, – not

knowing which would be the severest. – The Spanish tradition says Hell – but it is probably only an Allegory of the other state. – – You are now in possession of my notions on the subject' (*BLJ* VIII, 78; see also, Letter 151 below).

6. The Royal Society of Literature for the Encouragement of Indigent Merit and the Promotion of General Literature was founded in November 1820 under the patronage of George IV. Three prizes were to be awarded annually. The first prize offered in 1821 was the King's Premium of 100 guineas, 'for the best Dissertation on the Age, Writings, and Genius of Homer; and on the State of Religion, Society, Learning, and the Arts, during that period, collected from the writings of Homer'; the second, the Society's Premium of 50 guineas 'for the best Poem on Dartmoor'; and the third, the Society's Premium of 25 guineas 'for the best Essay on the History of the Greek Language; of the present Language of Greece, especially in the Ionian Islands; and on the Difference between Ancient and Modern Greek'. The winner of the second prize here was *Dartmoor; A Poem*, by Felicia Hemans, which was 'Printed by Order of the Society' by J. Brettell in July 1821 (see *The Gentleman's Magazine*, XC, Pt II [July–December 1820], 444, and XCI, Pt I [January–June 1821], 61 and 542). Needless to say, B did not submit an entry, nor did he comment on JM's information; but in October 1821 he sent his ruthlessly anti-George IV poem *The Irish Avatar* to JM saying: 'It is doubtful whether the poem was written by Felicia Hemans for the prize of the Dartmoor Academy – or by the Revd. W. L. Bowles with a view to a bishopric – your own discernment will decide between them' (*BLJ* VIII, 236; see also, Letter 162, n. 7 below).

7. Lord Archibald Hamilton's 'Motion respecting the Omission of the Queen's Name in the Liturgy' (which was intended to restore her name thereto) was debated in the Commons on Friday 26 January and was adjourned on a ministerial majority of 101 (*Parliamentary Debates, New Series*, IV [January–April 1821], 139–221).

8. This did not have a pretty outcome. Between May 1820 and January 1821, John Scott (1784–1821), formerly editor of *The Champion*, had, in his present capacity as editor of *The London Magazine*, attacked *Blackwood's Edinburgh Magazine* and more particularly John Gibson Lockhart as its joint-editor. Lockhart had come to London to challenge him, but had returned to Scotland before the issue was resolved on account of his wife's perilous pregnancy. His friend, however, John Henry Christie, pursued the matter, which eventually led to a duel between himself and Scott which took place by moonlight at 9 o'clock on 16 February 1821 at Chalk Farm. Scott was hit and died a lingering death on 27 February. As editor of *The Champion* he had been one of B's most vociferous antagonists during the Separation Proceedings, but they had recently met in Venice and resolved their differences. B did not immediately respond to JM's present news, but he was to write a touching tribute to Scott in *Observations upon Observations* (1821; pub. 1832), and on

JM's application sent a generous subscription to his widow (see Letter 152 below; see also, *CMP*, 171–72 and 472–73; Patrick O'Leary, *Regency Editor: Life of John Scott, 1784–1821* [Aberdeen: Aberdeen University Press, 1983], chs 8 and 9; and Marion Lochhead, *John Gibson Lockhart* [London: John Murray, 1954], 82–85).

9. Cornwall's (Procter's) printers were Shackell and Arrowsmith of Johnson's Court, Fleet Street, who appear to have used the same size and type of font as that used by JM's printer, Thomas Davison.

10. See Letter 132, n. 3 above; JM also alludes to Mungo Park (1771–1806), the surgeon and traveller who explored the course of the river Niger and published *Travels in the Interior of Africa* (1799). B replied on 16 February: 'Belzoni *is* a grand traveller and his English is very prettily broken' (*BLJ* VIII, 79).

Letter 149)   Tuesday 30 January 1821

London 30th. Jany^y 1821
Tuesday

Dear Lord Byron

You are much more a man of business that [*sic*] your publisher & I can bear testimony to the obliging punctuallity [*sic*] of your answers – this day brought me the Sheet of the Doge and those of the "Hints from Horace"[1] – I did not know until you pointed it out that this was not the whole for Hobhouse gave me two Copies – & I printed from that in the fairest Hand – I have now taken out the other & mind much more wch with the Notes &c I have <g> sent to the printer – I will also insert all respecting Pope from the Letter to Blackwood – & send Proofs of these parts in a few days.[2] – I am glad you have given me something to say to the Theatres in case they force your Muse on the Stage and you may rely upon my attention to it[3] – You are very kind in your admission of Cohens name for which he will feel both pride & gratitude[4] – You appear to estimate all our Poets with just appreciation down to Barry Cornwall whose tragedy will certainly not raise him in your estimation[5] – The injudicious commendations of the Ed. Rev. will do him no good[6] nor the tea drinkings wch Hunt Hazlitt – Reynolds &c – – who are all alternately allowed to praise each other in the Ed. Rev. – which is going down Hill[7] –

I told you what I had said to Galignani – Postage – do you mention – I would set aside half my Income to pay it in Letters from you[8] –

Well the Wigs [*sic*] have been most desperately beaten – never so compleatly – they want common knowledge of their Country-men – & almost Common Sense – <they> & to have their heels tripped up by an Alderman[9] –

By the way dining with my most excellent friend Freeling a few days since I put Yr Letters about – Waite – the Commandant &c in my pocket as he is a great admirer of any thing from you – well shays [*sic*] he All my Letters from Italy are <u>opened</u> – let me look at yours – <u>thats</u> been opened – <u>thats</u> opened – <u>thats</u> opened.[10]

Pray is there any hope of your coming to England in the Spring?[11]

I received with the Doge & Hints – a note for Lady B – wch I have forwarded[12] –

Yes the <u>Seal</u> was intended for you but it is vile & I have returned it & the other for Sir Walter Scott!!!!![13] Foscolo is to get me One well made in Italy[14] – No word of Torwalsteins Bust[15] – which my Room <u>yearns</u> for – I am Ever My Lord

Most faithfully
Your obliged Servant
John Murray

Kinnaird not arrived yet & I have not seen Canto 5[16] –

Notes to Letter 149)

<u>Cover</u>: Milord/Milord Byron/poste restante/Ravenna/Italie <u>arrived</u>: Forli 15? February

This Letter arrived at the same time as Letter 148.

1. B's three letters of 11 January, in each of which he told JM he had not sent him the whole proof of *Hints from Horace* (*BLJ* VIII, 59–61; for the various proofs, see *CPW* I, 425–26).

2. In letter (*c*) of 11 January, B had directed JM to put all that regarded Pope in *Some Observations* (1820) as a '*note*' to the first mention of his name in *Hints from Horace* (line 82), which in the event was not done (*BLJ* VIII, 61; see also, *CPW* I, 426 and *CMP*, 359–60).

3. See Letter 144, n. 15 above.

4. See Letter 143, n. 9 above.

5. JM may be alluding to B's letter of 4 January criticizing Procter's *Sicilian Story* and *Marcian Colonna* ('quite spoilt by I know not what affectation of Wordsworth – and Hunt – and Moore – and Myself – all mixed up into a kind of Chaos'), and discussing his own dramatic aims as against those of popular writers of the day (*BLJ* VIII, 56–57; see also, n. 6 below). But it

seems more likely that JM is referring to B's dire assessment of 'the present State of English Poetry' in *Some Observations* (see *CMP*, esp. 104–19).

6. Procter's *Marcian Colonna, an Italian Tale, with Three Dramatic Scenes, and Other Poems* was reviewed very favourably in the *Edinburgh Review*, XXXIV, lxviii (November 1820), 449–60, by Jeffrey who somewhat extraordinarily seems to have descended to the utmost namby-pamby ('He has a beautiful fancy and a beautiful diction – and a fine ear for the music of verse, and a great tenderness and delicacy of feeling ... His soul ... seems filled to overflowing with images of love and beauty, and gentle sorrows, and tender pity, and mild and holy imagination. The character of his poetry is to soothe and melt and delight: to make us kind and thoughtful and imaginative – to purge away the dregs of our earthly passions ...' and so on), before concluding with high expectations for Procter's forthcoming tragedy (i.e., *Mirandola*) (449–50 and 460).

7. A slight exaggeration. Hazlitt contributed to Hunt's *Examiner* and to the *Edinburgh Review*, to which he introduced John Hamilton Reynolds (who idolized him) and with whose 'Sonnet on Sherwood Forest' ('The trees in Sherwood Forest are old and good') he closes Lecture VII of his *Lectures on the English Poets* (1818–19). In turn, Reynolds reviewed Hazlitt's *Lectures on the English Comic Writers* in *The Scots Magazine*, his single contribution to the *Edinburgh Review* being a review of Walpole's *Letters* to George Montagu. (For his reviewing activities and his intimacy with Keats and Hazlitt, see Leonidas M. Jones, *The Life of John Hamilton Reynolds* [Hanover and London: University Press of New England, 1984], esp. 139–40 and 157–61). What JM is really driving at here is the self-praising circle of writers (including Hunt, Hazlitt, Keats, Reynolds and others) whom Lockhart had derisively dubbed 'the Cockney School of Poetry' in a series of articles beginning in October 1817 in *Blackwood's Edinburgh Magazine*, and indeed whose reference to them as 'fanciful dreaming tea-drinkers' in *Blackwood's Edinburgh Magazine*, III, xvii (August 1818), 521, JM echoes.

8. See Letter 146 above. B had again asked what JM had decided about Galignani in letter (*b*) of 11 January, at the conclusion of which he asked JM to 'excuse the severe postage – with which my late letters will have taxed you' (*BLJ* VIII, 60–61).

9. See Letter 148, n.7 above. In the debate on Lord Archibald Hamilton's Motion in the Commons on Friday 26 January, Alderman William Heygate, Whig MP for Sudbury, had stated that though he was 'no supporter of ministers, nor an enemy to the Queen', he objected to the motion because if carried it would 'be followed by others in endless succession', 'prolong the unhappy agitation of the public mind', and 'interrupt still further the important business of the nation' (*Parliamentary Debates, New Series*, IV [January–April 1821], 219).

10. Francis (later Sir Francis) Freeling (1764–1836), postal reformer and Secretary

to the General Post Office since 1797. B replied on 16 February: "'*Letters opened!*' to be sure they are – and that's the reason why I always put in my opinion of the German Austrian Scoundrels; – there is not an Italian who loathes them more than I do – and whatever I could do to scour Italy and the earth of their infamous oppression – would be done "con amore"' (*BLJ* VIII, 79). B's letters in question would have been those of 18 November, and 9 and 14 December 1820 (*BLJ* VII, 228–29, 247–48 and 250–51; see also, Letters 141, 144 and 145 above). In their present state, there is no way of telling that they had been opened; but certainly B's letter to Hobhouse of 21–25 September 1820 concerning the trial of the Queen and enclosing a letter from Hoppner to him on the same subject, was not only opened but copied, together with its enclosure, at the Foreign Office and sent by Lord Clanwilliam, the Under-Secretary for Foreign Affairs, to Lord Liverpool (*BLJ* VII, 177–79, 180–81 and 204; BL Add. 38287, ff. 254–57; see Andrew Nicholson, 'Byron, Hobhouse, Hoppner: Intercepted Letters', *The Byron Journal*, forthcoming).

11. B said nothing about returning to England.

12. B had written to Annabella on 11 January (*BLJ* VIII, 61).

13. In letter (*b*) of 11 January, B had asked: 'Is not one of the Seals meant for my Cranium? and the other who or what is he?'; and at the end of letter (*c*) of the same date: 'Is not the Seal of your second letter Walter Scott's bust?' (*BLJ* VIII, 60 and 61). Unfortunately, the seals on JM's recent letters to B are either obliterated or missing: but the seal with Scott's bust on it B gave to Teresa on 12 January thinking she would be 'curious to have the effigies of a man so celebrated' (*BLJ* VIII, 23). According to Teresa: 'As he handed it to her he told her that this portrait was far from doing Scott justice, because Scott had the most sharp-witted look about him, above all when reciting, whereas the seal did not convey anything of that' (*LBLI*, 260). Replying to JM on 16 February, B said: 'I did not think the second *Seal* so bad – surely it is far better than the Saracen's head with which you have sealed your *last letter*' (*BLJ* VIII, 79). The seal of JM's '*last letter*' (i.e., the present one) is not intact.

14. B continued his reply of 16 February: '[So] Foscolo says he will get you a [*seal*] cut better in Italy – he means a *throat* – that is the only thing they do dextrously' (*BLJ* VIII, 79).

15. B replied on 26 February saying he had 'written *twice* to Thorwaldsen without any answer!! – Tell *Hobhouse* so – he was *paid* four years ago – you must address some English at Rome upon the subject – I know none there myself' (*BLJ* VIII, 85–86).

16. Kinnaird was still in Paris and therefore JM had not yet seen *DJ* V.

Letter 150)   [Friday] 2 March 1821

London March 2.
1821

Dear Lord Byron

Your Letter of yesterday – Feb 12 – is like yourself & makes me perfectly easy[1] – I shall give Kinnaird a Thousand <u>Guineas</u> – for the Tragedy Dante & the Po[2] – which I am printing in one volume & publish next week – I have received the Fifth Canto of Don Juan & will now print the three together & publish[3] – adding the Pulci – translation & original – & Dante[4] – The Letter about Pope[5] was read yesterday by Mr Gifford to whom I took it the moment after its arrival – he likes it very much & told me to print it immediately & Mr Gifford will take care to see it carefully through the Press – I now inclose the first part of a third pamphlet by Bowles more insane if possible than the former ones – he has now found out that D Israeli is the writer of the offensive article in the Quarterly – but hitherto <without> he has abstained from naming him[6] – I shall observe strictly your instructions regarding the Tragedy if I observe any intention of acting it[7] – it is certainly a great oversight in our Copyright law

I shall send you some very interesting works in a few day [sic] Ld Waldegraves Memoirs are the most beautiful in the Language & Ld Orfords most delectable[8]

I fear the poor Italians will make a sad business of it[9] –

I remain Dearest Sir

Your Lordships faithful Servant

John Murray

Notes to Letter 150)

<u>Cover</u>: Milord/Milord Byron/poste restante/Ravenna/Italie <u>arrived</u>: Forli 25? March

1. B's letter of 12 February concerning the terms of the publication of *Marino Faliero* (*BLJ* VIII, 77; see Letter 147, n. 7 above).

2. 'To the Po' was not included in the publication.

3. Kinnaird had at last returned from Paris and delivered *DJ* V to JM who now proposed publishing it (as indeed he did do) in a single volume with Cantos III and IV.

4. That is, *Morgante Maggiore* and 'Francesca of Rimini', neither of which was published in B's lifetime.

5. B had sent his letter on the Bowles/Pope controversy (*Letter to John Murray Esqre*.) on 12 February, telling Kinnaird he had done so in his letter to him of that date (*BLJ* VIII, 76).

6. For D'Israeli's 'offensive article in the Quarterly', see Letter 141, n. 8 above. For the various pamphlets in the Bowles/Pope controversy, see *CMP*, 408–10: the pamphlet to which JM here refers would have been what is there designated 'Observations', which was to prompt B to write *Observations upon Observations*, which he later withdrew from publication (see *CMP*, 403–04, 409 and 459–60).

7. B's instructions to prevent the acting of *Marino Faliero* contained in letters (*a*) and (*b*) of 11 January, and reiterated in those of 19, 20 and 27 January (*BLJ* VIII, 59–61, 64–65, 66–67 and 69; see also, Letter 143, nn. 3 and 7, and Letter 144, n. 15 above). Between this Letter (150) and Letter 149 above, JM had evidently written another (no longer extant) in which he told B '"there is nothing to fear let them do what they please"', which did not please B (*BLJ* VIII, 89).

8. See Letter 144, n. 14 above. These had still not arrived by the end of June but perhaps had done so by the end of August 1821; at all events, B had decided as early as 1 February 1821 that the former's were 'trash of memoirs' (*BLJ* VIII, 71, 144 and 187).

9. JM feared aright: within the month the Neapolitans had surrendered to the Austrians without a blow. Replying to JM on 26 April, B said: 'You see the Italians have [*sic*] made a sad business<.> of it. – All owing to treachery and disunion amongst themselves. – It has given me great vexation. – The Execrations heaped upon the Neapolitans by the other Italians are quite in unison with those of the rest of Europe' (*BLJ* VIII, 102, corrected from MS BL Ashley 4747). That it had indeed given B 'great vexation' is also evident from his letters to Hobhouse, Kinnaird and Moore, and his Journal entry of 1 May 1821 (*BLJ* VIII, 99–100, 101, 104 and 106).

Letter 151) [Tuesday] 6 March 1821

London March 6
1821

Dear Lord Byron

I am very much obliged by your kind Letter of Feby. 16 and you may be assured that I will pay every attention of all kinds to your friends Signor Curioni & Signora Tarascelli – but <there> it is now so much the fassion [*sic*] to patronise persons of their class that they will soon grow beyond my reach but I may assist them with sober friendliness[1] – <I>Your history of the plan of the progress of Don Juan is very entertaining but I am clear for sending to Hell – because he may favour us with the Characters whom he finds there[2] – You are as you always have been compleatly liberal in my terms & you say with justice that I have had no cause for fighting shy upon this point[3] – – Hobhouse is also very gentlemanly but I dont know you when I negotiate with Mr Kinnaird.[4] Next week the Traged [sic] will be finally ready & Don Juan 3 – 4 – 5 in a few days after – & I will tell what is said –

Mrs Johanna Baillie has just put forth a Volume of Metrical Legends which is absolute trash – so much so that I hardly shall send it to you[5] –

It will make Belzoni very happy that you have mentioned him – he is now preparing to exhibit all his Egyptian Curiosities at Bullochs [sic] Musæeum [sic] – & to give a fac-simile of two Chambers of the Tombs of the Kings at Thebes[6] –

A very extraordinary trial took Place yesterday at Nottingham wch is not yet in the papers – a Man, marries his own daughter who having a Lover afterwards induces him to <kil> murder her father – & it is the trial for murder that has brought it out[7] – I will cut the best report of it out of the papers & inclose it I have just had Galignani with me another fellow has printed yr Works beautifully in 3 Vols 8vo like my Edition[8] – made Fac-similes of <Pla> Westalls plates – & sells it for 18 franks [sic] – I believe I must let Galignani have your Lordships assignment – & I will thank you to give me one to him for the Tragedy –

The Letter on Bowles I hope to have this night – I will make the alteration suggested by your Letter of today.[9]

With best Compliments & entreating that you will spare me & vowing never to empigramatize [sic] on you any more[10] I remain

    Dear Lord Byron
    Your obliged & faithful
    friend & Servant
    John Murray

Notes to Letter 151)

Cover: Milord/Milord Byron/poste restante/Ravenna/Italie

1. B's letter of 16 February announcing the imminent arrival from Barcelona of the Italian tenor Signor Alberico Curioni (c.1785–1832), in whose favour he requested JM's 'personal kindness and patronage', and of his companion, Signora Arpalice Taruscelli, 'a Venetian lady of great beauty and celebrity and a particular friend of mine', to whom B was sure JM's 'natural

gallantry' would induce him to pay 'proper attention' (*BLJ* VIII, 77). Writing to Kinnaird a little later, B was rather more particular about the Signora's accomplishments (*BLJ* VIII, 129–30).

2. A sound reason: see Letter 148, n. 5 above. Teresa wanted him to '*remain*' there (*BLJ* VIII, 145; see also *LBLI*, 595–96).

3. See Letter 147, n. 8 above. Writing to Kinnaird on 26 April, B told him that 'Murray complains to me that you are *brusque* with him' (*BLJ* VIII, 101), to which Kinnaird replied on 14 May: 'I was not aware I had been brusque – But I will avoid it ... I have never had a cross word with Murray'; and he went on to explain that in his dealings with JM he had taken the line that he would 'receive a proposition <u>from</u> him' but not '<u>seek</u> him', and would 'say <u>no</u> to his proposition' if he 'thought proper' but abstain from any '<u>bargaining conversations</u>'. He had said '<u>no</u> to his offer of £1050 for the Play & Dante', but as JM had said B 'had said <u>yes</u>', he had 'assigned the work & receiv'd his Bills' (MA; see also, n. 4 below).

4. 'You are ... Kinnaird.' B has drawn a line down the left and right margins of this passage, and on 2 June enclosed this Letter 'in confidence' to Kinnaird, telling him he would see from it what JM said 'of "*Negotiation*" or "*Negociation*" – how is this word spelt – with a *t* or a *c*?', which would enable Kinnaird to judge for himself whether JM was acting liberally or not (*BLJ* VIII, 131–32). Replying on 26 June, Kinnaird said he had received B's letter 'enclosing M's letter to you': 'I do not feel that his remark is just – Hobhouse's Gentlemanliness means that he has not interfer'd at all – I think Mr Murray thinks I have your interest & honor at once at heart, & that I deal <u>with him</u> as between a Gentleman & a Tradesman – but of any words I defy him to complain' (MA).

5. Joanna Baillie's *Metrical Legends of Exalted Characters* was published by Longmans in March 1821. JM did send it to B (see *CMP*, 246, lot 24).

6. See Letter 132, n. 3, and Letter 148, n. 10 above. The exhibition, which included replicas of two chambers in the tomb of King Sety I discovered at Thebes, opened at William Bullock's Egyptian Hall (formerly the London Museum) in Piccadilly on Tuesday 1 May 1821 (entrance fee, 2/6); at the preview on Friday 27 April it received the highest commendations (*London Chronicle*, CXXIX, 9730 [Saturday 28-Monday 30 April 1821], 403, and *The Times*, Tuesday 1 May 1821; see also, *The Gentleman's Magazine*, XCI, Pt I [January–June 1821], 447–50). JM published the Exhibition Guidebook at one shilling: *Description of the Egyptian Tomb, discovered by G. Belzoni* (1821).

7. JM has taken some liberties with the truth. The trial took place not at Nottingham but at Northampton Assizes: '*Philip Haynes* and *Mary Clarke*, for the wilful murder of John Clarke, husband of Mary Clarke, at Charwelton, each received sentence of death, and were to suffer on Saturday, and their bodies to be afterwards dissected and anatomised' (*The Times*, Wednesday

14 March 1821). The execution took place on Saturday 17 March and was reported at some length in the *London Chronicle* where it transpired that Haynes was the 'paramour' of Mary Clarke at whose instigation he had murdered John Clarke whom she had married against her will. Letters indicating her 'extreme ferocity' and 'diabolical mind' were subjoined, but nothing was said about incest (*London Chronicle*, CXXIX, 9713 [Tuesday 20-Wednesday 21 March 1821], 268). JM did not send any report to B.

8. See Letter 146, n. 2 above. A letter from Galignani to JM of 4 April 1821 indicates that he had been in London the previous month (MA), but this particular pirated edition has not been identified. B made no reference to this subject in his reply, and JM told Galignani on 9 April that he could not yet send him 'a regular assignment of the Copyright from the Author' (MS Pforzheimer Library).

9. In his letter of 16 February, B had asked JM to make a minor addition to his *Letter to John Murray Esqre.*, which was printed in the first edition (see *BLJ* VIII, 79, and *CMP*, 414, n. 13).

10. See 148, n. 2 above.

Letter 152)   [Tuesday] 20 March 1821

Albemarle Street
March 20. 1821

Dear Lord Byron

The pamphlet on Bowles is deemed excellent & is to be published on Saturday – the Note on Lady Montague though also very good, Mr Gifford recommends to be suppressed[1] – The Letter about the Helespont [*sic*] will appear in the next London Magazine[2] – The fatal death of its late editor,[3] poor Scott <your>, in a Duel<el>, your Lordship will have read of – he has left a widow – a very superior Woman & two infant Children without a Shilling – <if y> A Committee of wch Sir Ja^s Mackintosh is the head & yr humble Servant the tale [*sic*] – are endeavouring to form a subscription for them & if you please I shall be glad to put your Lordships name down for £10 –

The Doge of Venice will now come out, with the Prophecy of dante [*sic*], at a most happy time when we are just now interested for Italy – nothing could be better – it is nearly worked off & will be out next week.[4]

I long to know what you propose to do will these wars – to which our lives may not see the End – for all Europe will mingle indiscriminately[5] – bring you to England or will Lady Noels Death

– wch they tell me from good authority must immediately take place[6] –

By the way Hobhouse spoke to Lord Grey about the impropriety of allowing – a Play not intended for performance to be Acted on the Stage Earl Grey spoke to the Lord Chancellor – who said that he would grant an injunction[7] –

We as yet can get no certain News from Italy[8] –

I am My Lord

yr faithful Servant

Jno Murray

Notes to Letter 152)

Cover: Milord/Milord Byron/Poste restante/Ravenna/Italie

1. B's *Letter to **** ******, on the Rev. W. L. Bowles' Strictures on the Life and Writings of Pope* was published on Saturday 31 March 1821. On 26 February he had sent an additional note on Lady Mary Wortley Montagu, leaving JM 'complete discretionary power of *omission altogether* or curtailment ... since it may be scarcely chaste enough for the Canting prudery of the day' (*BLJ* VIII, 85). The note, which deals in part and most sympathetically with the amatory passions of 'deformed persons', was not published in his lifetime (see *CMP*, 125–26, 400 and 417, n. 27).

2. B's long letter of 21 February 1821 addressed to JM, which he told Hobhouse the following day was 'for publication (in any Magazine or in the Examiner)' (*BLJ* VIII, 80–83). This had been provoked by another work JM had incautiously published at the very same time as Miss Waldie's *Sketches* (see Letters 138 and 140 above), William Turner's *Journal of a Tour in the Levant*, 3 vols (1820). In this Turner denigrated B's swimming of the Hellespont with Lieutenant Ekenhead in May 1810, and challenged various assertions he had made as to its 'practicability' in his note to 'Written after swimming from Sestos to Abydos' published with *CHP* I in 1812 (*CPW* I, 422–23). Writing of Leander's feat, Turner observed:

> This had excited my curiosity more than ever, since the experiment of Lord Byron, who, when he expressed such confidence of having proved its practicability, seems to have forgotten, that Leander swam over both ways, with and *against* the tide, whereas he only performed the easiest part of the task, by swimming *with* it from Europe to Asia. For the tide does not here run strait down, parallel with the banks, but having been dashed violently into the Bay of Maito, is by the reaction thrown to the opposite shore lower down; and thus in the narrowest part of the gulf, flows transversely from the European to the Asiatic coast, whence it is again thrown off with vehemence into the Archipelago. Whatever, therefore, is thrown into the stream, on this part of the European bank, *must* arrive at the Asiatic shore.

> Both the emulators of Leander quoted by Lord B. did only this. I attempted to swim across from Asia to Europe, starting from the northerly side of the castle; but the current was so completely in my teeth, that with the most unremitted and violent exertion, I did not, in twenty-five minutes, advance more than one hundred yards, and was then obliged to give it up from utter exhaustion. Having been accustomed to swimming from my childhood, I have no hesitation in asserting, that no man could have strength to swim a mile and a half, (the breadth of the strait in the narrowest spot, a little northerly of the castles) against such a current; and higher up or lower down, the strait widens so considerably, that he would save little labour by changing his place of starting. I therefore treat the tale of Leander's swimming across both ways, as one of those fables, to which the Greeks were so ready to give the name of history (I, 44–45).

B answered each of these points firmly but graciously in his reply which was published in *The London Magazine*, III, xvi [April 1821], 363–65, under the headline 'Swimming Across the Hellespont./*Letter from the Right Honourable Lord Byron to Mr. Murray*', and was reprinted from that source in, for instance, the *London Chronicle*, CXXIX, 9719 [Tuesday 3–Wednesday 4 April 1821], 316; Marchand's note [*BLJ* VIII, 83n.], following Prothero's [V, 251n.], is incorrect: B's letter did not appear in the *Monthly Magazine*). Turner, 'unshaken still', wrote a reply to B but did not publish it at the time; he gave it to Moore who published it in an Appendix to B's *Life* from where Prothero reprinted it (see *Byron's Life and Works*, VI, 280–83, and Prothero, V, Appendix VII, 601–03).

3. See Letter 148, n. 8 above (JM's 'fatal death' is his own whimsicality). John Scott (formerly editor of *The London Magazine*) had been buried on 9 March and an appeal committee including Sir James Mackintosh, Robert Baldwin (the publisher of *The London Magazine*) and JM himself set up to raise a subscription for his wife Caroline and family. Among the numerous contributors were Bowles, Jeffrey, Lord Holland, Charles Lamb and Haydon (see O'Leary, *Regency Editor*, 163). B replied on 21 April: 'You may make my subscription for [*sic*] Mr. Scott's widow &ᶜ. <u>thirty</u> – instead of the proposed <u>ten</u> pounds – but do not put down <u>my name</u> – put down N.N. [*sic*] only. – The reason is, that as [*sic*] I have mentioned him in the enclosed pamphlet – it would look indelicate' (MA, correcting *BLJ* VIII, 99; 'N.N.' stands for 'No Name'; B did not begin to use 'N.B.' for 'Noel Byron' until February 1822; the 'enclosed pamphlet' was *Observations upon Observations*).

4. *Marino Faliero* and *The Prophecy of Dante* were published together in a single volume on 21 April 1821.

5. JM refers to the increasing unrest in Europe, which was now spreading through Spain, southern France, Sardinia, Sicily, Naples and Piedmont, and would shortly reach Moldavia, Wallachia and Greece.

6. JM's 'good authority' was almost certainly Augusta, who had told B herself. B wrote to Kinnaird on 26 April: 'I hear from Mrs. L[eigh] that Lady N[oel] *has been* "dangerously ill" – but it should seem by *her* letter that She is now getting dangerously well again'; and replying to JM on the same date, he told him: 'Mrs. Leigh writes that Lady *No-ill* is getting *well* again – See what it is to have luck in this world' (*BLJ* VIII, 101 and 102).

7. See Letter 154 below. Hobhouse does not mention having approached Lord Grey on the subject either in his Diary or in any letter to B.

8. See Letter 150, n. 9 above. The uncertainty is well illustrated by Hobhouse's Journal entries for the week: Sunday 25 March, 'rumour of an engagement between Piedmontese & Austrians near Pavia – rumour of insurrections in France'; Wednesday 28 March, 'Report of Austrians being beaten in Italy'; Thursday 29 March, 'Report of Naples being taken by Austrians'; Friday 30 March, 'appears that Naples is taken – and fear of a counter-revolution in Piedmont'. Confirmation eventually arrived on Tuesday 3 April: 'Naples certainly taken – and without a struggle – soldiers 120.000 dispersed without a shot – a Count Santorre Santa Rosa trying to keep the Revolutionists together in Pied-mont' (BL Add. 56542, ff. 12*v*, 13*r* and 14*r*; see also, Moore, *Journal*, II, 437–39). The Italian patriot, Count Santorre Santa Rosa (1783– 1825), was a leading Constitutional Monarchist and revolutionary in the Piedmont and Minister for War in the provisional government of March 1821. After the defeat of the revolutionists by the Austrians at the Battle of Novaro on 8 April 1821, he fled to Lausanne and thence to Paris where his *De la Révolution Piémontaise*, describing in detail the movements Hobhouse here records, was published anonymously in November 1821 (an English translation appeared the following year in *The Pamphleteer*, XIX, xxxvii [1822], 9–77). Unjustly suspected of anti-French activity he took refuge in England, arriving in late October 1822 and renting Green Cottage from Foscolo before settling in Nottingham. In November 1824, he left England to join the Greek War of Independence and, having taken part in the relief of Navarino on 21 April 1825 with Mavrocordatos, he was killed defending the Island of Sphacteria on 9 May 1825 (see *Della Rivoluzione Piémontese nel 1821, versione eseguita sulla terza edizione francese riveduta e corredata di annotazioni coll' Aggiunta della Biografia del Conte di Santarosa e di importanti documenti* [Genoa, 1849]; see also, Margaret C. W. Wicks, *The Italian Exiles in London 1816–1848* [Manchester: Manchester University Press, 1937], ch. 4, and Vincent, *Ugo Foscolo: An Italian in Regency England*, 168–69).

Letter 153)   [Tuesday] 27 March 1821

London March 27
1821

Dear Lord Byron

Yours of the 1st March[1] – & a later one of the 3rd – have reached
me,[2] the latter half an hour ago – the first contained an addit[1] Stanza
to Juan – & the Letter from Balfour, from [sic] Gifford[3] – I will make
enquiry about the man before I send the £20 to him – I gave your love
to Sir Walter who reciprocates with the most faithful steady warmth[4]
– I sent the addition to the Letter, without reading it to the printer
for the Letter was advertised for publication this day & was on the
point of issuing[5] – It is very gratifying to me to be able to say that
Gifford, Scott, Merivale Sotheby, Morritt & other few who have seen
it consider it admirably done[6] – Your prose is in the very happiest &
most original taste & Style & you have in the most lively & convincing
& gentlemanly manner compleatly proved your point – Indeed yr prose
is excellent[7] – the Preface to the Doge equally in good taste – I am
not sorry for this elegant tract's preceeding by a few Days the Doge
– I got all the<ir> fair Sheets compleat on Saturday of this Tragedy
– I was alone on Sunday & devoted my quiet to it – and I assure you
I could not stop until I had finished it – it is monstrously fine & very
interesting – The Doge is admirably portrayed & his Wife perfectly
original & beautiful – I account for a little disappointment in my first
& second reading from the peculiar expectations which I had previously
conceived of it as a <u>Tragedy</u> – I now read it as a Poem & have been
compleatly delighted – I shall launch it with the fullest confidence that
it will weather the Storm of any Criticism & as being fully worthy of
you – besides its whole tone & character – discovers a new Vein in your
Genius – I shall long to get some fair opinion of it to send you from
the public – I believe I told you that Gifford desired me to tell you how
very highly he estimates your Prose – & he always dwells with delight
upon the unrivalled purity of the Blank Verse of this Tragedy –

Gifford does not agree in your estimation of the <English> Hints
from Horace[8] – but I will print it – Don Juan 3 – 4 – 5 – in one Vol
– & Pulci – Dante – Horace in another – & let the [sic] float on the
Waters of Public Opinion.

I send a parcel with Waverley &c I will be glad to have your
Lordships opinion of Lord Waldegrave? [sic] How like you Kenilworth?[9]

I am afraid that Mr Rogers will be sadly mortified at the notice of
him in the pamphlet & I would gladly have omitted the "Venerable"

& Nestor if I had dared – perhaps in subsequent Editions you will give countervailing praise[10] – he has just been here & taken it in his pocket odds Squibs & Crackers[11] – I am convinced that your Tragedy is beautiful –

Ever Dearest Sir
yr Lordships obliged &
faithful Servant
Jno. Murray

Notes to Letter 153)

<u>Cover</u>: Milord/Milord Byron/poste restante/Ravenna/Italie <u>arrived</u>: Forli 12 April

1. B's letter of 1 March enclosing an additional stanza for *DJ* V (stanza 158), which JM 'forgot' to print in the first edition – much to B's displeasure (*BLJ* VIII, 87 and 192; see also, Letter 164 below).

2. B did not write on 3 March, though he did on 2 March; but as JM never refers to that letter here or elsewhere he must mean B's letter of 9 March (see n. 5 below).

3. Unfortunately, neither Balfour's letter nor his connection with Gifford (if any) is forthcoming; and all we can gather about the matter is from B's letter to JM of 1 March enclosing the letter, which he thought would make JM laugh and which he asked him to answer '*secretly*' so as 'not to mortify' Balfour, and to tell him that he 'never wrote for a *prize*' in his life. He added: 'As for the twenty pounds he wants to gain – [you may] *send* them to him for me' (*BLJ* VIII, 88).

4. Scott was in London from the end of January to the beginning of April 1821 (Lockhart, *Life of Scott*, 444–46). In his letter of 1 March, B had written: 'Give my love to Sir W. Scott – & tell him to write more novels; – pray send out Waverley and the Guy M[annering] – and the Antiquary – It is five years since I have had a copy – – I have read all the other forty times' (*BLJ* VIII, 88).

5. See n. 2 above. In his letter of 9 March, B enclosed a long '"Addenda"' to his Bowles/Pope *Letter*, which was initially appended to the second issue of the first edition, and in the second and subsequent editions embodied in the text (*BLJ* VIII, 90; see also, *CMP*, 136–40, 400, 430, n. 94, and 434, n. 117).

6. For the critical reception of B's *Letter*, see *CMP*, 407–08: Shelley and Moore were not so impressed, but Hobhouse thought it 'very good', and Kinnaird told B on 14 May: 'Your <u>letter</u> is a complete hit – The dispute may be of less consequence than to enlist your pen – But you shew your wit & power – & fun – & your earnest hatred of hypocrisy, & real love for Pope' (MA).

7. B replied on 26 April: 'As you say my "*prose*" is good – why don't you treat with *Moore* for the reversion of the Memoirs – *conditionally* – *recollect* – not to be published before decease' (*BLJ* VIII, 103).

8. For JM's initial slip here, '<English>' (for *EBSR*), cf. Letter 145, n. 8 above. In his letter of 1 March, B said he regarded *Hints from Horace* 'and my Pulci as by far the best things of my doing – *you* will not think so – and *get* frightened for fear I shall charge accordingly – but I know that they will *not* be popular – so don't be afraid – publish them together' (*BLJ* VIII, 88).

9. B replied on 26 April: 'Your latest packet of books is on its way here but not arrived. Kenilworth excellent' (*BLJ* VIII, 103; see also, Letter 156 below).

10. In his Bowles/Pope *Letter*, B had referred to Rogers as 'our venerable host ... the last Argonaut of Classic English poetry – and the Nestor of our inferior race of living poets' (*CMP*, 121 and 413, n. 10). JM's fears were justified. Kinnaird told B on 10 April: 'Do you know that Rogers cuts Hobhouse, conceiving that to his radical suggestions he is indebted for the <u>venerable</u> you have affix'd to his hospitality in your Bowleian letter' (MA). Replying to Kinnaird on 26 April, B said that he 'meant but a compliment': 'He and Dryden – and Chaucer – are the oldest upon record who have written so well at that advanced period. – His age is a credit to him'; and writing to JM on the same date, he said: 'I hear that Rogers is not pleased with being called "venerable" – a pretty fellow – if I had thought that he would have been so absurd – I should have spoken of him as defunct'; to Hobhouse also on the same date he wrote: 'I hear "Rogers cuts *you*" – because I called him "Venerable" – the next time I will state his age without the respectable epithet annexed to it – which in fact he does not deserve' (*BLJ* VIII, 100, 101 and 102). B believed, or chose to believe, that Rogers was 73, which was pensioning him off prematurely as he was only 58 (b. 1763); but he gave no 'countervailing praise' in subsequent editions.

11. JM slips delightfully into the exclamations of Bob Acres: cf. 'Odds hilts and blades!', 'Odds flints, pans, and triggers!', 'Odds balls and barrels!', 'Odds bullets and blades!', 'Odds sparks and flames!', 'Odds crowns and laurels!', 'Odds fire and fury!' (Sheridan, *The Rivals*, III, iv, 72, 81–82, 90 and 99, and IV, i, 4–5, 25 and 48). B had slipped into the same Acreage when writing to JM on 29 August 1819 (*BLJ* VI, 220).

Letter 154) [Tuesday] 24 April 1821

April 24 – 1821

My Lord

I have waited to see what effect Your Letter would produce and the four inclosures are the result.[1]

I have received the additions[2] & have forwarded them with a Printed Answer with Copies of the Doge in a parcel[3] –

The Doge is admired beyon [sic] my most sanguine as P^r my re cantation [sic] Letter I expected[4] –

I have just come to town to prevent Elliston from Acting the Tragedy & tomorrow hope to succeed[5] – on friday You shall hear – if you had <N>written nothing but this Tragedy you would be where you now are

Most truly yr Lordships

faithful Ser^t

Jno Murray

Notes to Letter 154)

Cover: Milord/Milord Byron/Poste Restante/Ravenna/Italie arrived: Forli 10 May

1. These four enclosures were Bowles' letters to JM of 6, 15, 17 and 22 April. In the first he asked him to thank B 'for the kind terms in which he introduces my name, and also for the pleasure I have receiv'd from a work as much mark'd by good sense, liberal principles, and just thinking as by its peculiar tone of good-humour and urbanity', adding that he would 'probably have to discuss these points further' with B. Subsequently he asked JM whether he would be the publisher of his reply to B (to which JM was happy to accede), and in his final letter sent its proposed title asking JM to let him know immediately if he objected to the motto, '"He that plays at BOWLS, must expect RUBBERS." Old Proverb' (which parried B's motto, '"I'll play at Bowls with the Sun and Moon." Old Song') (Garland Greever, A Wiltshire Parson and his Friends: The Correspondence of William Lisle Bowles [London, 1926], 124–33: see also, CMP, 120, 405–06, and 411, and Letter 156 below). Replying to JM on 10 May, B said: 'I have just got your packet. – I am obliged to Mr. Bowles – & Mr. B. is obliged to me – for having restored him to good humour. – He is to write – & you to publish what you please – motto and subject – I desire nothing but fair play for all parties'; and having instructed JM not to publish Observations upon Observations now as 'it would be brutal to do so – after his urbanity', he proceeded to relate in full a story about Bowles that he had only touched on in his Letter. He returned Bowles' letters to JM on 14 May (BLJ VIII, 111–12 and 116; see also, CMP, 127–28).

2. B had sent an '*addenda*' and various additions to his *Letter* on 12 and 13–16? March, of which only two of the additions were added in the third edition (*BLJ* VIII, 92–94 and *CMP*, 142, 150, 400, 436, n. 131, and 448, n. 191).

3. Receiving this parcel on 14 June, B remarked that the 'whole volume looks very respectable – and sufficiently dear in price'. But he wished to know, firstly, why JM had printed 'the face of M[argarit]a C[ogn]i by way of fron-tispiece? – It has almost caused a row between the Countess G[uiccioli] and myself'; and secondly, why he had included the note about 'the Kelso woman's "Sketches" – Did I not request you to omit it – the instant I was aware that the *writer* was a *female*?' (*BLJ* VIII, 136; for JM's 'mistake about the Kelso-woman', which still rankled B two months later, see *BLJ* VIII, 178; see also, Letter 138, n. 9 and Letter 140, n. 8 above, Letter 158, n. 7 below, and *BLJ* IX, 67). With regard to the 'frontispiece', there was none in any published edition of *Marino Faliero*. But in the copy JM sent B (which B gave to the American Joseph Coolidge on 26 June 1821, and which is now in the Boston Public Library), he had inserted an engraving of Harlow's portrait of Margarita Cogni, 'complete even to the pencilled autograph notation: "... This drawing was done at the request of G. G. Byron L. B. Venice, August 6, 1818."' (against which, on the title-page opposite, B has written: '"This drawing was so, but why the devil Murray has placed it here – I neither know nor can imagine. – It was done by Mr. Harlowe."') (see Ellen M. Oldham, 'Lord Byron and Mr. Coolidge of Boston', *The Book Collector*, 13, 2 [Summer 1964], 211–13; see also, Letter 128, n. 12, above).

4. JM's 'recantation Letter' was Letter 153 above. In an undated fragment in MA, which almost certainly belongs to May 1821, B replied: 'You say that the play pleases "beyond your &c. &c." – You now See the good of <u>not</u> puffing before hand – if you had <u>pronè</u>-d it too much – it would not have done half so well – (<u>if</u> it does well even now) the<y must>best way is to say little before hand – & let things find their way fairly. – – – ' (cf. *BLJ* VIII, 53; *prôner* = to praise or flatter).

5. JM was unsuccessful. *Marino Faliero* was published on Saturday 21 April. Writing from Drury Lane Theatre on Sunday 22 April, Elliston submitted the acting version of the play (promiscuously cut and maimed almost beyond recognition) to John Larpent, examiner of plays in the Lord Chamberlain's Office (see headnote to Letter 5 above), with the accompanying letter: 'I have been anxiously waiting for the publication of the Tragedy, which I now send to you, & which we have so curtailed that I believe not a single objectionable line can be said to exist – Despatch you will observe my dear Sir is to me of the greatest consequence, as all my artists will work all this night & will be employed also all Monday night [23 April]. I wish to produce it on Wednesday next [25 April], & as upon all occasions of emer-gency, you have been so obliging to put yourself out of the way, & this is a circumstance in which we are deeply interested, perhaps you will do me the favour to send me the license as soon as possible' (Larpent Collection

2224, Huntington Library; BL microfiche copy 254/464). The 'license' was
duly granted and the play was performed for the first time at Drury Lane
Theatre on Wednesday 25 April 1821. Prior to the performance, JM had
handbills distributed which read: 'The public are respectfully informed, that
the representation of Lord Byron's tragedy, *The Doge of Venice*, this evening,
takes place, in defiance of the injunction of the Lord Chancellor, which
was not applied for until the remonstrance of the publisher, at the earnest
desire of the noble author, had failed in protecting that drama from its
intrusion on the stage, for which it was never intended.' At the conclusion
of the performance, Mr Russell announced that there would be no future
performance until further notice (*The Times*, Thursday 26 April 1821; see
also, *London Chronicle*, CXXIX, 9729 [Thursday 26-Friday 27 April 1821],
394). On Friday 27 April, the case of Murray vs. Elliston was heard before
the Lord Chancellor, who was extremely sympathetic to JM's representations
and commended his conduct in the matter, but decided that the question
was one of law and should be settled once and for all; and that, unless the
parties could come to an accommodation, it would have to go through the
court of law (reported in full in *The Times* for Saturday 28 April 1821; see
also, *London Chronicle*, CXXIX, 9730 [Saturday 28-Monday 30 April 1821],
404 and 407). The play was performed each evening the following week and
frequently thereafter; the performance on Monday 14 May was unexpectedly
honoured by the presence of the Queen (*London Chronicle*, CXXIX, 9737
[Tuesday 15-Wednesday 16 May 1821], 459).

Letter 155)   [Friday] 11 May 1821

London May 11 – 1821

Dear Lord Byron

I yesterday received safely the Second Letter on Pope – which I
immediately sent to Mr Gifford[1] – upon whom I called this morning
and he told me <th> he thought it very interesting & exceedingly clever
– there were <u>parts</u> certainly wch could not be published, but he desired
me to get it set up instantly in print & then he would go over it with
great care & give your Lordship his opinion –

I wrote <la> at different times lately[2] acknowledging additions &c &
I am [*sic*] now nearly compleated a packet containing all that has been
written respecting the Tragedy which that <u>No</u>-Gentleman Elliston has
so shamefully & vilely attempted to perform Mr Kinnaird wrote to you
the history & I am prosecuting a Law Suit[3] – I will send you documents
immediately

The Tragedy is greatly admired

I am Dear Lord Byron

most faithfully y[rs]
Jno Murray

Notes to Letter 155)

Cover: Milord/Milord Byron/poste restante/Ravenna/Italie

1. B's *Observations upon Observations*, which he had sent to JM on 21 April saying he was unsure 'how *much* – if *any* of it – should be published. Upon this point you can consult with Mr. Gifford – and think *twice* before you publish it at all' (*BLJ* VIII, 99; see also, *CMP*, 161–83, and 459–60, Letter 154, n. 1 above, and Letter 156, n. 4 below).

2. In his relatively short reply of 31 May, B remarked: 'You say you have written often – I have only received yrs. of the eleventh – which is very short … You write so seldom & so shortly – that you can hardly expect from me more than I receive' (*BLJ* VIII, 128–29).

3. See Letter 154, n. 5 above. Kinnaird had written to B on 26 April telling him about the first performance of *Marino Faliero*, and went to see the play on 30 April and 3 May. He was deeply impressed and wrote to say so on 1 and 4 May. In his letter of 1 May he also explained the legal position very simply to B: 'With regard to the law, I am convinc'd it is against you & your publisher – Were it otherwise, no man could with impunity read any of Poetry [*sic*] or prose or that of any one else, aloud in a room for money – Common law is out of the question – <u>Authors</u> were not known before the art of printing – I mean as being property, transferable, saleable – the Statute recognizes their property in their works – But then the words of the Statute must be referr'd to – & these speak alone of Printing &c – not of reciting – If I have learnt a Printed book by heart – which book I have bought, the devil is in it if I may not repeat what I remember' (MA).

Letter 156)   [Tuesday] 29 May 1821

London 29. May 1821

Dear Lord Byron

I have this day been favoured with your Lordships obliging communication of May 8 – 10 containing in particular a note to be added to the New Edition of the Letter or to be printed Separately which I will do referring to M[r] Giffords revision.[1] Some time ago I sent a parcel with all the newspapers containing opinions upon Faliero and the infamous conduct of M[r] Elliston but I find that I was wrong in so doing for that papers can go only through the Post office & the brobability [sic] is that my parcel has been ripped up as contraband, as I took care to get two Copies of the Papers on this occasion I have now cut out from them all that relates to this subject and have sent them in a parcel this day² – and as the communication from Venice to Ravenna is probably uncertain I have now addressed the parcel to your Lordship – to the care of Mr Hoppner whom you will probably advise of this immediately³ – I have added a Copy of the Second Letter with Mr Giffords remarks – he says "I hope however Lord B will not continue to squander himself away thus – when will he resume his majestic march, & shake the earth again"?⁴

If you intend proceeding, wait for Bowles's answer a new edition of which I expect tomorrow – he prints in the country⁵ – & let us have the whole digested against the winter for nothing will be attended too [sic] now but the Coronation⁶ – Your Lordships Letter is certainly very much liked.

I have ever since the nefarious performance of the Tragedy been engaged in attending my Solicitor & Council [sic] in arguing & drawing up cases – and the Trial for I have determined to have a decision – and then having felt the Sense of so many members of parliament to be in our favour I hope to get a clause to this effect inserted in the new Copyright Act⁷ – Your Lordship will see by the Arguments at length inserted in the Times – the opinion of the Chancellor – at whose own suggestion to Lord Grey I applied & obtained an injunction – & yet who allowed the play to be performed in spite of it –

On the 2d of April last I sent a parcel containing Mannering – Waverley – Antiquary & Letter on Bowles – May 2 Doge &c May 11 – 1 Doz Boxes Soda Powder – 11 Parrys Voyage to the North Pole – Today I have sent Waldegrave⁸ – Lady Hervey (not yet published) &c⁹ Ant [sic] it monstrous good Bowles cringing to you & thinking he may kick Hobhouse as he likes – Hobhouse does not like it – & thinks of cutting his (Bowless) throat¹⁰ – Bowles too making an apology for the liberty he has taken [with] your "Lordship's Motto" [and] mistaking your Lines f[or tho]se written by Hobhouse¹¹

I have lately had the misfortune to lose my Second Son¹² – but I can not expect to go through the world with out participating in the Misfortunes of all around me –

God Bless you
Prays Your Lordships
obliged & faithful Servt
Jno Murray

[On back cover] I shall look out for the <u>Bust</u>¹³

Notes to Letter 156)

<u>Cover</u>: Milord/Milord Byron/Poste restante/Ravenna/Italie

1. B's letter of 8 May containing an additional note to his *Letter* which he said was of such 'importance to the question in dispute' that JM should even print it 'on a separate page and distribute it to the purchasers of the former copies' (*BLJ* VIII, 109–10; see also, *CMP*, 400 and 431, n. 103). The note was not published in his lifetime. In his letter of 10 May, B cancelled the publication of *Observations upon Observations* (see Letter 154, n. 1 above).

2. As a sample of newspaper 'opinions' of *Marino Faliero*, on the day of its publication and before it was acted, one writer observed, having quoted B's prefatory disclaimer as to its representation: 'From what we have seen, however, of the Tragedy, it does strike us that Lord Byron has had some eye to representation. He seems to have fitted Mr. KEAN in the character of the *Doge*, almost as well as if he had taken his measure' (*London Chronicle*, CXXIX, 9727 [Saturday 21–Monday 23 April 1821], 379). After its first performance, however, both the *London Chronicle* and *The Times* deplored its having been staged against B's express wishes, *The Times* observing that only 'fragments, violently torn from that noble work, were presented to the audience': '*Procrustes-like*, they have irreverently lopped and disfigured the body of the *Doge of Venice*, to fit him for the narrow bed of torture at Drury-lane … Many of the finest and most spirited passages have been omitted altogether, and others have been so jumbled together that Lord Byron himself would hardly recognise them. The poetry of the piece, *as we read it*, is of the highest order' (*The Times*, Thursday 26 April 1821; see also, *London Chronicle*, CXXIX, 9729 [Thursday 26–Friday 27 April 1821], 394).

3. B wrote to Henry Dorville at Venice on 24 June asking him to forward this parcel when it arrived (*BLJ* VIII, 142).

4. Of *Observations upon Observations*, Gifford had written to JM on 26 May: 'I send Lord B. with a good deal cut out – but it will be unsafe to publish it – a little more may yet be spared, but that he will probably see himself. The <letter> matter is not very refined, but it is vigorous, & to the purpose. Bowles requires checking. I hope however Lord B. will not continue to squander himself away thus. When will he resume his majestic march, & shake the earth again?' (MA; Gifford aptly fuses Pope on Dryden, who 'taught to join/The varying verse, the full resounding line,/The long majestic march, and energy divine' [*Imitations of Horace*, Epistle I, Bk II, 267–69], and B on Napoleon: 'thou seek'st/Even now to re-assume the imperial mien,/And shake again the world, the Thunderer of the scene!' [*CHP* III, stanza 36]). B replied on 14 June: 'I *have* resumed my "majestic march" (as Gifford is pleased to call it) in "Sardanapalus" which by the favour of Providence and the Post Office should be arrived by this time'; B had sent *Sardanapalus* to JM on 2 June, 'avising' Kinnaird of its 'expedition' the same day (*BLJ* VIII, 131 and 136).

5. With this Letter (156) JM had clearly sent Bowles' *Two Letters to the Right Honourable Lord Byron* (dated 30 April, 1821), which was printed by Richard Cruttwell of St James's-Street, Bath and published by JM. A '*Third Edition with Alterations, exclusively for the Pamphleteer*' (dated 25 May, 1821), was published in the *Pamphleteer*, XVIII, xxxvi (June 1821), 331–400. B replied on 14 June: 'I have read Bowles's answer – I could easily reply – but it would lead to a long discussion – in the course of which I should perhaps lose my temper – which I would rather not do with so civil & forbearing an antagonist. – I suppose he will mistake being *silent* for *silenced*'; he said almost exactly the same to Moore on 22 June (*BLJ* VIII, 136 and 141).

6. The much delayed Coronation of George IV was now fixed for 19 July 1821. Replying to this on 29 June, B remarked: 'By the time you receive this letter the Coronation will be over – & you will be able to think of business' (*BLJ* VIII, 144).

7. JM's efforts proved unavailing; Copyright law remained unaltered from 1814 until the Dramatic Copyright Act of 1833 and the Copyright Act of 1842 (see John Russell Stephens, *The Profession of the Playwright* [Cambridge: Cambridge University Press, 1992], esp. 88–95; see also, Letter 154, n. 5 above).

8. B received *Marino Faliero*, his Bowles/Pope *Letter*, and Bowles' *Two Letters* on 14 June, and 'Scott's novels all safe' on 29 June; the other works, however, had not arrived by then (*BLJ* VIII, 136 and 144); he had last requested soda powders, 'for the Summer dilution', on 21 and 26 April and 10 May (*BLJ* VIII, 99, 102 and 112).

9. *Letters of Mary Lepel, Lady Hervey. With a Memoir, and Illustrative Notes* was published by JM in June 1821; B's copy forms lot 95 in his Sale Catalogue (1827) (*CMP*, 249).

10. See n. 5 above. In his Bowles/Pope *Letter* B had acknowledged that Hobhouse was the author of the lines on Bowles in the first edition of *EBSR*, and that he had substituted his own lines in the second edition (*CMP*, 123 and 415, n. 20). Bowles picked this up at the close of his *Two Letters*, referring to Hobhouse as the 'gallant and puissant KNIGHT OF WESTMINSTER' and attacking him with a parody of B's lines, substituting for 'Do thou essay' (*EBSR*, 369), 'HOBHOUSE, essay', and commenting: 'The gallant *knight* for Westminster and I are now even' (*Two Letters*, 103–04). Hobhouse was indignant, telling B on 7 May that had Bowles not been a clergyman he would have challenged him, adding: 'L'ami Murray tells me as God is his judge he never saw it until it was published – but that's a bounce [a fib] no doubt' (*BB*, 306–07). But instead of 'cutting his (Bowless) throat' literally, he cut it poetically, sending his dissection to JM and later to B (MA; see also, Smiles, I, 421, and *BB*, 318).

11. Words in square brackets torn off with seal. See Letter 154, n. 1 above. In

his prefatory 'Advertisement' to his *Two Letters* Bowles expressed the hope that B would excuse him '*for having made somewhat free with the singular Motto to his book*'; and went on to explain that by '*a somewhat ludicrous coincidence*' the arms of his family were, '*literally*', '*a "sun and moon" a* Sun, OR, *and a* Moon, ARGENT, secundùm ARTEM': '*It is, therefore, with this* SUN *and* MOON, *that Lord* BYRON, *I have no doubt, plays at* "BOWLS!" *Not with the* SUN *and* MOON *in* NATURE' (see *CMP*, 411; '*freee*' should there read '*free*').

12. On 23 May 1821 in the Obituary columns of *The Gentleman's Magazine* appeared the simple announcement: 'William, youngest son of John Murray, esq. of Albemarle-street' (*The Gentleman's Magazine*, XCI, Pt I [January–June 1821], 571). B replied sympathetically and as philosophically as JM on 14 June: 'I am truly sorry to hear of yr. domestic loss – but (as I know by experience) all attempts at condolence in such cases are merely varieties of solemn impertinence. – There is nothing in this world but *Time*' (*BLJ* VIII, 136).

13. This postscript is written on the outside of the back of the cover. In his letter of 8 May, B had told JM that Thorwaldsen had 'sent off the bust to be shipped from Leghorn last week. As it is addressed to your house and care you may be looking out for it, though I know not the probable time of the voyage in this Season of the year' (*BLJ* VIII, 111).

Letter 157)   [Friday] 22 June 1821

London June 22.
1821

Dear Lord Byron

Late on Tuesday night I received your Lordships valuable packet containing the Tragedy of Sardanapalus[1] – As it was written not as legibly as formerly I sent it the next morning to the printer with orders to put all hands upon it & the result is that I am enabled to send you a proof of the first Act – Mr Hobhouse called just as it came in & I gave him a Copy of it for himself & Kinnaird[2] & Since I have given another to Mr Gifford – I am amazingly anxious to read it for its Title promises great Originality & entertainment –

By every post you may I think calculate upon receiving an Act. Pray be so good as to put all packets under cover to John Barrow Esq Secretary to the Admiralty – as the name will insure security[3] –

I shall tell you Giffords opinion in my next.

Most truly

Your Lordships Servant
John Murray

I have sent Plutarch &c[4]

Notes to Letter 157)

1. On Tuesday 19 June JM had received *Sardanapalus*, which B had sent on 31 May saying it was written 'in a rough hand – perhaps Mrs. Leigh can help you to decypher it. – You will please to acknowledge it by *return* of post' (*BLJ* VIII, 128).

2. B wrote to Kinnaird on 31 May telling him he had sent *Sardanapalus* to JM and asking him to read it (*BLJ* VIII, 129). Accordingly, Kinnaird asked JM on 19 June to transmit it to him, and told B on 26 June that he had read 'the two first acts' (MA). Hobhouse mentions nothing about *Sardanapalus* in his Journal at the time, nor did he say anything to B about it until 12 August when he told him that to his 'poor way of thinking' he did not like it 'as well as the Doge & certainly it will not do so well for acting' (*BB*, 314).

3. B followed this direction when returning the proofs of *Sardanapalus* and enclosing *The Two Foscari* on 14 July: 'According to yr. wish I have expedited by this post two packets addressed to J. Barrow Esqre. Admiralty &c.' (*BLJ* VIII, 151; see also, Letter 159, n. 1 below).

4. In his letter of 28 May, B had asked JM to send him '"*Wrangham's*" reformation of "*Langhorne's Plutarch*"' (*BLJ* VIII, 127). A second edition of the Rev. Francis Wrangham's revised and corrected edition of John and William Langhorne's *Plutarch's Lives, translated from the Original Greek; with Notes Critical and Historical, and a Life of Plutarch*, 6 vols, was published corporately by JM and others in 1813; B never mentions having received the work, nor does it appear in his Sale Catalogue (1827). In the same letter he had also requested 'a life published some years ago of the *Magician Apollonius* of T[yana] ... & I think edited or written by what "Martin Marprelate" calls "*a bouncing priest*"' (*BLJ* VIII, 127). 'Martin Marprelate' was the *nom de guerre* under which a group of fanatical Puritans wrote anti-episcopalian pamphlets in 1589–90. B's source would have been D'Israeli, to whom he had only recently dedicated *Some Observations* (1820; see *CMP*, 88): 'They declared their works were "printed in Europe, not far from some of the bouncing Priests;" or they were "printed over sea, in Europe, within two furlongs of a bouncing Priest, at the cost and charges of Martin Mar-prelate, Gent."' (*Calamities of Authors*, 2 vols [1812], II, 7–8; D'Israeli gives a fuller account of the Marprelate Controversy in his *Quarrels of Authors*, 3 vols [1814], III, 201–82). B's 'bouncing priest' was the Rev. Edward Berwick (b. 1750), classical scholar and Vicar of Leixlip in Ireland, whose *The Life of Apollonius of Tyana, translated from the Greek of Philostratus. With Notes and Illustrations* was published by T. Payne in 1809.

Though reviewed somewhat tepidly by Thomas Middleton in the *Quarterly Review*, III, vi (May 1810), 417–31, it remained the first and only full English translation of the work until 1912. Berwick had in fact offered it to B when, writing to JM on 22 September 1813 to thank him for a letter which had been franked by B ('an autograph of Lord Byron has its value in this country – for we look on him as the Most original poet of the age'), he asked him to ask B, 'if he had ever looked into my life of Apollonius – I am inclined to think he would be amused with it – & if he wished to have it – I should feel honoured in his accepting it from me' (MS Bodleian, Dep. Lovelace Byron 155, f. 15); but there is no indication that JM ever communicated this to B. According to Philostratus, Apollonius was a Pythagorean philosopher gifted with miraculous and prophetic powers who flourished during the first century AD. He travelled throughout Asia and the East teaching and healing and leading the exemplary life of an ascetic. His cult was celebrated at his birthplace of Tyana in Cappadocia, and in the later struggle between paganism and Christianity his life was held up as the counterpart to that of Christ. However, by translating the whole, and without disputing whether or not Apollonius was, as he had been considered during his lifetime and subsequently by Origen and others, a 'false prophet' and 'celebrated magician', Berwick aimed to expose what he regarded as the 'uncandid insinuation' fostered especially by Gibbon that Philostratus himself had written the life as a counterblast to Christianity (*Life of Apollonius*, v–ix). B repeated his request on 9 October 1821 and the volume forms lot 157 in his Sale Catalogue (1827) (*BLJ* VIII, 238, and *CMP*, 251).

Letter 158)   [Tuesday] 24 July 1821

London July 24 – 1821

Dear Lord Byron

I have this instant received your Letters of July 6. 7 – & on Saturday I got one of the 29th June[1] – You ought not to be angry that I addressed the Newspaper extracts to you addressed to Mr Hoppner – for my intention was well designed – & I have no doubt yet of its safe delivery – One parcel wch you missed before I applied about & paid 18/ & they said it would be forwarded[2] – Don Juan is now printed and I will cancel the leaf containing the Stanza wch your letter desires[3] – & publish immediately – I have sent you <a> the first rough Copy in a parcel (wch goes tomorrow) with Soda powders[4] –

It is a most infamous trick of Valpy to write to get Pamphlets gratis to sell for his own advantage[5] – & Mr Stockdale who wishes to sell you Justice is a compleat a S. — l as ever breathed[6] – Shall I now print the Hints & Pulci anonymously – Gifford does not like the Hints & so let them take their chance[7] –

I have just received the inclosed letter from M[r] Moore[8] – the Subject of it is every way worthy of your Lordship's usual liberality – & I had not a moments hesitation in acceeding [sic] to a proposal which enabled me in any way to join in assisting so excellent a fellow – I have told him <t> wch I suppose your Lordship will think fair that he should give me all additions that you may from time to time make – & in case of survivorship he Should edit the whole – & I will leave it as an Heir loom to my Son – please to return so curiously a valuable and honourable a Letter –

I wonder that yr Lordship has not received the Proofs of Sardanapaulus [sic] – Shall we publish the New Tragedy & it in one Volume[9] – their Stories will form a fine contrast –

I have written to acceed [sic] to M[r] Moores proposal[10] –

I remain
Dear Lord Byron
Your grateful
& faithful Servant
John Murray

Notes to Letter 158)

Cover: Milord/Milord Byron/Poste Restante/Ravenna/Italie

Between the preceding Letter (157) and the present Letter (158) JM must have written again; but his letter is no longer extant; see Letter 161, n. 2 below.

1. B's letters of 29 June, which JM would have received on Saturday 21 July, and 6 and 7 July (*BLJ* VIII, 144–45, 147–48 and 149).

2. For the parcels in question, see Letter 156 above. At the end of his letter of 29 June, B had said crossly that the 'packet or letter you addressed to Mr. H[oppner] has never arrived & never will. – You should address directly to *me here* & by the *post*'; and he reiterated this even more threateningly at the close of his letter of 6 July. It seems to have arrived on 9 July when B wrote tersely: 'I have at length received your packet' (*BLJ* VIII, 145, 148 and 150; see also, Letter 161 below).

3. In his letter of 6 July, B had told JM that in accordance with Hobhouse's wishes he would omit 'the Stanza upon the *horse* of *Semiramis*' (*BLJ* VIII, 147). This was stanza 61 of *DJ* V which was not printed in the first edition – its absence being indicated on p. 165 by its number ('LXI') followed by a blank stanza whose opening and closing lines are represented by asterisks. The so-called 'first issue of the first edition', which B gave to Joseph Mawman, is an entire misnomer: this was never published (see Letter 159,

n. 4 below). When B later complained to Kinnaird of the misprints and other liberties JM had taken with his text, he specifically excluded from his complaints the stanza 'upon the Queen – *that* I *ordered* to be omitted at Hobhouse's desire'; and Hobhouse himself writing on 12 August told B it was 'very kind & considerate of you to leave out about Semiramis & her Courier' (*BLJ* VIII, 194 and *BB*, 315; cf. *CPW* V, 693–95 and 708).

4. B had asked for soda powders again in his letter of 6 July (*BLJ* VIII, 148).

5. Abraham John Valpy (1787–1854), publisher and the proprietor of the *Pamphleteer*, had written to B on 25 April asking him permission to republish his Bowles/Pope *Letter* in the next number of the *Pamphleteer* (MA). In his letter to JM of 19 May, B said he was enclosing Valpy's letter as it was for him to answer; but perhaps he forgot to enclose it as he seems to have sent it in his letter of 7 July (*BLJ* VIII, 118 and 149; see also, n. 6 below; his *Letter* was not reprinted in the *Pamphleteer*).

6. 'S. — l' stands for 'Scoundrel'. JM takes great umbrage at what B treats lightheartedly. In his letter of 7 July, he had enclosed 'two letters from two of yr. professional brethren' (one of whom must have been Valpy; see n. 5 above): 'By one of them you will perceive that if you are disposed to "*buy justice*" it is to be sold (no doubt as "*Stationary*") at his Shop. – – Thank him in my name for his good will – however – and good offices – and say that I *can't* afford to "purchase justice" – as it is by far the dearest article in these very dear times' (*BLJ* VIII, 149). The letter was from John Joseph Stockdale (1770–1847), later the publisher of Harriette Wilson's *Memoirs* (1825), who had written to B from 33 Pall Mall on 1 June saying that it had long seemed strange to him that among B's 'numberless readers, none <of> should have taken up the pen of vindication': 'Indeed I am surprised that Murray himself should not, were it necessary, have <u>bought</u> [B's underlining] that Justice <to>for your lordship's fame.' He had therefore 'stepped forward' to supply the deficiency, and enclosed a Newspaper of which he was 'half-proprietor, ... sometimes Editor & frequently a correspondent'. In a postscript he said he 'was too late for the Mail' and had therefore sent 'another inclosure', adding: 'I do not consider D. <as> a very formidable Antagonist' (MA; I regret that 'D.' remains unidentified).

7. Replying to this on 13 August, B merely reminded JM to omit from *Hints from Horace* all that touched on Jeffrey and the *Edinburgh Review*: 'Your late mistake about the Kelso-woman induces me to remind you of this – which I appended to your power of Attorney six years ago' (*BLJ* VIII, 178; see also, Letter 138, n. 9, Letter 140, n. 8, and Letter 154, n. 3 above; for the 'power of Attorney', see *CMP*, 218 and 543–45).

8. Moore's letter is not extant; but B had written to him as early as 9 December 1820 suggesting he might try making something of the memoirs '*now* in the way of *reversion*': 'Would not Longman or Murray advance you a certain sum *now*, pledging themselves *not* to have them published till after *my* decease ...?'

(*BLJ* VII, 244). Clearly Moore's letter was couched in these terms (see n. 10 below). Returning it to JM on 10 August 1821, B said: 'Your conduct to Mr. Moore is certainly very handsome', and agreed to the 'additions, &c ... and any continuation'. He added that he would rather be edited by Moore than any one else, saying he thought his letter 'very creditable to him, and you, and me' (*BLJ* VIII, 176–77).

9. B had asked JM 'to forward the proofs of "Sardanapalus" as soon as you can' in his letter of 29 June, by which time they were already on their way (*BLJ* VIII, 144; see Letter 157 above). On 6 July, B told JM that he was 'in the *fifth* act of a play on the subject of the Foscaris – father and son. – Foscolo can tell you their story' (*BLJ* VIII, 147).

10. In his Journal for Friday 27 July 1821, Moore records receiving 'a letter from Murray consenting to give me Two thousand guineas for Lord Byron's memoir's [*sic*], on condition that in case of survivorship, I should consent to be the Editor' (Moore, *Journal*, II, 472; see also, n. 8 above).

Letter 159) [Tuesday] 31 July 1821

London July 31 – 1821

Dear Lord Byron

I have great satisfaction in announcing the safe arrival of the Proof Sheets of Sardanapalus and the MSS of the new Tragedy[1] – I have sent the latter – within an hour of its arrival to day, to the printer and I hope to send a proof of a portion of it by fridays Post – & I will give another copy of it to our old friend Mr Gifford who is now at Ramsgate –

I hope you will not be angry at a liberty which I have ventured to take in retaining until I can be favoured with your Lordships reiterated [*sic*] commands – the Letter – however trifling its Contents may be wch may connect your name with that of J. J. Stockdale – who is a very wretch and not by the possibility of any accident – do you otherwise than discredit – I entreat you let me put it into the fire – or into my collections[2] –

I sent you the first Sheets of Don Juan which is now ready to be published on Wednesday[3] – the Stanza is cancelled – in all the other Copies[4] – I am sorry that your ardour for the Compleation of this poem has been so frequently damped[5] –

Holmes is so great a man with the King & has so much occupation here that he can not venture to travel[6] –

I inclose a letter which I have just received from James Smith[7]

I remain Dearest Sir
Your Lordships
faithful Servant
John Murray

Notes to Letter 159)

Cover: Milord/Milord Byron/poste restante/Ravenna/Italie <u>arrived</u>: Forli 16?
August

1. B had sent *The Two Foscari* and returned the proofs of *Sardanapalus* in 'two
   packets addressed to J. Barrow Esqre. Admiralty &c.' on 14 July (*BLJ* VIII,
   151; see also, Letter 157 above).

2. See Letter 158, n. 6 above. This is curious. When sending Stockdale's letter,
   B had asked JM merely to thank him 'in my name'; yet replying to JM's
   present request on 16 August he said: 'You may do what you will with my
   answer to Stockdale − of whom I know nothing − but answered his letter
   civilly − you may open it − & burn it or not − as you please. − It contains
   nothing of consequence to any-body. − How should I − or at least *was* I then
   to know that he was a rogue? − I am not aware of the histories of London
   and it's inhabitants' (*BLJ* VIII, 181). This suggests that B himself replied to
   Stockdale and enclosed it to JM when sending Stockdale's letter to him, but
   no such reply survives nor does any appear in *Stockdale's Budget* (1826–27);
   JM must have 'put it into the fire' rather than into his 'collections'.

3. That is, Wednesday 8 August, but in fact published on Tuesday 7 August
   (see Letter 160, n. 3 below).

4. For the cancellation of *DJ* V, 61, see Letter 158, n. 3 above. This would
   confirm that 'the Sheets of Don Juan' that JM was now sending did not
   represent the contents of the first edition as published: in effect they form a
   final proof before copy. This was what B gave Joseph Mawman on his way
   through Ravenna on 1 September with an inscription requesting him 'to
   show this copy to the publisher and to point out the gross printer's blunders',
   to which JM evidently took great exception (*BLJ* VIII, 196; see also, interim
   note below).

5. In his letter of 6 July, B had told JM that at Teresa's request he had 'promised
   not to continue Don Juan' and he could therefore look upon *DJ* III–V 'as
   the last of that poem' (*BLJ* VIII, 147). See also, *LBLI*, 288–91 and 595–96.

6. B had asked JM as early as March 1821 to ask Holmes to come out and take
   the pictures of Allegra and Teresa, 'and the head of a peasant Girl − which
   latter would make a study for Raphael' (*BLJ* VIII, 95). He told Kinnaird on
   8 June that JM had never answered his request, and reiterated it to JM on 14
   June (*BLJ* VIII, 135 and 136). He was not pleased with this response; replying

to JM on 16 August, he said, 'I regret that Holmes can't or won't come – it is rather shabby – as I was always very civil & punctual with him – but he is but one rascal more – one meets with none else, amongst the English' (*BLJ* VIII, 181; see also, Letter 162, n. 7 below). Holmes was friendly with George IV partly on account of his musical accomplishments for which he was dubbed 'the King's hobby'.

7. James Smith, co-author with his brother of the *Rejected Addresses* (1812). His letter is not extant; but B returned it to JM on 16 August asking him to thank Smith 'for his good opinion' – which 'opinion' may have concerned B's Bowles/Pope *Letter* in which B had alluded good-naturedly to the 'Authors of the "Rejected Addresses"' and to 'the "Rejected Addresses" Scene in 1812' (*BLJ* VIII, 182, and *CMP*, 145 and 146).

Letter 160)   [Wednesday] 8 August 1821

London Aug. 8
1821

Dearest Sir

I now send your Lordships [*sic*] two Acts of "the Foscari" & I have inclosed a duplicate to Mr Gifford at Ramsgate – hear what a critical friend says[1]

"Never mind his plays not being Stage-worthy: in these times, it signifies not much – but he has the true dramatic turn, & fails only in his plots. If he could but get a little into the bustle of our old dramatists, absurd as it sometimes was, it would do:– otherwise he must die a martyr to his simplicity or singleness. I profess myself much taken with the gay & sprightly dialogue of Sardanapalus – we have had very little like it since Fletcher & Shirley. They would however have crowded the canvas more – After all he is a wonderful creature – if I had him, I would keep him up carefully, & shew him only on high days and holydays."

Don Juan was published yesterday[2] – and as far as I have yet heard – it is said to contain most splendid passages –

The Two Tragedies will make a handsome & interesting Volume – not much larger & not to sell for more than the Doge – & may I have them for a Thousand Guineas? – And for the 3. 4 & 5th Canto [*sic*] of Don Juan which I have printed only in the sizes sent to your Lordships [*sic*][3] will you accept Another Thousand Guineas[4] –

The Queen died last night – <G> The Lord have Mercy on her Soul[5] –

God Bless your Lordship prayeth thy dutiful Servant
John Murray

Notes to Letter 160)

1. JM's 'critical friend' and Gifford were one and the same person. Writing to JM from Ramsgate on 4 August, Gifford remarked: 'Lord Byron will have a pretty collection of dramas by & by – Let him proceed, he will do something at last. Never mind his plays not being stage-worthy; in these times, it signifies not much – but he has the true dramatic turn, & fails only in his plots. If he could but get a little into the bustle of our old dramatists, absurd as it sometimes was, it would do: otherwise he must die a martyr to his simplicity and singleness. I profess myself much taken with the gay & sprightly dialogue of the last [*Sardanapalus*] – We have had very little like it since Fletcher & Shirley. They would however, have crowded the canvass [*sic*] more. – After all he is a wonderful creature – if I had him, I would keep him up carefully, & shew him only on high-days and holydays' (MA; cf. Smiles, I, 412). B replied on 23 August: 'Your friend – like the public is not aware that my dramatic Simplicity is *studiously* Greek – & must continue so – *no* reform ever succeeded at first. – – I admire the old English dramatists – but this is quite another field – & has nothing to do with theirs. – I want to make a *regular* English drama – no matter whether for the Stage or not – which is not my object – but a *mental theatre*' (*BLJ* VIII, 186–87; see also, n. 4 below).

2. That is, Tuesday 7 August. The story retailed by Smiles, and unfortunately repeated by Prothero and Marchand, as to 'parcels of books' being 'given out of the window' of Albemarle Street, 'in answer' to the 'obstreperous demands' of 'booksellers' messengers', is quite unsubstantiated (Smiles, I, 413, Prothero, V, 351n, and *BLJ* VIII, 193n.)

3. *DJ* III–V, the last Cantos of the poem to be published by JM, appeared anonymously together in a single volume octavo; no quarto edition was issued.

4. B sent this letter to Kinnaird on 23 August saying: 'I have received the enclosed proposal from Mr. Murray which I can *not* accept. – – He offers me for *all* – the sum he once offered for <separate> two cantos of D[on] Juan. – I will accept nothing of the kind – unless he advances very considerably, [or] – unless the things have completely failed … With regard to what his friend says of "Simplicity" – I study to be so. – It is an experiment whether the English *Closet* – or *mental* theatre will or will not bear a *regular* drama instead of the melo-drama. – – Murray's offer falls short by *one half* of the fair proposal' (*BLJ* VIII, 185; see also, n. 1 above). To JM himself, however, on the same date B replied superbly in verse and prose saying he should arrange the matter with Kinnaird: 'To him you can state all your mercantile

reasons which you might not like to state to me personally – such as "heavy season" ["]flat public" "don't go off" – ["]Lordship writes too much – Won't take advice – declining popularity – deductions for the trade – make very little – generally lose by him – pirated edition – foreign edition – severe criticisms. &c.["] with other hints and howls for an oration – which I leave Douglas who is an orator to answer' (*BLJ* VIII, 187; see also, *BLJ* VIII, 191).

5. The Queen died at 10.25 p.m. on Tuesday 7 August 1821. B replied on 23 August: 'I am sorry for the Queen – and that's more than you are' (*BLJ* VIII, 187).

Letter 161)   [Sunday] 12 August 1821

Cheltenham
Aug. 12. 1821

Most dear Sir

I have this day received your Lordships most obliging Letter[1] with a packet inclosing notes for Sardanapalus & the Foscari, which go immediately to the printer. As your Lordship so particularly desires the immediate publication of these two tragedies it shall be done – at present Drury Lane Theatre – the most ravenous – is opened – for the summer Season – & therefore I presume that I am acting according to the spirit of your Lordships wishes, in having the plays ready to put forth as soon as both Theatres are closed[2] – I told your Lordship in my last what M^r G – had said privately to me about Sardanapalus[3] – <Of> The two first Acts of the Foscari – he thinks have more life than the first Doge – Mr Gifford is at Ramsgate – but it is doing him no good, and I begin to entertain serious apprehensions about him[4] – and how I am to supply his place I know not in all my range of Literary acquaintances <I kn>There is not one that is the least like him in the union of so many & such variety of quallifications [*sic*] –

You think of leaving Ravenna & perhaps of quitting Italy; <and> indeed, after the State in which it is placed it has become almost necessary – but where does your Lordship think of taking up your abode?[5] is there any hope of your returning to England?

Hobhouse is revising his translation of Francisca di Rimini [*sic*] and I shall publish it with the original in the winter[6] – Did you read a paper in the Quarterly two or three Numbers back on Petrarch & how did you like it & the translations – the Article was by Foscolo & the versions by Lady Dacre[7] – the latter are thought to be particularly happy –

Then I am to understand that your Lordship has at length received my parcel of cuttings from the various Newspapers &c?[8] – I have sent you some Copies of Juan &c since.[9] – Our friend Hen. Matthews is just married & going out to Ceylon as a kind of a Judge with an appointment of £2000 certain & whatever he may make by practice[10] – You have charmed one or two Americans whom you have admitted to your acquaintance & attentions[11] – Irving who has lately returned from france, read me a letter from one – they are improving in Education & its consequence Manners – with great strides – & the urbanity of Irvings Mind is delightful – He is preparing two new Volumes[12] – Milman has also another Drama, which I expect to receive from him in a Week.[13]

I expect every day to receive your Lordships Busts which are now in the River[14] – Chantry [sic] has made a most exquisite one of Scott[15] – I had the good fortune to sit by Sir W Scott in the Hall during the Coronation – a Sight wch I would not have Missed for any thing – & he declared it had infinitely surpassed all that he could have conceived possible[16] – Scott never ceases to talk of you with the most firm regard –

I am here – for a month – on account of my wifes health which has been precarious since her late severely [sic] & dangerous illness[17] – – I suspect that Drury Lane will not close as it has within these ten days only – presented a most superb imitation of the Coronation[18] – at a most enormous expense – & it will require a Month to repay them – & [sic] Queens death too interfered & every body has escaped from town – Copleston is here & Professor Monk[19]

I have great doubts if Heber will succeed in his election for Oxford – Sir Jno Nichol his opponent is a violent Anti-Catholic[20] – & vigourously [sic] supported by the bigoted in this way & by the Ld Chancellor & his brother.

I remain Dear Lord Byron
Your grateful & faithful Servt
Jno Murray

Notes to Letter 161)

Cover: Milord/Milord Byron/poste restante/Ravenna/Italie

1. JM had received B's letter of 22 July informing him that by that post he had 'expedited a parcel of notes – addressed to J. Barrow Esqre. &c.' (*BLJ* VIII, 155).

2. JM understood B's wishes very well. In his letter of 22 July, B had said: 'I *oppose* the "delay till Winter" – I am particularly anxious to print while the *Winter theatres* are *closed* – to gain time in case they try their former piece of

politeness' (*BLJ* VIII, 155; '"delay till Winter"' evidently echoes JM's use of the phrase and indicates, as does other evidence elsewhere, that one of JM's letters is missing; B sent it to Kinnaird on 23 July [*BLJ* VIII, 158]; see also, headnote to Letter 158 above). In this same letter B told JM to 'publish the two tragedies ... together'; but by 10 September he had completed *Cain* and sent it saying: 'If *there is time* – publish it with the other *two*'; and thus the three were published later in the year (*BLJ* VIII, 157 and 205).

3. See Letter 160, n. 1 above; JM gives the game away as to the identity of his 'critical friend'. In fact Gifford said rather more than what JM chooses to tell B. Writing to JM at Cheltenham on 7 August from Ramsgate, he asked: 'What can Lord Byron propose to himself by forcing the publication of these cantos [*DJ* III–V]? They will not add to his fame; and this is what he should now take care of. Our friend Sir Walter [Scott], makes an occasional sacrifice – but then he has a powerful motive: and besides, though he may play with his talents, he never trifles with his character. I could say more, but alas! cui bono? [what's the use?] You forgot to put up the revise of the Assyrian monarch [*Sardanapalus*]. The two acts of Foscari have more life than the other Doge; but these are tame & stiffly measured lines, which might be wished away. Our old poets, and even Massinger, did not always make the end of one speech, & the beginning of another a metrical line, as Lord Byron does – sometimes very feebly. I have said something of this in the second Edition of Massinger' (MA; cf. Smiles, I, 422; Gifford discusses these technicalities in the 'Advertisement' to *The Plays of Philip Massinger*, 4 vols, 2nd edn [1813], I, xxiv–xxviii). Writing again to JM in Cheltenham from Ramsgate on Tuesday 15 August, Gifford animadverted once more on the publication of *DJ* III–V: 'I knew Lord Byron would not be satisfied till he saw himself in print. He must occupy the public eye, & all that his friends have to lament is that his taste of fame is so indiscriminate. I have often heard Lord Grosvenor say, when a young man, that he did not know the difference between bull-beef [*sic*] & a delicate loin of veal! – Lord Byron's case is worse' (MA; cf. Smiles, I, 422).

4. Gifford, who had gone to Ramsgate in early July and remained until late August, was very far from well and never fully recovered; he was feverish, had a facial complaint and was experiencing breathing difficulties: 'The few teeth I have seem taking their leave – I wish they would take a French one; and after so long an acquaintance they do not like to part without pain' (see Smiles, II, 54–56). B was too angry to allude to Gifford's health until 4 September when he wrote: 'Let me hear that Gifford is *better* – he can't be spared either by you or me' (*BLJ* VIII, 198; see also, n. 17 below).

5. In his letter of 22 July, B had said that the government had 'exiled about a thousand people of the best families all over the Roman States': 'As many of my friends are amongst them – I think of moving too – but not till I have had your answers – continue *your address* to me *here* as usual – & quickly'; replying to JM's present query on 4 September, B told him he was 'going

to *Pisa* in a few weeks', but to address to him '*here*' (Ravenna) (*BLJ* VIII, 156 and 197–98). In an unpublished fragment in MA, which must have been written between 22 July and late August, B repeated his directions:

> When you write – direct here as usual – I have no idea of returning to England without some strong provocation. – – – I shall prob-ably go into Tuscany – but do you still address here – till you know further. – – I had some things – books – coins – &ᶜ. which I wanted to send – (if you chose to accept them) but have no safe opportunity – till I light upon a traveller of trust=worthiness. – – –

The 'traveller of trust=worthiness', as B told JM on 4 September, would have been Joseph Mawman had not B by the time of his visit already packed his 'books & every thing' ready for Pisa: 'It regretted me ... I could not send you a few things I meant for you but they were all sealed & baggaged – so as to have made it a Month's work to get at them again' (*BLJ* VIII, 197; for Joseph Mawman, see Letter 159, n. 4 above, and Interim Note below).

6. Hobhouse had written to JM on 8 August saying he would write out his translation of Francesca da Rimini for him so that JM could show it to whom he pleased 'previously to publication', which he suggested 'had better wait until next season' (MA). He also wrote to B on 12 August saying that he was thinking of employing the recess 'in writing a little essay on Italian tragedy & appending it to a translation of Francesca da Rimini which if you recollect we began together at Milan – I wish you would help me ... Your opinion for instance of Alfieri's plays' (*BB*, 314–15; see also, Hobhouse's Journal entry for 22 October 1816: 'Byron and I translated part of "Francesca da Rimini"' [*Recollections*, II, 52]). It came to nothing; but this would explain why B told JM in his letter of 20 September: 'Hobhouse in his preface to "Rimini" will probably be better able to explain my dramatic system – than I could do – ... It is more upon the Alfieri School than the English' (*BLJ* VIII, 218).

7. Ugo Foscolo's review of Madame de Genlis's *Pétrarque et Laure* (1819) in the *Quarterly Review*, XXIV, xlviii (January [pub. April] 1821), 529–66, included three of Petrarch's sonnets translated by the poet and dramatist Barbarina Lady Dacre (formerly Mrs Wilmot), which were later collected with her many other translations from Petrarch in Vol. I, pp. 205–49 of her *Dramas, Translations and Occasional Poems*, which was printed privately in two volumes by JM in 1821. Foscolo also included all her Petrarch translations in Appendix VII (pp. 279–325) of his enlarged *Essays on Petrarch*, which was published by JM in 1823 and dedicated to Lady Dacre.

8. In his letter of 9 July, B told JM: 'I have at length received your packet' (*BLJ* VIII, 150; see also, Letter 158, n. 2 above).

9. B received these copies of *DJ* III–V on 31 August, and was outraged at the omissions, inaccuracies and carelessness in printing (*BLJ* VIII, 192–93; see also, Letter 163 below).

10. See Letter 131, n. 6 above. Henry Matthews was called to the Bar in 1821 and appointed Advocate-fiscal of Ceylon; he seems to have left England to take up the appointment in November (in his 'Advertisement' to the third edition of *The Diary of an Invalid*, 2 vols [1822], he states that he would have made 'greater use' of the 'opportunity for revisal and correction' were he not 'called away from the task of superintendence to a distant part of the globe'; this is dated 29 October 1821).

11. One of these Americans was Joseph Coolidge (1798–1879), a friend of Washington Irving's, who had visited B in Ravenna in June 1821 (see Letter 154, n. 3 above). B told Moore that he thought Coolidge 'a very pretty lad ... only somewhat too full of poesy and "entusymusy"': 'I was very civil to him during his few hours' stay, and talked with him much of Irving, whose writings are my delight. But I suspect that he did not take quite so much to me' (*BLJ* VIII, 146; see also, *BLJ* IX, 20–21).

12. Washington Irving left Paris for London on 11 July 1821 (Moore, *Journal*, II, 467). He was at work on his next novel *Bracebridge Hall*, which JM published in June 1822.

13. JM published Milman's *The Martyr of Antioch: A Dramatic Poem* in March 1822, and his *Belshazzar: A Dramatic Poem* in June 1822.

14. Thorwaldsen's bust of B was *on* the river at the Custom's House in Lower Thames Street (between London Bridge and Tower Bridge) (see Letters 162 and 163 below).

15. Francis (later Sir Francis) Chantrey (1781–1841), the sculptor, made his bust of Scott during Scott's visit to London in March 1820; but he added the finishing touches when Scott came to London for the Coronation in 1821. Writing to his wife in March 1820, Scott told her: 'Chantrey's bust is one of the finest things he ever did. It is quite the fashion to go to see it'; and Chantrey himself later told Peel that 'about forty-five casts were disposed of among the poet's most ardent admirers' (Lockhart, *Life of Scott*, 425–26, 457 and 763). One of those lucky 'ardent admirers' was JM, whose copy now stands in 50 Albemarle Street (see Letter 162 below).

16. Scott does not mention sitting by JM during the Coronation, but the day after it (20 July) he sent his exuberant 'Eye-Witness' account of the ceremony to the Editor of the *Edinburgh Weekly Journal* from where it was reprinted in *The Gentleman's Magazine*, XCI, Pt II (August 1821), 107–10 (see also, Lockhart, *Life of Scott*, 454–56, and Scott, *Letters*, VI, 494–502).

17. Annie's 'illness' after William's stillbirth (see Letter 156, n. 12 above). B replied on 9 September: 'Let me hear that Gifford is better & your family well' (*BLJ* VIII, 204; see also, Letter 162, n. 11 below).

18. JM was quite right: Drury Lane Theatre did not close at all for the whole winter. On Wednesday 1 August it mounted *The Coronation* (a '*fac-simile*'

of the ceremony itself), which ran as an afterpiece for every single night until Saturday 10 November and was greeted with universal acclamation: 'it is one of the most, if not the most, magnificent spectacles ever witnessed on the boards of either of the Winter Theatres' (*London Chronicle*, CXXX, 9771 [Thursday 2-Friday 3 August 1821], 114); it 'does more credit to the liberality, the taste, and the powers of Drury-lane, than any thing we have witnessed in it since it was built' (*The Literary Gazette*, 237 [Saturday 4 August 1821], 493–94); the banqueting-scene in particular was 'one of the most superb scenes ever exhibited in a theatre' (*The Times*, Thursday 2 August 1821). See also, *The Gentleman's Magazine*, XCI, Pt II (August 1821), 174.

19. Edward Copleston (1776–1849), Provost of Oriel College, Oxford and later (1828–49) Bishop of Llandaff, was a contributor to the *Quarterly Review*. For Professor Monk, see Letter 70, n. 2 above.

20. The seat for the University of Oxford had become vacant when the Lord Chancellor's elder brother Sir William Scott (1745–1836), the sitting MP since 1801, was created Baron Stowell in 1821. It was contested by Richard Heber and Sir John Nicholl (1759–1838), who was strongly opposed to Roman Catholic Emancipation. After some rancorous electioneering, voting took place on Wednesday 22 August when Heber won by a majority of 93 (*The Gentleman's Magazine*, XCI, Pt II [August 1821], 103–04). See also Letter 162, n. 15 below.

Letter 162)   [Thursday] 6 September 1821

Cheltenham
Sepr. 6 – 1821

Most dear Sir

I am much delighted by your Lordships kind letter of the 16th Aug. which allows me to hope that your rage against me has abated[1] – the same post brings me a letter from town in answer to my constant enquiries after the Bust[2] "The Busts of Lord B are arrived – the Ship is now under quarantine [*sic*] – I inclose an order for their delivery for you to sign" – so that I expect to find them on my return – it is curious that after waiting for this bust for years it should at length arrive in the same week with one of Sir Walter Scott (a <bus> very fine bust) which Chantry [*sic*] (whom Moore can tell you, your Lordship would be Delighted to know) has obligingly presented to me[3] – Stockdale shall not have the honour of your correspondence whilst it is in my power to prevent it.[4]

Proofs of the whole of the Foscari have been forwarded to your

Lordship during my absence[5] – Copies have also been sent to M^r
Gifford – who will tell me on Monday when I shall be in town,
what he thinks of it – Sardanapalus is already half set up in the
regular 8vo form – I will send you revises of the Hints &c for fear of
error[6] –

Dont be offended with Holmes, you were of great essential service in
putting him the way [sic] to make a livelihood, but it is very long before
in his profession, he can gain one – if you wanted me to come out to
you it would be very different[7] – Neither be thou afraid of our funds
breaking – when they go – there will be so many on the highway that
a Noble free booter will have a bad chance[8] – I bet Sixpence they last
our time – I will send your thanks to James Smith – who will be much
pleased.[9]

Many persons besides your Lordship have at first supposed that I
was the person of the same name connected with the Constitutional
Association[10] – but without consideration for on what occasion have I
identified myself with a party – I have studiously avoided every party
publication & this more strenuously every year and my connexions
are I believe even more numerous amongst the Whigs than the Tories
– indeed the Whigs have nearly driven away the Tories from my room
– and Jeffray [sic] said "if you wish to meet the most respectable of Whe
[sic] Whigs you must be introduced to Mr Murrays room [sic] –

You hint that I am a little ungrateful to you, I think – but upon my
soule [sic] you will find that my occasional apparent inattention arises
from no causes but constitutional indolence – & now distaction [sic]
from having so many correspondents – & such incessant interruption to
my writing to them – but in essentials I trust you can never find me
wanting.[11]

I forgot in my former letter to notice a hint in yours respecting
an additional sum to Mr Moore – the purchase wch I have made of
the Memoirs is perfectly con amore[12] – as a matter of mere business
if I placed the £2000 in the funds (supposing they did not break)
in 14 Years (the least annuity value of the Autors [sic] life) it would
become 4000£ & so on – Moore should not shew the Memoirs to any
one – now, I think[13] –

Gifford always mentions you with unabated regard[14] as do Scott
– Rose &c &c

Heber (Rich^d) has succeeded in his long desired election for
Oxford[15] –

The Jerseys are gone abroad – to resuscitate[16]

Did you receive a Copy of Richardetto [sic] Canto I – translated – &
presented to your Lordship by Lord Glenbervie?[17]

I have sent the <u>Blue Stockings</u> to amuse M^r G – & it shall be forwarded in proof on my return – – if you had the <u>local</u> knowledge – it would become an excellent moreceau [*sic*]^18

Accept my very kindest compliments and be assured that I always am Dearest Lord Byron

Your Lordships

faithful servant

John Murray

Notes to Letter 162)

<u>Cover</u>: Milord/Milord Byron/poste restante/Ravenna/Italie <u>arrived</u>: Forli 20? September

1. In the postscript to his letter of 7 August, B had said: 'I am extremely angry with *you* – I beg leave to add for several reasons too long for present explanation'; and again, in his letter of 10 August: 'Your conduct to Mr. Moore is certainly very handsome; and I would not say so if I could help it, for you are not at present by any means in my good graces' (*BLJ* VIII, 173 and 176). On 16 August, however, he was rather more merciful: 'You are very good as times go – and would probably be still better but for "the March of events" (as Napoleon called it) which won't permit anybody to be better than they should be' (*BLJ* VIII, 182, quoting Napoleon's letter to Tsar Alexander of 2 February 1808: 'Il est de la sagesse et de la politique de faire ce que le destin ordonne et d'aller où la marche irrésistible des événements nous conduit' [It is wise and politic to do what Destiny ordains and to follow whither the irresistible march of events leads us]).

2. See Letter 161 above and Letter 163 below.

3. See Letter 161, n. 15 above. Moore and Chantrey were very friendly; they had dined and visited galleries together in Rome and Paris in 1819 (see Moore, *Journal*, I, 240–68 *passim*).

4. See Letter 158, n. 6, and Letter 159, n. 2 above.

5. In his letter of 13 August, B said he was expecting 'with anxiety the proofs of the two Foscaris', which he was still awaiting 'with proper impatience' on 16 August (*BLJ* VIII, 178 and 181). He had certainly received, 'corrected' and 'returned them to England' by 13 September (*BLJ* VIII, 208; see also, *CPW* VI, 625–26).

6. JM is being very cautious; in his letter of 13 August, B had merely wished to 'remind' him to '*omit* all that could touch upon Jeffrey' in *Hints from Horace* (*BLJ* VIII, 178; see also, Letter 158, n. 7 above).

7. See Letter 159, n. 6 above. B did not respond to JM's tender for a similar offer; but in an undated fragment in MA, probably written on or shortly

after 20 October 1821 (cf. *BLJ* VIII, 245), he returned to Holmes, and to some other matters:

> What you say of Holmes hath in no degree softened me; – he was not asked to come without being <feed> paid for his trouble – a base Mechanic – – "painting the king" as you call it! – <why don't he white=wash him? he wants it –> paint a sepulchre – – why don't he white=wash him – he wants it. – – His Irish palace! at sixty – "Et Sepulchri immemor struis domos." – – – –
> Ask Moore (I sent it to Paris but he left it before) to shew you "the Irish Avatar" – a congratulatory poem on the late Irishisms. – – – – –
> It is by M^r. Bowles – & written for a bishopric. – – – – – – – – –
> Send me Scott's next novel. – –

The Irish Avatar was prompted by the craven reception George IV had been given by the Irish on his visit to Ireland in August 1821, and his own hypocritical conduct and speeches whilst there: hence B's allusion to Horace (*Odes*, II, xviii, 18–19: 'et sepulcri/immemor struis domos [and build a palace forgetful of the tomb]; cf. *DJ* V, 63), and to the 'whited sepulchres' of Matthew 23.27. He had sent the poem to Moore in Paris on 17 September (followed by an '"Addenda"' three days later), and sent a second copy for him to JM on 9 October. In both cases he employed the same jocular attribution to Bowles, though he gave JM the alternative of Felicia Hemans (*BLJ* VIII, 213, 219 and 236; see also, Letter 146, n. 6 above). Scott's 'next novel' was *The Pirate*, published on 24 December 1821, which B was still expecting on 27 January 1822, and which he never acknowledges receiving (*BLJ* IX, 87).

8. In his letter of 16 August, B had said he was 'in a [*sic*] great discomfort about the probable war' and his 'damned trustees' not getting him out of the funds, adding jocularly: 'If the funds break – it is my intention to go upon the highway – all the other English professions are at present so ungentlemanly by the conduct of those who follow them – that open robbery is the only fair resource left to any man of <honour> principles' (*BLJ* VIII, 182, corrected from MS MA).

9. See Letter 159, n. 7 above.

10. Apropos of JM's publishing *DJ* III–V, B had written on 16 August: 'an't you afraid of the Constitutional Association of Bridge street? – when first I saw the name of *Murray*, – I thought it had been yours – but was solaced by seeing that your [*sic*] Synonime is an Attorneo – and that you are not one of that atrocious crew' (*BLJ* VIII, 181–82; corrected from MS [MA]; see also, Prothero, V, 344n.–45n.) '"The Constitutional Association, for opposing the progress of disloyal and seditious principles"' (dubbed 'the Bridge Street Gang' by B [*BLJ* X, 98] and by *The Examiner*, 762 [Sunday 1 September 1822], 558), was a self-appointed watchdog committee whose secretary and solicitor was a Mr. Charles Murray. Since its formation in

December 1820, it had brought prosecutions for libel against a number of printers and booksellers for issuing lampoons, pamphlets and caricatures, and was to prosecute John Hunt in December 1823 for publishing *The Vision of Judgment* (see *CPW* VI, 671). It was welcomed by some (see, for example, *The Gentleman's Magazine*, XCI, Pt I [January–June 1821], 81 and 640), but not by others. *The Times* for Wednesday 23 May 1821, for instance, under the rubric 'Mock Constitutional Association', wrote scathingly: 'As some of our readers may not have heard of this "worshipful society," we may here mention that there [*sic*] are a set of persons calling themselves a constitutional association, who have instituted in their own names, or rather in their own behoof without names, prosecutions against certain individuals for the publication of libels. No matter who the persons prosecuted may be: tyranny never or but rarely makes its first essay upon unblemished characters.'

11. B seems to have responded to this in a postscript attached to his letter to JM of 12 September: 'you are the most ungrateful and ungracious of correspondents. – But there is some excuse for you – with your perpetual levee of politicians – parson-scribblers – & loungers – – some day I will give you a *poetical* Catalogue of them' (*BLJ* VIII, 207). The MSS of this letter and the postscript are in MA. The postscript is written on the inside of a separate sheet, which forms the cover of a letter that arrived in London on 8 October, only the day before the arrival on 9 October of B's letter of 20 September. From this and various other indications, it would appear that either the postscript does not belong to B's letter of 12 September, or else B posted the whole simultaneously with that of 20 September; see also, n. 15 below. (Incidentally, in the second line of the three additional lines to Eve's Ovidian curse in *Cain* [III, i, 441–43], which B enclosed in his letter of 12 September, 'thee' should read 'the<ir>e', and in the third line, 'light!' should read '<warmth!> light!'; these corrections are not reproduced in *BLJ* VIII, 206, nor are they recorded in *CPW* VI, 291. See Plate 16; see also, Andrew Nicholson, 'Byron and Ovid', *The Byron Journal*, 27 [1999], 77–78.)

12. See n. 1 above.

13. JM seems to be alluding to B's letter of 10 August in which B had said that if he ever consented to publication of his Memoirs he supposed JM would 'make Moore some advance, in proportion to the likelihood or non-likelihood of success. You are both sure to survive me however' (*BLJ* VIII, 177). Replying to JM's present remarks on 20 September, B directed him to letters and additional material in the care of Hobhouse and others; but perhaps more to JM's purpose wrote on 27 September: 'Moore & you can settle between you about the "Memoranda" – *I* can only do what I can to accommodate your arrangements – as fixed between you – which I shall do readily & Cheerfully' (*BLJ* VIII, 216–17 and 225). He did not comment on whether or not Moore should 'shew the Memoirs to any one – now' – Moore having allowed numerous people in Rome and Paris to read them,

many of whom had made copies.

14. For Gifford's most recent written remarks, see Letter 161, n. 3 above.

15. For Heber's success, see Letter 161, n. 20 above. B seems to have replied to this at the close of the postscript to his letter of 12 September: 'My Compliments to Mr. Heber upon his Election' (*BLJ* VIII, 207, and see n. 11 above; in the MS, this sentence does not form part of the postscript itself but is written on the outside of the cover above the seal).

16. The Jerseys had gone to Paris, where Moore first visited them when he returned there on Tuesday 13 November (Moore, *Journal*, II, 504). They had to 'resuscitate' from the strains of the Coronation, the death of the Queen and that of the Earl's mother, Frances Dowager Lady Jersey, at Cheltenham on 25 July (*The Gentleman's Magazine*, XCI, Pt II [August 1821], 180; see also, Ilchester, ed., *The Journal of the Hon. Henry Edward Fox*, 74–75 and 79).

17. Lord Glenbervie's *Translation from the Italian of Forteguerri of the First Canto of Ricciardetto; with an Introduction concerning the principal Romantic, Burlesque, and Mock-heroic Poets* was printed by Thomas Davison in 1821. It was unpublished and anonymous. This would explain why B replied to JM on 27 September: 'I thought Ricciardetto was *Rose's* – but pray thank Lord Glenbervie there*for*. – He is an old & kind friend of mine – if [it] be the *old* man you mean' (it was) (*BLJ* VIII, 224). The volume contains a number of references to B and an 'Additional Note', written in May 1821, in high praise of *The Prophecy of Dante*: 'Reader! if you have already had the delight of perusing the last productions of Lord *Byron's* Muse, how must you have admired those exquisitely poetical and affecting portraitures of *Ariosto* and *Tasso* which conclude the 3d Canto of the "Prophecy of *Dante*." We there see them contrasted without invidious comparison, or depreciation of the one to exalt the other; and characterized in numbers, style, and sentiment, so wonderfully *Dantesque*, that – mastering our uncongenial language, and habitual modes of thought as well as expression – they seem to have been inspired by the very genius of the "*inarrivabilé*" [unmatchable] *Dante* himself' (p. 93). The same note appears in pp. 106–07 of *The First Canto of Ricciardetto: translated from the Italian of Forteguerri: with an Introduction, concerning the principal Romantic, Burlesque, and Mock-heroic Poets; and Notes, Critical and Philological*, by Sylvester (Douglas) Lord Glenbervie, which was published by JM in 1822, and which B received on 18 April 1822 when he told JM: 'I have got Lord Glenbervie's book which is very amusing and able upon the topics which he touches upon – & part of the preface pathetic' (*BLJ* IX, 146). B's copy forms lot 71 in his Sale Catalogue (1827) (*CMP*, 248).

18. B had sent JM *The Blues* on 7 August saying it was 'a mere buffoonery' and that if published 'it must be *anonymously*'; it was 'too short for a separate publication', but JM could send him a proof of it if he thought it 'worth the

trouble' (*BLJ* VIII, 172). By '<u>local</u> knowledge' JM may mean Cheltenham specifically; whether or not this is the case, his implication is that he does not think much of the piece. B replied on 20 September telling him he 'need not send "the Blues"' and repeating that it was 'a mere buffoonery never meant for publication'; it was first published in 1823 in the third number of *The Liberal* (*BLJ* VIII, 216; see also, *CPW* VI, 664–65).

Letter 163)   [Friday] 28 September 1821

I will write fully by next post – but I would not lose a moment

London 28 Sepr. 1821

Dearest Sir

I have this instant arrived in town & find an accumulation of packets from your Lordship which I have just time merely to acknowledge – the last three containing the Tragedy of Cain has [*sic*] <th> come to hand this instant[1] – My Mind is filled with this subject wch I think most happily chosen & of which I form the very highest expectations – I will instantly send it to the printer & forward proofs to you.

Pray let me entreat you to trust to my honour about prices[2] –

The mistakes in printing Don Juan – I will prove to exist in the <u>MSS</u>[3] – & Hobhouse read every proof[4]

Moore is in town & incog – I have the precious Memoirs[5] –

Most faithfully your Lordships

obliged Servant

J. Murray

[On back cover] The Bust still detained at the Custom House[6]

Notes to Letter 163)

<u>Cover</u>: Milord/Milord Byron/poste restante/Ravenna/Italie <u>arrived</u>: Forli 18 October

1. For the superscription, see Letter 164, n. 8 below. JM had returned from Cheltenham to find several letters awaiting him, and *Cain* which B had sent in three packets on 10 September telling JM to send 'a proof of the whole by return of *post*' and to publish it 'with the other *two*' (*Sardanapalus* and *The Two Foscari*) if there was time (*BLJ* VIII, 205).

2. In his letter of 12 September, B remarked that JM would no doubt 'avoid saying any good of it [*Cain*] – for fear I should raise the price upon you

– that's right – stick to business!' (*BLJ* VIII, 206). Replying on 20 October, he stated: 'As to "*honour*" I will trust no man's honour in affairs of barter', and proceeded to tell JM why in almost exactly the same words he had used when writing to Kinnaird on 14 July (*BLJ* VIII, 153 and 244–45; see also, IX, 62).

3. Having received the published edition of *DJ* III–V on 31 August, B was enraged to find it 'printed so *carelessly* ... as to be disgraceful to me – & not creditable to you', and with omissions he had not sanctioned. He insisted (twice) that the whole 'be *gone over again* with the *Manuscript*' and that Hobhouse should 'correct the press': 'I copied the *Cantos* out carefully – so there is *no* excuse – as the Printer reads or at least *prints* the M.S.S. of the plays without error'. He ordered JM to 'Replace what is omitted – & correct what is so shamefully misprinted' and concluded: 'I am in such a humour about this printing of D[on] J[uan] so inaccurately – that I must close this' (*BLJ* VIII, 192–93). He wrote a little more coolly on 4 September (*BLJ* VIII, 197–98). The misprints chiefly affected Canto V from which also were omitted stanza 158 and the long note to stanza 147 (for which, see *CPW* V, 291 and 710–13 respectively, and Letter 164, n. 3 below).

4. Hobhouse, having heard either from Kinnaird or JM himself, wrote to B on 24 September: 'You complain of faults in the last cantos of the Don. I looked over the proofs but not with the manuscript before me – Some difficult passages I did see but imputed that circumstance to a certain habitude of my own rather than to a printer's blunder, but I did not see any thing very outrageous. As to leaving out passages I made one or two pencil marks concluding the proofs would go to you previously to publication, but I presume that my desperate hooks have not slashed out any of your good things. If this enormity has been committed some other hand has, I should think, been at work; for I too well know your paternal propensities to interfere in the last instance with your offspring' (*BB*, 317; see also, *BLJ* VIII, 194–95).

5. Moore had arrived in London from Paris on Tuesday 25 September. He was 'incog' to avoid creditors, and had even bought 'a pair of mustachios, by advice of the women, as a mode of disguising myself in England' (*Journal*, II, 486). He had seen JM on Thursday 27 September who 'agreed to all my arrangements about the payment of the sum for the Memoirs' and 'took away the MS.'. (Bearing in mind that JM had clearly read the whole of B's Alpine Journal [see Letter 99, n. 4 above], it is hardly credible that he would not also have read 'the precious Memoirs' now that they were in his possession, despite his claim at the time of their destruction that he had 'scrupulously refrained from looking into' them [Smiles, I, 448].) Moore also noted that JM 'says that Lord Bs. two last Tragedies (Sardanapalus & Foscari) are worth nothing – that nobody will read them – offered Lord B. £1000 for the continuation of Don Juan & the same for the 2 Tragedies, which he refused – advised Murray not to speak too freely of his transactions with Lord B. nor

of the decrease which he says has taken place in the attraction of his works' (*Journal*, II, 488). B replied to JM on 20 October: 'So – Thomas M[oore] is in town incog. – Love to *him*. – I except him from my regretted morsures – for I have always found him the pink of honour – and honesty' (*BLJ* VIII, 245).

6. This is written on the back cover below the seal. The bust had arrived at Albemarle Street by Thursday 25 October when Moore called and saw 'a bust of Lord Byron ... by Thorwalsen – does not do him justice' (*Journal*, II, 497). When Hobhouse heard that JM had the bust, he wrote to claim it on 31 October. But JM, quite understandably, thought it was for himself and questioned Hobhouse's right to it; to which Hobhouse replied somewhat stiffly on 2 November: 'To be sure the bust is mine & how the deuce it came into your possession I am at a loss to conjecture'; and he directed JM to deliver it to Kinnaird who would 'give house-room to it until I can get it safely conveyed to Whitton' (MA; see also, Interim Note below).

Letter 164)   [Wednesday] 14 November 1821

London <Oct^r> Novr. 14 – 1821

My Lord

I received your Letter of the 20th Octr. on Saturday last[1] – I will send you the MSS of Juan in wch you will find some of the faults & another wch was doubtful as you omitted to erase for what you substituted. The omitted Stanza I certainly plead guilty too [*sic*], but intending to have it extracted from your letter,[2] I forgot to do it & so it became mingled with your Lordships other letters – but where there is no <u>mala anamus</u> [*sic*] you should be less enraged – I have cancelled what I had & am printing the whole correctly.[3] I have received two Copies of Juan from you by post each costing £6. 7 – 8 – postage[4] – I have now sent you all the books you wrote for & amongst them your own Copy of Burton wch I got at yr sale – the bible I have sent you is one with a selection of the best commentaries.[5] As to new books I am sure you know very well that I do not send them to you as a matter of <u>trade</u> – for my dealings are for MSS – & with booksellers – but they were sent merely to give you a specimen of modern literature[6] –

I did receive the printed Sheet to <a> be appended as a note to the next edition of the Doge, wch shall carefully be done[7] –

At this place I am interrupted by the arrival of your Lordships Letter dated R^a Octr 26 – it surprises me very much indeed to find by it that you had not received the proofs of Cain which were sent regularly as

I had previously announced to your Lordship – addressed as you have constantly enjoined me <u>Pisa</u>[8] – & this being the case how could you expect to receive it [*sic*] in course at Ravenna whence I perceive you continue to date – since that I have also a fortnight ago sent you even the proofs of the Vision of Judgment[9] – I hope you will find that at least the neglect is not mine, for I sent the proof as soon as it could be compleated – A <u>Third</u> Copy of Juan[10] – a Visitation – £6. 7 – 8 – more[11] –

I have now settled with Mr Moore for the Memoirs & I inclose the paper with his signature for the addition, if you approve, of yours, in the presence of two witnesses.[12] I am very much obliged indeed for the recollections of Persons which your Lordship tells me you are preparing[13] – these can not fail of being very interesting & valuable & will give great variety to the work.

I sent you various Scraps of Prose[14] <fo> but I would advise the mere publication of the Tragedies & Mystery this winter[15] – for these & Juan III. IV – V I have proposed Two Thousand Five Hundred Guineas to Mr Kinnaird. The Copyright of Juan I can not substantiate without endless litigation & giving up the name of the Author – there are already two pirated editions of the whole[16] – if any new Stanzas or episode occur to you pray give it me to render mine at least the most perfect Edition.[17]

I remain Dearest Sir
Your Lordships
faithful Servant
John Murray

Every Post I have expected to receive back the corrected Proofs of Cain – so long have they been sent – if they do not arrive by Tuesday next I will send another Copy

Notes to Letter 164)

<u>Cover</u>: Milord/Milord Byron/poste restante/Pisa/Italie

1. B's letter of 20 October (which would have arrived on Saturday 10 November) in which he responded to JM's statement in Letter 163 above: '*If* errors *are* in the *M.S.S.* – write me down an Ass – they are *not* – & I am content to undergo any penalty if they be' (*BLJ* VIII, 244, quoting Dogberry in *Much Ado About Nothing*, IV, ii, 70: 'O that he were here to write me down an ass'; see also, Letter 163, nn. 3 and 4 above).

2. In his letter of 20 October, B asked: 'Besides, the *omitted* Stanza (last but

one or two) sent *afterwards* – was that in the M.S.S. too?' (*BLJ* VIII, 244). This was stanza 158 of Canto V, which he had sent in his letter of 1 March 1821 and supposed JM had omitted because of its final couplet (*BLJ* VIII, 87 and 192; see also, Letter 153, n. 1 above; incidentally, for the '*Wedlock*' and '*Padlock*' parallel in this stanza, cf. Massinger, *The Fatal Dowry*, IV, i, 70–72: 'I marry? were there a queen o' the world, not I./Wedlock? no, padlock, horselock, I wear spurs/To keep it off my heels').

3. *malus animus*: evil intent (cf. *DJ* I, 30). Stanza 158 was replaced and extensive corrections were made in the 'Fifth Edition, Revised and Corrected' published in 1822 (see *CPW* V, 695).

4. Although B had told JM to 'acknowledge all packets by *name*' at the close of his most recent letters of 9 and 20 October, he does not say exactly when he sent any copy of *DJ* 'by post'. In his letter (*b*) of 26 October, however (whose arrival is about to interrupt JM's present writing), he sent 'a *third copy corrected* – with some alteration', which he told JM to collate 'with the other two copies both sent by the post' and to 'print any future impression' therefrom (*BLJ* VIII, 237, 245 and 248; see also, n. 10 below).

5. In his letter of 9 October, B had sent a list of books he desired JM to send him, amongst which were '"Burton's Anatomy of Melancholy"' and a 'common bible of a good legible print (bound in Russia)' (*BLJ* VIII, 237–38). JM sent B's own copy of the former (2 vols, 1806) which JM himself had bought at B's book sale in 1816 (see *CMP*, 233, lot 41). For B's youthful observations on the work (which echo the testimonies of various authors quoted in Vol. I, xxii–iv of his copy), see *CMP*, 6–7; see also, *CMP*, 197–98, where he has copied into his Harrow Notebook almost all the disabled persons named by Burton in Part 2, Sec. 3, Mem. 2 (Vol. II, 9–10). These points I failed to note in *CMP*, 268–69 and 507–11.

6. In his letter of 24 September, B had issued not quite Ten Commandments as to what JM should or should not send him, the third of these being: 'That you shall *not* send me any modern or (as they are called) *new* publications in English – whatsoever' (to which edict of course he made several exceptions), adding: 'You have also sent me a parcel of trash of poetry for no reason that I can conceive – unless to provoke me to write a new "English Bards"' (*BLJ* VIII, 219–21).

7. In his letter of 27 September, B had asked whether JM had received 'a new Italian account of M[arino] Faliero's Conspiracy for a note – sent two months ago by the post? & printed for the first time?', which question he repeated in his letter of 20 October (*BLJ* VIII, 225 and 244). He had sent this to JM on 30 July telling him to 'Get it translated and append it as a note to the next edition'; but it does not appear to have been added to any edition (*BLJ* VIII, 161).

8. B wrote angrily to JM on 26 October from Ravenna: 'I waited here another

week to receive the proofs of "Cain" which have *not* arrived – though your letter announced them for next post ... Upon my word – you will provoke me to play you some trick one of these days that you won't like' (*BLJ* VIII, 248; see also, Letter 163 above). This was grossly unfair: since 20 September B had repeatedly directed JM to address to him at Pisa ('Address to me at *Pisa* – whither I am going'; 'Address to *Pisa*'), as indeed he had done so in his letter of 20 October (*BLJ* VIII, 218, 224, 232, 235, 237 and 245). Obeying B's directions would explain JM's apparently 'dilatory' conduct with regard to *Cain* (see *CPW* VI, 647). For some of JM's letters, none of which is extant, see the Interim Note below.

9. B had sent *The Vision of Judgment* to JM on 4 October, instructing him to 'address the proof to me at *Pisa*', and reiterated, with the same instruction to 'Address to Pisa', that 'By last post I sent the "Vision of Judgeme[nt] [*sic*] by Quevedo Redivivus"' in his letter of 9 October (*BLJ* VIII, 232 and 236, corr. MS MA. See Plate 17).

10. B sent 'a *third copy corrected*' of *DJ* III–V to JM on 26 October with a covering letter (see n. 4 above) and a note written in the inside of the volume itself (*BLJ* VIII, 248–49; in the note, 'R[*avenn*]a' should read 'Bⁿ.', 'kindly' should read 'humbly', and 'M.S.S. of their humble Servant' should be underlined; see the reduced facsimile in Mrs James T. Fields, *A Shelf of Old Books* [1894], 75). This copy should be distinguished from the copy B gave to Mawman to '*show*' to JM (see Letter 158, n. 3, and Letter 159, n. 4 above, and the Interim Note below).

11. JM likens B's flood of letters to an official examination. B felt some compunctions about this 'Visitation', telling Kinnaird on 28 November that he had sent JM '*three* copies of Juan per post to *correct him* for not *correcting* them. – – But of these *I* will pay the postage of *two* – which deduct. – I leave him to pay the other – as a warning to be more precise in printing another time' (*BLJ* IX, 71–72).

12. See Letter 163, n. 5 above. Moore had written to JM on Sunday 30 September saying he thought it as well for both of them 'that there should be some *regular* agreement' between them and asked to see him the following day (Moore, *Letters*, II, 495). The result was this 'paper' which B signed and enclosed to Kinnaird on 29 November asking him to forward it to JM whom he wished to 'spare' the postage having 'sweated him lately'; he told JM he had done this on 4 December (*BLJ* IX, 72 and 74).

13. At the close of his letter of 20 October, B said he was filling another copy-book for JM 'with little anecdotes to my own knowledge or well authenticated – of Sheridan – Curran &c. and such other public men – as I recollect to have been acquainted with' (*BLJ* VIII, 245). This was his 'Detached Thoughts', which he had begun on 15 October and continued until 18 May 1822 (see *BLJ* IX, 11–52, and Letter 167, n. 8 below).

14. Writing on 9 October, B said that JM had a good deal of his 'prose tracts in
M.S.S.' and requested 'proofs of them *all* again', including 'the *controversial*
ones' and 'The Epistle of St. Paul' he had translated from the Armenian (*BLJ*
VIII, 237). These would have been 'To the Editor of the *British Review*' (1819),
Some Observations (1820), and the 'The Epistle of the Corinthians to St. Paul
the Apostle' and 'Epistle of Paul to the Corinthians', which he had translated
from the Armenian in 1817 (for which, see *CMP*, 70–76 and 343–44).

15. That is, *Sardanapalus, The Two Foscari* and *Cain, A Mystery*.

16. These were *Don Juan. Cantos III. IV. and V.* piratically published by Sherwin
and Co. of Paternoster Row in 1821, which was uniform with their octavo
edition of the first two Cantos they had pirated in 1820; and *Don Juan. Cantos
I. to V.* piratically published by Benbow of Castle Street, Leicester Square in
12mo. in 1821.

17. 'I sent ... Edition.': B has drawn a line down the left and right margins of
this passage, and sent this letter to Kinnaird on 28 November from Pisa
saying: 'Murray's offer in his letter to *me* is for the *three* cantos of Don Juan
– and the *three* plays ... – As you think it right that I should accept it (he
says two thousand five hundred *guineas* – recollect *not* pounds is the *word*) I
accept it accordingly for the *above named* works – but distinctly understood
that it is *not* for "the Vision of Judgement" nor *any other* M.S. of mine now
in his or other hands ... Murray's plea is that the *Juans* are *pirated* – but this
is none with me – as it is his *own* fault – – what business had *he* to affect
not to put his name on the title page? – I enclose you his letter to prevent
mistakes ... I shall by no means be guided by *him* about *not* publishing except
the three plays this winter – on the contrary I desire that the "Pulci" in
particular be published – and "the Vision" if not by him – by some other
– but separately'. The following day he added that they 'ought to have had
three thousand G[uinea]s for the three plays and Cantos only', but nevertheless
he would do as Kinnaird pleased (*BLJ* IX, 71–72). Kinnaird replied on 16
December: 'I understand you to limit, as I perceive Mr Murray does by his
letter, the purchase he has made for 2500 <u>guineas</u> to the three last Cantos
of Juan, & to the three Plays – I think the assignments of these had better
be made & the money paid 'ere [*sic*] I talk to him about the Pulci'; and he
added: 'You are quite right in what you say about Mr Murray's Complaint
about Pirating the Juan – All this would have been avoided had the M.S.S.
been sent to Hobhouse or myself, & either of us had given him a copy to
read & buy or not as he pleased – <u>After</u> he had made the purchase he was
perhaps entitled to hurt the sale by his folly – but he is not entitled to injure
the work, & <u>afterwards</u> plead that injury, of his own doing, in diminution
of the price he is to offer' (MA).

Interim Note

Between Letter 164 above and Letter 165 below, a number of JM's letters to B are missing. B had arrived in Pisa on 1 November 1821 where he evidently found three letters awaiting him which JM would have written in early October after receiving B's instructions to address him 'at *Pisa*' (*BLJ* VIII, 218; see Letter 164, n. 8 above). Replying on 3 November, B said JM's 'first note was queer enough', but his 'two other letters with Moore's & Gifford's opinions set all right again' (*BLJ* IX, 54). These 'opinions' would have concerned *Cain* – Gifford apparently expressing some '"alarms"' as to its impiety, and either JM himself or Gifford again, objecting to 'two passages' in the dialogue between Cain and Lucifer, which B said could not be altered (*BLJ* IX, 53–54). Moore's opinion can be gleaned from his letter to B of 30 September: 'Cain is wonderful – terrible – never to be forgotten. If I am not mistaken, it will sink deep into the world's heart; and while many will shudder at its blasphemy, all must fall prostrate before its grandeur. Talk of Æschylus and his Prometheus! – here is the true spirit both of the Poet – and the Devil' (Moore, *Letters*, II, 494–95; see also, *Byron's Life and Works*, V, 318 and *BLJ* IX, 64). JM had also complained of B's inscription in the copy of *DJ* III–V he had given to Mawman. Joseph Mawman (1764?–1827), formerly an eminent bookseller of York and subsequently of the Poultry and Ludgate Hill, was the author of *An Excursion to the Highlands of Scotland and the English Lakes*, published by himself in 1805, and was 'a very intelligent man and spirited publisher; and was honoured with the friendship of Dr. Parr, Dr. Lingard, and numerous other learned individuals' (*The Gentleman's Magazine*, XCVII, Pt II [September 1827], 283). JM was clearly galled at having been degraded in the eyes of such a respected fellow-publisher and friend. B replied that he had 'received him civilly as *your* friend – and he spoke of you in a friendly manner': 'I gave him that book with the inscription to show to *you* – that you might correct the errors. – With the rest I can have nothing to do – but he served you very *right*. – You have played the Stepmother to D[on] J[uan] – throughout ... You seem hurt at the words "*the publisher*" what! *you* – who won't put your name on the title page – would have had me stick J. M. Esqre. on the blank leaf' (*BLJ* IX, 54; for the inscription, see *BLJ* VIII, 196; see also, Letter 158, n. 3, and Letter 159, n. 4 above).

On 16 November, B asked Kinnaird whether Hobhouse had got the bust by Thorwaldsen yet: 'Murray has lately asked me for it – for *himself*!! tell Hobhouse to claim his property – for it is his own' (*BLJ* IX, 63). By 23 November he had received 'a not very temperate' letter (no longer extant) from Hobhouse himself to which he replied, quite unfairly, that JM 'must have been crazy or tipsy to imagine that the Bust could be for *him!*', and the following day wrote to JM to clarify the misunderstanding (*BLJ* IX, 67 and 69–70; see also, Letter 163, n. 7 above, and see below).

By 28 November, B had received Letter 164 above. Thereafter, on 4 December he wrote saying he had 'received safely the parcel containing the Seal, – the E[dinburgh] Review – and some pamphlets &c.', and asked JM: 'Are there not designs from *Faust*? send me some – and a translation of it – if such there is' (*BLJ* IX, 75). Such there was: *Faustus: From the German of Goethe*, anonymously translated and published by Boosey and Sons in quarto and octavo in late 1821, was 'designed to serve also as an accompaniment to the *Series of Outlines*, illustrative of "Faust"' (p. 85, in both editions). These were 26 quarto designs engraved by Henry Moses (d. 1870) from the originals of Friedrich August Moritz Retzsch (1779–1857), which could be had separately. B gave his copy to Mrs Catherine Potter Stith (1795?–1839) of Philadelphia (wife of Major Townsend Stith [d. 1824] of Petersburg, Virginia, American Consul at Tunis) in May 1822; his presentation copy is now in the Goethe Collection at Yale University (*BLJ* IX, 162, and see Adolph B. Benson, 'Catherine Potter Stith and Her Meeting with Lord Byron', *South Atlantic Quarterly*, XXII, 1 [January 1923], 10–22). See also, *CPW* VI, 730, and Shelley, *Letters*, II, 376 and 407.

On 14 December (not November), B sent *Heaven and Earth* to JM, telling Kinnaird he had done so on the same day and JM again, in an undated letter, that he had done so 'by last post' (*BLJ* IX, 58–60 and 81. The MSS of these three letters are in MA. From a number of indications it is evident that B has himself misdated his letter to JM of 'Novr. 14th.', and that Marchand's conjectural though logically consequent dating of the undated letter '[November 15–16?]' is incorrect: in both cases the month should be December. This would serve to clarify the issue raised in *CPW* VI, 679 as to when *Heaven and Earth* was actually sent).

B had received proofs of *Heaven and Earth* by 22 January 1822, when he told JM he had returned them by that post to Kinnaird to whom he said he would also send his new drama *Werner* when 'fairly c[opied] out', but which he eventually sent to Moore in Paris (see below and Letter 165, n. 1 below). Crucially, however, he added very tactfully: 'As you have lately published more of mine than you seem to think convenient – it is probable that I shall not trouble you with the publication of these – but transfer them to some other publisher ... I merely apprize you of this – because it may be proper after the length of the connection – not to terminate it abruptly without such advice of my intention' – which 'intention' he confirmed in the 'P.S.' of his letter of 8 February (*BLJ* IX, 90, 91 and 104, and see below; effectively this announced his breaking off his publishing relationship with JM). He also promised to send JM 'In a post or two ...

a version of the extract from "Petrarch" as you wished' (*BLJ* IX, 90) – which Medwin tells us he translated for B who 'forwarded [it] by the next courier to England', and 'Almost by return of post' received 'a furiously complimentary epistle in acknowledgment' (*Medwin's Conversations*, 99 and n.; although the translation is attributed to B in Ugo Foscolo's *Essays of Petrarch* [1823] it is not by him [see *CPW* VII, 160, D10]).

On 23 January, B received *Sardanapalus, The Two Foscari, and Cain, A Mystery* (published together on 19 December 1821) from which he was 'greatly surprized to see' that JM had 'omitted the dedication of "Sardanapalus" to Goethe', which he asked him to restore 'if any opportunity of replacing it occurs' (*BLJ* IX, 91; see also, *CPW*, VI, 607). He was rather more angry about the matter three days later when he wrote to Kinnaird asking him whether the omission was JM's 'insolence or negligence', and enclosing two of JM's letters (neither of which is extant), 'in which he expressly says that "as far as he is concerned the tragedies are all sold"' – – In the other he speaks of the '"outcry &c."' (*BLJ* IX, 93–94). The '"outcry &c."' was over *Cain*, which had prompted, amongst other attacks, a 20-page pamphlet entitled *A Remonstrance addressed to Mr. John Murray, respecting a Recent Publication* signed by Oxoniensis (who may well have been a member of the Constitutional Association; see Letter 162, n. 10 above) and printed by F. C. & J. Rivington in January 1822. With the exception of seven pages touching on the play itself, this was addressed exclusively and in menacing language to JM, intending to prevent him 'henceforward from becoming the agent of so much mischief as must result from the wide dissemination of works like "'CAIN, a Mystery"' and concluding with the veiled threat: 'I trust you will not persevere; but if you do, neither your courtly locality and connections, nor the demi-official character with which you are invested, will avail to protect you' (pp. 6–7 and 20). B had seen this, or extracts from it, 'in the papers', and wrote most liberally to JM on 8 February exonerating him from all blame, accepting full responsibility himself and offering to refund the copyright, and inviting JM to 'Make any use of this letter which you please' (*BLJ* IX, 103–04, and see below). JM did make use of it; and *this* portion of the letter ('Attacks upon me … which you please', *not* the 'P.S.') was published in, for instance, *The Times*, Thursday 7 March 1822, the *London Chronicle*, CXXXI, 9865 (Saturday 9-Monday 11 March 1822), 238, and, together with a commentary and a parody, *The Literary Gazette*, 269 (Saturday 16 March 1822), 166–67.

By 19 February, B told Moore that he and JM were 'but little in correspondence' (*BLJ* IX, 110). On that very day, however, JM was writing a letter to B, which when it arrived on 6 March clearly disarmed him. He agreed to 'make peace' with JM, promised him *Werner*, and released him from making any proposal for that and *Heaven and Earth*, 'till we see if they succeed'. He also promised him Bartolini's busts of himself and Teresa, 'to show you that I don't bear malice – and as a compensation for the trouble and squabble you had about Thorwaldsen's' (*BLJ* IX, 121–22, and see above, and Letter 163, n. 6 above; for Bartolini's busts, see Letter 168 below). On the same day, B sent JM's letter to him to Moore in Paris saying that it had 'melted' him, and that though he thought it against JM's own interest 'to wish that I should continue his connexion', asked Moore to send JM *Werner* (*BLJ* IX, 120, and see above, and Letter 165, n. 1 below); two days later, however, he told Moore to tell JM that 'one of the conditions of peace is, that he publisheth (or obtaineth a publisher for)' Taaffe's *A Comment on the Divine Comedy of Dante Alighieri*, which he had been soliciting JM to do since November 1821, and which JM eventually did publish in octavo at 18 shillings on 21 December 1822 (*BLJ* IX, 63–64, 90, 122, 123 and 126, quotation from 123 [corr. *Byron's Life and Works* (1832), V, 325, and Prothero, VI, 39]; *The Times*, Saturday 21 December 1822; see also, *CMP*, 253, lot 207 for B's copy in quarto).

On 15 March, B received a letter from JM that must have been written at the end of February or beginning of March, thanking B for his letter of 8 February and evidently asking if he might give it 'publicity' (to which B replied: 'you may give it what publicity you think proper in the circumstances' – by which time JM had already done so; see above), resuming publication plans for B's works, enquiring whether the 'Noel affairs' would bring B to England (which B hoped they would '*not*'), and requesting '"a poem in the old way to interest the women"', which met with a prompt refusal (*BLJ* IX, 125–26).

On 31 March, B wrote to JM acknowledging 'the receipt of several books &c.', which he promised to acknowledge at more length later, being 'very much occupied at present' with what has become known as the 'Pisan Affray' (*BLJ* IX, 132; see Letter 165, n. 2, and Letter 166, n. 3 below). On 9 April, apparently in fulfilment of his promise, he told JM that the busts by Bartolini would be sent 'when completed', suggested the 'best way' to publish *The Vision of Judgment*, and asked JM to thank Henry Luttrell (for *Letters to Julia, In Rhyme. Third Edition. To which are added Lines Written at Ampthill-Park*, published by JM in February 1822; see also, *CMP*, 250, lot 122), and D'Israeli (for the third edition of *The Literary Character*, 2 vols [1822]), to the latter of whom he said he would himself 'write ... soon', which he did on 10 June (*BLJ* IX, 136–67; see also, IX, 171–73, and *CMP*, 219–21 and 546–49).

Although B continued to write, this seems to have been the last communication he received from JM before receiving Letter 165 below.

On 13 April, B told JM his 'congratulations on the Noel accession'

were 'somewhat premature' as Annabella was on a '"Milk diet"', and asked
him to send him the defence of *Cain* he had heard about from Kinnaird
(*BLJ* IX, 141–42). This was an 85-page pamphlet, welcoming *Cain* as a
contribution to philosophical debate, entitled *A Letter to Sir Walter Scott,
Bart., in answer to the Remonstrance of Oxoniensis on the Publication of Cain,
A Mystery, by Lord Byron*, signed by Harroviensis, dated London, February
1822, and published by Rodwell and Martin. On receiving this (from
Kinnaird) on 18 April, B wrote to JM saying he thought it 'conclusive
– and if you understood your own interest – you would print it together
with the poem', which he reiterated on 1 May (*BLJ* IX, 145, 146, and 151).
In the same letter he told JM he had got Lord Glenbervie's book (see Letter
162, n. 17 above), but added significantly: 'It is very odd that I do not hear
from you' (*BLJ* IX, 146).

Letter 165)   [Tuesday] 16 April 1822

London 16. April 1822

My Lord

I have been in dayly [*sic*] expectation of being able to announce the
arrival of Werner – but by a letter just received from Mr Moore I find
that he has been disappointed in his intention of returning to England &
he has inclosed it in our Ambassadors dispatches so that every moment I
may now expect to receive it.[1]

I am glad to learn from the tone of our Florentine Ministers letter
to your Lordship that your portion in the unlucky affray at Pisa
appears to be very small[2] – but I feel sufficient interest to wish to hear
the story & to be prepared with the true statement in case a false one
shall appear –

The division of Ld Wentworths property is indeed most liberal on
your Lordships part, who has but a life interest in it.[3]

We are all as dull here as possible, after humbug Row about Cain[4]
– nothing having succeeded to it – & there has been no Lion even this
season.

I inclose a Letter to you from Sir Walter Scott who is your Lordships
fast friend[5]

I remain My Lord

Your Lordships

faithful Servant

John Murray

Notes to Letter 165)

<u>Cover</u>: Milord/Milord Byron/Poste Restante/Pisa/Italie <u>arrived</u>: 1 May

1. With a view to its being published there by Galignani, B had sent *Werner* to Moore in Paris on 29 January, telling Kinnaird he had done so by the same post (*BLJ* IX, 94). Moore received it on 12 February and told B on 19 February that he had 'written to the Longmans to try the ground, for I do *not* think Galignani the man for you' (Moore, *Journal*, II, 541, and *Letters*, II, 503; see also, *Byron's Life and Works*, V, 319). B received Moore's letter on 4 March; but two days later JM's melting letter arrived, and he therefore told Moore to send the drama to JM, telling JM he had done so the same day (*BLJ* IX, 118, 120 and 121; see also, Interim Note above). Moore's letter to JM is not extant; but by a curious coincidence he arrived in London the very evening of JM's present writing, though he does not record having seen JM 'soon after' his arrival until 22 April (Moore, *Journal*, II, 554 and 556–57). B replied on 1 May that he would 'expect the proof of "Werner"' (*BLJ* IX, 151).

2. Returning from pistol-shooting outside Pisa in the evening of Sunday 24 March, B, Shelley and their party were rudely overtaken by an Italian Sergeant-Major, Stefani Masi. They accosted him at the gates and much argument and violence ensued, and Masi was severely wounded. (This was the 'Pisan Affray', for full details of which, see C. L. Cline, *Byron, Shelley and their Pisan Circle* [London: John Murray, 1952], chs 6 and 7; Marchand, III, 980–90; Moore, *Lord Byron: Accounts Rendered*, ch. 9; Iris Origo, The *Last Attachment* [London: John Murray, 1949], 301–11; and *LBLI*, 429–38 and 451–58; see also, *BLJ* IX, 128–61, *passim*, and *CMP*, 225–26 and 558–60). B had informed JM on 31 March that he was 'very much occupied at present with a squabble between some English (myself for one) and some Soldiers of the Guard at the Gate and a dragoon who wanted to arrest us', adding very cautiously that he could not send 'an ex parte statement' at that time, as the matter was 'before the British Minister at Florence' whose letter to him, however, had been 'very handsome & obliging' (*BLJ* IX, 132; the 'British Minister' was Edward James Dawkins, Secretary of Legation to Tuscany at Florence [1816–23], and later [1828–35], Minister Plenipotentiary to Greece). Replying to JM on 1 May, B told him that the 'chief documents' of 'the Pisan affray' were in the hands of Kinnaird (copies to Hobhouse), to whom he had sent them on 28 March and 2 April (*BLJ* IX, 130, 134–35 and 151; see also, Letter 166, n. 4 below).

3. Lady Noel had died on 28 January 1822. According to the terms of the Separation Agreement, at her death the estate of her brother, Lord Wentworth, was to be divided between Annabella and B by arbitration. Annabella had appointed Lord Dacre; B, Sir Francis Burdett. B had said nothing about the decision to JM (whose informant was almost certainly Kinnaird), nor

did he learn of it until 18 April when he received Kinnaird's letter of 4 April informing him of it: 'Lord Dacre & S F. Burdett met yesterday & this morning; & have given their decision "<u>that Lady B. have one moiety of the net proceeds of the Wentworth Estates for her sole use</u>" – It is also agreed, that Lady B. shall never have any claim upon you for any expences <of>for the maintenance or education &c of your daughter, as long as she remains under Lady B's care & protection – This of course she cannot do longer than you consent to it – By this decision the estates are placed under Your controul & management –, & are your's for Ldy B's life' (MA). Replying to this on 18 April, B said the decision was 'quite satisfactory' to him, and proceeded to discuss various issues it raised (*BLJ* IX, 144–45; see also, Marchand, III, 970–71); he did not respond to JM's allusion to the matter.

4. For the 'humbug Row about Cain', see Interim Note above. In fact it was not quite over: a 60-page pamphlet entitled '*A Vindication of The Paradise Lost from the Charge of Exculpating "Cain," A Mystery.* By Philo-Milton', dated April 1822, was printed by F. C. & J. Rivington. In his reply of 1 May, B merely reiterated that JM ought to get the defence of *Cain* 'circulated as much as you can' and asked him who was the author (i.e., Harroviensis). Replying to this question sometime in May, in a letter that is no longer extant, JM told B he was '"a tyro in literature"' (i.e., a novice) (*BLJ* IX, 167), and he remains unidentified.

5. Scott's long and friendly letter is dated 28 March 1822 from Abbotsford (see Scott, *Letters*, VII, 116–22; the original is now in the Berg Collection at the New York Public Library). Receiving it on 1 May, B told JM he would answer it shortly, which he duly did on 4 May (*BLJ* IX, 151 and 153–55).

Letter 166)   [Thursday] 2 May 1822

London May 2. 1822

My Lord

I have received Werner & expect proofs of it in a post when they sh<ould>all be forwarded to you – Shall I print it in a plain form without the Authors name, to take its chance – Heaven & Earth may follow it – but just say no – & your Lordships former wish shall be fulfilled – Pulci &c shall be put in One Volume & published in November[1] – for nothing whatsoever has made the least impression this <year> Season

<There is an Article in the present N° of the>[2] I was very glad to observe by the obviously official Statement in the papers that the affair at Pisa turns out very much to your own judgement & honour[3] – Yesterday the Dukes of Buckingham and Bedford fought a Duel in

Kensington Gardens – Bedford fired in the Air – & they shook hands & parted friends[4] –

I remain My Lord
Your faithful Servant
Jno Murray

Notes to Letter 166)

Between the present Letter (166) and the following Letter (167) numerous letters, especially from JM, are missing, with which it seems best to deal as occasion arises in the notes.

1. Having written impatiently to JM only the day before, B received this letter on 17 May and replied somewhat stiffly: 'As the Mystery [*Heaven and Earth*] is not in many pages – you had better add it to Werner – – and let them take their chance – I do not mean the Pulci – to be published in the same volume with "the Vision" – the latter of course ought to be a separate publication. – As I take the risk upon myself – you will permit me to decide upon the *time* of publication which must be sooner than what you say – for I care nothing about what you call "the Season"' (*BLJ* IX, 159).

2. JM was almost certainly about to say that there was a review by Jeffrey of *Sardanapalus, The Two Foscari, and Cain*, in the *Edinburgh Review*, XXXVI, lxxii (February 1822), 413–52, but had second (and better) thoughts about doing so. Jeffrey was far from enthusiastic: as poems, he thought them 'heavy, verbose, and inelegant – deficient in the passion and energy which belongs to the other writings of the noble author – and still more in the richness of imagery, the originality of thought, and the sweetness of versification for which he used to be distinguished'; and as plays, 'wanting in interest, character, and action ... dramatic effect and variety' (419–20). B had heard of this review from Kinnaird ('The Edinburgh is free with your volume of Tragedies – Be they right or wrong, I see nothing but good feeling towards you') but had not seen it himself (*BLJ* IX, 158; Kinnaird to B, 3 May 1822 [MA]). Replying to JM on 17 May, B said that he had heard 'that the Edinburgh has attacked the three dramas – which is bad business for *you*; and I don't wonder that it discourages you'; and he told him to send it to him if he thought it 'necessary': 'should there be any thing that requires an answer – I will reply but *temperately* and *technically*'. On 6 June, however, he said that he had read it 'in Galignani's magazine' but had 'not yet decided whether to answer them or not'; he did, in a manner, but it was not published (*BLJ* IX, 159–60 and 167, and see Letter 170, n. 5 below). Hobhouse records on 17 September that B was 'much hurt' at the article (*Recollections*, III, 5).

3. See Letter 165, n. 2 above. JM would have read the 'official Statement' which Kinnaird told B on 3 May he had made out from the documents B had sent him and which he had had inserted in *The Observer* whence it was reprinted

in *The Times* and the *Morning Chronicle*. He also told B that the 'misstatement appeared the <u>preceding day</u> in an extract from the Courier Français
– & on that day your last packet reached me' (MA). This 'misstatement',
which is ludicrous enough and which Medwin also records reading in the
Courier Français in Rome (*Conversations*, 242), was naively reported in the
Morning Herald for Saturday 27 April 1822 under the title 'LORD BYRON':
'We copy the following paragraph from a Paris paper, without the means
of giving any opinion upon its truth or falsehood:– "A letter from Italy
gives the following details:– 'Lord Byron inhabited for some time past a
country-house in the environs of Pavia, where he employed himself, it is
said, in writing memoirs of himself. A superior officer called upon him a
few days since. A very lively altercation, of which the subject is unknown,
soon took place between this Officer and the English Poet. The menaces
of the Officer became so violent, that the servant of Lord Byron ran to his
master's assistance. A sort of struggle ensued, in which the Officer received
from the servant a stroke of a poniard, of which he died on the spot. The
servant instantly fled. Lord Byron remained in his house, and was taken
into custody after a few hours. He is at this moment in one of the prisons
of Pavia.'" – *Courier Francais*'. (*The Times* for Saturday 27 April 1822 was
much terser and more dismissive: 'The French papers contain a ridiculous
story respecting Lord Byron, which we give in their own words: – "After an
assassination committed on a Colonel by a domestic and in the house of Lord
Byron, the noble Peer of Great Britain is at present in prison: but they do
not name the Colonel. One account lays the scene at Pisa, another at Pavia,
and to complete the improbability, they make the news come from Rome."
If it had been true, says the *Journal des Debats*, it would probably have come
direct from Milan.') The statement that Kinnaird prepared appeared in *The
Observer* for Sunday 28 April 1822 under the title 'LORD BYRON':

> The following statement, transmitted to us by a friend of Lord
> Byron, may be relied upon as authentic:– "On the 24th of March
> last, as Lord Byron, with four other English gentlemen, followed by
> a servant, were returning on horseback to Pisa, and were within a
> quarter of a mile of Porta la Piaggie [*sic*], they were overtaken by a
> man on horseback, in the dress of a dragoon, riding at full gallop,
> who rushed through the party at speed, so as to endanger their
> safety. One of the gentlemen's horses was so excited, that he could
> with difficulty restrain him, and lost his hat; Lord Byron, (followed
> by the rest of the party, and the servant) conceiving the person to
> have been a commissioned officer, (he proved to be only a sergeant-
> major) pursued him at speed, and overtook him just at the Porta la
> Piaggie, where there is a guard. They rode up to the dragoon and
> asked his name and address, Lord Byron at the same time offering
> to him his card. The reply consisted of the most gross abuse, and
> threats of personal violence, accompanied with the act of laying his
> hand on his sword, as if to carry his threats into execution. This

took place in the presence of some of the guard, one of whom called
out to the dragoon to give them in charge to the guard, – on which
he immediately called out to the guard to arrest the whole party.
Lord Byron, on this, put spurs to his horse, and was followed by one
of his companions. His Lordship rode directly to his house, and sent
his secretary to the police, to acquaint them with the outrage; and,
without dismounting, returned towards the guard. On his way he
met the dragoon, who rode up to his Lordship, and asked him, in
an insulting manner, if he was satisfied? Lord Byron replied he was
not satisfied, and desired to know his name. The other stated it to
be Sergeant Major Masi. At this moment a servant of Lord Byron
came up to the dragoon, and laid hold of the bridle of his horse,
which Lord Byron desired him instantly to release. The dragoon
put spurs to his horse and proceeded along the street by the Aono
[*sic*], through a large number of people who were collected near the
Casa Lanfranchi. There, it appears, the dragoon received a wound;
from whom is uncertain. Several have been arrested on suspicion,
amongst the rest one of Lord Byron's servants. The story of Lord
Byron being arrested is not only a pure invention; but it has never
been pretended, that his Lordship was either present at, or had in
any way instigated, or countenanced any attack on the dragoon, who
is, however, beyond all danger. After his Lordship quitted the gate,
it appears that a most brutal attack was made by the dragoons and
soldiers, armed with swords, on the persons of the three unarmed
English gentlemen. One was knocked off his horse, another was
wounded in the face, and the servant was severely ill-used. The
conduct of the soldiers is at present referred to the civil tribunals.
Lord B. and the English gentlemen made immediately a report and
deposition to the governor of Pisa, and through the medium of Mr.
Dawkins, the English Charge d'Affaires, at Florence, have demanded
satisfaction for the injuries they have received. The Tuscan
Government have in the readiest manner intimated, through Mr.
Dawkins, that they do not entertain the remotest suspicion that Lord
Byron was in any manner cognisant of the attack on the dragoon,
although his Lordship's servant is necessarily retained till the affair is
fully investigated & judgment given".

(Reprinting this the following day, *The Times* for Monday 29 April 1822
sadly miscopied this last clause: 'although his lordship is necessarily detained
till the affair is fully investigated and judgment given').

4. Henry Fox (who had dined in JM's company the preceding evening)
records in his Journal for Thursday 2 May that the Dukes of Bedford
and Buckingham had fought a duel that morning at 7 a.m. in Kensington
Gardens, 'about some foolish, hot phrases at Bedford': 'They fired at the
same moment, Buckingham missed and Bedford fired in the air' (Earl of

Ilchester, *The Journal of the Hon. Henry Edward Fox*, 114–15; according to *The Times* for Friday 3 May 1822, the duel had arisen from some words used by Bedford at the Bedfordshire County meeting on 20 April but had terminated amicably).

5. At some point over the next six weeks or so, JM evidently sent B a parcel of books to which the following unpublished fragment in MA refers. It is written by B on the inside of the cover of a letter addressed to JM, the receiving postmark of which indicates that it arrived in London on 19 or 29 July 1822; it must have been written therefore from Pisa around the beginning of the month:

> recollect that the latter is lost. − − −
> There were some poems by M^r. Brooke^i − and a thing of Milman's^ii
> − − travels of Burchardt^iii & one or two small volumes besides by
> different writers − but <u>not</u> <u>the</u> Novel^iv − however −
> Iriving^v will be a consolation in the interim. − − −

Notes

    i. Arthur Brooke, the pseudonym of John Chalk Claris (1797–1866), poet and journalist of Canterbury, whose *Retrospection; with Other Poems* was published by John Warren in 1822 (see also, *CMP*, 246, lot 26).

    ii. Henry Hart Milman's *The Martyr of Antioch: A Dramatic Poem* and *Belshazzar: a Dramatic Poem* were published by JM in March and June 1822 respectively.

    iii. John Lewis Burckhardt's *Travels in Syria and the Holy Land*, edited by William Martin Leake, was published by JM in April 1822 (see also, *CMP*, 253, lot 201).

    iv. The 'Novel', to which 'recollect that the latter is lost' obviously refers, was almost certainly one of Scott's, and would have been either *The Pirate*, published on 24 December 1821, or, more likely, *The Fortunes of Nigel*, published on 30 May 1822: although B told Scott on 27 January 1822 that the former was 'under way' but had 'not yet hove in sight', he does not mention it in his next letter to him of 4 May (*BLJ* IX, 87 and 153–55; see also, Letter 162, n. 7 above). Indeed, he never mentions receiving either, nor does he ever allude to them again, and neither is among his books in his Sale Catalogue (1827).

    v. Washington Irving's *Bracebridge Hall* was published by JM in June 1822 (B sent his copy to Mr Ingram in January 1823, but whether he got it back is another matter; it seems to have become one of the items circulated in the 'reading Association' formed in Genoa in 1823; see *BLJ* X, 83 and 171, and Andrew Nicholson, 'Byron: A Manuscript Fragment and a Note', *Byron Journal*, 29 [2001], 79–80).

Letter 167)   [Wednesday] 25 September 1822

Albemarle Str
Septr. 25th 1822

Dear Lord Byron

On my return from paying the last offices to Allegra I found your
Letters of Aug. 27. 31 – & this day I have received a third dated Sepr. 10.[1]

I did, certainly, omit in the published Copies of Cain the lines quoted
by your Lordship, I could not venture to give them to the public,
and I even hoped tha<n>t when their omission should be discovered,
<that> you would <be> feel surprise rather than dissatisfaction.[2] I have
so often and so publicly acknowledged my obligation for the fame and
profit which I have gained by the publication of your writings, that
your Lordship cannot <I> imagine that I am not sensible of the heavy
sacrifice which I should make in losing so invaluable a friend – and it
is <to> this circumstance alone which has rendered my recent, (not
as you I think, <you> unjustly term it "shuffling" & "timeserving"
which would imply sinister motives, for it is obvious than [*sic*] I have
none but a regard to your fame & my own character – but, certainly,
I must allow,) <u>indecision</u> – for this there would have, I think, been no
occasion were you still in this country for then you would have been
more sensible to those public animadversions which at present fall upon
me. If you are so kind <and so generous as> so nobly generous as to
allow me the honour of continuing to be the publisher of such of your
writings as are of your former glorious class – I shall feel more than
ever grateful – But, I beg leave to repeat, that no adverse determination
of yours can diminish – at any time – my sense of obligation to you,
nor of the most sincere personal attachment – and as you have avowed
that, when an occasion offered you did not find me mercenary or
indisposed to practical gratitude[3] I trust that our mutual feelings will
be such as to leave the door open to a speedy renewal of the most
delightful <interco> connexion which I ever formed in my life; – but if
you should acce<ed>de to my proposal it will really leave undestroyed a
very considerable portion of my happiness.[4]

With regard to my reception of Mr John Hunt whom I was not aware
that your Lordship had ever seen,[5] he sent up word that "a Gentleman"
wished to deliver into my own hands a Letter from Lord Byron, &,
with instantaneous joy, I went down to receive him – there I found M^r
Hunt & a person obviously brought there as a <u>witness</u> – He delivered
the letter in the most tipstave formal manner to me staring me, fully &
closely in the face as if having <given a Cup> administered a dose of

Arsnick he wished to see its minute operations – & to all that I civilly
& simply replied – with the same assassin look, he ever repeated "are
these your words Sir" – "is that your answer Sir" – "am I to write these
words to Lord Byron" – in fact if you knew the insulting behaviour
of this man – you would I am sure excuse me for having directed my
confidential Clerk to tell him when he called again that, he might be
assured that whatever papers Lord Byron directed Mr Murray to send
to him would be carefully and, as speedily as possible delivered at his
house – but that personal intercourse was not agreeable & could not
be necessary. A friend of yours!!! – My heart & soul are & ever have
been with any & every friend of yours – After so long an interval it
is not very extraordinary that some of the Slips of Letter to Pope [sic]
– Blackwood &c should have been mislaid – but this man can make no
allowances but conceives that mystery, deceit or fraud, can be the only
[exc]use – There have now been sent to him[6]

1		The Blues
2	–	Pulci – orig^l & Eng
3	–	Francesca
4		Hints from Horace
5		Part of Letter to Blackwood

Yet wanting
I   Armenian Epistles
II – Lines on the Po (wch Mr Kinnaird has)
III   remainder of Letter to Blackwood

all these, I know I have, & my papers are undergoing diligent
investigation to find them. – The inclosed notice has been just put
into circulation – the association which it unfolds, thus publicly – your
friends will view with regret.[7] I have received the very interesting
Journal which your Lordship was so good as to send me by your most
gentlemanly friend Lord Clair [sic][8] & it is deposited in the Iron Box
containing all your other papers.

I inclose <a> specimes [sic] of two Editions of Your Lordships Works
which I am printing in the most beautiful manner that modern Art can
effect[9] – the best proof of my honouring your Writings – I have sent for
the Don Juan

I open the Letter to say that I called immediately upon Mr Kinnaird
– he is in Paris – but I saw that all your Lordships packets had arrived
safely[10] – I entreat you to believe that I remain My Lord

Yours most sincerely & faithfully

John Murray

Notes to Letter 167)

<u>Cover</u>: Milord/Milord Byron/poste restante/Genoa/ <u>arrived</u>: 9 October

1. None of these letters is extant. B's natural daughter Allegra had died at the Convent of Bagnacavallo on 20 April 1822. B had informed JM of this on 22 April, saying he wished her body to be buried at Harrow Church and asking JM whether he would 'have any objection to give the proper directions on it's arrival' (*BLJ* IX, 146–47). On 26 May he wrote from Montenero telling JM the body was embarked and giving him detailed instructions as to the exact spot for its burial in the churchyard and for the placing of the commemorative tablet inside the church; he wished the funeral 'to be as private as is consistent with decency – and I could hope that Henry Drury will perhaps read the service over her' (*BLJ* IX, 163–64). Evidently Drury said he was willing to do so as JM enclosed a letter from him with a 'scrap' of his own (neither of which is extant) upon which B commented on 3 August: 'It is just like him – always kind and ready to oblige his old friends' (*BLJ* IX, 189). After much delay and many objections raised by the parishioners, Allegra was buried at the entrance to Harrow Church on 10 September without any commemorative tablet (see Smiles, I, 430–32, and Marchand, III, 1000–001). The funeral was 'performed' by B. Palmer & Son, Upholsterers [*sic*], of 175 Piccadilly whose bill, amounting to £58 6s od, was disbursed by JM on 18 September, B having directed Kinnaird on 27 May to reimburse him (MA and *BLJ* IX, 166; Upholsterers and Cabinetmakers also acted as Undertakers). To judge from the expenses, the ceremony was conducted in as dignified and decorous a manner as B could have wished: there were numerous funeral assistants (pall-bearers, pages, porters, coachmen and ushers), and both Drury and 'the Clergyman of the Parish' (the Rev. J. W. Cunningham) were in attendance. B's 'long Inscription' (his memorial originally intended for the marble tablet inside the church) was inscribed on 'a planished [beaten] plate' affixed to the 'strong Elm case made to contain the 3 Packages' of Allegra's remains (MA). B was never to know this. What he did learn, however, upset him profoundly; and without the least justification he blamed JM, accusing him on 21 December (evidently repeating what he had earlier aspersed in a letter no longer extant – perhaps that of 9 December of which only a portion survives [*BLJ* X, 52]) of having allowed 'calumnies ... to circulate in the papers on the subject of the funeral of Allegra': 'You *knew* and *know* how desirous I was that the funeral might be private – and you also knew or might have known – that I had not the most distant idea that Lady B[yron] was a frequenter of Harrow Church'; and he added: 'Why not tell me what were or are the objections to the inscription over poor little Allegra' (*BLJ* X, 64–65; see also, X, 54–55). These latter 'objections' he would have heard about from Mary Shelley, who had written to him on 21 October quoting a passage from a letter to her from Maria Gisborne: '"When Mr Gisborne went to

Harrow ... he saw the grave of poor Allegra. This was precisely the day your father called on me, the funeral had taken place the day preceding. There was a great outcry among the Ultra priests on the occasion, and at the time they seemed resolved that the inscription intended by her father, should not be placed in the church. These Gentlemen would willingly cast an eternal veil over King David's infirmities & their own, but the world will peep through, even though poor Allegra should be without the honours of her inscription'" (Betty T. Bennett, ed., *The Letters of Mary Wollstonecraft Shelley*, 3 vols [Baltimore: Johns Hopkins University Press, 1980–88], I, 284). But he had clearly also read one or all of the three extraordinarily tasteless stories circulated in the papers, the first of which, opening with a crude glance at the subtitle of his most recent compositions, appeared in The *Morning Herald* for Thursday 21 November 1822:

ANOTHER MYSTERY. – It is whispered at the west end of the town, that a package, containing a "pledge of love," was lately received in London, by a person whose name is familiar to the public, from an eccentric but distinguished genius, who for some time has not resided on this side of the Alps. It is reported that a letter had previously reached the Agent alluded to, informing him such a package would arrive, and directing him to take proper steps for having it, as soon after being landed as possible, deposited some feet below the surface of the earth, at the root of a particular tree on Harrow-hill, which was specifically pointed out for that purpose. Application, it is said, was accordingly made to a public, but religious character [Cunningham], for permission to comply with this request, which having been granted after a short hesitation, the package, on its arrival, was buried on the appointed spot. It is further hinted, in a still more obscure manner, that the package probably contained something which was once dear to an English Lady now abroad – perchance not unconnected by tender ties to the eccentric but distinguished genius who resides on the other side of the Alps.

The second appeared in *The Observer* for Monday 25 November 1822:

SINGULAR CONSIGNMENT. – In the course of the last 10 days, a very interesting little girl, about eight years of age, arrived from the Continent in London, specially consigned, and almost indorsed, to the firm of a highly respectable upholsterer in Piccadilly. The instructions were simply to take proper and fitting care of the child, and to place the expenses to the account of the consignor. The consignees have attended with becoming promptness to the order of their correspondent, and having, in the first instance, furnished the exterior of their charge, have taken steps to obtain the more essential furniture of the mind. The child is stated to be the offspring of an eccentric nobleman long self-banished from his country.

The third appeared in *The Times* for Friday 29 November 1822:

> The following is, we understand, an elucidation of the mysterious story relating to a noble exile, of great poetical fame, which was copied into our paper last week. The noble Lord consigned from Italy, to a certain Bibliopolist in London, three cases, in which were preserved the heart, the intestines, and the body of an infant, dear to his Lordship, with a request that their remains should be deposited in Harrow church, and that a monument to the memory of this infant, with an appropriate inscription, written by his Lordship, should be erected there. The most extraordinary injunction was, that the *hic jacet* should be placed on the wall in the front of and immediately opposite to a pew which is regularly frequented by the lady of the poet. The faithful Bibliopolist, true to his trust, communicated the whole matter to his cheerful and rotund friend [Henry Drury], one of the Masters of Harrow School, who, in the exercise of a prudent and well-regulated judgment, advised that the contents of the three cases should be consigned to one coffin, and quietly and unostentatiously interred in the churchyard. This was done, and the Bibliopolist and the Knight of the *Rod* were the only mourners.

2. These lines were *Cain*, I, i, 163–66, containing Lucifer's mocking prophecy of the crucifixion, which were omitted from all editions and first printed as a variant in 1833 (see *CPW* VI, 237 and apparatus, and 657). Replying on 9 October, B said he had no objection on JM's account to the omissions from *Cain*, or from *Heaven and Earth* 'which were marked in the half sheet sent the other day to Pisa', but reproved him for not being open and saying so 'at *first*' (*BLJ* X, 12).

3. In his letter to JM of 8 October 1820, B had said: 'I never met but three men who would have held out a finger to me – one was yourself ... who offered it while I *really* wanted it ... when I was in actual uncertainty of five pounds. – I rejected it – but I have not forgotten it although you probably have' (*BLJ* VII, 195; see also, Letter 137, n. 1 above).

4. To this B replied on 9 October: 'I have no wish to break off our connection – but if you are to be blown about with every wind – what can I do? – You are wrong – for there will be a *re-action* – you will see that by & bye – and whether there is or not – I [*sic*] cannot alter [*sic*] my opinions – though I am ready to make any allowance in a *trade* point of view – which unpalateable [*sic*] speculations may render necessary to *your* advantage' (*BLJ* X, 12, corrected MS MA).

5. B had never 'seen' or even met John Hunt, but had sent him via his brother Leigh Hunt his letter to JM of 3 July instructing JM 'to deliver to the bearer, Mr. John Hunt, the *Vision of Judgment* ... with the preface' (*BLJ* IX, 179). Leigh Hunt forwarded this letter to his brother from Pisa on Saturday 6 July

saying: 'The enclosed is a letter from Ld Byron to Murray, directing him to put into your hands a poem of his upon Southey & the late king, entitled *A Vision of Judgment*. His Lordship has made me a present of it, & I trust it will do away all I owe to you & to those whom you undertook to see paid' (Eleanor M. Gates, ed., *Leigh Hunt: A Life in Letters* [Essex, Connecticut: Falls River Publications, 1998], 116. In his very last letter to Mary of 4 July 1822, Shelley told her that this gift was '*more* than enough to set up the Journal' and would 'set every thing right' [Shelley, *Letters*, II, 720]). On 6 July, B wrote directly to JM telling him to give the poem to Hunt 'which will relieve you from a dilemma': 'Give him the *corrected* copy which Mr. K[innair]d had – as it is mitigated partly – and also the preface' (*BLJ* IX, 181–82). On 8 July he wrote again saying: 'I have consigned a letter to Mr. John Hunt for the "Vision of Judgment" – which you will hand over to him. – Also the Pulci – original and Italian – and any *prose* tracts of mine – for Mr. Leigh Hunt is arrived here & thinks of commencing a periodical work – to which I shall contribute – – I do not propose to you to be the publisher – because I know that you are unfriends – but all things in your care except the volume now in the press [*Werner* and *Heaven and Earth*] – and the M.S.S. purchased of Mr. Moore [the Memoirs] – can be given for this purpose – according as they are wanted – and I expect that you will show fair play – although with no very good will on your part' (*BLJ* IX, 182; this last letter was evidently in reply to a letter from JM that is no longer extant in which JM had spoken of his own '"want of memory"', which prompted B to remind him of various instances illustrative of that deficiency, and to suggest ways JM might circumvent it in future, before adding rather more promisingly: 'It is not impossible that I may have three or four cantos of D[on] Juan ready by autumn or a little later' [ibid.; see also, n. 10 below]). This was B's first intimation to JM of his joining the *Liberal* project, for a thorough account of which, see William H. Marshall, *Byron, Shelley, Hunt, and The Liberal* (Philadelphia: University of Pennsylvania Press, 1960), esp. chs III and IV.

6. Square brackets indicate portion of word torn off with seal. The following undated memorandum in MA from John Hunt to JM was perhaps sent around this time:

List of Imperfect Papers sent by M^r. Murray to M^r. John Hunt.

———

1. A Proof Sheet entitled "Observations upon an Article in Blackwood's Edinburgh Magazine, August 1819". Dated March 15, 1820. Half a sheet, ending abruptly –

2. A Proof of some matter on the subject of the Pope & Bowles Controversy, without any title, beginning "Dear Sir." Two half sheets, ending abruptly. –

———

N.B. The only other now <u>unpublished</u> papers M^r. Murray has delivered to M^r. Hunt are –

1. Hints from Horace. Proof sheet.
2. Morgante Maggiore, 1st. Canto, Italian & Translation.
   MS. Proof.
3. The Blues, a literary Eclogue.
   Proof sheet.

7. 'The inclosed notice' would have been the following from the *Morning Chronicle* for Wednesday 25 September 1822: 'The long promised periodical work from *Pisa* is nearly ready for publication. Lord BYRON's main portion of it is, we hear, entitled "*The Vision of Judgment*," and is a direct *quiz* upon the Laureate. – LEIGH HUNT has merely a few minor Poems in the first Number.' B replied on 9 October: 'That d——d advertisement of Mr. J. Hunt is out of the limits I did not lend him my name to be hawked about in this way'; he also expressed his dissatisfaction to Leigh Hunt (*BLJ* X, 13 and 32). Incidentally, neither of the two notices cited by Prothero (VI, 125n.) and repeated by Marshall (op. cit. [see n. 5 above], 78–79) could have been the one that JM enclosed, as both post-date his present Letter (167); cf. however: 'Mr John Hunt will shortly publish "The Vision of Judgment," by Quevedo Redivivus, suggested by the composition of Mr Southey. We understand this production is from the pen of Lord Byron' (*Blackwood's Edinburgh Magazine*, XII, lxvii [August 1822], 236).

8. On his way back to England from Rome, B's 'earliest and dearest friend' Lord Clare had visited him for a day only on 6 June (*BLJ* IX, 167 and 169). Writing to JM on 8 June, B said he had sent by him 'a common-place book – about half filled – which may serve *partly* hereafter – in aid of the Memoirs' (*BLJ* IX, 168). This was B's 'Detached Thoughts', begun on 15 October 1821 and concluded on 18 May 1822 (see *BLJ* IX, 11–52, and Letter 164, n. 13 above). JM clearly intends to distinguish B's old 'gentlemanly' friend from his new ungentlemanly associates (the Hunts).

9. B did not comment on these 'specimens' [*sic*]. Under 'New Editions' in the *Monthly Literary Advertiser*, 212 (10 December 1822), 92, JM advertised: 'The POEMS of the Rt. Hon. Lord BYRON, a New Edition, handsomely printed in 4 Vol. 8vo, 2l 2s. A New Edition also in 5 Vol. small 8vo, 1l 15s. ⋆⋆⋆ The Tragedies to complete the above, may be had separately.' I have been unable to trace either of these editions, and they are not recorded in the Bibliographies. Coleridge records an octavo edition published by JM in 1823, with an engraving by Charles Warren of Phillips' portrait of B, entitled *The Works of Lord Byron. In Four Volumes* (*Poetry*, VII, 99–100); and I have seen a small octavo edition of *The Works of Lord Byron. In Five Volumes* also published by JM in 1823 (but with no engraving), which is merely a new edition of *The Works of Lord Byron*, 5 vols (1821), containing none of the 'Tragedies' nor *The Prophecy of Dante*. As *Werner*, published in 1822, is also dated 1823 (see Letter 168, n. 4 below), these are almost certainly the editions in question.

10. Kinnaird had gone to Paris without telling B or JM and did not return until
    mid-October. B had sent him four new Cantos of *DJ* (Cantos VI–IX) on 7
    and 10 September, and had told JM he had done so on 11 September (*BLJ*
    IX, 204 and 206; see also, Letter 169 below).

Letter 168)   [Friday] 11 October 1822

London 11th Octr. 1822

Dear Lord Byron

I wrote to you last week – since wch I have received two Short
Letters from you – the last date is Sep. 23rd.[1]

I entreat as a most particular favour that you will not place me in
personal intercourse with Mr John Hunt – for I have invicible [*sic*]
reasons for not wishing to know him – As to my giving myself airs
in the matter – I can assure you that no one can charge me with any
alteration <since> in this respect since I had first the good fortune
of seeing you – and as to my going about talking of my losses – it is
utterly destitute of all foundation[2] – I always consider & speak of myself
as a most fortunate man – I have had to pay £16.000 for an insane
brother-in-law[3] – it is true – but I am less hurt at the loss (for I can
never hope to have One Pound of it repaid) than joyful that it was
no greater – I beseach you not to set me down for such an incurable
Blockhead as not to thing [*sic*] of you with every body around me as far
superior as a Man of Genius to any man breathing – that that [*sic*] all
the other work together which I publish as a matter of business – would
keep in the balance of my mind – with yours – this is my opinion from
the bottom of my heart & Soul – & do what you please misconceive my
real character – nothing can eradicate this opinion nor any thing alter
my firm devoted dutiful & respectfully affectionate friendship for your
Lordship.

May I dash out Werner alone by the way Poems are always ten times
more read when published separately[4] –

I send you a Copy of the Lines[5] – pray do not fire them off rashly
– death must be the inevitable consequence you must be aware how
honourably I have kept your secret.

Pray dont attend to what evil tongues tell you I will be sworn falsely
of Mr Hobhouse & me [*sic*][6] — come over & see the truth

Poor Godwin has been suddenly called upon for £400 – of Rent
– wch would ruin him – Shelley would have paid it – there is a
Committee – of which I am one – for raising this Sum – I have given

<10g> 10Gˢ – I dare say you will give your Lordships name for £25.[7]

Poor Gifford was very nearly dead three days ago – he is now out of danger – he ever continues your firm admirer[8]

There is a Review of Cain the next quarterly – wch I will inclose[9]

I am & ever shall remain Dear Lord Byron

Your grateful & faithful

friend & Servant

John Murray

Every day of my life I sit<e> opposite to your Lordships Portrait – Pray send me both Busts[10]

Notes to Letter 168)

Cover: Milord/Milord Byron/Poste restante/Genoa/Italie arrived: 25 October

1. B's two short letters of 11 and 23 September: the first advising JM of having sent *DJ* VI–IX to Kinnaird; the second complaining of not having heard from JM but saying that he had seen his brother, 'who – I must say – by no means loses in the comparison – I like him very much' (*BLJ* IX, 206–07 and 212–13). This was JM's half-brother, Archie Murray, RN, Purser of *HMS Rochfort*, which had put in at Leghorn towards the end of August. He and B had in fact met twice – once in Pisa and again in Genoa – and their feelings for one another were evidently mutual. Writing from Florence on 31 August to his wife at Naples, Archie reported:

> We arrived at Pisa yesterday afternoon [in fact, 28 August], and stopped there for the night on my account, that I might see if Lord Byron, who is still there, was accessible. I sent him a billet doux, to which a very civil answer was immediately returned, but without waiting an answer, I proceeded to his mansion soon after my note, sent up my card, and was admitted tout de suite, which was the more civil as I have now reason to believe that I called at an unreasonable hour, and was not expected, he having written to appoint another. However, as soon as his Lordship was appareled [sic] (for I could perceive that my card had caught him in deshabille) he received me, & was very courteous, agreeable, and gay; I was with him about an hour; and on parting, had his permission not only graciously but cordially, (as I thought) to renew my visit on returning to Pisa. He seemed in good spirits, and careless of the evil reports against his works. If I could have presumed upon the reception he gave me, I would have made Pisa my abode for his sake, for I cannot but think that, (if he has not designedly deceived me) we should have got into a friendly intercourse. His Lordship intends removing to Genoa in a few weeks, and his furniture is now

packed up for conveyance. I learnt in the course of our conversation
that Charles Parker is a cousin of his (MA; Charles, later Admiral
Sir Charles Parker [1792–1869], was the brother of Sir Peter Parker
[1785–1814], the subject of B's 'On the Death of Sir Peter Parker,
Bart.').

Writing again to his wife, this time from Genoa on 29 September, Archie
commented:

> My Lord B. is not tall, but of moderate stature – he is rather stout
> than thin – he is considered handsome – I have heard him called
> <u>very</u> handsome – and he <is> certainly has very comely features
> – but his countenance is not on the Grecian or Roman model of
> elegance – it is round and full, and might be less agreeable in a
> different person – the emotions of his poetical spirit animate and
> beautify it – his eye has the expression of a man of genius – he
> wears the hair rather longer than is <customary> the present
> costume for gentleman, which in him is not unpleasing – it is just
> long enough to curl gracefully – the defect in one of his feet is so
> well concealed by his dress there that it is not observable when he
> sits or stands – The portrait<s> prefixed to his works resembles him
> very well – and a statue of him which I saw at Florence is also a
> very good likeness (it is a bust intended for John Murray) – I am
> not so well able to give a description of his person as another might
> be, because I approached him both times with some commotion,
> and because in both my interviews, <I was> my ears were far more
> greedy than my eyes – I was much more intent upon his conversa-
> tion than his person – more anxious to penetrate his character than
> to scrutinize his form. I was moreover restrained from gazing at him
> by a feeling of delicacy, and had ample employment for my attention
> in our colloquies (MA; for the 'bust', by Bartolini, cf. n. 10 below).

These cheering accounts were somewhat marred by a false report put about
a little later by a certain unidentified Major in Malta, whence Archie wrote
to JM himself on 25 June 1823:

> I am told that Lord Byron says, in one of his letters to you, that
> "he has seen me, and treated me with more civility than you ever
> treated him" (I omit the epithet alledged for energizing the position)
> – This may pass between friends, as a piece of familiar wit – but
> if meant as any thing more, I should have a right to be displeased
> at it both for you and for myself – and should be ready to offer an
> animadversion upon it – which, however, I shall forbear until quite
> sure of the premises. – I had it from an Etonian schoolfellow [sic] of
> his Lordship's, a Major in a regiment here. – His Lordship's reputa-
> tion is sadly on the wane with all sorts of people – occasioned by
> his superabundance of dark themes, and too frequent exhibition

of reprobate personages – which no longer pass for fine poetical inventions, but are considered by most folks as the habitual emanations of his mind, the types of his own nature – In this opinion I do not fully concur; but I think he has in some measure deserved it by identifying himself with his own Childe Harold, to the destruction of the potent poetical charm, and to the conferring of his own example, & consequently authority, upon the world to identify him with other of his heroes. – Be this as it may, his Dramas are admirable; they appear to me much the best of his compositions, the first part of Childe Harold always excepted. – I hope he will give us more of them; and I wish he might engage in more prose composition, in which he is excellent (MA).

2. In his letter of 23 September, B had said: 'If you can't be civil to Mr. John Hunt – it means that you have ceased to be so to me – or mean to do so. I have thought as much for some time past – but you will find in the long run (though I hear that you go about talking of yourself like Dogberry "as a fellow that hath had losses") that you will not change for the better. – – I am worth any "forty on fair ground" of the wretched stilted pretenders and parsons of your advertisements' (*BLJ* IX, 213). B received JM's present Letter (168) just as he had finished writing angrily to him on 24 October. He therefore added a kindlier postscript (superscribing the first page of his letter 'See Postscript'): 'I have since the above was written – received yrs. of the 11th. – and as I am "a pitiful-hearted negro" [Gifford, *Baviad*, 263n., adapting *I Henry IV*, II, iv, 114] and can't keep resentment – it hath melted my flint. – It is *you* who force yourself into contact with Mr. J[ohn] H[unt] – if you deliver the M.S.S. mentioned – in their complete state you will have no more trouble on that score' (*BLJ* X, 18, and MA for superscription; see also, Letter 170, n. 1 below).

3. This was Annie's brother, William Elliot, who was a constant drain on JM's resources. JM must have mentioned this before in an earlier letter (no longer extant) which was either rather garbled or which B read rather carelessly, confusing brother with brother-in-law; for, writing to Kinnaird on 26 September, he told him: 'There is I doubt something wrong about M[urray] ... He told me months ago – that he had lost *fifteen* thousand pounds by a *brother*. – I saw his brother not long ago (purser of the Rochefort) who said he never owed him a farthing. So you [see] there is something queer in all this' (*BLJ* IX, 218).

4. In his postscript to his letter of 24 October, B merely repeated his earlier instructions: 'You must not separate Werner from the Oratorio H[eaven] & E[arth]' (*BLJ* X, 18); and this is how they were advertised both prior to and even on the day of their (supposed) publication: 'This day is published, in 8vo, price 5s. 6d. WERNER, a Tragedy; Heaven and Earth, a Drama. By the Right Hon. Lord BYRON. Published by John Murray, Albemarle-

street' (*The Times*, Thursday 21 November 1822; see also, the *Monthly Literary Advertiser*, 211 [9 November 1822], 87). However, a letter from Kinnaird to B of 15 November helps to clarify the position: 'Werner & Heaven & Earth have been for some days advertized to be published by M^r. Murray. Availing myself of the discretion allowed me & of the best reflection, I have sanctioned Mr Murray's proceeding with the publication of Werner alone. He states that the one will clog the sale of the other – not only from the subjects being so entirely different but that the fanciful public buy more readily a single poem than two together – He mentioned he had thrown off 2000 copies of the two together but that of Werner, if printed separately he would throw off 5 or 7000 at once' (MA). To this B replied on 28 November: 'About Werner – you are to decide also – I mean as to letting Murray publish – for as to any profit from it – our friend of Albemarle Street would sacrifice even his *own* – (far more mine) to gratify his unintelligible spite against the Hunts – and me for having assisted – or endeavoured to assist them' (*BLJ* X, 42). In the meantime, however, on 22 November Kinnaird had written again saying: 'This day Werner is out. Murray has a Sale, & a Dinner, & ere this has probably sold some thousand Copies'; and on 26 November: 'Murray – whom I saw yesterday says he has sold six Thousand Copies of Werner and he sacrificed the two thousand copies he had printed of Werner and Heaven and Earth' (MA). Despite the date of publication, the date on the title-page of *Werner* is 1823 (cf. Letter 167, n. 9 above). For further publishing details, see *CPW* VI, 691 and 693–94; see also, Letter 170, n. 6 below).

5. These were the lines on Rogers that B had sent JM in 1820 (see Letter 140, n. 2 above). At the close of his letter of 23 September, B had requested JM to send him 'a copy of the M.S.S. lines on *Samiel*', as Hobhouse, who had just visited him for five days before going on to Rome, had told him that Rogers 'hath said something which is like him – it is time to teach him – and if I take him in hand – I'll show him what he has been these sixty years' (*BLJ* IX, 213; 'Samiel' is Turkish for the Simoom or sirocco – the 'Blast of the Desert' that kills the Sorcerer in Southey's *Thalaba the Destroyer* [1801], bk II, st. 40, and to which Southey very naturally appends a long explanatory note, but which B borrows appropriately enough here from Moore's *Lalla Rookh* [1817], which is dedicated to Rogers, where the Impostor's 'thousands of Believers' are described as 'blind,/Burning and headlong as the Samiel wind' [*Lalla Rookh* (1817) 'The Veiled Prophet of Khorassan', p. 90]).

6. JM's hand has become progressively illegible in the course of writing this letter and at this point is almost indecipherable. He may have intended to write: 'It will be sworn falsely of Mr Hobhouse & me'.

7. Godwin had in fact been in arrears with rent to the tune of £400 since May 1822 when he was evicted from 41 Skinner Street (see Shelley, *Letters*, II, 423–26, esp. 424n.–25n. where William Godwin junior succinctly summarizes the position in a letter to the Shelleys of 24 June 1822). With the death of Shelley his last hope for financial support vanished and an appeal

committee was set up by JM, Sir James Mackintosh, Charles Lamb and others to assist him (see Peter H. Marshall, *William Godwin* [New Haven & London: Yale University Press, 1984], 353–55). B replied on 24 October: 'Put me down twenty five pounds for Godwin' (*BLJ* X, 18).

8. Gifford had suffered what D'Israeli called an 'alarming attack', and his state of health remained 'precarious'; the pressing question now was who would succeed him as editor of the *Quarterly Review* (Smiles, II, 156–57). He may indeed have continued B's 'firm admirer'; but from an undated note to JM, which must have been written around this time, he was clearly disappointed in him: 'What can make a man of Lord Byron's extraordinary pre-eminence so careless of his name, as to venture it upon every caprice? What purpose can be answered by his bringing forward such a person as Hunt, who is sinking every hour, & cannot be upheld even by his strong arm? – but tis no purpose to talk – your part is to do as he desires, & mine to grieve to no end' (MA).

9. Reginald Heber's balanced, but reasonably severe review of *Sardanapalus, The Two Foscari* and *Cain* appeared in the *Quarterly Review*, XXVII, liv (July [pub. October] 1822), 476–524. B replied on 24 October: 'You had better not send me the Quarterly on Cain – as it can only be in the preaching style – & may make me answer or say something disagreeable'; and although JM did send it later, B returned it 'uncut and unopened' on 23 November (*BLJ* X, 18 and 40). However, he could not escape it. Writing to JM on 25 December, he told him that since he had returned it, Galignani had 'forwarded a copy of at least one half of it', and that to his surprise, 'upon the *whole* – that is the whole of the *half* ... it is extremely handsome & any thing but unkind or unfair'; indeed he was so impressed that he said he would 'erase two or three passages in the latter 6 or 7 Cantos' of *DJ*, adding: 'I like what I read of the article much' (*BLJ* X, 67–68 and 69).

10. In his letter of 23 September, B had said: 'The bust does not turn out a very good one – though it may be like for aught I know – as it exactly resembles a superannuated Jesuit. – – I shall therefore not send it as I intended – but I will send you *hers* [Teresa's] – which is much better – and you can get a copy from Thorwaldsen's. – I assure you Bartolini's is dreadful – though my mind misgives me that it is hideously like. If it is – I can not be long for this world – for it overlooks seventy' (*BLJ* IX, 213; cf. Archie's opinion, n. 1 above). B replied briefly on 24 October: 'You shall have the busts'; but in the event neither was sent (*BLJ* X, 18; see also, Peach, *Portraits of Byron*, 100–06). Teresa's bust is now in the Biblioteca Classense, Ravenna.

Letter 169)   [Tuesday] 29 October 1822

London 29th. Octr. 1822

Dear Lord Byron

I was truly gratified by the favour of your kind letter from Genoa
dated the 9th which reassures me of that confidence which will enable
me to write to you openly.[1] Werner and the Myster<ie>y I can &
will publish – and immediately – for I observe the Announcement of
"The Loves of the Angels" a poem by Moore wch must be on the
same subject as the Mystery[2] – and because they will dimish [sic] (as
far at least as your Lordship is supposed to be concerned,) the universal
disappointment and condemnation which has followed the publication
of the first number of the "Liberal"[3] – do not let others deceive you
– I pledge my honour to the truth of what I tell you, that never since I
have been a publisher did I ever observe such a universal outcry as this
work has occasioned & it is deemed to be no less dull than wickedly
intended – finding all this attributed to you & moreover that you were
accused of mercenary motives – I felt it a duty that I owed to you to
read that part of your Letter in which you communicate the cause of &
your motives for contributing to this work to every gentleman who is in
the habit of visiting at my house.[4] The consequence of which has been
the instant insertion of the inclosed paragraph by Mr John Hunt in his
Examiner of Sunday last.[5] You see the result of being forced into contact
with wretches who take for granted that every one must be as infamous
as themselves – really Lord Byron it is dreadful to think upon your
association with such outcasts from Society, it is impossible, I am sure,
that you can conceive any thing like the horrid sensation created in the
mind of the public by this connexion, unless you were here to feel it.

Mr Kinnaird sent me the 3 Cantos of Don Juan and with them,
very ungenerously I think, your angry Letter[6] – <a> having read it
– I returned the MSS unopened – I refrained from writing you [sic]
expecting to find by a subsequent letter that nothing but momentary
irritation could have induced you to have penned it But, though I did
not read any part of the MSS – Mr Kinnaird read to me, a few days
before, the Preface & many extracts from the Poem – and I declare
to you, these were so outrageously shocking that I would not publish
them – if you would give me your estate – Title – & Genius[7] – For
heavens sake revise them, they are equal in talent to any thing you have
written,[8] & it is therefore well worth while to extract what would shock
the feeling of every man in the Country – & do your name everlasting
injury.

My Company used to be courted for the pleasure of talking about you – it is totally the reverse now – &, by a re-action,[9] <y> even your former works are considerably deteriorated in Sale – It is impossible for you to have a more purely attached friend than I am, my name is connected with your fame – and I beseach you to take care of it – even for your Sister's Sake for we are in constant alarm lest She should be deprived of her situation about the court – Do let us have your good humour again & put Juan in the tone of Beppo – Werner & the Mystery shall be published immediately. I entreat you to believe that nothing but the most devoted regard could have induced me to write this Letter & that I ever <u>will</u> remain[10]

> Your Lordships
> devoted friend
> Jno. Murray

Notes to Letter 169)

Cover: Milord/Milord Byron/poste restante/Pisa/Italie arrived: [Pisa] 15 November

Despite B's direction 'Address to *Genoa*' at the end of his letter of 11 September (*BLJ* IX, 207), JM addressed this Letter (169) to Pisa, and it did not arrive at Genoa until after B had received JM's next Letter (170) below, by which time the damage to their relationship was beyond repair. As B told JM on 18 November in reply to the present Letter (169): 'I have – since I received yr. letter of the 5th received yrs. of the 29 – which you had directed to Pisa. – It puts the affair in a different aspect'; and on the same date he sent both Letters (169 and 170) to Kinnaird saying: 'Since I wrote the enclosed I have received another letter from Murray – which he had directed to Pisa. – Of the truth of both you can judge as well as any one ... You see that M. is frightened or pretends to be so – so – the truth comes out at length' (*BLJ* X, 35 and 36).

1. B's letter of 9 October in reply to JM's letter of 25 September (see Letter 167 above).

2. For *Werner* and *Heaven and Earth*, see Letter 168, n. 4 above, and Letter 170, n. 6 below. Moore's *The Loves of the Angels, A Poem* was published by Longmans in January 1823, and was indeed on the same subject as B's *Heaven and Earth* – a point not only discussed, but proclaimed by their being reviewed together by Jeffrey, in the *Edinburgh Review*, XXXVIII, lxxv (February 1823), 27–48, who clearly preferred B's. Both were also reviewed separately by John Wilson in *Blackwood's Edinburgh Magazine*, XIII, lxxii (January 1823), 63–71 and 72–77, who was disgusted at Moore's irreverence, impiety and bad taste. When he came to *Heaven and Earth*, however, he could not resist comparing the two: 'The first is all glitter and point, like a piece of Derbyshire spar – and the other is dark and massy, like a block of marble.

In the one, angels harangue each other, like authors wishing to make a great public impression; in the other, they appear silent and majestic, even when their souls have been visited with human passions ... The one is extremely pretty, and the other is something terrible. Moore writes with a crow-quill, on hot-press wire-wove card-paper, adorned with Cupids sporting round Venus on a couch. Byron writes with an eagle's plume, as if upon a broad leaf taken from some great tree that afterwards perished in the flood. The great power of this "Mystery" is in its fearless and daring simplicity. Byron faces at once all the grandeur of his sublime subject' (72).

3. The first number of *The Liberal* was published by John Hunt on Tuesday 15 October 1822. *The Examiner*, 768 (Sunday 13 October 1822), contained a preview of its contents with substantial passages from *The Vision of Judgment* (pp. 648–52). The 'universal disappointment and condemnation' burst forth in *The Literary Gazette* for Saturday 19 October 1822 (pp. 655–58), which sally was noted with contempt in *The Examiner*, 769 (Sunday 20 October 1822), p. 666. In a footnote to his review of B's *Heaven and Earth* (see n. 2 above), John Wilson referred to *The Liberal* as 'a paltry periodical' (p. 72n.) For a full account of its reception, see Marshall, *Byron, Shelley, Hunt, and The Liberal*, ch. IV.

4. This was the final paragraph of B's letter of 9 October: 'I am afraid the Journal *is* a *bad* business – and won't do – but in it I am sacrificing *myself* for others – *I* can have no advantage in it. – I believe the *brothers* H[unt] to be honest men – I am sure that they are poor ones. – They have not a rap – they pressed me to engage in this work – and in an evil hour I consented – still I shall not repent if I can do them the least service. – I have done all I can for Leigh Hunt – since he came here – but it is almost useless – his wife is ill – his six children not very tractable and In the affairs of this world he himself is a child. – The death of Shelley left them totally aground – and I could not see them in such a state without using the common feelings of humanity – & what means were in my power to set them afloat again' (*BLJ* X, 13; see n. 5 below).

5. The 'inclosed paragraph' was from *The Examiner*, 770 (Sunday 27 October 1822), 679:

> We heard last night that a report is industriously circulated in certain circles, that Mr. Murray the Bookseller *shews about* a pretended letter from Lord Byron to himself, in which his Lordship speaks in the most disparaging manner of some friends connected with him in the *Liberal*. Now we know, that the savage fury into which that publication has put the corrupt faction is so great, that they will spare no means, however false, daring, and desperate, to cast odium upon any persons concerned in it. We do not therefore affect any *surprise* at this report; but we know enough of certain recent circumstances (*of which Mr. Murray is also quite conscious*) to be able to declare,

that if the said Mr. Murray does really (as reported, perhaps *falsely*) shew about a letter answering this description, it is a *forgery*, and we hereby dare him to publish it, if he denies the charge. This is truly an entertaining exhibition of corrupt spleen, and affords a pretty idea of the sort of feeling existing in the circles in which such reports are caught up and repeated with eager delight! We repeat, that report *may* wrong Mr. Murray on this occasion; but as it *is* in circulation, it becomes him to exonerate himself, if he is misrepresented. Mr. John Murray can, however, play some odd tricks at a pinch, some of which we shall forthwith expose, if we should find he is misbehaving himself in the manner attributed to him.

JM did not publish B's letter, but his showing it about had already caused friction between Leigh Hunt and B by the time his present Letter (169) arrived, and Mary Shelley was trying to conciliate them. Writing to B on Saturday 16 November, she suggested his saying a few words of explanation to Hunt, 'since you would stop effectually the impertinence of Murray, by shewing him that he has no power to make you quarrel with your friend, & that you do not fear his treason' (Bennett, *The Letters of Mary Wollstonecraft Shelley*, I, 288; see also, *BLJ* X, 25–26, 32–33 and 34; a note in John Murray III's scrapbook of reminiscences indicates that the following passage was omitted by Moore from B's letter to Mary Shelley of 16 November 1822: 'Friendships arise from community of pursuits, and an equality of ranks neither of which I share with Mr Hunt' [MA]). B replied to JM on 18 November: 'prima facie – your showing my letter – without permission – was to say the least of it indiscreet enough, – though I should wish repelled the attribution of a mercenary motive … As to any other motives – they will of course attribute motives of all kinds – but I shall not abandon a man like H[unt] because he is unfortunate' (*BLJ* X, 36; see also, X, 68–69; see also, Letter 170, n. 1 below).

6. B had written to Kinnaird on 6 September enclosing a letter for JM (which is no longer extant), which he asked him to 'present if you do not deem it too harsh. – At any rate it contains my opinions – & I wish you to act upon them in dealing with the absolute John' (*BLJ* IX, 203: the absence of this letter is unfortunate to say the least, as it probably contains the key to the final breakdown in publishing relations between B and JM; its general tenor, however, can be gathered from Kinnaird's letter to JM and JM's reply to Kinnaird below). The following day, B sent Kinnaird Cantos VI and VII of *DJ*, and on 10 September Cantos VIII and IX saying: 'I have no objection to listen to any suggestion of omissions *here & there* – but I *wont* be dictated to by *John Murray Esqre* – remember' (*BLJ* IX, 203 and 204; see also, Letter 167, n. 9 above). Kinnaird did not return from Paris until 11 October, when he found all B's letters from 29 August to 24 September and the four new Cantos of *DJ* awaiting him. Writing to B on 15 October, he said: 'I deliver'd your letter to Mr M. & had an interview with him when

I deliver'd the 4 Cantos – He is to give me an answer by Friday's Post – I think you have adopted the proper manner of dealing on a plain matter of business' (MA; whether or not that 'interview' included reading to JM, as B had instructed Kinnaird to do on 18 September, 'the *bookseller's* letter to the Welch Clergyman in the *introduction*' to Smollett's *Humphry Clinker* – 'it will be a good lesson to him' [*BLJ* IX, 209], Kinnaird does not say, and at any rate 'the *bookseller's* letter', though extremely apropos, is hardly obnoxious, indeed rather the reverse). The 'interview' and the delivery of the Cantos took place on 14 October. Sending B's letter to JM on 15 October, Kinnaird wrote:

> In transmitting to you the enclosed letter address'd to you by Lord Byron, & which was sent to me in its present state without envelope, I think it my duty to let you know that his Lordship desired me not to deliver it if I thought it harsh. With that Commentary from Lord Byron, which assures you that he <u>meant not</u> to have written any thing unkind, I think it better to put the letter into your hands, as it is on business & to the point – directing however your attention to <u>my want of judgement</u>, not to Lord Byron's feelings, as the cause of your annoyance if you be annoyed by it – For my own part I take the liberty to add that I should & do see in it nothing but one more proof of the propriety with which the epithet <u>irritabile</u> has been applied to the Genus Vatum [Horace, *Epistles*, II, ii, 102: 'genus irritabile vatum'; the irritable tribe of poets] – I hope you give me credit for preferring the kinder office of a peace-maker to that of a Channel for communicating angry letters – If so, you will beleive [*sic*] me to have none but the best intentions in sending the enclosed letter, as it is right you should know Lord B's wishes on the subject of the new Cantos [*DJ* VI–IX] – & his own words speak plainest – After what I read to you yesterday from a private letter of Lord B to me [possibly 10 or 18 September; see above], you will of course not take <u>literally</u> all that he says about <u>not altering</u> – I offer myself most readily to further any of your wishes in such a matter in any manner in my power. (MA; apart from other minor differences this letter is misdated 18 October in Prothero, VI, 126n.).

For all that Kinnaird says, his delivering of B's letter can only be seen as a deplorable lack of judgment on his part, or as a deliberate act of provocation; it elicited the following reply from JM dated Thursday 17 October: 'The tone, of the whole, of Lord Byrons Letter is such as I hope no part of our connexion can justify but there is one passage so peculiarly ungracious that I have not thought it necessary to look over the new Cantos of Don Juan, which I have brought from the country and now return to you unread for I will not be the publisher of any work that is accompanied by a condition so degrading to my feeling & character as that contained in Lord Byrons Letter' (MA). On receiving this, Kinnaird enclosed it to B on Friday 18

October saying: 'I sent your letter to Mr Murray together with the 4 Cantos – after Keeping them two days he returned them to me with the enclosed – I do not recollect the condition to which he alludes – For my own part I rather suspect he wishes to back out, from other feelings or motives than any excited by Your letter – I recollect nothing offensive in it, provided the charges be true – In the case of his thinking them false he should reply to them' (MA). B did not understand what this 'condition' was either. Writing to JM on 31 October (in a letter he enclosed again to Kinnaird), he said: 'I have received a note addressed by you to Mr. Kinnaird – in which you complain of some letter of mine and talk of a "condition" what condition? I invoked none nor does Mr. Kinnaird. – If there is anything unjust in the letter it will be now easy to answer it – if on the other hand it is a new excuse – I regret that you should have recourse to such expedients – which were unnecessary'; and he told him to deliver 'all' his compositions, including *Werner* and *Heaven and Earth* but not the Memoirs, to Kinnaird (*BLJ* X, 21–22 and 24). In a second letter of the same date, which he may also have sent via Kinnaird (it has no cover), B was rather more decided: 'I have received and answered through Mr. Kinnaird your enigma of a note to him – which riddle as expounded by Œdipus – means nothing more than an evasion to get out of what you thought perhaps a bad business – either for fear of the Parsondom – or your Admiralty patrons – or your Quarter*lyers* – or some other exquisite reason – but why not be sincere & manly for once – and say so?' (*BLJ* X, 22).

7. B glances wryly at JM's phraseology here when writing to him on 25 December with reference to the Hunts: 'As it is – I will not quit them in their adversity – though it should cost me – character – fame – money – and the usual et cetera' (*BLJ* X, 68). The new Cantos of *DJ* cover the Harem episode and the Siege of Ismail and Juan's arrival at the court of Catherine the Great. Kinnaird was 'delighted with them' (MA), but does not say exactly which 'extracts' he read to JM to provoke quite such an outburst – though certainly JM would have found the Preface to Cantos VI–VIII, with its brutal attack on Castlereagh and his suicide, 'outrageously shocking', as he would have the stanzas on Wellington at the opening of Canto IX.

8. See headnote. B referred to this passage when writing to Kinnaird on 16 December: 'on ye. 14th. inst. I sent you the 12th. C[ant]o of D[on] J[uan] which perhaps is equal to the former. Even M[urray] in the letter which I sent to you – allows that "in talent they have not been heretofore exceeded by me" that is something' (*BLJ* X, 60).

9. JM retorts B's own word in his letter of 9 October: 'You are wrong – for there will be a *re-action* – you will see that by & bye' (*BLJ* X, 12; see also, Letter 167, n. 4 above).

10. Without alluding to any of the particulars in this paragraph, B replied on 18 November: 'With regard to the rest of your letter – I dare say that it is

true – and that you mean well. – I never courted popularity – and cared little or nothing for the decrease or extinction thereof… I care but little for the opinions of the English – as I have long had Europe and America for a Public and were it otherwise I could bear it. – – My letters to you were written under the impression that you had acted unfairly by Hunt – and *when* that is cleared up – of course I have no complaint against you. – – I shall withdraw from you as a publisher – on every account even on your own – and I wish you good luck elsewhere'; and he closed saying: 'I send you my letter written previously to the receipt of yours from Pisa [i.e., Letter 169] (direct to *Genoa* if you write again) if you do not deserve it – it is harsh – & would have been written more mildly had I got yrs. of the 29th. before that of the 5th.' (*BLJ* X, 36; no such letter 'written previously' from B to JM is extant).

Letter 170)　[Tuesday] 5 November 1822

Albemarle S^t
<Oct> Nov. 5 – 1822

My Lord

I have received your Letter of the 24 Octr in reply to wch & to every other of the same kind I shall only reply that your suspicions are as groundless as they are unworthy of you.[1]

I told you that some of the papers wch you wanted were mislaid but that they should be sent as soon as found[2] – the preface I could not find the printer <I> could not find a Copy – but Mr Kinnaird had had copies of it & consequently there could have been no motive for my retaining it[3] – Mr Kinnaird must have received his Copies of the Said Preface <t> 2 Monts [*sic*] ago!! I reollect [*sic*] that I gave him an order upon the printer to deliver every thing – & consequently it was out of my Hands – The Lines to the Po were sent by you to Mr Kinnaird – I never had <your> the original of them.[4] Apply for these then to Mr Kinnaird – I declare upon my honour though I may have seen the preface I never read it

Remember Mr Kinnaird has also both dedications <<to>of Werner> to Goethe[5]

I am My Lord
yr obed^t. Servt
John Murray

I have just found the MSS of the Letter to Blackwood & have sen [*sic*] it to Bond St.[6] a Letter addressed to me & marked on the Outside from Mr John Hunt – was received by me <this morning> last night & returned <to> unopened this morning – What it could be about I pretend not to guess – I will have no connexion with this Man[7]

Notes to Letter 170)

<u>Cover:</u> Milord/Milord Byron/poste restante/<Pisa>Genoa/Italie <u>arrived:</u> 18? November

See headnote to Letter 169 above: this Letter (170) arrived before Letter 169, and is written with evident passion.

1. B's letter of 24 October, full of complaints and accusations and threatening to make JM's treatment of him public: 'I will show you that I am not disposed to permit you to take advantage of my absence – in a manner – which whatever may be your motive – can do little credit to you – & less to your instigators – for I firmly believe that there is some one behind the curtain playing you off upon this occasion. – I know enough of the baseness of Mr. Southey – and his employers to believe them capable of any thing – – and as for yourself – though I am very unwilling to believe you acting *wilfully* & *wittingly* – as their tool – you leave me no other supposition but that either by menaces or persuasions they are rendering you an instrument – of their purposes personal and political, – "on *fair* ground I could beat forty of them" but not if my Armourer proves treacherous – and spoils my weapons. – – I am truly sorry to be obliged to address you in such a manner – but you have forced me to do so.' Here he signed off; but receiving JM's Letter 168 soon afterwards, he added a much milder postscript which, despite his superscription ('See Postscript') at the head of his letter, JM seems to have ignored as he does not allude to anything it contains (*BLJ* X, 17–18; see also, Letter 168, n. 2 above). The following fragment in MA, conjecturally dated by Marchand 'July 30, 1811?', and printed – incomplete and incorrectly and with no addressee – in *BLJ* II, 63, clearly forms part of a reply by B either to this Letter (170) or to Letter 169 above, and may belong to his letter to JM of 18 November or of 9 December 1822, more probably the former (*BLJ* X, 36 and 52). It is in fact two fragments from the same letter: the first portion is written at the bottom of one leaf, recto ('have been ... mislaid') and verso ('Your showing ... in='); the second ('=discreet only ... cases. – ') at the top of the adjacent page numbered '2/' by B:

> have been forthcoming amongst my posthumous MS.S? – In short you have lost them you say – or mislaid
> Your showing about my letter – I thought in the first instance – <u>base</u> – but as you explain it – it was indiscreet only – since you heard a bad motive attributed to me – and thought this the readiest way of repelling it. – But you should have asked my leave – this is but fair in such cases. –

2. In his letter of 24 October, B accused JM of not having forwarded to Hunt the Preface to *The Vision of Judgment*, which had now appeared without it, and of sending other things to Hunt 'also incomplete' (*BLJ* X, 17; see also, nn. 3 and 7 below). JM had already told him that various items were 'Yet wanting' in his letter of 25 September (see Letter 167 above).

3. JM has underlined 'Mʳ Kinnaird' very heavily. This was the Preface to *The Vision of Judgment* concerning which JM was having to face not only B's accusations but also those of Hunt, who printed the following notice under the title of 'The Liberal' in *The Examiner*, 771 (Sunday 3 November 1822), 697:

> In the First Number of this work, just published, there ought to have been a Preface to the Vision of Judgment, which would have explained the full spirit of one or two passages that may be misconstrued, and shewn more completely how Mr. Southey has subjected himself and his cause to this sort of attack, – if indeed any such evidence be wanting. The author was somewhat anxious on the former point, lest he should be thought to bear harder than he wished on the late Sovereign. The latter, perhaps, may be explained at once by quoting and applying to Mr. Southey the famous line about "fools rushing in where angels fear to tread." But the fact is, that for some reasons best known to himself, Mr. Murray the bookseller, who was to have been the original publisher of the Vision, contrived to evade sending the preface to the present publisher.

This was entirely unjust and untrue. All the indications suggest that Kinnaird was the culprit: almost exactly a year before he had acknowledged receiving 'the corrected proofs of Quevedo Redivivus & a preface & a note to Ditto', when writing to B on Sunday 16 December 1821 (MA), and B himself had told JM on 6 July 1822 to give Hunt 'the *corrected* copy which Mr. K[innair]d had ... and also the preface' (*BLJ* IX, 182; see also, Letter 167, n. 5 above and Letter 171 below); but now, writing to B on 15 November 1822, Kinnaird was curiously circumspect: 'I do not believe that Mʳ. Murray gave to Mʳ Hunt any wrong copy intentionally of the "vision of judgment" – This is my conviction – He had no interest in so doing. The fact is – having sent the MSS both of the preface & the poem to Mʳ Davison his printer, he invested me with full authority over them & he was so frightened of having a copy of either in his house that I recollect applying to him sometime afterwards & he had none. In consequence of an interview with Mʳ Henry Leigh Hunt this morning I have given him a letter to Mʳ Davison desiring he may be furnished with the copy corrected by yourself & the preface. I recollect thinking the latter excellent' (MA). Again, on 22 November he wrote to acknowledge B's letter of 6 November with its enclosure for JM (*BLJ* X, 27–28), 'which you will approve of my not delivering. It turns out that Mʳ Murray did send the corrected copy of the Vision to Mʳ Hunt. There may have been neglect on his part – but I am satisfied of no male fides [bad faith] towards you. It was very unbecoming on his part to be so ready to take offence at Mr Hunt or any one who came from you. But I think Mr Hunt may have been equally disposed to brusques [*sic*] Mr Murray' (MA). Finally, on 26 November, he told B: 'I have just received from him [JM] a packet of your Manuscripts − It turns out that the Copy of the Vision he gave to Mr Hunt was not the copy corrected by you − wether [*sic*] the fault of its not forthcoming lie with him or me I cannot determine − I am fully impress'd with the belief that he is only to be charged with slovenliness' (MA).

4. B told Kinnaird to 'Give Murray the Po verses' on 10 October 1820, and Kinnaird told B he had done so on 14 November 1820; perhaps he had only given JM a copy, not 'the original of them' (*BLJ* VII, 191, and MA; see also, Letter 136 and n. 12, and Letter 138).

5. This was a precautionary move on JM's part. B had not mentioned the dedication to Goethe, originally intended for *Sardanapalus*, in his most recent letters. His last instruction concerning it was in his letter to JM of 3 July, which he sent via John Hunt, telling him 'to append it to *Werner*, making only the necessary alteration in the title of the work dedicated' (*BLJ* IX, 179, and see IX, 167; for the vexed question of the dedications, see *CPW* VI, 604, 607 and 689–91, and E. M. Butler, *Byron and Goethe* [London: Bowes & Bowes, 1956], esp. 81–85). However, writing to JM on 21 December, B complained that he had seen 'by some extracts in a paper' that JM had omitted from *Werner* 'both the *conclusion* to the preface … referring to the E[dinburgh] R[eview] and also the inscription to Goëthe' (*BLJ* X, 63–64; for the *Edinburgh Review*, see Letter 166, n. 2 above). The 'inscription' to Goethe *was* printed in *Werner*, but *not* the 'dedication' nor the '*conclusion* to the preface'. Although this conclusion can be read in its manuscript state in *CPW* VI, 713–14, the following letter from JM to John Hunt, dated simply 'Saturday', indicates that it had been printed but was cancelled by JM in the proof: 'I send you a proof of the Preface to Werner − I submit to you if the paragraph alluding to the Edinb. Rev. might not be omitted − as he is more pointed about it in the new Cantos of Don Juan. My only meaning is that it were better not to allow him to appear too (Q^y two) anxious about criticism'; and he added: 'Will you send me the dedication to Goethe<s>?' (MA). When Hunt published *Werner* in *The Works of Lord Byron. In Two Vols.* (1824), the preface and inscription remained the same as in JM's edition; neither the remainder of the preface nor the 'dedication' appeared.

6. That is, *Some Observations upon an Article in Blackwood's Edinburgh Magazine* (1820), which was not published in B's lifetime. Hunt's premises were at 22 Old Bond Street.

7. See also, Letter 171 below. It is unfortunate that JM should have reacted in this way, as it was to have embarrassing repercussions two years later. Hunt's 'Letter' enclosed B's letter to JM of 22 October 1822, in which B states more savagely and tersely what he says in his letter of 24 October

and which he sent 'To John Murray Esqre./to ye care of John Hunt Esqre/ London', telling JM he had done so in his letter of 24 October (*BLJ* X, 16 and 17; MA for cover direction). When JM later claimed (*Notes on Captain Medwin's Conversations of Lord Byron* [1824], 10; see also, *The Gentleman's Magazine*, XCIV, Pt II [November 1824], 440), that 'nothing had occurred to subvert' the 'friendly sentiments' subsisting between himself and B, the Hunts printed B's letter of 22 October 1822 in *The Examiner* as evidence to the contrary, with the following pertinent note:

> There is a laughable little history connected with the delivery of this letter ... It was sent from Italy, without seal or wafer, enclosed in a letter to Mr. John Hunt, who was directed to 'take a copy and forward it *open*.' Nevertheless, Mr. Hunt put the letter in an envelope, which he sealed and directed to Mr. Murray, and forwarded to Albemarle-street; not wishing to inflict on Mr. M. the humiliation of receiving an open letter through his servants. Mr. Murray, however, unluckily 'rode the high horse' at that moment; and thinking perhaps to annoy Mr. Hunt by a piece of affected scorn and real rudeness, returned the double letter *unopened*. (It had 'From Mr. J. H.' on the outside.) There was no alternative; the intended mercy had been unconsciously spurned; Lord Byron's letter was taken out, and delivered open at Mr. Murray's counter; whence (not perhaps without being first perused by his clerks and shopmen) it was of course expedited to the inner *sanctum*, where the scornful Bookseller sat wrapped in his proud contempt! It was impossible to pity him – the retribution was so entirely the fruit of arrogance and ill-manners (*The Examiner*, No. 876 [Sunday 14 November 1824], 723 and n.).

At JM's earnest request, Hobhouse tried to persuade the Hunts from printing this letter 'but found them exasperated against Murray & could do nothing. The letter is genuine & certainly convicts Murray of a mistake – but it is a pity publishing it'; on the day of its publication he remarked laconically: 'read Examiner – alas poor Murray!!' (Journal entries for Friday 12 and Sunday 14 November 1824; BL Add. 56549, ff. 65r and 66r).

Letter 171) [Friday] 8 November 1822

London – 8th. Novemb^r. 1822 –

My Lord,

Since I last wrote, – a letter (unsealed) from you! was flung on the floor of my shop.[1] – I have now before me M^r. Kinnaird's order[2] upon the Printer for Copies of the Preface to the Vision dated Jan^ry 14th.

1822 – He had taken the whole upon himself, by your order to get it published elsewhere, consequently the care of it was dismissed from my mind. – I enclose what the Printer and I have been able to recover of the Letter to Blackwood[3] which I naturally concluded to be of no use when the occasion of it was gone. – The verses on the Po – were not sent to me.[4] –

I am

My Lord,

Your Obedient Servant

(signed –) John Murray[5]

Notes to Letter 171)

This Letter is written in the hand of JM's clerk, who was probably writing at JM's dictation. It may have accompanied 'a parcel of books' for which B thanked JM in his letter of 23 November, and which he said were 'very welcome, especially Sir Walter's gift of *Halidon Hill*' (*BLJ* X, 40). Scott's metrical drama, *Halidon Hill; A Dramatic Sketch from Scottish History*. By Sir Walter Scott, Bart., was published by Constable in June 1822; B's *'presentation copy, with an inscription on the fly-leaf'* forms lot 180 in his Sale Catalogue (1827) (*CMP*, 252).

1. B's letter of 22 October, which he told JM in his letter of 24 October he had addressed to him 'through the care of Mr. J. Hunt' (*BLJ* X, 16 and 17; see also, Letter 170, n. 6 above).

2. This 'order' is not forthcoming (see Letter 170, n. 3 above).

3. Presumably JM means what he and his printer (Thomas Davison) had been able to recover of the proof rather than the MS of *Some Observations* (see Letter 170, n. 7 above).

4. See Letter 170, n. 4 above.

5. This is the last surviving Letter from JM to B and there is no indication that he ever wrote again. B's penultimate letter to JM was written appropriately enough perhaps on Christmas Day, 25 December 1822, and though censorious and critical still, is written in a much lighter and more amicable vein, concluding (apart from the inevitable postscript) with a wonderful tribute to Shelley and with B telling JM a few plans of his own: 'I have some thoughts of taking a run down to Naples – (solus – or at most – *cum sola*) this Spring – and writing (when I have studied the Country) a fifth & sixth Canto of Ch[ild]e Harolde [*sic*] – but this is merely an idea for the present – and I have other excursions – & voyages in my mind. – – The busts are finished – are you worthy of them?' (*BLJ* X, 69; for the 'busts', see Letter 168, n. 10 above). Unfortunately, though quite understandably, JM seems to have taken this as an intimation that had B gone to Naples and written

another two Cantos of *Childe Harold* he might have been their publisher. But when Hobhouse wrote to B saying how glad he was to hear he was going to Naples, B replied irritably on 19 March 1823: 'I am *not* going to Naples – I thought of it for an instant – being invited there – and Mr. Murray has set the report afloat – with a story about a New Childe Harold – because I said that *if* I went there – I *might* write another Canto' (*BLJ* X, 126, and *BB*, 324); and writing to Kinnaird the next day he was even more emphatic and final: 'As to more Childe Harolds – and Naples – it was a mere hypothetical case – which now that Murray has thought proper to hint it about – I would *not* write – at all – and least of all for such as him. – He went about saying that "*perhaps he* &c. &c. ["] – does the fellow think that he is or ever will be on the same terms with me as formerly?' (*BLJ* X, 127; see also, X, 108). In the event anyway, 'other excursions – & voyages' materialized; and although he told Hobhouse on 11 September that he understood JM was behaving 'infamously – circulating facsimiles of my letters &c.' – which Hobhouse tactfully skirted in his reply of 6 December, saying JM had asked him 'to give your Lordship assurances of his unabated attachment', and adding 'I hope the story of the *letters* is not true' (*BLJ* XI, 24, and *BB*, 339), B never wrote to JM again – save once. On 22 November 1823, Kinnaird wrote to B: 'I saw Mʳ Murray yesterday … He said he had heard of a Satire from Italy on Gifford & – that it was said to be from you – But he did not credit that – but thought it Came from L. Hunt' (MA). It did: Leigh Hunt's *Ultra-Crepidarius; A Satire on William Gifford* was published under his name by John Hunt in 1823. At first B replied solely to Kinnaird on 21 February 1824 saying: 'It is not true that I ever *did* – *will* – *would* – *could* or *should* write a *satire* against Gifford – or a hair of his head – and so tell Mr. Murray' (*BLJ* XI, 117). Four days later, however, on 25 February 1824, he wrote directly to JM himself: 'I have heard from Mr. Douglas K[innair]d that you state "a report of a satire on Mr. Gifford having arrived from Italy – *said* to be written by *me*! – but that *you* do not believe it." – I dare say you do not nor any body else I should think – whoever asserts that I am the author or abettor of anything of the kind on Gifford – lies in his throat. – I always regarded him as my literary father – and myself as his prodigal son; … *you* know as well as any body upon *whom* I have or have not written – and *you* also know whether they *do* or did not deserve that same – – and so much for such matters. – You will perhaps be anxious to hear some news from this part of Greece', and he proceeded to give him a personal account (*BLJ* XI, 123–25). This was his last letter to JM; two months later he was dead.

APPENDICES

APPENDIX A

How Murray became Byron's Publisher

For the circumstances as to how JM came to be the publisher of *CHP*, biographers and editors from Moore to the present day have been obliged to rely upon Dallas's account.[1] Indeed, our knowledge of what took place in the first 15 days or so, between B's arrival in town from Greece on Sunday 14 July 1811 and his departure for Newstead on Friday 2 August 1811, has been governed almost exclusively by what Dallas has told us. Briefly, he tells us that on the very first morning after B's arrival in town, Monday 15 July 1811, B gave him *Hints from Horace* to read, which he took home, read overnight, and by which he was 'grievously disappointed'. Returning the next day, Tuesday 16 July, he asked B whether he had not written anything else, whereupon B produced *CHP* which, though deprecating the poem himself, he 'gave' to Dallas. No sooner had Dallas read *CHP* than he recognized its merits, and immediately wrote to B to tell him so, and then informed him in person that as he had 'given' it to him he would certainly publish it. Impressed by Dallas's 'perseverance', B eventually acquiesced and desired Dallas to offer it to William Miller, who declined it. Thereupon Dallas, wishing to 'oblige' JM, who had with his father before him published for Dallas and had also asked Dallas soon after B's return from Greece to 'obtain some work of his Lordship's for him', offered it to him. And so on.

There is scarcely a word of truth in this. It is a little unfortunate for Dallas, who sought only to magnify his own consequence and the role he played in bringing *CHP* before the public, and thus the obligation that both B and JM owed to him and his impeccable literary judgement for their fame and success, that the manuscripts of his letters to B which he chose to publish in his account, as well as those he chose *not* to publish, are in the Murray Archives; and they, together with unimpeachable evidence from elsewhere (not least from B himself), tell a very different story – one of fraud, forgery and blackmail. In a word, as JM told Hobhouse in 1824, 'the man was a swindler'.[2] A full exposure of all his impostures is beyond the compass of this volume. I shall therefore set forth here, in their baldest outline and without further elaboration, the facts pertinent only to *CHP* and the opening of negotiations with JM, the actual circumstances of which I regret to say still remain uncertain:

1. Dallas had never even seen or read *Hints from Horace* before it had been set up in proof and withdrawn from publication – that is to say, no earlier than October 1811: it was already 'transcribing at Cawthorn's' by Monday 15 July when Dallas claims he was reading it;[3] and Dallas himself, in a letter to B of Monday 26 August 1811 (which he naturally chose not to publish), told him: 'Your remarks on the Romaic are unquestionably the right of Childe Harold – they are far from being so appropriate to the "Hints from Horace". Though, by the way, I say this on supposition, from the recollection of the Art of Poetry, and what passed with you in conversation respecting your paraphrase of it, for I have not seen the "Hints"'.[4]

2. B did not 'give' *CHP* to Dallas; Dallas asked him for it. In a sentence he suppressed in the published version of his letter to B of Tuesday 16 July 1811, he writes: 'As you are resolved to keep your Muse pure of mercenary aims, I wish you would make me a present of this Childe'.[5]

3. B eventually gave the copyright, but not the manuscript, of *CHP* to Dallas, and had apparently done so by 19 January 1812 when Dallas first informed JM that he had – though it was not formalized until 17 March 1812.[6]

4. B gave the manuscripts of both *CHP* and *Hints from Horace* (as well as the manuscript of a Burns letter) to Henry Drury in May 1813, in fulfilment of a promise he had made him sometime earlier.[7]

5. B himself offered *CHP* to William Miller.[8] In his *Biographical Sketches of British Characters Recently Deceased*, Miller gives a sketch of B to which he appends the following note:

> It has been frequently stated in print, that the Author of this work [ie. Miller], when in business, refused the publication of "Childe Harold," because it contained an offensive note against the EARL OF ELGIN. This is only a slight part of the fact. When the original manuscript was placed by LORD BYRON in Mr. MILLER'S hands, it contained several notes of a like nature to that against the Scotch EARL; and at LORD BYRON'S request, Mr. M. took the liberty to point them out; but his LORDSHIP did not *at that time* choose to make any alteration: in consequence of which, the manuscript was returned to the noble Author. When, a few months after, the poem was

published by Mr. MURRAY, most of the objectionable notes *were omitted*.

Had "Childe Harold" created less public notice, this paragraph would not have been obtruded on the reader; but whatever relates to LORD BYRON, or his productions, however trivial, creates a literary interest.[9]

6. Dallas had no reason to 'oblige' JM; and except for one work of his, neither JM nor his father before him had published for him.[10] Nor does he appear to have been personally acquainted with JM prior to the negotiations over *CHP*.[11]

7. If B himself of his own accord did not think of offering *CHP* to JM (and there is no reason to believe he did not do so), it may just as well have been Miller as Dallas who suggested that he should: Miller and JM were on good terms with each other, they each had a quarter share in *Marmion*, and Miller was to offer JM his business when he retired.[12] Otherwise it could have been Hodgson.[13] However, this does not rule out the possibility that it was indeed Dallas.

8. At some point between Miller's declining to publish *CHP* and B's hasty departure for Newstead on account of his mother's ill-health, B did indeed put the poem into Dallas's hands, who placed it for him with JM; and as B could not return immediately to London, he subsequently accepted Dallas's offer of 'mediation' between himself and JM.[14]

Notes to Appendix A

1. His account is given in *Recollections* (1824), 103–23, and in *Correspondence* (1825), II, 46–65. Extracts may also be found in Ernest J. Lovell, Jr., ed., *His Very Self and Voice: Collected Conversations of Lord Byron* (New York: Macmillan, 1954), 39–41; see also, Marchand I, 278–85.

2. Hobhouse's diary entry for Saturday 3 July 1824 (BL Add. 56549, f. 12v).

3. Letter to Hobhouse of Monday 15 July 1811 (*BLJ* II, 59).

4. Unpublished letter from Dallas to B of 26 August 1811 (MA).

5. MA; in the manuscript of this letter the date reads simply '16th July' (uncharacteristically, without the year) and is itself unsafe, the '16' being written in heavy ink over another indecipherable date.

6. MA; unpublished letter from Dallas to JM of 19 January 1812; copyright agreement of 17 March 1812 (see Letter 1, n. 5).

7. MA; unpublished letters from Drury to B of 9 and 23 May 1813; Drury's inscription on the first flyleaf of each manuscript. Incidentally, B's note on the last flyleaf of the manuscript of *CHP* is addressed to 'Dear D^y' (i.e., Drury), not 'Dear D^s.' (i.e., Dallas) as Coleridge has unfortunately misread it (*Poetry*, II, xxviii). The manuscript of the Burns letter, dated 6 April 1793 and endorsed by B 'Given to me by y^e. Lady Charlotte Rawdon Octr. 23^d. 1812 Byron', is also in MA, and is published in J. De Lancey Ferguson, ed., *The Letters of Robert Burns*, 2nd edn ed. G. Ross Roy, 2 vols (Oxford: Clarendon Press, 1985), II, 201–03.

8. B may have offered it to Miller either on his own initiative – he had an outstanding bill to settle with him and had seen him on 16 July promising its settlement on 30 July (*BLJ* II, 62 and 63) – or on the advice of Hodgson, who regarded him as 'the only eligible publisher' (*BLJ* II, 61).

9. William Miller, *Biographical Sketches of British Characters Recently Deceased*, 2 vols (Henry Colburn, 1826), II, 129–30n. Miller also gives a short account of Dallas in which there is no mention of Dallas's being connected in any way with B, or of his having been the medium through whom Miller received the manuscript of *CHP*; nor, indeed, is there the slightest suggestion that Miller knew or had ever met Dallas. Of Dallas's *Recollections* he merely says that 'the publication was suppressed in this Country by the same influence which, aided by the additional power of the law, destroyed the celebrated "Memoirs"' – which act appalled him (II, 193–94). Moreover, that Miller may have had yet other reasons for not publishing *CHP*, and would have retained the manuscript and reserved his opinion until he saw B in person, is suggested by a letter from him to George Cumberland of 20 February 1812, concerning the publication of one of his works: 'I know not how it happened but I got it into my head that I was to keep the MSS. & my remarks until I had the pleasure of seeing you in town ... I shall at some future time be most willing to meet your wishes relative to the publication of it – but at present the times, & State of trade, is [*sic*] So bad, that Literature, is at a Stand – & I acknowledge my unwillingness to enter into new Speculations at this Moment' (BL Add. 36503, f. 131. George Cumberland [1754–1848], artist and writer and intimate friend of Blake's, lived in Bristol).

10. Dallas's *Elements of Self-Knowledge* was published by Murray and Highley in 1802. Otherwise his publishers were Cadell and Davies, Cawthorn, and Longman.

11. There is, however, a single grumbling letter in MA from Dallas to Murray and Highley, dated 13 June 1802 and opening 'Dear Sirs', from which it is evident that he had at least been to 32 Fleet Street.

12. Smiles I, 76 and 233–34.

13. Hodgson was on friendly terms with Gifford who had praised *EBSR* to him shortly after its publication. In an unpublished letter to B of 21 April

1809, Hodgson told him: 'I saw Gifford after you had left Town, and he expressed himself highly pleased with the Satire, & personally obliged by your commendation. He told me you were generally known to be the author – so I have not withstood the propagation of the Truth' (MA).

14. Letter to Dallas of 21 August 1811 (the second only to him from B since his return from Greece, and the first to him in which *CHP* is mentioned at all) (*BLJ* II, 75 and 70–71; see headnote to Letter 1). Miller had declined *CHP* by Tuesday 30 July 1811; B left London for Newstead on Friday 2 August 1811 (*BLJ* II, 63 and 67).

APPENDIX B

The Newspaper Attacks on Byron in 1814
(See Letters 30–33)

'Lines to a Lady Weeping' were first printed anonymously, under the title of 'Sympathetic Address to a Young Lady', in the *Morning Chronicle* for Friday 7 March 1812, and were remarked upon that evening by the *Courier* in an editorial on what it called the 'overweening Aristocracy': 'Who has not read with disgust their attempts to wound every feeling of the heart – None of the relations of private life, however delicate, are to be held sacred – and even the daughter is desired to view her father as an object of suspicion and disgrace!!' (*Courier*, Friday 7 March 1812). When B republished the 'Lines' in *The Corsair* on Tuesday 1 February 1814, thus acknowledging himself as their author, the *Morning Chronicle* for the same day merely extracted the whole of the Dedication to Moore commending it as 'an elegant Eulogium'. The *Courier*, however, immediately pounced on the 'Lines' again (item 1), briefly repeating its disgust the following day (item 2). On Thursday 3 February, the *Morning Chronicle* responded to the *Courier* in support of B (item 3), to which the *Courier* in turn retorted that evening (item 4). The following day *The Sun* intervened in the argument (item 5), and on Tuesday 8 February the *Morning Post* delivered its first lucubrations on the subject (item 6). By this time, however, the *Courier* had begun a series of strictures on B, entitled '*BYRONIANA*', which ran with increasing ferocity for five numbers from Saturday 5 February to Saturday 19 February (items 7–11; the references to *EBSR* therein being to one of the first four editions). Meanwhile, between 5 and 17 February there also appeared in the *Morning Post*, *The Sun* and the *Herald* (no copy forthcoming), various hostile poetical, parodic or epigrammatic responses to the 'Lines' (see, for example, *BLJ* IV, 49, 51 and 63; one alone defending B appeared in the *Morning Chronicle* for Tuesday 8 February signed 'B.B.' [Bernard Barton?]). On 11 February the *Morning Post* announced the intention (never realized) of a peer (unidentified) to bring the matter before Parliament (item 12; cf. *BLJ* III, 242, and IV, 53 and 62; *The Sun* quoted the announcement from the *Morning Post* the same day), and on 18 February gave its final deliberation in the affair (item 13; cf. *BLJ* III, 242). *The Times*, incidentally, was entirely silent on the whole subject.

B was at Newstead when *The Corsair* was published. Before his return to London late in the evening on Wednesday 9 February, he had seen no *Courier* whatsoever (see *BLJ* IV, 45 and 50). On Thursday 10 February, however, he told JM he had received '*two*' unspecified items (very possibly items 3 and 4), but requested others – which clearly included items 1 and 2 (see *BLJ* IV, 41 and 52 [note esp. the 'parody on the *Skull*']). It was therefore after that date, and indeed after the appearance of the *Courier* for 12 February (item 9: 'impudent doggerel', cf. *BLJ* IV, 42), that he drafted his 'Answer to the *Courier*', which he neither completed nor sent (ibid., 41–43, and cf. 53). Subsequently, in the wake of the particularly poisonous aspersions in the *Courier* of 17 February in which JM's name was introduced (item 10), and after some discussion amongst B, JM and Dallas, Dallas wrote a reply which was printed in both the *Morning Chronicle* and *Morning Post* for Monday 21 February (item 14; text from the *Morning Post*). This effectively silenced recrimination for the time being.

Printed here are items 1–14. In a Coda I have added Sir James Mackintosh's 'defensive letter' in the *Morning Chronicle* for Saturday 12 March 1814, and the *Courier*'s brief response thereto. For the whole episode, see also, *BLJ* IV, 41–76, Dallas, *Correspondence*, III, 60–70 and *LLLM*, 164–68.

Item 1: *Courier*, Tuesday 1 February 1814

LORD BYRON.

———

A new Poem has just been published by the above Nobleman, and the *Morning Chronicle* of to-day has favoured its readers with his Lordship's Dedication of it to THOMAS MOORE, Esq. in what that paper calls "an elegant eulogium." If the elegance of an eulogium consist in its extravagance, the *Chronicle's* epithet is well chosen. But our purpose is not with the Dedication, nor the main Poem, *The Corsair*, but with one of the pieces called Poems, published at the end of the *Corsair*. Nearly two years ago (in March, 1812), when the REGENT was attacked with a bitterness and rancour that disgusted the whole country; when attempts were made day after day to wound every feeling of the heart; there appeared in the *Morning Chronicle* an anonymous Address *to a Young Lady weeping*, upon which we remarked at the time (*Courier* of March, 7, 1812), considering it as tending to make the Princess CHARLOTTE of WALES view the PRINCE REGENT her father as an object of suspicion and disgrace. Few of our readers have forgotten the disgust which this address excited. The author of it, however, unwilling that it should sleep in the oblivion to which it had been consigned with the other trash of that day, has republished it, and, placed the first of what are called Poems at the end of this newly published work the *Corsair*, we find this very address:––

> Weep daughter of a *royal* line,
> A Sire's disgrace, a realm's decay;

Lord BYRON thus avows himself to be the Author.

To be sure the Prince has been extremely *disgraced* by the policy he has adopted, and the events which that policy has produced; and the realm has experienced *great decay*, no doubt, by the occurrences in the Peninsula, the resistance of Russia, the rising in Germany, the counter-revolution in Holland, and the defeat, disgrace, and shame of BUONAPARTE. But, instead of continuing our observations, suppose we parody his Lordship's Address, and apply it to February 1814:

TO A YOUNG LADY.

February, 1814.

> View! daughter of a royal line,
>   A father's fame, a realm's renown:
> Ah! happy that that realm is thine,
>   And that its father is thine own!
>
> View, and exulting view, thy fate,
>   Which dooms thee o'er these blissful Isles
> To reign, (but distant be the date!)
>   And, like thy Sire, deserve thy People's smiles.

––––

On reading the Lines written by Lord BYRON, and engraven on the Silver Mounting of a Human Skull, formerly used as a Goblet, at his residence Newstead Abbey:––

> Why hast thou bound around with silver rim
>   This once gay peopled "palace of the soul?"

Look on it now – deserted, bleach'd and grim –
Is this, thou feverish Man, thy festal bowl?

Is this the cup in which thou seek'st the balm
Each brighter chalice to thy breast denies?
Is the oblivious bowl, whose floods becalm. [*sic*]
"The worm that will not sleep, and never dies?"

Woe to the lip to which this Cup is held; –
The lip that's pall'd with every purer draught;
For which alone, the rifled grave can yield,
A Goblet worthy to be deeply quaff'd.

Strip then this glitt'ring mockery from the skull, –
Restore the relic to its tomb again;
And seek a healing balm within the Bowl,
The *blessed Bowl*, that never flow'd in vain.

St.

Item 2: *Courier*, Wednesday 2 February 1814

Lord BYRON, as we stated yesterday, has discovered and promulgated to the world, in eight lines of choice doggrel, that the realm of England is in decay, that her Sovereign is disgraced, and that the situation of the country is one which claims the tears of all good patriots.

Item 3: *Morning Chronicle*, Thursday 3 February 1814

The Courier is indignant at the discovery now made by Lord BYRON, that he was the author of "the Verses to a Young Lady weeping," which were inserted about a twelvemonth ago in *The Morning Chronicle*. The Editor thinks it audacious in a hereditary Counsellor of the KING to admonish the *Heir Apparent*. It may not be *courtly* but it is certainly *British*, and we wish the kingdom had more such honest advisers.

[On the page facing this paragraph, the *Morning Chronicle* extracts *The Corsair*, I, 2, 47–82]

Item 4: *Courier,* Thursday 3 February 1814

"The *Courier* is indignant," says the *Morning Chronicle*, "at the discovery now made by Lord BYRON, that he was the author of 'the Verses to a Young Lady weeping,' which were inserted about a twelvemonth ago in the *Morning Chronicle*. The Editor thinks it audacious in a hereditary Counsellor of the KING to admonish the *Heir Apparent*. It may not be *courtly* but it is certainly *British*, and we wish the kingdom had more such honest advisers."

The discovery of the author of the verses in question was not made by Lord BYRON. How could it be! When he sent them to the *Chronicle, without* his name, he was just as well informed about the author as he is now that he has published them in a pamphlet, *with* his name. The discovery was made by the public. They did not know in March 1812 what they know in February 1814. They did not suspect then what they now find avowed, that a Peer of the Realm was the Author of the attack upon the PRINCE; of the attempt to induce the Princess CHARLOTTE of WALES to think that her father was an object not of reverence and regard, but of disgrace.

But we "think it audacious in a hereditary Counsellor of the KING to admonish the Heir Apparent." No! we do not think it audacious: it is constitutional and proper. But are anonymous attacks the constitutional duty of a Peer of the Realm? Is that the mode in which he should admonish the Heir Apparent? If Lord BYRON had desired to admonish the PRINCE, his course was open, plain, and known – he could have demanded an audience of the PRINCE; or, he could have given his admonition in Parliament. But to level such an attack – – – What! – – – "Kill men i' the dark!" [*Othello*, V, i, 63 (Iago speaking)] This, however, is called by the *Chronicle* "certainly *British*," though it might not be *courtly*, and a strong wish is expressed that "the country had many more such honest advisers" or admonishers – – –

Admonishers indeed! A pretty definition of admonition this, which consists not in giving advice but in imputing blame, not in openly proffering counsel but in secretly pointing censure.

Item 5: *The Sun*, Friday 4 February 1814

LORD BYRON and the MORNING CHRON.

————

That poetical Peer, Lord BYRON, knowing full well, that any thing insulting to his Prince or injurious to his country, would be most thankfully received and published by the *Morning Chronicle*, did in March 1812, send the following loyal and patriotic lines to that loyal and patriotic Paper, in which of course they appeared.

"TO A LADY WEEPING.

"Weep, daughter of a Royal line,
  A Sire's disgrace, a realm's decay:
Ah! happy! if each tear of thine
  Could wash a father's *fault* away!

"Weep – for thy tears are Virtues tears –
  Auspicious to these suffering isles:
And be each drop, in future years,
  Repaid thee by thy people's smiles!"

These lines the *Morning Chronicle*, in the following paragraph of yesterday, informs us were aimed at the PRINCE REGENT, and addressed to the Princess CHARLOTTE:–

"*The Courier* is indignant at the discovery now made by Lord BYRON, that he was the author of "the Verses to a Young Lady weeping," which were inserted about a twelvemonth ago in *The Morning Chronicle*. The Editor thinks it audacious in a hereditary Counsellor of the King to admonish the *Heir Apparent*. It may not be *courtly*, but it is certainly *British*, and we wish the kingdom had more such honest advisers."

No wonder the *Courier*, and every loyal man, should be indignant at the discovery (made by the republication of these worthless lines, in the Noble Lord's new Volume), that this gross insult came from the pen of "a hereditary Counsellor of the KING!" No wonder every good subject should execrate this novel and disgraceful mode of "*admonishing* the Heir Apparent," which is further from being British than it is from being Courtly; for, from Courtier baseness may be expected, but from a Briton no such infamous dereliction of his duty as is involved in a malignant, *anonymous* attack by a Peer of the Realm upon the person exercising the Sovereign Authority of his Country. – But the assertions of Lord BYRON are as false as they are audacious. What was the "Sire's Disgrace" to be thus bewept? He preferred the independance [sic] of the Crown to the arrogant dictation of a haughty Aristocracy, who desired to hold him in Leading-strings. It was then, amid a "Realm's (fancied) decay," because this Faction were not admitted to supreme power, that his Royal Highness's early friends drunk his health in contemptuous silence, while their more vulgar partizans "at the lower end of the Hall" hissed and hooted the royal name. But mark the reverse since March 1812, a reverse which it might have been thought would have induced the Noble Lord, from prudent motives, to have withheld this ill-timed publication! How is his Royal Highness's health toasted *now?* With universal shouts and acclamations. Treason itself dare not interpose a single discordant sound save in its own private orgies! Where is *now* the realm's decay? oh short-sighted prognosticators of prophecies! look around, and dread the fate of the speakers of falsehood among the Jews of old, who were stoned to death by the people! The wide world furnishes the answer to your selfish Croakings, and tells Lord BYRON that he is destitute of at least one of the qualities of an inspired Bard.

Perhaps we might add another, viz. honesty in acknowledging his plagiarisms, one of which (as we have already said more than his silly verse above quoted deserves, except from the rank of its author) we shall take the liberty of stating to the Public.

The *Bride of Abydos* begins, something in the stile of an old ballad, thus:–

> "Know ye the land where the cypress and myrtle
> Are emblems of deeds that are done in their clime,
> Where the rage of the vulture – the love of the turtle –
>   Now melt into sorrow – now madden to crime? –
> Know ye the land of the cedar and vine?
> Where the flowers ever blossom, the beams ever shine,
> Where the light wings of Zephyr, oppress'd with perfume,
> Wax faint o'er the gardens of Gúl in her bloom;
> Where the citron and olive are fairest of fruit;
> And the voice of the nightingale never is mute;
> Where the tints of the earth, and the hues of the sky,
> In colour though varied, in beauty may vie,
> And the purple of Ocean is deepest in dye."

[*The Bride of Abydos*, I, 1–13]

The whole of which passage we take to be a paraphrase, and a bad paraphrase too, of a song of the German of Göthe [Mignon's song in Goethe's *Wilhelm Meisters Lehrjahre* (1795–96): 'Kennst du das Land, wo die Zitronen blühn'], of which the following translation was published at Berlin in 1798:–

> "Know'st thou the land, where citrons scent the gale,
> Where glows the orange in the golden vale,
> Where softer breezes fan the azure skies,
> Where myrtles spring and prouder laurels rise?"

> "Know'st thou the pile, the colonnade sustains,
> Its splendid chambers and its rich domains,
> Where breathing statues stand in bright array,
> And seem, 'What ails thee, hapless maid?' to say?"

> "Know'st thou the mount, where clouds obscure the day;
> Where scarce the mule can trace his misty way;
> Where lurks the dragon and her scaly brood;
> And broken rocks oppose the headlong flood?"

Item 6: *Morning Post*, Tuesday 8 February 1814

LORD BYRON.

————

We are very much surprized, and we are not the only persons who feel disgust as well as astonishment, at the uncalled for avowal Lord BYRON has made of being the Author of some insolent lines, by inserting them at the end of his new Poem, entitled "*The Corsair.*" The lines we allude to begin "*Weep, Daughter of a Royal Line.*" Nothing can be more repugnant to every good heart, as well as to the moral and religious feelings of a country, which we are proud to say still cherishes every right sentiment, than an attempt to lower a father in the eyes of his child. Lord BYRON is a young man, and from the tenor of his writings, has, we fear, adopted principles very contrary to those of Christianity. But as a man of honour and of *feeling*, which latter character he affects *outrageously*, he ought never to have been guilty of so unamiable and so unprovoked an attack. Should so gross an insult to her Royal Father ever meet the eyes of the illustrious young Lady, for whose perusal it was intended, we trust her own good sense and good heart will teach her to consider it with the contempt and abhorrence it so well merits. Will she *weep for the disgrace of a Father* who has saved Europe from bondage, and has accumulated, in the short space of two years, more glory than can be found in any other period of British history? Will she *"weep for a realm's decay,"* when that realm is hourly emerging under the Government of her father, from the complicated embarrassments in which he found it involved? But all this is too evident to need being particularised. What seems most surprising is, that Lord BYRON should chuse to avow Irish trash at a moment when every thing conspires to give it the lie. It is for the *organ of the Party* alone, or a few insane admirers of BONAPARTE and defamers of their own country and its rulers, to applaud him. We know it is now the fashion for our young Gentlemen to become Poets, and a very innocent amusement it is, while they confine themselves to putting their travels into verse, like *Childe Harolde* [*sic*], and Lord NUGENT'S *Portugal* [*Portugal. A Poem. In two parts* (London, 1812)]. Nor is there any harm in Turkish tales, nor wonderful ditties of ghosts and hobgoblins. We cannot say so much for all Mr. MOORE'S productions, admired as he is by Lord BYRON. In short, the whole galaxy of minor poets, Lords NUGENT and BYRON, with Messrs. ROGERS, LEWIS, and MOORE, would do well to keep to rhyme, and not presume to meddle with politics, for which they seem mighty little qualified. We must repeat, that it is innocent to write tales and travels in verse, but calumny can never be so, whether written by poets in St. James's-street, Albany, or Grub-street.

Item 7: *Courier*, Saturday 5 February 1814

BYRONIANA.

No. I.

The Lord BYRON has assumed such a poetico-political and such a politico-poetical air and authority, that in our double capacity of men of letters and politicians, he forces himself upon our recollection. We say *recollection* for reasons which will, bye and by, be obvious to our readers, and will lead them to wonder why this young Lord, whose greatest talent it is to forget, and whose best praise it would be to be forgotten, should be such an enthusiastic admirer of Mr. SAM. ROGERS'S "*Pleasures of Memory.*"

The most virulent satirists have ever been the most nauseous panegyrists, and they are for the most part as offensive by the praise as by the abuse which they scatter.

His Lordship does not degenerate from the character of those worthy persons, his poetical ancestors –

> "The mob of Gentlemen who wrote with ease."
> [Pope, *Imitations of Horace*, II, i, 108]

Who of all authors dealt the most largely in the alternation of flattery and filth. He is the severest satirical and the civilest dedicator of our day; and what completes his reputation for candour, good feeling, and honesty, is that the persons whom he most reviles, and to whom he most fulsomely dedicates, are identically the same.

We shall indulge our readers with a few instance [*sic*]: – the most obvious case, because the most recent, is that of Mr. THOMAS MOORE, to whom he has dedicated, as we have already stated, his last pamphlet; but as we wish to proceed orderly, we shall postpone this and revert to some instances prior in order of time; we shall afterwards shew that his Lordship strictly adheres to HORACE'S rule, in maintaining to the end the ill character in which he appeared at the outset. His Lordship's first dedication was to his guardian and relative, the Earl of CARLISLE. So late as the year 1808 [*Poems Original and Translated*], we find that Lord BYRON was that Noble Lord's "most affectionate kinsman, &c. &c."

Hear how dutifully and affectionately this ingenuous young man celebrates, in a few months after (1809), the praises of his friend:

> "No Muse will cheer with renovating smile,
> The *paralytic puling* of CARLISLE;
> What heterogeneous honours deck the Peer,
> Lord, rhymester, petit-maitre, pamphleteer.
> So *dull* in youth, so *drivelling* in age,
> *His* scenes alone had damn'd our sinking stage.
> But Managers, for once, cried "hold, enough,"
> Nor drugg'd their audience with the tragic stuff.
> Yet at their judgment let his Lordship laugh,
> And case his volumes in *congenial calf!*
> Yes! doff that covering where Morocco shines,
> And hang a calf-skin on those recreant lines."
> [*EBSR*, 725–40 (with omissions)]

And in explanation of this affectionate effusion, our lordly
dedicator subjoins a note to inform us that Lord CARLISLE'S
works are splendidly bound, but that "the rest is all but leather
and pranella [*sic*]," and a little after, in a very laborious note [*CPW*
I, 416], in which he endeavours to defend his consistency he
out-Herods Herod, or to speak more forcibly, out-Byrons Byron,
in the virulence of his invective against his "guardian and relative,
to whom he dedicated his volume of puerile poems." Lord
CARLISLE has, it seems, if we are to believe his word [*sic*], for a
series of years, beguiled "the public with reams of most orthodox,
imperial *nonsense*" and Lord BYRON concludes by asking,

> "What can ennoble knaves, or *fools*, or cowards?
> "Alas! not all the blood of all the Howards."

"So says POPE," adds Lord BYRON. But Pope does not say
so; the words "*knaves and fools*," are not in POPE, but interpolated
by Lord BYRON [for 'sots, or slaves' (*Essay on Man*, IV, 215), and
borrowing from Sheridan's *The School for Scandal*, II, iii, 54], in
favour of his "guardian and relative." Now all this might have slept
in oblivion with Lord CARLISLE'S Dramas, and Lord BYRON'S
Poems; but if this young Gentleman chooses to erect himself into
a spokesman of the public opinion, it becomes worth while to
consider to what notice he is entitled; when he affects a tone of
criticism and an air of candour, he obliges us to enquire whether
he has any just pretensions to either, and when he arrogates the
high functions of public praise and public censure, we may fairly
enquire what the praise or censure of such a being is worth ––

> "Thus bad begins, but worse remains behind."
> [*Hamlet*, III, iv, 179]

Item 8: *Courier*, Tuesday 8 February 1814

BYRONIANA.

––––

No. II.

"Crede Byron," is Lord Byron's armorial motto; *Trust Byron*,
is the translation in the Red-book. We cannot but admire the
ingenuity with which his Lordship has converted the good faith of
his ancestors into a sarcasm on his own duplicity.

"Could nothing but your chief reproach,
Serve for a motto on your coach?"

[Swift, 'Whitshed's Motto on his Coach', 3–4]

Poor Lord Carlisle; he, no doubt, *trusted* in his affectionate ward
and kinsman, and we have seen how the affectionate ward and
kinsman acknowledged, like *Macbeth*, "*the double trust*" [*Macbeth*,
I, vi, 12] only to abuse it. We shall now show how much another
Noble Peer, Lord Holland, has to trust to from his *ingenuous*
dedicator.

Some time last year Lord Byron published a Poem, called *The
Bride of Abydos*, which was inscribed to Lord Holland, "*with every
sentiment of regard and respect by his gratefully obliged and sincere friend,
BYRON.*" "*Grateful and sincere!*" Alas! alas; 'tis not even so good
as what Shakespeare, in contempt, calls "the sincerity of a cold
heart." [*I Henry IV*, II, iii, 1–32] "*Regard and respect!*" Hear, with
what *regard*, and how much *respect*, he treats this identical Lord
Holland. In a tirade against literary assassins (a class of men which
Lord Byron may well feel entitled to describe), we have these lines
addressed to the Chief of the Critical Banditti:

"Known be thy name, unbounded be thy sway,
Thy *Holland's* banquets shall each toil repay,
While grateful Britain yields the praise she owes,
To *Holland's hireling*, and to *learning's foes!*"

[*EBSR*, 518–21]

By which it appears, that

" — These wolves that still in darkness prowl;
This coward brood, which mangle, as their prey,
By hellish instinct, all that cross their way;" [*EBSR*, 429–31]

are hired by Hord [*sic*] Holland, and it follows, very naturally, that
the "*hirelings*" of Lord Holland must be the "*foes of learning.*"

This seems sufficiently caustic; but hear how our dedicator
proceeds—

"Illustrious Holland! hard would be his lot,
His *hirelings* mention'd, and himself forgot!
Blest be the banquets spread at Holland House,
Where Scotchmen feed, and Critics may carouse!
Long, long, beneath that hospitable roof
Shall *Grub-street* dine, while duns are kept aloof,
And *grateful* to the founder of the feast

Declare the Landlord can *translate*, at least! [*sic*]

[*EBSR*, 540–51 (with omissions)]

Lord Byron has, it seems, very accurate notions of *gratitude*, and the word *"grateful"* in these lines, and in his dedication of the Bride of Abydos, has a delightful similarity of meaning. His Lordship is pleased to add, in an explanatory note to this passage, that Lord Holland's Life of Lopez de Vega, and his translated specimens of that author, are much "BEPRAISED *by these disinterested guests.*" Lord Byron well knows that *bepraise* and *bespatter* are almost synonimous. There was but one point on which he could have any hope of touching Lord Holland more nearly; and of course he avails himself, in the most gentlemanly and generous manner, of the golden opportunity.

When his club of literary assassins is assembled at Lord Holland's table, Lord Byron informs us

> "That lest when heated with the unusual grape,
> Some *glowing* thoughts should to the press escape,
> And tinge with red the *female* readers' cheek,
> MY LADY skims the *cream* of each critique;
> Breathes o'er each page *her purity* of soul,
> Reforms each error, and refines the whole."

[*EBSR*, 554–59]

Our readers will, no doubt, duly appreciate the manliness and generosity of these lines; but to encrease their admiration, we beg to remind them that the next time Lord Byron addresses Lord Holland, it is to dedicate to him, in all friendship, *sincerity*, and gratitude, the story of a young, a pure, an amiable, and an affectionate bride!

The verses were bad enough, but what shall be said, after *such* verses, of the insult of *such* a dedication!

We forbear to extract any further specimens of this peculiar vein of Lord Byron's satire; our "gorge rises at it;" [*Hamlet*, V, i, 178–91] and we regret to have been obliged to say so much. And yet Lord Byron is, "with all regard and *respect*, Lord Holland's sincere and grateful friend!" It reminds us of the *respect* which Lear's daughters shewed their father, and which the poor old king felt to be "worse than murder." [*King Lear*, II, ii, 22]

Some of our readers may perhaps observe that, personally, Lord Holland was not so ill-treated as Lord Carlisle; but let it be recollected, that Lord Holland is only an acquaintance, while Lord

Carlisle was "guardian and relation," and had therefore *peculiar* claims to the ingratitude of a mind like Lord Byron's.

Trust Byron, indeed! "him," as *Hamlet* says

> "*Him*, I would trust as I would *adders* fang'd."
>
> [*Hamlet*, III, iv, 203]

Item 9: *Courier*, Saturday 12 February 1814

BYRONIANA.

———— No. III.

Crede Byron — Trust Byron.

————

We have seen Lord Byron's past and present opinions of two Noble Persons whom he has honoured with his satire, and villified by his dedications; let us now compare the evidence which he has given at different and yet not distant times, on the merits of his third *Dedicatee*, Mr. Thomas Moore. To him Lord Byron has inscribed his last poem as a person "of unshaken *public principle*, and the most undoubted and various talents; as the firmest of the Irish *patriots*, and the first of Irish bards."

Before we proceed to give Lord Byron's own judgment of this "firmest of patriots," and this "best of poets," we must be allowed to say, that though we consider Mr. Moore as a very good writer of songs, we should very much complain of the poetical supremacy assigned to him, if Lord Byron had not qualified it by calling him the first only of *Irish* poets, and, as we suppose his Lordship must mean, of *Irish* poets of the *present* day. The title may be, for aught we know to the contrary, perfectly appropriate; but we cannot conceive how Mr. Moore comes by the high-sounding name of "*patriot*;" what pretence there is for such an appellation, by what effort of intellect or of courage he has placed his name above those idols of Irish worship, Messrs. Scully, Connell [*sic*], and Dromgoole [Denys Scully (1773–1830), Irish political writer; Daniel O'Connell (1775–1847), Irish politician and lawyer (the 'Liberator'); and Thomas Dromgoole (1750?–1826?), Irish physician – all agitators for Catholic Emancipation]. Mr. Moore has written words to Irish tunes; so did Burns for *his* national airs; but who ever called Burns the "firmest of patriots" on the score of his contributions to the Scots Magazine?

Mr. Moore, we are aware, has been accused of tuning his harpsichord to the key-note of a faction, and of substituting, wherever he could, a party spirit for the spirit of poetry; this, in the opinion of most persons, would derogate even from his *poetical* character, but we hope that Lord Byron stands alone in considering that such a prostitution of the muse entitles him to the name of patriot. Mr. Moore, it seems, is an Irishman, and, we believe, a Roman Catholic; he appears to be, at least in his poetry, no great friend to the connexion of Ireland with England.

One or two of his ditties are quoted in Ireland as *laments* upon certain worthy persons whose lives were terminated by the hand of law, in some of the unfortunate disturbances which have afflicted that country; and one of his most admired songs begins with a stanza, which we hope the Attorney-General will pardon us for quoting:

> Let Erin remember the days of old,
>   Ere her *faithless sons betrayed her*,
> When Malachy [*sic*] wore the collar of gold,
>   Which he won from her proud Invader;
> When her Kings, with standard of green unfurl'd,
>   Led the Red Branch Knights to danger,
> Ere the emerald gem of the western world,
>   *Was set in the crown of a Stranger.*
> ['Let Erin Remember the Days of Old', *Irish Melodies* (1807)]

This will pretty well satisfy an English reader, that, if it be any ingredient of patriotism to promote the affectionate connexion of the English isles under the constitutional settlement made at the revolution and at the union; and if the foregoing verses speak Mr. Moore's sentiments, he has the same claims to the name of "*patriot*" that Lord Byron has to the title of "trustworthy;" but if these and similar verses do *not* speak Mr. Moore's political sentiments, then undoubtedly he has never written, or at least published any thing relating to public affairs; and Lord Byron has no kind of pretence for talking of the political character and public principles of an humble individual who is only known as the translator of Anacreon, and the writer, composer, and singer of certain songs, which songs do not (*ex hypothesi*) speak the sentiments even of the writer himself.

But, hold – we had forgot one circumstance; Mr. Moore has been said to be one of the authors of certain verses on the highest characters of the State, which appeared from time to time in the

Morning Chronicle, and which were afterwards collected into a little
volume [*Intercepted Letters: or, the Two-penny Post-bag; with some trifles
reprinted from the Morning Chronicle and the Examiner*, By Thomas
Brown, the Younger (13th edn, pub. Wed. 2 Feb. 1814)]; this may,
probably, be in Lord Byron's opinion, a clear title to the name of
patriot, in which case, his Lordship has also his claim to the same
honour; and indeed that sagacious and loyal person, the Editor of
the *Morning Chronicle*, seems to be of this notion: for when some
one ventured to express some, we think, not unnatural, indignation
at Lord Byron's having been the author of some impudent doggrels
[cf. *BLJ* IV, 42], of the same vein, which appeared anonymously
in that paper reflecting on his Royal Highness the Prince Regent
and her Royal Highness his daughter, the Editor before-mentioned
exclaimed — "What! and is not a Peer, an hereditary councillor of
the Crown, to be permitted to give his constitutional advice?!!!"

If writing such vile and anonymous stuff as one sometimes reads
in the *Morning Chronicle* be the duty of a good subject, or the
privilege of a Peer of Parliament, then indeed we have nothing
to object to Mr. Moore's title of Patriot, or Lord Byron's open,
honourable, manly, and constitutional method of advising the
Crown.

To return, however, to our main object, Lord Byron's *consistency*,
truth, and trust-worthiness.

His Lordship is pleased to call Mr. Moore not only Patriot and
Poet, but he acquaints us also, that "he is the delight alike of his
readers and his friends; the poet of all circles, and the idol of his
own."

Let us now turn to Lord Byron's thrice-recorded opinion of
"*this Poet of all circles*." We shall quote from a Poem which was
re-published, improved, amended, and re-considered, not more
than *three* years ago; since which time Mr. Moore has published
no Poem whatsoever; therefore, Lord Byron's former and present
opinions are founded upon the same data, and if they do not agree,
it really is no fault of Mr. Moore's, who has published nothing to
alter them.

> "Now look around and turn each *trifling* page,
> Survey the *precious* works that please the age,
> While Little's lyrics shine in hot-pressed twelves."
>
> [*EBSR*, 121–22, 128]

Here, by no great length of induction, we find that Little's,
i.e. Mr. Thomas Moore's, lyrics, are *trifling*, "*precious works*," his

Lordship ironically adds, that "please times from which," as his Lordship says, "taste and reason are passed away!" [*EBSR*, 120]

Bye and by his Lordship delivers a still more plain opinion on Mr. Moore's fitness to be the "*Poet of* ALL *circles*."

> "Who in soft guise, surrounded by a quire
> All virgins *melting*, not to *Vesta's* fire,
> With sparkling eyes, and cheek by *passion* flush'd,
> Strikes his wild lyre, while listening dames are hush'd?
> 'Tis Little, young Catullus of his day,
> As sweet, but as immoral, in his lay;
> Griev'd to condemn, the Muse must yet be just,
> Nor spare melodious *advocates of lust*!"   [*EBSR*, 283–90]

O cœlum et terra! as *Lingo* says;[*] what? this purest of Patriots is *immoral*? What, "the Poet of *all* circles," is "the advocate of lust!" Monstrous! but who can doubt Byron? and his Lordship, in a subsequent passage, does not hesitate to speak still more plainly, and to declare, in plain round terms (we shudder while we copy) that Moore, the Poet, the Patriot "Moore, is lewd!!!" [*EBSR*, 921 (edns 1–4 only)]

After this, we humbly apprehend that if we were to "trust Byron," Mr. Moore, however he may be the idol of his own circle, would find some little difficulty in obtaining admittance into any other.

Lord Byron, having thus disposed, as far as depended upon him, of the moral character of the first of Patriots and Poets, takes an early opportunity of doing justice to the personal honour of this dear "friend;" one, as his Lordship expresses it, of "the magnificent and fiery spirited" sons of Erin.

"In 1806," says Lord Byron, "Messrs. Jeffery [*sic*] and Moore met at Chalk Farm – the duel was prevented by the interference of the Magistracy, and on examination, the balls of the pistols, *like the courage of the combatants* [edns 1–4 only], were found to have *evaporated*!"

"Magnificent and fiery spirit," with a vengeance!

We are far from thinking of Mr. Moore as Lord Byron either did or does; not so degradingly as his Lordship did in 1810; not so

---

[*] 'O heaven and earth!' Lingo was a butler in variety entertainments whose songs were full of pseudo-Latin tags, such as 'Domino felix', 'Amo amas', 'Mallas homo' and 'Quid opies' in *Lingo's Triumph* ('Once more good friends with Latin grac'd'), sung by Mr. Davis, and printed for T. Skillern in *c.* 1785.

extravagantly as he does in 1813 [*sic*]. But we think that Mr. Moore
has grave reason of complaint, and almost just cause, to exert "his
fiery spirit" against Lord Byron, who has the effrontery to drag
him twice before the public, and overwhelm him, one day with
odium, and another with ridicule.

We regret that Lord Byron, by obliging us to examine the value
of his censures, has forced us to contrast his past with his present
judgments, and to bring again before the public the objects of his
lampoons and his flatteries. We have, however, much less remorse
in quoting his satire than his dedications; for, by this time, we
believe, the whole world is inclined to admit, that his Lordship can
pay no compliment so valuable as his censure; nor offer any insult
so intolerable as his praise.

Item 10: *Courier,* Thursday 17 February 1814

BYRONIANA.

—————   No. IV.

DON PEDRO. – What offence have these men done?
DOGBERRY. – Many, Sir; they have committed false
reports; moreover they have spoken untruths; secondarily,
they are slanders; sixthly and lastly, they have belied a Lady;
thirdly, they have verified unjust things, and, to conclude,
they are lying knaves.
MUCH ADO ABOUT NOTHING [V, i, 203–08].

We have already seen how scurvily Lord Byron has treated
three of the four persons to whom he has successively dedicated
his Poems: but for the fourth he reserved a species of contumely,
which we are confident our readers will think more degrading
than all the rest. *He has uniformly praised him! and him alone!!!*
– The exalted rank, the gentle manners, the polished taste of his
guardian and relation, Lord Carlisle – The considerations due to
Lord Holland, from his family, his personal character and his love
of letters – The amiability of Mr. Moore's society, the sweetness of
his versification, and the vivacity of his imagination; all these could
not save their possessors from the *brutality* of Lord Byron's personal
satire.

It was, then, for a person only, who should have *none* of these
titles to his *envy* that his Lordship could be expected to reserve

the fullness and the steadiness of his friendship; and if we had any respect or regard for that small poet and disagreeable person, Mr. Sam Rogers, we should heartily pity him for being "*damned*" to such "*fame*" as Lord Byron's uninterrupted praise can give [Pope, *An Essay on Man*, IV, 284, and *The Dunciad*, III, 158].

But Mr. Sam Rogers has another cause of complaint against Lord Byron, and which he is of a taste to resent more – His Lordship has not deigned to call *him* "the firmest of patriots," though we have heard that his claims to that title are not much inferior to Mr. Moore's. Mr. Sam Rogers is reported to have clubb'd with the Irish Anacreon in that scurrilous collection of verses, which we have before mentioned, and which were [*sic*] published under the title of the "Twopenny Post-bag," and the assumed name of "Thomas Brown." The rumour may be unfounded; if it be, Messrs. Rogers and Moore will easily forgive us for saying, that, much as we are astonished at the effrontery with which Lord Byron has acknowledged his lampoon, we infinitely prefer it to the cowardly prudence of the author or authors of the "Twopenny Post-bag," lurking behind a fictitious name, and "devising impossible slanders," [cf. *Much Ado About Nothing*, III, i, 84] which he or they have not the spirit to avow.

But, to return to the more immediate subject of our lucubrations: It seems almost like a fatality, that Lord Byron has hardly ever praised any thing that he has not at some other period censured, or censured any thing that he has not, by and bye, praised or *practised*.

It does not often happen that booksellers are assailed for their too great liberality to Authors; yet, in Lord Byron's satire, while Mr. Scott is abused, his publisher, Mr. Murray, is sneered at, in the following lines:

> "And think'st thou, Scott, by vain conceit perchance,
> On public taste to foist thy stale romance;
> Though *Murray* with his Miller may combine,
> *To yield thy Muse just* HALF-A-CROWN A LINE?
> No! when the sons of song descend to trade,
> Their bays are sear, their former *laurels fade.*
> Let such forego the poets' sacred name,
> Who *rack* their *brains* for *lucre*, not for fame:
> Low may they sink to *merited contempt*
> And *scorn* remunerate the *mean* attempt."   [*EBSR*, 171–80]

Now, is it not almost incredible that this very Murray (the only remaining one of the booksellers whom his Lordship had attacked; Miller has left the trade;) is it not, we say, almost incredible, that this very Murray should have been soon after selected, by this very Lord Byron, to be his own publisher? But what will our readers say, when we assure them, that not only was Murray so selected, but that his magnanimous young Lord has actually *sold* his works to this same Murray; and what is a yet more singular circumstance, has received and pocketted, for one of his own "stale romances," a sum amounting, not to "*half-a-crown*," but to *a whole crown, a line!!!*

This fact, monstrous as it seems in the author of the foregoing lines, is, we have the fullest reason to believe accurately true; and the "*faded laurel*," "*the brains rack'd for lucre*," "*the merited contempt*," "*the scorn*," and the "*meanness*," which this impudent young man dared to attribute to Mr. Scott, appear to have been a mere anticipation of his own future proceedings; and thus,

> ———— Even-handed Justice
> Commends the ingredients of his *poison'd* chalice
> To his own lips.   [*Macbeth*, I, vii, 10–12]

How he likes the taste of it we do not know; about as much, we suspect, as the "incestuous murderous damned Dane" did, when *Hamlet* obliged him to "*drink off the potion*" which he had treacherously drugged for the destruction of others [*Hamlet*, V, ii, 317–18].

Item 11: *Courier*, Saturday 19 February 1814

BYRONIANA.

————   No. V.

"He professes no keeping oaths; in breaking them he is stronger than Hercules. He will lie, Sir, with such volubility, that you would think truth were a fool."

ALL'S WELL THAT ENDS WELL [IV, iii, 233ff.]

We have, we should hope, sufficiently exposed the audacious levity and waywardness of Lord Byron's mind, and yet there are a few touches which we think will give a finish to the portrait, and add, if it be at all wanting, to the strength of the resemblance.

————

It must be amusing to those who know any thing of Lord Byron in the circles of London, to find him magnanimously defying in very stout heroics,

> "——— all the din of *Melbourn* [*sic*] House
> "And Lambes' [*sic*] resentment ———" [*EBSR*, 1045–46]

and adding, that he is "*unscared*" even by "*Holland's spouse.*"

———

To those who may be in the habit of hearing his Lordship's political descants, the following extract will appear equally curious:—

"Mr. Brougham, in No. 25. of the *Edinburgh Review*, throughout the article concerning Don Pedro Cevallos, has displayed more politics than policy; many of the worthy burgesses of Edinburgh being so *incensed at the* INFAMOUS *principles it evinces*, as to have withdrawn their subscriptions;" and in the text of this poem, to which the foregoing is a note, he advises the Editor of the Review to

> "Beware, lest *blundering Brougham* destroy the sale;
> Turn beef to bannacks, cauliflower to kail." [*EBSR*, 524–25]

Those who have attended to his Lordship's progress as an author, and observe that he has published *four* poems, in little more than two years, will start at the following lines:

> " ——— Oh cease thy song!
> A bard may chaunt too often and too long;
> As thou art strong in verse, in mercy spare;
> A FOURTH, alas, were more than we could bear."
>
> > [*EBSR*, 225–28]

And as the scene of each of these *four* Poems is laid in the Levant, it is curious to recollect, that when his Lordship informed the world that he was about to visit "Afric's coast," and "Calpe's height," and "Stamboul's minarets," and "Beauty's native clime," [*EBSR*, 1019–21] he enters into a voluntary and solemn engagement with the public,

> "That should he back return, no letter'd rage
> Shall drag *his* common-place book on the stage;
> Of Dardan tours let Dilettanti tell,
> He'll leave topography to classic Gell,

And, *quite content*, no more shall interpose,
To *stun* mankind with *poetry* or *prose*."
[*EBSR*, 1023–24 (edns 1–4 only), 1033–36]

And yet we have already had, growing out of this "Tour," four
volumes of *poetry*, enriched with copious notes in *prose*, selected
from his "*common-place book*." The whole interspersed every here
and there with the most convincing proofs that instead of being
"*quite content*," his Lordship has returned, as he went out, the most
discontented and peevish thing that breathes.

But the passage of all others which gives us the most delight is
that in which his Lordship attacks his critics, and declares, that

"Our men in buckram shall have blows enough,
"And feel they too are penetrable stuff."

[*EBSR*, 1049–50]

And adds,

———— "I have —
"Learn'd to deride the Critic's stern decree,
"And *break him on the wheel he meant for me*."

[*EBSR*, 1059–60]

We should now with all humility ask his Lordship whether *he*
yet feels that "he *too* is penetrable stuff," and we should further
wish to know how he likes being "*broken on the wheel he meant for
others?*"

When his Lordship shall have sufficiently pondered on those
questions, we may perhaps venture to propound one or two more.

Item 12: *Morning Post*, Friday 11 February 1814

We are informed from very good authority, that as soon as the
House of Lords meets again, a Peer of very independent principles
and character intends to give notice of a motion occasioned by the
late spontaneous avowal of a copy of verses, by Lord BYRON,
addressed to the Princess CHARLOTTE of WALES, in which he
has taken the most unwarrantable liberties with her august Father's
character and conduct; this motion being of a personal nature,
it will be necessary to give the Noble Satirist some days' notice,
that he may prepare himself for his defence, against a charge of
so aggravated a nature, which may perhaps not be a fit subject for

a criminal prosecution, as the laws of the country, not foreseeing the probability of such a case ever occurring, under all the present circumstance, have not made a provision against it; but we know that each House of Parliament has a controul over its own Members, and that there are instances on the Journals of Parliament where an individual Peer has been suspended from all the privileges of the high situation to which his birth entitled him, when by any flagrant offence against good order and government, he has rendered himself unworthy of exercising so important a trust.

Item 13: *Morning Post*, Friday 18 February 1814

LORD BYRON

––––––

If it was the object of Lord BYRON to stamp his character, and to bring his name forward by a single act of his life into general notoriety, it must be confessed that he has completely succeeded. We do not recollect any former instance, in which a Peer has stood forth as the libeller of his Sovereign. If he disapproves the measures of his Ministers, the House of Parliament, in which he has an hereditary right to sit, is the place where his opinions may with propriety be uttered. If he thinks he can avert any danger to his country by a personal conference with his Sovereign, he has a right to demand it. The Peers are the natural advisers of the Crown, but the Constitution which has granted them such extraordinary privileges, makes it doubly criminal in them to attack the authority from which it is derived, and to insult the power which it is their peculiar province to uphold and protect. What then must we think of the foolish vanity, or the bad taste of a titled Poet, who is the first to proclaim himself the Author of a Libel, because he is fearful it will not be sufficiently read without his avowal. We perfectly remember having read the verses in question a year ago [*sic*]; but we could not then suppose them the offspring of patrician bile, nor should we now believe it without the Author's special authority. It seems by some late quotations from his Lordship's works, which have been rescued from that oblivion to which they were hastening with a rapid step, by one of our co-equals [the *Courier*], that this peerless Peer has already gone through a complete course of private ingratitude. The inimitable HOGARTH has traced the gradual workings of an unfeeling heart in his progress of cruelty.

He has shewn, that malevolence is progressive in its operation, and that a man who begins life by impaling flies, will find a delight in torturing his fellow creatures before he closes it [alluding to Domitian; see Suetonius, *Lives of the Caesars*, VIII, 'Domitian', iii]. We have heard that even at school these poetical propensities were strongly manifested in Lord BYRON, and that he began his satirical career against those persons to whom the formation of his mind was entrusted ['On a Change of Masters, at a Great Public School' (*CPW* I, 132)]. From his schoolmaster he turned the oestrum [fury] of his opening genius to his guardian and uncle, the Earl of CARLISLE. We cannot believe that the Noble Person's conduct has in this instance been a perfect contrast to the general tenor of his life. We have heard, that during his guardianship he tripled the amount of his nephew's fortune. If the Earl of CARLISLE was satisfied with his own *conscia mens recti* [Ovid, *Fasti* IV, 311: 'Conscia mens recti famae mendacia risit' (a mind conscious of its right laughs at the lies of rumour)], if he wanted no thanks, he must at least have been much surprised to find such attentions and services rewarded with a libel, in which not only his literary accomplishments, but his bodily infirmities, were made the subject of public ridicule. The Noble Earl was certainly at liberty to treat such personal attacks with the contempt which they deserve, but since his Sovereign is become the object of a vile and unprovoked libel, he will no doubt draw the attention of his Peers to a new case of outrage to good order and government, which has been unfortunately furnished by his own nephew.

Item 14: Dallas's letter in the *Morning Chronicle* and *Morning Post*, Monday 21 February 1814

(text from the *Morning Post*)

LORD BYRON

———

TO THE EDITOR OF THE MORNING POST.

Sir – – I have seen the paragraph in an Evening Paper, in which Lord BYRON is *accused* of "receiving and pocketing" large sums for his works [cf. item 7]. I believe no one who knows him has the slightest suspicion of this kind, but the assertion being public, I think it a justice I owe to Lord BYRON to contradict it publicly.

I address this letter to you for that purpose, and I am happy
that it gives me an opportunity, at this moment, to make some
observations which I have for several days been anxious to do
publicly, but from which I have been restrained by an apprehension
that I should be suspected of being prompted by his Lordship.

I take upon me to affirm, that Lord BYRON never received a
shilling for any of his works. To my certain knowledge the profits
of the *satire* [*EBSR*] were left entirely to the Publisher of it. The
gift of the copyright of *Childe Harold's Pilgrimage*, I have already
publicly acknowledged, in the dedication of the new edition of
my novels [*The Miscellaneous Works and Novels of R. C. Dallas Esq.*,
7 vols, New Edition (Longman, 1813), I, iii–iv]; and I now add
my acknowledgement for that of *The Corsair*, not only for the
profitable part of it, but for the delicate and delightful manner
of bestowing it, while yet unpublished. With respect to his two
other poems, *The Giaour* and *The Bride of Abydos*, Mr MURRAY,
the publisher of them, can truly attest that no part of the sale
of these has ever touched his hands, or been disposed of for his
use. Having said thus much as to facts, I cannot but express my
surprise, that it should ever be deemed a matter of reproach that
he should appropriate the pecuniary returns of his works. Neither
rank nor fortune seems to me to place any man above this; for
what difference does it make in honour and noble feelings, whether
a copyright be bestowed, or its value employed in beneficent
purposes; I differ with my Lord BYRON on this subject, as well
as some others, and he has constantly, both by word and action,
shown his aversion to receiving money for his productions.

The pen in my hand, and affection and grateful feelings in my
heart, I cannot refrain from touching upon a subject of a painful
nature, delicate as it is, and fearful as I am that I shall be unable
to manage it with a propriety of which it is susceptible, but of
which the execution is not easy. One reflection encourages me,
for if magnanimity be the attendant of rank (and all that I have
published proves such a prepossession in my mind) then have I the
less to fear from THE MOST ILLUSTRIOUS, in undertaking to
throw into its proper point of view, a circumstance which has been
completely misrepresented, or misunderstood.

I do not purpose to defend the publication of the two stanzas
at the end of *The Corsair*, which has given rise to such a torrent
of abuse, and of the insertion of which I was not aware till it
was published: but most surely they have been placed in a light
which never entered the mind of the author, and in which men of

dispassionate minds cannot see them. It is absurd to talk seriously of their ever being meant to disunite the parent and child, or to libel the Sovereign. It is very easy to descant upon such assumed enormities; but the assumption of them, if not a loyal error, is an atrocious crime. Lord BYRON never contemplated the horrors that have been attributed to him. The lines alluded to were an impromptu, upon a single well-known fact; I mean the failure in the endeavour to form an administration in the year 1812, according to the wishes of the author's friends; on which it was reported that tears were shed by an illustrious female. The very words in the context show the verses to be confined to that one circumstance, for they are in the singular number, *disgrace, fault.* What disgrace? What fault? Those (says the verse) of not saving a sinking realm (and let the date be remembered, March 1812,) by taking the writer's friends to support it. Never was there a more simple political sentiment expressed in rhyme. If this be libel, if this be the undermining of filial affection, where shall we find a term for the language often heard in both Houses of Parliament?

While I hope that I have said enough to show the hasty misrepresentation of the lines in question, I must take care not to be misunderstood myself. The little part I take in conversing on politics is well known among my friends to differ completely from the political sentiments which dictated these verses; but knowing their author better than most who pretend to judge of him, and, with motives of affection and admiration, I am shocked to think that the hasty collecting of a few scattered poems, to be placed at the end of a volume, should have raised such a clamour. – I am, Sir, your obedient servant,

Feb. 18, 1814.   R. C. DALLAS.

CODA

In his Journal for Tuesday 15 March 1814, B remarks: 'Mackintosh is, it seems, the writer of the defensive letter in the Morning Chronicle. If so, it is very kind, and more than I did for myself' (*BLJ* III, 251). This refers to a letter signed 'S. H.', which appeared in the *Morning Chronicle* for Saturday 12 March 1814. Although Mackintosh seems never to have acknowledged the letter openly, there is no reason to doubt B's ascription: he had dined with Mackintosh the preceding evening (Monday 14 March; *BLJ* III, 250); and in a letter to her niece, Elizabeth Wedgwood, dated 24 March 1814, Fanny Allen, Mackintosh's pet sister-in-law, told her that B had 'called at

M.'s [Mackintosh's] yesterday': 'You have heard that it was Mackintosh who wrote that letter in his favour in the *Morning Chronicle*. Lord Byron knows from whence it came and is so thankful, he does not know how sufficiently to express his thanks. This is a secret, as 'tis called' (Henrietta Litchfield, ed., *Emma Darwin: A Century of Family Letters 1792–1896*, 2 vols [London: John Murray, 1915], I, 50). Mackintosh's letter elicited a brief response from the *Courier* on Tuesday 15 March 1814; both are given here:

A) Sir James Mackintosh's letter in the *Morning Chronicle*, Saturday 12 March 1814:

LORD BYRON.

————

TO THE EDITOR OF THE MORNING CHRONICLE.

SIR,

I am desirous of calling the attention of men of honour and delicacy of all parties to some attacks which have lately been made in *The Courier* on a young nobleman of great celebrity. Had they been directed against his poetry I might have ascribed them to jealousy of his fame, and I should have left them to be repelled by the admiration of his country. If his political conduct had been aimed at, I should have thought the most important part of it sufficiently secured by its apparent independence and disinterestedness. To call the most popular poet of our times, "an impudent young man," is an insult to the public taste, pretty sure of being punished by the disgust with which vulgar scurrility never fails to inspire all men of liberal education and sentiments. But if Lord Byron has employed his talents in the disputes of party, I should not have blamed any severity of retaliation expressed in the language of gentlemen, confined as nearly as possible to himself, and consistent with the usages of fair contest.

I charge the writer in *The Courier* with a breach of all these conditions.

Lord Byron at the age of twenty-one, smarting under a sharp provocation, and probably misled about its source, published a satire, which he himself condemned almost as soon as he could calmly consider it. He suppressed it on his return from Greece, and he is said to have refused the offer of large sums of money for permission to re-publish it, a circumstance which I should have disdained to mention in a contest with a generous adversary, especially after the purposes to which Lord Byron is now publicly known to have applied the sums which have been paid for the copyright of his works. In the following words of the dedication of the Corsair, he has publicly announced the suppression, and avowed his indelible regret for having published the suppressed production, "*Compositions whose* FORMER CIRCULATIONS [*sic*] *is part of my present and will be of my future regret.*"

Nothing, it is evident, could have limited a generous mind to this general disavowal, but an apprehension (well or ill founded) that more particular language might revive the pain formerly inflicted, or, perhaps, wound where the shaft might not before have reached. This delicacy, perhaps, originally overstrained, soon proved wholly unavailing.

The writer in *The Courier*, to whom I have alluded, chose to republish all those parts of the disavowed poem which had been directed against the nearest relations of the writer, and against those who had become his most intimate friends. Is there any example of such a proceeding in the civilized and honourable warfare of English parties?

Offensive language in private conversation is considered as unsaid by all mankind as soon as the speaker desires to recal it. If warm words used to a relation or friend in society were not revocable, every infirmity of temper might dissolve the dearest and most sacred relations of human life. The deliberate and cold repeater of the words, after their recal, is justly regarded as being equally the enemy of both parties. He does his utmost to convert momentary warmth into everlasting hatred, to render explanation vain, forgiveness disreputable, and reconciliation impossible.

Is the case changed because the offensive words are printed? Has the author lost by publication the right to deliver himself from the effects of his own inconsiderate language? Has he no right to relieve his mind, and gratify his sense of justice by reparation to others? Shall a common enemy be entitled to render the reparation unavailing, precisely where the injury is most extensive? Are the hot words of youth, anger, and mistake to be made irrevocable at the pleasure of every malevolent antagonist?

Had a bookseller re-published the Poem in spite of Lord Byron's prohibition, he would have been universally reprobated as an invader of the author's rights. But what is the difference between a bookseller and the writer to whom I advert? Only this: that the bookseller would publish the whole for profit, and this writer has published parts from malice. To publish the whole, or any part, of a disavowed work, is morally the same with publishing the whole or part of a purloined manuscript. The moral right of the writer to withdraw his work is as clear as his original right to withhold it. It is vain to say that, however unjustifiable the re-publication may be, the author has too deeply offended to have any right to complain. In truth the author is rarely the greatest sufferer. If he be malicious it may be agreeable to him – if he be careless of the feelings of others, it may be indifferent. It is a suffering so unjust as only to be felt by a generous author, and in exact proportion to his generosity.

But the principal sufferers must generally be those whom the writer in *The Courier* affects to compassionate, and whose wrongs he pretends to deplore. Because respectable and amiable persons have been once attacked, this writer, under pretence of punishing the original assailant, again tears open their wounds and invades the privacy of their domestic life. It is his triumph that he throws disquiet into families – that he contributes to exasperate and perpetuate the divisions of those whom nature and friendship have joined. He avowedly exults in having inflicted pain by wounding the dearest and most sacred sentiments of those whom he is compelled to represent as already suffering under unprovoked injury. No man who felt such sentiments in his own breast could have wounded them in others. Such writers are sufficiently punished by the privation of all that is noble and delightful in human feeling. But they must also be condemned by men of honour, without distinction of party, and without regard to the merit or demerit of Lord Byron. They have rendered themselves the authors of the republished satire. As such they would be considered by a court of justice. As such they must be regarded by the parties against whom they have adopted the *offensive* language disclaimed by the original author. As such they must be reprobated by all those who value fairness and decency in political contest, who condemn the dragging of private feeling and conduct before the public, and who esteem literary property as inviolable for purposes of honour and morality, as it is for these of pecuniary profit. Nothing can be wanting to the condemnation of such writers but the proof evidently supplied by the circumstances and objects of their abuse, that they have not the excuse of resentment, but are actuated by the base policy of infusing suspicion and confirming prejudice against the opponents of their employers in the minds of those whose cause they dishonour by their means of defence.

Feb. 21, 1814.   S. H.

B) Response in the *Courier*, Tuesday 15 March 1814:

The republication of some *Satires*, which the humour of the
moment now disposes the writer to recall, was strenuously
censured, the other day, in a Morning Paper. It was there said,
amongst other things, that such a republication "contributes to
exasperate and perpetuate the divisions of those, whom *nature*
and friendship have joined!" – This is within six weeks after the
deliberate *republication* of "Weep, daughter," &c. &c.: and thus we
are informed of the exact moment, at which all retort is to cease;
at which mis-representation towards the public and outrage towards
the Personages much more than insulted in those lines, is [*sic*] to
be no longer remembered. What privileges does this writer claim
for his friends! They are to live in all "the swill'd [*sic*] insolence"
[misquoting *Paradise Lost*, I, 501–02: 'the Sons/Of Belial, flown with
insolence and wine'] of attack upon those, on whose character,
union, and welfare, the public prosperity mainly depends; they
are to instruct the DAUGHTER to hold the FATHER disgraced,
because he does not surrender the prime Offices of the State to
their ambition; and if after this, public disgust make the author feel,
in the midst of the little circle of flatterers, that remains to him,
what an insight he has given into the guilt of satire *before* maturity,
before experience, *before* knowledge; if the original unprovoked
intruder upon the peace of others be thus taught a love of privacy
and a facility of retraction; if Turnus have found the time,

> "magno cum optaverit emptum
> Intactum Pallanta, et cum spolia ista, diemque
> Oderit;"
> [Virgil, *Aeneid*, X, 503–05: 'A time shall come for Turnus
> when he will wish he had left Pallas untouched, and will
> hate this day and its spoils']

if triumphing arrogance be changed into a sentimental humility,
O! then *Liberality* is to call out for him in the best of her hacknied
tones; the contest is to cease at the instant when his humour
changes from mischief to melancholy; *affetuoso* is to be the only
word; and he is to be allowed his season of sacred torpidity, till the
venom, new formed in the shade, make him glisten again in the
sunshine he envies!

APPENDIX C

Sale Catalogue (1813)
(see Letter 67, n. 1, and Letter 76, n. 4)

When B was intending to leave England again in 1813, his Library was catalogued for a sale by auction, which was to have taken place at the house of R. H. Evans in Pall Mall on Thursday 8 and Friday 9 July 1813. In the event he did not leave England at the time and the auction did not take place. However, a very rare – indeed, I believe, unique – copy of the Sale Catalogue is preserved in MA. It is an octavo pamphlet, containing the title-page, a page of 'CONDITIONS OF SALE', and nine pages listing the books and other items to be auctioned, a number of which do not reappear in his Sale Catalogues for 1816 and 1827 (for which see *CMP*, 231–54).

The title-page of the Catalogue serves in part to explain B's objection in the following undated letter to JM written at the time (July? 1813), here transcribed from the MS in MA (cf. *BLJ* XI, 184–85, where it is conjecturally dated '[June, 1813?]', and XIII, 40, where it is misdated and misprinted):

> Dr. Sir
>
> I hope the Catalogue of the books &c. has not been published without my seeing it – I must reserve several – & many ought not to be printed. – The advertisement is a very bad one – I am not going to the <u>Morea</u> – & if I was – you might as well – advertise a man in Russia as going to <u>Yorkshire</u> – –
>
> ever yrs
>
> B

The title-page of the Catalogue runs:

> A CATALOGUE OF BOOKS,/THE PROPERTY OF A NOBLEMAN,/ABOUT TO LEAVE ENGLAND/ON A TOUR TO THE MOREA./TO WHICH ARE ADDED/A SEPULCHRAL URN,/CONTAINING/RELICS BROUGHT FROM ATHENS IN 1811,/AND/A SILVER CUP,/THE PROPERTY OF THE SAME NOBLE PERSON;/WHICH WILL BE/SOLD BY AUCTION,/

BY R. H. EVANS,/AT HIS HOUSE, No. 26, PALL-MALL,/On Thursday July 8th, and following Day./Catalogues may be had, and the Books viewed at the/Place of Sale./[rule]/*Printed by W. Bulmer and Co. Cleveland-row, St. James's.*/1813.

CATALOGUE OF BOOKS.
FIRST DAY'S SALE.
Octavo et Infra.

LOT

1 Ducarel's Poems. – Kirke White's Poems. – Girdlestone's Anacreon. – Baker's Poems. – Royal Eclipse, in all 5 vols. *russia.*

2 Memoirs of Talleyrand, 2 vols. – Flowers of Literature. – Moral Narratives. – Pleasures of Love. – Cowley's Works, 2 vols. – Ovid's Metamorphoses, by Garth. – Cartwright's Letters, – and Mayne's Poems, in all 10 vols.

3 Lord Chatham's Letters. – Penn's Bioscope. – Butler's Lives of Fenelon and Bossuet, 4 vols.

4 Translations fron [*sic*] the Greek Anthology. – Xenephon's Expedition of Cyrus. – Rejected Addresses. – Licida da Mathias. – Œuvres de Cazotte, 3 vols. in all 7 vols.

5 Bacon's Essays. – Man of Feeling. – Lord Lyttelton's Letters, 2 vols. – 4 vols.

6 Oldham's Works, 2 vols. – Letters of a Mameluke, 2 vols. – Williams's State of France, 2 vols. – Spirit of the Public Journals. – Flowers of Literature. – Hobhouse on the Origin of Sacrifices, six copies. – Lettres du Prince de Ligne, 2 vols. – Macauley's Poetical Effusions, and Jones's Epistles.

7 Cornelius Nepos, Oxon. 1803. – Sallustii Opera, Glasg. 1777. Horatius, Eton 1791.

8 Coleridge's Poems. – Milton's Paradise Lost. – Edgeworth's Modern Griselda.

9 Akenside's Poems. – Poems of Addison, Pomfret, Mallet, Collins, Smollett, Gray, Goldsmith, Armstrong, &c. – Poetry of the Anti-Jacobin. – Adventures of an Atom. – Holloway's Poems.

10 Watson's Apologies for the Bible and Christianity. – Lord Baltimore's Tour to the East. – Temple's Account of the Netherlands. – Bland's Edwy and Elgiva, and seven others.

11 Demosthenis Orationes selectæ a Mounteney. – Ciceronis Orationes Selectæ Delphini.

12 Selecta ex Poetis Græcis – Xenophontis Cyropædia Hutchinsoni, and Sophoclis Electra.

13 Hurd's Horace, 2 vols. – Busbequius's Travels. – Gifford's Baviad and Mæviad. – Veneroni's Grammar and six more.

14 Wright's Horæ Ionicæ. – Elgin's Pursuits in Greece. – Simpson's Euclid, – Mackenzie on the Authenticity of Ossian, and five more.

15 Gazetteer of Scotland. – Wilson's Isle of Palms. – Hay's History of the Insurrection of Wexford. – Penal Laws of Ireland, and six others.

16 Paterson's Book of Roads 1811. – Metrical Effusions. – Hutton's Battle of Bosworth Field. – Wood's Mechanics. – Angelo's School of Fencing, and twelve others.

17 Alciphronis Epistolæ, Bergleri.

18 Art of Tormenting, *russia*.

19 Aikin's Annual Review for 1806, 1807, and 1808, 3 vols.

20 Aikin's Annual Review for 1807.

21	Adam's Summary of Geography, *russia*.		1802
22	Æschylus a Porson, 2 vols. *russia*,	*Glasg.*	1806
23	Æschylus a Schutz, 3 vol. *russia*,	*Halæ*	1798
24	Aristotelis Poetica a Tyrwhitt.	*Oxon.*	1794
25	Anacreon a Forster, *morocco*,	*Lond.*	1802
26	Anacreon by Moore, 2 vols. *russia*,		1806
27	Anderson's British Poets, 14 vols.		1795
28	Ancient British Drama, 3 vols.		1810
29	Annual (New) Register for 1807.		
30	Arabian Nights by Scott, with an additional set of plates inserted, 6 vols. *green morocco.*		1811
31	Account of the most celebrated Pedestrians,		1813
32	Another, (2 copies)		1813
33	Another, (2 copies),		1813
34	Biographical Anecdotes of the Founders of the French Republic. 2 vols.		1799
35	Barker's Classical Recreations,		1812
36	Byron's (Lord) Child [*sic*] Harold, *russia*,		1812
37	British Novelists with Prefaces, by Mrs. Barbauld, 50 vols.		1810
38	British Essayists by Chalmers, 45 vols.		1808
39	Biographical Peerage, 2 vols.		1808
40	Barry's History of the French Consulate,		1804
41	Biographie Moderne, or Lives of distinguished Characters in the French Revolution, 3 vols.		1811
42	Beloe's Anecdotes of Literature, 2 vols.		1807
43	Boswell's Life of Johnson, 4 vols.		1807
44	Burn's [*sic*] Works, 5 vols.		1806

45 Burton's Anatomy of Melancholy, 2 vols, *russia*, 1806
46 Blackstone's Commentaries, by Christian, 4 vols. *russia*, 1803
47 Bisset's History of George III. 6 vols. *russia*, 1803
48 Buffon's Natural History, by Smellie, 18 vols. *russia*, 1792
49 Beauties of England and Wales, 11 vols. 1801, &c.
50 Bonnycastle's Astronomy, *russia*, 1807
51 Bruce's Travels, 8 vols. LARGE PAPER, 1805
52 Browne's British Cicero, 3 vols. 1808
53 Bisset's Life of Burke, 2 vols. 1800
54 Biographical Dictionary by Chalmers, 9 vols, 1812
55 Bland's Collections from the Greek Anthology, 1813
56 Cumberland's John de Lancaster, 3 vols. 1809
57 Count Fathom, Humphry Clinker and Launcelot Greaves, 5 vols.
58 Crabbe's Poems, 2 vols. 1809
59 Cowper's Poems, 2 vols.
60 Citizen of the World, 2 vols. 1790
61 Camilla, 5 vols. *russia* 1802
62 Corinna or Italy, 3 vols. 1807
63 Cobbett's Parliamentary Debates from 1803 to 1812, 21 vol.
64 Cobbett's Parliamentary History, 13 vols. 1806
65 Carleton's Memoirs, 1808
66 Chesterfield's Miscellaneous Works, 4 vols. *russia*, 1779
67 Cumberland's Memoirs of his Life, 2 vols. *russia*, 1807
68 Churchill's Poetical Works, 2 vols. *russia*, 1804
69 Catullus, Tibullus, et Propertius, Variorum. *Tr. ad Rhen.* 1680
70 Creed, Grammatica Linguæ Græcæ Hodiernæ, *Veronæ* 1782
71 Caliph Vathek, *red morocco*, 1786
72 Critical Review from 1795 to 1807, 38 vols.
73 Dallas's Knights, a Tale, 3 vols. 1808
74 Dutens's Memoirs of a Traveller, 5 vols. *russia*, 1806
75 Don Quixote, 4 vols. Cooke's edition, *fine paper.*
76 Dryden's Poems, 3 vols. 18mo.
77 D'Israeli's Calamities of Authors, 2 vols. 1812
78 Dallas's Novels, 7 vols. 1813
79 D'Israeli's Curiosities of Literature, 2 vol. 1807
80 Demosthenes a Mounteney, 1799
81 Demosthenes ab Allen, *russia*, *Oxon*, 1807
82 Demosthenes, by Leland, 2 vol. *russia*, 1806
83 Dryden's Works, by Scott, 18 vol. LARGE PAPER, *russia*, 1808
84 Drake's Literary Hours, 2 vol. 1800
85 Edgeworth's Fashionable Tales, 6 vol. 1809
86 Eugene's Memoirs, 1811

87	Elegant Extracts in Verse,		1805
88	Euripidis Medea et Phœnissæ a Piers,	*Cantab.*	1703
89	Euripidis Tragœdiæ 4 [*sic*] a Porson, *russia*,	*Lips.*	1802
90	Euripides Troades a Burges, LARGE PAPER, *russia*,	*Cant.*	1807
91	Edinburgh Review, 8 vol.		
92	Edinburgh Review, 12 odd numbers.		
93	Epictetus, by Carter, 2 vol.		1807
94	Edinburgh Annual Register for 1810, 2 vol.		
95	Elegant Extracts in Verse, 2 vol.		
96	Flim Flams, 3 vol. *russia*,		1805
97	Ford's Dramatic Works, 2 vol.		1811
98	Falconer's Shipwreck, by Clarke,		1804
99	Fernandez's Spanish Grammar, *russia*,		1805
100	Gil Blas, 4 vol. Cooke's edition, FINE PAPER.		
101	Granger's Biographical History of England, and Noble's Continuation, 7 vol. LARGE PAPER,		1804
102	Gibbon's Decline and Fall of the Roman Empire, 12 vol.		1807
103	Gisborne's Familiar Survey of Christianity,		1801
104	Gifford's Baviad and Mæviad,		1797
105	Grammont's Memoirs, 3 vol.		1809
106	Genlis's Siege of Rochelle, 3 vol.		1808
107	Grahame's Poems, 2 vol. *russia*,		1807
108	Grant on the Superstition of the Highlanders, 2 vol.		1811
109	History of the Bucaneers [*sic*], 2 vol.		
110	Historic Gallery of Portraits and Paintings, 7 vol.		1807
111	Hooke's Roman History, 11 vol.		1810
112	Hume's History of England, 8 vol.		1807
113	Homer's Iliad and Odyssey, by Cowper, 4 vol. *russia*,		1802
114	Hayley's Life of Cowper, 4 vol. *russia*,		1806
115	Hardy's Life of Lord Charlemont, 2 vol.		1812
116	Herodotus, by Beloe, 4 vol.		1806
117	Homeri Ilias, a Clarke, 2 vol.		1760
118	Horatius Gesneri, LARGE PAPER, *morocco*,		1806
119	Homeri Ilias, Græcè LARGE PAPER,	*Oxon.*	1758

Quarto.

120	Ainsworth's Latin Dictionary,		1796
121	Aiken and Enfield's General Biography, 7 vol.	1799, &c.
122	Austin on Rhetorical Delivery, *russia*,		1806
123	Broughton's Letters from a Marhatta Camp,		1813
124	Blair's Grave, with Blake's Designs,		1808
125	Browne's Travels in Africa,		1806

126   Blomfield's General View of the World, 2 vol.   1804
127   Clarke's Travels, vol. 2,   1812
128   Carr's Stranger in France   1803
129   Carr's Travels through Denmark, Sweden, &c.   1805
130   Carr's Tour through Scotland,   1809
131   Chaucer's Canterbury Tales, by Tyrwhitt, 2 vol.
         LARGE PAPER,   Oxf. 1798
132   Coxe's History of the House of Austria, 3 vol.   1807
133   Coxe's Memoirs of the Bourbon Kings of Spain, 3 vol.   1813
134   Campbell's Gertrude of Wyoming,   1809
135   Colman's Poetical Vagaries,   1802
136   Costume of Turkey, *red morocco*,   1802
137   Decker's Gull's Hornbook, by Nott,   1812
138   Davila, Historia delle Guerre Civili di Francia, 2 vol.   *Lond.* 1755
139   Edinburgh Encyclopædia, 4 vol. and vol. 5, part I.
140   Fox's History of James the Second, ELEPHANT PAPER,
         russia,   1808
141   Galt's Life of Wolsey, LARGE PAPER,   1812
142   Hodgson's Juvenal,   1807
143   Holinshed's Chronicles, 6 vol.   1807
144   Hope's Costume of the Ancients, 2 vol.   1809
145   Hederici Lexicon Græcum, *russia*,   1803
146   Juvenal, by Gifford,   1802

Folio.

147   Biographia Britannica, by Kippis, 5 vol.   1778, &c.
148   General Dictionary, Historical and Critical, including Bayle,
         10 vol. half bound, uncut,   1734
149   Herbelot Bibliothèque Orientale,   *Maest.* 1776
150   Meletii Geographia Antiqua et Moderna, *in* Lingua Græca,
         Hodierna, *russia*,   *Ven.*

151   A Silver Sepulchral Urn made with great taste. Within it are
         contained human bones and relics taken from a tomb within
         the long wall of Athens in the month of February, 1811. The
         Urn weighs 187 oz. 5 dwt.
152   A Silver Cup, containing
         "Root of hemlock gathered in the dark,"
         according to the directions of the Witches in Macbeth [cf.
         Macbeth, IV, i, 25]. The Hemlock was plucked at Athens by the
         Noble Proprietor in 1811. The silver cup weighs 29 oz. 8 dwt.

SECOND DAY.
Octavo et Infra.

153	Hodgson's Lady Jane Grey,	1809
154	History of Pugilism, 1812. – Pride and Prejudice, 3 vols. 1813. – Sense and Sensibility, 3 vols. 1811. – Despotism, 2 vols. 1811. – Volume of Plays.	
155	Jones's Beauties of the Poets,	1800
156	Junius's Letters, 2 vols. *russia,*	1806
157	Junius's Letters by Woodfall, 3 vols. LARGE PAPER,	1812
158	Johnson's Dictionary, 4 vols. *russia,*	1805
159	Johnson's Lives of the Poets, 3 vols. *russia,*	1806
160	Juvenal and Persius, by Madan, 2 vols.	1807
161	Juvenal et Persius, Variorum,	*L. Bat.* 1664
162	Inchbald's British Theatre, 25 vols. FINE PAPER,	1808
163	Inchbald's Collection of Farces, 7 vol. FINE PAPER,	1809
164	Italian by Mrs. Radcliffe, 3 vol.	1811
165	Kaim's Elements of Criticism, 2 vol. *russia,*	1805
166	Louvet, Vie de Faublas, 4 vol.	*Par.* 1807
167	Lewis's Romantic Tales, 4 vol.	1808
168	Lebrun's Monsieur Botte, 3 vol.	1803
169	Lebrun's Barons of Felsheim, 3 vol. *russia,*	1804
170	Lebrun's My Uncle Thomas, 4 vol. *russia,*	1801
171	Locke on Understanding, 2 vol. *russia,*	1805
172	Lempriere's Classical Dictionary, *russia,*	1801
173	Luciani Opera, 10 vol.	*Bipont,* 1789
174	Lyre of Love, 2 vol. *russia,*	
175	Meiner's History of the Female Sex, 4 vols. 1808. – Dangerous Connections, 4 vol. – Life of Faublas, 4 vol.	
176	Miseries of Human Life, 2 vol. *plates, russia,*	1807
177	Montaigne, Essais de, 3 vol.	1802
178	Mrs. Moore's Coelebs, 2 vol.	1808
179	Memoirs of the Margravine of Bareith, 2 vol.	1812
180	Middleton's Life of Cicero, 3 vol. *russia,*	1804
181	Milton's Prose Works, 7 vol. LARGE PAPER,	1806
182	Montaigne's Essays, 3 vols.	1811
183	Mirabeau de la Monarchie Prussienne sous Frédéric le Grand, 7 vol.	1788
184	Mitford's History of Greece, 6 vol. *russia,*	1795
185	Murphy's Life of Garrick, 2 vol. *russia,*	1801
186	Montesquieu's Spirit of Laws, *russia,*	1793
187	Monumens de la Vie Privée des douze Césars, *russia,*	1782

188	Massinger's Plays by Gifford, 4 vol.		1805
189	Another copy, 4 vol.		1813
190	Nichols's Literary Anecdotes of the 18th century, 7 vol.		1812
191	Ossian's Poems, 3 vol. *russia*,		1805
192	Ossian's Poems, Gaelic and Latin, 3 vol. *russia*,		1807
193	Poets of Great Britain from the time of Chaucer to Sir William Jones. Bagster's edition, bound in 61 vol. *russia*, in a travelling case,		1807
194	Petrarca, 2 vol. *morocco*,	*Lond.*	1807
194★	Poetry of the Anti-Jacobin,		
195	Peregrine Pickle, 4 vol. Cooke's ed. FINE PAPER,		1813
196	Philosophy of Nature, 2 vol.		1813
197	Peter Pindar's Works, 5 vol.		1794
198	Public Characters, 8 vols. *russia*,		1799
199	Public Characters for 1806,		1806
200	Pinkerton's Modern Geography, *russia*,		1803
201	Pope's Works by Bowles, 10 vol.		1806
202	Poetical Register, 4 vol. *russia*,		1802
203	Paley's Philosophy, 2 vol. *russia*,		1806
204	Parke's Chemical Catechism,		1808
205	Petronius Arbiter Variorum,	*Amst.*	1669
206	Pratt's Poems,		1807
207	Pursuits of Literature,		1808
208	Portroyal Greek Grammar, *russia*,		1797
209	Plutarch's Lives by Langhorne, 6 vol.		1809
210	Potts's Gazetteer of England,		1810
211	Polybius by Hampton, 3 vol.		1809
212	The Ring and the Well, 4 vol.		1808
213	Revolutionary Plutarch, 3 vol.		1806
214	Roderic Random, 2 vol.		
215	Roscoe's Life of Lorenzo de Medici, 3 vol.		1806
216	Rolliad and Probationary Odes,		1799
217	Another copy		1812
218	Rogers's Poems,		1812
219	Secret History of the Court of St. Cloud, 3 vol.		1806
220	Southey's Madoc, 2 vol.		1807
221	Shakspeare's Poems, 2 vol.		1804
222	St. Pierre's Studies of Nature abridged,		1799
223	Spirit of the Public Journals,		1808
224	Salluste par Delamalle, 2 vol.	*Par.*	1808
225	Lettres de Sevigné, 11 vol.	*Par.*	1806
226	Shakspeare's Plays, 20 vols. Bell's edition,		1788

227	Strangford's Camoens, *russia*,	
228	Secret History of Bonaparte's Cabinet,	1811
229	St. Pierre's Studies of Nature, 3 vol.	1799
230	Scott's Lay of the Last Minstrel, *russia*,	1807
231	Scott's Ballads, *russia*,	1806
232	Scott's Border Minstrelsy, 3 vol.	1802
233	Sheridan on Elocution, *russia*,	1798
234	Saugnier and Brisson's Voyages to Africa,	1792
235	Œuvres de Saint-Simon, 13 vol.	*Strasb.* 1791
236	Ségur's History of Women, 3 vol.	1800
237	Ségur's Reign of Frederic II., 3 vol.	1801
238	Sturm's Reflections, 2 vol.	1804
239	Sheldrake on Distortion in Children, 2 copies,	1806
240	Sheldrake on Inclined Plane Wheels,	1811
241	Sinclair's Code of Health, 4 vol.	1807
242	Another Copy, 4 vol.	1807
243	Smither's Poems, *russia*,	1807
244	Stephens's Life of Horne Tooke, 2 vol.	1813
245	Stewart's Philosophy of the Human Mind, *russia*.	
246	Stewart's Outlines of Moral Philosophy.	
247	Seward's Memoirs of Darwin, 1804. Christian Knowledge, 1795. Memoirs of Gen. Lee, 1792. Tracts, by Thyers, 1712. Nicholl's Anecdotes of Hogarth, 1781.	
248	Turnbull's Voyage round the World, 3 vol.	1805
249	Tasso's Jerusalem, by Hoole, 2 vol. *russia*,	1803
250	Tom Jones, 3 vol. *Cooke's edition, fine paper.*	
251	Thiebault's Anecdotes of Frederic II., 2 vol.	1805
252	Taylor's Travels to India, 2 vol.	
253	Tiraboschi Vocabolario Italiano-Latino,	*Milan,* 1794
254	Tacitus, by Murphy, 8 vol.	1807
255	Tales of the East, 3 vol.	1812
256	Tasso, Gerusalemme Liberata, 2 vol. *mor.*	*Lond.*
257	Voltaire's Works, by Francklin, and Smollet [*sic*], &c. 36 vol.	1778
258	Vigerus de Idiotismis Græcis, Hermanni, *russia*,	1802
259	Walker's (Commodore) Voyages, 2 vol.	
260	Wordsworth's Poems, 2 vol. Wordsworth's Lyrical Ballads, 2 vol. *in russia, uniform.*	
261	White's (Kirke) Remains, 2 vol.	1808
262	Walsingham, by Mrs. Robinson, 4 vol. *russia*,	1805
263	Warton on the Genius of Pope, 2 vol.	1806
264	Wanley's Wonders of the Little World, 2 vol.	1806

Quarto.

Folio.

298 Thomson's Collection of Original Scottish Airs, 4 vol. in 2.
     – Violincello [*sic*] Accompaniment, and Violin
     Accompaniment.

299 Thomson's Collection of Original Welsh Airs, 2 vol. and
     Violin and Violencello [*sic*] Accompaniment.

300 Atlas de la Monarchie Prussienne,   1788

301 Tindal's Continuation of Rapin, 2 vol.   1751

302 The Large Plates to Boydell's Shakspeare, 2 vol. Imperial
     Folio, fine impressions, *bound in red morocco,*

303 Danville's Ancient Geography,   1805

Select Bibliography

A Biographical List of the House of Commons, Elected in October, 1812 (London: Longman, 1813).

Adam, R. B., ed., *Works, Letters and Manuscripts of James Hogg* (Buffalo, 1930).

Altick, Richard D., *The Shows of London* (Cambridge, Mass., Harvard University Press, 1978).

Anderson, W. E. K., ed., *The Journal of Sir Walter Scott*, rev. edn (Edinburgh: Canongate Books, 1998).

Anglesey, The Marquess of, *One Leg: The Life and Letters of Henry William Paget, First Marquess of Anglesey* (London: Jonathan Cape, 1961).

Ashton, Rosemary, *The Life of Samuel Taylor Coleridge* (Oxford: Blackwell, 1996).

Ashton, Thomas L., *Byron's Hebrew Melodies* (London: Routledge & Kegan Paul, 1972).

Aspinall, A., ed., *Letters of the Princess Charlotte 1811–1817* (London: Home and Van Thal, 1949).

Authentic Memoirs ... of the Most Eminent Physicians and Surgeons of Great Britain; with ... An Account of the Medical Charities of the Metropolis, 2nd edn, enlarged (London, 1818).

Bagot, Captain Josceline, ed., *George Canning and His Friends*, 2 vols (London: John Murray, 1909).

Bakewell, Michael & Melissa, *Augusta Leigh. Byron's Half-Sister – A Biography* (London: Chatto & Windus, 2000).

Balayé, Simone, *Les Carnets de voyage de Madame de Staël* (Genève: Librairie Droz, 1971).

Bamford, Francis, and Wellington, The Duke of, eds, *The Journal of Mrs. Arbuthnot 1820–1832*, 2 vols (London: Macmillan, 1950).

Barber, Giles, 'Galignani's and the Publication of English Books in France from 1800 to 1852', *The Library*, 5th series, XVI (December 1961), 267–86.

[Barrow, Sir John] *An Auto-Biographical Memoir of Sir John Barrow, Bart., Late of the Admiralty* (London: John Murray, 1847).

Barrow, John, *The Life and Correspondence of Admiral Sir William Sidney Smith*, 2 vols (London, 1848).

Bartlett, William A., *The History and Antiquities of the Parish of Wimbledon, Surrey* (London, 1865).

Baylen, Joseph O., and Gossman, Norbert J., eds, *Biographical Dictionary of Modern British Radicals, Vol. I: 1770–1830* (Hassocks, Sussex: Harvester Press, 1979).

Beattie, William, ed., *Life and Letters of Thomas Campbell*, 3 vols (London, 1850).

Beatty, Bernard, *Byron's Don Juan* (London: Croom Helm, 1985).

Beloe, the Rev. William, *The Sexagenarian, or Recollections of a Literary Life*, 2 vols (London, 1817).

Bennett, Betty T., ed., *The Letters of Mary Wollstonecraft Shelley*, 3 vols (Baltimore: Johns Hopkins University Press, 1980–88).

Benson, Adolph B., 'Catherine Potter Stith and Her Meeting with Lord Byron', *South Atlantic Quarterly*, XXII, 1 (January 1923), 10–22.

Bickley, Francis, ed., *The Diaries of Sylvester Douglas (Lord Glenbervie)*, 2 vols (London, 1928).

Bishop, Morchard, ed., *Recollections of the Table Talk of Samuel Rogers* (London, 1952).

Boswell, James, *The Life of Samuel Johnson, LL.D.*, 2 vols (London: Dent, 1949).

Boyle's Fashionable Court and Country Guide, and Town Visiting Directory (London, 1803).

Brown, Eluned, ed., *The London Theatre 1811–1866. Selections from the Diary of Henry Crabb Robinson* (London, 1966).

Buckingham and Chandos, the Duke of, *Memoirs of the Courts and Cabinets of George the Third*, 4 vols (London, 1853–55).

——, *Memoirs of the Court of England during the Regency, 1811–1820*, 2 vols (London, 1856).

——, *Memoirs of the Court of George IV. 1820–1830*, 2 vols (London, 1859).

Buckland, C. S. B., 'Richard Belgrave Hoppner', *The English Historical Review*, XXXIX, clv (July 1924), 373–85.

Burke, Edmund, *On Empire, Liberty, and Reform: Speeches and Letters*, ed. David Bromwich (New Haven & London: Yale University Press, 2000).

Burnett, T. A. J., *The Rise and Fall of a Regency Dandy: The Life and Times of Scrope Berdmore Davies* (London: John Murray, 1981).

——, ed., *The Manuscripts of the Younger Romantics. Lord Byron, Volume VII. Childe Harold's Pilgrimage, Canto III. A Facsimile of the Autograph Fair Copy Found in the 'Scrope Davies' Notebook* (New York & London: Garland Publishing, 1988).

Burwick, Frederick, and Douglass, Paul, eds, *A Selection of Hebrew Melodies, Ancient and Modern, by Isaac Nathan and Lord Byron* (Tuscaloosa and London: University of Alabama Press, 1988).

Bury, Lady Charlotte, *The Diary of a Lady-in-Waiting*, ed. A. Francis Steuart, 2 vols (London, 1908).

Butler, E. M., *Byron and Goethe* (London: Bowes & Bowes, 1956).

Campbell, J. Menzies, 'An Exhibition of Early Dentistry', *British Dental Journal*, 99, 7 (4 October 1955), 239–43.

Chancellor, E. Beresford, trans. and ed., *The Diary of Philipp von Neumann 1819 to 1850*, 2 vols (London, 1928).

Chilcott, Tim, *A Publisher and His Circle* (London: Routledge & Kegan Paul, 1972).

Cholmondeley, R. H., *The Heber Letters 1783–1832* (London: Batchworth, 1950).

Clark, Roy Benjamin, *William Gifford: Tory Satirist, Critic, and Editor* (New York, 1930).

Clayden, P. W., *Rogers and His Contemporaries*, 2 vols (London, 1889).

Cline, C. L., *Byron, Shelley and their Pisan Circle* (London: John Murray, 1952).

Cochran, Peter, 'New Byron Letters', *The Newstead Byron Society Review* (July 2000), 7–11.

——, 'Did Byron Take Money for his Early Work?', *The Byron Journal*, 31 (2003), 72–76.

Cockburn, Lord, *The Life of Lord Jeffrey with a Selection from his Correspondence*, 2 vols (Edinburgh: Adam and Charles Black, 1852).

Cole, Richard Cargill, *Irish Booksellers and English Writers 1740–1800* (London: Mansell Publishing, 1986).

Constable, Thomas, *Archibald Constable and His Literary Correspondents*, 3 vols (Edinburgh, 1873).

Cooper, Barry, *Beethoven's Folksong Settings: Chronology, Sources, Style* (Oxford: Clarendon Press, 1994).

Corson, James C., *Notes and Index to Sir Herbert Grierson's Edition of the Letters of Sir Walter Scott* (Oxford: Clarendon Press, 1979).

Courtney, William Prideaux, *Eight Friends of The Great* (London, 1910).

[Dallas, Mrs. A. R. C.] *Incidents in the Life and Ministry of the Rev. Alex. R. C. Dallas, A.M.* (1871).

[Dallas, R. C.] *The Miscellaneous Works and Novels of R. C. Dallas, Esq.*, 7 vols, new edn, (London: Longman, 1813).

De Lancey Ferguson, J., ed., *The Letters of Robert Burns*, ed. G. Ross Roy, 2nd edn, 2 vols (Oxford: Clarendon Press, 1985).

Dibdin, the Rev. Thomas Frognall, *Bibliomania* (1811).

Dibdin, the Rev. T. F., *The Bibliographical Decameron*, 3 vols (London, 1817).

[Dibdin, Thomas] *The Reminiscences of Thomas Dibdin*, 2 vols (London: Henry Colburn, 1827).

Edgcumbe, Richard, *The Diary of Frances Lady Shelley 1787–1873*, 2 vols (London: John Murray, 1912).

Elmes, James, *A Topographical Dictionary of London* (1831).

Elwin, Malcolm, *Lord Byron's Wife* (London: Macdonald, 1962).

——, *The Noels and the Milbankes* (London: Macdonald, 1967).

——, *Lord Byron's Family: Annabella, Ada and Augusta 1816–1824* (London: John Murray, 1975).

Erdman, David V., and Worrall, David, eds, *The Manuscripts of the Younger Romantics. Lord Byron. Volume VI. Childe Harold's Pilgrimage: A Critical, Composite Edition* (New York & London: Garland Publishing, 1991).

[Erskine, Lord] *The Speeches of the Right Hon. Lord Erskine ... Collected by the Late James Ridgway*, 4 vols (London, 1847).

Espinasse, F., 'The House of Murray', *Harper's New Monthly Magazine*, LXXI, ccccxxiv (September 1885).

Evans, John, *Richmond and its Vicinity*, 2nd edn, corr. (Richmond: James Darnill, 1825).

Fairweather, Maria, *Madame de Staël* (London: Constable, 2005).

[Farington, Joseph] *The Diary of Joseph Farington 1795–1821*, 16 vols (New Haven and London: Yale University Press, 1978–84): vols I–VI, ed. Kenneth Garlick and Angus Macintyre (1978–79); vols VII–XVI, ed. Kathryn Cave (1982–84).

Faulkner, Thomas C., ed., *Selected Letters and Journals of George Crabbe* (Oxford: Clarendon Press, 1985).

Feldman, Paula R., and Scott-Kilvert, Diana, eds, *The Journals of Mary Shelley* (Baltimore: Johns Hopkins University Press, 1995).

Field, John, *The King's Nurseries. The Story of Westminster School* (London: James & James, 1987)

Fields, Mrs. James T., *A Shelf of Old Books* (1894).

Fontana, Biancamaria, *Rethinking the Politics of Commercial Society: the Edinburgh Review 1802–1832* (Cambridge: Cambridge University Press, 1985).

Forman, Maurice Buxton, ed., *The Letters of John Keats*, 3rd rev edn, (Oxford: Geoffrey Cumberlege, 1947).

Franklin, Caroline, *Byron: A Literary Life* (Basingstoke: Macmillan, 2000).

Franklin, Robert, *Lord Stuart de Rothesay. The Life and Times of Lord Stuart de Rothesay of Highcliffe Castle 1779–1845* (Upton-upon-Severn, Worcestershire: Images, 1993).

Franklin, Robert, *Private and Secret: The Clandestine Activities of a Nineteenth-century Diplomat* (Lewes, Sussex: Book Guild Publishing, 2005)

Fraser, Flora, *The Unruly Queen. The Life of Queen Caroline* (London and Basingstoke: Macmillan, 1996).

Frere, W. E. and Frere, Sir Bartle, eds, *The Works of John Hookham Frere, in Verse and Prose, now first collected, with a prefatory Memoir*, 2 vols (London: Pickering, 1872).

Fulford, Roger, *Samuel Whitbread 1764–1815. A Study in Opposition* (London: Macmillan, 1967).

[Galignani's] *A Famous Bookstore* (Paris: Galignani Library, 1920).

Galt, John, *The Life of Lord Byron* (London: Henry Colburn and Richard Bentley, 1830).

Gell, Sir William, *Reminiscences of Sir Walter Scott's Residence in Italy, 1832*, ed. James C. Corson (London: Thomas Nelson, 1957).

Giazotto, Remo, *Giovan Battista Viotti* (Milan, 1956).

Giles, Frank, *Napoleon Bonaparte: England's Prisoner* (London: Constable & Robinson, 2001).

Gillies, R. P., *Memoirs of a Literary Veteran*, 3 vols (London, 1851).

Giuliano, Cheryl Fallon, ed., *The Manuscripts of the Younger Romantics. Lord Byron, Volume XI: Ode to Napoleon Buonaparte* (New York & London: Garland Publishing, 1997).

Gordon, Pryse Lockhart, *Personal Memoirs*, 2 vols (London, 1830).

Gordon, Mrs, *'Christopher North'. A Memoir of John Wilson* (Edinburgh, 1879).

Gotch, Rosamund Brunel, *Maria, Lady Callcott* (London: John Murray, 1937).

Greever, Garland, *A Wiltshire Parson and his Friends: The Correspondence of William Lisle Bowles* (London, 1926).

Greig, James Alexander, *Francis Jeffrey of the Edinburgh Review* (Edinburgh, 1948).

Griggs, Earl Leslie, ed., *Collected Letters of Samuel Taylor Coleridge*, 6 vols (Oxford: Clarendon Press, 1956–71).

Gronow, Captain R. H., *Celebrities of London and Paris; Being a Third Series of Reminiscences and Anecdotes* (London, 1865).

Groves, David, *James Hogg: The Growth of a Writer* (Edinburgh, 1988).

Gunn, Peter, *My Dearest Augusta. A Biography of the Honourable Augusta Leigh, Lord Byron's Half-Sister* (London: Bodley Head, 1968).

Hadden, J. Cuthbert, *George Thomson, The Friend of Burns: His Life and Correspondence* (London: Nimmo, 1898).

Halls, J. J., *The Life and Correspondence of Henry Salt*, 2 vols, (London: Richard Bentley, 1834).

Halsband, Robert, ed., *The Complete Letters of Lady Mary Wortley Montagu*, 3 vols (Oxford: Clarendon Press, 1966).

——, *Lord Hervey: Eighteenth-Century Courtier* (Oxford: Clarendon Press, 1973).

Hamilton, Sir William, ed., *The Collected Works of Dugald Stewart*, 10 vols (London, 1854–58).

Harben, Henry A., *A Dictionary of London* (1918).

Harcourt, the Rev. Leveson Vernon, ed., *The Diaries and Correspondence of the Right Hon. George Rose*, 2 vols (London, 1860).

Hawes, Frances, *Henry Brougham* (London: Jonathan Cape, 1957).

Hayden, John O., *The Romantic Reviewers 1802–1824* (London: Routledge & Kegan Paul, 1969).

——, ed., *Romantic Bards and British Reviewers* (London: Routledge & Kegan Paul, 1971).

Hemlow, Joyce, ed., *The Journals and Letters of Fanny Burney (Madame d'Arblay), 1791–1840*, 12 vols (Oxford: Clarendon Press, 1972–84).

Herold, J. Christopher, *Mistress to an Age. A Life of Madame de Staël* (London: Hamish Hamilton, 1959).

Hodgson, the Rev. James T., *Memoir of the Rev. Francis Hodgson, B.D.*, 2 vols (London, 1878).

Hogg, James, *Memoir of the Author's Life and Familiar Anecdotes of Sir Walter Scott*, ed. Douglas S. Mack (Edinburgh: Chatto & Windus, 1972).

——, *Anecdotes of Sir W. Scott*, ed. Douglas S. Mack (Edinburgh: Scottish Academic Press, 1983).

Holland, Henry Richard, Lord, *Foreign Reminiscences*, ed. Henry Edward Lord Holland, 2nd edn (London, 1851).

Holland, Sir Henry, *Recollections of Past Life* (London, 1872).

Holmes, Richard, *Coleridge: Darker Reflections* (London: Harper Collins, 1998).

Houtchens, Lawrence Houston, and Houtchens, Caroline Washburn, eds, *Leigh Hunt's Literary Criticism* (New York, 1956).

——, eds, *Leigh Hunt's Political and Occasional Essays* (New York, 1962).

Howse, Ernest Marshall, *Saints in Politics: The "Clapham Sect" and the Growth of Freedom* (London: George Allen & Unwin, 1952).

Huish, Robert, *Memoirs of George the Fourth*, 2 vols (1831).

[Hunt, Leigh] *The Correspondence of Leigh Hunt*, ed. by His Eldest Son, 2 vols (London: Smith & Elder, 1862).

Ilchester, the Earl of, ed., *The Journal of the Hon. Henry Edward Fox (afterwards fourth and last Lord Holland) 1818–1830* (London: Butterworth, 1923).

——, *The Home of the Hollands, 1605–1820* (London: John Murray, 1937).

Isaac, Peter, 'Byron's Publisher and His Printers', *The Newstead Byron Society Review* (July 2000), 86–96.

Jackson, J. R. de J., ed., *Coleridge: The Critical Heritage* (London: Routledge & Kegan Paul, 1970).

Jeffrey, Francis, *Contributions to the Edinburgh Review*, 4 vols (London, 1844).

Jenkins, Elizabeth, *Lady Caroline Lamb* (London: Sphere Books, 1972).

Jennings, Louis J., ed., *The Croker Papers: The Correspondence and Diaries of the late Right Honourable John Wilson Croker*, 3 vols (London: John Murray, 1884).

Johnson, Edgar, *Sir Walter Scott: The Great Unknown*, 2 vols (London: Hamish Hamilton, 1970).

Johnson, Samuel, *A Dictionary of the English Language*, 2 vols, 5th edn (London: W. & A. Strahan, 1784).

Jones, Frederick L., ed., *Maria Gisborne & Edward E. Williams, Shelley's Friends: Their Journals and Letters* (Norman: University of Oklahoma Press, 1951).

Jones, Leonidas M., *The Life of John Hamilton Reynolds* (Hanover & London: University Press of New England, 1984).

Joyce, Michael, *My Friend H. John Cam Hobhouse, Baron Broughton of Broughton de Gyfford* (London: John Murray, 1948).

Kaye, John William, *The Life and Correspondence of Major-General Sir John Malcolm, G.C.B.*, 2 vols (London, 1856).

Kelsall, Malcolm, ed., *John Cam Hobhouse: A Trifling Mistake and Reform of Parliament* (Cardiff: University College Cardiff Press, 1984).

Kempe, John A., ed., *Autobiography of Anna Eliza Bray* (London: Chapman and Hall, 1884).

Knight, Charles, *Passages of a Working Life during half a Century*, 3 vols (London, 1864).

Koch, Edward H. A., *Leaves from the Diary of a Literary Amateur. John Herman Merivale 1819–1844* (Hampstead: Priory Press, 1911).

Lambert, B., *The History and Survey of London and its Environs*, 4 vols (London, 1806).

Lane-Poole, Stanley, *The Life of the Right Honourable Stratford Canning, Viscount Stratford de Redcliffe*, 2 vols (London, 1888).

Lansdown, Richard, *Byron's Historical Dramas* (Oxford: Clarendon Press, 1992).

Lewis, Lady Theresa, ed., *Extracts from the Journals and Correspondence of Miss Berry*, 3 vols, 2nd edn (London, 1866).

Litchfield, Henrietta, ed., *Emma Darwin: A Century of Family Letters 1792–1896*, 2 vols (London: John Murray, 1915).

Lochhead, Marion, *John Gibson Lockhart* (London: John Murray, 1954).

Lovelace, Ralph Milbanke, Earl of, *Astarte: A Fragment of Truth Concerning George Gordon Byron, Sixth Lord Byron*. Recorded by his Grandson. New Edition, with many additional letters, edited by Mary Countess of Lovelace (London: Christophers, 1921).

Lovell, Ernest J., Jr., ed., *His Very Self and Voice: Collected Conversations of Lord Byron* (New York: Macmillan, 1954).

——, *Captain Medwin: Friend of Byron and Shelley* (London: Macdonald, 1962).

——, ed., *Lady Blessington's Conversations of Lord Byron* (Princeton: Princeton University Press, 1969).

MacCarthy, Fiona, *Byron: Life and Legend* (London: John Murray, 2002).

Mackerras, Catherine, *The Hebrew Melodist: A Life of Isaac Nathan* (Sydney: Currawong Publishing, 1963).

Mackintosh, Robert James, ed., *Memoirs of the Life of the Right Honourable Sir James Mackintosh*, 2 vols (London, 1835).

Marshall, Peter H., *William Godwin* (New Haven and London: Yale University Press, 1984).

Marshall, William H., *Byron, Shelley, Hunt, and The Liberal* (Philadelphia: University of Pennsylvania Press, 1960).

Martineau, Gilbert, *Napoleon's Last Journey* (London: John Murray, 1976).

——, *Madame Mère. Napoleon's Mother* (London: John Murray, 1978).

Mathews, Mrs, *Memoirs of Charles Mathews, Comedian*, 4 vols (London, 1839).

Maxted, Ian, The London Book Trades 1775–1800: A Preliminary Checklist of Members (Folkestone: Dawson, 1977).

Maxwell, the Right Hon. Sir Herbert, ed., *The Creevey Papers*, 3rd edn (London: John Murray, 1905).

Mayne, Ethel Colburn, *Byron*, 2nd rev. edn (London: Methuen, 1924).

——, *The Life and Letters of Anne Isabella, Lady Noel Byron* (London: Constable, 1929).

McClary, Ben Harris, ed., *Washington Irving and the House of Murray* (Knoxville: University of Tennessee Press, 1969).

Merivale, Anne W., *Family Memorials* (printed for private circulation) (Exeter: Thomas Upward, 1884).

Miller, William, *Biographical Sketches of British Characters Recently Deceased*, 2 vols (London: Henry Colburn, 1826).

Moore, Doris Langley, *The Late Lord Byron* (London: John Murray, 1961).

——, *Lord Byron: Accounts Rendered* (London: John Murray, 1974).

Moore, Thomas, *Letters and Journals of Lord Byron: With Notices of the Life of Lord Byron*, 2 vols (London: John Murray, 1830).

[Morgan, Lady] *Lady Morgan's Memoirs*, 2 vols, 2nd rev edn (London, 1863).

Morley, Edith J., ed., *Henry Crabb Robinson on Books and their Writers*, 3 vols (London: Dent, 1938).

Morpurgo, J. E., ed., *The Autobiography of Leigh Hunt* (London: The Cresset Press, 1948).

Murray, John, *Notes on Captain Medwin's Conversations of Lord Byron* (London: John Murray, 1824).

Nicholson, Andrew, ed., *The Manuscripts of the Younger Romantics: Lord Byron. Vol. VIII: Don Juan, Cantos III–IV Manuscript* (New York & London: Garland Publishing, 1992).

——, Byron: 'A Manuscript Fragment and a Note', *The Byron Journal*, 29 (2001), 79–86.

——, 'Napoleon's "last act" and Byron's *Ode*', *Romanticism*, 9, 1 (2003), 68–81.

——, 'Byron's Introduction to the Prince Regent in 1812', *The Byron Journal*, 34, 2 (2006), 147–54.

Normington, Susan, *Lady Caroline Lamb: This Infernal Woman* (London: House of Stratus, 2001).

O'Donoghue, Freeman, *Catalogue of Engraved British Portraits Preserved in the Department of Prints and Drawings in the British Museum*, 4 vols (London, 1908–14).

Ogden, James, *Isaac D'Israeli* (Oxford: Clarendon Press, 1969).

Oldham, Ellen M., 'Lord Byron and Mr. Coolidge of Boston', *The Book Collector*, 13, 2 (Summer 1964), 211–13.

O'Leary, Patrick, *Regency Editor: Life of John Scott (1784–1821)* (Aberdeen: Aberdeen University Press, 1983).

Oliphant, Mrs, *Annals of a Publishing House. William Blackwood and His Sons, Their Magazine and Friends*, 2 vols, 2nd edn (Edinburgh, 1897).

Origo, Iris, *Allegra* (London: Hogarth Press, 1935).

——, *The Last Attachment* (London: Jonathan Cape & John Murray, 1949).

——, *A Measure of Love* (London: Jonathan Cape, 1957).

Partington, Wilfred, ed., *The Private Letter-Books of Sir Walter Scott* (London: Hodder and Stoughton, 1930).

——, ed., *Sir Walter Scott's Post-Bag* (London: John Murray, 1932).

Paston, George, and Quennell, Peter, *"To Lord Byron": Feminine Profiles* (London: John Murray, 1939).

Patterson, M.W., *Sir Francis Burdett and His Times (1770–1844)*, 2 vols (London, 1931).

Peach, Annette, *Portraits of Byron* (London: The Walpole Society, LXII, 2000).

Perrin, W.G., 'The Navy List. I. The Forerunners of the Official Navy List', *The Mariner's Mirror*, I, 10 (October 1911), 257–64.

——, 'The Navy List. II. – The Official Navy List and Its Competitors', *The Mariner's Mirror*, I, 12 (December 1911), 321–29.

Peteinaris, Petros, 'The Bey Apologises', *The Newstead Byron Society Review* (July 2000), 13–19.

Phipps, The Honourable Edmund, ed., *Memoirs of the Political and Literary Life of Robert Plumer Ward, Esq.*, 2 vols (London: John Murray, 1850).

Pigott, Charles, *A Political Dictionary* (London: D. I. Eaton, 1795).

Pope, W. J. Macqueen, *Theatre Royal Drury Lane* (London: W. H. Allen, 1945).

Pope, Willard Bissell, ed., *The Diary of Benjamin Robert Haydon*, 5 vols (Cambridge, Mass.: Harvard University Press, 1960–63).

Polwhele, the Rev. R., *Reminiscences in Prose and Verse*, 3 vols (London: John Nichol, 1836).

Quérard, J. M., *La France Littéraire, ou Dictionnaire Bibliographique* (Paris, 1827).

Radziwill, The Princess, ed., *Memoirs of the Duchesse de Dino (Afterwards Duchesse de Talleyrand et de Sagan), 1831–1835* (London: Heinemann, 1909).

[Raikes, Thomas] *A Portion of the Journal of Thomas Raikes, Esq. From 1831–1847*, 4 vols (London, 1856–57).

Raymond, John, ed., *The Reminiscences and Recollections of Captain Gronow* (London: Bodley Head, 1964).

Redpath, Theodore, *The Young Romantics and Critical Opinion 1807–1824* (London: Harrap, 1973).

Richardson, Joanna, ed., *Letters from Lambeth. The Correspondence of the Reynolds family with John Freeman Milward Dovaston* (Woodbridge, Suffolk, 1981).

Rivington, Septimus, ed., The Publishing House of Rivington (London, 1894).

——, *The Publishing Family of Rivington* (London, 1919).

Robberds, J. W., *A Memoir of the Life and Writings of the late William Taylor of Norwich*, 2 vols (London: John Murray, 1843).

Roberts, Arthur, ed., *The Life, Letters, and Opinions of William Roberts, Esq.* (London, 1850).

Robinson, John Robert, *The Last Earls of Barrymore, 1769–1824* (London, 1894).

[Romilly, Sir Samuel] *Memoirs of the Life of Sir Samuel Romilly, written by himself; with a Selection from His Correspondence. Edited by His Sons*, 3 vols (London, 1840).

Romilly, Samuel Henry, ed., *Romilly–Edgeworth Letters 1813–1818* (London: John Murray, 1936).

——, *Letters to 'Ivy' from the First Earl of Dudley* (London, 1905).

Roper, Derek, *Reviewing before the Edinburgh 1788–1802* (London: Methuen, 1978).

Rose, C. Marshall, *Nineteenth Century Mortlake and East Sheen* (privately printed, Albert Clark, 1961)

Rossetti, William Michael, ed., *The Diary of John William Polidori* (London, 1911).

Ruskin, John, *Praeterita. The Autobiography of John Ruskin* (Oxford: Oxford University Press, 1978).

Sadler, Thomas, ed., *Diary, Reminiscences, and Correspondence of Henry Crabb Robinson*, 2 vols, 3rd edn (London, 1872).

Sargeaunt, John, *Annals of Westminster School* (London: Methuen, 1898).

Schrader, Richard J., ed., *The Reminiscences of Alexander Dyce* (Ohio: Ohio State University Press, 1972).

Scott, John, *Journal of a Tour to Waterloo and Paris, in company with Sir Walter Scott in 1815* (London, 1842).

Sebba, Anne, *The Exiled Collector: William Bankes and the Making of an English Country House* (London: John Murray, 2004).

Shattock, Joanne, *Politics and Reviewers: the Edinburgh and the Quarterly in the Early Victorian Age* (Leicester: Leicester University Press, 1989).

Shine, Hill, and Shine, Helen Chadwick, *The Quarterly Review Under Gifford: Identification of Contributors 1809–1824* (Chapel Hill: University of North Carolina Press, 1949).

Sichel, Walter, ed., *The Glenbervie Journals* (London: Constable, 1910).

Sim, Katharine, *Desert Traveller. The Life of Jean Louis Burckhardt* (London: Gollancz, 1969).

Simmons, Jack, *Southey* (London: Collins, 1945).

Smith, D. Nichol, ed., *Jeffrey's Literary Criticism* (London: Oxford University Press, 1910).

Smith, E. A., *A Queen on Trial. The Affair of Queen Caroline* (Stroud: Alan Sutton, 1993).

Smith, G. Gregory, ed., *The Spectator*, 4 vols (London: Dent, 1945).

Solovieff, Georges, *Madame de Staël, ses amis, ses correspondants, Choix de Lettres (1778–1817)* (Paris, 1970).

Southey, the Rev. Charles Cuthbert, ed., *The Life and Correspondence of the late Robert Southey*, 6 vols (London, 1849–50).

Stabler, Jane, *Byron, Poetics and History* (Cambridge: Cambridge University Press, 2002).

Stephens, John Russell, *The Profession of the Playwright* (Cambridge: Cambridge University Press, 1992).

Stockdale, J. J., *Stockdale's Budget* (London, 1826–27).

Stocking, Marion Kingston, ed., *The Journals of Claire Clairmont* (Cambridge, MA: Harvard University Press, 1968).

——, ed., *The Clairmont Correspondence*, 2 vols (Baltimore: Johns Hopkins University Press, 1995).

Storey, Mark, *Robert Southey: A Life* (Oxford: Oxford University Press, 1997).

Strout, Alan Lang, *The Life and Letters of James Hogg, the Ettrick Shepherd* (Texas, 1946).

Sultana, Donald, *From Abbotsford to Paris and Back. Sir Walter Scott's Journey of 1815* (Stroud: Alan Sutton, 1993).

Sutherland, John, *The Life of Walter Scott* (Oxford: Blackwell, 1995).

Thorne, R. G., *The History of Parliament. The House of Commons 1790–1820*, 4 vols (London, 1986).

Timperley, C. H., *Encyclopaedia of Literary and Typographical Anecdote*, 2 vols (London, 1842).

Toynbee, Paget, and Whibley, Leonard, eds, corr. H. W. Starr, *Correspondence of Thomas Gray*, 3 vols (Oxford: Clarendon Press, 1971).

Usick, Patricia, *Adventures in Egypt and Nubia. The Travels of William John Bankes (1786–1855)* (London: British Museum Press, 2001).

Vail, Jeffery W., *The Literary Relationship of Lord Byron & Thomas Moore* (Baltimore and London: Johns Hopkins University Press, 2001).

Vassall, Henry Richard, Third Lord Holland, *Further Memoirs of the Whig Party 1807–1821*, ed. Lord Stavordale (London, 1905).

Vincent, E. R., *Byron, Hobhouse and Foscolo* (Cambridge: Cambridge University Press, 1949).

——, *Ugo Foscolo: An Italian in Regency England* (Cambridge: Cambridge University Press, 1953).

Warter, John Wood, ed., *Selections from the Letters of Robert Southey*, 4 vols (London, 1856).

Wheatley, Henry B., *London Past and Present*, 3 vols (London: John Murray, 1891).

White, R. J., *Waterloo to Peterloo* (London: Heinemann, 1957).

Wicks, Margaret C. W., *The Italian Exiles in England 1816–1848* (Manchester: Manchester University Press, 1937).

Zachs, William, *The First John Murray and the Late Eighteenth-Century London Book Trade* (Oxford: Oxford University Press, 1998).

Zegger, Robert E., *John Cam Hobhouse. A Political Life, 1819–1852* (Columbia: University of Missouri Press, 1973).

Newspapers and magazines

The Annual Register; The Champion; Courier; The Examiner; The Gentleman's Magazine; The Lady's Magazine; London Chronicle; London Gazette; Monthly Literary Advertiser; Morning Chronicle; Morning Herald; Morning Post; The Observer; Parliamentary Debates; St James's Chronicle; The Star; The Stationers' Hall Register; The Statutes at Large; The Sun; The Times.

Miscellaneous Collection of Newspaper Cuttings, etc. Relating to Lord Byron 1812–80, 2 vols (BL 1764a11).

MURRAY, John II (JM)

birth, xxin.; intended for Navy, xxin.; loss of right eye, xxin.; publishing apprentice-ship, xxin.; partnership with Samuel Highley, xxin., dissolved, xxin.; publishes the *Edinburgh Review*, xxin.; establishes the *Quarterly Review*, xvii, xxin.; relations with Constable, Ballantyne and Blackwood, xvii, xxin.; in Fleet Street, xvii; removes to Albemarle Street, xviii, 13n., 20n., 21, 26n., 28, 28n.; his drawing-room, xviii, xxin.; relations with B, xvii, xviii, xix, xx; *CHP* I and II, objections to, 3, 4n., 'Orthodox', xviii, 3, 5n., copyright arrangements for, 5n., 6n.; first known meeting with B, 7 (int. n.); sends B books and reviews, 8, 9, 9n., 18, 20n., 21n., 27, 28, 29n., 30, 121, 122n., 124, 125n., 128, 130n., 131, 131n., 148, 149n., 169n., 170n., 171n., 182, 186n., 187, 189, 190, 193n., 195, 196, 196n., 198n., 229, 230n., 234, 235, 238n., 260, 261, 262n., 263, 264, 265n., 269, 270n., 298, 299n., 301, 302n., 321, 322n., 323n., 326, 327n., 334, 336n., 345, 351, 335, 359n., 360n., 400, 401, 403n., 404, 405n., 419, 410, 423n., 424n., 426, 427, 428n., 430n., 441n.; and George Thomson, 8, 12n., 15, 17n., 85, 85n., 126n.; and Lucien Buonaparte, 8, 13n., 38n., *Charlemagne*, 8, 13n., 37, 38n., Hodgson's translation of, 37, 38n., 39n.; and Madame de Staël, 37, 37n., 42, 45n., 81, 83n., *De l'Allemagne*, 37n., *Germany*, 50, 50n., 51n., *Considérations sur ... la Révolution Françoise*, 208, 210n., health of, 219, 220n., 232, 233n., death of, 234, 238n.; and B's Drury Lane Address, 15, 15n., 18, 27, 28n.; *Rejected Addresses*, 15, 16n., 27, 29n.; Albion Tavern Sale dinners, 21, 26n., 181, 183n., 184n., 453n.; and 'The Book', 31, 31n., 32n., 33n.; sends Gifford's letter to B, 33, 34n., 35n.; becomes publisher to the Board of Longitude, 35n.; in Brighton, 39, 40n., 115, 116n.; applies for ship for B, 46n., 47n.; proud to be B's publisher, 48; and B's portrait, 48, 49n., 50n., 99, 99n., 100n., 121, 122n., 123, 124n., 187, 211, 264, 266n., 450, reads B's letters under, 187, every day sits opposite, 450; and feud with Dallas, 62, 63n., 64n., 65, 65n., 66n., 67n., 68n., 80, 81, 82n., 83n.; asks B to procure *The Lay of the Scottish Fiddle*, 62, 63n.; concern for B's safety, 70; 'melancholny', 83, 84n.; accepts B's offer of 'Cyder', 83, 84n.; asks B's opinion of *The Wanderer*, 86, 86n., 87, 87n., 88n.; informs B of Napoleon's abdica-tion, 89, 89n., 90n.; B's fame invaluable to, 95, 95n.; distracted from business by drawing-room, 102; lends B Penrose's *Journal*, 109, 109n.; introduces B to Blackwood, 110n.; Augusta says 'how well he writes', 115n.; B sends game to, 115, 116n.; goes to Scotland, 105, 108n., 117., 119n., 260, 261n.; visits Newstead en route, 117, 119n.; fêted in Edinburgh, 117; negotiations with James Hogg, 110, 112n., 113n., 120n.; conveys Scott's gift to B, 121, 122n.; his wedding present to B, 123, 123n.; anecdotes of Napoleon, 127, 129n.; on Scott's *Lord of the Isles*, 128,

448n.; requests Goethe's *Faust*, 432 (int. n.); breaks off publishing relationship with JM, 432 (int. n.); the 'Pisan Affray', 434 (int. n.), 435, 436n., 437, 438n., 439n.; hurt by Jeffrey's review of tragedies, 438n.; Archie Murray on, 450n., 451n., 452n., B confuses with JM's brother-in-law, 452n.; sends JM letter via John Hunt, 442, 446n., 447n., 461, 462, 464n., 465, 465n., 466n.; sends JM letter via Kinnaird, 455, 458n., 459n., 460n.; on Hunt's advertisement in *The Morning Chronicle*, 448n.; Bartolini's busts of Teresa and B, 434 (int. n.), 450, 454n., 466n.; subscription for Godwin., 449, 450n.; on Heber's review of tragedies, 454n.; at Genoa, 450n., 456n.; on *The Liberal*, 457n.; and the Hunts, on assisting, 457n., on JM's showing about his letter concerning, 457n., 458n., 462n., will not quit, 460n., quarrel with Leigh Hunt, 457n., 458n.; mislaid manuscripts, 461, 462n., 463n., 464n., 466, 466n.; intends visiting Naples, 466n.; on a fifth and sixth Canto of *CHP*, 467n.; denies satire on Gifford, 467n.; final letter to JM, 467n.

Works

'Address, Spoken at the Opening of Drury-lane Theatre', 15, 15n., 16n., 18, 19n., 20n., 22n., 23n., 24n., 27, 28n., 29n., 49n.; Lord Holland asks B to write, 15n.; spoken by Elliston, 18, 19n., 20n., 22n., JM reports on, 18, Lord Holland reports on, 20n.; printed in the *Morning Chronicle*, 20n., criticized in the *Morning Chronicle*, 20n., 22n.; defended by 'Candidus', 22n.; defended by 'Petroniculus', 23n.; *The Examiner* on, 24n.; *A Critique on*, 27, 28n., 29n.; *The Antijacobin* on, 29n.; publication of, 49n.; and the Busbys, 22n., see also, 'Parenthetical Address, by Dr. Plagiary'

Armenian Translations, 430n., 443

Beppo, xx, 195n., 249 (int. n.), 251, 252, 254n., 255n., 256n., 257, 258, 259n., 263, 265n., 456; B sends, 249 (int. n.); publication, 249 (int. n.), 254n., anonymous, 254n.; Shelley mislays B's copy, 249 (int. n.); Frere on, 251, 254n., 255n.; and 'bustling Botherby', 133n., 252, 256n.; 5th edn, 259n.; payment for, thrown into the balance with *CHP* IV, 240n., 261, 262n.

Blues, The, 324n., 420, 423n., 424n., 443, 448n.; B sends, 420, 423n.; and John Hunt, 443, 448n.

Bride of Abydos, The, xviii, 44n., 45n., 48n., 49n., 50, 50n., 51, 51n., 52, 52n., 53, 53n., 56, 57n., 58, 58n., 59n., 60n., 62, 62n., 73, 74n., 81, 82n., 83n., 84n., 89n., 95n., 96, 96n., 101n., 105, 108n., 111, 114n., 121, 122n., 482, 487, 488, 500 App. B; published with *The Giaour*, 48n., 49n.; published separately, 48n., 52, 52n.; proofs for, 50n., 51n., 52, 53n., 57n., 62, 62n.; additions, 53, 53n., 58, 59n., 62, 62n., 'Ovidian hiatus', 59n.; errata page, 58, 59n.; note on Madame de Staël, 50, 50n., 51n.; 4th edn, 62, 63n.; dedication to Lord Holland, 57n., 487, 488, 500 App. B; payment for, 48, 49n., 51, 58, 59n., 81, 82n., 83n., 96, 96n.; premature notice of in the *Morning Chronicle*, 60n.; Gifford on, 51, 52n.; Heber on, 51, 52n.; George Canning on, 52, 53n.; Frere on, 56, 57n.; Lord Holland on, 57n.; Hay on, 58, 60n.; reviews of, in *The British Critic*, the *New Monthly Magazine*, *The Satirist*, 76n., *The British Review*, 84n., *The Antijacobin*, 89n., the *Edinburgh Review*, 108, 108n.; in first collected edition, 111, 114n.; quoted, 121, 122n.; plagiarism in, 482 App. B

Cain, 415n., 422n., 424, 424n., 425n., 426, 427, 428n., 429n., 430n., 431, 433 (int. n.), 435, 435n., 437, 437n., 438n., 442, 446n., 450, 454n.; B sends to JM, 424,

Collected Editions

Foreign Collected Editions

Spurious Works

The Right Honourable Lord Byron's Pilgrimage to the Holy Land; to which is added, The Tempest, 181, 184n., 185n., and James Johnston, 184n., 185n., injunction against, 181, 184n., 185n., 188, 192n., and Scrope Davies's affidavit, 181, 184n., 185n.

The Vampyre (1819), 269, 270n., 271n., and Polidori, 269, 270n., 271n.

General index

C